The Memoirs Of Philip De Commines, Lord Of Argenton: Containing The Histories Of Louis Xi. And Charles Viii. Kings Of France And Of Charles The Bold, Duke Of Burgundy: To Which Is Added, The Scandalous Chronicle, Or Secret History Of Louis Xi....

Philippe de Commynes, Jean de Roye

Russia, History of, by WALTER K. KELLY. *Portraits.* In 2 vols.

Schiller's Works. Translated into English. In 5 vols.
  Vol. 1. Thirty Years' War, and Revolt of the Netherlands.
  Vol. 2. *Continuation of* the Revolt of the Netherlands; Wallenstein's Camp; the Piccolomini; the Death of Wallenstein; and William Tell.
  Vol. 3. Don Carlos, Mary Stuart, Maid of Orleans, and Bride of Messina.
  Vol. 4. The Robbers, Fiesco, Love and Intrigue, and the Ghost-Seer.
  Vol. 5. Poems. Translated by EDGAR BOWRING, M.P.

Schlegel's Philosophy of Life and of Language, translated by A. J. W. MORRISON.

———— **History of Literature,** Ancient and Modern. Now first completely translated, with General Index.

———— **Philosophy of History.** Translated by J. B. ROBERTSON. *Portrait.*

———— **Dramatic Literature.** Translated. *Portrait.*

———— **Modern History.**

———— **Æsthetic and Miscellaneous** Works.

Sheridan's Dramatic Works and Life *Portrait.*

Sismondi's Literature of the South of Europe. Translated by Roscoe. *Portraits.* In 2 vols.

Smith's (Adam) Theory of the Moral Sentiments; with his Essay on the First Formation of Languages.

Smyth's (Professor) Lectures on Modern History. In 2 vols.

———— **Lectures on the French Re-** volution. In 2 vols.

Sturm's Morning Communings with God, or Devotional Meditations for Every Day in the Year.

Taylor's (Bishop Jeremy) Holy Living and Dying. *Portrait.*

Thierry's Conquest of England by the Normans. Translated by WILLIAM HAZLITT. *Portrait.* In 2 vols.

———— **Tiers Etat, or Third Estate,** in France. Translated by F. B. WELLS. 2 vols. in one. *5s.*

Vasari's Lives of the Painters, Sculptors, and Architects. Translated by Mrs. FOSTER. 5 vols.

Wesley's (John) Life. By ROBERT SOUTHEY. New and Complete Edition. Double volume. *5s.*

Wheatley on the Book of Common Prayer. *Frontispiece.*

II.

Uniform with Bohn's Standard Library.

Bailey's (P. J.) Festus. A Poem. Seventh Edition. revised and enlarged. *5s.*; with Portrait, *6s.*

British Poets, from Milton to Kirke WHITE. Cabinet Edition. In 4 vols. *14s.*

Cary's Translation of Dante's Hea- ven, Hell, and Purgatory. *7s. 6d.*

Cervantes' Galatea. Translated by GORDON GYLL.

Chillingworth's Religion of Pro- testants. *3s. 6d.*

Classic Tales. Comprising in One volume the most esteemed works of the imagination. *3s. 6d.*

Demosthenes and Æschines, the Orations of. Translated by LELAND. *3s.*

Dickson and Mowbray on Poultry. Edited by Mrs. LOUDON. *Illustrations by Harvey. 5s.*

Hawthorne's Tales. In 2 vols., *5s. 6d.* each.

  Vol. 1. Twice Told Tales, and the Snow Image.
  Vol. 2. Scarlet Letter, and the House with the seven Gables.

Henry's (Matthew) Commentary on the Psalms. *Numerous Illustrations.* *4s. 6d.*

Hofland's British Angler's Manual. Improved and enlarged, by EDWARD JESSE, Esq. *Illustrated with 60 Engravings.* *7s. 6d.*

Horace's Odes and Epodes. Translated by the Rev. W. SEWELL. *3s. 6d.*

Irving's (Washington) Life of Wash- ington. *Portrait.* In 4 vols. *3s. 6d.* each.

———— **(Washington) Life and Let-** ters. By his Nephew, PIERRE E. IRVING. In 2 vols. *3s. 6d.* each.

4

Irving's (Washington) Complete Works. In 11 vols. 3s. 6d. each.
  Vol. 1. Salmagundi and Knickerbocker. *Portrait of the Author.*
  Vol. 2. Sketch Book and Life of Goldsmith.
  Vol. 3. Bracebridge Hall and Abbotsford and Newstead.
  Vol. 4. Tales of a Traveller and the Alhambra.
  Vol. 5. Conquest of Granada and Conquest of Spain.
  Vols. 6 and 7. Life of Columbus and Companions of Columbus, with a new Index. *Fine Portrait.*
  Vol. 8. Astoria and Tour in the Prairies.
  Vol. 9. Mahomet and his Successors.
  Vol. 10. Conquest of Florida and Adventures of Captain Bonneville.
  Vol. 11. Biographies and Miscellanies.
For separate Works, see Cheap Series, p.15.

Joyce's Introduction to the Arts and Sciences. With Examination Questions. 3s. 6d.

Lawrence's Lectures on Compara- tive Anatomy, Physiology, Zoology, and the Natural History of Man. *Illustrated.* 5s.

Lilly's Introduction to Astrology. With numerous Emendations, by ZADKIEL. 5s.

Miller's (Professor) History Philoso- phically considered. In 4 vols. 3s. 6d. each.

Political Cyclopædia. In 4 vols. 3s. 6d. each.

——— Also bound in 2 vols. with leather backs. 15s.

Uncle Tom's Cabin. With Introductory Remarks by the Rev. J. SHERMAN. *Printed in a large clear type. Illustrations.* 3s. 6d.

Wide, Wide World. By ELIZABETH WETHERALL. *Illustrated with 10 highly-finished Steel Engravings.* 3s. 6d.

III.

Bohn's Historical Library.

UNIFORM WITH THE STANDARD LIBRARY, AT 5s. PER VOLUME.

Evelyn's Diary and Correspondence. *Illustrated with numerous Portraits, &c.* In 4 vols.

Pepys' Diary and Correspondence. Edited by Lord Braybrooke. With important Additions, including numerous Letters. *Illustrated with many Portraits.* In 4 vols.

Jesse's Memoirs of the Reign of the Stuarts, including the Protectorate. With General Index. *Upwards of 40 Portraits.* In 3 vols.

Jesse's Memoirs of the Pretenders and their Adherents. 6 *Portraits.*

Nugent's (Lord) Memorials of Hampden, his Party, and Times. 12 *Portraits.*

Strickland's (Agnes) Lives of the Queens of England, from the Norman Conquest. From official records and authentic documents, private and public. Revised Edition. In 6 vols.

——— Life of Mary Queen of Scots. 2 vols.

IV.

Bohn's Library of French Memoirs.

UNIFORM WITH THE STANDARD LIBRARY AT 3s. 6d. PER VOLUME.

Memoirs of Philip de Commines, containing the Histories of Louis XI. and Charles VIII., and of Charles the Bold, Duke of Burgundy. To which is added, The Scandalous Chronicle, or Secret

History of Louis XI. *Portraits.* In 2 vols.

Memoirs of the Duke of Sully, Prime Minister to Henry the Great. *Portraits.* In 4 vols.

V.

Bohn's School and College Series.

UNIFORM WITH THE STANDARD LIBRARY.

Bass's Complete Greek and English Lexicon to the New Testament. 2s.

New Testament (The) in Greek. Griesbach's Text, with the various readings of Mill and Scholz at foot of page, and

Parallel References in the margin; also a Critical Introduction and Chronological Tables. *Two fac-similes of Greek Manuscripts.* (650 pages.) 3s. 6d.; or with the Lexicon, 5s.

5

VI.

Bohn's Philological and Philosophical Library.

UNIFORM WITH THE STANDARD LIBRARY, AT 5s. PER VOLUME
(EXCEPTING THOSE MARKED OTHERWISE).

Hegel's Lectures on the Philosophy of History. Translated by J. SIBREE, M.A.

Herodotus, Turner's (Dawson W.) Notes to. With Map, &c.

—————— **Wheeler's Analysis and** Summary of.

Kant's Critique of Pure Reason. Translated by J. M. D. MEIKLEJOHN.

Logic; or, the Science of Inference. A Popular Manual. By J. DEVEY.

Lowndes' Bibliographer's Manual of English Literature. New Edition, enlarged, by H. G. BOHN. Parts I. to X. (A

to Z). 3s. 6d. each. Part XI. (the Appendix Volume). 5s. Or the 11 parts in 4 vols., half morocco, 2l. 2s.

Smith's (Archdeacon) Complete Col- lection of Synonyms and Antonyms.

Tennemann's Manual of the History of Philosophy. Continued by J. R. MORELL

Thucydides, Wheeler's Analysis of.

Wheeler's (M.A.) W. A., Dictionary of Names of Fictitious Persons and Places.

Wright's (T.) Dictionary of Obsolete and Provincial English. In 2 vols. 5s. each; or half-bound in 1 vol., 10s. 6d.

VII.

Bohn's British Classics.

UNIFORM WITH THE STANDARD LIBRARY, AT 3s. 6d. PER VOLUME.

Addison's Works. With the Notes of Bishop HURD, much additional matter, and upwards of 100 Unpublished Letters. Edited by H. G. BOHN. *Portrait and 8 Engravings on Steel.* In 6 vols.

Burke's Works. In 6 Volumes.
  Vol. 1. Vindication of Natural Society, On the Sublime and Beautiful, and Political Miscellanies.
  Vol. 2. French Revolution, &c.
  Vol. 3. Appeal from the New to the Old Whigs; the Catholic Claims, &c.
  Vol. 4. On the Affairs of India, and Charge against Warren Hastings.
  Vol. 5. Conclusion of Charge against Hastings; on a Regicide Peace, &c.
  Vol. 6. Miscellaneous Speeches, &c. With a General Index.

Burke's Speeches on Warren Hast- ings; and Letters. With Index. In 2 vols. (forming vols. 7 and 8 of the works).

—————— **Life.** By PRIOR. New and revised Edition. *Portrait.*

Defoe's Works. Edited by Sir WALTER SCOTT. In 7 vols.

Gibbon's Roman Empire. Complete and Unabridged, with Notes; including, in addition to the Author's own, those of Guizot, Wenck, Niebuhr, Hugo, Neander, and other foreign scholars; and an elaborate Index. Edited by an English Churchman. In 7 vols.

VIII.

Bohn's Ecclesiastical Library.

UNIFORM WITH THE STANDARD LIBRARY, AT 5s. PER VOLUME.

Eusebius' Ecclesiastical History. With Notes.

Philo Judæus, Works of; the contemporary of Josephus. Translated by C. D. Yonge. In 4 vols.

Socrates' Ecclesiastical History, in continuation of Eusebius. With the Notes of Valesius.

Sozomen's Ecclesiastical History, from A.D. 324-440: and the Ecclesiastical History of Philostorgius.

Theodoret and Evagrius. Ecclesiastical Histories, from A.D. 332 to A.D. 427, and from A.D. 431 to A.D. 544

IX.

Bohn's Antiquarian Library.

UNIFORM WITH THE STANDARD LIBRARY, AT 5s. PER VOLUME.

Bede's Ecclesiastical History, and the Anglo-Saxon Chronicle.

Boethius's Consolation of Philoso- phy. In Anglo-Saxon, with the A. S. Metres, and an English Translation, by the Rev. S. Fox.

Brand's Popular Antiquities of Eng- land, Scotland, and Ireland. By Sir HENRY ELLIS. In 3 vols.

Browne's (Sir Thomas) Works. Edited by SIMON WILKIN. In 3 vols.
  Vol. 1. The Vulgar Errors.
  Vol. 2. Religio Medici, and Garden of Cyrus.
  Vol. 3. Urn-Burial, Tracts, and Correspondence.

Chronicles of the Crusaders. Richard of Devizes, Geoffrey de Vinsauf, Lord de Joinville.

Chronicles of the Tombs. A Collection of Remarkable Epitaphs. By T. J. PETTIGREW, F.R.S., F.S.A.

Early Travels in Palestine. Willibald, Sæwulf, Benjamin of Tudela, Mandeville, La Brocquiere, and Maundrell; all unabridged. Edited by THOMAS WRIGHT.

Ellis's Early English Metrical Ro- mances. Revised by J. O. HALLIWELL.

Florence of Worcester's Chronicle, with the Two Continuations: comprising Annals of English History to the Reign of Edward I.

Giraldus Cambrensis' Historical Works: Topography of Ireland; History of the Conquest of Ireland; Itinerary through Wales; and Description of Wales. With Index. Edited by THOS. WRIGHT.

Handbook of Proverbs. Comprising all Ray's English Proverbs, with additions; his Foreign Proverbs; and an Alphabetical Index.

Henry of Huntingdon's History of the glish, from the Roman Invasion to Henry II.; with the Acts of King Stephen, &c.

Ingulph's Chronicle of the Abbey of Croyland, with the Continuations by Peter of Blois and other Writers. By H. T. RILEY.

Keightley's Fairy Mythology. *Frontispiece by Cruikshank.*

Lamb's Dramatic Poets of the Time of Elizabeth; including his Selections from the Garrick Plays.

Lepsius's Letters from Egypt, Ethio- pia, and the Peninsula of Sinai.

Mallet's Northern Antiquities. By Bishop PERCY. With an Abstract of the Eyrbiggia Saga, by Sir WALTER SCOTT. Edited by J. A. BLACKWELL.

Marco Polo's Travels. The Translation of Marsden. Edited by THOMAS WRIGHT.

Matthew Paris's Chronicle. In 5 vols.
  FIRST SECTION: Roger of Wendover's Flowers of English History, from the Descent of the Saxons to A.D. 1235. Translated by Dr. GILES. In 2 vols.
  SECOND SECTION: From 1235 to 1273. With Index to the entire Work. In 3 vols.

Matthew of Westminster's Flowers of History, especially such as relate to the affairs of Britain; to A.D. 1307. Translated by C. D. YONGE. In 2 vols.

Ordericus Vitalis' Ecclesiastical His- tory of England and Normandy. Translated with Notes, by T. FORESTER, M.A. In 4 vols.

Pauli's (Dr. R.) Life of Alfred the Great. Translated from the German.

Polyglot of Foreign Proverbs. With English Translations, and a General Index, bringing the whole into parallels, by H. G. BOHN.

Roger De Hoveden's Annals of Eng- lish History; from A.D. 732 to A.D. 1201. Edited by H. T. RILEY. In 2 vols.

Six Old English Chronicles, viz.:— Asser's Life of Alfred, and the Chronicles of Ethelwerd, Gildas, Nennius, Geoffrey of Monmouth, and Richard of Cirencester.

William of Malmesbury's Chronicle of the Kings of England. Translated by SHARPE.

Yule-Tide Stories. A Collection of Scandinavian Tales and Traditions. Edited by B. THORPE.

X.

Bohn's Illustrated Library.

UNIFORM WITH THE STANDARD LIBRARY, AT 5s. PER VOLUME (EXCEPTING THOSE MARKED OTHERWISE).

Allen's Battles of the British Navy. Revised and enlarged. *Numerous fine Portraits.* In 2 vols.

Andersen's Danish Legends and Fairy Tales. With many Tales not in any other edition. Translated by CAROLINE PEACHEY. *120 Wood Engravings.*

Ariosto's Orlando Furioso. In English Verse. By W. S. ROSE. *Twelve fine Engravings.* In 2 vols.

Bechstein's Cage and Chamber Birds. Including Sweet's Warblers. Enlarged edition. *Numerous plates.*
    ⁎⁎ All other editions are abridged.
    With the plates coloured. 7s. 6d.

Bonomi's Nineveh and its Palaces. New Edition, revised and considerably enlarged, both in matter and Plates, including a Full Account of the Assyrian Sculptures recently added to the National Collection. *Upwards of 300 Engravings.*

Butler's Hudibras. With Variorum Notes, a Biography, and a General Index. Edited by HENRY G. BOHN. *Thirty beautiful Illustrations.*

———; or, *further illustrated with 62 Outline Portraits.* In 2 vols. 10s.

Cattermole's Evenings at Haddon Hall. *24 exquisite Engravings on Steel,* from designs by himself, the Letterpress by the BARONESS DE CARABELLA.

China, Pictorial, Descriptive, and Historical, with some Account of Ava and the Burmese, Siam, and Anam. *Nearly 100 Illustrations.*

Craik's (G. L.) Pursuit of Knowledge under Difficulties, illustrated by Anecdotes and Memoirs. Revised Edition. *With numerous Portraits.*

Cruikshank's Three Courses and a Dessert. A Series of Tales, *with 50 humorous Illustrations by Cruikshank.*

Dante. Translated by I. C. WRIGHT, M.A. New Edition, carefully revised. *Portrait and 34 Illustrations on Steel, after Flaxman.*

Didron's History of Christian Art; or, Christian Iconography. From the French. *Upwards of 150 beautiful outline Engravings.* Vol. I. (Mons. Didron has not yet written the second volume.)

Flaxman's Lectures on Sculpture. *Numerous Illustrations.* 6s.

Gil Blas, The Adventures of. 24 *Engravings on Steel, after Smirke, and 10 Etchings by George Cruikshank.* (612 pages.) 6s.

Grimm's Gammer Grethel; or, German Fairy Tales and Popular Stories. Translated by EDGAR TAYLOR. *Numerous Woodcuts by Cruikshank.* 3s. 6d.

Holbein's Dance of Death, and Bible Cuts. *Upwards of 150 subjects, beautifully engraved in fac-simile,* with Introduction and Descriptions by the late FRANCIS DOUCE and Dr. T. F. DIBDIN. 2 vols. in 1. 7s. 6d.

Howitt's (Mary) Pictorial Calendar of the Seasons. Embodying the whole of Aiken's Calendar of Nature. *Upwards of 100 Engravings.*

——— **(Mary and William) Stories** of English and Foreign Life. *Twenty beautiful Engravings.*

India, Pictorial, Descriptive, and Historical, from the Earliest Times to the Present. *Upwards of 100 fine Engravings on Wood, and a Map.*

Jesse's Anecdotes of Dogs. New Edition, with large additions. *Numerous fine Woodcuts after Harvey, Bewick, and others.*

———; or, *with the addition of 34 highly-finished Steel Engravings.* 7s. 6d.

King's Natural History of Precious Stones, and of the Precious Metals. *With numerous Illustrations.* Price 6s.

Kitto's Scripture Lands and Biblical Atlas. *24 Maps, beautifully engraved on Steel,* with a Consulting Index.

———; *with the maps coloured,* 7s. 6d.

Krummacher's Parables. Translated from the German. *Forty Illustrations by Clayton, engraved by Dalziel.*

Lindsay's (Lord) Letters on Egypt, Edom, and the Holy Land. New Edition, enlarged. *Thirty-six beautiful Engravings, and 2 Maps.*

Lodge's Portraits of Illustrious Per- sonages of Great Britain, with Memoirs. *Two Hundred and Forty Portraits, beautifully engraved on Steel.* 8 vols.

8

Hinchliff

Louis. XI.

THE MEMOIRS

OF

PHILIP DE COMMINES,

LORD OF ARGENTON:

CONTAINING THE

HISTORIES OF LOUIS XI. AND CHARLES VIII., KINGS OF FRANCE,

AND OF

CHARLES THE BOLD, DUKE OF BURGUNDY.

TO WHICH IS ADDED,

THE SCANDALOUS CHRONICLE,

OR

SECRET HISTORY OF LOUIS XI.,

BY JEAN DE TROYES.

EDITED, WITH LIFE AND NOTES,

BY ANDREW R. SCOBLE, ESQ.

IN TWO VOLUMES.

VOL. II.

LONDON:

HENRY G. BOHN, YORK STREET, COVENT GARDEN.

1856.

LONDON:
Printed by SPOTTISWOODE and Co.,
New-street-Square.

CONTENTS

OF

THE SECOND VOLUME.

BOOK THE SIXTH.

CHAPTER I.—How the King of France cajoled the English after the Duke of Burgundy's Death, for fear they should have interrupted him in the Conquest of the Territories belonging to the said Duke - - - - - - - Page 1

CH. II.—Of the Conclusion of the Marriage between the Princess of Burgundy and Maximilian Duke of Austria, and since Emperor 9

CH. III.—How King Louis, by the Management of Charles d'Amboise his Lieutenant, recovered many Towns in Burgundy, which the Prince of Orange had persuaded to revolt from him - - - 18

CH. IV.—How the Lord of Argenton was sent to Florence during the Wars in Burgundy, and how he received Homage of the Duke of Milan, in the King's Name, for the Duchy of Genoa - - 25

CH. V.—Of the Lord of Argenton's Return out of Italy into France, and of the Battle of Guinegaste - - - - 32

CH. VI.—How King Louis was surprised with a Malady that for some Time took away the Use of both his Senses and Tongue; how he recovered and relapsed several Times, and how he kept himself in his Castle at Plessis les Tours - - - - 36

CH. VII.—How the King sent for the Holy Man of Calabria to Tours, supposing he could cure him; and of the strange Things that were done by the King, during his Sickness, to preserve his Authority - - - - - - - - 54

CH. VIII.—Of the Conclusion of the Marriage between the Dauphin and Margaret of Flanders, and how she was brought into France; upon which Edward IV., King of England, died with Displeasure 58

CH. IX.—How the King behaved towards his Neighbours and Subjects during his Sickness; and how several Things were sent him from several Parts for the Recovery of his Health - - 65

CH. X.—How King Louis sent for his Son Charles a little before his Death; and the Precepts and Commands which he laid upon him and others - - - - - - - - 68

CH. XI.—A Comparison of the Troubles and Sorrows which King Louis suffered, with those he had brought 'upon other People; with a Continuation of his Transactions till the Time of his Death - - - - - - Page 70

CH. XII.—A Digression concerning the Miseries of Mankind, especially of Princes, by the Example of those who reigned in the Author's Time, and chiefly of King Louis - - - - 80

BOOK THE SEVENTH.

CH. I.—How Duke René of Lorraine came into France to demand the Duchy of Bar and the County of Provence, which King Charles had in his Possession; and how he failed to obtain the Kingdom of Naples, to which he laid Claim as well as the King; and what Right each had thereto - - - - - - 93

CH. II.—How the Prince of Salerno, a Neapolitan by Birth, came into France; and the Endeavours that were used by him and Ludovic Sforza, surnamed the Moor, to persuade the King to make War upon the King of Naples; and the Occasion of it - - - 100

CH. III.—How the Duchy of Milan is one of the finest and most valuable Territories in the World, if relieved from the heavy Tribute which oppresses it - - - - - - 106

CH. IV.—How King Charles VIII. made Peace with the King of the Romans and the Archduke of Austria; and returned the Lady Margaret of Flanders to them before his Expedition to Naples - 110

CH. V.—How the King sent to the Venetians, in order to induce them to enter into an Alliance with him, before undertaking his Expedition to Naples; and of the Preparations in order to it - - 119

CH. VI.—How King Charles set out from Vienne, in Dauphiny, to conquer Naples in Person; and the Action that was performed by his Fleet, under the Command of the Duke of Orleans - - 124

CH. VII.—How the King, being at Asti, resolved to go in Person into the Kingdom of Naples, by the Persuasion and Advice of Ludovic Sforza: how Philip de Commines was sent on an Embassy to Venice: and of the Duke of Milan's Death - - - - 129

CH. VIII.—How and by what Means the Lord Ludovic seized and usurped the Lordship and Duchy of Milan, and was received by the Milanese as their Sovereign - - - - - 132

CH. IX.—How Peter de Medicis put Four of his strongest Garrisons into the King's Possession; and how the King restored Pisa, which was one of them, to its ancient Liberty - - - 134

CH. X.—How the King departed from Pisa to go to Florence; and of the Flight and Destruction of Peter de Medicis - - 139

CH. XI.—How the King made his Entrance into Florence, and what other Towns he passed through in his March to Rome - - 143

CH. XII.—How the King sent the Cardinal of St. Peter ad Vincula (who was afterwards Pope by the name of Julius II.) to Ostia; what

the Pope did at Rome in the Meantime; and how the King entered
Rome, notwithstanding all the Endeavours of his Enemies to the con-
trary; and of the Factions between the Ursini and the Colonne in
Rome - - - - - - - Page 145

CH. XIII. — How King Alphonso caused his Son Ferrand to be crowned
King; his Flight into Sicily; and of the evil Life his Father (old Ferrand) and he had led during their Reigns - - - 149

CH. XIV. — How King Alphonso fled into Castile and did Penance 153

CH. XV. — How, after Ferrand the Younger was crowned King of Naples,
he encamped with his Forces at St. Germain, in order to oppose King
Charles; and of the Agreement King Charles made with the Pope
during his stay at Rome - - - - - 157

CH. XVI. — How the King departed from Rome to Naples; of the
Transactions in that Kingdom in the Meantime; and an Account of
the Places the King of France passed through in his March - 159

CH. XVII. — How King Charles was crowned King of Naples; the
Errors he committed in his Government of that Kingdom; and of the
Discovery of a Design in his Favour against the Turks by the Vene-
tians - - - - - - - - 163

CH. XVIII. — A Digression or Discourse, by no Means unconnected
with the main Subject, in which Philip de Commines, Author of this
present Book, speaks at some Length of the State and Government
of the Signory of Venice, and of what he saw, and what was done,
while he was Ambassador from the King of France in the City of
Venice - - - - - - - 168

CH. XIX. — What were the Subjects of the Embassy of the Lord of
Argenton to the Republic of Venice - - - - 173

CH. XX. — How the Lord of Argenton was informed that the King had
gained Possession of Naples and the Places round about; at which
the Venetians were displeased - - - - - 177

BOOK THE EIGHTH.

CH. I. — Of the Order in which the King left his Affairs in the Kingdom
of Naples upon his Return into France - - - 183

CH. II. — How the King departed from Naples, and returned to Rome,
from whence the Pope fled to Orvieto; of the Conference the King
had with the Lord of Argenton upon his Return from Venice; and
his Deliberation about the Restitution of the Florentine Towns - 186

CH. III. — Of the memorable Preachings of Friar Jerome of Florence 189

CH. IV. — How the King retained Pisa and several other Florentine
Towns in his Hands, while the Duke of Orleans on the other Side entered Novara, in the Duchy of Milan - - - - 191

CH. V. — How King Charles crossed several dangerous Passages over the
Mountains between Pisa and Sarzana; and how the Germans burned
Pontremoli - - - - - - - 194

CH. VI. — How the Duke of Orleans behaved himself in the City of
Novara - - - - - - - - 197

Ch. VII. — How the King passed the Apennine Mountains with his Train of Artillery, by the Assistance of the Swiss; and of the great Danger to which the Marshal de Gié and his whole Vanguard were exposed - - - - - - Page 199

Ch. VIII. — How the Marshal de Gié withdrew with his Army to the Mountains, and waited until the King came up to him - 202

Ch. IX. — How the King and his small Army arrived at Fornovo, near the Camp of his Enemies, who awaited him in very fine Order, and with a Determination to defeat and capture him - - 204

Ch. X. — The Arrangement of the two Armies for the Battle of Fornovo - - - - - - - - 207

Ch. XI. — How Parleys were vainly attempted; and the Beginning of the Battle of Fornovo - - - - - 211

Ch. XII. — Consequences of the Victory gained by the French at Fornovo; and the Danger to which King Charles VIII found himself exposed - - - - - - - 215

Ch. XIII. — How the Lord of Argenton went alone to parley with the Enemy, upon the Refusal of those that were deputed to go along with him, and of the King's safe Arrival with his whole Army at Asti - - - - - - - - 220

Ch. XIV. — How the Swiss secured the French Army in its Retreat - - - - - - - - 226

Ch. XV. — How the King fitted out a Fleet with an Intention to have relieved the Castles of Naples; and of the Miscarriage of that Design - - - - - - - 228

Ch. XVI. — Of the great Famine and Misery to which the Duke of Orleans and his Army were reduced at Novara: of the Death of the Marchioness of Montferrat: of the Death of the Duke of Vendôme; and the Conclusion of a Peace for the Preservation of the besieged after several Negotiations - - - - 232

Ch. XVII. — How the Duke of Orleans and his Army were delivered upon Terms of Accommodation from the dire Misery they suffered during their being besieged in Novara; and of the Arrival of the Swiss that came to the Relief of the King and the said Duke of Orleans - - - - - - - 242

Ch. XVIII. — How Peace was concluded between the King and the Duke of Orleans on the one Part, and the League on the other; and of the Conditions and Articles contained in that Treaty of Peace - - - - - - - - 245

Ch. XIX. — How the King sent the Lord of Argenton to Venice again, to invite the Venetians to accept the Terms of Peace that were offered, which the Venetians refused; and of the Tricks and Jugglings of the Duke of Milan - - - - - - 248

Ch. XX. — How the King forgot those that were left behind at Naples, upon his Return into France; and of the Dauphin's Death, which was a great Affliction to the King and Queen - 253

Ch. XXI. — How the King received News of the Loss of the Castle of Naples; of the selling of the Towns belonging to the Florentines to several Persons; of the Treaty of Atella in Apulia, much to the Prejudice of the French; and of the Death of Ferrand, King of Naples - - - - - - Page 257

Ch. XXII. — How several Plots were formed (in Favour of our King) by some of the Italian Princes, not only for the Recovery of Naples, but for the Destruction of the Duke of Milan; how they miscarried for want of Supplies; and how another Design against Genoa came to the same ill End - - - - - - 264

Ch. XXIII. — Of certain Differences that arose between Charles King of France and Ferrand King of Castile; and the Ambassadors whs were sent by both of them to accommodate the Affair - - 260

Ch. XXIV.—A Digression concerning the Fortunes and Misfortune9 which happened to the House of Castile in the Author's Time 277

Ch. XXV. — Of the magnificent Building which King Charles began not long before his Death; his good Inclination to reform the Church, the Laws, the Treasury, and himself; and how he died suddenly in this Resolution in his Castle at Amboise - - - 281

Ch. XXVI — How holy Friar Jerome was burned at Florence by the Malice and Solicitation of the Pope, and several Venetians and Florentines who were his Enemies - - - - 284

Ch. XXVII. — Of the Obsequies and Funeral of King Charles VIII., and the Coronation of his Successor Louis XII.; with the Genealogies of the Kings of France to King Louis XII. - - - 287

THE SCANDALOUS CHRONICLE.

THE Chronicles of the very Christian and very victorious Louis of Valois, late King of France (whom God absolve), with various other Adventures which occurred both in the Realm of France and in neighbouring Countries, from the Year 1460 until 1483 inclusively - - - - - - - 297

THE MEMOIRS

OF

PHILIP DE COMMINES,

LORD OF ARGENTON.

BOOK THE SIXTH.

CHAPTER I.—How the King of France cajoled the English after the Duke of Burgundy's Death, for fear they should have interrupted him in the Conquest of the Territories belonging to the said Duke.—1477.

THEY who shall read these Memoirs hereafter, and have a better knowledge of the affairs of this kingdom and its neighbouring States than I have, may perhaps wonder that, from the Duke of Burgundy's death to this time, which is little less than a year, I have not said a word of the English, nor of their suffering the king to seize upon those towns which were near them, as Arras, Boulogne, Hesdin, Ardres and several other castles, and to lie so many days before St. Omer. The reason of it was, because, in cunning and artifice, our king was much superior to King Edward, who was indeed a brave prince, and had won eight or nine battles in England, in which he had been always present himself, and had fought constantly on foot, which redounded much to his honour; but the two kings were placed in different circumstances, and the English king depended not so much upon his diligence or understanding, for upon the success of one battle he was absolute master till another rebellion disturbed him. In England, when any disputes arise, and occasion a war, the controversy is generally decided in eight or ten days, when one party or other gains the victory; but with us, on this side of the water, affairs are managed quite otherwise.

Our king is obliged, whilst he is carrying on any war, to keep a watchful eye upon his neighbours, as well as over the rest of his kingdom; and particularly to satisfy the King of England above all, who must be quieted at any cost, and cajoled with ambassadors, promises, and presents, lest he should attempt anything that might interrupt our king's designs. For our master was well aware that the nobility, commons, and clergy of England, are always ready to enter upon a war with France, being incited thereunto, not only upon the account of their old title to its crown, but by the desire of gain, for it pleased God to permit their predecessors to win several memorable battles in this kingdom, and to continue in the possession of Normandy and Guienne for the space of three hundred and fifty years *, before Charles VII. gave them the first blow †; during which time they carried over enormous booty into England, not only in plunder, which they had taken in the several towns, but in the richness and quality of their prisoners, who were many of them great princes and lords, who paid them vast ransoms for their liberty; so that every Englishman afterwards hoped to do the same thing, and return home laden with spoils. But this fortune was not to be looked for in our king's days, for he would never have ventured the whole kingdom upon the doubtful issue of a battle, nor have done anything so rashly as to dismount himself, with all his nobility, to fight on foot, as the English did at the battle of Agincourt ‡; and if he had been reduced to that extremity, he would certainly have managed his affairs with more prudence and

* The English became masters of the duchy of Guienne about the year 1159, in consequence of the marriage of King Henry II. with Eleanor of Guienne. Charles VII. regained possession of the duchy in 1451; but Bordeaux having placed itself once more in the hands of the English, the French king reduced it finally on the 17th of October, 1453.

† Commines here alludes to the series of successes obtained over the English by the French under Joan of Arc.

‡ The battle of Agincourt was fought on the 25th of October, 1415. The English army, under Henry V., did not consist of more than 15,000 men; the French were, at the least, 50,000, and, by some computations, still more numerous. They lost 10,000 killed, of whom 9000 were knights or gentlemen. Almost as many were made prisoners. The English, according to Monstrelet, lost 1600 men; but their own historians reduce this to a much smaller number.

caution, as may be presumed from the manner of his conduct when King Edward was in France.

The king accordingly found himself under an absolute necessity to caress and pacify the King of England, and the rest of his neighbours, whom he perceived inclinable to peace, in hopes of receiving his money; and therefore he paid a pension of fifty thousand crowns punctually in London, and allowed it to be called tribute by the English. He also distributed sixteen thousand more among the King of England's officers that were about his person, particularly to the Chancellor*, the Master of the Rolls† (who is now

* Thomas Rotherham, Bishop of Lincoln, was chancellor in February, 1475. "He owed his elevation," says Lord Campbell, "to his own merits. His family name was Scot, unillustrated in England at that time, and, instead of it, he assumed the name of the town in the West Riding of Yorkshire in which he was born. He studied at King's College, Cambridge, and was one of the earliest fellows on this royal foundation, which has since produced so many distinguished men. He was afterwards Master of Pembroke Hall, and Chancellor of this University. For his learning and piety he was at an early age selected to be chaplain to Vere, thirteenth Earl of Oxford, and he was then taken into the service of Edward IV. Being a steady Yorkist, he was made Bishop of Rochester in 1467, and translated to Lincoln in 1471. In 1480, he became Archbishop of York, and he received a cardinal's hat from the Pope." In April, 1476, he was removed from the chancellorship, but reinstated in the office in September of the same year; and he "continued chancellor and chief adviser of the Crown during the remainder of the reign of Edward IV. He was considered the greatest equity lawyer of the age." On the death of Edward IV., he delivered up the great seal; but though "he did not take any active part in the struggles which ensued, he was so strongly suspected by Richard III., that he was detained in prison till near the end of this reign. After the battle of Bosworth he quietly submitted to the new government, but he was looked upon with no favour by Henry VII. He died of the plague at Cawood, in the year 1500, aged 76, and was buried in his own cathedral. He was founder of Lincoln College, Oxford, and showed his affection to the place of his nativity by building a college there, with three schools for grammar, writing, and music."—CAMPBELL's *Lives of the Chancellors*, vol. i. pp. 393—403.

† "John Morton was born at Bere in Dorsetshire, of a private gentleman's family, in the year 1410. He received his earliest education at the Abbey of Cerne, from whence he was removed to Balliol College, Oxford, where he devoted himself to the study of the civil and canon law, and took with great distinction the degree of LL.D. He then went to London, and practised as an advocate in Doctors' Commons, where he soon became the decided leader, and rose to such distinction by his

chancellor), the High Chamberlain, the Lord Hastings (a man of honour and prudence, and of great authority with his master, and deservedly, upon account of the faithful service he had done him), Sir Thomas Montgomery, the Lord Howard (who afterwards espoused King Richard's interest, and was created Duke of Norfolk), the Lord Cheney, master of the horse, Mr. Chalenger, and a certain marquis*, who was the Queen of England's son, by her first husband.

learning and eloquence, that he gained the good opinion of Cardinal Bourchier, who recommended him to Henry VI. He was sworn of the Privy Council by that sovereign, was made prebendary of Salisbury, and had the rich living of Blakesworth bestowed upon him. On the accession of Edward IV. he made submission to the House of York, and the new king continued him a privy councillor, appointed him Master of the Rolls, and conferred on him great ecclesiastical preferment, crowned with the Bishopric of Ely. Richard III. imprisoned him, but he contrived to escape to the Continent. Immediately after the battle of Bosworth, Henry VII. recalled him, raised him to the see of Canterbury on the death of Cardinal Bourchier, procured a cardinal's hat for him from Pope Alexander VI., and made him Lord Chancellor. He continued in this office, and in the unabated favour and confidence of his royal master, down to the time of his death, a period of thirteen years, during which he greatly contributed to the steadiness of the government and the growing prosperity of the country. Several important statutes were passed on his recommendation, including that which protects from the pains of treason all who act under a *de facto* king. In 1494, Morton was made Chancellor of the University of Oxford, and on the 13th of September, 1500, he died, after a lingering illness. Notwithstanding some arbitrary acts of government, which should be judged of by the standard of his own age, he left behind him a high character for probity as well as talents. His munificence was great, and he was personally untainted by the vice of avarice which disgraced the sovereign. Sir Thomas More, who was brought up in his house, says of him: ' He was a man no less venerable for his wisdom and virtue than for the high reputation he bore. He was of a middle stature, in advanced years, but not broken by age; his aspect begot reverence rather than fear. He spoke both gracefully and mightily; he was eminently skilled in the law; he had a comprehensive understanding, and a very retentive memory; and the excellent talents with which nature had furnished him were improved by study and discipline. The king depended much on his counsels, and the government seemed to be chiefly supported by him; for from his youth he had been constantly practised in affairs, and having passed through many changes of fortune, he had, at a heavy cost, acquired a great stock of wisdom, which, when so purchased, is found most serviceable.' "—See LORD CAMPBELL's *Lives of the Chancellors*, vol. i. pp. 417—425.

* Thomas Gray, first Marquis of Dorset.

Besides these great presents, he was also very generous to ambassadors; and all who were sent to him from the English Court, though their messages were never so harsh and displeasing, he dispatched with such fair words and large presents, that they went away very well satisfied with him; and though they were certainly assured (at least some of them), that what he did was only to gain time to effect his designs, yet their private interest prevailed with them to wink at it, highly to the detriment and disadvantage of their public affairs.

To all the persons of quality above-mentioned, the king gave considerable presents, besides their pensions. To the Lord Howard, besides his pension, he gave, to my certain knowledge, in less than two years' time, in money and plate, above twenty-four thousand crowns; and to the Lord Hastings, who was King Edward's chamberlain, he gave at one time one thousand silver marks in plate; and all the receipts of every Englishman of quality, except the Lord Hastings, are still to be seen in the chamber of accounts at Paris. This Lord Hastings was at that time High Chamberlain of England (an office of great reputation, and executed singly by one man). It was with great difficulty and solicitation, that he was made one of the king's pensioners, and I was the cause of it: for at the time when I was in the Duke of Burgundy's service, I had brought him over to his interest, and he allowed him a pension of a thousand crowns a year.* Upon my telling our king what I had done, he employed me to try what I could do to bring him over to his interest; for he had been his particular enemy in the Duke of Burgundy's time, after which he became a favourer of the young Princess of Burgundy, and was once like to have prevailed with the King of England to cross the seas again to assist that princess. I began our amity by letters; the king granted him a pension of two thousand crowns per annum, which was double what had been paid him by the duke, and sent one of the stewards of his house, called Peter Clairet †, with it; giving him express orders to take his receipt, that here-

* On the 4th of May, 1471, the Duke of Burgundy granted a pension of twelve hundred florins to Lord Hastings.—LENGLET, ii. 198.

† Pierre Cleret, esquire, councillor, and steward to Louis XI. for many years.

after it might appear upon record, that the lord chamberlain, chancellor, admiral, master of the horse, and several other great lords of England, had been at the same time pensioners to the King of France. This Peter Clairet was a very cunning man, and was privately admitted to the lord chamberlain, at his house in London; and having delivered his compliments from the king, he presented his two thousand crowns in gold (for to foreign lords of great quality the king never gave any other coin). The chamberlain having received the gold, Peter Clairet desired his lordship would be pleased to give him a receipt for it; the lord chamberlain scrupling to do it, he repeated his request, and entreated him that he would give him only three lines under his hand, directed to the king his master, lest his majesty should think he had embezzled it himself, for he was of a very suspicious temper. The lord chamberlain seeing he persisted (though his demand was but reasonable), replied, "Master Clairet, what you desire is not unreasonable, but this present proceeds from your master's generosity, not from any request of mine; if you have a mind I should receive it, you may put it into my sleeve, but neither letter nor acquittance will you have from me; for it shall never be said of me, that the High Chamberlain of England was pensioner to the King of France, nor shall my receipt be ever produced in his chamber of accounts." Clairet urged the matter no farther, but left the money, and returned his answer to the king, who was highly displeased at his not bringing a receipt: but he commended and valued the lord chamberlain above all the King of England's ministers, ever after paid him his pension constantly, and never asked for his receipt.

In this posture were affairs between the King of England and our master: however, the King of England was earnestly solicited and urged to assist the young princess, and he sent several embassies to our master to remonstrate with him, and to press him either for a peace, or a cessation of arms. For some of the privy council of England, and of the Parliament (which is of the same nature as our three Estates), were persons of wisdom and penetration, who came out of the country, and were not pensioners of France like the rest, and these pressed hard, that the King of England would interpose vigorously for the Princess of Burgundy;

urging, that we did but dissemble with them, and amuse them
with hopes of a marriage, as it very plainly appeared: for
at the treaty at Picquigny * the two kings had mutually
sworn, that within the space of a year, the King of England's
daughter should be sent for; but though the King of France
had permitted her to be styled the dauphiness, yet the time
was elapsed, and the lady had not been sent for. But all
the arguments his subjects made use of could not prevail
with King Edward, for several reasons. King Edward was
a voluptuous prince, wholly addicted to his pleasures and ease;
and having been, in his former expeditions, reduced to great
straits and necessities, he had no mind to involve himself
in a new war on this side of the water: the fifty thousand
crowns, too, which were punctually paid him in the Tower,
softened his heart, and hindered him from concerning himself in this affair. Besides, his ambassadors were always
bribed, and entertained so nobly, that they left the French
court well satisfied; though the king's answers were always un-
certain, in order to gain time; for they were always told that in
a few days the king would send ambassadors of his own, who
would satisfy their master in every point which had been
left in doubt.

As soon as the King of England's ambassadors were returned, about three weeks or a month later, sometimes more,
sometimes less (which in such cases is a great matter), the
king our master would send his envoys; but always new persons, and such as had not been employed in any overture
with the English before, to the end that if anything had
been promised by their predecessors, but not afterwards
performed, they might pretend ignorance, and not be obliged
to give an answer. The ambassadors, therefore, who were
sent into England, used their utmost endeavours to persuade
King Edward of the good inclinations of the King of France,
so that he might remain quiet, and not give the least assistance to the Princess of Burgundy: for both the King and
the Queen of England were so desirous of the match with
their daughter, that upon that account, not to mention
several other reasons, the king was willing to wink at these
proceedings, and take no notice of the remonstrances that
were made to him by some of his privy council, who repre-

* See book iv. chap 9. of these Memoirs.

sented to him how prejudicial it would be to the interest of the whole nation. Besides, he was afraid the marriage might be broken off, as it began already to be laughed at in England, especially by such as were desirous of war.

But to clear up this matter a little more, the king our master never designed to effect this marriage, by reason of the disproportion in their years; for the young lady *, who is now Queen of England, was much older than the dauphin, who is now King of France. † So that a month or two were spent in sending ambassadors from one court to another; and these artifices were made use of purely to gain time, and hinder the English from declaring war against our king: for certainly, had it not been in hopes of this marriage, the King of England would never so tamely have suffered our king to have taken so many towns, without endeavouring to have defended them; and had he declared at the outset for the young Princess of Burgundy, as our king was so fearful of bringing anything to a hazard, he would not have encroached so far upon the dominions of the House of Burgundy, nor have weakened it so much. My chief design in narrating these transactions is, to show the method and conduct of all human affairs, by the reading of which such persons as are employed in the negotiation of great matters, may be instructed how to manage their business; for though their judgment may be good, yet a little advice sometimes does no harm. This I have been assured of, that if the Princess of Burgundy could have been persuaded to marry Earl Rivers, the Queen of England's brother, they would have succoured her with a considerable number of troops; but that marriage would have been very unequal, for he was only an earl, and she the greatest heiress of her time.

Many overtures and bargains were made between the Kings of England and France; among the rest the King of France offered, that if he would join with him, and come over in person, and invade the Low Countries, which belonged to the Princess of Burgundy, his majesty would con-

* The Princess Elizabeth, who afterwards was married to Henry VII., by which match the Houses of York and Lancaster were united, was born in 1466.

† Charles VIII. was born on the 30th of June, 1470.

sent that the King of England should have all Flanders for
his share, and hold it without homage, and the province of
Brabant besides, in which the King of France would engage to reduce four of the chief towns at his own expense,
and afterwards deliver them up to the King of England.
Besides, he proffered (to lessen his charge in the war), to
pay ten thousand of the King of England's troops for four
months; and to lend him a large train of artillery, horses,
and carriages, for their conveyance, upon condition the
King of England would invade Flanders, whilst he made
war upon Burgundy in another place.   The King of England's answer was, that the towns in Flanders were large and
strong, and not easy to be kept when they were taken, and that
Brabant was the same; besides which, the English had no
great inclination to undertake such a war, upon account of
the commerce that was betwixt them and the Low Countries; but since the king was so generously inclined, as to
allow him a share in his conquests, he desired he would give
him some of the places he had conquered already in Picardy,
such as Boulogne, and others; upon surrendering up of
which, he would be ready to declare on his side, and would
send an army to his assistance if he would engage to
pay it.

Ch. II.—Of the Conclusion of the Marriage between the Princess of
Burgundy, and Maximilian Duke of Austria, and since Emperor.—
1477.

AFTER this manner (as I have said before), transactions
were managed between the two kings for no other purpose
but to gain time, by which means the Princess of Burgundy's affairs began visibly to decay; for of the few
soldiers that remained after her father's death, many revolted
from her to the king, especially after the Lord des Cordes
had quitted her service, and carried several others along
with him. Some were forced to leave her because their
estates or abodes lay very near or within the towns
which had declared for the king; others left her in hopes
of preferment; for in that respect no prince was so

noble and generous to his servants as our master.   Besides,
commotions and factions discovered themselves daily in the
great towns, and particularly in Ghent, which wanted to
have everything its own way, as you have already heard.
Several husbands were proposed to the Princess of Burgundy, and every one was of opinion there was a necessity of
her marrying, to defend those territories that she had left to
her, or (by marrying the dauphin), to recover what she had
lost.   Several were entirely for this match, and she was as
earnest for it as anybody, before the letters she had sent by
the Lord of Humbercourt and the chancellor to the king
were betrayed to the ambassadors from Ghent.   Some opposed the match, and urged the disproportion of their age,
the dauphin being but nine years old, and besides engaged
to the King of England's daughter; and these suggested the
son of the Duke of Cleves.   Others recommended Maximilian, the emperor's son, who is at present King of the
Romans.

The princess herself had conceived an extreme hatred
against the king, ever since he had basely given up her
letters; for she looked upon him as the occasion of the
death of her two principal ministers of state, and of the
dishonour and shame that was put upon her, when the
letters were delivered to her publicly in her council, as you
have heard before.   Besides, it was that which gave the
Gantois confidence to banish so many of her servants, and
to remove her mother-in-law and the Lord of Ravestain
from about her, and put her maids of honour into such a
consternation, that not one of them durst open a letter without first showing it to the Gantois, nor speak to their
mistress in a low tone.   This made the princess carry herself very distantly to the Bishop of Liège, who was of the
House of Bourbon, and a great promoter of this match with
the Dauphin, which certainly would have been very honourable and advantageous for the princess, had it not been for
the extreme youth of the dauphin; but the bishop was
unable to effect his object, so he removed to Liège, and that
affair was laid wholly aside.   Without dispute, it would
have been a very difficult matter to have managed that negotiation to the satisfaction of both parties; and I am of
opinion that whoever had undertaken it, would have gained

but little credit by it in the end.   However (as I have been informed), a council was held about it, at which Madame de Hallewin*, first lady of the bed-chamber to the princess, was present; and being asked her opinion about the dauphin, she replied, " That there was more need of a man than a boy; that her mistress was capable of bearing a child, which was what her dominions wanted more than anything else;" and this opinion prevailed.   Some condemned the lady for answering so plainly, others commended her, alleging that what she spoke was purely in relation to marriage, and the necessity of her lady's dominions, so that now the only talk was, who should be the person.   I am verily persuaded, that if the king had been inclined to have had her marry the Count of Angoulesme†, who is now living, she would have consented to it, so desirous was she to continue her alliance with France.   God, however, thought fit to appoint her another husband, for reasons unknown perhaps to us, unless it were, that it might occasion greater wars and confusions on both sides than could possibly have happened, had she married the Count of Angoulesme, for by this match the provinces of Flanders and Brabant sustained great miseries and afflictions.   The Duke of Cleves was at this time in Ghent with the princess, making friends, and trying all arts to effect a marriage between the princess and his son, but she had no inclination to it, for the character of the young gentleman pleased neither her nor any person about her court.   At last a marriage was again proposed between her and the emperor's son, the present King of the Romans, of which there had formerly been some overtures between the Emperor and Duke Charles, and a match concluded between them.   The emperor had in his custody a letter written by the young lady, at her father's command, under her own hand, and a diamond ring of considerable value.   The purport of the letter was to acquaint his imperial majesty, that, in obedience to her father's commands, she promised to accomplish the marriage with his son the Duke of Austria,

---

* Jeanne de la Clite, Lady of Commines, and wife of the Lord of Halewyn. She was a cousin of the author of these Memoirs.
† Charles of Orleans, Count of Angoulême, and father of King Francis I.

in the same form and manner as her father the Duke of Burgundy should think fit to prescribe.

The emperor sent certain ambassadors* to the princess, who was at Ghent; but, upon their arrival at Brussels, letters were sent to them to remain there, and that commissioners should be sent thither to receive and answer their demands. This was only a contrivance of the Duke of Cleves, who was extremely displeased at their coming, and endeavoured to send them back again dissatisfied; but the ambassadors continued their journey, for they had intelligence in the princess's court, or, at least, with the Duchess Dowager of Burgundy, who had been removed from the princess, as you have heard before, upon occasion of the letter. This lady, as I have been since informed, advised them to proceed with their journey notwithstanding these letters, gave them instructions how they were to behave themselves upon their arrival at Ghent, and assured them that the young princess and the greatest part of her court were well disposed towards them. Upon this information the ambassadors advanced, and taking no notice of the orders which they had received, went directly to Ghent, at which the Duke of Cleves was highly offended; but he knew nothing as yet of the inclination of the ladies. It was resolved by the council that the princess should give them audience, and, after they had delivered their credentials, should let them know that they were very welcome, that she would acquaint her council with their desires, and order them to return her answer; but that she could not give any farther answer about it.

The ambassadors being admitted to a public audience, presented their credentials, and then delivered their embassy, which was only to remind her Highness that the marriage had been concluded formally between the emperor and her father, by her own consent and approbation, as appeared by the letter under her own hand, which they produced, and the diamond ring which they said had been sent as a pledge

---

* According to Molinet (ii. 94.) these ambassadors were " My Lord Bishop of Mayence, Duke Louis of Bavaria, and a very elegant prothonotary named George Hesler." To this list Lenglet adds a certain doctor, William Mortingle; and Oliver de la Marche (ii. 422.) substitutes the Bishop of Metz for the Bishop of Mayence.

of the said marriage. Upon which the ambassadors insisted, that the young princess should be pleased to consummate the marriage according to the engagement and promise both of her father and herself; and then they conjured her to declare before the whole assembly whether she had written the letter or not, and whether she designed to make good her promise. The young princess, without consulting any, replied that she had written the letter and sent the ring in obedience to her father's commands, and that she freely owned the contents of it. The ambassadors thereupon expressed their humble acknowledgments, and returned very joyful to their lodgings.

The Duke of Cleves was extremely dissatisfied with her answer, as being contrary to what had been agreed on in council, and he upbraided the young princess for having acted very indiscreetly in this affair. To which she replied, " That it was not in her power to do any otherwise, since it was a thing agreed on long before, and she could not gainsay it." On hearing her answer, and finding that many about the princess were of the same opinion, he resolved to give over his own solicitations, and retire in a few days into his own country. And thus was the marriage concluded; and Duke Maximilian came to Cologne, where several of the princess's servants went to meet him, and carry him money, with which, as I have been told, he was but very slenderly furnished; for his father was the stingiest and most covetous prince, or person, of his time.* The

* The character of this emperor is thus sketched by Mr. Hallam: " Frederic III. reigned fifty-three years—a longer period than any of his predecessors ; and his personal character was more insignificant. With better fortune than could be expected, considering both these circumstances, he escaped any overt attempt to depose him, though such a project was sometimes in agitation. He reigned during an interesting age, full of remarkable events, and big with others of more leading importance. The destruction of the Greek empire, and appearance of the victorious crescent upon the Danube, gave an unhappy distinction to the earlier years of his reign, and displayed his mean and pusillanimous character in circumstances which demanded a hero. At a later season he was drawn into contentions with France and Burgundy, which ultimately produced a new and more general combination of European politics. Frederic, always poor, and scarcely able to protect himself in Austria from the seditions of his subjects, or the inroads of the King of

Duke of Austria was conducted to Ghent, with about seven
or eight hundred horse in his retinue, and this marriage was
consummated*, which at first sight brought no great advantage to the subjects of the young princess ; for, instead of his
supporting her, she was forced to supply him with money.
His armies were neither strong enough, nor in a condition to
face the king's ; besides which, the humour of the house of
Austria was not pleasing to the subjects of the house of
Burgundy, who had been bred up under wealthy princes,
that had lucrative offices and employments to dispose of ;
whose palaces were sumptuous, whose tables were nobly
served, whose dress was magnificent, and whose liveries
were pompous and splendid. But the Germans are of quite
a contrary temper ; boorish in their manners, and rude in
their way of living.

It seems to me, that upon good and solid advice, and not
without the particular grace of God, that law was made in
France, whereby women are excluded from the succession,
and no daughter suffered to inherit the crown, to prevent its
falling into the hands of a foreign nation, or prince ; which
the French would hardly endure, nor, indeed, would any
other nation ; for there is no sovereignty whatever but at
length revolves upon the natives. This may be seen in
France, where the English had great possessions for forty
years together, and at this present time have nothing left
of all their conquests but Calais and two little castles †, which
cost them a great deal to keep ; the rest they lost much
more easily than they conquered it ; for they lost more in

Hungary, was yet another founder of his family, and left their fortunes
incomparably more prosperous than at his accession. The marriage of
his son Maximilian with the heiress of Burgundy began that aggrandisement of the house of Austria which Frederic seems to have anticipated.
The Austrian provinces were re-united, either under Frederic, or in the
first years of Maximilian : so that at the close of that period, which we
denominate the middle ages, the German empire, sustained by the patri-
monial dominions of its chief, became again considerable in the scale of
nations, and capable of preserving a balance between the ambitious
monarchies of France and Spain."—HALLAM's *Middle Ages*, vol. i. pp.
449, 450.

* On the 18th of August, 1477.—See Gachard's edition of BARANTE's
Dukes of Burgundy, vol. ii. p. 577.

† Guines and Hames.

one day than they had gained in a year.   The same thing
is observable in the kingdoms of Naples and Sicily, and
other provinces, of which the French had possession for
many years together; in all which there is now no monu-
ment of their power remaining but the sepulchres of their
fathers.   And, if it were possible for a nation to admit a
foreign prince whose wisdom was great, and his retinue
small and well-regulated, yet they could hardly be prevailed upon to receive him with a great train, or suffer that
he should send for great numbers of his other subjects,
upon pretence of making war upon his neighbours; because
animosities will certainly arise among them, by reason of
their diversity of manners and disposition, and the violences
the new-comers will commit; for they cannot feel so much
love and affection for the country as those who were born
in it; especially if they aspire and aim at offices or employments which belong more properly to the natives. So
that it is very requisite for a wise prince, upon his coming
into a foreign country, to adjust all differences in his towns;
and, if he be not master of this virtue (which proceeds more
immediately from God than anything else), the rest, though
called virtues, will be of no advantage to him: and, if he
reigns long, he and all his subjects will find themselves involved in troubles, especially when he comes to be aged,
and his ministers and servants have no hopes of amendment
in his condition.

This aforesaid marriage was performed with great pomp
and solemnity, but affairs were not placed by it in a much
better posture; for they were both very young. Duke
Maximilian was a person of no great knowledge, both in
consequence of his youth, and of his being in a foreign
country. Besides, his education had been but indifferent,
and not serviceable for the management of great affairs;
nor, if it had been better, had he a sufficient body of troops
ready to have attempted anything considerable: so that
his poor countries were involved in great troubles, which
have continued to this day, and are like to continue. For
which reasons, as I said before, it is a great misfortune
to any country to have to seek a foreign sovereign; and
God has been very merciful to France in establishing
that law against the inheritance of the crown by a daugh-

ter.* A private or insignificant family may be much aggrandised by it; but a great kingdom, like ours, will always be greatly inconvenienced, and incommoded. A few days after the consummation of this marriage (if not at the very time of its negociation), the whole country of Artois was lost. (It will be sufficient for me to narrate the substance of events, and if I fail in terms, or the just computation of times, I hope the reader will excuse me.) The king's affairs went on prosperously, without any manner of opposition, during the winter; only now and then some overture or proposition was made, which came to nothing; for both sides being high in their demands, the war could not but continue. Duke Maximilian and the Princess of Burgundy had a son the first year, namely, the Archduke Philip†, who is now

* The rule that a woman was incapable of succeeding to the crown of France — *quod in regno Franciæ mulier non succedit* — was first proclaimed when Philip the Long succeeded to the throne in 1317, to the exclusion of his niece. "French writers," says Mr. Hallam, "almost unanimously concur in asserting that this exclusion was built upon a fundamental maxim of their government. No written law, nor even, as far as I know, the direct testimony of any ancient writer, has been brought forward to confirm this position. The text of the Salic law, which has, indeed, given a name to this exclusion of females, can only by a doubtful and refined analogy be considered as bearing any relation to the succession of the crown. It is certain, nevertheless, that from the time of Clovis, no woman had ever reigned in France; but, on the other hand, the crown resembled a great fief, and the great fiefs were universally capable of descending to women. And it was scarcely beyond the recollection of persons living, that Blanche had been legitimate regent of France during the minority of St. Louis. For these reasons it may be fairly inferred that the Salic law, as it was called, was not so fixed a principle at that time as has been contended. But however this may be, it received at the accession of Philip the Long a sanction which subsequent events more thoroughly confirmed. Philip himself, leaving only three daughters, his brother Charles mounted the throne; and upon his death, the rule was so unquestionably established, that his only daughter was excluded by the Count of Valois, grandson of Philip the Bold." — HALLAM's *Middle Ages*, vol. i. pp. 43, 44.

† Philip, Archduke of Austria, was born on the 22nd of July, 1478. He married Joanna, the second daughter of Ferdinand and Isabella of Spain; their nuptials were celebrated with great pomp and solemnity in the city of Lisle, on the 21st of October, 1496; and the first fruit of their marriage was the celebrated Charles the Fifth. Philip succeeded to the throne of Castile in 1506, and after a reign of two months, he died, on the 25th of September, 1506.

reigning: the next year they had a daughter, called Margaret[*], who at present is our queen; the third year they had a son, called Francis, after the name of Francis[†] Duke of Bretagne, who was his godfather. The fourth year the princess died of a fall from her horse, or a fever[‡]; but it is certain she had a fall, and some say she was pregnant. Her death was a great loss to her subjects; for she was a person of great honour, affability, and generosity to all people, and she was more beloved and respected by her subjects than her husband, as being natural sovereign of their country. She was tenderly attached to her husband, and of singular reputation for modesty and virtue. Her death happened in the year 1482. [§]

In Hainault the king was possessed of two towns, Quesnoy le Comte and Bouchain, both which he restored; at which several persons were highly astonished, knowing his aversion to any peace, and how desirous he was to take all,

---

[*] The Princess Margaret had been affianced in her cradle to Charles VIII. of France, but their marriage never took place; and when her intended husband espoused Anne of Brittany, she was returned to her native land under circumstances of indignity never to be forgotten or forgiven by the House of Austria. In 1495 she was betrothed to Prince John, the heir of the Spanish monarchy, and on her passage to Spain, in 1497, to join her husband, she was nearly shipwrecked. She retained, however, sufficient composure amid the perils of her situation to indite her own epitaph, in the form of a pleasant distich:

"Ci gist Margot, la gentil' damoiselle,
Qu'a deux maris, et encore est pucelle!"

Fortunately, her epitaph was not needed, as she reached Spain in safety, and was married to the Prince of the Asturias on the 3rd of April, 1497. On the 4th of October, in the same year, her husband died; and shortly afterwards Margaret returned to her native land. She subsequently married the Duke of Savoy, who died without issue in less than three years; and Margaret passed the remainder of her life in widowhood, being appointed by her father, the emperor, to the government of the Netherlands, which she administered with great ability. She died in 1530.

[†] This boy, born at Brussels, on the 10th of September, 1481, died on the 26th of December in the same year.

[‡] She died at Bruges, at about two o'clock in the afternoon, on the 27th of March, 1481.—MOLINET, ii. 302

[§] Commines is here in error as to the date; the year 1482 (old style) did not begin until the 7th of April, and the princess died on the 27th of March.

and leave the house of Burgundy nothing; and my opinion is, if he could have done it undisturbedly, and destroyed or divided those territories at his ease, he would not have failed to have done so. But, as he told me afterwards himself, he surrendered those towns in Hainault for two reasons; the first was, because he thought a prince had more strength and importance in his own country, where he was anointed and crowned, than he could have out of his dominions; and these towns were not in his territory. The other was, because there had been solemn oaths and great confederacies between the emperors and the kings of France, not to invade or usurp upon one another's dominions; and these above-mentioned places belonging to the empire were restored in the year 1478.* Upon the same account Cambray was delivered up, or put into a state of neutrality, the king being content to lose it; but the truth is, the inhabitants had received him at first upon those terms.

CH. III.—How King Louis, by the Management of Charles d'Amboise his Lieutenant, recovered many Towns in Burgundy, which the Prince of Orange had persuaded to revolt from him.—1478.

THE war was still carried on in Burgundy; but the king could not accomplish his designs, because the Prince of Orange was chosen by the Burgundians to be their lieutenant, and was secretly assisted by the Germans, for the sake of his money, and not out of love to Duke Maximilian; for there was not a man in the whole country that espoused his interest, at least during the time I speak of. These Germans were Swiss troops in search of adventure, and the Swiss are neither friends nor well-wishers to the House of Austria. The Burgundians had little assistance from them, although their pay was good; and no prince could have paid them better than Duke Sigismond of Austria, Maximilian's uncle, whose territories lay near, especially the

* The treaty of Trèves, by which the king restored all that he held in Burgundy and Hainault, bears date on the 11th of July, 1478.— LENGLET, iii. 540.

county of Ferrete, which he had sold, not many years before, for ten thousand florins of the Rhine, to Charles Duke of Burgundy, and had afterwards repossessed himself of it, without returning the money; and he keeps it now by force. Sigismond was never a person of great penetration, nor was he very just and honourable in his dealings, and from such allies no great assistance is to be expected. He was of the number of those princes I mentioned before, who know nothing of their own affairs but what their ministers of state are pleased to represent; and they are always rewarded for their indolence and supineness in their old age, as Sigismond was in this case.

During these wars his ministers, who had the sole administration of affairs, engaged him on what side they pleased; and for the most part he entered into an alliance with the King of France against his own nephew, and in the end would have given his hereditary territories (which were very large) to a foreign family, and disappointed his own relations (for though he had been twice married, he never had any issue); but at last, about three years since*, by the persuasion of another set of ministers, he conveyed all his estates to his nephew Maximilian (at present King of the Romans)†, reserving only a pension of about a third part of the revenue, without any authority or power; but, as I have been informed, he has often repented of it since; and if the story be not true, it is at least very probable. And such is the fate of princes who live so carelessly, and like beasts; and who certainly are most highly to be condemned, upon account of the great responsibility and duty that God has laid upon them in this world. These errors and imprudent actions are not so much to be laid to the charge of weak and stupid princes, as of those who are endued with a sufficient share of sense and understanding, and yet squander away all their time in pleasure and folly; such princes have no claim on our compassion when any misfortune befals them. And, on the other side, those who divide their time according to their age, sometimes in

* Sigismund transferred his hereditary estates to his nephew, the Archduke Maximilian, in 1492.

† Maximilian was elected King of the Romans on the 16th February 1486.

council, and sometimes in festivities and diversions, are much to be commended; and those subjects are happy who have such princes to rule over them.

The war in Burgundy was carried on for some time by help of the little assistance they received from the Germans: yet the king's forces were too powerful for them; for the Burgundians wanted money, and their garrisons were corrupted. The Lord of Craon, who was the king's lieutenant in those parts, besieged Dole*, the chief town in the county of Burgundy; which he presumed he should quickly make himself master of, upon account of the weakness of the garrison†: but his confidence proved much to his disadvantage; for, being surprised by a sudden sally, he lost some few of his men, and a great part of his cannon; which so highly raised the king's displeasure against him, that, being vexed at this unfortunate action, he began to think of sending a new governor into the county of Burgundy, not only upon account of this misfortune, but for the great and excessive sums of money which had been exacted in those parts. However, before the Lord of Craon laid down the command of the army, he engaged and defeated a party of Germans and Burgundians‡, in which action Monsieur de Chasteau-

* Dôle, formerly the capital of Franche-Comté, is a very ancient town in the department of Jura, in France. It stands on the right bank of the Doubs, and is well placed for trade on the canal that joins the Rhone and Rhine. It is pleasantly situated on the crest and slope of a hill; the streets are rather steep, but well built, and ornamented with fountains; and the neighbourhood is prettily laid out in gardens, vineyards, and promenades. A ruined aqueduct and amphitheatre, and some remains of the old Roman road from Lyons to the Rhine, mark the place as having been a Roman station. After its capture by the French, as related in the text, it sustained several remarkable sieges. In 1530, it was strongly fortified by the Emperor Charles V., into whose hands it had come with the rest of Franche-Comté. In 1636 it was fiercely, but ineffectually, besieged by the Prince of Condé; but Louis XIV. took it in 1668, and again in 1674, when he demolished the fortifications. At length, by the treaty of Nimeguen, the town, together with the whole of Franche-Comté, was made over to France.

† The chief commander in Dole was the Lord of Montballon; with him was a Knight of Berne, with about 900 Swiss; the garrison consisted in all of about 2000 fighting men. In their sally, they slew 800 or 900 of the French.—MOLINET, ii. 49.

‡ On the 15th of June, 1478.

guyon * (the greatest lord in Burgundy) was taken prisoner; but besides that, nothing of importance was done that day. I speak only by hear-say; though, if we may believe report, the Lord of Craon behaved himself with a great deal of valour and intrepidity in that engagement.

As I was saying, the king, for the reasons above-mentioned, resolved to put a new governor into the county of Burgundy; but not to meddle with the profits or advantages of the Lord of Craon's places †; he only deprived him of his guards, and left him but six men-at-arms, and a dozen archers to attend him. The Lord of Craon was grown very unwieldy, and retired well satisfied to his country-seat, where he lived in great ease and plenty. The king put into his post the Lord Charles of Amboise, Lord of Chaumont, a valiant, discreet, and diligent officer, who at once endeavoured to dissuade the Germans from assisting the Burgundians, and to induce them to enter into the king's service (not that he valued their service, but in order to facilitate his conquest of the rest of that country.) To this purpose the king sent to the Germans or Swiss (whom he styled *Messieurs des Ligues*), and offered them very handsome terms: first, a pension of twenty thousand francs, to be paid annually to their four chief towns, Berne, Lucerne, Zurich, and I suppose Fribourg, with their three cantons (or villages upon the mountains) Schwitz, which now gives name to the whole country, Soleure and Unterwald: secondly, twenty thousand francs per annum to particular persons, whose assistance he used in his negotiations; and he also made himself one of their burgesses, and their principal ally, and desired it might be declared in writing; but they made some difficulty of consenting to that, because, from time immemorial, the Duke of Savoy had been their principal ally; yet at length they consented, and promised to furnish the king with a body of six thousand men, to be employed continually in his service, upon condition that he should pay to each man

* Hugh de Chalon, son of William Prince of Orange.

† This Lord de Craon was at that time Governor of Champagne, Brie, Burgundy, and Touraine: he was also in possession of the government of several cities in France, and chief chamberlain to the king, besides enjoying the whole revenue of the barony of Craon in Anjou, which was his own inheritance.

four Rhine florins and a half every month ; and that number
of Swiss were retained in the king's service till his death.

A poor prince could not have managed this affair, which
turned so much to the king's advantage at that time ; though
I am of opinion, in the end it will be a prejudice to the
Swiss; for they are now so used to money (which was
scarce with them before), especially gold, that it was like to
have raised a civil war among them.   Otherwise, nothing
was capable of ruining or doing them any mischief; for
their country is so poor and mountainous, and the inhabitants of such a martial temper, that few or none of the neighbouring princes could think it worth their while to endeavour to conquer them.   When these treaties were agreed
on, and all the Swiss in Burgundy had entered into the
king's service, the Burgundian power was utterly broken
and destroyed ; and to bring matters to a conclusion, the
governor, Monsieur de Chaumont, after performing several notable exploits, besieged Rochefort *, a castle near Dole,
commanded by Monsieur de Vaudray, and took it by capitulation.   He also besieged Dole (where, as I said before,
his predecessor had been repulsed), and took it by storm.
The newly enlisted Swiss designed to have got in and defended it ; but a body of Frank archers getting in amongst
them (not with any suspicion of their design, but merely
from a desire of plunder), when they were entered, all of
them fell to pillaging, and the town was burnt and destroyed.

Not long after he besieged Aussone†, a very strong town;
but he held intelligence with the garrison, and wrote to the
king for offices for his friends before investing the town;
which were readily granted.   I was not upon the spot myself, yet I was well informed of what was done ; both by the
reports which were made to the king, and the letters which
were sent to him, and which I saw, as I was employed by the
king to return answers to many of them.   Aussone had but
a small garrison in it, and the chief officers being in treaty
with the governor, in five or six days the place was surren-

* Rochefort, in the department of Jura, about four miles from Dole.
† Auxonne, a fortified town on the Saône, eighteen miles from Dijon ;
celebrated for its fine bridge and causeway. It surrendered to the king
on the 4th of June, 1479.

dered; so that there remained nothing in all Burgundy for
the king to take possession of, but three or four castles upon
the mountains, to wit, Jou* and others; and he had the
obedience of Bezançon†, which is an imperial town, not at
all, or very slightly, subject to the county of Burgundy; but,
being seated as it were in the middle of it, paying a sort of
obedience to the prince of that country.   The governor took
possession of the town, and the inhabitants having paid him
the homage which they were accustomed to pay to the
princes who formerly had possession of Burgundy, he immediately quitted it.   After this expeditious manner was
the whole province of Burgundy subdued; and the king
watched the business very closely, fearing the governor desired some place might still hold out, in order to continue
longer in his command, and not to be moved into another
country to serve the king upon some other expedition: for
Burgundy is a plentiful country, and he managed it as if it
had been his own inheritance, so that the Lord of Chaumont,
as well as the Lord of Craon, made his fortune there.

This province for some time continued in peace, under the administration of the Lord of Chaumont; but afterwards several
towns rebelled, as Beaune‡, Semur§, Verdun‖, and others.
(I was then present, having been sent thither by the king
with the pensioners of his household. This was the first
time the pensioners had any officer to command them, and
since then they have never been without one.) Which towns

* Joux, a strong fortress on a high mountain in the department of
Doubs, was eventually surrendered to the king by the treachery of its
governor, who sold it to Louis XI. for 14,000 crowns. In later times,
Joux has acquired celebrity as the prison of Fouquet, of Mirabeau, and
of Toussaint l'Ouverture.

† Besançon, now the chief town of the department of Doubs, is a very
ancient city. Julius Cæsar mentions it as one of the largest and strongest
cities of Gaul; it was then the capital of the Sequani. In 456 it was
devastated by the Burgundians, and in 937 by the Hungarians. From
1184 to 1664 it was an imperial city; but in 1668 it was captured by
Louis XIV., and it has since belonged to France.

‡ Beaune, an old Burgundian town in the department of Côte-d'Or,
23 miles from Dijon. It is now chiefly celebrated for its wines.

§ Semur, a considerable town in the department of Côte-d'Or, built on
a granite rock on the left bank of the Armançon, 45 miles west of
Dijon.

‖ Verdun-sur-Saône, in the department of Saône-et-Loire.

c 4

were reduced by the wisdom and conduct of our general, and the indiscretion of the enemy. By this one may plainly see the vast difference there is between men ; which proceeds from the grace of God, who gives wise ministers of state to that nation He designs to support, and imparts to the prince that governs it wisdom to choose them ; and He has made, and does still make it appear, that in all things He will maintain our monarchy, not only in the person of our late master, but of our present king. Those who lost these places the second time were strong enough to have defended them, had they assembled their forces sufficiently soon, and thrown them into the towns : but they gave the governor leisure to draw his troops together ; which they ought not to have done, for, having intelligence of his strength, and knowing the country was entirely in his interest, they ought to have thrown themselves into Beaune ; which was a strong town, and more defensible than the rest.

The very day on which the governor marched out to invest a little town called Verdun, upon information of their weak condition, the Burgundians entered it, in their march to Beaune. They were in all, both horse and foot, six hundred choice men out of the county of Ferrete, commanded by several good Burgundian officers, of whom Simon de Quingey was one. They halted at a time when they might have got into Beaune ; which, if they had done, the place had been almost impregnable ; but for want of good counsel, they stayed a night too long, were besieged in Verdun, and taken by storm : and after that, Beaune was reduced, and all the rest ; the loss of which towns the Burgundians could never recover. I was at this time with the king's pensioners (as I said before) in Burgundy ; from whence I was summoned by the king, upon an information he had received that I had favoured certain of the citizens at Dijon about the quartering of soldiers. This charge, with other little suspicions, was the cause why he sent me away very suddenly to Florence.*

* The Cardinal of Pavia wrote to the Pope : " I know that there is coming to us, on the part of the King of France, an ambassador of high esteem in Gaul, with a mission of overweening pride. He is charged to threaten us with the withdrawal of the allegiance of the French, and with an appeal to a council, if we do not revoke the censures pronounced against the Florentines ; if those who murdered Giuliano de' Medici,

I obeyed him, as in duty bound, and, upon the receipt of his letters set out immediately for Italy.

CH. IV. — How the Lord of Argenton was sent to Florence during the Wars in Burgundy, and how he received Homage of the Duke of Milan, in the King's Name, for the Duchy of Genoa. — 1478.

THE design of my going into Italy was, to adjust a difference between two illustrious families, very eminent in those days. One was the family of the Medicis, the other of the Pacis *; which last being supported by the Pope †, and Ferrand King of Naples ‡, endeavoured to cut off Laurence

and those even who abetted his murder, are not punished; and, finally, if we do not abandon the war which we have just commenced."—SIS-MONDI, xi. 110.

* The history of the Medici family is too well known to require reca-pitulation in this place. The family of the Pazzi was one of the noblest and most respectable in Florence: numerous in its members, and pos-sessed of great wealth and influence. Of three brothers, two of whom had filled the office of gonfaloniere, only one was living at the period referred to in the text; and this man, Giacopo de' Pazzi, who was re-garded as the chief of the family, though far advanced in years, was, if we may credit the account of Politiano, an unprincipled libertine, who having, by gaming and intemperance, dissipated his paternal property, sought an opportunity of averting or concealing his own ruin in that of the republic. For a full account of the conspiracy of the Pazzi, see ROSCOE's *Life of Lorenzo de' Medici*, in BOHN's *Standard Library*.

† Sixtus IV., previously called Francesco da Savona, or Della Rovere, was the son of a fisherman. By his talents he became general of the Franciscan order, and afterwards Cardinal. He was elected Pope on the 9th of August, 1471. "He was the first," says Machiavelli, "who be-gan to show how far a pope might go, and how much that which was previously regarded as sinful lost its iniquity when committed by a pontiff." He died on the 13th of August, 1484, in the seventy-first year of his age.

‡ Ferdinand I., King of Naples, succeeded to the throne on the death of his father in 1458. His claim was contested by John of Anjou, sup-ported by many of the chief barons of the kingdom; but Ferdinand sub-dued them, and reigned for thirty years, after the discomfiture of his competitor, with success and ability. His character was, however, dark and vindictive, and his government was marked by a degree of ill-faith as well as tyranny towards his subjects that rendered him deservedly odious. He died in 1494.

de Medicis*, and all his adherents.   They failed in their
design upon Laurence de Medicis; but they slew his brother
Julian † in the great church in Florence ‡; and with him one
Franquein Noli §, a servant of the house of Medicis, who
threw himself before Julian in hopes to have saved him.
Laurence was severely wounded ‖, but made his retreat into
the vestry of the church, whose doors were of copper, and
had been given to the church by his father.¶   A servant**,
whom he had delivered out of prison only two days before,
did him good service, and received several wounds which

* Lorenzo de' Medici, surnamed the Magnificent.   For a full account
of this illustrious man, no less celebrated as a politician than as an
author and patron of science and art, see his *Life*, by Mr. ROSCOE, in
BOHN's *Standard Library*.

† Giuliano de' Medici, a younger brother of Lorenzo, was born in the
year 1453.   Between him and his illustrious brother there subsisted a
warm and uninterrupted affection.   Educated under the same roof,
they had always participated in the same studies and amusements.
Giuliano was well acquainted with the learned languages; he delighted
in music and in poetry, particularly in that of his native tongue, which
he cultivated with success; and, by his generosity and urbanity, he
gained, in a great degree, the affections of the populace.   At the death
of his father he was associated with his brother Lorenzo in the government of Florence, and he therefore incurred the animosity of the Pazzi.
He was assassinated on Sunday, the 26th of August, 1478.

‡ In the Church of Santa Reparata at Florence, since called Santa
Maria del Fiore.—MACHIAVELLI, p. 359. (BOHN's *Standard Library*
edition.)

§ Francesco Nori, a most intimate friend of the Medici.—MACHIA-
VELLI, p. 360.

‖ The assassination of Lorenzo de' Medici had been committed, in the
first instance, to Giovan Battista Montesecco, a distinguished condottiere in the service of the Pope; and he had willingly undertaken the
office, whilst he understood that it was to be executed in a private
dwelling; but he shrank from the idea of polluting the house of God
with murder.   Two ecclesiastics—Stefano da Bagnone, an apostolic
scribe, and Antonio Maffei, a priest of Volterra—were therefore selected
for the commission of the bloody deed.   Maffei aimed a blow at Lorenzo's
throat, which took effect behind his neck, and only roused him to defend
himself.   Drawing his sword, he drove off his assailants, and made
good his retreat to the sacristy.—See ROSCOE's *Lorenzo de' Medici*, pp.
142—144.

¶ Piero de' Medici, who died in 1472.

** This was probably Francesco Nori.—ROSCOE, pp. 144. 501.   Sismondi (xi. 97.) mentions two esquires, Andrea and Lorenzo Cavalcanti,
as having assisted Lorenzo de' Medici to beat off his assailants.

were aimed at Laurence. This assassination was committed at the time of high mass; and the moment appointed for its execution was when the officiating priest should begin the Sanctus. But it fell out otherwise than was designed; for, supposing all sure, some of the conspirators* ran to the palace to kill the senators who were there (which senate, consisting of about nine persons, has the whole administration of the affairs of that city, and is changed every three months); but they were ill supported, and having run upstairs into the palace, somebody shut one of the doors behind them; so that when they were got up, there were not above four or five of them, and those in such a terrible consternation, that they knew not what to say or do.

The senators and their servants that attended them, perceiving the astonishment of the conspirators, looked out of the windows, saw all the town in confusion, and heard Signor James de Pacis † and his accomplices crying out in the palace-yard, " *Liberta! Liberta! Popolo! Popolo!* " thinking by this means to have stirred up the people to take their part; but they were mightily mistaken, for the mob kept themselves very quiet; upon which James de Pacis and his adherents, despairing of success, betook themselves to flight. The governors and magistrates of the city, who were then in the palace, finding how matters went, imme-

* Francesco Salviati, Archbishop of Pisa, with about thirty followers. —MACHIAVELLI, p. 360.

† Giacopo de' Pazzi was the head of the family of that name, and at the time of this conspiracy was far advanced in years. He escaped from the city during the tumult; but on the following day he was made prisoner by the peasants of Romagna, who, regardless of his entreaties to put him to death, brought him to Florence, and delivered him up to the magistrates. He was immediately hanged from the palace windows; but, in consideration of his rank, his relatives were allowed to inter his body in the church of Santa Croce. " But," says Machiavelli (p. 363), " as if to mark the event by some extraordinary circumstance, after having been laid in the tomb of his ancestors, he was disinterred like an excommunicated person, and thrown into a hole outside the city walls: from this grave he was taken, and with the halter in which he had been hanged, his body was dragged naked through the city, and, as if unfit for sepulture on earth, was thrown by the populace into the Arno, whose waters were then very high." Such was the fate of a man who had enjoyed the highest honours of the republic, and for his services to the state had been rewarded with the privileges of equestrian rank.

diately seized upon the five or six who had got up into the
room, with a design to murder them and so get command
over the city, and caused them to be hanged at the bars of
the palace windows ; and among them was the Archbishop of
Pisa.* The senators finding the people unanimously declare
for the House of Medicis, sent immediately to all the passes
upon the road, to stop and apprehend all persons that were
found flying, and to bring them before the senate. James de
Pacis was presently apprehended, and with him an officer †
of the Pope's, who had the command of a brigade of men-at-
arms under the Count Hieronymo ‡, who was concerned in
the plot. Pacis and his accomplices were hanged from the
windows, but the Pope's officer had the favour of being beheaded. Several more were discovered in the town (and
amongst them Francisco de Pacis §), and all were hanged

* Francesco Salviati was appointed Archbishop of Pisa by Pope Sixtus IV., in opposition to the wishes of the Signory of Florence, who had
for some time endeavoured to prevent him from exercising his episcopal
functions. Hence his hostility to the Medici family. He appears to
have been totally unfit for his high preferment ; and his last moments,
if we may credit Politiano, were marked by a singular instance of fero-
city. Being suspended close to Francesco de' Pazzi, he seized the
naked body with his teeth, and relaxed not his hold even in the agony
of death.—Roscoe, pp. 141. 146.

† Giovanni Battista de Montesecco, a distinguished captain of Condottieri in the service of Pope Sixtus IV.

‡ Girolamo Riario was either the son or nephew of Pope Sixtus IV.
He was dignified by the Pontiff with the appellation of count ; and that
it might not to be an empty title, 40,000 ducats were paid out of the
papal exchequer for the principality of Imola, which was at once conferred on him, and to which was afterwards added the dominion of
Forli. This dilapidation of the patrimony of the Church to aggrandise
the relatives of the Pope was one of the most scandalous examples of
what was afterwards called the nepotism of the Court of Rome. Girolamo Riario married a natural daughter of Galeazzo Sforza, Duke of
Milan ; and was assassinated by three of his subjects, over whom he
had shamefully tyrannised, on the 14th of April, 1488.

§ Francesco de' Pazzi, a nephew of Giacopo, seems to have been the
leader in this conspiracy. He it was who gave the death-stroke to Giuliano de' Medici ; and such was the violence of his rage that, in striking
his victim, he wounded himself severely in the thigh. He then hastened
to his house, and endeavoured to mount his horse, in order to ride
through the city, and call the people to arms ; but he found himself
unable to do so, from the nature of his wound, and the great effusion
of blood it had caused. Soon after he was dragged from his bed
by the infuriated populace, and hanged from the windows of the

immediately; so that in the whole I think there were about fourteen or fifteen persons of quality hanged, besides servants who were killed in the town.*

Not long after this occurrence I arrived at Florence, in quality of an agent for the king, having made no stay since I left Burgundy, unless it were two or three days with the Duchess of Savoy, our king's sister, who received me very graciously.† From thence I proceeded to Milan, where I continued two or three days likewise, to solicit supplies for the Florentines, with whom at that time the Milanese were in alliance. The Milanese granted them very freely, because it was their duty, as well as the king's request, and sent them immediately a reinforcement of three hundred men-at-arms, and afterwards a greater number. In short, the Pope, immediately upon hearing of this tumult in Florence, ex-communicated the Florentines ‡, and caused his own army, in conjunction with that of the King of Naples, to march against them. The Neapolitan army was numerous, made a fine appearance, and had abundance of brave soldiers in it. They first besieged Castellina §, not far from Sienna, and took it, with several other places; so that it was a great chance that the Florentines were not utterly ruined, for they had enjoyed a long peace, and were not conscious of their danger. Laurence de Medicis, who was the chief man of that city, was but young ‖, and managed by persons of his own years; yet his judgment was of great authority among them. They had but few officers, and their army was but small. The

---

palace. His brother Renato was also hanged; and the rest of this devoted family were condemned either to imprisonment or exile ; with the single exception of Guglielmo de' Pazzi, who was connected by marriage with the Medici family, and spared accordingly.

* "The executioner," says Sismondi, "did not rest till 200 Florentines had perished in consequence of the conspiracy of the Pazzi. All those who had any relation of blood or connection of friendship with them, all those who had shown any opposition to the government, were torn from their houses, dragged through the streets, and put to death."

† The duchess granted him a contingent of 300 men-at-arms, to assist the Florentines against the Pope.—GUICHENON, ii. 145.

‡ The bull of excommunication was dated at Rome, on the 1st of Jun 1478.

§ La Castellina, a fortress about eight miles from Sienna.

‖ Lorenzo de' Medici was thirty years old at this time : he was bo on the 1st of January, 1448.

armies of the Pope and King of Naples were commanded in chief by the Duke of Urbin *, a wise man and a brave commander; with him there were likewise the Lord Robert d'Arimini † (who has since become a great man), the Lord

* Federigo da Montefeltro, second Duke of Urbino, succeeded his natural brother Oddantonio, in 1444. His character is thus sketched by a writer in the *Edinburgh Review* (xciv. 348.) : " He was a man for whom every human being that becomes acquainted with him is bound to express his love and reverence. He himself was of a loving, a reverencing, and a thankful nature. He was a soldier, yet a lover of books ; religious, but not bigoted ; energetic, but superior to anger ; severely bred, yet cheerful ; voluptuous by temperament, but not by habit ; a prince at once magnificent and paternal ; a right gentleman and fellow-creature; and, above all, a man true to his word in an age of liars. He had the good fortune to receive an excellent education, as far as one person could give it. His master understood the training both of mind and body. At eight years of age he was affianced, and at fifteen he was married. He studied the art of war under Piccinino and Sforza, whose different systems of daring and caution he is said to have combined. He had long and successful contests with Sigismund Malatesta, his neighbour, a ferocious dilettante, who committed murders, and struck medals. He had also the honour of being excommunicated by Pope Eugene the Fourth for adhering to an unfortunate friend ; became successively Captain-General of the Florentines, of the Duke of Milan, and of the King of Naples ; the last of whom he delighted by his honesty : was then general in the service of the Church ; refused to break his word with the most faithless of his enemies ; built a splendid palace and library, and kept a stately court. which did not hinder him from mixing in the pleasantest manner with his people; was chosen commander of the first National Confederation, prototype of the measure so often since desired by Italians, and so invariably nullified by their divisions ; helped to procure for his country, nevertheless, twenty-eight years of comparative tranquillity; attended with pomp the convocation of Pope Sixtus IV., who invested him with the dukedom, and married a nephew to his daughter ; received the order of the Garter from our Edward IV., which, though truly fit for such a mirror of knighthood, was bestowed with an eye to his good offices with the Pope; indulged his love of scholarship and philosophy, and patronised art and science ; rejected with scorn and horror a proposal to aid the Roman Court in the assassination of Lorenzo de' Medici and his brother, yet thought it no dishonour to conceal the plot from its objects, and to conduct troops against them for his papal employer; found himself, nevertheless, in a short time fighting on the side of Lorenzo against papal encroachment ; and on the 10th of September, in the year 1482, died of a fever, caught during a campaign, and rendered fatal by his refusal to quit his post."— See DENNISTOUN's *Memoirs of the Dukes of Urbino.*

† Roberto Malatesta, Lord of Rimini, one of the most celebrated among the condottieri captains of this period.

Constantine de Pesaro *, and several other officers, with two of the king's sons (that is, the Duke of Calabria †, and Don Frederick ‡, both of them still living), and many other persons of quality. They took all places which they besieged, but not with the same expedition as we do in France, for they were not so well skilled in the art of taking or defending a town; but for encamping and supplying their army with provisions, and providing all things necessary for a campaign, they understood that better than we do. The king's favourable inclination toward them was in some measure serviceable to them; but not so much as I could have wished, for I had no army with which to reinforce them beyond my own retinue. I stayed in Florence and its territories a whole year, and was nobly treated at their expense all the while, and with more civility at last than at first § ; but being recalled by the king, I returned home. At Milan I received homage of John Galeas ‖, Duke of Milan, for the duchy of Genoa; which homage was performed to me for my master by the duke's mother, in her son's name. After which I returned to my master, who received me very graciously, and admitted me more freely to his affairs than ever before, permitting me to lie with him, though I was unworthy of that favour, and many persons were more deserving of such a familiarity than myself. But he was so discreet and sagacious a prince, that no minister of his could possibly mis-

* Costanzio Sforza, Prince of Pesaro, another eminent condottiere, nephew of Francesco Sforza, Duke of Milan.

† Alphonso II., Duke of Calabria, succeeded his father on the throne in May, 1494. On the 23rd of January, 1495, he was forced to abdicate; and he died on the 19th of November following.

‡ Frederic, Prince of Tarento, became King of Naples in 1496, and died on the 9th of November, 1504.

§ It is not surprising that Commines was pleased at his treatment by the Florentines, when he took leave of them; for Ammirato (iii. 126) informs us that, at his departure, the Signory presented him with fifty-two pounds weight of wrought silver for the use of his table.

‖ Giovanni Galeazzo Maria Sforza became Duke of Milan on the death of his father in 1476. In 1488 he married Isabella, granddaughter of Ferdinand, King of Naples. He died on the 22nd of October, 1494, at the age of twenty-five; and the popular belief of the time was that he was poisoned by his uncle. At the period referred to in the text the young Duke was only nine years old, and it was on this account that his mother did homage for him.

carry in any negotiation in which he was employed, provided he acted directly according to his master's instructions,
and added nothing of his own.

Ch. V.—Of the Lord of Argenton's Return out of Italy into France,
and of the Battle of Guinegaste.—1479.

UPON my return from Italy I found the king our master
somewhat aged, and inclined to be sickly; yet not so much
as to neglect his affairs, which he managed himself, with
great prudence. He was still engaged in his wars in Picardy,
upon which his heart was mightily set, and the enemy would
have been no less fond of that country, if they could have
got it into their possession. The Duke of Austria (at present King of the Romans) having that year the Flemings at
his command, invested Therouenne*; upon which the Lord
des Cordes, the king's lieutenant in Picardy, assembled all
the forces that were in that province, and in the frontier
towns, together with eight thousand Frank archers, and
marched to relieve it. Upon news of his approach, the
Duke of Austria raised the siege, and, advancing to meet
him, they came to an engagement at a place called Guinegaste.† The duke had twenty thousand men or more out of
the country of Flanders, besides some few Germans and
about three hundred English, under the command of Sir
Thomas Abrigan‡, an English knight, who had been in the
service of Charles Duke of Burgundy. The king's cavalry,
who were much more numerous than the duke's, broke them
immediately, and drove them and their commander, the lord
Philip of Ravestain, as far as Aire.§ The duke took part in
the battle with his infantry.‖ In the king's army there were

* On Thursday, July 29, 1479.—MOLINET, ii. 200.
† Guinegatte, a small village in the department of the Pas-de-Calais.
The battle was fought on the 7th August, 1479. A detailed account
of it will be found in MOLINET (ii. 220.). The battle of the Spurs was
fought on the same ground between the English and the French in
1513 — See HUME, ii. 589.
‡ Elsewhere called Thomas D' Orican or D'Aurican.
§ Aire, a town on the Lys, in the department of the Pas-de-Calais.
‖ Molinet tells several stories of the duke's prowess in the fight. He
says that " he charged a man-at-arms so violently that he broke his

about eleven hundred men-at-arms of his standing forces.
They did not all follow the chase, but the Lord des Cordes,
who commanded in chief, pursued, and Monsieur de Torcy
with him; but though they behaved themselves very bravely,
yet it is not the duty of any commanding officer to follow the
pursuit.   Some of the van-guard and rear-guard retreated,
under pretence of defending their own towns; others fled
downright.   The duke's infantry kept their ground, though
they were vigorously attacked; but they had with them on
foot fully two hundred gentlemen, all good officers and brave
men, to lead them; and among these were the Count de Romont, a son of the house of Savoy, the Count of Nassau *, and
several others, who are still living   The bravery and conduct of these gentlemen kept the whole body together, which
was very marvellous, after they had witnessed the defeat of
their cavalry.   The king's Frank archers fell to plundering
the duke's waggons, and all that attended them, such as sutlers
and others; which being observed, some of the duke's forces
attacked them, and cut off a great number of them.   On the
duke's side the slaughter was greater, and more prisoners
were taken than on the king's side, but he remained master
of the field of battle; and I am of opinion, that if he had
marched back immediately to Therouenne, he would not have
met with the least opposition either there or at Arras: yet
he durst not venture to make the attempt, which proved
highly to his disadvantage; but in such cases no one knows
always what measures are best to be taken; and indeed the
duke had some reason to fear.   I speak of this battle only
by hearsay, for I was not present at it; but to continue my
discourse, I found it necessary to mention it.

    I was with the king when he received the news of this
defeat; he was extremely concerned at it, for he had not
been used to lose, but had been so successful in all his enterprises, that it seemed as if everything turned out according
to his pleasure.   Indeed, to speak truth, his judgment and

lance in three pieces; after which he knocked down a Frank archer with
a stick which he had in his hand; and, finally, he took prisoner a native
of Brittany named Alexander."
    * Engelbert, Count of Nassau and Vianden, Knight of the Golden
Fleece, and Governor of Brabant.   He was chief chamberlain to Duke
Maximilian.   He died in 1504.

penetration in state affairs contributed very much to his
success: for he would never risk anything, and always endeavoured to avoid a battle; nor was this fought by any
positive orders from him.   His armies were always so
numerous, that few princes were able to cope with him, and
he had a larger train of artillery than any of his predecessors.
His method was to assemble his troops on a sudden, and
attack those places that were ill provided and slenderly
fortified; and when he had taken them, he immediately put
into them such a strong garrison, with so much artillery,
that it was almost impossible to retake them; and if there
were any officer in the town able and willing to betray it for
money, he was sure to have the king for a customer, and
needed not to be afraid to demand an extravagant sum; for,
however exorbitant, his majesty would certainly have paid
it rather than venture a battle, or undertake a siege.   He
was mightily alarmed at the first news of this battle, supposing he had lost all, and that they durst not tell him the whole
truth; for he was aware that, had it been an absolute defeat,
all that he had got from the house of Burgundy in those
marches and elsewhere, would certainly have been lost, or at
least placed in very great danger.   However, as soon as he
was informed of the whole truth, he was better satisfied, but
gave orders that, for the future, no battle should be fought
without his knowledge and consent; and so he was reconciled to the Lord des Cordes.

From this very hour the king resolved to make a treaty of
peace with the Duke of Austria, but to manage the whole
negotiation purely to his own advantage; and so to curb the
duke by means of his own subjects (who, he knew, were
desirous to clip the wings of his authority), that it should
never again be in his power to disturb or injure him.   He
was likewise very desirous to make some new regulations in
the affairs of his own kingdom, particularly in regard to
delays in processes of law, in order thereby to control the
court of parliament; not to diminish their number or authority; but there were many things which occasioned his
hatred against them.   He was also desirous to establish in
his kingdom one general custom as to weights and measures;
and that all the laws should be written in French, in one
book, so as to prevent the frauds and prevarications of the

lawyers, which are greater in France than in any other nation in Europe, as the nobility have often experienced to their cost. And, doubtless, had God graciously permitted him to live five or six years longer, without being too much affected by disease, he would have done much good to his kingdom; and it was but reasonable he should do so, for he had oppressed and tyrannised over his subjects more than all his predecessors. But no man's authority or remonstrance could persuade him; it must have come of his own accord, as certainly it would, if God had not afflicted him with sickness: wherefore it is best to do good while we have time and God gives us health.

The treaty which the king designed to make with the Duke of Austria, his duchess, and their dominions, was, by the mediation of the Gantois, to make a match between his son the Dauphin (who is now our king) and the daughter of the duke and duchess, in consideration of which they should give him the counties of Burgundy, Auxerrois, Maconnois, and Charolois; and in exchange he would restore to them the province of Artois, retaining only the city of Arras*, in the same posture of defence as he had put it in; for the town was of no importance since the new fortifications had been added to the city. Before Arras fell into the king's hands, the town was much stronger than the city, with a large ditch and thick walls between them; but now the city was in a much better posture of defence, and was held of the king by the bishop of the place; contrary to the practice of the Dukes of Burgundy (at least for above a hundred years), who had always made whom they pleased bishop, and put in a governor of the city besides: but the king, to increase his authority, proceeded in a quite different manner, caused the town walls to be demolished, and new ones to be raised about the city, which before (as I said) was weaker than the town, with great ditches betwixt them; so that in effect the king gave nothing by the treaty; for he that was master of the city could command the town when he pleased. There was not the least mention made of the duchy of Burgundy, the county of Boulogne, the towns upon the Somme, or the chastellanies of Peronne, Roye, and Mon-

* These projects were afterwards realised by the Treaty of Arras, concluded on the 23rd December, 1482.

didier. The Gantois were extremely pleased with these proposals, and behaved themselves very disrespectfully to the Duke and Duchess of Austria; and some of the other great towns in Flanders and Brabant were equally importunate, particularly Brussels; which was very remarkable, for Dukes Philip and Charles of Burgundy had always resided there, and the Duke and Duchess of Austria had their residence there at that very time. But the long ease and pleasures that they had enjoyed under the above-mentioned princes, made them so far forget both God and their sovereign, that at last they brought down misfortunes upon their heads, and occasioned their own ruin, as you shall see.

CH. VI.—How King Louis was surprised with a Malady that for some time took away the Use of both his Senses and Tongue; how he recovered and relapsed several Times, and how he kept himself in his Castle at Plessis les Tours.—1479.

IN the year 1479, in the month of March, a truce was concluded between the two princes; and the king was very solicitous for a peace, especially in the quarter I have mentioned, provided that it proved very advantageous for his affairs. He began now to decline in age, and to be subject to infirmity; and as he was sitting at dinner one day at Forges, near Chinon, he was seized on a sudden with a fit that took away his speech. Those who were about him took him from the table, placed him near the fire, and shut up the windows; and though he endeavoured to get to them for the benefit of the air, yet some of them, imagining it for the best, kept him away. It was in March, 1480, when this fit seized upon him after this manner, which deprived him of his speech, understanding, and memory. As soon as you arrived, my Lord of Vienne, who were then his physician, you ordered him a clyster, and caused the windows to be opened to give him fresh air, and he came to himself immediately, recovered his speech and his senses in some measure, and mounting on horseback, he returned to Forges, for he was taken with this fit in a small village about a quarter of a league off, whither he had gone to hear mass.   He was diligently attended, and made signs for everything he wanted; among other things, he desired the official of Tours to come and take his confession, and made signs that I should be sent for, for I was gone to Argenton, which is about ten leagues off.

Upon my return I found him at table, and with him Master Adam Fumée * (physician to the late King Charles, and at present Master of the Requests), and Master Claude †, another physician.   He made signs that I should lie in his chamber; he understood little that was said to him, and could form no words; but he felt no manner of pain.   I waited on him fifteen days ‡ at table, and attended on his person like a valet-de-chambre, which I took for a great honour, and it gave me great reputation.   At the end of two or three days he began to recover his speech and his senses; and he fancied no one understood him so clearly as myself, and therefore would have me always to attend him.   He confessed himself to the official in my presence, for otherwise they could not have understood each other.   There was no great matter in his confession, for he had confessed a few days before; because whenever the kings of France touch for the king's evil, they confess themselves beforehand, and he never missed touching once every week. and if other princes do not the same, I think they are highly to blame, for there are always great numbers of sick people to be touched.   As soon as he was a little recovered, he began to inquire who they were who held him by force from going to the window; and being told their names, he banished them from court, took away their employments from some of them, and never would see them again.   From some, as the Lord de Segre §, and Gilbert de Grassay, Lord of Champeroux ‖,

* Adam Fumée, Knight, Lord of Roches St. Quentin in Touraine, councillor of the king, Master of Requests in the royal household, and Commissioner of the Great Seal of France.   He died in November, 1494.—ANSELME, vi. 420.
† Claude de Molins, physician and councillor to the king.
‡ The other editions erroneously say "forty days."
§ Jacques d'Espinay, Lord of Segre and Ussé, and captain of the town of Saint-Macaire, was the son of Richard d'Espinay, one of the chamberlains of Francis II., Duke of Bretagne.   He was afterwards appointed one of the councillors and chamberlains of King Charles VIII.
‖ See Vol. I. p. 258.

he took away nothing, but banished them from his presence.

Many wondered at this caprice, condemned his conduct, and affirmed they had done what, in their opinion, they thought for the best; and they spoke the truth; but the imaginations of princes are different, and all those who undertake to account for them are not able to understand them. He was afraid of nothing so much as of the loss of his regal authority, which was then very great indeed; and he would not suffer his commands to be disobeyed in the most trivial point. On the other hand, he remembered that his father, King Charles, in the illness of which he died, believed that his courtiers intended to poison him, at the request of his son; and this made so deep an impression upon him, that he refused to eat, and by the advice of his physicians, and of his chief favourites, it was concluded he should be forced to eat; and so, after great deliberation, they forced soup down his throat, upon which violence he died. King Louis, who had always condemned that proceeding, took it very angrily that they should use any violence with him; and yet he pretended to be more angry than he was, for the great matter that moved him was an apprehension that they would attempt to govern him in everything else, and pretend he was unfit for the administration of public affairs, by reason of the imbecility and unsoundness of his senses.

After he had thus severely handled the persons abovementioned, he made inquiry into what had been done in council, and what orders had been made during the ten or twelve days he had been sick; of which matters the Bishop of Alby*, his brother the Governor of Burgundy†, the Marshal de Gié‡, and the Lord du Lude, had the principal charge, as they were with him when he fell ill, and all lodged under his room, in two little chambers. He also insisted on seeing all letters and despatches which had arrived, and those also which arrived every hour; they showed him the most im-

---

* Louis d'Amboise, Bishop of Alby, was the son of Pierre d'Amboise, Lord of Chaumont. In 1480 he was appointed the king's lieutenant-general in Burgundy; and he died in 1505.

† See Vol. I. p. 34.

‡ See Vol. I. p. 271.

portant, and I read them to him. He would pretend to understand them, take them into his own hand, and make as if he were reading them to himself, when in truth he did not understand one syllable of them. Yet he would offer now and then a word, and make signs what answers should be given; but little business was despatched during his illness, till we could see what would be the event; for he was a master with whom it was necessary to deal straightforwardly. This indisposition continued about a fortnight; at the end of which he recovered his speech and senses pretty well; but he remained very weak, and in great fear of a relapse, for naturally he was not inclined to put confidence in his physicians.

As soon as he was a little recovered, he released Cardinal Balue *, whom he had kept a prisoner for fourteen † years, though the Pope and other princes had many times interceded for his liberation; of which crime he was absolved afterwards by an express bull from his Holiness, which the king had earnestly requested. When he was first seized with his illness, those who were about him took him for dead, and orders were issued for remitting an excessive and cruel tax, which, at the instigation of the Lord des Cordes (his lieutenant in Picardy), he had lately laid upon his subjects, for raising ten thousand foot as a standing force, and two

* The order for the cardinal's deliverance was in these terms :—" My Lord Chancellor,—After dinner assemble the whole council, and deliver Cardinal Balue from my hands, and give him up to the Archpresbyter of Lodau, in the name of the Legate, who has express commission from our Holy Father to receive him : that is to say, I give him into the hands of our Holy Father, or to the Legate for him, or to the Archpresbyter for the Legate, until he shall come. I have written to him to come with all haste, and accordingly I believe he will be at Orleans at Christmas; whither you will go, as well as the greatest personages I can find, to require justice at his hands. Look to the protestations which you have to make after dinner, and give them up when you deliver him. And God keep you, my Lord Chancellor. Written at Plessis du Parc, on the 20th day of December, 1480."

† Cardinal Balue was a prisoner for eleven years only, as he was arrested in April, 1469. See Vol. I. p. 165. of these Memoirs. He was confined in an iron cage of his own invention, in which it was impossible for him to stand upright, or to stretch himself at length. A special cage was made for his reception, at a cost of sixty livres.—DUPONT, ii. 217.

thousand five hundred pioneers, who were to be called the "Gens du Champ;" to which force he added one thousand five hundred men at arms, of his old standing forces, who were to fight on foot upon occasion, among the rest; besides which he caused a vast number of tents and pavilions to be made, and wagons to inclose all, in imitation of the army of the Duke of Burgundy; and this camp cost him fifteen hundred thousand francs a year.* When it was ready he went to review it, in a large plain near Pont de l'Arche in Normandy. In this camp there were the six thousand Swiss I mentioned before, and this number he never saw but this once. From thence he returned to Tours, where he was taken with a new fit, and lost his speech again, and for two hours everybody thought him dead; he lay upon a straw-bed in a gallery, with several people about him: the Lord du Bouchage and I devoutly recommended him to St. Claude, and all that were present concurred with our prayers; and immediately he recovered his speech, and walked up and down the house, but he was very weak and feeble; and this second fit took him in 1481. He still went into the country as formerly, and particularly with me to Argenton†, where he continued a month, and was very ill; from thence he went to Thouars, where he was also very sick; and he then undertook a journey to St. Claude, to whom we had recommended him, as you

* This armament awakened the suspicions of the King of England, as is proved by the following letter from Louis XI. to Lord Hastings: —" My good cousin,—I have been informed by some merchants of Normandy just returned from England, that there is a report in your country that I was at Boulogne, and intended to lay siege to Calais. My good cousin, as this matter affects me and my honour, I beg you to be so good as to tell my cousin your king, that I have no such thought, nor will I do or suffer any damage to the smallest village in the territory of Calais, and if any one should attempt to injure it, I would defend it to the best of my power. And I did not go from Plessis du Parc until the 26th day of May; but I am going to see my camp at Pont de l'Arche, which I have not yet seen; and I have ordered the Lord des Cordes and the Picards to be there at the end of this month; and I assure you that this is the truth, and my cousin the king shall find no departure from what I have promised him."—DUPONT, ii. 219.

† He was at Argenton in November, 1481; at Thouars in the months of January and February following; and at Saint-Claude in April.

have already heard.   At his departure from Thouars he sent me into Savoy, to oppose the Lords de la Chambre*, Miolans†, and Bresse (though he was privately their friend), for having seized upon the person of the Lord de Luy‡ in Dauphiny, whom he had recommended to be governor to his nephew, Duke Philibert.   He sent a considerable body of troops§ after me, whom I led to Macon against Monsieur de Bresse; however, he and I were agreed underhand.   Having taken the Lord de la Chambre‖ in bed with the Duke of Savoy at Turin, in Piedmont, he gave me notice of it, and I caused our soldiers to retire; for he brought the Duke of Savoy to Grenoble, where the Marshal of Burgundy, the Marquis de Rothelin, and myself, went to receive and compliment his highness.   The king sent for me to meet him at Beaujeu, in Beaujolois.   I was amazed to find him so thin and weak, and wondered how he had strength enough to bear the fatigue of travelling as he did; but his great spirit carried him through all difficulties.

At Beaujeu he received advice that the Duchess of Austria was dead of a fall from her horse.   She had been set upon a hot-headed young nag, that threw her down against a piece of timber, which was the occasion of her death.   Others said she died of a fever, not of her fall; but be it as it may, she died not many days after, to the great detriment of her friends and subjects; for after her death they never had peace or prosperity.   The people of Ghent and other towns had a greater love and respect for her than her husband, as she was their natural sovereign.   This misfortune happened in

---

* Louis, Count of La Chambre and Léville, and Viscount of Maurienne, in Savoy.

† Louis de Myolans, appointed Marshal of Savoy in 1478.

‡ Philibert de Grolée, Knight, Lord of Huis, councillor and chamberlain of Louis XI., and Governor of Lyons.

§ Two hundred Frank archers of the King's guard.

‖ "The Count de Bresse, being informed of the king's intention, proceeded to Turin at daybreak on the day before St. Sebastian's day, the 19th of January, 1480, accompanied by Thomas de Saluces, brother of the marquis.   They entered the Castle of Turin, and went into the duke's bed-chamber, where the Count de la Chambre was sleeping; whom Thomas de Saluces, by command of the Count de Bresse, seized, saying, 'You are prisoner of the King of France;' and he had him put in prison."—GUICHENON, ii. 42.

the year 1482.* The king told me the news with a great deal of joy and satisfaction; being extremely pleased that the two children† were under the tutelage of the Gantois, who (he knew) were inclined to any mischief that might weaken the power of the house of Burgundy; and now he thought this was the time to attempt something, because the Duke of Austria was young, with his father still living, involved in war on every side, a stranger, and his forces very weak, because of the covetous temper of his father the emperor.

From that time the king began to deal with the Gantois by means of his agent the Lord des Cordes, about the marriage of his son the dauphin with the Lady Margaret, the duke's daughter, who is at present our queen. The Lord des Cordes applied himself in this affair to one William Ryn ‡, pensionary of the town (a cunning, subtle man), and to Coppenol §, the town-clerk, who was a hosier, and a person of great reputation among the people, who, in times of trouble, are soonest wrought upon by such folk.

The king returned to Tours, and kept himself so close, that very few were admitted to see him; for he was grown marvellously jealous of all his courtiers, and afraid they would either depose him, or deprive him of some part of his authority.‖ He removed from about him all his old servants,

---

* On the 27th of March. Her feminine delicacy was so great, that she preferred to die rather than allow a surgeon to examine her wounds.

† Margaret and Philip. See pp. 16, 17.

‡ William Ryn, appointed tenth echevin of Ghent in 1476, and town councillor in 1482; beheaded on the 8th of August, 1484.

§ John Coppenolle, a hosier of Ghent, "a man of no better condition than William Ryn, and nevertheless appointed steward to the king of France, with a pension of six hundred francs a year." He was beheaded at Ghent on the 11th of August, 1491.

‖ "He immured himself," says Sir Walter Scott, "in his castle of Plessis, intrusting his person to the doubtful faith of his Scottish mercenaries. He never stirred from his chamber; he admitted no one into it; and wearied Heaven and every saint with prayers, not for the forgiveness of his sins, but for the prolongation of his life. With a poverty of spirit totally inconsistent with his shrewd worldly sagacity, he importuned his physicians, until they insulted as well as plundered him. Bodily health and terrestrial felicity seemed to be his only object. Making any mention of his sins when talking on the state of his health was strictly prohibited; and when, at his command, a priest recited a

especially if they had any extraordinary familiarity with him; but he took nothing from them, and only commanded them to retire to their posts or country seats: but this lasted not long, for he died soon after. He did many odd things, which made some believe his senses were impaired; but they knew not his character. As to his suspicion, all princes are prone to it; especially those who are wise, and who have many enemies, and have offended many people, as our master had done. Besides, he knew he was not beloved by the nobility of the kingdom, nor by many of the commons; for he had taxed them more than any of his predecessors, though he now had some thoughts of easing their burdens, as I said before; but he should have begun sooner. King Charles VII. was the first prince who (by the assistance of several wise and good knights, who had served him in the expulsion of the English out of Normandy and Guienne) gained that point of laying taxes upon the country at his pleasure, without the consent of the three Estates of the kingdom; but then his occasions were great, as it was indispensable to secure his new conquests, and to disperse the free companies who were pillaging the kingdom. Upon which the great lords of France consented to what the king proposed, upon promise of certain pensions in lieu of the taxes which were to be levied upon them.

Had this king lived long, and kept with him those who were then of his council, without dispute he would by this time have enlarged his dominions very considerably; but, considering what has already occurred, and what is likely to follow upon it, he has laid a great load both upon his own soul, and the souls of his successors, and has given his kingdom a cruel wound, which will bleed a long time; namely, by establishing a terrible band of paid soldiers, in imitation of the princes of Italy. King Charles at his death had laid taxes upon all things in his kingdom, amounting to one million eight hundred thousand francs, and maintained about

prayer to St. Eutropius, in which he recommended the king's welfare both in body and soul, Louis caused the two last words to be omitted, saying it was not prudent to importune the blessed saint by too many requests at once. Perhaps he thought, by being silent on his crimes, he might suffer them to pass out of the recollection of his celestial patrons, whose aid he invoked for his body."

one thousand seven hundred men at arms, constantly in pay, and in the nature of guards, to preserve the peace, and secure the provinces of the kingdom ; by which means, for a long while before his death, there was no free quarter, nor riding up and down the country, which was a great ease to the people. At the death of our master, he raised annually four million seven hundred thousand francs ; and had about four or five thousand men at arms, and above twenty-five thousand foot soldiers ; so that it is no wonder if he entertained such jealousies and fears of his subjects, and fancied he was not beloved by them. √ Yet he made one very great mistake : he had no confidence in those who had been brought up and received their preferments under him ; of whom he might have found many that would have died before they would have forsaken him in anything. ⌐ In the first place, nobody was admitted into the Plessis du Parc (which was the place where he resided) but his domestic servants and his archers, who were in number four hundred, some of whom kept constant guard at the gate, while others patrolled continually about to prevent its being surprised. No lord nor person of quality was permitted to lodge in the castle, nor to enter with any of his retinue ; nor, indeed, were any of them admitted but the Lord de Beaujeu, the present Duke of Bourbon, who was his son-in-law. Round about the castle of Plessis he caused a lattice of iron bars to be set up, and spikes of iron to be planted in the wall, with several points projecting along the ditch, wherever there was a possibility for any person to enter. Besides which, he caused four watch-houses to be made of thick iron and pierced with holes, out of which his archers might shoot at their pleasure ; and these were a very clever invention and cost above twenty thousand francs ; in them he placed twenty of his crossbow men, who were upon guard night and day, with orders to fire upon any man that ventured to come near, before the opening of the gate in the morning. He also persuaded himself that his subjects would be apt to divest him of his power, and take the administration of affairs upon themselves, when they saw their opportunity ; and, indeed, there were some persons about the court that consulted together how they might get into the Plessis, and despatch affairs according to their own wishes ; but they durst not attempt it, and they acted wisely, for the king had provided against every attack. He often changed his bed-chamber attendants, and all the rest of his servants, alleging that nothing was more agreeable to nature than novelty. For conversation he kept only one or two with him, and those of inferior condition, and of no great reputation; who, if they had been wise, would have clearly seen that as soon as he was dead, the best they could expect would be to be turned out of all their employments; and so it happened. Those persons never acquainted him with anything that was sent or written to him, unless it concerned the preservation of the State, or the defence of the kingdom; for he concerned not himself for anything, but to live quietly and peaceably with all men. He gave his physician * ten thousand crowns a month, and within the space of five months he received of his majesty above fifty-four thousand. He also gave large estates to the church; but this gift was never ratified, for the church was thought to have too much already.

A Treaty between Louis XI. of France, and Maximilian Duke of Austria, as well for himself as his Children, made at Arras, December 23. 1482.

1. THERE shall be a perpetual peace, union, and alliance between the king, dauphin, and kingdom, their countries, territories, and subjects on the one part; and Duke Maximilian of Austria, Duke Philip, and the Lady Margaret of Austria, his children, their countries, territories, and subjects, on the other; laying aside all rancour and enmity towards one another, and any or all manner of injuries, either in word or deed.

2. For the more firm establishing of the peace, a treaty of marriage is agreed to between the dauphin, the king's son and heir-apparent to the crown, and the Lady Margaret of Austria, only daughter of the said duke, and of the late Mary of Burgundy, only daughter of Duke Charles of Burgundy, to be solemnised when the said lady shall be of fit age.

3. As soon as the peace is proclaimed, the said lady shall

* His physician in ordinary was named Jacques Coitier. He also held the office of Vice President of the Chambre des Comptes, of which he became President in 1482. He died on the 29th of October, 1506.

forthwith be conducted to Arras, and be put into the hands of Monsieur de Beaujeu, or another prince of the blood authorised by the king for that purpose; and the king shall take care to bring her up as his eldest daughter, the wife of the said dauphin.

4. Upon the delivery of the said lady, Monsieur de Beaujeu shall swear solemnly, in the presence of the princes and lords who shall conduct her, in the king's name, that the dauphin, when she comes of age, shall take her in marriage, and proceed to the consummation of the same.

5. The like oath Monsieur de Beaujeu shall take in the name of the dauphin, being authorised thereunto by the king, upon the account of his youth.

6. In consideration of this marriage, the Duke of Austria and the states of his country, agree in their own names, and in that of Duke Philip, that the countries of Artois, Burgundy, the lands and signories of Maconnois, Auxerrois, Salins, Bar-sur-Seine, and Noyers, shall be given in dower with her to the dauphin, to be enjoyed by them, their heirs by that marriage, whether male or female, for ever; but in failure thereof, to return to Duke Philip and his heirs. And seeing these countries, and the greatest part of the province of Artois, are at present in the king's possession, it is agreed they shall be the dowry and inheritance of the said lady, to be enjoyed by the dauphin her intended husband, and her heirs. But in case those countries should come into any other hands than those of the dauphin and the issue of this marriage, the king, dauphin, and their successors, kings of France, may in that case retain the said counties of Artois and Burgundy, with the other signories, till the king's pretensions to Lisle, Douay, and Orchies are determined. And in case they are not adjudged to return to him, he and his successors shall pretend no right to them; but the earls and countesses of Flanders shall enjoy them as formerly. Moreover, as soon as the said lady shall arrive at Arras, she shall be there received and declared Countess of Artois and Burgundy, and lady of the other territories.

7. From thenceforward the said county of Artois, except the castle and bailiwick of St. Omer, shall be governed according to its ancient rights and privileges, as well the cities as the open country, by and in the name of the dauphin

her future husband; and the domain and revenue, with the administration of justice, and other privileges, shall appertain to him.

8. The same thing shall be done in respect to the county of Burgundy and the other signories.

9. The king, at the request of the said duke and states, shall restore Arras to its ancient government, under the administration of the dauphin, by appointing officers for that purpose; the king is content that the dauphin shall do so.

10. As to the town, castle, and bailiwick of St. Omer (which is in the province of Artois), it is comprehended with the said county of Artois in the dower of the said Lady Margaret, and so shall be forthwith delivered into the possession of the dauphin, upon the completing and consummation of the marriage with her.

11. The guarding and government of the said town, castle, and bailiwick from henceforward is to be put into the hands of the inhabitants, in order to be given up to the dauphin upon the consummation of his marriage; and they shall make solemn oath before the king or his commissioners, that during the minority of the lady they will not deliver them up to the Duke of Austria, Duke Philip, or their agents.

12. The like oath shall be taken by them to the Duke of Austria, that they shall not deliver them up to the king, dauphin, or their agents, during the minority, and till the consummation of the marriage.

13. For the better support of the town, the domain thereof, &c., shall be applied towards it during the minority; neither shall the town and bailiwick pay the tax called the Ordinary Aid of Artois.

14. As to the appointing of officers, such as bailiff, &c., the duke, as father of the lady, shall have the nomination during the said time, and the dauphin, as her intended husband, the institution: but if the said lady should happen to die before the consummation of the marriage, the inhabitants shall restore the town, with its appendages, to the Duke of Austria, and Duke Philip, his son, or successors.

15. The privileges of the town shall be maintained, and justice administered in the same manner as formerly; and the estates of the place shall take care to provide for the guard of it.

16. As to the neighbouring forts and castles, the lords of them shall bind themselves not to injure, but to assist them in defence of the same.

17. If a war should break out between the king and the duke, they shall not intermeddle, or receive a garrison from either.

18. It shall be free for the inhabitants of all conditions to go and traffic, or otherwise, into France, or the dominions of the Duke of Austria, and other neighbouring kingdoms and countries.

19. Upon the surrendering of the town to the dauphin and the Lady Margaret, upon their marriage, those princes shall make oath to maintain it, as a member of the county of Artois, and the county of Artois, in all its privileges, as their predecessors the counts and countesses of Artois have done, without innovation in the government there.

20. The king resigns the provision made for the town by the late Duchess of Austria, and the duke her husband, for the discharge of the debts and rents due from it.

21. The king and the dauphin oblige themselves to pay the debts contracted by the duchess, the Duke of Burgundy her father, and their other predecessors, by mortgaging the revenues of the said county.

22. The yearly pensions assigned by the duchess, Duke Charles, &c., upon the domain of the said counties and signories of Burgundy and Artois, shall be continued.

23. In consideration of this lady's dowry, the king and dauphin renounce all claims and pretensions upon the duchies, counties, goods, moveables and immoveables whatsoever, remaining after the death of the duchess, the lady's mother.

24. In case, upon the account of death, or otherwise, the said marriage should not be consummated, the dowers, and the said counties and signories shall be restored to the Duke of Austria; but at the same time with a salvo to the king's pretensions to the towns and chastellanies of Lisle, Douay, and Orchies.

25. If, after the consummation of the marriage, the dauphin should die (whether he leaves children or not by the said lady), she shall enjoy the counties of Artois and Burgundy as her portion, and withal fifty thousand livres of

Tournay yearly as dower, assigned to her in Champagne, Berry, and Touraine.

26. If she should happen to die before the Dauphin, the children shall succeed in those territories that are her portion; and in case there are no children, they shall revert to the next heirs.

27. Neither the King nor Dauphin shall, during the minority of Duke Philip, claim to have the government of the said countries of Brabant, Flanders, &c., but shall leave them in the condition they are now in.

28. If Duke Philip should die under age, and the said lady becomes his heir, the King and Dauphin shall agree that the government of the said countries shall continue upon the same footing.

29. In case Duke Philip die without issue of his body, and that his dominions fall to his sister and her heirs, who shall also be heirs to the crown of France, the King and the Dauphin shall engage that the said countries shall be maintained in all their ancient rights and privileges.

30. The King's sovereignty over the country of Flanders is acknowledged by the Duke and the States, and Duke Philip, when he comes of age, shall do homage for the same in the usual form.

31. The King confirms all the ancient and modern privileges of the three members of Flanders, and particularly the towns and corporations of the country of Flanders, the towns and chatellanies of Lisle, Douay, and St. Omer.

32. The inhabitants of Antwerp shall also have their privileges maintained.

33. Customs and tolls shall be paid as usual.

34. Margaret, Duchess of Burgundy, widow of the late Duke Charles, is comprehended in this treaty, and she shall have the full enjoyment of the lands of Chaussins and La Pierrière, upon the repaying of twenty thousand crowns in gold to the country of Burgundy; and in case, by the death of the young duke, those countries should come into the hands of France, she shall be maintained fully in her dower, and find all kind assistance, as a cousin and relation, from the King and Dauphin.

35. A general act of indemnity is agreed to on both sides, in as ample manner as could be desired by offenders.

36. The subjects and adherents of both parties shall be reinstated in their dignities, benefices, fiefs, lands, signiories, and other inheritances, rents, &c., without being called in question for any thing that happened during the war, and notwithstanding any declarations, confiscations, and arrests, to the contrary whatsoever.

37. If the inheritances of any persons who followed the fortune of the adverse party have been sold in court for the payment of their debts, they shall forthwith re-enter upon the peace, and pay their debts within a year after; if not, the order of court shall stand.

38. In case the debts were purely personal, for which the inheritance of the followers of the opposite party have been sold, the debtor shall return to his inheritance, without making any compensation to the purchaser.

39. The subjects on both sides shall return to the possession of their immoveable goods, as well before the troubles begun in Duke Charles's time, as after.

40. As to the profits and income of estates, which have been levied by the commanders of the respective parties, those that received them shall never be accountable for them, and no prosecution in law, upon that account, shall take effect against them.

41. All personal debts granted by the princes, or pursuant to their order, shall be theirs who had the grant of them. As to all other moveables in being upon the peace, they shall belong to those that had them before the war, without any molestation or any impediment whatsoever.

42. The town of St. Omer and its dependencies, are fully discharged of all rewards, remissions, &c., which have been granted them.

43. The Duke of Austria and his children are, by this treaty, fully discharged of all debts they may owe to those who adhered to the contrary party, and they and their descendants shall never be molested for them.

44. Upon returning to their possessions, nobody shall take any oath to the prince or lord under whom the said possessions are, saving vassals and feoffees.

45. The widow of the late Peter of Luxemburg, and the ladies Mary and Frances, her daughters, shall be restored to their estates, as well those which they enjoyed in the

lifetime of Lewis de Luxemburg, Count of St. Paul, Madame Jane de Bar his wife, and John de Luxemburg, Count of Marle, their eldest son. In like manner, Monsieur de Croy, Count of Porcien, is restored particularly to the County of Porcien, the granaries belonging to the castle of Cambarsay, Montcornet, and other appanages, in the signiory of Bar-sur-Aube, and other places in Picardy.

46. The King shall favour the Count de Romont, in his pretensions to the county of Romont, and the county of Vaux; and as for the Princes and Princesses of Orange, the Count of Joigny, Liepart de Chalon, the Lord of Lorme, Messieurs William de la Beaume, Du Lain, Claude de Toulongeon, and the Sieur de la Bastie, they are comprehended in this peace, and shall be re-instated.

47. In like manner, the monks of Anchin are restored to their abbey; so are those of the church and abbey of St. Wast d'Arras, and the inhabitants of Arras, whether they have withdrawn into the one or the other prince's country, shall freely return home, and follow their respective occupations, without any let or hindrance, as before the war.

48. The heirs of those who have been put to death for adhering to the party opposite to him under whom they lived, shall return to their estates and succeed. The widows also of such shall have their rights and dowries.

49. As to persons enjoying their own, they shall not be obliged to go and reside where their estates are, either in the one or the other countries.

50. The King consents to free the county of Artois, the towns of Arras, Aire, Lens, Bapaume, Bethune, their villages, and the chastellany of Lilliers, from the tax called the ordinary aid of Artois, and all other extraordinary aids, for the space of six years, from the day of the date of the peace: and seeing the late Duchess of Austria hath exempted the hospitals of Douay, &c., from paying any taxes to the county of Artois for their inheritances, the King and Dauphin confirm the same privileges.

51. Those who shall return to their possessions shall not be accountable for any rent due during the war; and the lands which, by reason of the war, have been untilled, shall have no rent paid for them till next Christmas.

52. Those who, at their entry upon fiefs and inheritances,

are obliged to pay fines and other duties to their lords, shall have three months allowed them to do it, after the peace, and so remain unmolested.

53. The nobility and feoffees of the territories of the Duke of Austria, and his son Philip, shall not be obliged to serve under any but them, or their lieutenants; and in case that they, or one of them, should be in the King's service, if they are not there in person, the other shall not be obliged to serve in person, but may send another.

54. The decrees and sentences made in the court of Malines, as also of the grand council of the Dukes Philip and Charles, the Duchess Mary and the present duke, shall stand good, and not be brought into question before the Parliament of Paris, or any other sovereign court. But those suits and clauses which are not yet decided in the said courts, shall be brought before the Parliament of Paris, and there be determined.

55. In like manner, mortmains, compositions, new acquests, and ennoblings, made by the said dukes and duchess, shall remain good; only the subjects of the county of Artois shall be obliged to take new patents for their nobility, which shall be granted without any charge to them.

56. The abolitions, remissions, and pardons, granted by Duke Charles, his daughter, and the dukes of Austria, to the counties of Flanders, Lille, Douay, Artois, and Burgundy, shall be valid; only the subjects of Artois shall sue them out as before.

57. The inhabitants on the frontiers of the duke, and others subject to the French crown, cited to appear in person in the court of Parliament, or before the royal judges, shall appear only by their proctors, during the minority of the said lady; and the same privilege is granted to St. Omer. Those preferred to livings by Duke Charles, his daughter, &c., shall remain in quiet possession of them, notwithstanding any pretence of a pragmatic sanction, or the like, to the contrary.

58. Tournay, Tournesis, St. Amand, and Mortagne, are comprehended in this treaty; and any places the King may have in the duchy of Luxemburg, shall be restored to the Archduke, and his son Philip; so shall also the houses of Flanders, and of Conflans, and the house of Artois in the said country.

59. After the lady shall be delivered into the hands of those appointed to receive her for the Dauphin, the troops, for the benefit of trade, shall be withdrawn by the King from the little places on the frontiers; and for the larger ones, the garrisons shall be regulated to the satisfaction of the Duke of Austria, and the States of the country.

60. As for the Duke's desiring to have the King of England and Duke of Bretagne comprehended in the treaty, it is answered, "the English are in truce with France, and for the Duke of Bretagne, the King is at peace with him."

61. The King, after the peace, will assist the duke against William of Aremberg, the Liégeois, and all others that shall invade Brabant, &c.

62. The Duke's subjects shall have all manner of protection and encouragement, in respect to navigation and commerce, equally with those of France.

63. Any prizes taken after the publication of the peace shall be restored, for the prevention whereof, the peace shall on both sides be proclaimed without delay.

64. Such as are malefactors and delinquents, after the peace, shall be seized on both sides, and returned to be punished by the parties to whom they belong.

65. The infractors and violators of this peace, be they who they will, shall be punished unfeignedly for an example to others, in the places where they are taken.

66. In case this peace should in any way be contravened, it shall not be reputed an infraction or rupture; but the breach shall forthwith be made up, and reparation made, without coming to hostilities either by sea or land, before the King and the Duke's ambassadors have met together to adjust the difference in an amicable way.

67. It is agreed, that as soon as the said lady is brought to Lisle or Douay, and before she be conducted to Arras, the promises and sureties which follow shall be given the Duke and States. That in case the Dauphin do not accomplish the marriage in due time, the said lady shall be returned, at the King's or Dauphin's charge, to her father or brother, in one of the good towns of Brabant, Flanders, or Hainault, in the Duke's possession; and the King and Dauphin, in that case, shall quit all pretensions for keeping the territories and countries of Artois, Burgundy, Charolois,

Maconnois, Auxerrois, the lordships of Salins, Bar-sur-Seine, and Noyers, and surrender them to the Duke in the name of his son Philip, while under age, or to Philip when of age, reserving only the homage and sovereignty to him.

68. The King shall also, upon the failure of the marriage, renounce his right to Lisle, Douay, and Orchies, and consent they shall belong for ever to the Counts and Countesses of Flanders.

69. The signing, sealing, and ratifying of all the premises in ample and due form, shall be done by the parties on either sides. The treaty shall also be registered and verified in the court of the Parliament of Paris, and in the Chambers of Accompts, and of the Finances.

The rest of the articles being mere matter of form, concerning the observation of the treaty, are omitted.

Ch. VII. — How the King sent for the Holy Man of Calabria to Tours, supposing he could cure him; and of the strange Things that were done by the King, during his Sickness, to preserve his Authority.—1482.

AMONG men renowned for devotion, King Louis sent into Calabria for one Friar Robert*, who, for the holiness and purity of his life, was called the "Holy Man;" and in honour to whom our present King erected a monastery at Plessis-du-Parc, in compensation for the chapel near Plessis at the end

---

* In previous editions it is erroneously stated that the name of this holy man was Friar Robert; but there can be no doubt, that the personage alluded to in the text was St. Francis de Paulo, the founder of the Minims, or lowest order of monks. He was born at Paulo in Calabria in the year 1416. He began his career by retiring to a cave on a desert part of the coast, where his sanctity soon obtained for him many followers, who ere long constructed a monastery round his cell. His rule was extremely rigorous; he enjoined his disciples to abstain from wine, fish, and meat, never to sleep on a bed, to go always barefooted, and to practise many other bodily mortifications. He died in France, on the 2nd of April, 1507, at the age of ninety-one, and he was canonised by Pope Leo X. in 1519. By the confession of his admirers, he was perfectly illiterate.

of the bridge. *   This hermit, at the age of twelve years, was put into a hole in a rock, where he lived until the age of three and forty years and upwards, when the King sent for him by a steward of his household†, in the company of the Prince of Tarento, the son of the King of Naples.   For this hermit would not stir without leave from his Holiness, and from his king, which was great discretion in a man so inexperienced in the affairs of the world, though he had built two churches in the place where he lived; and he never had eaten flesh, fish, eggs, milk, or any thing that was fat‡, since he undertook that austerity of life, nor has he yet; and truly I never saw any man living so holy, nor out of whose mouth the Holy Ghost did more manifestly speak; for he was not illiterate, though he had never been taught; only his Italian tongue was a great assistance to him.

This hermit passed through Naples, where he was respected, and visited (with as much pomp and ceremony, as if he had been the Pope's Legate) both by the King of

* By letters patent, dated on the 6th of May, 1491, Charles VIII. ordains "that the furniture, vestments, and ornaments which decorate the chapel of St. Matthew in the lower court of his house at Plessis, and which belong to Francis de Paulo and his companions, shall be removed to the place where, at their prayer and request, he has recently caused a church to be built for them, behind the enclosure of the park of Montils, and dedicated to Jesu Maria."

† Guynot de Boussière, or Guynot de Lauzière, as he is called in a letter from Louis XI. to Francis de Genas, superintendent of the finances. The letter is as follows:—"Mr. Superintendent,—The seneschal of Quercy, Guynot de Lauzière, who brought to me the good holy man, complains that you have deprived him of half of his pension, which amounts to 600 livres tournois, and that you told him I had ordered it, which I did not, and never intended to do.   And I assure you I am not pleased with you, wherefore take care (and fear to disobey me), that as soon as you see these letters, the matter may be entirely settled, and the pension paid in such a manner that I may hear no more about it; for if you fail ⟨to⟩ obey, you shall be lodged in the hands of my Lord of Alby; and from this time forth, and until he is satisfied, I detain in my hands the wages and pensions which you receive from me.   Written at Plessis du Parc, on the 15th day of May, 1482."—DUPONT, ii. 229.

‡ Another letter from Louis XI. to Francis de Genas illustrates the holy man's mode of life :—"Mr. Superintendent,—I beg you to send me some limes and sweet oranges and muscadel pears and water melons, for the holy man who eats neither flesh nor fish: and you will thereby give me very great pleasure.   Written at Clery on the 29th of June, 1483."

Naples and his children, with whom he conversed as if he had been all the days of his life a courtier. From thence he went to Rome, where he was visited by all the cardinals, had audience three times of the Pope, and was every time alone with him three or four hours, sitting beside him in a rich chair (which was great honour for a person of his low condition), and answering so discreetly to everything that was asked him, that everybody was astonished at it, and his Holiness gave him leave to institute a new order, called the Hermits of St. Francis. From Rome he came to our king *, who paid him the same honour as he would have done to the Pope himself, falling down upon his knees before him, and begging him to prolong his life: to which he replied as a prudent man ought. I have heard him often in discourse with the present king, in the presence of all the nobility of the kingdom, and that not above two months ago; and it seemed to me that whatever he said or remonstrated, was suggested by inspiration, or else it would have been impossible for him to have spoken of some things that he discoursed of. He is still living, and may grow either better or worse, and therefore I will say nothing. There were some of the courtiers that made a jest of the king's sending for this hermit, and called him the Holy Man, by way of banter; but they knew not the thoughts of that wise king, and had not seen what it was that induced him to do it.

Our king was at Plessis, with little company but his archers, and the suspicions I mentioned before, against which he had carefully provided; for he allowed no person, of whom he had any suspicion, to remain either in the town or country; but he sent his archers not only to warn, but to conduct them away. No business was communicated to him but what was of great importance, and highly concerned him. To look upon him one would have thought him rather a dead than a living man. He was grown so lean, it was scarce credible: his clothes were now richer and more magnificent than they had ever been before; his gowns were all of crimson satin, lined with rich martens' furs, of which he gave several away, without being requested; for no person durst ask a favour of him, or scarce speak to him of any

* He arrived at the castle of Plessis on the 24th of April, 1482.

thing. He inflicted very severe punishments to inspire dread, and for fear of losing his authority, as he told me himself. He removed officers, disbanded soldiers, retrenched pensions, and sometimes took them away altogether; so that, as he told me not many days before his death, he passed his time in making and ruining men; which caused him to be talked of more than any of his predecessors, and he did this that his subjects might take notice he was not yet dead; for few were admitted into his presence (as I said before), and when they heard of his vagaries, nobody was willing to believe he was sick.

He also sent agents to all foreign courts. In England, their business was to carry on the treaty of marriage *, and pay King Edward and his ministers of state their pensions very punctually. In Spain, their instructions were to amuse that court with fair words, and to distribute presents as they found it necessary for the advancement of his affairs. In remoter countries, where he had no mind his indisposition should be known, he caused fine horses or mules to be bought at any rate whatever; but this was not done in France. He had a mighty curiosity for dogs †, and sent into foreign countries for them; into Spain for mastiffs; into Bretagne for greyhounds and spaniels; to Valentia for little shaggy dogs; and bought them at a dearer price than the people asked. He sent into Sicily to buy a mule of an officer of that country, and paid him double the value. At Naples he bought horses; and purchased strange creatures wherever they could be found, such as a sort of lions from Barbary ‡ no bigger than foxes, and which are called adits. He sent into Sweden and Denmark for two sorts of beasts those

* The marriage of the Dauphin with the Princess Elizabeth of England.

† The accounts of Jehan Raguier for the year 1479 inform us that he gave " to a Portuguese, who had brought some dogs to the King, six gold crowns; to an Englishman, who brought him a great dog, ten gold crowns; to a man who brought him a little dog, one crown; to six men who brought him some live hares, thirty crowns."

‡ In 1482, a sum of 160 livres was paid to Master Macé Bastard, for the expenses of a journey he had made into Provence, by the King's order, " to await the coming of certain galleys with strange and savage beasts, and other things, which the King had ordered to be brought from the countries of Barbary."—FONTANIEU, 142.

countries afforded; one of them called an elk, of the shape
of a stag, and the size of a buffalo, with short and thick
horns; the other, called reindeers, of the shape and colour
of a fallow deer, but with much larger horns; indeed I have
seen reindeers with fifty-four horns; for six of each of
which beasts he gave the merchants four thousand five hundred Dutch florins.*   Yet, when all these rarities were
brought to him, he never valued them, and many times would
not so much as see the persons who brought them to him.
In short, he behaved himself after so strange a manner, that
he was more formidable, both to his neighbours and subjects,
than he had ever been before; and indeed that was his
design, and the motive which induced him to act so unaccountably.

Ch. VIII. — Of the Conclusion of the Marriage between the Dauphin
and Margaret of Flanders, and how she was brought into France;
upon which Edward IV., King of England, died with displeasure.—
1482-3.

But to return to our principal design, and to the conclusion
of these Memoirs, and the affairs of all the illustrious persons of the age in which they were transacted, it is abso-
lutely necessary for us to speak of the conclusion of the marriage between our present king (then Dauphin of France)
and the daughter of the Duke and Duchess of Austria,
which was effected by the mediation of the citizens of Ghent,
to the great displeasure of the King of England, who found
himself deluded in the hopes he had entertained of marrying
his daughter to the Dauphin, of which marriage both himself
and his queen were more ambitious than of any other match
in the world; and never would believe any man, whether
subject or foreigner, that endeavoured to persuade them that
our king's intentions were not sincere and honourable.   For

* In the accounts of Pierre de Lailly for the year 1479, the following
entry occurs:—" To Bernard More, an Easterling merchant, 750 livres,
as agreed upon, for bringing to the King six beasts named elks, three
males and three females, and six others named reindeer, also three males
and three females."—Dupont, ii. 234.

the Parliament of England had remonstrated to King Edward several times, when our king was in Picardy, that after he had conquered that province he would certainly fall upon Calais and Guynes, which are not far off. The ambassadors from the Duke and Duchess of Austria, as also those from the Duke of Bretagne, who were continually in England at that time, represented the same thing to him, but to no purpose; for he would believe nothing of it*, and he suffered greatly for his incredulity: yet I am entirely of opinion his conduct proceeded not so much from ignorance as avarice, for he was afraid to lose his annual pension of fifty thousand crowns, which our master paid very punctually; and, besides, he was unwilling to leave his ease and pleasures, to which he was extremely given.

There was a conference held at Halots, in Flanders, about this marriage, at which the Duke of Austria (now King of the Romans) was present, with several commissioners from the three Estates of Flanders, Brabant, and other territories belonging to the Duke and his children. There the Gantois did several things contrary to the Duke's inclination; for they banished his officers, removed old servants from about his son, told him their desire to have the marriage concluded, in order to establish peace, and forced him to an accommodation, whether he would or not. The Duke was very young, and but scantily provided with sense; for all belonging to the house of Burgundy were either slain or revolted to France, or at least the greatest part, I mean of such as were capable of advising him; so that coming thither with a small retinue, and having lost his duchess, who was sovereign in those provinces, he durst not speak so boldly to his subjects as when she was alive. In short, the King was informed of all these proceedings by the Lord des Cordes, and was very well pleased; and a day was set for the young lady to be conducted to Hesdin.

A few days before, in the year 1481, Aire was delivered up, for a sum of money †, to the Lord des Cordes, by the Lord

---

* He was probably satisfied by the letter of Louis XI. to Lord Hastings. See p. 40.

† Aire surrendered on the 28th July, 1482. It was sold by the Lord de Cohen for an annual pension of ten thousand crowns. — MOLINET, ii. 306.

de Cohem (a gentleman of Artois), who had held it under his captain, the Lord de Beurs*, for the Duke of Austria, a good while.   The surrender of this town, which was very strong, and situated in Artois, at the very entrance into their country, helped the Flemings to hasten the marriage, for though they were well enough pleased at the diminution of the Duke's power, yet they did not care to have the King so near them upon their frontiers.   As soon as measures were concerted, as I said before, ambassadors were sent to the King from Flanders and Brabant†; but all depended upon the Gantois, by reason of their strength, and because the Duke's children were in their hands, and they were always the most forward in every commotion.   With them there came in behalf of the King of the Romans, certain young noblemen much about his own age, and but indifferently qualified to make terms of peace for their country; Monsieur John de Berghes ‡ was one, and Monsieur Baudouin de Lannoy§ was the other, besides some few secretaries.   Our king was then very ill, and had no inclination to be seen, and pretended great difficulty about swearing to the treaties in the manner agreed on ; but it was only because he was unwilling they should see him.   However, he swore to them at last, which was much to his advantage ; for whereas in all his former overtures for the match, he demanded only the county of Artois or Burgundy, or whichever of the two they pleased to assign him : now, the States of Ghent (as he called them) were contented he should have both, and the counties of Maconnois, Charolois, and Auxerrois, into the bargain; and if they could have delivered Hainault, Namur, and all the subjects of that family who speak the French language,

---

* Philip of Burgundy, Lord of Bevres and La Vère, councillor and chamberlain of Maximilian, King of the Romans, Knight of the Golden Fleece, and Governor of Artois.

† These ambassadors arrived at Paris on Saturday, the 3rd of January, 1483, and proceeded on the following Monday to Amboise, where the King was then residing.—LENGLET, ii. 168.

‡ John de Berghes, knight, Lord of Cohen and Olhain, and governor of the town of Aire for the Archduke Maximilian.

§ Baudoin de Lannoy, second of the name, Lord of Molembrais, Knight of the Golden Fleece, chamberlain and steward of the Archduke Maximilian.   He died on the 7th of May, 1501.

they would willingly have done so, on purpose to weaken their sovereign.

Our master was a cunning politician, and understood well enough that Flanders was of little importance to him, unless he could have Artois with it, which lies betwixt France and them, and is as it were a bridle to the Flemings, affording good soldiers upon occasion, to correct their wantonness and folly; and therefore in taking from the Earl of Flanders the county of Artois, he would leave him the most inconsiderable prince in Europe, without either subjects or authority, except by the permission of the Gantois; whose commissioners, William Ryn and Coppenole, whom I mentioned before (governors of Ghent), were at that time principal in the embassy. Upon the return of the ambassadors, the Lady Margaret was conducted to Hesdin, and delivered into the hands of the Lord des Cordes, in the year 1483, and with her came Madame de Ravestain, Duke Philip of Burgundy's natural daughter, and they were received by the present Monsieur and Madame de Bourbon*, the Lord d'Albret†, and others from the king; and they brought her to Amboise, where the dauphin met her.‡   If the Duke

* Anne of France, daughter of Louis XI. and Charlotte of Savoy, married Pierre de Bourbon, Lord of Beaujeu, in 1474, and assumed the title of Duchess of Bourbon in 1488. She died on the 14th of November, 1522, after having governed the kingdom with great prudence and energy during the minority of Charles VIII.

† Alain le Grand, son of Jean d'Albret, Viscount de Tartas, succeeded his grandfather Charles II. in 1471. He married Frances, daughter of Jean de Blois, Count of Penthievre; and in virtue of this marriage, set up a claim to the duchy of Brittany, and became a competitor for the hand of Anne of Brittany. He died in October, 1522.

‡ Margaret was then three years and a half old, and the Dauphin rather more than twelve. Their meeting took place on Sunday, the 22nd of June, 1483, at a place called Metairie le Rayne, near Amboise. "The Dauphin," says a contemporary letter, "left the Castle of Amboise, dressed in a robe of crimson satin, lined with black velvet, and mounted on a hackney, and attended by thirty archers. At the bridge he dismounted, after having saluted the ladies, and changed his dress and put on a long robe of cloth of gold. . . Presently the Dauphiness arrived, and descended from her litter; and immediately they were betrothed by the prothonotary, nephew of the Grand Seneschal of Normandy, who demanded of the Dauphin in a loud voice, so that all could hear him, If he would have Margaret of Austria in marriage? and he answered, Yes; and a similar question was put to the

of Austria could have taken her from her convoy, he would willingly have done it before she left his dominions; but the Gantois had placed too strong a guard about her, for they had begun to abate much of their obedience to him, and many considerable persons joined with them, as having the custody of the young heir, and power of placing and displacing whom they pleased. Among the nobility who were resident in Ghent, there was the Lord of Ravestain, brother to the Duke of Cleves, and chief governor to the young prince, whose name is Philip, still living, and like to possess vast territories, if it please God to spare his life.

But whoever was pleased with this match, the King of England was highly affronted; for he thought himself disgraced and baffled, and in danger of losing his pension or tribute, as the English called it. He feared likewise it would render him contemptible at home, and occasion some rebellion, more especially because he had rejected the remonstrances of his council. Besides, he saw the King of France ready to invade his dominions with a very great force; which made such a deep impression upon his spirits, that he fell sick immediately upon hearing the news, and died not long after, though some say he died of a catarrh. But let them say what they please, the general opinion was, his grief at the consummation of this marriage, caused the illness which killed him in the month of April, 1483.* It

---

Dauphiness, who gave the same answer. Upon which, they joined hands, and the Dauphin kissed the Dauphiness twice; and then they returned to their lodgings. And the streets of Amboise were hung with cloth, and in the market place was a figure of a Siren, who spouted forth white wine and red from her breasts." The next day, the young couple went through the ceremony of marriage in the chapel of the castle.—DUPONT, iii. 345, 352.

* King Edward IV. died on the 9th of April, and the Dauphin's marriage did not take place until the 22nd of June, more than two months later; so that the supposition of Commines that he died of grief at the disappointment of his own daughter, who had long been contracted to the Dauphin, is evidently erroneous. His dissolute mode of life renders it exceedingly probable that he died of a surfeit, according to the popular report. "He was a prince," says Hume, "more splendid and showy than either prudent or virtuous; brave, though cruel; addicted to pleasure, though capable of activity in great emergencies, and less fitted to prevent ills by wise precautions, than to remedy them after they took place, by his vigour and enterprise."

is a great fault in a prince to be obstinate, and rely more
upon his own judgment than on the opinion of his council;
and sometimes it occasions such losses and disappointments
as are never to be repaired.

Our King was quickly informed of King Edward's death;
but he expressed no manner of joy upon hearing the
news.   Not long after, he received letters from the Duke of
Gloucester, who had made himself king*, styled himself
Richard III., and barbarously murdered his two nephews.†
This King Richard desired to live in the same friendship
with our king as his brother had done, and I believe would
gladly have had his pension continued; but our king looked
upon him as an inhuman and cruel person, and would neither
answer his letters nor give audience to his ambassador; for
King Richard, after his brother's death, had sworn allegiance to his nephew, as his king and sovereign, and yet
committed that inhuman action not long after; and, in full
Parliament, caused two of his brother's daughters to be
degraded and declared illegitimate, upon a pretence which
he justified by means of the Bishop of Bath, who, having
been formerly in great favour with King Edward, had incurred his displeasure, was dismissed, imprisoned, and fined
a good sum for his releasement.‡   This bishop affirmed,
that King Edward being in love with a certain lady whom
he named, and otherwise unable to have his desires of her,
had promised her marriage; and caused the bishop to marry

* Richard III. did not assume the title of King until the 26th of June,
1483, after the death of his nephew Edward V.

† Molinet (ii, 402.) gives the following account of the murder of the
princes: "The eldest was simple and very melancholy, aware of the
wickedness of his uncle, but the youngest was joyous and witty, nimble,
and ever ready for dances and games; and he said to his brother, who
wore the order of the garter, 'My brother, learn to dance:' and his
brother answered, 'It would be better for us to learn to die, for I think
we shall not long remain in the world!' They were prisoners for
about five weeks; and Duke Richard had them secretly slain by the
captain of the Tower.   And when the executioners came, the eldest was
asleep, but the youngest was awake, and he perceived their intention,
and began to say, 'Ha! my brother, awake, for they have come to kill
you.'   Then he said to the executioners, 'Why do you kill my brother?
kill me, and let him live.'   But they were both killed; and their bodies
cast into a secret place."

‡ See notes, vol. i. pp. 395, 396.

them, upon which he enjoyed her person, though his promise
was only made to delude her ; but such games are dangerous,
as the effects frequently demonstrate. I have known many
a courtier who would not have lost such a fair lady for want
of promises.

This malicious prelate smothered this revenge in his heart
near twenty years together, but it recoiled upon himself, for
he had a son, of whom he was extremely fond, and to whom
King Richard designed to give a plentiful estate, and to
have married him to one of the young ladies whom he had
declared illegitimate (who is now Queen of England, and
has two fine children). *   This young gentleman being on
board ship by commission from King Richard, was taken upon
the coast of Normandy, and upon a dispute between those that
took him, he was brought before the Parliament at Paris, put
into the Petit Chastellet, and suffered to lie there till he was
starved to death. This King Richard himself lived not long,
no more did the Duke of Buckingham †, who had put the two
children to death, for King Richard himself, a very few days
afterwards, ordered his execution ; and against King Richard
God on a sudden raised up an enemy ‡, without power, without money, without right to the crown of England §, and
without any reputation but what his person and deportment
obtained for him ; for he had suffered much, and had been,
from the eighteenth year of his age, prisoner in Bretagne
to Duke Francis, who treated him as kindly as the necessity
of his imprisonment would permit. The King of France
having supplied him with some money, with about three
thousand Normans, the loosest and most profligate persons in
all that country, he passed into Wales, where his father-in-
law, the Lord Stanley, joined him with twenty-five thousand

* Arthur, born on the 20th of September, 1486, and Margaret, born
in 1488.

† Molinet (ii. 403) also asserts that Buckingham was implicated in
the murder of the princes ; but there is no evidence to be found in support of the statement, which rests probably on the fact that the duke was
a prominent supporter of Richard's usurpation, and was therefore
likely to have been concerned in the assassination of his nephews.

‡ The Earl of Richmond, afterwards Henry VII.

§ Richmond was considered as representing the line of Lancaster by
right of his mother, Margaret Beaufort, who was daughter of a Duke of
Somerset, and a great-granddaughter of John of Gaunt.

men at the least; in three or four days' time he met cruel
King Richard, who was slain on the field of battle; and he
was crowned King of England, and reigns at this present
time.*   I have discoursed on this subject already, but it is
not improper to mention it again, if only to show that God
in our times has taken vengeance for such cruelties immediately, without delaying his judgments.   Several other
princes besides have met with the same reward of their
villanies, in our days; but who could enumerate them?

CH. IX.—How the King behaved towards his Neighbours and Subjects during his Sickness; and how several Things were sent him from
several Parts, for the Recovery of his Health.—1483.

AFTER the consummation of this marriage, which our King
had so earnestly desired, the Flemings were perfectly at his
command: Bretagne (which he hated so bitterly) was at
peace with him, but he kept them in great awe and terror
by the number of his forces, which he quartered upon their
frontiers.   Spain was quiet, and her king and queen desired nothing more than to live in peace and amity with him,
for he kept them, likewise, in perpetual fear and expense
about the country of Roussillon, which he held of the
House of Arragon, and which had been given him by John
King of Arragon, father to the present King of Castile, as
security for some conditions† which have never yet been
performed.   The princes of Italy all courted his friendship;

* Henry left Harfleur on the 1st of August, 1485, with an army of
about 2,000 men, and landed at Milford Haven on the 7th of August.
He met with little opposition in Wales, and at Shrewsbury he was joined
by Sir Gilbert Talbot and all his vassals. Marching onwards, through
the midland counties, he came up with his rival at Bosworth, in Leices-
tershire, on the 22nd of August. Henry was at the head of 6,000 men,
and Richard had an army of above double the number. But during
the action Lord Stanley joined Henry with 7,000 men, and decided the
battle in his favour.

† By letters dated on the 23rd of May, 1462, the King of Arragon
pledged the counties of Roussillon and Cerdagne to Louis XI. for the
sum of 300,000 golden crowns, on condition that Louis should supply
him with a sufficient number of troops to reduce Catalonia, and to carry
on the war in Arragon and Valencia. These counties were restored to

and some of them had entered into alliance with him, and
sent ambassadors often to his court. In Germany the Swiss
were as obedient to him as his own subjects. The Kings
of Scotland* and Portugal † were his allies. Part of Navarre ‡ was perfectly at his disposal. His subjects trembled
before him; whatever he commanded was instantly executed,
without the least difficulty or hesitation.

Whatever was thought conducible to his health §, was sent
to him from all corners of the world. Pope Sixtus‖ (who
died lately) being informed of the King's illness, and that he,
in his devotion, desired to have the corporal, or vest, which
the Apostle St. Peter used when he sung mass, sent it immediately, and several relics ¶ besides, which were returned
to him. The holy vial at Rheims, which had never been
moved before, was brought to his chamber at Plessis, and
stood upon his buffet when he died, for he designed to be
anointed with it again, as he was at his coronation. Some
were of opinion that he designed to have anointed himself
all over, but that was not likely, for the vial is but small,
and there is no great store of oil in it.** I saw it myself at

Castile by the Treaty of Barcelona, signed on the 19th of January, 1493.
—PRESCOTT'S *Ferdinand and Isabella*, vol. ii. p. 249.

* James III. See note, Vol. I. p. 398.

† John II., son of Alphonso V., King of Portugal. He succeeded to
the throne in 1481, and died on the 25th of October, 1495. It was to
him that Columbus first submitted the theory on which he had founded
his belief in the existence of a western route; but the foolish monarch
refused his patronage to the adventure.

‡ Navarre was then divided by two opposing factions; that of Queen
Catherine, the niece of Louis XI., and that of the Viscount of Narbonne,
who wished to gain possession of the crown. It is to the former of these
parties, doubtless, that Commines alludes.

§ Among other things, he tried *aurum potabile*, and paid dearly for
it, though it does not seem to have done him much good.

‖ Sixtus IV. died on the 13th of August, 1484. See note, p. 25.

¶ Nor was this the full extent of the Pope's benevolence. He sent
two briefs to Francis de Paulo, ordering him to pray for the restoration
of the King's health, under penalty of excommunication in case of refusal.
—RAYNALDUS, xix. 29.

** The supposition of Commines is correct: the King did not dare to
ask, in the first intance, to be entrusted with the phial itself. "Dear
and well-beloved," he wrote to the Abbot of St. Rémy at Rheims, on the
17th of April, 1483, "we should much wish, if it were possible, to have
a *little drop* from the Holy Ampulla; wherefore we pray you to consult

the time I speak of, and also when our Lord the King was
interred in the church of Notre Dame de Clery.*   The
Great Turk† that now reigns, sent an ambassador‡ to him,
who came as far as Riez, in Provence; but the King would
not hear him, nor permit him to proceed any farther, though
he brought him a large roll of relics which had been left at
Constantinople in the hands of the Turk; all which, and a
considerable sum of money besides, he offered to deliver into
the king's hands, if he would keep guard over a brother§ of

and inquire whether a little could be taken from the phial in which it is
contained, without sin or danger."   This humble and modest request
having been refused, Louis XI. had recourse to the authority of the
Pope, from whom he obtained the desired permission.   Three commissioners, the Bishop of Seez, the Governor of Auvergne, and the Lord
de la Heuze, were sent to fetch the Holy Ampulla from Rheims.   It was
escorted into Paris, on the 31st of July, 1843, with great pomp; and on
the following day it was taken to the King.

* Notre Dame de Clery, a pretty little town on the left bank of the
Loire, nine miles from Orleans.

† Bajazet II., son of Mahomet II., succeeded his father in 1481; and
was dethroned and died in 1512.

‡ The name of this ambassador was Hussein.—HAMMER, iii. 361.

§ Djem, or Zizim, brother of Bajazet II., on hearing of his father's
death, resolved to make a vigorous effort for the empire; but finding
that his forces were far inferior to those of his brother, he applied to the
Knights Hospitallers at Rhodes for assistance, who resolved to concede
his demands, and sent a squadron to escort him to Rhodes, where he was
received with all the honours due to a powerful sovereign.   Bajazet, in
great alarm, hastened to negotiate a treaty with the Order; the Knights,
however, dared not violate the laws of hospitality by giving up Zizim;
but the Grand Master concluded a secret compact with the Sultan, in
which, for the annual pension of 45,000 ducats, he engaged to detain
the prince a prisoner.   The subsequent fate of the unfortunate captive
was truly calamitous.   He was held in durance for a long time in France,
constantly mocked with false hopes, until Pope Innocent VIII. bribed
the Grand Master D'Aubusson with a cardinal's hat to resign to him the
guardianship of his profitable prisoner.   In 1489 Zizim was removed
to Rome, where he was tormented by frequent proposals to change his
religion, all of which he peremptorily rejected.   When Alexander Borgia
ascended the papal throne, he sent an embassy to the Sultan, demanding
the continuation of the pension for the custody of Zizim, and offering
also to put him to death for 300,000 ducats, paid in one sum.   Before an
answer could arrive from Constantinople, the Pope was forced to resign
his prisoner to Charles VIII., King of France; but Borgia soon procured
the death of the unfortunate prince by poison.   After ten years' captivity
among Christians, he was murdered in 1495.

F 2

the Turk's, who was then in France, in the custody of the Knights of Rhodes, and is now at Rome, in the hands of the Pope. From all which one may be able to judge of the wisdom and greatness of our King, and of the great esteem and character he bore in the world, when spiritual things, dedicated to devotion and religion, were employed for the lengthening of his life, as well as things temporal and secular. But all endeavours to prolong his life proved ineffectual; his time was come, and he must needs follow his predecessors. Yet in one thing God Almighty favoured him in a peculiar manner, for, as he had made him more prudent, liberal, and virtuous in all things than the contemporary princes, who were his neighbours and enemies, so he suffered him to survive them, though not for a very long time. For Charles Duke of Burgundy, the Duchess of Austria his daughter, King Edward of England, Duke Galeas of Milan, and John King of Arragon, were all dead a few years before him; but King Edward and the Duchess of Austria died very shortly before his decease. In all of them there was a mixture of bad as well as good, for they were but mortals. But, without flattery, I may say of our King, that he was possessed of more qualifications suitable to the majesty and office of a prince than any of the rest, for I had seen most of them, and knew the extent of their abilities.

Ch. X.—How King Louis sent for his Son Charles a little before his Death; and the Precepts and Commands which he laid upon him and others.

In the year 1482 the King desired to see the Dauphin his son, whom he had not seen for several years; for besides his being of opinion that it was better for his son's health to have but few come near him, he was afraid lest he should be taken out of his management, and made the occasion for some conspiracy against him, as had been done by himself against his father, King Charles VII., when, at eleven* years of age, he was taken away by some lords of the kingdom,

* Louis XI. was nearly seventeen years old at the time of the Praguerie. having been born in July, 1423.

and engaged in a war called the Praguerie*, which lasted not long, and was merely a court faction.

Above all things, he recommended to the Dauphin certain of his servants, and laid his commands expressly upon him not to change any of his officers, declaring that upon the death of his father Charles VII., and his own accession to the throne, he had imprudently dismissed all the good officers of the kingdom, both military and civil, who had assisted his father in the conquest of Normandy and Guyenne, served him in the expulsion of the English, and contributed much to the restoration of peace and tranquillity throughout the kingdom; which rash method of proceeding proved highly to his prejudice, for it was the foundation of the war called the Public Good, which I mentioned before†, and which had like to have cost him his crown. Soon after the King had given this advice to his son, and concluded the marriage ‡ above mentioned, upon a Monday § the illness seized him of which he died, and it lasted until the Saturday following, the last day but one of August, 1483; I was present at the termination of his illness, and therefore I think myself entitled to say something of his death.

Not long after his being seized with this last fit, he was deprived of his speech, as he had been formerly; and though he recovered that again, yet he found himself much weaker than he had ever been (though indeed he was so weak before that he had scarce strength to lift his hand to his mouth), and he became so meagre and lean, that every one who saw him pitied him. The King, perceiving he had not long to live, sent for the Lord de Beaujeu (who had married his daughter, and is now Duke of Bourbon), and commanded him to go to Amboise, to his son the king, as he called him. He recommended his son to him, and all his servants, and gave

* The Praguerie (so called in allusion to the Hussite wars in Bohemia) was a rebellion of the nobles against Charles VII., in consequence of his having established a regular army, in order to drive the marauding free-companies out of the kingdom. The vigorous measures taken by Charles to suppress this insurrection put an end to the war in less than six months.

† See Book I. Chaps. 2—14. of these Memoirs.

‡ The marriage of the Dauphin to the Princess Margaret of Flanders.

§ Monday, the 25th of August, 1483. The King died on Saturday, the 30th of August.

him the charge and government of the young king, and made him promise, for several good reasons, not to permit certain persons to come near him; and, if the Lord de Beaujeu had observed his commands strictly, or at least the best part of them, (for some were contradictory and not to be observed,) I am of opinion, considering what has since happened, it had been much better both for the kingdom and himself.

After this he sent the chancellor*, with all that were under him, to carry the seals to the king his son. He also sent him some archers of his guard, several of his captains, the officers of his hounds and hawks, and all others in charge of his sports; and he desired all that were going to Amboise to pay their respects to the king his son, to be faithful and true to him; and by every one he sent him some message or other, but more especially by Stephen de Vers†, who had brought up the young king, serving him in quality of first gentleman of his bed-chamber, and had been made Bailiff of Meaux by King Louis. After the recovery of his speech, his senses never failed him, and indeed were never so quick, for he had a continual looseness upon him, which kept the vapours from ascending to his head. In all his sickness he never complained, as most other people do when they are ill; at least I am of that nature, and I have known many of the same temper; and the common opinion is that complaining alleviates our pain.

CH. XI.—A Comparison of the Troubles and Sorrows which King Louis suffered, with those he had brought upon other People; with a Continuation of his Transactions till the Time of his Death.—1483.

HE was continually discoursing on some subject or another, and always with a great deal of sense and judgment. His

* William, Lord of Rochefort. See Vol. I. p. 16.

† Stephen de Vesc, knight, belonged to a noble family of Lower Dauphiny. He was one of the chamberlains of Charles VIII., who appointed him Seneschal of Beaucaire and Nismes, on the 3rd of March, 1490. He afterwards became President of the Chamber of Accounts; and was dignified with the baton of Constable of France on the King's entrance into Naples. He died on the 6th of October, 1501.

last illness (as I said before) continued from Monday to Saturday night. Upon which account I will now make comparison between the evils and sorrows which he brought upon others, and those which he suffered in his own person: for I hope his torments here on earth, have translated him into Paradise, and will be a great part of his purgatory: and if, in respect of their greatness and duration, his sufferings were inferior to those he had brought upon other people, yet, if you consider the grandeur and dignity of his office, and that he had never before suffered anything in his own person, but had been obeyed by all people, as if all Europe had been created for no other end, but to serve and be commanded by him; you will find that little which he endured was so contrary to his nature and custom that it was more grievous for him to bear.

His chief hope and confidence was placed in the good hermit I spoke of (who was at Plessis, and had come thither from Calabria); he sent continually to him, believing it was in his power to prolong his life if he pleased; for, notwithstanding all his precepts, he had great hopes of recovering; and if it had so happened, he would quickly have dispersed the throng he had sent to Amboise, to wait upon the new king. Finding his hopes rested so strongly upon this hermit, it was the advice of a certain grave divine*, and others who were about him, that it should be declared to him that there was no hope left for him but in the mercy of God; and it was also agreed among them, that his physician, Master James Coctier (in whom he had great confidence), should be present when this declaration was made him. This Coctier received of him every month ten thousand crowns, in the hope that he would lengthen his life. This resolution was taken to the end that he should lay aside all other thoughts, and apply himself wholly to the settlement of his conscience. And as he had advanced them, as it were, in an instant, and against all reason, to employments beyond their capacities, so they took upon them fearlessly to tell him a thing that had been more proper for other people to com-

---

* M. de Barante (x. 82.) says this divine was Jean de Rely, doctor in theology, and canon of Paris. Gabriel Naudé asserts, on the contrary, that his name was Philippe, and that he was a monk of the Abbey of St. Martin.

municate ; nor did they observe that reverence and respect towards him, which was proper in such a case, and would have been used by those persons who had been brought up with him, or by those whom, in a mere whim, he had removed from court but a little before.   But, as he had sent a sharp message of death to two great persons whom he had formerly beheaded (the Duke of Nemours*, and the Count of St. Paul †), by commissioners deputed on purpose, who in plain terms told them their sentence, appointed them confessors to arrange their consciences, and acquainted them that in a few hours they must resolve to die ; so with the same bluntness, and without the least circumstance of introduction, these imprudent persons told our King : "Sire, we must do our duty; do not place your hopes any longer in this holy hermit, or anything else, for you are a dead man. Think therefore upon your conscience, for there is no remedy left."   Every one added some short saying to the same purpose; to which he answered, "I hope God will assist me, for perhaps I am not so ill as you imagine."

What sorrow was this to him to hear this news !   Never man was more fearful of death, nor used more means to prevent it.   He had, all his life long, commanded and requested his servants, and me among the rest, that whenever we saw him in any danger of death, we should not tell him of it, but merely admonish him to confess himself, without ever mentioning that cruel and shocking word Death ; for he did not believe he could ever endure to hear so cruel a sentence. However, he endured that virtuously, and several more things equally terrible, when he was ill; and indeed he bore them better than any man I ever saw die. · He spoke several things, which were to be delivered to his son, whom he called king ; and he confessed himself very devoutly, said

* See note, Vol. I. p. 16.

† See Book IV. Chap. 12.   The constable's trial lasted from the 27th of November, 1475, to the 19th of December following.   His sentence was read to him in these terms :—" You have been long in the custody of the King, and you have been diligently interrogated with regard to the extreme offences you have committed.   The sentence of the Court of Parliament against you is, that you be publicly beheaded and put to death to-day on the Grève, opposite the Hotel de Ville."   At these words the constable cried aloud and said : " My God ! what news ! this is a hard sentence !"—MOLINET, i. 183.

several prayers suitable to the sacraments he received, and
called for the sacraments himself. He spoke as judiciously as
if he had never been ill, discoursed of all things which might
be necessary for his son's instruction, and among the rest gave
orders that the Lord. des Cordes should not stir from his
son for six months; and that he should be desired to attempt
nothing against Calais, or elsewhere, declaring, that though
he had designed himself to undertake such enterprises for
the benefit of both the king and the kingdom, yet they were
very dangerous, especially that against Calais, because the
English might resent it; and he left it in especial charge,
that for five or six years after his death, they should, above
all things, preserve the kingdom in peace, which during his
life he had never suffered. And indeed it was no more than
was necessary; for, though the kingdom was large and fer-
tile, yet it was grown very poor, upon account of the marching and counter-marching of the soldiers up and down, in
their passage from one country to another, as they have done
since, to an even worse extent. He also ordered that nothing
should be attempted against Bretagne, but that Duke Francis
should be suffered to live in peace; that both he and his
neighbours might be without fear, and the king and kingdom remain free from wars, till the king should be of age,
to take upon himself the administration of affairs.

You have already heard with what indiscretion and bluntness they acquainted the king with his approaching death;
which I have mentioned in a more particular manner,
because in a preceding paragraph I began to compare the
evils, which he had made others suffer, who lived under his
dominion, with those he endured himself before his death;
that it might appear that, though they were not perhaps of
so long a duration, yet they were fully as great and terrible,
considering his station and dignity, which required more
obedience than any private person, and had found more; so
that the least opposition was a great torment to him. Some
five or six months before his death, he began to suspect everybody, especially those who were most capable and deserving
of the administration of affairs. He was afraid of his son,
and caused him to be kept close, so that no man saw or discoursed with him, but by his special command. At last he
grew suspicious of his daughter, and of his son-in-law the

Duke of Bourbon, and required an account of what persons came to speak with them at Plessis, and broke up a council which the Duke of Bourbon was holding there, by his order.

At the time that the Count of Dunois* and the said Duke of Bourbon returned from conducting the ambassadors, who had been at Amboise to attend the marriage of the Dauphin and the young queen, the King being in the gallery at Plessis, and seeing them enter with a great train into the castle, called for a captain of the guards, and commanded him to go and search the servants of those lords, to see whether they had any arms under their robes; and ordered him to do it in discourse, so as no notice might be taken. Behold, then, if he had caused many to live under him in continual fear and apprehension, whether it was not returned to him again; for of whom could he be secure when he was afraid of his son-in-law, his daughter, and his own son? I speak this not only of him, but of all other princes who desire to be feared, that vengeance never falls on them till they grow old, and then, as a just penance, they are afraid of everybody themselves; and what grief must it have been to this poor King to be tormented with such terrors and passions?

He was still attended by his physician, Master James Coctier, to whom in five months' time he had given fifty-four thousand crowns in ready money, besides the bishopric of Amiens for his nephew†, and other great offices and estates for himself and his friends; yet this doctor used him very roughly indeed; one would not have given such outrageous language to one's servants, as he gave the King, who stood in such awe of him, that he durst not forbid him his presence. It is true he complained of his impudence afterwards, but he durst not change him as he had done all the rest of his servants; because he had told him after a most audacious manner one day, "I know well that some time or other you will dismiss me

* Francis of Orleans, Count of Longueville and Dunois, was born in 1447; married Agnes of Savoy; was appointed Governor of Dauphiny by Charles VIII. in 1483, and Grand Chamberlain of France in 1485; and died on the 25th of November, 1491. He was a son of the celebrated Bastard of Orleans, so distinguished in the wars against the English in the time of Joan of Arc.

† Pierre Versé, appointed to the bishopric of Amiens, on the 16th of August, 1482.

from court, as you have done the rest.; but be sure (and he confirmed it with a great oath) you shall not live eight days after it* ;" with which expression the king was so terrified, that ever after he did nothing but flatter and bribe him, which must needs have been a great mortification to a prince who had been humbly obeyed all his life by so many good and brave men.

The King had ordered several cruel prisons to be made; some were cages of iron, and some of wood, but all were covered with iron plates both within and without, with terrible locks, about eight feet wide and seven high; the first contriver of them was the Bishop of Verdun†, who was immediately put in the first of them that was made, where he continued fourteen years. Many bitter curses he has had since for his invention, and some from me as I lay in one of them eight months together in the minority of our present King. He also ordered heavy and terrible fetters to be made in Germany, and particularly a certain ring for the feet, which was extremely hard to be opened, and fitted like an iron collar, with a thick weighty chain, and a great globe of iron at the end of it, most unreasonably heavy, which engines were called the King's Nets. However, I have seen many eminent and deserving persons in these prisons, with these nets about their legs, who afterwards came forth with great joy and honour, and received great rewards from the King. Among the rest, a son‡ of the Lord de la Grutuse,

* The same, or nearly the same story is told of Tiberius, who demanded of a soothsayer, Thrasullus, if he knew the day of his own death, and received for answer, it would take place just three days before that of the emperor. On this reply, instead of being thrown over the rocks into the sea, as had been the tyrant's first intention, he was taken great care of for the rest of his life.—TACITI *Annales*, vi. 21.

† Guillaume de Haraucourt. See Vol. I. p. 165.

‡ Jean de Bruges, Lord of Avelghem and Espières, and afterwards Lord of La Gruthuse, and Prince of Steenhuys, in Flanders. He was knighted by Duke Maximilian of Austria, on the 7th of August, 1479, just before the battle of Guinegatte, in which he was taken prisoner. Louis XI. afterwards appointed him one of his chamberlains, and married him to Renèe de Bueil, daughter of the Count of Sancerre. In 1484, Charles VIII. appointed him Seneschal of Anjou; in 1498 he was made Grand Master of the crossbow-men of France; and in 1491 he was raised to the office of Captain of the Louvre. He died on the 8th of August, 1512. In regard to his father, see note, Vol. I. p. 193.

in Flanders (who was taken in battle), whom the king married very honourably afterwards, made him his chamberlain, and seneschal of Anjou, and gave him the command of a hundred lances. The Lord de Piennes*, and the Lord de Vergy†, both prisoners of war, also had commands given them in his army, were made his or his son's chamberlains, and had great estates bestowed on them. Monsieur de Richebourg‡, the constable's brother, had the same good fortune, as did also one Roquebertin§, a Catalonian, likewise prisoner of war; besides others of various countries, too numerous to be mentioned in this place.

This by way of digression. But to return to my principal design. As in his time this barbarous variety of prisons was invented, so before he died he himself was in greater torment, and more terrible apprehension than those whom he had imprisoned; which I look upon as a great mercy towards him, and as part of his purgatory; and I have mentioned it here to show that there is no person, of what station or dignity soever, but suffers some time or other, either publicly or privately, especially if he has caused other people to suffer. The king, towards the latter end of his days, caused his castle of Plessis-les-Tours to be encompassed with great bars of iron in the form of thick grating, and at the four corners of the house four sparrow-nests of iron, strong, massy, and thick, were built. The grates were without the wall on the other side of the ditch, and sank to the bottom. Several spikes of iron were fastened into the wall, set as thick by one another as was possible, and each furnished with three or four points. He likewise placed ten bow-men in the ditches, to shoot at any man that durst

* Louis de Halewin, Lord of Piennes, having been made prisoner by the French, some time after the siege of Neuss, entered the service of Louis XI., who appointed him Captain of Montlhery in 1480. In 1486 Charles VIII. gave him the government of Bethune; and in 1512 Louis XII. appointed him Governor and Lieutenant-General of Picardy. He died in 1518.

† The Lord of Vergy was made prisoner in 1477. See note, Vol. I. p. 362.

‡ The Lord of Richebourg, brother of the Constable of St. Paul, was made prisoner in 1475. See Vol. I. pp. 245—249.

§ Pierre de Roquebertin, Knight, Councillor and Chamberlain of Louis XI., Governor of Roussillon and Cerdagne, and Lord of Sommières.

approach the castle before the opening of the gates; and he ordered they should lie in the ditches, but retire to the sparrow-nests upon occasion. He was sensible enough that this fortification was too weak to keep out an army, or any great body of men, but he had no fear of such an attack; his great apprehension was, that some of the nobility of his kingdom, having intelligence within, might attempt to make themselves masters of the castle by night, and having possessed themselves partly of it by favour, and partly by force, might deprive him of the regal authority, and take upon themselves the administration of public affairs; upon pretence he was incapable of business, and no longer fit to govern.

The gate of the Plessis was never opened, nor the drawbridge let down, before eight o'clock in the morning, at which time the officers were let in; and the captains ordered their guards to their several posts, with pickets of archers in the middle of the court, as in a town upon the frontiers that is closely guarded: nor was any person admitted to enter except by the wicket and with the king's knowledge, unless it were the steward of his household, and such persons as were not admitted into the royal presence.*

* Sir Walter Scott's description of the Royal Castle of Plessis is sufficiently accurate to deserve insertion. "There were three external walls, battlemented and turreted from space to space, and at each angle; the second enclosure rising higher than the first, and being built so as to command the exterior defence, in case it was won by the enemy; and being again, in the same manner, itself commanded by the third and innermost barrier. Around the external wall was sunk a ditch of about twenty feet in depth, supplied with water by a dam-head on the River Cher, or rather on one of its tributary branches. In front of the second enclosure there ran another fosse, and a third of the same unusual dimensions was led between the second and the innermost enclosure. The verge, both of the outer and inner circuit of this triple moat, was strongly fenced with palisades of iron, serving the purpose of what are called *chevaux-de-frise* in modern fortification; the top of each pale being divided into a cluster of sharp spikes, which seemed to render any attempt to climb over an act of self-destruction.

"From within the innermost enclosure arose the castle itself, containing buildings of different periods, crowded around, and united with the ancient and grim-looking donjon-keep, which was older than any of them, and which rose like a black Ethiopian giant, high into the air, while the absence of any windows larger than shot-holes, irregularly disposed for defence, gave the spectator the same unpleasant feeling

Is it possible then to keep a prince (with any regard to his quality) in a closer prison than he kept himself? The cages which were made for other people were about eight feet square; and he (though so great a monarch) had but a small court of the castle to walk in, and seldom made use of that, but generally kept himself in the gallery, out of which he went into the chambers on his way to mass, but never passed through the court. Who can deny that he was a sufferer as well as his neighbours, considering how he was locked up and guarded, afraid of his own children and relations, and changing every day those very servants whom he had brought up and advanced; and though they owed all their preferment to him, yet he durst not trust any of them, but shut himself up in those strange chains and enclosures. If the place where he confined himself was larger than a common prison, he also was much greater than common prisoners.

which we experience on looking at a blind man. The other buildings seemed scarcely better adapted for the purposes of comfort, for the windows opened to an inner and enclosed courtyard; so that the whole external front looked much more like that of a prison than a palace.

" This formidable place had but one entrance; at least none could be seen along the spacious front, except where in the centre of the first and outward boundary arose two strong towers, the usual defences of a gateway, with their ordinary accompaniments, portcullis and drawbridge. Similar entrance-towers were visible on the second and third bounding wall; but not on the same line with those on the outward circuit, because the passage did not cut right through the whole three enclosures at the same point, but, on the contrary, those who entered had to proceed nearly thirty yards betwixt the first and second wall, exposed, if their purpose were hostile, to missiles from both; and again, when the second boundary was passed, they must make a similar digression from the straight line, in order to attain the portal of the third and innermost enclosure; so that, before gaining the outer court, which ran along the front of the building, two narrow and dangerous defiles were to be traversed under a flanking fire of artillery, and three gates, defended in the strongest manner known to the age, were to be successively forced.

" The environs of the castle, except the single winding path by which the portal might be safely approached, were surrounded with every species of hidden pitfall, snare, and gin, to entrap the wretch who should venture thither without a guide; and upon the walls were constructed certain cradles of iron, called *sparrow-nests*, from which the sentinels, who were regularly posted there, could, without being exposed to any risk, take deliberate aim at any who should attempt to enter without the proper signal or pass-word of the day."

It may be urged that other princes have been more given to suspicion than he, but it was not in our time; and, perhaps, their wisdom was not so eminent, nor were their subjects so good. They might too, probably, have been tyrants, and bloody-minded; but our king never did any person a mischief who had not offended him first, though I do not say all who offended him deserved death. I have not recorded these things merely to represent our master as a suspicious and mistrustful prince; but to show, that by the patience which he expressed in his sufferings.(like those which he inflicted on other people), they may be looked upon, in my judgment, as a punishment which our Lord inflicted upon him in this world, in order to deal more mercifully with him in the next, as well in regard to those things before-mentioned, as to the distempers of his body, which were great and painful, and much dreaded by him before they came upon him; and, likewise, that those princes who may be his successors, may learn by his example to be more tender and indulgent to their subjects, and less severe in their punishments than our master had been : although I will not censure him, or say I ever saw a better prince; for though he oppressed his subjects himself, he would never see them injured by anybody else.

After so many fears, sorrows, and suspicions, God, by a kind of miracle, restored him both in body and mind, as is His divine method in such kind of wonders; for He took him out of this miserable world in perfect health of mind, and understanding, and memory; after having received the sacraments himself, discoursing without the least twinge or expression of pain, and repeating his paternosters to the very last moment of his life. He gave directions * for his own burial, appointed who should attend his corpse to the

---

* These directions will be found in Dupont, iii. 339—344. Master Colin of Amiens is therein directed to represent the king " on his knees on a cushion, with his dog beside him, his hat in his clasped hands, his sword by his side, and his horn hanging behind his shoulders. Let him be dressed in a hunting suit, with boots on his feet; and withal the handsomest countenance you can make him, young and smooth; with his nose rather long and turned-up a little, as you know; and do not make him bald." This effigy was to be made of molten copper, and gilt with ducat gold; and the sum to be paid for it was a thousand gold crowns.

grave, and declared that he desired to die on a Saturday of all days in the week; and that he hoped Our Lady would procure him that favour, for in her he had always placed great trust, and served her very devoutly. And so it happened; for he died on Saturday, the 30th of August, 1483, at about eight in the evening, in the Castle of Plessis, where his illness seized him on the Monday before. May Our Lord receive his soul, and admit it unto His kingdom of Paradise!

CH. XII.—A Digression concerning the Miseries of Mankind, especially of Princes, by the Example of those who reigned in the Author's Time, and chiefly of King Louis.

SMALL hopes and comfort ought poor and inferior people to have in this world, considering what so great a king suffered and underwent, and how he was at last forced to leave all, and could not, with all his care and diligence, protract his life one single hour. I knew him, and was entertained in his service in the flower of his age, and at the height of his prosperity, yet I never saw him free from labour and care. Of all diversions he loved hunting and hawking in their seasons; but his chief delight was in dogs. As for ladies, he never meddled with any in my time; for about the time of my coming to his court he lost a son*, at whose death he was extremely afflicted, and he made a vow to God in my presence never to have intercourse with any other woman but the queen; and though this was no more than what he was bound to do by the canons of the church, yet it was much that his self-command should be so great, that he should be able to persevere in his resolution so firmly, considering that the queen (though an excellent princess in other respects) was not a person in whom a man could take any great delight.

In hunting, his eagerness and pain were equal to his pleasure, for his chase was the stag, which he always ran down.

* This son's name was Joachim. He was born on Tuesday, the 17th of July, 1459, at the Castle of Genappes; and he died on the 29th of November in the same year.

He rose very early in the morning, rode sometimes a great distance, and would not leave his sport, let the weather be never so bad; and when he came home at night he was often very weary, and generally in a violent passion with some of his courtiers or huntsmen; for hunting is a sport not always to be managed according to the master's direction; yet, in the opinion of most people, he understood it as well as any prince of his time. He was continually at these sports, lodging in the country villages to which his recreations led him, till he was interrupted by business; for during the most part of the summer there was constantly war between him and Charles Duke of Burgundy, and in the winter they made truces.

He was also involved in some trouble about the county of Roussillon, with John, King of Arragon, father of Peter of Castile, who at present is King of Spain; for though both of them were poor, and already at variance with their subjects in Barcelona and elsewhere, and though the son had nothing but the expectation of succeeding to the throne of Don Henry of Castile, his wife's brother (which fell to him afterwards), yet they made considerable resistance; for that province being entirely devoted to their interest, and they being universally beloved by the people, they gave our king abundance of trouble, and the war lasted till his death, and many brave men lost their lives in it, and his treasury was exhausted by it; so that he had but a little time during the whole year to spend in pleasure, and even then the fatigues he underwent were excessive. When his body was at rest his mind was at work, for he had affairs in several places at once, and would concern himself as much in those of his neighbours as in his own, putting officers of his own over all the great families, and endeavouring to divide their authority as much as possible. When he was at war he laboured for a peace or a truce, and when he had obtained it, he was impatient for war again. He troubled himself with many trifles in his government, which he had better have let alone: but it was his temper, and he could not help it; besides, he had a prodigious memory, and he forgot nothing, but knew everybody, as well in other countries as in his own.

And, in truth, he seemed better fitted to rule a world than

to govern a single kingdom. I speak not of his minority, for then I was not with him ; but when he was eleven years old, he was, by the advice of some of the nobility, and others of his kingdom, embroiled in a war with his father, Charles VII., which lasted not long, and was called the Praguerie. When he was arrived at man's estate, he was married, much against his inclination, to the King of Scotland's daughter* ; and he regretted her existence during the whole course of her life. Afterwards, by reason of the broils and factions in his father's court, he retired into Dauphiny † (which was his own), whither many persons of quality followed him, and indeed more than he could entertain. During his residence in Dauphiny he married the Duke of Savoy's daughter ‡, and not long after he had great disputes with his father-in-law, and a terrible war was begun between them. His father, King Charles VII., seeing his son attended by so many good officers, and raising men at his pleasure, resolved to go in person against him, with a considerable body of forces, in order to disperse them. While he was upon his march he put out proclamations, requiring them all, as his subjects, under great penalties, to repair to him ; and many obeyed, to the great displeasure of the Dauphin, who, finding his father incensed, though he was strong enough to resist, resolved to retire, and leave that country to him ; and accordingly he removed, with but a slender retinue, into Burgundy, to Duke Philip's court, who received him honourably, furnished him nobly, and maintained him § and his principal

---

* Margaret, daughter of James I., King of Scotland. She was married to the Dauphin on the 24th of June, 1436; and died on the 16th of August, 1444. Her lot in France was singularly wretched, as she was treated by her husband with marked contempt and dislike. The story of her adventure with Alain Chartier is well known. Finding the famous poet asleep in a saloon of the palace, she stooped down and kissed him, observing to her ladies, who were somewhat astonished at her proceeding, that she did not kiss the man, but the mouth which had uttered so many fine things.

† In the year 1446. See Vol. I. p. 60.

‡ Charlotte, daughter of Louis, Duke of Savoy, was married to the Dauphin in March, 1451; and died on the 1st of December, 1483.

§ The Duke of Burgundy granted the Dauphin a monthly pension of 2000 francs; to the Dauphiness he allowed 1000 gold crowns per month; to the Lord of Montauban, 500 crowns; to the Marshal of Dauphiny, a similar sum; and to others according to their degree.

servants (as the Count de Comminges*, the Lord de Montauban †, and others), by way of pensions, and to the rest he
gave presents, as he saw occasion, during the whole time of
their residence there.   However, the Dauphin entertained so
many at his own expense, that his money often failed, to his
great disgust and mortification; for he was forced to borrow ‡, or his people would have forsaken him, which is
certainly a great affliction to a prince who was utterly unac-
customed to those straits.   So that during his residence at
the court of Burgundy he had his anxieties, for he was con-
strained to cajole the duke and his ministers, lest they should
think he was too burdensome, and had laid too long upon
their hands, for he had been with them six § years, and his
father, King Charles, was constantly pressing and soliciting
the Duke of Burgundy, by his ambassadors, either to deliver
him up to him, or to banish him out of his dominions.‖   And
this, you may believe, gave the Dauphin some uneasy thoughts,
and would not suffer him to be idle.   In which season of his
life, then, was it that he may be said to have enjoyed himself?
I believe from his infancy and innocence to his death, his
whole life was nothing but one continued scene of troubles
and fatigues¶; and I am of opinion, that if all the days

* John, Bastard of Armagnac, was created Count of Comminges and
Marshal of France in 1461, and died in 1473.

† See Vol. I. p. 19.

‡ He once borrowed thirty crowns from the Lord de Sassenage, to
whom he gave the following receipt: "We, Louis, eldest son of the King
of France, Dauphin of Viennois, confess that we owe to James, Lord
of Sassenage, the sum of thirty crowns for a black horse, which he has
handed over and delivered, by our order, to Henry Guerin, to whom we
have given it: which sum of thirty crowns we promise to pay him before
Christmas next.   In witness whereof we have signed these presents."
The Dauphiness, on her accession to the throne of France, was obliged
to borrow the palfreys of the Countess of Charolais for her journey.—
DUPONT, ii. 275.

§ He remained there only five years.

‖ On learning the reception given to Louis by the Duke of Burgundy,
Charles VII. said: "Our brother Philip has taken home a fox who will
eat his chickens."

¶ Chastellain (129.) reports this speech of Louis XI. on his accession
to the crown: "Only yesterday I held myself to be the poorest son of a
king that ever was, and one who, from my infancy to the present day,
have had nought but suffering and tribulation, poverty, anguish, and
want; and, what is more, expulsion from my inheritance, and loss of my

of his life were computed in which his joys and pleasures outweighed his pain and trouble, they would be found so few, that there would be twenty mournful ones to one pleasant. He lived about sixty-one years, yet he always fancied he should never outlive sixty, giving this for a reason, that for a long time no king of France had lived beyond that age. Some say, since the time of Charlemagne; but the king our master was far advanced in his sixty-first year.*

What ease or what pleasure did Charles, Duke of Burgundy, enjoy more than our master King Louis? In his youth, indeed, he had less trouble, for he did not begin to enter upon any action till nearly the two-and-thirtieth year of his age; so that before that time he lived in great ease and quiet. His first quarrel was with his father's chief officers; and as his father took their part, he immediately withdrew from court, and retired into Holland †, where being well received, he fell immediately into intelligence with the Gantois, and went and visited his father sometimes. He had no allowance from his father; but Holland, being a rich country, made him great presents, as did several other great towns, hoping thereby to insinuate themselves into his favour, and reap the advantage after Duke Philip's death. And it is the common custom of the world to worship the rising sun, and court him whose future authority will be great, rather than him who is already at the height of his fortune, and can never be higher. For this reason, when Duke Philip was informed that the Gantois had expressed great kindness for his son, and that he understood how to manage them, he answered, "They always love him who is to be their sovereign; but as soon as he is their lord they will hate him." And his saying was true, for from the time of Duke Philip's death and Charles's accession, their love began to decline, and they showed it openly, and he, on the other side, cared as little for them; yet they did more mischief to his posterity than they could possibly do to him.

father's love, so as to be obliged, my wife and myself, to live by borrowing and begging, without a foot of land, a house to cover us, or a penny in our pockets, except by the goodness and charity of my good uncle, who has maintained me thus for the space of five years."

* The exact age of Louis XI. at the time of his death was sixty years, one month, and twenty-seven days.

† In the year 1462.

But to continue these Memoirs. From the time Duke Charles undertook his war to recover the towns in Picardy, (which our master had redeemed from Duke Philip), and joined himself with the lords of the kingdom in the war called the Public Good, what pleasure, what tranquillity had he? He had continual trouble and labour, without the least cessation or refreshment, either to his body or mind; for glory got entire possession of his heart, and constantly spurred him on to attempt new conquests. He was always in the field during summer, exposing his person to the greatest danger, taking the care and command of the whole army upon himself; and yet he thought his work too little. He was the first that rose, and the last that went to bed in the camp; and he slept in his clothes, like the poorest foot-soldier in the army. In winter, when the campaign was over, he was busily employed about raising money; six hours every morning he set apart for conferences, and for giving audience to ambassadors; and in this perpetual hurry of affairs he ended his days, and was killed by the Swiss in the battle of Nancy, as you have already heard; so that it cannot be said that he enjoyed one happy day from the time of his beginning to aggrandise himself to the hour of his death; and then what were the fruits of all his pains and labour? Or what necessity was there of his doing so? since he was a rich prince, and had towns and territories large enough already to have made him happy, if he could have been contented with them.

The next prince whom we shall have occasion to mention is Edward IV., King of England, a great and powerful monarch. In his minority he saw his father the Duke of York * defeated and slain in battle, and with him the father † of the Earl of Warwick, who governed the king in his youth, and managed all his affairs; and, to say the truth, it was the Earl of Warwick who made Edward king, and dethroned his old master, King Henry VI., who had reigned many years in England, and (in my judgment, and the judgment of the world,) was the lawful king; but, in such cases, the disposal of kingdoms and great states is in the hands of

* See Vol. I. p. 48.
† Richard Neville, Earl of Westmoreland and Salisbury.

God, who orders them as He pleases, for indeed all things proceed from Him. The reason of the Earl of Warwick's espousing the interest of the House of York against King Henry, who was of the Lancastrian family, was upon a difference that happened at court betwixt the Duke of Somerset and the Earl of Warwick. The king not having wisdom enough to compose it, it grew to that height that the queen* (who was of the house of Anjou, and daughter to René, King of Sicily) interposed in it, and inclined to the duke's party against the Earl of Warwick; for all had acknowledged Henry, his father, and his grandfather, for their lawful kings. The queen would have acted much more prudently in endeavouring to have adjusted the dispute between them than in saying, "I am of this party, and will maintain it;" and it proved so by the event, for it occasioned many battles in England, and a war which continued nine-and-twenty years†; and in the end nearly all the partisans of both sides were destroyed; so that factions and parties are very perilous and fatal, especially to the nobility, who are too prone to propagate and foment them. If it be alleged that by this means both parties are kept in awe, and the secret minds of his subjects are discovered to the prince, I agree that a young prince may encourage faction among his ladies, and it may be pleasant and diverting enough, and may give him opportunity of finding out some of their intrigues; but nothing is so dangerous to a nation as to nourish such factions and partialities among men of courage and magnanimity; it is no less than setting one's own house on fire; for immediately some or other cry out, " The king is against us," seize upon some fortified town, and correspond with his enemies. And certainly the factions of Orleans and Burgundy ought to make us wise on this point; for they began a war which lasted seventy-two years‡, in which the English were concerned, and thought by those unhappy divisions to have conquered the kingdom.

* Margaret of Anjou, daughter of René, King of Naples and Sicily. She was born on the 23rd of March, 1429; married to King Henry VI in 1444; and died on the 25th of August, 1482.

† The first battle was fought in 1455, and the last in 1471. See Vol. I. p. 181.

‡ See Vol. I p. 273.

But to return from this digression.   King Edward was a
very young prince, and one of the handsomest men of his
age, at the time he had overcome all his difficulties; so he
gave himself up wholly to pleasures, and took no delight in
anything but ladies, dancing, entertainments, and the chase;
and in this voluptuous course of life, if I mistake not, he
spent about sixteen years, till the quarrel happened between
him and the Earl of Warwick.   In which contest, though
the king was driven out of the kingdom, yet his misfortune
lasted not long; for he quickly returned, obtained a victory,
and afterwards fell again to his pleasures, and indulged himself in them more recklessly than before.   From this time
he feared nobody: but he grew very fat, and his excess inclining him to diseases, in the very flower of his age, he died
suddenly (as it was reported) of an apoplexy*, and his family
perished after him (as you have heard), as regarded the succession in the male line.

In our time also, there reigned two wise and valiant
princes, Matthias, King of Hungary†, and Mahomet Ottoman, Emperor of the Turks.‡   This King Matthias was the
son of a very valiant gentleman, called the White Knight
of Wallachia §, a person of great honour and prudence, who

* This is the third explanation given by Commines of the cause of
Edward's death.   At Vol. I. p. 394., he says he died of *melancholy*, and
at p. 62. of this volume he ascribes his decease to a *catarrh*.   Apoplexy
is the most probable explanation of the event.

† Matthias I., surnamed Corvinus, was the son of John Hunniades,
and was proclaimed King of Hungary in 1458, at the age of sixteen
years.   He reigned for thirty-two years with considerable reputation, to
which his patronage of learned men, who repaid his munificence with
very profuse eulogies, did not a little contribute.   He died in 1490.

‡ Mahomet II., son of Amurath II., was proclaimed Sultan in 1451,
and died in 1481.   He is usually distinguished by European historians
by the title of Mahomet the Great, first Emperor of the Turks.   His
reign was signalised by the capture of Constantinople, and the fall of
the Byzantine empire.

§ John Hunniades, Voyvode of Transylvania, was Regent of Hungary during the minority of King Ladislaus.   This hero stood in the
breach for twelve years against the Turkish power, frequently defeated,
but unconquered in defeat.   "If the renown of Hunniades," says Mr.
Hallam, "may seem exaggerated by the partiality of writers who lived
under the reign of his son, it is confirmed by more unequivocal evidence, by the dread and hatred of the Turks, whose children were taught
obedience by threatening them with his name, and by the deference of a

for a long time had governed the kingdom of Hungary, and had gained several battles over the Turks, who are neighbours to that country, by reason of the territories which they have usurped in Sclavonia, Bosnia, and Greece. Not long after his death, Lancelot * came to man's estate, who was heir to that kingdom, and to the kingdoms of Bohemia and Poland besides. This Lancelot was advised by some persons (as was reported) to seize upon the two sons of the White Knight, on the pretence that, as their father had obtained and exercised so much power and authority in that kingdom during his infancy, it was not improbable that his sons might do the same. Upon which the said Lancelot resolved to have them both apprehended, which was accordingly done. He put the eldest † to death, and sent the other, which was Matthias, a prisoner to Buda, the chief town in Hungary; but he did not remain long in confinement (God Almighty being perhaps pleased with the services of his father), for, awhile after, King Lancelot was poisoned at Prague, in Bohemia, by a lady of quality (whose brother I have seen), with whom he had been in love, and she with him; but being incensed at his intended marriage in France, with the

---

jealous aristocracy to a man of no distinguished birth." Hunniades was a Wallachian, of a small family. His last and most splendid service was the relief of Belgrade. That strong city was besieged by Mahomet II., three years after the fall of Constantinople; its capture would have laid open all Hungary. A tumultuary army, chiefly collected by the preaching of a friar, was entrusted to Hunniades. He penetrated into the city, and having repulsed the Turks in a fortunate sally, wherein Mahomet was wounded, had the honour of compelling him to raise the siege in confusion. The relief of Belgrade was more important in its effects than in its immediate circumstances: it revived the spirits of Europe, which had been appalled by the unceasing victories of the infidels. Mahomet himself seemed to acknowledge the importance of the blow, and seldom afterwards attacked the Hungarians. Hunniades died in 1456, soon after this achievement.

* Ladislaus V., King of Hungary, was the posthumous son of Albert, Duke of Austria, who acquired the crown of Hungary for his progeny by marrying Elizabeth, daughter of the Emperor Sigismund. Ladislaus was born on the 22nd of February, 1440; became king on the 13th of February, 1453; and died on the 23rd of November, 1457.

† Ladislaus, the eldest son of John Hunniades, was beheaded on the 8th of March, 1456, for having assassinated the Count of Cillei during the preceding year.

daughter * of King Charles VII. (called now the Princess of Vienne), which was contrary to his engagement to her, she poisoned him in a bath, by giving him an apple to eat, and conveying poison into the haft of his knife. Upon the death of Lancelot, the barons of Hungary assembled at Buda for the election of a king, according to an ancient privilege which they have, to elect their king when his predecessor has died without issue. Whilst they were mightly divided, and in great controversy about the election, the widow of the White Knight, and mother of Matthias, entered the town with a very splendid equipage; for she was very rich, especially in ready money, which her husband had left her, by means of which she was able to raise men immediately; and, besides, it is not improbable that she had partisans in the town, and among the electors, upon account of the influence and authority her husband had had in that kingdom. As soon as she came into the city, she marched directly to the prison, and released her son; upon which some of the barons and prelates who were assembled fled in terror out of the town, and those that remained chose Matthias for their king; and he reigned among them in great prosperity, with as much applause and esteem as any of his predecessors, and in some things with even more. He was a man of as much courage as any of that age, and obtained many signal victories over the Turks, without any loss to his kingdom, which he much enlarged, as well towards Turkey as towards Bohemia (most of which was in his possession), and also in Wallachia (where he was born) and Sclavonia; and on the side towards Germany he took the greatest part of Austria from the Emperor Frederic, and kept it till his death, which happened in Vienna, the chief city of Austria, in the year 1491. He was a prince who managed his affairs discreetly, both in peace and in war. Towards the latter end of his days, finding he was become formidable, he began to affect a pompous and splendid way of living, and provided great store of rich hangings, jewels, and plate, for the adornment of his palace. All his business was dispatched by himself, or by his direc-

* Madelaine of France, daughter of King Charles VII., was born on the 1st of December, 1443, and betrothed to the King of Hungary in 1457. In 1461 she married Gaston de Foix, Prince of Viane; and she died in 1486.

tion : he had also an inclination to make himself terrible to his own subjects, and became a very tyrant towards his latter end ; after which he fell into a grievous and incurable distemper, as it were in his youth (for he was but eight-and-twenty* years of age), and died : his life having been one continued scene of labour and sorrow, without any great pleasure or ease.

The Turk, whom I mentioned before, was a wise and valiant prince, but he made more use of his cunning than of his courage. His father† also was a valiant prince, who took Adrianople (that is to say, the city of Adrian), and left his son very great; and this son, at the age of twenty-three, took Constantinople‡, or the city of Constantine; I have seen his portrait painted at that age, which represented him vigorous and sprightly. It was a great disgrace to all Christendom to suffer that city to be lost; he took it by assault, and the Emperor of the East § (whom we called Emperor of Constantinople) was slain in the breach. Many brave men were killed with him in this assault, many great ladies ravished, and no manner of cruelty was omitted. This was his first exploit, but he continued to perform great actions, and so many, that I heard a Venetian ambassador say once in the presence of Charles, Duke of Burgundy, that this Mahomet had conquered two empires, four kingdoms, and two hundred cities; he meant, indeed, the empires of Con-

---

* As might have been expected, from his having no personal knowledge of Hungarian affairs, Commines falls into many inaccuracies about Matthias Corvinus, who was forty-eight years old when he died, in the year 1490. His election to the kingdom is to be ascribed far less to any intrigues of his mother than to the aversion felt by the Hungarian nobles to the character and Austrian connections of the Emperor Frederic III., the other candidate for the crown.

† Amurath II. succeeded his father Mahomet I. in 1421, and died in 1451.

‡ The siege of Constantinople began on the 6th of April, 1453, and the city was taken on the 29th of May following. — See GIBBON's *Roman Empire*, chap. 68.

§ Constantine Palæologus XIV., surnamed Dragases, was born in February, 1403, and succeeded to his father's throne in November, 1448. He fought bravely in defence of his capital, and when he found resistance unavailing, " he folded around him the imperial mantle, and remembered the name which he represented in the dignity of heroic death."

stantinople and Trebizond *; the kingdoms of Bosnia, Syria, Armenia, and I think Morea was the fourth. He conquered likewise many fair islands in the Archipelago (where the Venetians have two† settlements), among others, Negropont and Mitylene; besides which he subdued nearly all Albania and Sclavonia: and as his conquests were great over the Christians, so were they no less considerable over those of his own religion, among whom he destroyed several great princes, as the Prince of Caramania‡, and others.

The greatest part of his affairs were transacted by himself, according to the practice of our king and of the king of Hungary; and these three were without all dispute the wisest princes that had reigned for a hundred years. But the generosity of our master's conversation, and his liberality to his servants, as well as to foreigners and others, distinguished him very much from the other two; and it is no wonder, for he was styled the most Christian King. As to worldly pleasures and enjoyments, this Turk had his share, and spent most of his time in them; and, indeed, he would have done more mischief to Christendom, had he not been so employed. He indulged himself in all kinds of sensuality, and was strangely given to gluttony, which brought him numberless diseases, which continued upon him as long as he lived. Every spring he had a swelling in his legs, that made them as big as a man's waist (as I have heard from those who have seen it); and the swelling never broke, but dispersed of its own accord, and no surgeon could tell what to make of it, but all agreed his gluttony was the occasion of it, though perhaps it was a judgment from heaven; and one reason why he suffered himself to be seen so seldom, and kept himself shut up in his seraglio, was, lest he should discover that infirmity, and grow contemptible to his subjects. He died about the fifty-second year of his age, and suddenly; yet he made a will, and I have seen it, and, if it be true, he

---

* The empire of Trebizond was overthrown by Mahomet in 1461.

† The Venetian settlements of Modon and Coron in the Morea were surrendered to the Turks in the year 1500.

‡ Caramania, a province of Asiatic Turkey, on the south of Anatolia. Its emirs were formerly powerful princes; but Mahomet II. greatly weakened them in 1440, and his son Bajazet incorporated their dominions with the Turkish empire in 1488.

seemed to have some remorse for a tax which he had lately laid upon his subjects.   Let Christian princes therefore consider what they do, since they have no reasonable power to raise money, without the permission and consent of their people.

Thus have you seen the death of many illustrious persons in a short time, who had borne so much sorrow, and endured so many fatigues, only to extend their dominions, and advance their fame and glory, as perhaps tended not only to the shortening of their lives, but to the endangering the welfare of their immortal souls.   I am not speaking here of the Turk, for I question not but that he is gone to his predecessors, but of our king and the rest, on whom I hope God will have mercy.   But to speak freely (as one that is no great scholar or genius, but has had some experience in the world), would it not have been better for them, and for all other great princes and subjects whatever, to choose a middle course in all their desires ; that is, not to be so solicitous and careful about temporal things, and have such vast and unreasonable designs in view; but to be more cautious of offending God, oppressing their subjects, and invading their neighbours, by so many cruel and unchristian ways, as I have mentioned before, and rather employ their time in tranquillity and innocent diversions? Their lives would be longer, their infirmities the later in coming, their deaths less desirable to other people, and less terrible to themselves. Can we desire any clearer examples to prove how poor and inconsiderable a creature man is, how short and miserable his life, and how little difference there is betwixt princes and private persons, since as soon as they are dead, whether rich or poor, their bodies become abominable, all people fly and shun them, and their souls are no sooner separated but they prepare to receive their doom, which is given by God at that very instant of time, according to every man's works, and bodily deserts.

BOOK THE SEVENTH.

CH. I.—How Duke René of Lorraine came into France to demand the Duchy of Bar and the County of Provence, which King Charles had in his Possession; and how he failed to obtain the Kingdom of Naples, to which he laid Claim as well as the King; and what Right each had thereto.—1484—6.

To continue these Memoirs, which were begun by me, Philip de Commines, concerning the exploits and reign of our late king, Louis XI. (whom God absolve!), I will now give you an account how it came to pass that his son, Charles VIII., undertook his expedition into Italy, in which I was engaged. The king set out from Vienne*, in Dauphiny, on the 23rd of August, 1494, and returned into his kingdom in October of the year 1495. Before he undertook this enterprise, it was warmly debated whether he should go or not, for by all persons of experience and wisdom it was looked upon as a very dangerous undertaking; nor indeed was anybody in favour of it but himself, and one Stephen de Vers, a native of Languedoc, a man of mean extraction, and who had never seen or had the least knowledge of military affairs. It was also promoted at first by one Brissonet†, who was one of the generals of the finances, but his heart soon failed him. However,

---

* Charles VIII. set out from Grenoble, on his journey into Italy, on the 29th of August, 1494. He had previously resided for four months at Vienne, and left that city for Grenoble on the 23rd of August, as is stated in the text.

† Guillaume Briçonnet was the son of Jean Briçonnet, Lord of Varennes, Secretary to the King, and Receiver-General of the Finances. He at first embraced his father's profession, and was appointed General of the Finances in Languedoc by Louis XI. In 1490 he was installed in the bishopric of St. Malo, and created Chief Superintendent of the Finances. In 1495 he received a cardinal's hat; in 1497 he was translated to the archbishopric of Rheims, and performed the ceremony of consecrating Louis XII.; and he died at Narbonne, of which he was archbishop, in 1514.

this expedition turned much to his advantage afterwards, for he obtained great preferment in the church, was made a cardinal, and was endowed with several benefices. De Vers had acquired a plentiful estate before, and was seneschal of Beaucaire, and president of the accounts at Paris, for he had served the King in his youth faithfully, in quality of gentleman of the bed-chamber; and, by his persuasion, Monsieur Brissonet was brought over to his party, so that they two were the chief promoters of this expedition, for which few persons praised them, and many censured them; because not only were all things necessary for so great an enterprise wanting, but the king was young, foolish, and obstinate, without either money, officers, or wise councillors. So that before he began his march he was forced to borrow a hundred thousand francs from the bank of Soly at Genoa* at an extravagant interest, and from mart to mart, besides what he collected in other places, as you shall hear hereafter. They had neither tents nor pavilions, though it was winter when the army entered into Lombardy: one thing, indeed, was very handsome, and that was a brigade of young gentlemen, who were lively and brisk, but under little command or discipline. So that we may conclude this whole expedition, both going and coming, was conducted purely by God; for, as I said before, the wisdom of the contrivers of this scheme contributed but little. However, they may boast of this, that they were the occasion of highly advancing the honour and glory of their king.

As soon as the King was fourteen or fifteen years old, at which age he was crowned†, the Duke of Lorraine‡ came to him to demand the duchy of Bar, which King Louis XI. had kept from him, and the county of Provence, which King

* By letters patent, issued at Lyons on the 30th of April, 1494, Charles VIII. authorises Master Pierre de Lignac to receive and distribute at Milan a sum of 20,000 ducats "for the payment of the troops we are raising in that neighbourhood to serve in our army for the conquest of our kingdom of Naples." This money was borrowed from the bank of Paul Sauli at Genoa, as is proved by a receipt in the writing of Pierre de Lignac, which still exists, and is printed in DU-PONT, ii. 292.

† Charles VIII. was born on the 30th of June, 1470, and consecrated at Rheims on the 30th of May, 1484.

‡ René II. See note, Vol. I. p. 242.

Charles of Anjou, his cousin-german, dying without issue, left to Louis XI. by his last will and testament.* The Duke of Lorraine laid claim to it, as being son to the daughter of René, King of Sicily, Duke of Anjou, and Count of Provence, and alleged that the King of Sicily had highly injured him, for that the said Charles of Anjou was but his nephew, son of his brother, the Count du Maine, whereas he was descended from his daughter. But King Charles pretended that Provence could not be transferred by will to a daughter. The conclusion of this affair was, Bar was restored for a sum of money, which the king demanded; and the Duke of Lorraine being in great favour, and having many friends at court (especially John, Duke of Bourbon, who was old, and desirous to marry his sister †), had a lucrative post‡, and the command of a hundred lances given him by the king, and a pension of thirty-six thousand francs for four years§, during which time his title to Provence was to be examined into. I was one of the council‖ which was chosen for this purpose, partly by the King's relations, and partly by the three Estates of the kingdom. Stephen de Vers, whom I mentioned before, and who had got some estate in Provence, and who had in his head the expedition to Naples, persuaded the King, young as he was, to declare (in the presence of his sister, the Duchess of Bourbon¶) to the Count de Com-

* Dated December 10, 1481. See Lenglet, iii. 334.

† Of the three sisters of the Duke of Lorraine, two only were living in 1484; namely, Yolande, who married the Landgrave of Hesse in 1496; and Margaret, who married René, Duke of Alençon, in 1488. As the Duke of Bourbon did not lose his second wife, Catherine of Armagnac, until March, 1487, he must, if Commines be right, have formed the project of a matrimonial alliance with the Duke of Lorraine during her lifetime.

‡ By letters patent, dated on the 7th of August, 1486. King Charles VIII. appointed the Duke of Lorraine his Grand Chamberlain, "with all the perquisites and pre-eminence attaching to the office."

§ This pension was to become due on and after the 1st of October, 1483.

‖ The Lord of Argenton was included in the List of Councillors of the King, drawn up immediately after the death of Louis XI. He was also one of the fifteen persons suggested to the States-General as most worthy to constitute the council of the young King.—Masselin, 123.

¶ She did not obtain the title of Duchess of Bourbon until after the death of her brother-in-law, John II., which occurred on the 1st of April, 1488.

minges, the Lord du Lau (who were both likewise of the council), and myself, that we should have a care he did not lose the county of Provence; and this was done before the above-mentioned agreement was made.

Before the expiration of the four years, some clerks of Provence produced a new will of King Charles I.*, brother to St. Louis, and the wills of other kings of Sicily of the house of France. By these it was pretended, that not only the county of Provence belonged to the king, but the kingdom of Sicily also, and other places possessed by the house of Anjou, and that the Duke of Lorraine had no title to any of them (which other people denied). And those who were against the Duke of Lorraine's title, addressed themselves to this Stephen de Vers, who persuaded his master that the last King Charles, Count of Provence, son of Charles of Anjou, Count du Maine, and nephew to King René, had left it to him by his will; for King René had made him his heir before he died, and preferred him before the Duke of Lorraine, who was his daughter's son; and this, they urged, was done by King René, in consideration of the wills of Charles I. and his wife, the Countess of Provence, by which they had enjoined that that kingdom and the county of Provence should not be separated, nor descend to a daughter, whilst there was a son living of their line. And they affirmed that the wills of their immediate successors, and particularly the will of Charles II. †, were to the same effect.

* Charles I., King of Naples, was the son of Louis VIII. of France. He married Beatrice, Countess of Provence and Forcalquier, and died on the 7th of January, 1295. He was invested with the kingdom of Sicily by Pope Clement IV., who charged him to conquer it, which he did, after a severe struggle with Manfred and Conradin, the legitimate possessors of the crown. But his reign was of short duration: the Sicilian Vespers overthrew his tyranny in 1282, and separated the kingdom of Sicily from that of Naples.

† Charles II., son of Charles I., King of Sicily, was a prisoner in the hands of the Sicilians at the period of his father's death in 1285. He was set at liberty in 1288, in pursuance of a treaty by which he acknowledged the separation and independence of the two crowns of Naples and Sicily; but Pope Nicholas IV., by whose influence the treaty was made, broke it, released Charles from his oath, and authorised him to begin the war anew. This war, which lasted twenty-four years, occupied without lustre the whole reign of Charles II. He died on the 5th of May, 1309.

During these four years, they that had the management of the king (who were the Duke and Duchess of Bourbon, and a chamberlain named the Lord of Graville *, and other lords of his bed-chamber, who at that time had great power) sent for the Duke of Lorraine to court, and put him into places of great trust and authority, in order that, as he was a person of a more enterprising temper than most of the courtiers, he might aid and assist them in their undertakings†; besides, they questioned not to find a way to get rid of him when they had no further need of him, as they did afterwards, when they found they were strong enough to manage affairs by themselves, and that the power of the Duke of Orleans‡ and the rest of the nobility in his faction was weakened. But after the expiration of the four years, the Duke of Lorraine refused to stay any longer at court, unless they would either put him into possession of the county of Provence, or secure it to him in writing at a fixed time, and meanwhile continue his pension of thirty-six thousand francs: to which they would not agree; so the Duke of Lorraine left court, highly disgusted with their conduct.

Four or five months before his leaving the court, a very lucky adventure happened to him, if he had known how to make use of it. The whole kingdom of Naples rebelled § against King Ferrand ‖, for his and his son's tyranny; and all the barons, and three parts of the kingdom, submitted themselves to the Church. But King Ferrand, with the

* Louis Malet, Lord of Graville, and one of the king's chamberlains, was appointed Admiral of France in 1486, and resigned that post in favour of his son-in-law, Charles d'Amboise, Lord of Chaumont, in 1508. He died on the 30th of October, 1516, aged seventy-eight years.

† The Duke of Lorraine made a written promise to the Duke and Duchess of Bourbon, dated at Bar, on the 29th of September, 1484, that he would support the young king.

‡ Louis d'Orleans, son of Charles, Duke of Orleans, and Mary of Cleves, succeeded to the throne of France in 1498, under the title of Louis XII. He was born on the 27th of June, 1462; crowned on the 27th of May, 1498; and died on the 1st of January, 1514. He was the chief opponent to the Duchess of Bourbon's claim to the Regency, during the minority of Charles VIII.

§ This revolt broke out on the 25th of October, 1485.—SISMONDI, xi. 265.

‖ See note, Vol. I. p. 313.

assistance of the Florentines, pressed them very hard; upon which the Pope* and the rebel lords of the kingdom sent to the Duke of Lorraine, to make him king; and they were so far in earnest in the matter, that their galleys, and the Cardinal of Saint Peter ad Vincula†, waited for him a long time at Genoa, whilst he was quarrelling at the French court, though ambassadors from all the nobility of Naples were with him, pressing him daily to depart.

The result of all was, the king and his council expressed great readiness to assist him. He was promised sixty thousand francs, and received twenty thousand of them; the rest he lost. He had leave to carry his hundred lances along with him, and was told that the king would send ambassadors to foreign courts in his favour. However, though the king was now nineteen years of age, yet he was still governed by the persons above-named, who were always telling him of his undoubted title to the kingdom of Naples (which I insert the rather, because persons of little consideration are often capable of raising great troubles), as I learned from several of

---

* Gian Battista Cibo, Cardinal of Melfi, was elected Pope on the 29th of August, 1484, and assumed the title of Innocent VIII. At the time of his elevation to the supremacy he was about fifty-five years of age, and had several natural children. He was quite as corrupt as his predecessor, Sixtus IV., but endued with far less talent and energy. He married his son, Franceschetto Cibo, to a daughter of Lorenzo de' Medici; and this alliance afterwards procured to his posterity the duchy of Massa-Carrara. In 1489 he gave a cardinal's hat to Giovanni de' Medici, afterwards Leo X. By venality in the distribution of justice, by monopoly, and by the ignorance and carelessness of his administration, he brought Rome into a state of poverty and humiliation previously unexampled. He died on the 25th of July, 1492, the most despised, but not the most detested, of the Popes who had yet filled the chair of St. Peter.

† Giuliano della Rovere, Cardinal of St. Peter ad Vincula, and Bishop of Avignon, was elected Pope on the 1st of November, 1503, under the title of Julius II. Although violent and irascible, he had a strong sense of his duty as a pontiff and as an Italian. He was determined on preserving the States of the Church intact for his successors. He rejected all nepotism, all aggrandisement of his family; and would have accused himself of unpardonable weakness if he had suffered others to usurp what he refused to give his family. With these motives, he made his tiara a helmet and his crosier a sword. After having driven the French out of Italy, and restored the Medici at Florence, he died of an inflammatory disease on the 21st of February, 1513. See his life in RANKE's *History of the Popes*, in BONN's *Standard Library*.

the Duke of Lorraine's ambassadors to Rome, Florence, Genoa, and elsewhere, and also from the duke himself as he passed by Moulins, where I then resided with John Duke of Bourbon, upon account of a dispute with the court. At that time the Duke of Lorraine's opportunity was half lost already by his own delay; however, I went out to meet him, though I had no obligation to do so, for he was partly the occasion of my being driven from court, and had given me very abusive language. But nobody was now so dear to him as I; he caressed me at a most extravagant rate, and complained heavily of those who had the present administration of affairs. He continued two days with John Duke of Bourbon, and then he set out for Lyons.

In short, his friends were so weary and tired with waiting, that both Pope and barons came to an accommodation* with King Ferrand; in reliance upon which, when the barons ventured to Naples, they were all seized and imprisoned†, though the Pope, the Venetians, the King of Spain, and the Florentines, had all of them guaranteed the observance of the peace, and had promised and sworn to secure their safety. The Prince of Salerno‡ escaped into France, refusing to be comprehended in the treaty of accommodation, as he knew the revengeful temper of King Ferrand; and the Duke of Lorraine returned with great shame and dishonour into his own country. He never afterwards had any credit with our king, who took away his lances, stopped his pension of· thirty-six thousand francs for the county of Provence; and in that condition he stands to this very day, which is the year 1497.

* Peace was concluded on the 11th of August, 1486.

† In contempt of his plighted word, Ferdinand ordered the arrest of the Princes of Altamura and Bisignano, and of several other gentlemen, who were immediately put to death, and their bodies sewn up in sacks, and thrown into the sea.—SISMONDI, xi. 278.

‡ Antonio de Sanseverino, Count of Marsico and Prince of Salerno, was Grand Admiral of Naples in 1477, and died in 1497.

CH. II. — How the Prince of Salerno, a Neapolitan by Birth, came into France ; and the Endeavours that were used by him and Ludovic Sforza, surnamed the Moor, to persuade the King to make War upon the King of Naples ; and the Occasion of it. — 1486-92.

THE Prince of Salerno with three of his nephews, sons to the Prince of Bisignan *, fled to Venice, where he had great acquaintance. Their business was to consult the senate (as the prince told me himself), to know what prince they should address themselves to, whether to the Duke of Lorraine, the King of France, or the King of Spain. He told me their answer was, that the Duke of Lorraine was a dead man, and it was impossible for him ever to relieve them ; that the King of Spain would be too powerful if he had the kingdom of Naples in addition to the isle of Sicily and what he possessed already in the Gulf of Venice ; and that his strength at sea was very considerable : but they would rather advise them to apply to the King of France, for with the Kings of France who formerly reigned in Naples, the Venetians had held very good friendship and amity ; and this I believe was spoken without any anticipation of what happened afterwards. The conclusion of all was that these barons came into France, where they were well received, but indifferently supplied. They solicited very hard for two years together ; and all their applications were made to Stephen de Vers, at that time seneschal of Beaucaire, and chamberlain to the king.

One day they were in hopes, another in despair. However, their friends were active in Italy, especially in Milan, where John Galeas† was duke ; not the great Galeas ‡, who

* Girolamo de Sanseverino, Count of Tricario and Prince of Bisignano, was Grand Chamberlain to Ferdinand I. King of Naples. He was treachereously murdered by order of his sovereign in 1487.

† Gian Galeazzo Sforza succeeded to the dukedom of Milan on the assassination of his father, and died in 1494, at the age of twenty-five. He was succeeded by his uncle Ludovic the Moor, who was probably the cause of his death.

‡ Gian Galeazzo Visconti became Lord of Milan in 1378, on the death of his father Galeazzo. In 1395 he obtained from the Emperor Wenceslaus a diploma creating him Duke of Milan ; and by a subsequent imperial diploma the boundaries of his duchy were defined, and

is buried in the Chartreux at Pavia, but the son of Duke Galeas * and the Duchess Bona †, a daughter of the House of Savoy; which duke being a weak prince, the Duchess had the education of her children; and I saw her (when she was a widow) in great authority, but managed by one of her secretaries called Cico ‡, who had been a long time in that family, and had banished or imprisoned all the brothers § of this Duke Galeas, in order to secure the duchess and her children. Among the rest he banished one Ludovic ‖ (who has since become Duke of Milan), whom she afterwards recalled, though he was her enemy, and actually in arms against her; as she did also the Lord Robert di St. Severino ¶, a valiant captain whom this Cico had likewise banished.

At last, by the persuasion of one Anthony Tassini **, who was her carver (a native of Ferrara, and of mean extrac-

made to include twenty-five towns, from Verona and Vicenza on the east to Alessandria and Tortona on the west. In 1402 he was only waiting for the surrender of Florence to declare himself King of Italy, when he died suddenly of the plague.

* Galeazzo Maria Sforza, son of the eminent Francesco Sforza, succeeded his father as Duke of Milan in 1466. Ten years afterwards, on the 26th December, 1476, he was assassinated in a solemn procession, and in his ducal robes, as he was entering the Church of St. Stefano.

† Bona of Savoy assumed the regency of the dukedom on the death of her husband.

‡ Cecco or Francesco Simoneta was a native of Calabria, whose integrity and activity had recommended him to the patronage of Duke Francesco Sforza. He afterwards became prime minister of Duke Galeazzo Maria. On the 11th of September, 1479, he was arrested and conveyed to the Castle of Pavia, where he was beheaded on the 30th of October, 1480. He was brother to Giovanni Simoneta, whose elegant Latin history of the life of Francesco Sforza is one of the best records of the transactions of that period.

§ These were Sforza, Duke of Bari, Ludovic the Moor, Ottaviano, and Ascanio. Ottaviano soon after perished in attempting to cross the river Adde.

‖ Ludovico Maria Sforza, surnamed the Moor, was the second son of Francesco Sforza. He became Duke of Milan on the death of his nephew Gian Galeazzo Sforza, in 1494; and he died on the 16th of June, 1508.

¶ Roberto di Sanseverino, Count of Cajazzo, and Lieutenant-general of the armies of Italy.

** Antonio Tassini, a Ferrarese, Chamberlain to Galeazzo Maria, Duke of Milan.

tion), she recalled them very indiscreetly; presuming that, according to their oaths and promises, they would do no harm to Cico. But the third day after their return they took Cico, put him in a tub, and carried him through the town of Milan; for he was allied by marriage with one of the family of the Visconti, and had he been in the way, it is said they would not have dared to seize Cico; and the Lord Ludovic contrived that Robert di St. Severino, who was to pass that way, might have the pleasure of meeting him in that posture, for he knew he abhorred him: after which Cico was conducted to the castle of Pavia, where he died a prisoner.

They paid the lady all possible respect, and, as she thought, complied with her wishes in everything; but they held private councils among themselves, and never communicated anything to her but what they pleased; and she took it for the greatest kindness in them not to trouble her with anything. They gave her leave to give Anthony Tassini what presents she pleased: they assigned him an apartment near her own, and permitted him to carry her on horseback behind him through the town; and nothing but feasting and dancing went on in her palace. This way of living did not continue long, scarce half a year, during which time she made him many rich presents, and all packets were directed to him, which rendered him odious to the Lord Ludovic (uncle to the two children *), who intended to make himself sovereign, as he did afterwards. One morning† the children were both taken from their mother, and carried to a castle called "The Rock;" where they were confined by the appointment of the Lord Ludovic, Robert di St. Severino, one Pallevoisin ‡ (the young duke's governor), and the captain of the castle §, who, since the death of Duke Galeas, had never stirred out of it, nor did he for a long time after; till at length he was taken by the cir-

* Gian Galeazzo, mentioned in a previous note; and Hermes, who, after his brother's death, went to reside in Germany.
† They were conveyed to this castle in November, 1480, after the banishment of Antonio Tassini.
‡ Gian Francesco Pallavicini, one of the young duke's lieutenants.
§ Filippo Eustachio of Pavia, who was created a knight by the young Duke of Milan on Christmas-day in the year 1480.

cumvention of Ludovic, and the folly of his master, who took after his mother, and was far from wise.

When these persons had secured the children in the castle, they seized upon the treasury (which at that time was the richest in Christendom), and took an account of it; after which they caused three keys to be made, of which the duchess had one, but she never touched one farthing of the money afterwards. They made her renounce the guardianship of her son *, and the Lord Ludovic was appointed in her place; besides which they wrote letters to several places, and particularly into France, which I saw, and which contained severe remarks on her conduct, in relation to her favourite Anthony Tassini; yet they sent him away without any other punishment, for the Lord Robert was his friend, and would not suffer either his person or his estate to be touched. But these two great men could not as yet get admittance into the castle when they pleased; for the captain had a brother in it, and near a hundred and fifty men; and he always ordered the gate to be very strictly guarded when they entered, and would not suffer above one or two to come in with them; and this caution was used for a long time.

In the meanwhile a great dispute arose between the Lord Ludovic and Robert di St. Severino, as is usual, for it is impossible for two persons in authority to agree long together; but Ludovic getting the upper hand, the other quitted Milan, and went into the Venetian service. † Yet since that time, two of his sons, the Lord Galeas ‡ and the Count di Cajazzo§, came back into the service of the Lord Ludovic, and the state of Milan; some say they came with their

---

* The young duke was declared of full age on the 7th of October, 1480; and the duchess left Milan on the 2nd of November following. — SISMONDI, xi. 174.

† He was declared a rebel on the 27th of January, 1482; and in the month of March following, the Venetians appointed him their Lieutenant-general.

‡ Galeazzo di Sanseverino married Bianca, a natural daughter of Ludovico Sforza. He was killed in the battle of Pavia, in February, 1524.

§ Gian Francesco di Sanseverino, Count of Cajazzo, died on the 7th of September, 1502. He and his brother entered the service of the Duke of Milan in 1483.

father's consent, others say not : be it which it will, Ludovic entertained them very kindly, and they did, and do still *, serve him very faithfully. You must know that the Lord Robert, their father, was of the house of St. Severino †, but by a natural daughter, which in Italy is no great matter; for a natural daughter with them is as good as one lawfully begotten. I mention this because they assisted us in our enterprise in Italy, in favour of the Prince of Salerno (who is chief of the house of St. Severino), and for other reasons, which you shall hear afterwards.

The Lord Ludovic began presently to make it appear that he was resolved to establish his authority; and he caused money to be coined with the Duke's effigy on one side, and his own on the other, which caused abundance of the people of Milan to murmur. The duke was married to the Duke of Calabria's daughter‡, who, after the death of his father, Ferrand King of Naples, became king himself by the name of Alphonso; the young lady was very courageous, and would fain have stimulated her husband to vindicate his authority; but he was a weak prince, and merely disclosed all she said. The captain of the castle maintained his reputation for a long while, and never stirred from his fortress; for suspicions began now to arise, so that both the sons never went abroad together, but when one went forth the other stayed at home. In short, about a year or two before our expedition into Italy, this Lord Ludovic, having been abroad with the young duke, waited on him back to the castle, to receive homage of his subjects. The captain as usual ordered the drawbridge to be let down, and advanced a little way upon it with some of his officers to receive the duke and kiss his hand, according to the usual custom; the duke being at some distance from the bridge, the captain was forced to step forward a pace or two; upon which the two sons of St. Severino, and others that were with them,

---

* This was probably written in 1497.

† Instead of Sanseverino we should here read Sforza ; for Roberto di Sanseverino's mother was Lisa Attendolo, a natural daughter of Muzio Attendolo, the father of Francesco Sforza, Duke of Milan. See *note*, Vol. I. p. 52.

‡ Isabella, daughter of Alphonso II., King of Naples. She died in 1524.

seized on him and secured him.   Those of the castle pulled
up the drawbridge, upon which Ludovic, causing the end
of a candle to be lighted, swore he would cut off their heads
if they did not surrender the castle before the candle was
burnt out; upon which they submitted, and he fortified the
castle, and put a strong garrison in it for himself, though all
was done in the duke's name. Ludovic also caused a charge to
be made against the captain, upon pretence that he intended
to deliver up the castle to the emperor, and he seized upon
several Germans, who (as he gave out) were agents in the
business, but discharged them again; and he beheaded one
of his secretaries * as having been a principal manager of
that affair, and another for carrying messages betwixt them.
Ludovic kept the captain a long while in prison, but at last
he released him, stating that, when the Duchess Bona of
Milan had once upon a time corrupted one of the captain's
brothers, and hired him to kill him as he was entering into
the castle, the captain had prevented it; and upon that
account he now spared his life.†   Yet I am of opinion, had
he been guilty of a design of delivering that castle to the
emperor (who had a double title to it both as emperor‡ and
as Duke of Austria, which family claims it likewise), he
would scarce have pardoned him, for it would have produced
great disturbance in Italy, and the whole state of Milan
would have revolted in a day; for whilst they were under
the dominion of the emperors, they paid only half a ducat
taxes; but now, both clergy, nobility, and people are
cruelly oppressed, and are, to speak the truth, under a
perfect tyranny.

* Ludovico Terzago, a secretary and relative of Ludovico Sforza, was
sent by him to Pavia, where he was long kept a prisoner, and eventually
starved to death, according to popular rumour.—CORIO, p. 880.

† A plot against Ludovic was to have broken out on the 7th of December, 1485; among the conspirators were two brothers of Captain
Eustachio. — CORIO, p. 866.

‡ The duchy of Milan was then a fief of the empire.

CH. III.—How the Duchy of Milan is one of the finest and most valuable Territories in the World, if relieved from the heavy Tribute which oppresses it.—1492-3.

THE Lord Ludovic, being in possession of this castle, and finding all the soldiers belonging to the family devoted to his service, resolved to proceed; for he that is master of Milan has the whole government and signory at his mercy; because the principal senators, and those who have the charge of other places in that government, have their residence in that city. And, for the size of it, I never saw a richer or finer country than the duchy of Milan: and if the prince could content himself with a yearly revenue of five hundred thousand ducats, the subjects would grow only too wealthy, and the prince would be secure; but he raises six hundred and fifty or seven hundred thousand ducats every year, which is absolute tyranny, and makes the people prone to revolutions. Finding himself so near the completion of his wishes, as has been said before, the Lord Ludovic (who was married to the Duke of Ferrara's daughter*, by whom he had several children) took measures to strengthen himself with friends, both in Italy and abroad. He first entered into an alliance (for mutual preservation) with the Venetians†, to whom he was a great friend, to the prejudice of his father-in-law, from whom, not long before, the Venetians had taken a small territory called the Polesan‡, encompassed entirely with water, and wonderfully fruitful; which place (though but half a league distant from Ferrara) the Venetians keep to this day, and in it there are two pretty towns, Rovigo and Labadio§, which I have seen. This country was lost when the Duke of Ferrara made war upon the

---

* Beatrice d'Este was married to Ludovico Sforza on the 18th of January, 1491; and died on the 2nd of January, 1497. She was the daughter of Hercules d'Este, Duke of Ferrara, who succeeded his brother Borso in 1471.

† By a treaty dated on the 7th of August, 1484.—SISMONDI, xi. 243.

‡ Rovigo, the chief town of the Polesina, surrendered to the Venetians on the 17th of August, 1482.

§ Badia, a small town to the west of Rovigo, and near the right bank of the Adige.

Venetians at first by himself; but before the end of the war Alfonso, Duke of Calabria (whilst his father Ferrand was alive), Count Ludovic with the forces of Milan, the Florentines, the Pope *, and the city of Bologna, came in to his assistance: yet, when the Venetians were almost conquered, or at least very low, with their treasury exhausted, and several of their towns lost, Ludovic made an honourable and advantageous peace for them, by which all was to be restored to everybody but the poor Duke of Ferrara, who had begun the war at the instigation of Ludovic and Ferrand, whose daughter he had married; and the Duke of Ferrara was forced to let the Polesan remain in the hands of the Venetians, who keep it to this day.   It was reported that Ludovic had sixty thousand ducats for his pains; whether this be true or false I cannot state; but I know the Duke of Ferrara was of that opinion himself. Ludovic at this time was not married to his daughter; and therefore the friendship between him and the Venetians subsisted.

None of all the subjects or relations of John Galeas, Duke of Milan, gave the Lord Ludovic the least disturbance in his designs upon the duchy except the young duchess, who was a wise lady, daughter to Alphonso, Duke of Calabria (as I said before), eldest son to Ferrand, King of Naples. In the year 1493 the Lord Ludovic began to solicit King Charles VIII., now reigning in France, to undertake an expedition into Italy, to conquer the kingdom of Naples, and to supplant and exterminate those who possessed it; for, whilst they were in force and authority, Ludovic durst not attempt what he did afterwards; for at that time Ferrand, King of Sicily, and Alphonso his son, were both very rich, of great experience in war, and had the reputation of being very valiant princes, though it appeared otherwise afterwards.† This Ludovic was a wise man, but very timorous and humble where he was in awe, and false and deceitful when it was for his advantage; and this I do not speak by hearsay, but as one that knew him well, and had many transactions with him. But to proceed, in the year 1493 he began to tickle King Charles

---

* Pope Sixtus IV.

† The arrival of Charles VIII. in Italy, and his early successes, so terrified Alphonso, that he abdicated the crown in favour of his son.

(who was but twenty-two years of age) with the vanities and glories of Italy, remonstrating (as is reported) the right which he had to the fine kingdom of Naples, which he knew well enough how to blazon and display. He addressed himself in everything to Stephen de Vers (who was now become seneschal of Beaucaire, and was much enriched, though not yet to the full height of his ambitious desires) and to General Brissonet, who was rich and well skilled in the management of the finances, and a great friend of the seneschal of Beaucaire, by whose means the Lord Ludovic persuaded Brissonet to turn priest, and he would make him a cardinal; but the seneschal was to have a duchy.

For the better management of these affairs, the Lord Ludovic, in the year 1493, sent a great embassy to the king at Paris. The chief of the embassy was the Count di Cajazzo, eldest son of Robert di St. Severino (whom I mentioned before). At Paris the Count di Cajazzo met the Prince of Salerno, who was his cousin, and chief of the house of St. Severino, and who, having been banished his own country by King Ferrand, was then in France, pressing and soliciting our king to an enterprise against Naples. With the Count di Cajazzo came also Count Charles de Bellejoyeuse *, and the Lord Galeas Visconti † of Milan : both of them were well attended, and in great splendour; but their discourse was only in public, and then in general terms by the way of compliment and visitation; and this was the first solemn embassy that ever Ludovic sent to the king. He had formerly sent one of his secretaries to endeavour to procure that his nephew, the Duke of Milan, might be permitted to do homage for Genoa, by proxy, which was granted against all reason. It is true, the king was at liberty to do him that favour, and depute some person or other to receive his homage; for, when he was under the guardianship of his mother, I (being then ambassador at Milan for the late King Louis XI.) received it by commission from the king in the castle of Milan; but then Genoa was out of his hands,

---

* Carlo Balbiano, Count of Belgioioso.

† Galeazzo Visconti was one of those Milanese nobles who nominated Ludovic the Moor, Duke of Milan, in 1494, to the prejudice of Francesco Sforza.

and in the possession of Baptista di Campoforgoso *, and
now the Lord Ludovic had recovered it, and gave eight
thousand ducats (to some chamberlains of the king) to have
the investiture of it. But they did their master a mighty
injury thereby, for they might have had Genoa for him if
they had wished; or, if it must be sold, why for so little;
as Duke Galeas paid my master, King Louis, fifty thousand
ducats at one payment, of which sum I had thirty thousand
crowns given me by his majesty,' whom may God pardon!
and yet they pretended they received the eight thousand
ducats by the king's consent. Stephen de Vers was one of
the number of those that received the money, and I think he
beat down the price to prepare and oblige Ludovic to back
his interest, when his design should be fit for execution.

The ambassadors having arrived at Paris (as I said before), and having had their public audience, the king took
the Count di Cajazzo into his closet, and had a private conference with him for some time. This Count di Cajazzo
was in great reputation in Milan, and his brother Galeas di
St. Severino was in greater credit, especially in military
affairs; and he began to make large offers of his service and
assistance to the king, both in men and money; for his
master had already as absolute a command of the state of
Milan as if it had been his own, and could dispose of it as
he pleased. He represented the business very easy to the
king, and a few days after, he and the Lord Galeas took
their leave of his majesty and departed; but Count Charles
de Bellejoyeuse remained behind, to promote the business,
and immediately after they were gone, he dressed himself in
the French habit, and managed the affair so dexterously,
that several of the courtiers began to approve of the design.
The king sent into Italy one Peron de Bashe† (educated in
the family of Anjou, under John, Duke of Calabria) as his
ambassador to Pope Innocent, the Venetians, and the Florentines. These embassies from one court to another, and
secret negotiations, continued seven or eight months, and

* In 1478 the Genoese revolted from Milan, proclaimed their independence, and elected Baptista Fregosi as their doge; but in 1487
they were again reduced to subjection to the dukes of Milan.

† Perron de Bachi, son of Berthol de Bachi, one of the equerries of
Louis, King of Naples.

among those who were privy to it, the enterprise was talked of in several ways; but none of them ever imagined that the king designed to go himself in person.

CH. IV. — How King Charles VIII. made Peace with the King of the Romans and the Archduke of Austria ; and returned the Lady Margaret of Flanders to them, before his Expedition to Naples.—1493.

DURING this suspension of affairs, a peace was negotiated at Senlis * betwixt the king and the Archduke of Austria, heir to the house of Burgundy, for, though a truce was already concluded †, yet new occasion of difference had arisen ; for the king forsook the daughter of the King of the Romans, and sister to the archduke (upon account of her being too young ‡), and married the daughter § of Francis, Duke of Bretagne, that he might keep that duchy peaceably ; the greatest part of it at the time of the treaty was in his possession, except the town of Rennes, where the young lady lived, under the guardianship of her uncle, the Prince of Orange, who had been instrumental in making the match between her and the King of the Romans, and married her by proxy publicly in the church, about the year 1492.   In favour of the archduke, the Emperor Frederick sent a solemn embassy, and offered his mediation.   The King of the Romans, the Count Palatine, and the Swiss did the like, in order to compose this difference ; for they all were of opinion great disputes would arise ‖, and that the King of

---

* This treaty was dated at Senlis, on the 23rd of May, 1493.   It is printed at the end of this chapter.
† At Frankfort, on the 22nd of July, 1489.
‡ Margaret was then thirteen years old.
§ Anne, Duchess of Bretagne, was born on the 26th of January, 1476 ; in 1490 she was married by proxy to the Archduke Maximilian ; but, preferring Charles VIII., she was married to him on the 6th of December, 1491 ; she became a widow in April, 1497, and on the 8th of January following she married Louis XII., her deceased husband's successor on the throne of France.   She died on the 9th of January, 1574.
‖ It is evident, from contemporary documents, that the emperor was

the Romans had had very great injury done him; not only to take from him a person whom he thought was his wife, but to send back his daughter who had been lawfully Queen of France for several years together.

In the end, a peace was concluded; for everybody was weary of war, especially Archduke Philip's subjects, who had suffered so much both by their wars with the king and their distractions and divisions at home, that they were not able to carry it on any longer. The peace was made only for four years, to give some repose; and Maximilian's daughter was to be sent back, though with some difficulty; for there were some persons about both the king and the lady who strenuously opposed it. I was present at this treaty myself, with the rest of the commissioners, who were Peter, Duke of Bourbon, the Prince of Orange, the Lord des Cordes, and several other persons of quality. It was concluded, that all the king was possessed of in the province of Artois should be restored to Duke Philip, according to the agreement made in the treaty of marriage in 1482, that if that marriage were not accomplished, then all the lands which went in dower with the daughter, should be restored, either to her or Duke Philip. But the archduke's subjects had already taken Arras and St. Omers *, so that there remained nothing to be restored but Hesdin, Aire, and Bethune; the revenue and lordship of which places were immediately delivered to the archduke's envoys, and they put in what officers they pleased, only the king was to remain in possession of the castles for the term of four years; during which time he might put what garrisons he pleased into them; but at the end of four years, which were to expire on St. John's Day, 1498, the king was obliged, both by oath and promise, to restore them to the archduke.

Whether these changes of marriages were according to the laws and canons of the church or not, I cannot resolve, and, therefore, shall leave it without any determination; for

really making preparations for war with the King of France on account of this twofold insult to his family.—See Dupont, iii. 360.

* Arras was taken by the Burgundians on the 5th of November, 1492. They had recovered St. Omer on the 11th of February, 1488.— Molinet, iii. 447.

I find the theological doctors divided about this point, and some have told me they were not lawful, but others have maintained that they were. Be it which way it will, the ladies were all unfortunate in their children. Our queen had three sons * successively in four years, but all of them died, though one lived to be three years old. The Lady Margaret of Austria was married to the Prince of Castile †, only son to the King and Queen of Castile and several other kingdoms; which prince died in the first year of his marriage, (which was in the year 1487), leaving his princess with child, and she miscarried of a son not long after his death, to the unspeakable affliction of the King and Queen of Castile, and the whole kingdom.

Presently after these changes, the King of the Romans married the daughter ‡ of Galeas, Duke of Milan, sister to the above-mentioned Duke John Galeas; which marriage was contracted by the Lord Ludovic, highly to the dissatisfaction of the princes of the empire, and several other of the King of the Romans' friends, who looked upon the lady as not of an extraction illustrious enough for him. For, as for the Visconti, from whom the present Dukes of Milan are descended, there is no great matter of nobility among them, and less among the Sforzi; for the first of that house was Duke Francis, whose father was a shoemaker § in a little town called Cotignole; but he was a brave and magnificent person, and his son was even greater; for he made himself Duke of Milan, by the assistance and management of his wife ‖ (who was the natural daughter of Duke Philip

---

* These sons were Charles Orlando, born on the 10th of October, 1492, and died on the 6th of December, 1495; Charles, born on the 8th of September, 1496, and died on the 2nd of October following; and Francis, who lived only a few days.—ANSELME, i. 125.

† John, Infante of Castille, died on the 4th of October, 1497. See *note*, Vol. I. p. 394.

‡ Bianca Maria, widow of Philibert I., Duke of Savoy, after twelve years' widowhood, married the King of the Romans on the 16th of March, 1494, and died on the 31st of December, 1510.

§ Muzio Attendolo, surnamed Sforza, was born at Cotignola, in Romagna, on the 28th of May, 1369. At first distinguished for prodigious strength of body and undaunted bravery, he soon became equally distinguished in military tactics, and was one of the greatest condottieri of the fourteenth century. He died on the 4th of January, 1424.

Bianca Maria Visconti married Francesco Sforza on the 28th of

Maria) conquered it, and possessed it, not as a tyrant, but as a good and lawful prince; being equal in virtue and goodness with most (and those of the best) princes of his time. Thus much I have written that I might show what has already been the consequence of these changes of marriages; nor can I tell what there is still remaining behind.

A Treaty of Peace between King Charles VIII. and Maximilian I., King of the Romans, and his Son, Philip, Archduke of Austria, concluded at Senlis, May 23. 1493.

1. A good peace, firm friendship, and perpetual alliance, is and shall ever remain between the most Christian king, the dauphin, their kingdom, territories, and subjects, and the King of the Romans, and Archduke Philip his son, as well in their own name, as in the name of the Lady Margaret of Austria, the said king's daughter, and the archduke's sister, for themselves, their countries, territories, subjects, &c., laying aside all malevolence, and forgetting all past injuries.

2. Seeing that the most Christian king, after his marriage to the queen, hath notified by his ambassadors to the King of the Romans and the archduke, his desire to send back the said Lady Margaret, and to have her conducted suitably to her quality, to any place agreed on, and for this end hath sent her as far as Amiens; he does still offer, at his own charge, to conduct her suitably to her quality, from the town of Meaux, where she now resides, before the 3rd of June next, to St. Quentin, and to put her from thenceforward into the hands of the ambassadors of the King of the Romans and the archduke.

3. Upon such a delivery of the said lady into the hands of the commissioners appointed by the King of the Romans and the archduke, the said princes shall give proper instruments to the king, freeing him from all obligations of marriage with her, and he shall also do the same by her.

4. The most Christian king and the archduke reserve to themselves the liberty of recovering any rights in an amica-

October, 1441, and died on the 23rd of October, 1469, it is believed of poison.

ble way, and by course of law, to such matters as are not adjusted by this peace.

5. The counties of Burgundy, Artois, and Charolois, and the lordship of Noyers, with all their appurtenances, shall be delivered up to the King of the Romans, as guardian to his son the archduke; and also the towns and castles of Hesdin, Aire, and Bethune, now in possession of the King of France, shall be deposited in the hands of the Marshal des Querdes, who shall keep them without any charge to the archduke, save the usual profits taken by the commanders of the said places; and he shall take an oath to both the king and archduke for the due maintenance of their several rights, and shall keep no guard therein, that may be prejudicial to either party; who shall engage not to force him thereunto on either side: and if they do, he shall then be discharged of all his oaths, till the archduke shall arrive at the age of twenty, which will be on St. John Baptist's Eve, in 1498.

6. The archduke, after he is of age, having done homage to the king in due form, those towns and places shall be given up to him by the marshal or others appointed to do it, and to have the command therein.

7. The officers shall continue in their places, having commissions from the archduke till he comes of age and does homage. ~

8. As to the city of Arras, its revenue and temporalities, it shall be deposited in the hands of the bishop and chapter, to whom it belongs, under the ordinary jurisdiction of the bailiwick of Amiens, in the usual manner; and as to the captainship, which is in the king's disposal, he shall be content to appoint the person that now is, or shall be, nominated by the archduke till of age, under the usual obligations; but the city shall be entirely in the king's power, when the archduke comes of age.

9. The houses of Flanders, Artois, and Conflans, in and near Paris, shall be delivered to the archduke.

10. The archduke shall not be obliged to do homage till he is of age; but the king shall, at the same time, enjoy his usual rights and prerogatives.

11. The counties of Maconnois, Auxerrois, and Bar-sur-Seine, shall be enjoyed by the king, till the pretensions of the claimants are decided.

12. Whatever rights the archduke pretends to have acquired by the treaty of 1482, shall remain in being, and the king shall be free to controvert the same.

13. The ecclesiastical preferments conferred by the king in Artois, Burgundy, Charolois, and Noyers, shall remain as they are.

14. Free commerce shall be restored both by sea and land, and on fresh waters, paying the usual customs due before the breaking out of the war.

15. The cities, towns, and villages of Tournay, Tournesis, Mortagne, St. Amand, &c., as the king's subjects, are expressly comprehended in this peace; so are the allies of both parties.

16. Cambray and the Cambresis, with all its inhabitants, are, by common consent, included in the peace, and maintained in all their rights under either prince to whom they belong; and infractors on either side shall be punished by the conservators of the peace.

17. A general act of indemnity shall be granted by both parties, to all who have taken up arms, for the contrary side, no process being ever to be brought against them: and to those who have a mind to sue out a pardon, it shall be freely granted.

18. All persons, as well ecclesiastics as laymen, shall, by this peace, return to the peaceable possession of their dignities, benefices, and inheritances, wherever situated, on either side, and be kept in the peaceable possession of the same, notwithstanding any declarations, confiscations, sentences, and decrees to the contrary; and the judges, magistrates, &c., shall be obliged to assist herein.

19. Under this article of returning to their estates and rights are comprehended the old servants of the late Dukes Philip and Charles, who, after the death of Duke Charles, went over to the king; by virtue of this peace, they shall enjoy their pensions assigned them in his lifetime, upon the demesnes of the counties of Artois and Burgundy.

20. If any inheritance have been sold for contumacy, or on the account of personal debts owing, the debtors shall, within a year after the proclaiming of the peace, return to their possessions, paying the said debts, &c.

21. As to the rents, profits, and incomes of those in-

heritances, granted in a way of reward, or the like, by either party, all that has been done of that kind since 1470, to the present peace, shall never be accounted for; but yet with an exception to any inheritances that, in due course of law, have been adjudged to creditors for arrearages of rents, which arrearages have been given away or remitted, such gifts or releasements shall not take place, but only for such arrearages as have escheated in time of war.

22. As to moveables which have not been made away, but are found upon the premises which the subjects of either party shall return to, the debts and arrearages that have not been given away nor adjudged by law, shall belong to the said subjects, and not to those who have a general list of their moveables.

23. The enjoyment of dignities, benefices, inheritances, &c., by the subjects of either party, shall not oblige them to reside where those possessions are; neither are they thereby bound to take an oath to the prince in whose dominions they are situated, unless they are fiefs, and their vassals.

24. Those who shall return to their estates by virtue of this peace, shall not be prosecuted for rent charges escheated during the war; and those lands which lay waste and uncultivated during the war, shall be liable to the payment of no rents.

25. No reprisals shall be made after the peace, upon the account of damages sustained by the subjects of either party, nor any letters of mart, contramart, or the like granted.

26. By this peace all the people of Arras, of whatever condition, that have absented themselves since the surprise of that city, wherever they are, are free to return and traffic there, notwithstanding any promises or otherwise to the contrary. And whether they do return or not, they shall, as much as any of the other subjects, enjoy their estates, rights, benefices, moveables, and utensils yet in being, without any molestation whatsoever.

27. In like manner the people of St. Omer, of what calling or quality soever, who resided therein while it was neutral, and afterwards by reason of the taking and retaking of it, absented themselves from it, shall, notwithstanding any interdiction or sentence against them, return, and enjoy their estates, benefices, &c., without any manner

of molestation; and all offences and injuries shall be entirely remitted.

28. The Lady Margaret, widow of Charles, late Duke of Burgundy, is comprehended in this treaty. The king consents that she shall enjoy the lands and signories of Chauchnis and la Perrière, with all their appurtenances in the viscounty of Auxonne, in the same manner as the late Duchess Isabella, the mother of Duke Charles, enjoyed them, upon the payment of twenty thousand crowns in gold.

29. The most Christian king names for his allies, his imperial majesty, the kings of Castile, England, Scotland, Hungary, Bohemia, and Navarre, the Duke of Bavaria, the Count Palatine, and all the dukes and branches of the house of Bavaria, the electors of the Holy Empire, the duke and house of Savoy, the duke and house of Milan, the doge and republic of Venice, the Duke of Lorraine, the Duke of Guelderland, the marquis and house of Montferrat, the bishop and city of Liége, the Swiss Cantons, the commonwealths of Florence and Genoa. And, on the part of the said King of the Romans and archduke, his most sacred imperial majesty, the kings of Castile, Hungary, Portugal, Denmark, England, and Scotland, the electors of the Holy Roman Empire, as the king of Bohemia, and others, the marquis and house of Montferrat, the bishop and city of Liége, and all the princes of the empire, the Swiss Cantons, cities and communities of the empire are comprehended.

30. In this peace are also compreheded the king's counsellor William de Haraucourt, bishop and count of Verdun, as well in his own person as for his bishopric and county of Verdun, lordships, subjects, &c. So are also, by the consent of the said princes, the archbishop, and all the inhabitants of Briançon.

31. The respective parties oblige themselves, in the most solemn manner, to the observance of this treaty; so they do also their subjects, vassals, &c.

32. Any contravention which may happen of this treaty on either side, shall be repaired at farthest in the space of six weeks.

33. For the greater confirmation of this peace, the King of France will procure for the King of the Romans and the archduke, the instruments and seals of the dukes of Orléans,

Bourbon, Némours; the counts of Angoulême, Montpensier, and Vendôme; of the Prince of Orange; of the marshals and admirals of France: and of the cities, towns, and communities, of Paris, Rouen, Lyons, Poitiers, Tours, Angers, Orléans, Amiens, and Tournay. And the King of the Romans and archduke engage to procure those of the Duke of Saxony, Margrave of Baden, the Lord of Ravestein, Counts Nassau and Zollern, the Prince of Chimay, and the Lords de Bevres, Egmont, Fiennes, Chievres, Walhain, Molembais, du Fay, Fresnoy, the great bailiff of Hainault, and the towns and communities of Louvain, Brussels, Antwerp, Boisleduc, Ghent, Bruges, Lisle, Douay, Arras, St. Omer, Mons, Valenciennes, Dort, Middleburg, and Namur. And if any shall contravene this treaty, without making reparation in six weeks, these guarantees shall be obliged to leave the contravener, and give assistance to the injured party, and be discharged of their oaths.

34. The instruments on both sides shall be registered and verified in the most regular and authentic manner.

35. The conservators of this peace for the marches on the side of the country of Burgundy, on the king's part, are, the Prince of Orange, M. de Baudricourt, governor of Burgundy, and the bailiffs of Dijon, Chalons, Autun, and Macon, or their lieutenants. For the marches of Champagne and Rhetelois, M. de Orvat, governor of Champagne, the bailiffs of St. Peter le Moustier, Troyes, and Vitry, or their lieutenants; and for the marches of Picardy, the Marshal des Querdes, the bailiffs of Amiens and Vermandois, the seneschals of Ponthieu and Boulonnois, and the governors of Montdidier and Roye, or their lieutenants; and for the sea, the admiral, &c. The conservators on the King of the Romans and the archduke's part, for the marches of Flanders and Artois, are, M. de Nassau, with the governors of Lisle, Arras, and the bailiffs of the said countries respectively; for the marches of Hainault, the princes of Chimay, and the grand bailiff of Hainault; for Luxemburg, the Margrave of Baden; for Burgundy, the governor of the county of Burgundy, and the bailiffs of Damont, Daval, and Dole; and for the sea, Monsieur de Braves, admiral, &c.

36. No manner of protection or shelter shall be given to vagrants, thieves, and robbers, on either side; but they

shall be banished, or otherwise brought to condign punishment, wherever they are found.

37. The same thing is to be done in respect to rovers, or pirates by sea.

38. Neither party shall receive or support those who shall in any way contravene this peace; but they shall be punished for the infractions they make; but the peace at the same time shall not be held to be violated.

39. The said princes and their officers shall assist one another against all those who shall delay or refuse to keep this peace; and they shall on both sides be taken for common enemies; and those who shall in any way assist or favour them, shall in like manner be answerable for the mischiefs done by them, and be punished as violators of the peace.

———

Ch. V.—How the King sent to the Venetians, in order to induce them to enter into an Alliance with him, before undertaking his Expedition to Naples; and of the Preparations in order to it. —1493.

To return to our principal matter: you have already been informed how the Count di Cajazzo, and the other ambassadors, took their leave of the king at Paris; how several secret negotiations were carried on in Italy; and how the heart of our king (though he was very young) was strangely bent upon this expedition; which, however, he discovered to none but the two persons * above-mentioned. His request to the Venetians was that they would give him their assistance and counsel in his expedition; and they returned this answer: That he should be very welcome in Italy, but that they were wholly incapable of assisting him, upon account of their continual apprehensions of the Turk † (though at that time they were at peace with him); and to undertake to advise so wise a king, who had so grave a council, would

* Stephen de Vesc and Briçonnet.
† The Emperor Bajazet II.

savour of too much presumption on their part; but they
would rather assist than disturb him in his designs.

This they believed a very discreet answer, and truly so it
was; and I am of opinion that their affairs are managed
with more prudence and discretion at this day, than the
affairs of any other princes or states in the world : but God
will still have us know, that the wisdom and policy of man
is of no avail where He pleases to interpose ; for He orders
things many times quite otherwise than were expected. The
Venetians did not imagine that the king would come in
person, and (whatever they pretended) they had no apprehension of the Turk; for the Turk who then reigned was
a man of no courage nor activity. But their design was
to be revenged upon the House of Arragon, both father and
son, for whom they had a mortal hatred, because (as they
said) it was at their instigation that the Turk fell upon them
at Scutari.* I mean the father of this present Turk, called
Mahomet Ottoman, who conquered Constantinople, and did
abundance of mischief besides to the Venetians. They had
several complaints also against Alphonso, Duke of Calabria,
and, among the rest, they said that he had been the occasion
of the war which the Duke of Ferrara had made upon them,
which was very expensive, and had like to have proved their
ruin. They complained also that he had sent a man to
Venice, expressly to poison their cisterns, at least such as he
could come at; for some are kept under lock and key. In
that city they use no other water (for they are wholly surrounded by the sea); but that water is very good, and I
drank of it eight months together, in my first embassy
thither (for I have been there once since). But these were
not the true reasons of their animosity to the House of

* The treaty of peace concluded in 1478 between the Sublime Porte,
Ferdinand of Arragon, and the King of Hungary, enabled Mahomet II.
to concentrate all his forces against the Venetians. The republic in
vain attempted to enter into negociations. Mahomet, certain of the
success of his arms, refused to treat unless Scutari were surrendered to
him, and, without waiting for any answer to this proposition, marched
into Albania. On the 8th of June, 1478, he laid siege to Scutari ; and
on the 26th of January, 1479, the town and its territory were ceded to
him by the Venetians. This Scutari must not be confounded with the
suburb of Constantinople, which bears the same name : it is a large
town, the capital of a pashalic in Northern Albania.

Arragon; the real occasion was, because the father and son restrained them, and kept them from extending their conquests both in Italy and Greece; for their eyes were upon them on every side, and yet, without any title or pretence, they had lately subdued the kingdom of Cyprus.* Upon these considerations the Venetians thought it would be highly for their advantage if a war should be begun between our king and the House of Arragon; hoping it would not be brought to a conclusion so soon as it was, and that it would only weaken the power of their enemies and not utterly destroy them: and then (let what would happen) one side or the other would give them towns in Apulia (which borders upon their gulf) in order to have their assistance; and so it happened †, but they had like to have been mistaken in their reckoning. Besides, they thought to have transacted affairs so secretly, that nobody could have accused them of inviting our king into Italy, since they had neither given him counsel nor assistance, as appeared to the world by their answer to Peron de Basche.

In the year 1493, the king advanced to Lyons, to examine into his affairs; but nobody ever imagined he would have passed the mountains himself. He was met there by

* The title of the Venetians to the kingdom of Cyprus rested on the following grounds. Catharine Cornaro, the sister of Marco Cornaro, a Venetian gentleman, had married Jacopo de Lusignan, King of Cyprus, on condition that the republic of Venice should adopt her as a daughter. Two years after his marriage, on the 6th of June, 1473, the King of Cyprus died, leaving his widow pregnant of a son, who died in infancy. The Venetians thus became guardians of the kingdom, and soon rendered themselves odious to the Cypriotes, who made several attempts to shake off their yoke, but in vain. In consequence of these revolts and of a report that the queen was about to contract a new marriage, the Venetians resolved to take full possession of Cyprus: they accordingly declared that, by the decease of the heir to the crown, the queen had inherited the rights of her son, and that the republic in its turn would succeed to the rights of the queen, as she was a daughter of St. Mark. This decision was conveyed to Catherine, with orders that she should come at once to Venice, and deliver up the reins of government into the hands of the Venetians. She obeyed; and on the 26th of February, 1489, the standard of St. Mark floated over the palace of Famagosta and all the fortresses of the island.—SISMONDI, x. 398.

† In return for certain assistance which they promised him, Ferdinand II. made over the towns of Otranto, Brindisi, Trani, Monopoli, and Puglinano to the Venetians.—SISMONDI, xii. 386.

the Lord Galeas di St. Severino, brother to the Count di Cajazzo, with a numerous retinue, on the part of the Lord Ludovic, whose lieutenant and chief minister he was. He brought with him arms, and abundance of fine horses trained on purpose for tournaments. He tilted very well himself, for he was young and a fine gentleman; and the king entertained him with great honour and good cheer, and made him a knight of his own order; after which he returned into Italy, but the Count de Bellejoyeuse still stayed with the king to promote his expedition. By this time a great army was preparing at Genoa, where the Lord d'Urfé, master of the horse, and several others, were negotiating the king's affairs. At length, about the beginning of August, in that year, the king removed to Vienne in Dauphiny, and the nobility of Genoa resorted to him daily. The king also sent to Genoa at that time Louis, Duke of Orléans, now King of France, a young prince, and very handsome, but much addicted to his pleasures: of him enough has been said in these Memoirs. It was the opinion of everybody at that time, that he was to conduct the army by sea; and that it was to be embarked and landed in the kingdom of Naples, by the assistance and direction of the banished princes of Salerno and Bisignano, whom we have mentioned before. They had gotten fourteen great ships, besides several galleys and galleons, ready at Genoa; and the king was as much obeyed in those parts as at Paris, for the city belonged to the state of Milan, where the Lord Ludovic governed, without any competitor but the duke his nephew's wife, daughter to King Alphonso (for at that time his father King Ferrand was dead). But the poor lady had no great power, since the king's army was ready to march, and her husband was a weak prince, and discovered whatever she said to his uncle, who had already caused a messenger to be drowned whom she had sent to her father.

The equipping of this fleet was very expensive, and I believe cost no less than three hundred thousand francs, which quite exhausted the king's treasury; and yet it did him no great service after all, for, as I observed before, neither his exchequer, his understanding, nor his preparations were sufficient for such an important enterprise, and yet he succeeded in it by the mere favour of Providence, as was visibly manifest to all the world. I do not say that the king wanted wisdom, considering his age; but he was but two-and-twenty years old*, and not as yet capable of understanding state affairs. Those who were the chief managers of this affair (I mean Stephen de Vers, seneschal of Beaucaire, and Monsieur Brissonet, at present cardinal of St. Malo) were two persons of indifferent fortune, and less experience, which made the power of God more conspicuous, for our enemies were reputed wise, warlike, and rich, well furnished with good counsellors and officers, and in possession of the whole kingdom; I speak of Alphonso of Arragon (newly crowned by Pope Alexander†), who was supported by both the Florentines and the Turks. King Alphonso had a son called Don Ferrand, a hopeful gentleman of about two or three-and-twenty years old, who wore his harness very well, and was extremely beloved in that kingdom; and a brother called Don Frederic (who was king after the death of Ferrand), a wise prince, and admiral of their fleet, who was educated a long time in our country, and whom you, my Lord of Vienne, have often (by your skill in astrology) assured me would be king; and he promised me (upon my telling him of it) a pension of four thousand livres, if it proved true, as it did twenty years afterwards.

But to proceed. The king changed his resolution, being prevailed upon by the Duke of Milan's letters, and by the importunity of Charles de Bellejoyeuse, his ambassador, and of the two ministers above-mentioned; but by degrees Brissonet's courage began to fail him, finding that all sober and rational persons condemned the expedition, as it was to begin in August, without money, tents, and everything else that was necessary to carry it on; so that the seneschal was the only man that was consulted; for the king looked coldly upon Monsieur Brissonet for three or four days, but was reconciled to him afterwards. About this time one of the seneschal's servants died, it was said, of the plague, and he

---

* He was twenty-four years old at this time. — See *note*, p. 94.

† Roderic Borgia, a native of Valencia in Spain, was elected Pope under the title of Alexander VI, on the 11th of August, 1492, and died on the 18th of August, 1502. He was a monster of profligacy and wickedness, and has been well called by Roscoe "the scourge of Christendom, and the opprobrium of the human race."

durst not appear at court; which was a great mortification to him, for there was nobody else to carry on the design. The Duke and Duchess of Bourbon were with the king, and used all their interest to hinder this expedition, and Monsieur Brissonet did the same; so that one day it was laid aside, and the next revived. At last the king resolved to march, and, thinking to pass the mountains more commodiously in small bodies, I mounted on horseback, and advanced before; but I was countermanded, and assured that the design was given over. The same day fifty thousand ducats were borrowed of a merchant of Milan, but the Lord Ludovic was the real lender. I was surety for six thousand ducats, and others for the rest; but it was borrowed without interest. Before that, we had borrowed of the bank of Soly, in Genoa, a hundred thousand francs, the interest of which in four months amounted to fourteen thousand francs; but some people said the persons above mentioned kept part of the money for their own private use.

Ch. VI.—How King Charles set out from Vienne, in Dauphiny, to conquer Naples in Person; and the Action that was performed by his Fleet, under the Command of the Duke of Orleans.—1494.

In short, the King, on the 23rd of August, 1494, set out from Vienne, and marched straight towards Asti.* At Suza the Lord Galeas di St. Severino came post to meet his majesty, who advanced from thence to Turin†, where he borrowed the jewels of Madame de Savoy ‡, daughter to the late William, Marquis of Montferrat §, and widow to

* Asti, a city of Piedmont, about twenty-six miles east of Turin. Charles VIII. arrived there on Tuesday, the 9th of September, 1494. Susa is also a Piedmontese town, at the junction of the two routes across the Alps by Mont Cenis and Geneva.
† The king reached Turin on the 5th of September.
‡ Bianca de Montferrat married Charles I. Duke of Savoy, in 1485; became a widow on the 13th of March, 1489; and died on the 31st of March, 1509.
§ William VI., Marquis of Montferrat, succeeded his brother, John IV., in 1464, and died on the 28th of February, 1483.

Charles Duke of Savoy.   Having pawned them for twelve
thousand ducats, he removed a few days after to Casale *,
the residence of the Marchioness of Montferrat †, widow of the
late Marquis of Montferrat, a young and prudent lady, and
daughter to the King of Servia.   The Turk having overrun
her country, the emperor (in respect of the relation betwixt
them) took care of her, and married her there.   She also
lent the king her jewels, and they also were pawned for
twelve thousand ducats ; by which you may see what an
unprosperous beginning there was of this war, had not God
himself directed the enterprise.

The king continued at Asti for some time.   The wines
in Italy were sour this year, and therefore not at all agreeable to the French, any more than the excessive heat of the
atmosphere.   The Lord Ludovic and his wife came with a
numerous retinue to wait on his majesty ; they staid there
two days, and then removed to a castle called Annone, about
a league from Asti, belonging to the duchy of Milan, to which
place the king's council resorted to him daily.

King Alphonso had two armies in the field, one in Romagna, towards Ferrara, under the command of his son ; who
was attended by the Lord Virgil Ursini ‡, the Count de Pit-
telhane §, and the Lord John James di Trivulce ||, who at
this time is in our interest.   To face this body of forces,
there was the Lord d'Aubigny ¶ on the king's side, a wise
man and a brave officer, and with him at least two hundred
French men-at-arms, and five hundred Italians in the king's

* Casale, a city of Piedmont, on the right bank of the Po, thirty-
eight miles east of Turin.

† Mary, daughter of Stephen, despot of Servia, married Boniface IV.,
Marquis of Montferrat, on the 17th of October, 1485; became a widow
in 1493; and died in 1495.—See *infrà*, Book VIII. Chap. xvi.

‡ Virgilio Orsini, Count of Tagliacozzo, Lord of Bracciano, and constable of the kingdom of Naples.

§ Niccolo Orsini, Count of Nola and Pitigliano.

|| Gian Giacopo Trivulzio, surnamed the Great, Marquis of Vigevano
and Duke of Musocci.   He was afterwards created a marshal of
France.

¶ Beraut Stuart, Lord of Aubigny, and a Knight of the Order of St.
Michael, was one of the numerous gentlemen of Scottish descent then
in the service of the King of France.   Charles VIII. subsequently
created him Count of Arci, Marquis of Squilazzo, and constable of the
kingdom of Naples.   He died in 1504.

service, commanded by the Count di Cajazzo above-mentioned, as an officer under the Lord Ludovic: he was in great alarm for this brigade, for if it had been defeated, we should have retired, and have left him to shift for himself; and the enemy had a strong party in the duchy of Milan.

The other army, which was commanded by Don Frederick, King Alphonso's brother, was at sea, and the fleet that had this body of forces on board lay off Pisa and Leghorn (for the Florentines espoused their interest), and with it a certain number of galleys, commanded by Breto di Flisco *, and other officers of Genoa, by whose assistance they were in hopes of making themselves masters of that city; and they missed it but narrowly. They landed some thousand men at Specie and Rapalo †, and had they not met with a timely opposition, it is probable they would have carried their point; but that very day, or the next, the Duke of Orléans arrived there with some ships, a good number of galleys, and one great galeass, which was mine, and commanded by Albert Mely. The duke and chief persons of the army were on board my galeass, with several great pieces of cannon (for she was very strong); and getting as near the shore as possible, they cannonaded the enemy so briskly with their great guns (which till that time were unknown in Italy), that they beat them from their post, and landed what soldiers they had in their ships. And from Genoa, where the whole army lay, there came by land a considerable body of Swiss, commanded by the bailiff of Dijon.‡ There were other reinforcements also sent from the Duke of Milan, under the command of Lord John Lewis di Flisco §, brother to the above-mentioned Breto, and the Lord John Adorni ‖; but these were not in the engagement, yet they did their duty, and held several passes with great courage and resolution. In short, when joined by these reinforcements, our

* Obietto de Fieschi, who died at Verceil on the 25th of August, 1497.—FEDERICI, 78.
† La Spezzia, a maritime town in the Sardinian dominions, at the head of the Bay of Spezzia, in the Gulf of Genoa. Rapallo, another Sardinian seaport, fifteen miles east of Genoa.
‡ Antoine de Bessey, Baron of Trichastel, and Bailiff of Dijon.
§ Giovanni Ludovico de Fieschi, brother of Obietto.
‖ Giovanni Adorni, brother of Agostino, at that time Governor of Genoa.—GUICCIARDINI, i. 164.

army attacked and utterly defeated the enemy, of whom about a hundred or six-score were killed in the pursuit, and about eight or ten taken prisoners; among whom there was one Signor Forgosa*, son to the Cardinal of Genoa.† Those who were taken were stripped to their shirts by the Duke of Milan's soldiers, and dismissed without other injury! for in Italy that is the law of arms. I had a sight of all the letters which brought an account of this victory to the king and the Duke of Milan; and after this manner was the army defeated, and never after durst approach us. Upon our return to Genoa the citizens began to rise in arms, and slew several Germans, that were in the city; but the tumult was soon appeased, after some of the ring-leaders of the insurrection were killed.

Something must now be said of the Florentines, who sent two embassies to the king of France before his setting out upon this expedition; but their design was only to dissemble with him. The first time the seneschal of Beaucaire, Monsieur Brissonet, and myself were deputed to treat with their ambassadors, who were the Bishop of Arezzo‡, and one Peter Soderini. § Our demands were only that they should grant us passage for our troops, and a hundred men-at-arms, to be paid by them after the Italian rate (which is but ten thousand ducats a year). The ambassadors replied according to the instructions that were given them by Peter de Medicis, a young man of no extraordinary parts, son of Laurence de Medicis, lately deceased, who had been one of the wisest men of his time, governed the city almost as a prince, and left it in the same condition to his son. Their family had been of about two generations, Peter, the father of this Laurence, and Cosmo who founded it, and was worthy to be reckoned among the chief of that age: indeed, consi-

* Giovanni Fregosi, natural son of Cardinal Paolo Fregosi.

† Paolo Fregosi, Archbishop of Genoa, filled the office of doge of that city several times between the years 1462 and 1488; he was created a cardinal by Pope Sixtus IV. in 1480, and died on the 2nd of March, 1498.

‡ Gentile Becchi, the tutor of the sons of Cosmo de Medici, was appointed Bishop of Arezzo on the 21st of October, 1473, and died in 1497.

§ Piero Soderini was appointed Gonfalonier of Florence in 1502, and died on the 13th of June, 1522.

dering their profession (which was merchandising), I think this family was the greatest in the world; for their factors and agents had so much reputation upon their account, that it is scarce credible. I have seen the effect of it in England and Flanders: I saw one Gerard Quanvese, who kept King Edward IV. upon his throne, almost upon his own credit, during the time of the civil wars in that kingdom; for he furnished the king at different times with more than six-score thousand crowns, but not at all to his master's advantage, though at length he got his money back again. I knew also another, named Thomas Portunay*, who was security between King Edward and Charles Duke of Burgundy, for fifty thousand crowns, and at another time for eighty thousand. I cannot commend merchants for doing so; but it is highly commendable in a prince to be punctual with them, and keep his promise exactly; for he knows not how soon he may want their assistance, and certainly a little money at a critical juncture of affairs does great service.

This family of Medicis was thought to be in a declining condition (as is the case with all kingdoms and governments), for the authority of his predecessors was a great prejudice to Peter; though indeed Cosmo, the first of the family, was mild and gentle in his administration, and behaved himself as he ought to do in a free city. Laurence, the father of Peter (of whom we are now speaking), upon occasion of the difference betwixt him and the Pisans†, mentioned in a former part of this book (in which several of them were hanged), had a guard of twenty soldiers assigned him, for the security of his person, by an order from the Signory, which at that time did nothing without his direction and approbation. However, he governed very moderately; for (as I said before) he was a wise man; but his son Peter thought it his due, and employed his guards to the terror and vexation of his people, committing great injuries and insolencies by them in the night, and invading

---

* Thomas Portinari was agent to Lorenzo de Medici at Bruges, where he kept a bank.—SISMONDI, xi. 80. He is often mentioned in Rymer as having money transactions with Edward IV.

† See Book VI. Chap. iv. The allusion here is manifestly to the conspiracy of the Pazzi.

the common treasure, which his father indeed had done
before him: but he managed it so prudently, that the people
were almost satisfied with his proceedings.

The second time Peter sent, as his ambassadors to Lyon,
Peter Caponi* and others, excusing himself, as he had
done before, on the ground that King Louis XI. had commanded the Florentines to make a league with King Ferrand,
in the time of John Duke of Anjou, and to forsake the
alliance of the said duke; and alleging that, since it was by
command of the late King of France that they had entered
into alliance with the House of Arragon, and the term of
the said alliance was not to expire for some years†, they
could not in justice desert it: however, if his majesty entered their territories, they would be of service to him; but
they no more thought he would come in person than the
Venetians did.   In both these embassies there was always
somebody who was an enemy to the Medicis, and at this
time more particularly Peter Caponi, who often informed us
secretly what measures were to be taken in order to make
the city of Florence revolt from Peter de Medicis, traducing
him more sharply than he really deserved: indeed, he advised the king to banish all Florentines out of our kingdom,
which he did.   I mentioned this particular, that you may
more easily understand the sequel of these Memoirs; for
the king had conceived a great enmity against Peter de
Medicis; and the Seneschal and Monsieur Brissonet held
great intelligence with his enemies in the city, especially
with this Caponi, and with two of Peter's cousins-german,
who bore his own name.

Ch. VII.—How the King, being at Asti, resolved to go in Person into
   the Kingdom of Naples, by the Persuasion and Advice of Ludovic
   Sforza: how Philip de Commines was sent on an Embassy to Venice:
   and of the Duke of Milan's Death.—1494.

I have already given an account of the naval engagement
off Rapalo.   Don Frederic (upon this defeat) retired to Pisa

* Pietro de Gino Capponi, created Gonfalonier of Florence in 1493.—
Gamurrini, ii. 471.

† The treaty was made in March, 1480.—Sismondi, xi. 185

and Leghorn, without staying for the forces which he had
put on shore ; at which the Florentines were highly disgusted, as they were always in their own minds more inclinable to favour the French than the house of Arragon : and
our army in Romagna, though the weaker of the two, yet had
better fortune than the other, and forced the Duke of Calabria to give ground by degrees ; which the king observing,
he took a resolution to march forward, being solicited to do
so by the Lord Ludovic and others whom I have mentioned
before ; and at his arrival, Ludovic saluted him after this
manner :—

" Sir, do not fear for the success of this enterprise ; Italy
consists but of three powers that are at all considerable :
Milan, which is one of them, is yours already ; the Venetians
are neutral ; and you will therefore have to deal only with
Naples. When we were united, and joined together in a
mutual alliance, several of your predecessors have been too
powerful for us. If you will be ruled by me, I will assist in
making you greater than Charlemagne ; for, when you have
conquered the kingdom of Naples, we will easily drive the
Turk out of the empire of Constantinople." If he meant
the Turk who now reigns*, it was likely enough ; but to in-
sure success, affairs on our side needed to have been managed
more wisely. Upon this the king began to be wholly
governed by the Lord Ludovic, which highly displeased some
of our courtiers, among whom there was one of the gentlemen of the bed-chamber, and I know not who besides ; but
their resentment was to no purpose, for the king could not
do without him, and what they did was but in complaisance
to the Duke of Orleans, who pretended to the duchy of
Milan.† But, above all, none was so much disgusted as
Monsieur Brissonet, who now began to look upon himself as
a considerable person, and was become the seneschal's rival
in power ; and Ludovic having proposed to the king and the
seneschal to leave him behind, he was highly incensed against
him, and endeavoured to persuade all people that he meant
to leave them in the lurch. It had been more wise in him

* The Emperor Bajazet.
† As the descendant of Louis, Duke of Orleans, who had married
Valentina, daughter of Gian Galeazzo, Duke of Milan, during the reign
of Charles VL

to have been silent; but he was never employed in, nor indeed was he fit for, any affairs of state; for he had not the command of his tongue, though otherwise he was very well affected to his master. The conclusion of all was, that several ambassadors should be sent; and I, among the rest, was sent to Venice.

I put off my journey for some days, because the king was fallen sick of the small-pox, and being taken with a high fever besides, was thought to be in danger; but it lasted not above five or six days, so that I went upon my journey, and others went to other places. I left the king at Asti, not suspecting in the least that he would have proceeded any farther. In six days' time I arrived, with my mules and train, at Venice; for the road was the best in the world. I was very unwilling to depart, fearing the king would go back; but God had otherwise appointed. The king marched directly for Pavia*, by the way of Casale, where he visited the Marchioness of Montferrat, a lady much in our interest, but a great enemy to Lord Ludovic, and he hated her also. The king was no sooner at Pavia, than suspicions began to arise; they would have had the king to lodge in the town, and not in the castle; but nothing would serve his turn but the castle, and lie there he did, and his guards were doubled that night, as some have told me since, who were then with him. The Lord Ludovic was much surprised at it, and questioned the king about it, asking whether he was suspicious of him. In short, things were so carried on both sides, that amity was not like to last long: but our people were the most indiscreet in their language; not the king, but some of his nearest relátions. In this Castle of Pavia there was at that time John Galeas, Duke of Milan (whom I have mentioned before), and his wife, the daughter of King Alphonso. The duchess looked very melancholy; for her husband was dangerously sick, and kept in that castle under guard with herself, her son, and one or two of her daughters. Her son is still living, and was then about five years of age. Nobody might see the duke, but any one might see the child. I passed that way three days before the king, but was unable to see the duke, and was told he was very ill indeed. How-

---

* Charles VIII. entered Pavia on the 14th of October, 1494.

ever, the king visited him when he came, for he was his cousin-german. His majesty told me afterwards, the subject of their discourse was only in general terms, for he was unwilling to offend Count Ludovic in anything; yet he had a great mind (as he said) to have given him notice of the designs against him. At the same time the duchess threw herself at Ludovic's feet, and begged of him to have compassion on her father and brother; he replied it was not in his power; but she had more reason to have petitioned for her husband and herself, for she was still young and very beautiful.

From thence the king marched to Placentia*, where Ludovic was informed that his nephew, the Duke of Milan, lay a dying; so he took his leave of the king, and, being pressed to return, he promised faithfully to do so. Before he reached Pavia the duke was dead†, upon which he went post immediately to Milan. This I saw in a letter which the Venetian ambassador that was with him wrote to Venice, assuring the Signory of his design to make himself duke. And it is certain both the Doge of Venice and the Signory were much against it, and asked me if the king my master would not espouse the young duke's interest. Though the thing was but reasonable, yet knowing how necessary Ludovic's interest and assistance were to the king's designs, my answer was in doubtful terms.

Ch. VIII.—How and by what Means the Lord Ludovic seized and usurped the Lordship and Duchy of Milan, and was received by the Milanese as their Sovereign.—1494.

In short, he made himself Duke of Milan, and, as many affirmed, that was his design in inviting and drawing us into Italy. He was charged also with the death of his nephew, whose friends and relations put themselves in a condition to wrest the government out of his hands; and they might easily have done it, had it not been for his alliance with our king; for they had already assembled their forces in Romagna,

* The king arrived in Piacenza on the 18th of October.
† The Duke of Milan died on the 22nd of October.

as you have heard ; but the Count di Cajazzo, and Monsieur
d'Aubigny made them retire. For when Monsieur d'Aubigny,
with about a hundred and fifty or two hundred French men-
at-arms and a good body of Swiss, advanced upon them, Don
Ferrand retreated towards his friends, keeping about half
a day's march before us towards Forli*, which belonged to a
lady† that was a bastard of the house of Milan, and widow
of Count Hieronimo, who was, or said he was, a nephew to
Pope Sixtus. It was reported that she favoured their party,
but our men battered a small town‡ of hers for half a day, and
took it by storm ; upon which and the inclination she had
to us before, she came over to our side. The people of Italy
began generally to assume new courage, and be desirous of
change ; for they saw a thing that they had never seen
before, and that was the use of great guns, which had never
been so well understood in France till then. Don Ferrand
retreated towards his own kingdom, and marched for Cesenna§,
a strong city of the pope's, in the marquisate of Ancona ;
but the people stripped and plundered all the stragglers they
could meet with, for they were disposed all over Italy to
revolt, had things been managed wisely on our part, without
violence and plunder. But all was done quite contrary, at
which I was extremely concerned, for, by this way of proceeding, we lost all the honour and renown that the French
nation might otherwise have gained in that expedition. At
our first entrance into Italy we were regarded like saints, and
everybody thought us people of the greatest goodness and
sincerity in the world ; but that opinion lasted not long, for
our own disorders, and the false reports of our enemies,
quickly convinced them of the contrary ; for they accused us
of all imaginable rapacity, plundering and robbing their
houses, and ravishing their wives and daughters, whenever
they fell into our hands. Nor could they have invented any.

* Forli, the chief town of the Legazione di Forli, a province of the
Papal States.
† Catherine Sforza, equally celebrated for her courage and her beauty.
See Notes, Book VI. Chap. iv.
‡ Mordano, in the county of Imola, all the inhabitants of which were
put to the sword.—SISMONDI, xii. 163.
§ Cesena, a pretty town in the province of Forli, near the foot of the
Apennines.

thing to render us more odious, for the people of Italy are the most jealous and avaricious of any in Europe. As to our ravishing of the women they wronged us ; but for the rest, there was too much truth in what they said.

Ch. IX.—How Peter de Medicis put Four of his strongest Garrisons into the King's Possession; and how the King restored Pisa, which was one of them, to its ancient Liberty.—1494.

THE king, as you have heard, was at Placentia, where he ordered a solemn funeral service to be performed for his cousin-german the Duke of Milan ; and indeed he knew not how else to spend his time, since Ludovic, the new Duke of Milan, had left him. Those who had an opportunity of being well acquainted with these affairs have told me, that the whole army, understanding how ill they were provided with everything necessary for such an expedition, had a great inclination to return home ; and that those who were the chief promoters of it at first, began now to condemn it ; as, for instance, the Lord d'Urfé, master of the horse, (though he was at that time sick at Genoa), for he wrote a letter upon some intelligence that he pretended to receive, which increased and heightened their former fears and apprehensions. But God, as I said before, conducted this enterprise, for the king suddenly received news that the new Duke of Milan was upon his return, and that the Florentines were disposed to an alliance with us, in opposition to Peter de Medicis, who played the tyrant amongst them, to the great dissatisfaction of his nearest relations, and other considerable families in that city, as the Capponi, Soderini, and Nerli, and almost the whole town ; upon which the king left Placentia, and marched towards the territories of the Florentines, to force them to declare for him, or to seize upon their towns, which were but in an ill posture of defence, and take up his winter-quarters in them, as the cold weather had already begun. Several small places received him very readily, and so did the city of Lucca, which at that time was at war with Florence. The Duke of Milan had always advised the king to take up his quarters in those parts, and advance no farther that winter, in hopes, by the king's interest and favour, to get into his own possession Pisa, a strong and fair city, Sarzana, and Pietrasanta, for the two last had belonged lately to' Genoa, and had been taken from them by the Florentines, in the time of Laurence de Medicis.

The king marched by Pontremoli, which belongs to the duchy of Milan, and besieged Sarzana, the strongest castle the Florentines had, but ill provided, by reason of their divisions; and, to say truly, the Florentines never fight willingly against the French, for they have been always faithful and serviceable. to them, in respect of their trade and interest in France, and also upon account of their being Guelphs.* Had Sarzana been furnished as it ought to have been, the king's army had certainly been ruined in besieging it, for the country is mountainous and barren, full of snow, and not able to supply us with provisions. The king lay before it but three days, and the Duke of Milan came to him before any composition was made. Having passed through Pontremoli, the citizens and garrison fell out with our Germans, who were commanded by one Buser, and in the dispute some of our Germans were slain. I was not present at this action myself, but I was informed of it both by the king, the duke, and several others that were there; and this accident produced great inconveniences, as you will find hereafter. Our affairs went smoothly on at Florence, and were brought to that height, that fifteen or sixteen persons were deputed to attend the king, as the citizens publicly declared they would not expose themselves to the displeasure of the king and the Duke of Milan, who had a resident ambassador in Florence; and Peter de Medicis was forced to concur in this embassy, for, as matters then stood, he knew not how to avoid it, and to have done otherwise would have ruined them, considering how ill they were both provided and disciplined. Upon the arrival of their ambassadors, they offered to receive the king into Florence, and what other places his majesty pleased; but the designs of most of them were fixed upon his journey

---

* The Guelphs and the Ghibellines were two factions that began in Italy in the reign of the Emperor Frederic II. The former espoused the pope's interest, and the latter that of the emperor.

to Florence, which they thought would conduce to the expulsion of Peter de Medicis, and they pressed it very earnestly by means of those who then conducted the king's affairs, whom I have often mentioned before.

On the other hand, Peter de Medicis managed his affairs as diligently, by means of one Laurence Spinoli, his factor, who governed his bank at Lyons, and was a man of integrity, and had lived a considerable time in France; but he could get no intelligence of the secret affairs of our court, nor indeed could those who lived constantly in it rely positively upon anything, their counsels were so various. However, Spinoli practised with those who had authority there, such as the Lord de Bresse (who has since become Duke of Savoy,) and the Lord de Myolans, who was chamberlain to the king. As soon as the Florentine ambassadors were returned, Peter de Medicis, and some of his friends, waited on the king, with their answers to what had been demanded. They perceived that their inevitable ruin in the city would be the consequence of disputing anything the king thought fit to require; wherefore they resolved to gain his favour, by doing something extraordinary, beyond what the rest had done.

Upon the news of his approach, the Lord de Piennes, a native of Flanders, and chamberlain to the king, and Monsieur Brissonet (whom I have so often mentioned before), were sent to meet him. They proposed the surrender of Sarzana to Peter de Medicis, which was immediately done. They demanded farther, that he would give the king possession of Pisa, Leghorn, Pietrasanta, and Librefatta, and he granted it, without communicating with his colleagues, who were told, that the king was to be received into Pisa, and stay there some time to refresh his troops; but they never thought those places were to be left in his hands. However, their whole power and strength were put into our hands. Those who managed this treaty with Peter de Medicis have often told me and other people, with smiles and laughter, of his condescensions; for they were astonished at them, and he made several concessions, which they had scarce the confidence to demand. In short, the king entered Pisa *; and the ambassadors returned to Florence, where Peter de

* On the 9th of November, 1494.

Medicis ordered lodgings to be prepared for the king in his own house, which is the fairest and best furnished house for a merchant and man of his quality that I have ever seen.

We must now say something of the Duke of Milan, who was already grown weary of the king, and heartily wished him out of Italy, so that he might keep in possession of such places as had been delivered up by the Florentines. He pressed the king very hard to have Sarzana and Pietra-santa, which, he said, belonged to the Genoese, and, at the same time, he lent the king thirty thousand ducats, upon which (as he told me, and several others afterwards) he was promised that he should have them; but, finding he could not get them, he was highly disgusted, and pretending his affairs required him at home, he left the king, who never saw him afterwards. But he ordered the Lord Galeas di St. Severino to stay with the king, giving him instructions that he should be present in all councils with the Count Charles de Bellejoyeuse, whom I have mentioned before. During the king's stay at Pisa, the said Lord Galeas, at his master's instigation, invited several of the chief citizens of the town to his lodging, and advised them to rebel against the Florentines, and petition the king to restore them to their liberty; hoping, by this means, that the city would fall again into the Duke of Milan's hands, as had formerly* been the case in the time of Duke John Galeas, the first Duke of Milan of that name; which John was a great and wicked tyrant, but lived very honourably. His body lies in the Chartreux at Pavia, not far from the park, and is laid much higher than the altar; the monks showed it me, or, at least, his bones (and I mounted a ladder to see them), which were no sweeter than nature permitted. One of the monks, who was born at Bourges, in discourse, called him a saint; I whispered him in the ear, and asked him why he gave him the title of Saint; for one might see, painted about him, the arms of several cities which he had wrongfully usurped; be-sides which, his horse and himself, carved in fine marble, were placed above the altar, and his body lay under the feet of his horse. He answered me softly, "In this country we call all saints who do us any good; and he built us this

* In 1399.

church;" which is of fair marble, and, indeed, the handsomest I ever saw in my life of that kind.

But to proceed: this Galeas di St. Severino had an ambition to be a great man, and Ludovic, Duke of Milan (whose bastard daughter he had married), seemed ambitious of making him so, and took as much interest in him as if he had been his son, for his own children were not of age as yet. The Pisans had been cruelly treated by the Florentines, who used them as their slaves; for they had been conquered by them about one hundred years *, much about the same time as the Venetians subdued Padua†, which was their first acquisition upon the main land. These two cities were much alike; they had been long enemies to those who had the government of them; they were almost equal in power, and it was a great while before they could be conquered. The Pisans now called a council, and, finding themselves encouraged by so great a person, and being naturally desirous of liberty, as the king was going to mass, a great number of men and women cried out to him, "Liberty, Liberty," begging of him, with tears in their eyes, that he would vouchsafe to restore it to them. There was at that time one Rabot‡, a counsellor of the parliament of Dauphiny, and then either actually Master of the Requests, or executing that office for somebody else, who (having promised to do so, or not well understanding the nature of their demands) acquainted the king (as he was walking before him) with the deplorable condition of the Pisans, and told his majesty he ought in pity to redress their wrongs, for never people had been so tyrannically dealt with. The king not understanding what they meant by that word liberty, and beginning to commiserate the afflictions of Italy, and the miseries the poor subjects endured, both under princes and commonwealths, replied, he was willing it should be so; though (to speak truth) he had no authority to grant it, for the town was not his own, and he was received into it only in friendship, and to relieve him in his great necessities. Monsieur

---

* The Florentines became masters of Pisa on the 9th of October, 1406

† The Venetians conquered Padua on the 17th of November, 1405.

‡ Jean Rabot, knight, Lord of Uppi, and a man of great influence with Charles VIII.

Rabot told them the king's answer, and the people began immediately to fill the streets with acclamations of joy; and running to the end of the bridge upon the River Arno, they pulled down a great lion, called Marzocchi, which stood upon a marble pillar, and represented the government of Florence, and threw it into the river. When they had so done, they caused a statue of the King of France to be set on the pillar, with his sword in his hand, and the Marzocchi, or lion, under his horse's feet. After that, when the King of the Romans came to that town*, they served the King of France's statue as they had served the lion; for it is the nature of the Italians to side always with the strongest; but these Pisans were, and are still, so barbarously treated, that they ought to be excused for what they did.

Ch. X.—How the King departed from Pisa to go to Florence; and of the Flight and Destruction of Peter de Medicis.—1494.

THE king stayed not long there †, but departed for Florence; where they complained to him of the injury he had done to the Florentines, and that it was contrary to his promise, to restore the Pisans to their liberty. Those whom he appointed to answer their complaint, excused his conduct in the best manner they could; alleging, that his majesty had not been rightly informed, and they entered into another agreement, of which I shall say something hereafter. But, in the first place, I must speak of the fate of Peter de Medicis, and of the king's entrance into Florence, and of the garrisons that his majesty left in Pisa and other places, which the Florentines had lent him.

After Peter de Medicis, by the consent of some few of his colleagues, had delivered up the above-mentioned towns to the king, he returned to Florence, where the people supposed the king would not keep them, but that after he had refreshed himself for three or four days, and had left Pisa,

* In 1496.
† The king remained six days in Pisa, and entered Florence on the 17th of November, 1494.

they would be delivered up again. I am of opinion that, had the king proposed to them to remain there the whole winter, they would easily have consented to it; though Pisa, except in the numbers of the people, and the richness of their furniture, is of greater value and importance to them than Florence itself. However, Peter de Medicis, upon his return to Florence, was but coldly received by the people, who looked discontentedly upon him, and not without reason; for he had disarmed them of all their power and authority, and robbed them of all the conquests they had gained for a hundred years before; so that their hearts seemed to presage the calamities which have happened to them since. For this cause (which I believe was the principal, though they never declared it), for the hatred they bore him (as I have said before), and for the recovery of their liberties, of which they believed themselves deprived (without any respect to the services done them by Cosmo and Laurence his predecessors), they resolved to drive him out of the town. Peter de Medicis having some suspicion, but no certain knowledge, of their designs, went to the palace to announce the king's approach, who was within three miles of the city; but coming, according to his usual custom, with his guards, and knocking boldly at the palace gate, he was denied entrance by one of the Nerli * (of whom there were several brothers, with whom I was well acquainted, and also with their father, all very wealthy people), who told him he might enter alone if he pleased, but otherwise not; and he that gave him this answer was armed. Upon which Peter de Medicis returned at once to his house, put himself and his retainers in arms, and sent word to one Paul Ursini †, who was in the Florentine service; for by his mother's side Peter de Medicis was akin to the Ursini, and both his father and himself had always had several of that family in their service; and he resolved to stand upon his guard, and oppose any insurrection that might happen in the city. But, not long after, hearing a great cry of "Liberty, Liberty,"

* Giacopo de Nerli, gonfalonier of one of the city companies.— SISMONDI, xii. 147.

† Paolo Orsini, Marquis of Tripalda, and Lord of Lomentana; he was strangled, by order of Cæsar Borgia, on the 18th of January, 1503. His sister, Clarissa Orsini, was the mother of Pietro de' Medici.

and seeing the people assembled in' arms, he left the city according to the prudent advice that was given him by Ursini; but it was a sad parting for him, for in power and riches he and his predecessors, since the time of Cosmo, had been equal to the greatest princes, and on that day fortune began to be adverse, and he lost both authority and estate. I was at Venice myself, but the news was communicated to me by the Florentine ambassador, who was there, and I was extremely concerned at it; for I had a great affection for his father.　Had this Peter believed me formerly, he had not then been in that condition; for upon my first arrival at Venice I wrote to him, and offered to make his peace with the king, and it was in my power to have done it; for I had verbal commission, from both the Seneschal of Beaucaire and Brissonet, to do it, and the king would have been contented with passage for his troops, or, at the worst, to have had Leghorn put into his hands, in return for which, he would have done whatever Peter could have desired; but, by the persuasion and ill counsel of Peter Capponi, whom I have mentioned before, he did but laugh at me for the offer I made him.

The next morning the Florentine ambassador delivered a letter to the Signory of Venice, importing that Peter de Medicis was banished from Florence for endeavouring to make himself sovereign of that city, by the assistance of the Ursini, and of the house of Arragon; with other complaints besides against him, which were not true.　But such are the accidents of this world; he who is beaten and flies, is not only sure to be pursued by his enemies, but is forsaken, and perhaps persecuted by his friends; as was too visible in the behaviour of this ambassador, Paul Anthony Soderini * (one of the wisest statesmen in all Italy).　The day before the delivery of this letter he mentioned Peter de Medicis to me with the respect due to his sovereign lord, but now he declared himself his enemy by order from the State; but, to do him justice, he said nothing of his own feelings. The next day I was informed that Peter de Medicis was coming to

* Paolo Antonio Soderini, born in 1448, was appointed one of the Council of Ten in 1494, and Gonfalonier of Justice in 1497.　He was afterwards sent as ambassador to Venice, with Giambattista Ridolfi as his colleague.

Venice, that the king had made his triumphal entry into Florence, and that the senate had recalled their ambassador, telling him, that " he must sail with that wind." I saw their letter myself, for he showed it me upon his leaving Venice. Two days after his departure, Peter de Medicis arrived at Venice, in the disguise of a servant in livery. The Venetians were at a loss how to behave themselves towards him; they were afraid of disobliging the king, and yet they could not in reason refuse to give him protection; however, they made him wait outside the town for two days, and desired to know of me how my master would take it : I had never received any orders from the king to resent it, and, being willing to serve him, I answered, " That I supposed his flight was for fear of the people, not of the king." Upon which he was received, and the next day after his appearance before the Signory I made him a visit. The Signory ordered a handsome apartment for him, permitted him and about twenty of his retinue to wear their swords, and showed him a great deal of honour and respect; for, though his grandfather Cosmo had formerly hindered them from making themselves masters of Milan *, yet they had a reverence for the honour of his family, which had been so renowned and triumphant all over Christendom.

When I came into his presence, methought he seemed not to answer my expectation. He gave me a long narrative of his misfortunes, and I gave him the best consolation I could. Among the rest of his complaints, he told me he had lost all; but that which made the deepest impression on his spirits was, that, having written to his factor in that town to furnish him with cloth for himself and his brother, though only to the value of a hundred ducats, he had been refused. Not long after he had good news from the Lord de Bresse, who has since become Duke of Savoy; and the king wrote to him to come to him. However, the king left Florence about the same time, as you will find hereafter; but I was forced to say something of this Peter de Medicis, for he was

---

* Cosmo de Medici had greatly encouraged and assisted his friend Francesco Sforza in subjugating Milan and its territory, saying " it was far better to have a powerful friend for one's neighbour than a formidable foe."—See MACHIAVELLI's *History of Florence*, p. 284.

a great man, considering his estate and authority, which his family had enjoyed in its fullest extent for threescore years.

CH. XI.—How the King made his Entrance into Florence, and what other Towns he passed through in his March to Rome.—1494.

THE next day the king made his entrance into the city of Florence, where Peter de Medicis had prepared apartments for him in his own palace, and appointed the Lord de Ballassat to attend him; but, as soon as that nobleman was informed of the flight of Peter de Medicis, he fell to rifling the palace, upon pretence that the bank of Lyons was in arrear to him for a considerable sum of money; and among other things he seized upon a whole unicorn's horn *, valued at six or seven thousand ducats, besides two great pieces of another, and several other things; and other people followed his example.   The best of his furniture had been conveyed into another house in the city; but the mob plundered it. The Signory got part of his richest jewels, twenty thousand ducats in ready money, that he had in his bank in the city; several fine agate cups, besides an incredible number of cameos admirably well cut, which I had formerly seen, and three thousand medals of gold and silver, weighing near forty pounds' weight, and I believe there were not so many fine medals in all Italy besides: so that his losses in the city that day might be computed at a hundred thousand crowns, if not more.

But the king being arrived in the city of Florence, a treaty † was made between him and the Florentines, and I

* The unicorn's horn was highly valued in the middle ages, because it was believed to possess the power of detecting poison in meat and drink.   Cuvier is of opinion that the animal whose horn was supposed to be endowed with this precious quality was the *Oryx*, or Egyptian antelope, which is remarkable for its long, straight, and tapering horns.

† This treaty was published in the Cathedral of Florence during the celebration of mass on the 26th of November, 1494.   It was at one time very near being broken off; for Charles at first insisted on conditions disgraceful to the Florentines, which his secretary read as his ultimatum.   But the gonfalonier Pietro Capponi suddenly snatched the paper from the secretary's hand, and, tearing it up, exclaimed, " Well,

am of opinion the citizens embraced it very heartily. They gave the king sixscore thousand ducats, of which they paid him fifty thousand down, and the rest in two short payments afterward. They lent him all the above-mentioned fortresses, and changed their arms, which were the red fleur-de-lis, and adopted those of the king, who took them under his protection, and swore upon the altar of St. John to restore the towns which they had put into his possession, within four months after his arrival at Naples, or sooner, if he should return to France; but matters happened otherwise, as you will find in the sequel of these Memoirs.

The king made but a short stay at Florence; but advanced with his army to Sienna, where he was well received; thence he advanced to Viterbo*, where the enemy (Don Ferrand), having retreated towards Rome, designed to post and fortify themselves, and fight, if they saw an advantageous opportunity, as King Alphonso's and the Pope's ambassadors at Venice told me; and truly I expected the arrival of King Alphonso in person there (for he had the reputation of being a man of courage), and that he would have left his son in the kingdom of Naples to manage affairs in his absence. According to my judgment the place would have been most advantageous for him; for he would have had his own kingdom and the States of the Church, and the towns and places belonging to the Ursini behind him. And I was extremely surprised to receive letters from the king announcing that he was at Viterbo, and that one of the commanders had delivered up the castle upon the intercession of the Cardinal of St. Peter ad Vincula (who was governor of it) and of the Colonne. I fancied then that God would put an end to this affair, and began to repent of having advised and written to the king to come to an accommodation; for they offered him very fair terms. Aquapendente, Montefiascone, and all the adjacent towns, were delivered up before the surrender of Viterbo, as I was informed by letters from the king and the Signory of Venice, who had daily intelligence of what passed from their ambas-

---

if it be thus, sound your trumpets, and we will ring our bells!" This energetic movement daunted the French king, who at once abated his pretensions, and peace was concluded.—SISMONDI, xii. 168.

* Charles VIII. entered Siena on the 2nd of December, and reached Viterbo on the 10th of the same month.

sadors, which they either showed me, or else ordered their secretaries to give me an account. From Viterbo the king marched towards Rome, and thence through the dominions of the Ursini, which were all surrendered to him by the Lord Charles Ursini*, who pretended that he had orders from his father to do so (who was still in Alphonso's service), and said that, whilst Don Ferrand was entertained in the territories of the Church, so long would he wait on the king, and no longer. This was exactly according to the custom in Italy, both among princes and captains, and all persons; for there they carry fair with their very enemies, for fear it should be their misfortune to be of the weakest side. The king was accordingly received into Bracciano, the chief place belonging to Virgil Ursini; it was a strong and beautiful castle, and well furnished with provisions. I have heard the king often commend the place, and the entertainment he met with there; for at that time his army was in great distress for want of provision, and indeed they could hardly have been in greater want; so that, if we do but consider how often this army was inclined to disband since its first arrival at Vienne in Dauphiny, and the many unexpected accidents by which it was supplied and advanced, it must of necessity be acknowledged that God Almighty conducted the enterprise.

CH. XII.—How the King sent the Cardinal of St. Peter ad Vincula (who was afterwards Pope, by the name of Julius II.) to Ostia; what the Pope did at Rome in the Meantime; and how the King entered Rome, notwithstanding all the Endeavours of his Enemies to the contrary; and of the Factions between the Ursini and the Colonne in Rome.—1494.

FROM Bracciano the king sent the Cardinal of St. Peter ad Vincula to Ostia, of which he was bishop. Ostia is a town of great importance, possessed by the Colonne, who had taken it formerly from the Pope; but not long before, it had been recovered from the said cardinal by the forces of the Church.†

* Charles, Count of Anguillara, a natural son of Virgilio Orsini.
† Cardinal Julian della Rovere surrendered Ostia to the Papal troops on the 23rd of April, 1494, and fled into France.—SISMONDI, xii. 116.

It is a town of no great strength, and yet it kept. Rome in subjection a long time afterwards, by means of the said cardinal, who was a great friend to the Colonne, which family embraced our interest, at the instigation of Cardinal Ascanio* (the Duke of Milan's brother, and vice-chancellor to the Pope), and in opposition to the Ursini, with whom they have been always at difference. The faction of these two houses has occasioned as great troubles in the states of the Church as the animosity betwixt the Luce and Grandmont families have been to us, or the Houcs and Caballans to the Dutch† ; and were it not for this dissension, the territories of the Church would be one of the best habitations for subjects in the world ; for they pay no taxes, their duties are few, and they would be sure to be well governed, for the popes are always wise, and have good councillors about them. But because of these emulations, they are subject to many calamities, as murders and plundering, of which we have seen frequent examples within these last four years; for since that time‡ the Colonne have been our enemies, much to their loss, for the king had given them estates of twenty thousand ducats a year and more in the kingdom of Naples, such as the county of Tagliacozzo, and other places (which were formerly the estates of the Ursini), besides whatever else they demanded, whether in men or money; so that what they did was done treacherously and unhandsomely, without any manner of provocation; but they had been always for the house of Arragon against the French, as being Ghibellines, and the Ursini (being Guelphs) were always on our side with the Florentines.

The king sent with the Cardinal of St. Peter ad Vincula to Ostia, Peron de Basche, the steward of his household, who three days before had brought the king twenty thousand

* Ascanio Sforza, born on the 3rd of March, 1445, was appointed Bishop of Pavia in 1479, and elected cardinal on the 6th of March, 1484. Having taken an active part in the election of Alexander VI. to the Popedom, he was appointed vice-chancellor by that pontiff; and he died at Rome on the 28th of March, 1505.

† The families of Luz and Grammont were celebrated in Navarre for their long-continued rivalry. The Houcs and Caballans were two factions which arose in the Netherlands about the middle of the fourteenth century.

‡ The Colonne became enemies to the French in 1495.

ducats by sea, which was part of the money lent him by the
Duke of Milan.   This Peron de Basche landed at Piombino,
and left the fleet (which was but small) under the command
of the Prince of Salerno, and the Baron of Sernon* in Provence; but being overtaken suddenly by a storm, their ship
was much shattered, and driven upon the coast of Sardinia,
where they lay a long time without doing us any service till
they could be repaired, though they cost us a vast expense,
and came not to us till the king was in Naples.

There were with the Cardinal at Ostia about five hundred
men-at-arms, and two thousand Swiss under the command
of the Count de Ligny† (the king's cousin-german by his
mother's side), the Lord of Allegre‡, and others.   Their
design was to have passed the Tiber, and enclosed Don
Ferrand in Rome, by the favour and assistance of the
Colonne, of whom the chief were Prospero and Fabritio
Colonna, and the Cardinal Colonna§, who had two thousand
foot under their command, to pay whom the king remitted
money by Peron de Basche, though they had raised and mustered them at their own pleasure at Sansonna ‖, a town
belonging to them.

We must here observe that several affairs are coincident in
this place, and of every one of them something must be said.
Before the king had made his entrance into Viterbo, he had
sent the Lord de la Tremouille⁑, his chamberlain, the Presi-

* Louis de Villeneuve, Lord of Serenon, and Marquis of Trans, in
Provence.

† Louis de Luxembourg, Prince of Altramura, Duke of Andria and
Venusia, Count of Ligny, and Governor of Picardy; afterwards Lord
High Chamberlain to Louis XII.

‡ Yves, Baron of Alegre, and captain of the hundred gentlemen of
the king's household.

§ Prospero Colonna, Duke of Traetta, and Count of Fondi; Fabri-
zio Colonna, Duke of Pagliano and Tagliacozzo, Constable of Naples,
and cousin-german to Prospero; Giovanni Colonna, brother of Prospero, created a cardinal on the 15th of May, 1480.—IMHOFF, 218, 219,
222.

‖ Genzano, a town in the Papal States.—SISMONDI, xii. 182.

⁑ Louis II., Lord of La Tremouille, Viscount of Thouars, and Prince of
Talmont, surnamed the *Chevalier sans reproche*; created Governor of
Burgundy and Admiral of Guienne in 1502; and killed in the battle of
Pavia, on the 24th of February, 1524.   The estates of this nobleman
had been conferred on Commines by Louis XI., and a full account of

dent of Gannay *, who had the seal, and Monsieur Bidaut †, to Rome, to treat with the Pope, who was never without some underhand practices, according to the mode of the Italians. While they were at Rome, the Pope in the night received Don Ferrand and his whole army into the town, so that our people were seized for a short time, but dismissed the same day by the Pope; only the Cardinal Ascanio, vice-chancellor and brother to the Duke of Milan, and Prospero Colonna, were detained (some say by their own consent). I had news of all this immediately, by letters from the king, and the Signory of Venice had a more ample account of it from their agents; and it happened before the king got into Viterbo, for he never stayed above two days in any place, and all things succeeded better for our interest than we could have expected or hoped, and no wonder, for God's providence appeared so visibly for our assistance, that nobody could deny it.

The badness of the weather had rendered the army in Ostia utterly unserviceable. But you must understand that the forces under the command of the Lord d'Aubigny had been marched back, and he himself had no further employment there. The Italians were likewise dismissed, who had been raised in Romagna, and brought to the army by Count Rodolph of Mantua‡, the Lord Galeot de la Mirandola§, and Fracasse‖, brother to Galeas di St. Severino; who were well paid by the king, and were in all about five hundred men. At his departure from Viterbo the king advanced to Naples ⸸ of which the Cardinal Ascanio was then governor. And it

---

the law-suits which arose from this gift will be found in the " Life of Commines," prefixed to the first volume of this edition of his Memoirs.

* Jean de Ganay, Lord of Persan, apponted Fourth President of the Parliament of Paris in 1490, First President in 1505, and Chancellor of France in 1507. He died at Blois in 1512.—ANSELME, vi. 442.

† Denis Bidault, notary and secretary of the king, was appointed Receiver-General of the Finances in 1481, and President-Clerk of the Chamber of Accounts in Paris in 1495. He died on the 18th of June, 1506.

‡ Rodolph, son of Ludovic III., Duke of Mantua; born in 1451, and killed in the battle of Fornovo, on the 6th of July, 1495.

§ Galeotto Pic de la Mirandola, brother-in-law of Rodolph of Mantua.

‖ Gasparo, surnamed Fracasso de Sanseverino, son of Robert Count of Cajazzo.

⸸ Nepi, or Nepete, a small town about twenty-six miles from Rome.

it is most certain that, whilst our forces were in Ostia, twenty fathoms of the wall fell down at Rome, on that side where we designed to enter.

The Pope, observing this young prince advance so briskly, and with such unexpected success, consented to receive him into Rome (and to speak truth he could not help it), upon condition he would give safe conduct under his hand and seal to Don Ferrand, Duke of Calabria, and only son to Alphonso; but Ferrand marched away in the night towards Naples, and the Cardinal Ascanio conducted him to the very gate. The king entered Rome* in arms, as a prince who had authority to do what he pleased wherever he came. There came out to meet him several cardinals, and the governors and senators of the town, who attended him to his lodgings in the palace of St. Mark (which belonged to theColonne, who were then his servants and friends); and the Pope himself retired to his castle of St. Angelo.

Ch. XIII.—How King Alphonso caused his Son Ferrand to be crowned King; his Flight into Sicily; and of the evil Life his Father (old Ferrand) and he had led during their Reigns.—1495.

COULD any man have imagined that so imperious a prince as Alphonso, inured all his lifetime to wars, and his son and the Ursini, who had so great a party in Rome, should have been afraid to make a stand there? Especially when they perceived the Duke of Milan and the Venetians wavering, and a secret alliance on foot, which would certainly have been concluded, had any resistance been made, either at Viterbo or Rome, that might have stopped the progress of the king's arms, though but for three or four days. But God was willing to demonstrate to the world that all these things were beyond the contrivance and comprehension of human wisdom; and, as we said before, that above twenty fathoms of the city wall fell down, so now there fell down above fifteen fathoms of the outer wall of the castle of St. Angelo, as I have been told by several persons, and particularly by

* Charles VIII. entered Rome on the 31st of December, 1494.

two cardinals who were there.   But now we must say something of King Alphonso.

As soon as the Duke of Calabria, called the young Ferrand (whom we have already often mentioned), was returned to Naples, his father, King Alphonso, abdicated the crown, thinking himself unworthy of it on account of the mischiefs and cruelties he had committed against several princes and lords who had trusted to his and his father's honour, causing them to be put to death (to the number of four-and-twenty), after the decease of his father, who had kept them alive for some time after their wars against him. Two more he also caused to be executed, who had surrendered upon his father's security; one was the Prince of Rossano, Duke of Sessa *, a person of great authority.   This Prince of Rossano had married King Ferrand's sister, and had by her a son † of very great parts and understanding. To make sure of him, he had been married to a daughter of King Ferrand (for the Prince of Rossano had been engaged in a most abominable treason against his king, and had deserved the worst punishment that could have been inflicted, had he not surrendered himself upon assurance of a pardon). As soon as he had surrendered, the king ordered him to be closely confined in a stinking prison, where he continued for the space of four-and-twenty years, and whither his son was sent, when he was about fifteen or sixteen years old, to bear him company.   Alphonso, immediately upon his accession to the throne, ordered all the prisoners to be removed to a small island not far from Naples, called Ischia (of which

* Marino de Marzano, Prince of Rossano, and Duke of Sessa, who had married Eleanor, a natural daughter of Alphonso I., King of Naples, sided with John, Duke of Anjou, in 1459, against his brother-in-law, Ferdinand I., whom the Duke of Anjou was striving to deprive of the crown of Naples.   He was declared a rebel in 1460, but made his peace in 1462, on condition that his son should marry Ferdinand's daughter. Regardless of his oath, however, Ferdinand imprisoned Marino in the castle of Naples in 1464; and after twenty-two years' captivity he was put to a violent death in 1486.

† Giambattista de Marzano, son of the preceding, was born in 1459, and betrothed to Beatrice, the daughter of Ferdinand I., in 1462; but Ferdinand broke off the match, and married his daughter to Matthias, King of Hungary.   In 1464 Marzano was sent to join his father in prison, and remained a captive until the arrival of Charles VIII. at Naples in 1495, when he was liberated by Ferdinand II.

you shall hear further hereafter), and put all of them to death after a most barbarous and inhuman manner, except Rossano's son and the noble Count of Popoli*, whom he still kept prisoners in the castle of Naples.

I inquired very carefully how they were so cruelly murdered (because many people believed them alive when the king entered Naples), and I was told by their principal servants that they were horribly and villanously knocked on the head by a Moor of Africa, who, immediately after their execution, was dispatched into Barbary, that no notice might be taken of it. I was informed he did not even spare those ancient princes, some of whom had been kept in prison for four or five-and-thirty years. Never was any prince more bloody, wicked, inhuman, lascivious, or gluttonous than he. Yet his father was more dangerous, because no man knew when he was angry or pleased; for he would betray men in the midst of his entertainments and caresses, as he betrayed Count James †, whom he caused on a sudden to be apprehended, and put to a horrible death, though he was in the quality of an ambassador at his court from Francis, Duke of Milan, whose natural daughter he had married; but to that barbarous action Francis was consenting, for they were both afraid of his courage and interest with the Bracci ‡, for he was son to Nicolo Picinino. § In the same manner (as

---

* Pietro Giovanni Paolo Cantelini, Duke of Sora, and Count of Popoli, was one of the barons who revolted from Ferdinand in favour of the Duke of Anjou, and was forced to surrender when the duke abandoned his pretensions to the kingdom of Naples. According to some authorities, he succeeded in making his escape, and baffling the vengeance of Ferdinand.

† Jacopo Piccinino, a celebrated condottiere, served the Duke of Anjou against Ferdinand, who afterwards appeared to have forgotten the offence, for he gave him the command of the armies of his kingdom, and the principality of Sulmona, and other estates. After his marriage to Drusiana, a natural daughter of Francesco Sforza, Ferdinand invited Piccinino to return to Naples, which he did, in the capacity of an ambassador from the Duke of Milan. Ferdinand entertained him nobly for twenty-seven days, at the end of which he ordered him to be arrested, thrown into a dungeon, and put to death.—SISMONDI, x. 267.

‡ *Bracceschi*, the partisans of Braccio de Montone, a celebrated condottiere captain, long the rival in renown of Sforza Attendolo.

§ Niccolo Piccinino was the favourite pupil of Braccio, and succeeded to the command of his party at his death.

report goes) he served several others; for this Ferrand had
nothing of tenderness or compassion in him, as I have been
informed by his nearest friends and relations, nor was he
ever known to take the least pity of his own necessitous subjects in relation to their taxes.   The whole trade of buying
and selling he engrossed to himself all through his kingdom.
He delivered hogs to his people to feed, and required them
to make them fat, that they might fetch a good price; and if
any of them chanced to die, the people were forced to pay for
them.   In Apulia and other countries which are plentiful
in olives, he and his son bought up all the oil, almost at
their own price; the same they did with their corn, buying it
at a cheap rate before it was ripe, and then selling it again
as dear as they could; but if the price of any of their commodities happened to fall in the meantime, they obliged the
people to take them off their hands; and whilst they were
disposed to sell, nobody durst buy of any one else.

If a baron, or the lord of any country, was a thrifty man,
and saved anything out of his revenue by management and
industry, they sent presently to borrow it, and the owners
were forced to comply with their unreasonable demands.
They also took away their breed of horses (of which in
those parts there are several), and caused them to be managed
and trained for them and their use; so that they had in
horses, mares, and colts many thousands, which they sent up
and down the kingdom to be kept for them, to the great detriment of the masters.   Both father and son had ravished
several women; they made no conscience of sacrilege, nor
did they retain the least respect or obedience for the church.
They sold their bishoprics, as that of Tarento, which
the father sold for thirteen thousand ducats to a Jew for
his son, who the Jew pretended was a Christian.   He
gave abbeys to falconers and others for their children, telling them, " You shall keep me so many hawks, and mew
them, and keep me such a number of soldiers at your expense."   The son never kept Lent in his life, nor so much
as pretended to do it; and for many years he never was at
confession, nor ever received the Sacrament of the Lord's
Supper.   In short, it is scarce possible that any prince could
be guilty of greater villanies than they were.   Some will
have the young Ferrand to be the worst of the two; though

at his death he grew humble and civil, but then indeed he was in distress.

CH. XIV.—How King Alphonso fled into Castile, and did Penance.— 1495.

PERHAPS the reader may think that what I have written of these two princes proceeds from some particular pique against them; but upon my conscience that is not the motive that induces me to do it; for I have given you this history of their lives, only to continue my Memoirs, in the beginning of which I freely declared my opinion that I thought it impossible for those who had the management of our affairs to have carried on this expedition so prosperously, had not God himself undertaken to conduct it for our young king, whom he supplied with provisions in the extremity of his wants, that he might make him his instrument to scourge and chastise these Italian princes, who were wise, rich, powerful, and experienced in the affairs of the world; had wise and able ministers to defend and take care of their dominions, and were supported by powerful alliances; and, though they beheld the storm afar off, yet had they not courage or wisdom enough at that time either to resist or avoid it. For, except the castle of Naples, there was not one place which stopped the progress of the king's arms for a day, which occasioned Pope Alexander VI. to say that the French came into Naples with wooden spurs, and chalk in their harbingers' hands to mark out their lodgings, which they took up without any more trouble. The wooden spurs he mentioned because it was the custom at that time, when young gentlemen rode about the streets, for their pages to put a sharp piece of wood into the heels of their shoes, with which they pricked their mules forward. In short, this expedition into Italy was performed with so much ease, and so little resistance, that our soldiers scarce ever put on their armour during the whole expedition, and the king marched with his army from Asti to Naples in four months and nineteen days;

an ambassador with his retinue could hardly have got thither sooner.

I conclude, therefore, with several pious and religious men, and the general voice of the people (which is the voice of God), that God intended to make an example of these princes, that by their chastisement others might be excited to conform their lives according to his commandments. For these princes of Arragon lost their honour, their kingdom, and their treasure, besides their rich furniture of all sorts, which has been so strangely dispersed, it is hardly to be known what is become of it; and, finally, they died themselves, three in one year*, or a little more; but I hope their souls are in paradise. For King Ferrand, who was natural son to Alphonso the Great† (a wise, good, and honourable prince), was highly concerned to see his kingdoms invaded with such a powerful army, and to find himself not in a condition to oppose it. He was also sensible of the notoriously bad lives that he and his son had led, and that they had become odious to the people. And besides, in the pulling down of a chapel (as I have been assured by several of his nearest relations), there was a book found with this title, *Truth, with its secret Counsel*‡, in which (it is said) was contained a full prophecy of his misfortunes; but there were only three persons who had a sight of it, for as soon as he had read it, he committed it to the flames.

Another thing that troubled him was, that neither his son Alphonso, nor his grandson Ferdinand, could be persuaded of the king's coming into Italy; but they talked arrogantly and contemptuously of him, hectoring and threatening that they would go as far as the mountains to meet him. But some were so wise as to make it their solemn petition to God Almighty that a king of France might never come into Italy; for they had only seen a poor indigent prince of the family of Anjou, who had troubled all

* Ferdinand I. died in 1494; Alphonso II. in 1495; and Ferdinand II. in 1496. See previous notes.

† Alphonso V., surnamed the Wise, King of Arragon, who inherited the throne of Naples from Queen Joanna in 1420, and left it to his bastard son.

‡ Lenglet says it was a book written by St. Cotade, Bishop of Tarentum.

Italy before it could get rid of him, namely, Duke John, King Réné's son. Ferrand laboured hard, by means of his ambassador Camillo Pandone*, to stop the king's expedition into Italy before he left France, offering him a tribute of fifty thousand ducats a year, and to do him homage for his kingdom. But finding he could neither purchase his peace with the King of France, nor compose the differences of the city of Milan, he fell sick, confessed his sins, and died †, and, I hope, repented of his wickedness. His son Alphonso, who was so cruel and terrible, and in such reputation for his experience in military affairs before the King of France's departure from Rome, renounced the crown, and was seized with such a panic fear, that in the night he would cry out he heard the French, and that the stones and trees shouted, "France, France." Nor durst he ever stir boldly out of Naples; but upon his son's return from Rome he resigned the government of his kingdom to him, and caused him to be crowned, and carried on horseback through the streets of Naples, attended by the chief persons of the city, to wit, his brother Don Frederic, and the Cardinal of Genoa (between whom the new king rode), and all the foreign ambassadors that were there; and after all this pomp and solemnity was performed, Alphonso himself fled into Sicily, and took with him the queen his mother-in-law ‡ (sister to Ferrand, King of Castile, who is now reigning, and heir to the kingdom of Sicily), to a place § where she had a strong garrison.

This was looked upon as a very surprising turn of affairs all over Europe, but especially at Venice, where I was then as the king's ambassador. Some said he had retired to the Turkish court, others that his resignation was only in favour of his son, who was less odious to the people; but I was always of opinion it proceeded from nothing but real cowardice; for no person that was cruel was ever cou-

---

* Camillo Pandone, Viceroy of Apulia during the reign of Ferdinand II; killed in an encounter with the French in 1495.

† On the 25th of January, 1494.

‡ Joanna, daughter of John II, King of Arragon, was married to Ferdinand I., King of Naples, in 1476, and died on the 9th of January, 1517.

§ Mazzara, a large town on the sea-coast, in the province of Trapani. —GUAZZO, 80.

rageous, as all histories inform us; for so Nero and several other tyrants perished in despair. In short, Alphonso was in so great a consternation, that (as I was informed by some who were about him) he told his mother-in-law, on the very day of their departure, that if she would not go he would leave her behind; and when she entreated him to put off his departure for three days longer, that it might be said she had been a whole year in his kingdom, he replied that, rather than not go then, he would throw himself out of the window; "For do not you hear (saith he), how everybody cries out, 'France, France?'" Upon which they immediately went on board their galleys. He took along with him all sorts of wines (which he loved above all things), and seeds for his gardens, without taking any care of his property or furniture, which was left mostly in the castle of Naples; some jewels and a little money he carried with him besides, and away they sailed for Sicily, to the place above mentioned; and from thence to Messina, where he sent for and carried along with him certain monks, to whom he pretended and swore he would have no further conversation with the world. Among the rest, he took a particular fancy to the monks of Mount Olivet, whose habit is white (as they told me at Venice, where the body of St. Helena is deposited in their monastery), and with them he lived a most strict and austere life, serving God at all hours both of the day and night, as the monks did in their convents, spending his time in prayers, fasting, and alms; by which austerity and severe way of living he contracted a sad distemper of excoriation and gravel; and the monks told me they never saw any man suffer greater misery, and yet he endured it with abundance of patience, having resolved to spend the remainder of his days in a monastery at Valentia, and to take upon him the monkish habit; but he was surprised with a violent illness, and died in a short time after. If we may judge from the greatness of his penitence, we may conclude his soul is glorious in paradise. His son outlived him not long, for he died of a fever and a flux, and I hope they are better where they are, than they were in this world. To conclude, in less than two years' time there were five kings crowned in Naples; the three I have mentioned before,

Charles VIII. of France, and Don Frederic*, Alphonso's brother, who now reigns.

CH. XV.—How, after Ferrand the Younger was crowned King of Naples he encamped with his Forces at St. Germain, in order to oppose King Charles; and of the Agreement King Charles made with the Pope during his stay at Rome.—1495.

Now for the better understanding of all these affairs, you must know that King Ferrand, after his coronation was over, became a new man, supposing all the odium and resentment of past injuries were buried in oblivion upon his father's abdicating the throne. He assembled all the forces he could raise, both of horse and foot, and marched with them to St. Germain †, which is a strong place, and easy to defend (though the French passed it twice), upon the frontiers of his kingdom. Having encamped there, and put a strong garrison, with all manner of provisions, into the town, his friends began to take heart. The town is defended in two ways, by a small river ‡ that is fordable sometimes, and by a great mountain which seems to hang over it.

The king in the meantime was at Rome, and continued there about twenty days, during which time several affairs of importance were transacted. There were with him about eighteen cardinals, and others from various parts; among whom there were the Lord Ascanio, vice-chancellor and brother to the Duke of Milan, and the Cardinal of St. Peter ad Vincula (great foes to one another, but mortal enemies to the Pope); the Cardinals of Gurce §, St. Dennis ‖, St. Seve-

---

* He was crowned King of Naples in 1495. He reigned but six or seven years before he was dethroned; after which he retired into France, where he died.

† San Germano, fifteen miles from the frontier of Naples.

‡ The Garigliano.

§ Raimond Perauld, a native of Surgères in Saintonge, became successively Bishop of Saintes, and Bishop of Gurce, in Germany; he was made a cardinal by Pope Alexander VI. in 1494, and died at Viterbo on the 5th of November, 1505.—AUBERY, ii. 629.

‖ Jean de Vilhères, Bishop of Lombez, and Abbot of St. Denis, was created a cardinal in 1493, and died on the 6th of August, 1499.—DESCAUSSET, 145.

rino*, Savelly †, Colonna, and others; all of them earnest
for a new election, and that the Pope might be deposed, who
was then in his castle.   Twice our great guns were made
ready to fire (as I have been told by several persons of
quality); but both times the king in his mercy opposed it.
The place is not defensible, being built upon a small hill,
and that merely artificial.   It was alleged that the walls
had fallen down by miracle, and they charged his Holiness
with having given money for the papacy, and they said the
truth; but Cardinal Ascanio was the principal merchant, for
it was he that drove the bargain and received most of the
money, besides the house in which the Pope lived when he
was vice-chancellor, with all the rich furniture, and his vice-
chancellorship, and several other places of St. Peter's patrimony besides; for they two were competitors for the popedom.   However, I am of opinion they would both have
consented to a new election at the king's pleasure, though it
had been to choose a Frenchman.   I will not pretend to say
whether the king acted well or ill, but I think his best way
was to compose matters amicably, as he did; for he was a
young man, and incapable of performing so important a
work as the reformation of the Church, though, perhaps, his
strength might have been sufficient.   Could he have undertaken and gone through with it, I question not but all men
of wisdom and reason would have acknowledged it to have
been a good, great, and holy work; but great mystery would
have been necessary.   However, the king's intentions were
good, and are so still, if he were vigorously assisted.

The king took another course, and came to an accommodation ‡ with the Pope, which could not possibly last long,
for it was too violent in some points, and there was great
talk of making an alliance, of which we shall speak more
hereafter.   By this agreement there was to be peace
between the Pope and his cardinals; and the said cardinals

* Federigo de Sanseverino, fourth son of Robert Count of Cajazzo,
was made a cardinal in 1489, and died on the 7th of August, 1516.—
AUBERY, ii. 600.

† Giambattista Savelli, a noble Roman, was made a cardinal on the
15th of May, 1480, and died on the 18th of September, 1498.—AUBERY,
ii. 518.

‡ Dated on the 15th of January, 1495.

were to receive all the rights and perquisites belonging to their dignities, as well absent as present; and the Pope was to deliver four towns to the king, Terracina, Civita Vecchia, Viterbo (which was in his hands already), and Spoleto; but this last he never delivered, notwithstanding his promise. All these towns were to be restored to the Pope upon the king's return out of Naples, which was performed on the king's part, though the Pope had not dealt fairly with him. By this agreement he also delivered the Grand Seignior's brother* to the king, for whom he received constantly every year of the Great Turk forty-five thousand ducats, for he was greatly afraid of him.   He further promised not to put a legate into any place under the jurisdiction of the Church without the king's approbation.   There were other articles relating to the consistory, for which and the rest, his son the cardinal of Valentia † was given in hostage, who attended the king instead of a legate.   The king on his part did his filial obedience with all imaginable humility, and the Pope created two cardinals at his request; one was Monsieur Brissonet, who had before been made Bishop of St. Malo; the other was the Bishop of Mans ‡, of the house of Luxembourg, and then resident in France.

Ch. XVI.—How the King departed from Rome to Naples; of the Transactions in that Kingdom in the Meantime; and an Account of the Places the King of France passed through in his March.—1495.

Matters being adjusted after this manner, the king left Rome § seemingly in great friendship with the Pope, but

* Zizim.   See note, p. 67. of this volume.

† Cæsar Borgia, a natural son of Pope Alexander VI., was created a cardinal on the 20th of September, 1493.   He resigned his hat in 1498, in the hope of making a great marriage; and received the titles of Duke of Romagna in Italy, and Valentinois in France.   He died on the 12th of March, 1507, having crowded into a comparatively short life all the worst crimes of which human nature is capable.

‡ Philippe de Luxembourg, Bishop of Térouenne and Mans, was created a cardinal on the 27th of January, 1497, and died on the 2nd of June, 1519.

§ On the 28th of January, 1495.

eight cardinals left the town in a rage, of whom six were partisans of the vice-chancellor and the cardinal of St. Peter ad Vincula, though it was supposed this was only a feint of Ascanio's, and that at bottom he was agreed with the Pope ; but his brother * had not then declared himself our enemy. The king marched with his army to Genzano, and from thence to Velitri, where the Cardinal of Valentia gave him the slip.

The next morning the king took Monte-fortino by storm, and put the garrison to the sword. The place belonged to James Visconti, who had entered into the king's service, and afterwards deserted him ; for the Visconti are of the faction of the Ursini. From thence the king marched to Valmontone, which belonged to the Colonne, and thence advanced to within four miles of Mount St. John, a strong place, which he battered seven or eight hours with his heavy cannon, and then took it by storm †, and put all or nearly all the garrison to the sword. It was church land, and belonged to the Marquis di Pescara ‡ ; and there our whole army joined. From thence the king marched about sixteen miles to St. Germain, where the new King Ferrand was encamped, as I said before, with all the forces he was able to assemble. There was now no remedy ; this was the place for him to fight in or not at all, for it was the entrance into his kingdom, and he was advantageously posted, both in respect of the river and the mountain. He had also sent a strong detachment to secure the pass at Cancello, which is in the mountains, about six miles from St. Germain ; but before the king's approach, Ferrand retired with great precipitation, and abandoned both the town and the pass. Monsieur de Guise § commanded the van that day, and the Lord de Rieux ‖ was ordered to take the pass at Cancello, which the

* The Duke of Milan.

† On the 11th of February, 1495.

‡ Alfonso de Avalos, Marquis of Pescara, and Lord Chamberlain to Ferdinand I., King of Naples.

§ Louis D'Armagnac, Duke of Némours and Count of Guise, afterwards appointed Viceroy of Naples; killed in the battle of Cerignola, on the 28th of April, 1503.—ANSELME, iii. 429.

‖ John, Lord of Rieux and Rochefort, Count of Harcourt, and Marshal of Bretagne, born on the 27th of June, 1447, and died on the 9th of February, 1518.

Arragonians ought to have defended; but they also abandoned their post, so that the king entered St. Germain * without any resistance.   King Ferrand retreated to Capua, where they received him and some few of his retinue, but refused to admit his whole army.   He made no long stay among them at that time, but only entreated them to continue faithful to him, promising to return the next day; and away he posted to Naples, suspecting the rebellion which afterwards happened there.   The greater part of his army he left behind, and commanded them to attend him at Capua; but when he came back the next day they were all fled.   Virgil Ursini, and his cousin the Count de Pettilane, went to Nola, where they and their party were taken by our men.   They affirmed that they had a safe-conduct, and that we did them wrong; and it was true enough, but their passport had not yet come to their hands; however, they paid nothing for their ransom, only they were plundered, and, to speak the truth, their loss was very considerable.

From St. Germain the king marched to Mignano and Teano, and encamped at Calvi, two miles from Capua, where the inhabitants of that city came to treat with him, and the king entered it with his whole army.†   From Capua he marched the next day to Aversa, midway between Capua and Naples, about five miles distant from both.   The chief of the Neapolitans waited on his majesty there, and they came to an accommodation, by which their ancient liberties and privileges were secured to them.   The king sent thither before him the Marshal de Gié, the Seneschal of Beaucaire, the President Gannay, who kept the seals, and his secretaries. King Ferrand, finding how matters went, and seeing the people and nobility in arms against him, and his great stables plundered before his face, got immediately aboard a galley, and made the best of his way to Ischia, which is a small island about eighteen miles from Naples.   And the King of France was received into the city of Naples with great solemnity and joy‡; all the people came out to meet him, and those who were under the greatest obligation to the house of Arragon came first, as particularly the family of

* On the 14th of February, 1495.
† On the 19th of February, 1495.
‡ On Sunday, the 22nd of February, 1495.

the Caraffi, who had at that time from the house of Arragon above forty thousand ducats a year, in lands and employments; for the kings in that country can dispose of their own demesnes, as well as other people's; and I am of opinion there are not three considerable estates in the whole kingdom which are not held of the crown or other persons.

Never people expressed so great zeal and affection to any king or nation as they did to ours; for they supposed themselves delivered from all tyranny, so that everywhere they willingly submitted to us. The whole country of Calabria yielded, and the Lord d'Aubigny and Peron de Basche were sent to command them, without any forces of their own. The Abruzzi revolted of their own accord, and the town of Aquila, which was always in the French interest, set them an example. In Apulia they did the same, all but the castle of Brindisi, which is strong and well-manned, and the town of Gallipoli, which had also a strong garrison in it, or else the inhabitants would have revolted. In Calabria there were three places which held out for King Ferrand; two of them were Amantea and Tropea, anciently devoted to the house of Anjou, and they at first set up the arms of France; but, because the king had given them to Monsieur de Persi*, and would not make them part of his own demesnes, they pulled down his arms, and erected the banners of Arragon. The third place was the castle of Reggio, which continued firm to the house of Arragon; but all that stood out did so for want of being summoned to surrender; for there was not a sufficient body of troops sent into Apulia and Calabria to have kept one castle for the king. Tarento voluntarily surrendered both castle and town, and so did Otranto, Monopoli, Trani, Manfredonia, Barletta, and all but those places which I excepted before. They came three days' journey to meet our army, and begged of us to receive their respective cities into our protection. They sent likewise all of them to Naples, and all the princes and great lords of the kingdom came thither to do homage to our king, except the Marquis de Pescara, but his brothers and nephews came. The Count d'Acri and

* François d'Alegre, Count of Joigny, Baron of Viteaux, and Lord of Precy, was Grand Master of the Woods and Forests of France in 1498.

the Marquis de Squillazzo fled into Sicily, because our king had given their estates to the Lord d'Aubigny.   There also arrived at Naples the Prince of Salerno, newly come from sea; but he had done nothing considerable. His cousin, the Prince of Bisignano, was there also with his brothers, and the Dukes of Melfi * and Gravina †, and the old Duke of Sora, who heretofore had sold his duchy to the Cardinal of St. Peter ad Vincula, whose brother ‡ enjoys it at this day.   The Counts of Monterio, Fondi, Tripalda, and Celano (which last had been banished a long time, and was returned with the king) came also to Naples.   The Count de Troye, a young Scottish gentleman, but educated in France, was there also, and the Count de Popoli, whom we found prisoner in Naples.   The young Prince of Rossano, who, as I said before, was long a prisoner with his father, who had been confined thirty-four years, was released, and accompanied King Ferrand to Ischia.   There came also to Naples the Marquis de Venafro, all the Caldoresques §, the Count de Matalon, and the Count de Merillano, whose predecessors had always governed the house of Arragon; and, in short, all the nobility of that kingdom, except the three persons whom I mentioned before.

Ch. XVII.— How King Charles was crowned King of Naples; the Errors he committed in his Government of that Kingdom; and of the Discovery of a Design in his Favour against the Turks by the Venetians.—1495.

KING Ferrand, when he fled from Naples, left the Marquis of Pescara and some Germans in the castle, and sailed himself into Sicily to demand succour of his father.   Don

* Trojanus Carracciolo, in whose favour the dukedom of Melfi was erected into a principality.
† Francesco Orsini, Duke of Gravina, strangled, by order of Cæsar Borgia, on the 18th of January, 1503.—Sismondi, xiii. 182.
‡ Giovanni della Rovere, Duke of Sora and Acri, and Prefect of Rome, died in 1501.
§ The Caldoreschi, or members of the Caldora family.

M 2

Frederic still kept at sea with some few galleys, and came twice (with a passport) to treat with our king. His demands were, that some part of the kingdom should be left to his nephew, with the title of king; and that he should himself enjoy all the lands which belonged to him and his wife. His request was not unreasonable, for his own estate was but small: the king offered to give both him and his nephew an equivalent in France; and I am of opinion his majesty would have given them some considerable duchy, but they did not think fit to accept it; besides, there was no trusting them in the kingdom of Naples; for they would have observed no articles of agreement any longer than it had been for their advantage. So we erected our batteries against the castle of Naples, and began to fire upon it. The Marquis de Pescara was gone out of it, and there were only a few Germans in it. Had we sent but four of our great guns into the island, we had certainly carried it; but from thenceforward our misfortunes returned. For all the rest of the towns (which were not above four or five) would have fallen into our hands of course; but we spent our time in gaiety, entertainments, dancing, and tournaments, and grew so insolent and vain, we scarce considered the Italians to be men. Our king was crowned, and had his lodgings in the castle of Capoana, and sometimes went to Mont-Imperial * : to the subjects of that kingdom he did many good acts, and abated their taxes; so that I believe the people would never have rebelled of themselves (though they are naturally inconstant), had we but obliged some few of the nobility; but they were slighted, and treated uncivilly at the very gates. Those of the house of Caraffa (though friends to the house of Arragon) were used the best; yet they escaped not quite without loss. Every one else was deprived of his offices and estate; and the partisans of the house of Anjou fared a great deal worse than the friends of Arragon. Orders were sent into the county of Merillano, and the President Gannay and the seneschal (lately made Duke of Nola, and grand chamberlain of the kingdom) were suspected to have taken money for obtaining them: by

* Probably Poggio Reale, a palace near Naples, which Charles VIII. frequently visited.

those orders every one was to be confirmed in his possessions, only the partisans of the house of Anjou were to be
excluded from their estates, unless they could make good
their titles by law ; and for such as had entered of their own
accord (as the Count di Celano) they were to be ejected by
force.   All estates and offices were conferred upon two or
three Frenchmen, and all the stores of provision in the
castle of Naples (which were found to be very considerable
upon the taking of it) were given to any man that asked,
with the king's knowledge and consent.

During these transactions the Germans capitulated, and
delivered up the castle, keeping all the goods that were in
it (to a vast value) for themselves. · Another castle, called
Castel del Ovo, was taken by storm ; by which it may be
perceived that what was done was not done so much by
the conduct or dexterity of the agents, as by the providence of God ; but the great faults that were committed
were the works of men puffed up by vain glory, and unwilling to acknowledge from whence their success and
honour proceeded ; and their misfortune was the pure
product of their own depraved nature and experience :
so that their fortune changed as suddenly and visibly
as the day rises in Norway or Iceland, where the days in
summer are longer than in other parts, and one day is
scarce ended until within a quarter of an hour before the
next begins to dawn.   In the same manner a wise man
might have observed the face of their good fortune alter,
and that enterprise miscarry (which, if had been ascribed to
the true manager of it), would have contributed mightily to
the honour and advantage of all Christendom.   For the
Turkish empire would have been as easily shaken as Alphonso's kingdom ; for the emperor is still alive, and is a
man of no reputation or courage, and his brother was in
our king's hands (though he lived but a few days after the
Cardinal of Valentia made his escape, and was supposed to ·
have been poisoned), and the sultan dreaded him above all
persons in the world.   Besides, in the very heart of his
empire there were thousands of Christians ready to take
up arms; and from Otranto to Valona* is not above sixty

* Avlona, or Valona, a town in Albania, situated on the headland
known as Cape Linguetta, in the Adriatic Sea.

miles, and from Valona to Constantinople about eighteen days' journey, as I have been informed by men who have often travelled between those places, and in all the way there are not above two or three strong towns, the rest having been dismantled. The countries that lie between are Albania, Sclavonia, and Greece, all of them very populous, and acquainted with the fame and character of our king by their correspondents in Venice and Apulia, to whom they wrote constantly, and awaited only their directions to rebel. The king sent thither to them the Archbishop of Durazzo*, who was an Albanian born; and, discoursing with multitudes of the children and grandchildren of several great lords, descendants of Scanderbeg†, one son of the Emperor of Constantinople‡, several of the nephews of the Lord Constantine§ (at present Governor of Montferrat), and some nephews or cousins to the King of Servia, he found them all inclinable to revolt. In Thessaly above five thousand men would have appeared, and Scutari and Croia would have been surprised by means of the Lord Constantine, who lay concealed several days in my house at Venice; for Macedonia and Thessaly, which formerly belonged to Alexander the Great, were his inheritance. Valona is situated in them; Scutari and Croia are not far off; but in his time his father or uncle‖ mortgaged them to the Venetians, who lost Croia, and Scutari was surrendered to the Turk upon articles of peace.¶ The said Lord Constantine was at that time within three leagues of them; and

* Paolo Angelo, Archbishop of Durazzo, a native of Drivasto in Albania, and a friend and councillor of Scanderbeg. — HAMMER, iii. 123.

† George Castriota, surnamed Iskender-beg, or the Lord Alexander, was an Albanian prince, celebrated for his heroic warfare against the Turks. He was born in 1404, and died in 1467. His death was soon followed by the entire submission of Albania to the Turkish yoke.

‡ Probably Thomas Palæologus, son of the Emperor Manuel, and brother of Constantine Dragases, the last Emperor of Constantinople.

§ Constantine Aranito, of the family of the Comneni, and uncle to Mary Duchess of Montferrat.

‖ George, son of Stracimer Balch, Prince of Scutari, gave that town to the Venetians in 1394.—MURATORI, xxii. 762.

¶ Croia, in Albania, was given to the Venetians by Scanderbeg, and surrendered to Mahomet II. on the 15th of June, 1478. Scutari was ceded by treaty on the 26th of January, 1479.—HAMMER, iii. 227.

the enterprise would have been executed, had not the Archbishop of Durazzo stayed at Venice some time after Constantine's departure. I pressed him hard to depart, for I thought him a person that could not keep a secret long; and he went up and down boasting that he was about an affair which would make him celebrated all over Christendom. By ill fortune, on the very day that the Venetians had news of the death of the Turk's brother, whom the Pope had delivered to our king, they resolved to give notice of it to the Sultan by one of their secretaries; and being assured that whoever brought the first news would be certain of a great reward, they ordered that no vessel should pass between the two castles in the night (which castles command the entrance of the gulf of Venice); to prevent which they posted guards at both of them, being fearful of nothing so much as the small vessels and grips*, as they call them, of which there are great numbers in the ports of Albania, and their islands in Greece.

The poor archbishop happened that very night to set out upon the Lord Constantine's enterprise, and carrying along with him abundance of swords, bucklers, and javelins, for the use of his confederates who wanted them; as he passed between the two castles he was stopped and taken, and himself and servants secured in one of them; but the vessels had leave to go on. They searched him, and found letters about him that discovered the whole plot; and the Lord Constantine has told me since that the Venetians sent immediate notice to all the Turkish garrisons that were near, and an express to the Grand Signor himself; so that, had it not been for the grip which they suffer to pass (whose master was an Albanian who gave him notice), the Lord Constantine had been taken; but he escaped by sea, and got away into Apulia.

* Small vessels corresponding with our modern brigantines.

CH. XVIII.—A Digressión or Discourse, by no Means unconnected with the main Subject, in which Philip de Commines, Author of this present Book, speaks at some Length of the State and Government of the Signory of Venice, and of what he saw, and what was done, while he was Ambassador from the King of France in the City of Venice. —1495.

IT is now high time for me to say something of the Venetians, and of the occasion of my being sent thither in an embassy while the king was employed in his affairs at Naples. I was sent from Asti to return them thanks for the civil and obliging answers they had given to two former ambassadors from his majesty, and to endeavour, if possible, to continue them in his friendship, and to cultivate a good understanding with them; for he saw their power, wisdom, and conduct was more like to disturb him than any other state in Italy. The Duke of Milan hastened my despatch, and wrote to his resident there (where he constantly had one) to assist me, and give me instructions to whom I should apply myself. His ambassador had an allowance from the Signory of a hundred ducats a month, his lodgings well furnished, and three gondolas to carry him about the town without expense; and the Venetian ambassador has the same at Milan, excepting the boats; for there they go on horseback, and at Venice in boats. In my journey thither I passed by several of their cities, Brescia, Verona, Vicenza, Padua, and other places. I was treated very civilly wherever I came, in honour to the monarch who sent me, and the people came out to meet me in great bodies, with their Podesta or captain *; both of them never came out together, but the captain met me at the gate. When I had entered the town I was conducted to my lodgings; the master of the house was commanded that I should want nothing, and my whole charges were borne, and mighty good words given me into the bargain; yet, if you compute what must necessarily be given to the drums, trumpets, and officers in those ceremonies, an ambassador will be found to save but little; however, my reception was most honourable.

* The Podestà was the civil governor of the town; the captain the military commandant.

The day that I made my entry into Venice they sent to meet me as far as Fusina, which is five miles from Venice; there you leave the boats which bring you down the river * from Padua, and get into little boats covered with tapestry and very neat, with fair carpets within, and velvet cushions to sit upon. To this place you come from Venice by sea, as it is the next place to Venice upon *terra firma;* but the sea (unless agitated by some storm) is very calm, which is the reason of the great abundance of all sorts of fish. I was extremely surprised at the situation of this city, to see so many churches, monasteries, and houses, and all in the water; and the people have no other passage up and down the streets but in boats, of which, I believe, they have near thirty thousand, but they are very small. About the city, within less than the compass of half a French league, there are seventy religious houses both of men and women, all situated in little islands, very beautiful and magnificent both in building and furniture, with fair gardens belonging to them; without reckoning those in the city, where there are the four orders of mendicants, and seventy-two parishes, besides several fraternities; and, indeed, it is most strange to behold so many stately churches in the sea.

I was met and complimented at Fusina by five and twenty gentlemen, richly dressed in silks and scarlets; they welcomed me with abundance of civility, and conducted me to St. Andrew's church, which was near the town, where as many other gentlemen met and complimented me. These were accompanied by the ambassadors of Milan and Ferrara; and after they had made another speech to me I was conducted into other larger boats, which they called Plats, two of which were covered with crimson satin, and spread with tapestry at the bottom, big enough to hold forty persons; and placing me between the two ambassadors (the middle being the most honourable place in Italy), I was conducted through the principal street, which they call the Grand Canal, and it is so wide that galleys frequently cross one another; indeed I have seen vessels of four hundred tons or more ride at anchor just by the houses. It is the fairest and best-built street, I think, in the world, and goes quite through the city; the houses are very large and lofty, and built of

* The Brenta.

stone; the old ones are all painted; those of about a hundred years standing are faced with white marble from Istria
(which is about a hundred miles from Venice), and inlaid
with porphyry and serpentine. Within they have, most of
them, two chambers at least adorned with gilt ceilings, rich
marble chimney-pieces, bedsteads of gold colour, their portals of the same, and most gloriously furnished. In short,
it is the most triumphant city that I have ever seen, the
most respectful to all ambassadors and strangers, governed
with the greatest wisdom, and serving God with the most
solemnity; so that, though in other things they might be
faulty, I believe God blesses them for the reverence they
show in the service of the church.

In the company of these fifty gentlemen I was conveyed
to St. George's (which is an abbey of reformed black friars),
where I had an apartment prepared for me. The next
morning they came to wait on me again, and conducted me
to the Signory, where I delivered my credentials to the
Doge *, who presides in all their councils, and is honoured
as a king. All letters are addressed to him, but of himself
he cannot do much; yet this one had greater authority than
any of his predecessors, for he had been Doge for above
twelve years; and I found him a prudent man, of great experience in the affairs of Italy, and civil and courteous in
his person. The first day of my arrival was spent in receiving their compliments, and viewing three or four chambers
in the duke's palace; in which the ceilings, beds, and portals
were all richly gilt; the apartments are very fine, but the
court is not large. The palace is splendid and rich in all it
contains, being built of finely carved marble, and the whole
front and facings are of stone, gilt an inch thick; and there
are in this palace four handsome saloons, richly gilt, and
very spacious. The Doge from his own chamber can hear
mass at the high altar in the chapel of St. Mark, which, for
a chapel, is the most magnificent piece of building in the
universe, being built of mosaic work in every part, of which
they pretend to be the inventors; and, indeed, it is a great
trade amongst them, as I have seen.

* Agostino Barberigo, elected Doge on the 30th of August, 1486,
held the office for fifteen years.

In this chapel their treasure (of which so much is said) is kept, and intended only for the decoration of their churches; there are twelve or fourteen rubies, the largest I ever saw; one of them weighs seven, the other eight hundred carats, but both of them are unpolished; there are twelve other stones in cases of gold, with the edges and forepart set richly with very fine jewels. There are also twelve crowns of gold, wherewith, anciently, upon certain festivals in the year, twelve women of the city were crowned; and being styled and attended as queens, they passed in great pomp and solemnity through all the churches and islands. But, at length, certain robbers from Istria and Friuli (which are not far off), concealed about those islands, took their opportunity and surprised a number of the women of the city. Their husbands pursued, overtook, and recovered them; upon which they offered up their crowns to St. Mark, and founded a chapel, to which the Signory repairs every year upon the day of their victory. There is also great store of rich ornaments for the church, with several fair pieces of gold, many fine amethysts and agates, and some small emeralds. But this is not a treasure of equal value with ready money, and, indeed, they have not much of that kind of treasure; for the Doge told me in the Senate-house that it is a capital crime among them to suggest collecting a treasure of that nature; and they are right, for it might cause dissension among them. After they had shown me their treasure I was carried to see their arsenal, where their galleys are equipped, and all things necessary provided for their navies; which, perhaps, is even now the finest in the world, and was formerly under better order and regulation.

In short, I resided there eight months at their expense, and all the other ambassadors who were there had the same treatment; in which time I can assure you I found them so wise, and so intent upon enlarging their territories, that, if it be not prevented in time, all the neighbouring States may lament it too late. For since our king's expedition into Italy they have been much more dexterous and skilful in attacking and defending themselves than formerly; for they are still at war with him, and yet they have extended their dominions, and lent money upon the security of seven or eight cities in Apulia, which I am not sure will ever be restored.* Besides, at the king's first coming into Italy they did not imagine towns could have been taken so easily (contrary to their custom), nor in so short a time; but since they have been better instructed in the art of war, they have fortified their towns very strongly, and other commonwealths have done the same. It is not to be expected that they should attain to the perfection and grandeur of the old Romans, for their bodies are not so able to bear the fatigues of war, neither are they of such a martial genius; for they never make war upon the continent in their own persons, as the Romans did; but they send their Proveditori and other officers, with their general, to furnish his army with provisions, and assist him in his councils of war. But their naval expeditions are wholly managed by their own people; their fleet, both galleys and ships, being manned with their own subjects, and commanded by their own nobility. Another great advantage they have by not going in person to the wars upon *terra firma,* and that is, there is no man among them of that boldness or interest as to dare to make any attempt to seize the government, as they did in Rome; which is great wisdom, and prevents many civil contentions, against which they have provided in several ways, and all very wisely. They have no tribunes of the people, as they had in Rome (and those tribunes were in part the cause of its destruction); the people among them are of no authority, are consulted in no affair of state, and are incapable of bearing any office; for all their officers, except the secretaries, are chosen out of the gentry; and thus the greater part of the people have no share in the government. Titus Livius has acquainted them perfectly with the defects of the Roman government, and they have his history in great esteem, and his bones are preserved in their palace at Padua; so that, for these and many other reasons which I observed amongst them, I do once more affirm that they are in a fair way to be a very powerful people hereafter.

* In 1496 Ferdinand II. gave the towns of Otranto, Brindisi, Trani, Monopoli, and Pulignano to the Venetians as security for a debt of 200,000 ducats which he owed them. But all the Venetian possessions in the kingdom of Naples were restored to Ferdinand the Catholic in 1509.

CH. XIX.—What were the Subjects of the Embassy of the Lord of
Argenton to the Republic of Venice.—1495.

BUT to come to the business of my embassy: it was to thank
the Venetians for their civil answers which they had given
to two of our king's ambassadors who had been sent to
them before; by which answers he was encouraged to proceed boldly in his enterprise; and all this passed before his
majesty left Asti.*   I gave them a large discourse of the old
alliances between the kings of France and their republic,
and offered them Brindisi and Otranto, upon condition they
would engage to restore them, when my master should deliver them two better towns in Greece.   They spoke very
honourably both of the king and his affairs; for they did not
imagine he would proceed very far.   As to the offer which
I made them, they replied that they were his friends and
servants, and would not permit him to purchase their alliance (for our king had not yet these towns in his power);
and that they were not altogether unprovided for war, if
they thought fit to engage in it; but they were resolved not
to do it, though the Neapolitan ambassadors solicited them
daily, and offered them very advantageous terms.   And King
Alphonso (who then reigned) confessed he had behaved
himself very ill towards them, and laid before them the ill
consequences which would accrue to them if our master succeeded in his designs.

The Turk, on the other hand, sent an ambassador immediately to them (and I saw him several times), who, at the
Pope's request, threatened them heavily if they did not declare war against our king.   They gave fair answers to all
the ambassadors; for they had no apprehension of us at that
time, and did but laugh at our expedition.   For indeed the
Duke of Milan had told them, by his ambassador, that they
need not concern themselves in this affair, for he knew how
to send our king back again, without having got any footing
in Italy; and he sent the same message to Peter de Medicis,
who told me of it afterwards.   But when they and the Duke
of Milan saw the king had got those towns of the Floren-

* The king left Asti on the 6th of October, 1494.

tines in his possession, and especially Pisa, they began to
grow afraid of his designs, and to contrive how they might
hinder him from advancing farther; but their consultations were tedious, and in the meantime his majesty's affairs
went prosperously on. However, messengers passed constantly from one to the other, and the King of Spain began
to be afraid for his isles of Sicily and Sardinia. The King
of the Romans began also to be jealous of the imperial
crown, upon which he was persuaded by some persons that
our king had a design, and that he had requested it of the
Pope; but this was not true.

For these reasons the two kings sent formal ambassadors
to Venice during my residence there. The King of the
Romans, being their neighbour, first sent the Bishop of
Trent * as the chief in that embassy, and with him two gentlemen and a doctor-at-law; they were received with great
ceremony and respect, entertained as handsomely as myself,
had ten ducats a day allowed them for their expense, and
the charge of their horses (which were left at Treviso) was
borne besides. Not long after this there arrived a person of
quality† from Spain, with a numerous retinue, and in a very
splendid equipage, who was received as honorably as the
other, and his charges also borne. The Duke of Milan, besides the ambassador he had there already, sent the Bishop
of Como ‡, and Signor Francisco Bernardino Visconti.§
They began to have private conferences in the night, at
first by means of their secretaries; for they durst not declare
publicly against the king (especially the Duke of Milan and
the Venetians), not knowing what the success of this confederacy might be. The Duke of Milan's ambassadors made
me a visit, brought me letters from their master, and told
me their coming was in return for the visit of two ambassadors whom the Venetians had sent to Milan; whereas the
custom was only to have one resident there, and at last they
had no more. But all this was but artifice and deception;

* Ulrich von Lichtenstein, Bishop of Trent, who died on the 16th of
September, 1505.
† Lorenzo Suarez de Mendoza y Figueroa.—SISMONDI, xii. 266.
‡ Antonio Trivulzio, created a cardinal in 1500, died on the 18th of
March, 1508.—IMHOFF, 86.
§ Francesco Bernardo Visconti, elected a ducal councillor in 1484.

for they all came on purpose to make an alliance against our good king, and so many secret cabals could not be carried on long without becoming known.   They next asked me if I did not know what was the cause of the coming of the ambassadors from Spain and the King of the Romans, that they might give their master an account of it.   But I was informed before (by the servants of the ambassadors and others) that the Spanish ambassador had passed through Milan in disguise, and that the Germans were wholly managed by the duke.   Besides, I had notice that the Neapolitan ambassadors delivered several packets of letters hourly from their master (for all this was before our king's departure from Florence).   I was at some expense for my intelligence, but what I had I could depend on.   I had immediate notice of the treaty that was on foot, and what were the first proposals that were made, but not agreed to ; for in such consultations the Venetians are very long.   For these reasons, and seeing the alliance near its conclusion, I would not pretend ignorance, but answered the Milanese ambassador that, since they carried things so strangely, I would let them know that my master would not lose the friendship of the Duke of Milan if there was a possibility of preserving it, and that I would acquit myself as an ambassador, and excuse whatever ill reports might have been made to the Duke of Milan against my master.   The duke, I presumed, was misinformed, and I said that he would do well to consider (before he lost the recompense of so great a service as he had already done the king) that the kings of France did not use to be ungrateful, and that a rash or inconsiderate word ought not to break a friendship that was of such importance to both of them ; and then I desired that they would inform me of their grievances, that I might acquaint my master with them before they proceeded any further.   They swore to me all of them, with many imprecations, that they had no such thoughts ; but they did but equivocate, for they came thither on purpose to negotiate this alliance.

The next morning I went to the Signory to expostulate with them about it, and to say what I thought proper in the affair ; among other things I told them, that by their alliance with my master, and their former alliance with his father, it was mutually provided that neither should support the enemies of the other; and that therefore this new league that was so much talked of could not be entertained by them without infraction of their promises. I was desired to withdraw, and, being called in again by and by, the Doge told me that I ought not to believe all the flying reports of the town; for in Venice all people had the liberty of saying what they pleased. However, he assured me they never had any thoughts of entering into an alliance against the king, nor ever had heard of it; but that their designs were quite contrary, and rather to make a league between my master, the two other kings, and all Italy, against the Turk, and that each should bear his proportion in the charge of the war; and that if in Italy there should be any State or prince that refused to pay his share, the king and they together should compel him to do it. As to the war in which my master was at present engaged, they told me that they would endeavour to make an honourable peace for him; and the terms which they proposed were, that my master should accept of a good sum of ready money, which they would advance upon the caution of certain towns in Apulia (which are now in their possession); and that the kingdom of Naples should be held of him by the Pope's consent, and pay him an annual tribute; and that my master should keep three towns in his hands as a security. I wish to God he had accepted those advantageous offers.

I replied that I had no instructions to enter into any such treaty; and I desired that they would not be over-hasty in the conclusion of their alliance, that I might have time to acquaint my master with their proceedings, requesting them (as I had done the others), that they would acquaint me with their grievances, and not conceal them as the ambassadors of Milan had done. Then they plainly told me that they were not pleased with the king's having seized upon the Pope's towns, much less with what he had taken from the Florentines, and particularly Pisa; alleging that my master had written to several princes, and to them among the rest, that he would meddle with nothing in Italy but the kingdom of Naples, and that, having conquered that, he would undertake an expedition against the Turk; but that, nevertheless, he seemed desirous to get all he could conquer in Italy, and not meddle with the Turk at all. They told me also that the Duke of Orleans' continuance at Asti was a great terror to the Duke of Milan, and that the ministers of the Duke of Orleans had threatened him highly. However, they promised to conclude nothing before I had an answer from my master, or at least before a convenient time to receive it was past; and they showed me more respect than the Duke of Milan. I acquainted his majesty with every particular, but his answer was unsatisfactory; after which they had conferences every day, for they knew their designs were discovered. The King of France was at Florence in the meantime; and if he had met with any opposition at Viterbo, as was expected, they would have sent forces to Rome; and they would have done the same if King Ferrand had continued at Rome, for they could not imagine he would have abandoned the city; but, when they saw he was retired, they began to be afraid. Yet the ambassadors from the two kings pressed them hard to come to some resolution, declaring they would otherwise be gone; for they had been there four months, every day soliciting the Signory; and I was as diligent in making an interest against them.

Ch. XX.—How the Lord of Argenton was informed that the King had gained Possession of Naples and the Places round about; at which the Venetians were displeased.—1495.

WHEN the Venetians understood that several towns in Italy had surrendered, and were informed of the king's being at Naples, they sent for me to tell me the news, and pretended to be extremely pleased with it; yet they gave me to understand that the castle held out still against him; that there was a strong garrison in it, and provided with every thing necessary for its defence; and I could perceive they had great hopes it would never be taken. Upon which ground they had consented that the Neapolitan ambassador should raise forces in Venice to be sent to Brindisi, and were just upon the conclusion of their league, when their ambassadors acquainted them by letter of the surrender of the castle of Naples.* They sent for me again one morning and I found about fifty or sixty of them assembled in their Doge's chamber, who was at that time ill of the cholic. The Doge, with a composed countenance, rather inclining to joy, told me the news; but there was none in all the company could counterfeit so well as himself. Some of them sate upon low seats, with their elbows upon their knees, and their heads between their hands; others in other postures, but all expressing great sorrow at heart; and I believe after the battle of Cannæ there was not more terror felt by the senators of Rome; for not one of them had courage enough to look upon me or speak to me but the Doge himself, which I thought was very strange. The Doge asked me whether the king my master would now perform what he had always promised, and I had always told them. I assured them he would, and promised them to use my utmost endeavours, by way of mediation, in hopes by this means to pacify their fears and jealousies; and then I took my leave of them.

Their league as yet was neither broken off nor concluded; but the Germans were dissatisfied, and wished to be gone. The Duke of Milan would not consent to some of the articles; but at length he sent instructions to his ambassadors to dispatch, and in a short time the league was concluded. Whilst this affair was in agitation I wrote constantly to our king, advising him to make peace, or else to continue in that kingdom, and provide himself better with men and money; but, if he did not approve of my advice, that he would be pleased to make good his retreat towards France, and put strong garrisons into the chief towns, before the confederates had assembled their forces. I wrote also to the Duke of Orleans, who was at Asti, but attended by his own domestics only (for his forces were with the king), and advised him to throw more men into that town, assuring him that he would suddenly be besieged in it. I sent likewise to the Duke of Bourbon (whom the king had left as his lieutenant in France) to send what forces he could spare to reinforce the garrison of Asti; for if that town were lost, no supplies could be sent to the king. I also gave notice to the Marchioness of Mont-

* On the 13th of March, 1495.

ferrat (who was true to the French, and a great enemy to
the Duke of Milan), that she might be ready to assist the
Duke of Orleans with her forces, if there should be occasion;
for the taking of Asti would entail on her the loss of the two
marquisates of Montferrat and Saluzzo.

The league was concluded one night very late*; the next
morning I was sent for by the Signory somewhat earlier than
usual. As soon as I came thither, and had taken my seat,
the Doge told me, that in honour to the Holy Trinity they
had entered into an alliance with our Holy Father the Pope,
the Kings of the Romans and of Castile, and the Duke of
Milan, for three principal objects: one was to defend Christendom against the Turk; the second was the defence of
Italy; and the third the preservation of their territories,
which they desired I would notify to the king my master.
They were in all about a hundred or more, looked very gay,
and held their heads high, and there was no such sadness in
their countenances as upon the day when they heard of the
surrender of the castle of Naples. They also told me that
they had written to their ambassadors, who were attending
on our king, to take their leave, and return to Venice. One
of their ambassadors was Dominico Loredano, and the other
Dominico Trevisano. I was extremely troubled and concerned
for my master's person, as I feared that he and his whole
army were in great danger; for I thought the confederates
were much forwarder than they were (as they also thought
themselves), and that some German troops had been near at
hand. If it had been so, the king could never have got out
of Italy. I had resolved within myself to speak little in my
passion; but they provoked me beyond the bounds I had set
myself. I told them that the night before I had sent my
master notice of their alliance (as I had done often), and that
he had written me word he had news of it, both from Milan
and Rome. The Doge seemed to be surprised to hear I had
written concerning the alliance on the night before; for there
are no people in the world so jealous, nor who keep their
counsels so secret as they; and upon bare suspicion they
many times imprison their dearest friends. Upon that consideration I told them further, that I had written to the

* On the 31st of March, 1495.—SISMONDI, xii. 276.

Dukes of Orleans and Bourbon to take care to reinforce the
garrison of Asti; and I said this in hopes to discourage them
from attempting to surprise it, which they might certainly
have done, had they been as ready as they pretended; for it
was in a weak posture of defence a long time after. They replied that they had no hostile intentions against the king;
that what they had done, or should do, would be only in
defence of themselves; and they could not suffer that my
master should amuse all Europe with his fair words, as he
had done, saying that he wanted nothing but the kingdom of
Naples, and would next turn his arms against the Turk; and
that then he should falsify his word, act quite contrary, possess himself of what he could in the territories both of the
Florentines and the Pope, and endeavour to destroy the Duke
of Milan. To which I answered, that the kings of France
had been so far from defrauding the Church of any of its revenues, that, on the contrary, they had always augmented
them, and defended its rights; that those could not be the
reasons for their league, as they pretended, but that they had
a desire to involve Italy in new troubles, to make their advantage out of them, and that I thought they intended to do
it. They resented that expression of mine, as I was informed afterwards; however, it proved true, as appeared by
the towns which King Ferrand pledged to them in Apulia
to induce them to assist him against us. I rose up to take
leave, but they made me sit down again; and the Doge asked
me if I had any overtures of peace to make, because on the
day before I had said something to that purpose; but that
was only offered in case they would have protracted the conclusion of the league for fifteen days longer, that I might have
had time to write to his majesty, and receive his answer.

After this I retired to my lodgings, and they sent for the
rest of the ambassadors one after another. At my coming
out of the council I met the Neapolitan ambassador in a fine
new gown, and very gay; and indeed he had reason to be so,
for this was a lucky turn of affairs for him. After dinner
all the ambassadors of the league met together in boats upon
the water (which in Venice is their chief recreation); the
whole number of their boats (which are provided at the
charge of the Signory, and proportioned to every man's retinue) was about forty, every one of them adorned with the

arms of their respective masters; and in this pomp they passed under my windows with their trumpets and other instruments of music. The ambassadors of Milan (at least one of them), who had kept me company for many months, would take no manner of notice of me now. For three days together I and my domestics kept within doors; though indeed I cannot say either they or I were affronted all the while. At night there were extraordinary fire-works upon the turrets, steeples, and tops of the ambassadors' houses, multitudes of bonfires were lighted, and the cannon all round the city were fired. I was in a covered boat, rowing by the wharves to see this triumphal sight, about ten o'clock at night, especially before the ambassadors' houses, where there was great banqueting.

But this was not the day on which the league was proclaimed; for the Pope had sent to them to defer it for some days, till Palm-Sunday, at which time he had ordered that every prince in whose dominions it was published, and all the ambassadors then with him, should carry an olive-branch in their hand, in token of their alliance and peace; and that upon the same day it should be published both in Germany and Spain. At Venice they made a gallery of wood a good height above the ground (as they are wont to do at the inauguration of their Doges), which reached from the palace to the end of the piazza of St. Mark; upon which (after mass had been sung by the Pope's nuncio, who absolved all people who were present at the solemnity) they marched in procession; the Signory and the ambassadors all very splendidly dressed, several of them in crimson velvet gowns which the Signory had presented to them, at least to the Germans; and all their retinue in new gowns, but these were a little of the shortest. After the procession was ended, a great many pageants and mysteries were exhibited to the people: first of all, Italy, and then the allied kings and princes, and the Queen of Spain. At their return, at a porphyry stone, where such things are usually done, proclamation was made, and the alliance published. There was at that time a Turkish ambassador, who looked privately through a window and saw this solemnity. He had taken leave, but was asked to stay to see this festival; and at night, by the assistance of a Greek, he paid me a visit, and stayed four

N 3

hours in my chamber; and his great desire was to cultivate a friendship betwixt his master and mine. I was twice invited to this feast, but desired to be excused; yet I stayed nearly a month after in the town, and was all the while as civilly entertained as before the publication of this alliance. At length I was recalled; and, having had an audience of leave, they gave me a passport, and conducted me safely to Ferrara at their own expense. The Duke of Ferrara came in person to meet me, and entertained me two days very handsomely at his own charge. The same civility I received at Bologna from Prince John Bentivoglio; and, being sent for to Florence, I continued there in expectation of my master's coming, with the relation of whose affairs I shall now proceed.

BOOK THE EIGHTH.

CH. I.—Of the Order in which the King left his Affairs in the Kingdom of Naples upon his Return into France.—1495.

To continue my Memoirs, and for your better information, we must return to our discourse of the king, who, from his first arrival at Naples to his departure, minded nothing but his pleasures, and his ministers attended to nothing but their own advantage. His youth might excuse him in some measure; but nothing could excuse them, for the king referred all to their management; and if they only had had the discretion to advise him to put strong garrisons into three or four of the chief castles, such as that of Gaeta; nay, if he had only garrisoned the castle of Naples (whose magazines and furniture had been given away and embezzled, as you have heard), the kingdom of Naples had been his at this day; for, if he had been master of that castle, the town would never have revolted. Upon the conclusion of this Italian alliance, he assembled all his forces together, and ordered 500 French men-at-arms, 2,500 Swiss, and some French foot to remain to guard the kingdom; and with the rest he resolved to march back into France by the same way he came; while the confederates were determined to stop him. The King of Spain had sent, and was still sending, his caravels * into Sicily, though with but few men on board them. However, before our king's departure they had garrisoned Rheggio in Calabria, which is near to Sicily. I had often acquainted my master with their designs of sending supplies thither, for the ambassador of Naples had told me so, supposing they had got there already; and if the king had sent any forces thither in time, he would cer-

* A sort of vessels with sails and oars, much used in the Mediterranean.

tainly have taken the castle; and the town had declared for him before. For want of our sending thither, the enemy landed forces at Mantia and Tropea. The townsmen of Otranto in Apulia had set up our king's colours; but, being informed of the new alliance, and considering how near neighbours they were both to Brindisi and Gallipoli, and how difficult it would be to furnish themselves with troops, they pulled them down again, and erected the standard of Arragon; and Don Frederic, who was at Brindisi, supplied them with a garrison. There was a universal change in the minds of the people through the whole kingdom; and fortune, which had been so propitious but two months before, began now to frown upon us; both in relation to the alliance, the king's departure, and the great want in which he left the kingdom, and that rather in respect of officers than soldiers.

The supreme command was committed to Monsieur de Montpensier *, of the house of Bourbon, a brave soldier, and a noble gentleman; but his valour was greater than his wisdom, and, besides, he was so intolerably lazy, he would never rise till noon. In Calabria he left the Lord d'Aubigny, a Scotchman (a brave and worthy knight), to command in chief. The king had made him grand constable of the kingdom, and given him (as I said before) the county of Acri, and the marquisate of Squillazzo. At his first coming thither the king had made the seneschal of Beaucaire, Stephen de Vers, governor of Gaeta, Duke of Nola, and lord high chamberlain, and all the money in that kingdom passed through his hands; but he took more upon him than he was able to perform; yet he was very desirous of keeping the kingdom of Naples. The king created the Lord Dom Julian † of Lorraine, Duke of St. Angelo, in which post he behaved himself with a great deal of honour and reputation. He left Gabriel de Montfaucon‡ at Manfredonia. He was a person for whom the king had a great esteem; but he managed

* Gilbert de Bourbon, Count of Montpensier, Archduke of Sessa, and Viceroy of Naples. He died at Pozzuolo on the 5th of October, 1496.

† Antoine de Ville, Lord of Domjulien, and Duke of Saint' Angelo in the kingdom of Naples, died at Naples in 1504.

‡ Gabriel de Montfaucon, knight, Bailiff of Meaux, councillor and chamberlain to the King of France, and lieutenant of the hundred gentlemen-at-arms of the royal household.

things imprudently there ; for, though he found it well provided with corn and everything else, yet he delivered it
up in four days for want of provisions.   To all his followers
the king gave great estates in land ; but several sold whatever they found in their castles, and it was reported
that Gabriel did so too.   At Trani he left William de
Villeneuf * to defend the town ; but, being betrayed and sold
by some of his own servants to Frederic, he was kept by
him a long time in the galleys.   He left Tarento to the command of George de Suilly †, who behaved himself well, and
held out till he was forced by famine to surrender, and then
died there of the plague.   In Aquila he placed the bailiff of
Vitry‡, who discharged his duty as he ought to do ; and
Gratian des Guerres § did the same in Abruzzo.   The king
left them very little money, only assignments upon the
revenue, and of that but very little was ever raised.   The
king took care to make a handsome provision for the
princes of Salerno and Bisignano, who served him faithfully, as long as it was in their power to do so.   He also
gratified the Colonne in whatever they demanded, and gave
them and their friends the possession of about thirty towns ;
which, if they had defended as they ought and as they swore
to do, they would have done his majesty singular service, and
reaped the honour and advantage of it themselves ; for I do
not believe they had been so great for a hundred years
before.   But they had no patience to stay till the king had
left Italy, before they fell to caballing.   It is true they were
engaged with us upon the Duke of Milan's account, for
they are naturally Gibellines.   However, that ought not to
have led them to break their oaths, especially after they had
been so civilly treated ; besides, the king had done more for

---

* Guillaume de Villeneufve, knight, councillor and steward to King
Charles VIII., has left an account of his master's wars in Italy, in which
he states that, being left with forty men to guard Trani, thirty-two of
his party were suborned by Don Frederic to deliver up the castle.
Villeneufve was kept four months in the galleys; after which he was
confined for eight months in the Castel Nuovo at Naples, and released
on the 7th of August, 1496.
  † George de Sully, Lord of Cors and Romefort.
  ‡ Claude de Lenoncourt, Lord of Harouel, and Bailiff of Vitry from
1483 to 1497.
  § Garcin d'Aguerre, Lord of Aubenton.

them than this ; for, under pretence of friendship, he carried
prisoners with him the Lord Virgil Ursini and the Count de
Petillane, and several others of the Ursini who were their
enemies ; which, indeed, was a little severe, for, though they
were prisoners of war, yet the king knew they were to
have had passports. But his intention was to carry them no
farther than Asti, and then to dismiss them upon their
parole of honour. This he did at the request of the
Colonne ; and yet, before he could get thither, the Colonne
revolted, and appeared the first against him without the least
pretence or occasion.

CH. II.—How the King departed from Naples, and returned to Rome,
from whence the Pope fled to Orvieto; of the Conference the King
had with the Lord of Argenton upon his Return from Venice ; and
his Deliberation about the Restitution of the Florentine Towns.—1495.

As soon as the king had settled his affairs as he designed,
he began his march with what forces he could collect,
which, I believe, were about nine hundred men-at-arms (including his guards), and two thousand five hundred Swiss ;
in all, of his standing army about seven thousand men,
besides about fifteen hundred more who followed the camp
as servants, and were able to bear arms. The Count de
Petillane, who had reviewed them, and knew their number
better than I did, told me after the battle (of which I shall
speak presently) that they were nine thousand effective
men. The king bent his march directly towards Rome *,
where his Holiness, having no mind to attend him, determined to go to Padua, and put himself under the protection
of the Venetians, and lodgings were prepared for him in
that city ; but afterwards they changed their minds, and
both they and the Duke of Milan sent forces to him to Rome
for the defence of the town, which arrived in time enough ;
yet the Pope durst not stay, though the king had done him

* He left Naples on the 20th of May, 1495, and entered Rome on the
1st of June following.

all imaginable honour and service, and had sent ambassadors
on purpose to desire him to stay ; but he retired to Orvieto,
and from thence to Perusia, leaving the cardinals to receive
his majesty at Rome. The king was received very honourably by them ; but he made no stay among them, nor suffered
the least injury to be done to anybody. From thence I was
sent for to attend him at Siena*, where I waited on his
majesty, who received me graciously. He asked me, in a
jesting way, whether the Venetians had sent any forces to
fall upon his rear ; for his men were all young, and he
thought no troops were able to engage with them. I humbly replied that upon my leaving Venice the Signory informed me, in the presence of one of their secretaries called
Loredano, that they and the Duke of Milan would bring
forty thousand men into the field, not to molest him, but to
defend themselves ; and on the day I set out from Venice
they ordered one of their proveditors who was employed
against us to inform me, at Padua, that their army should
not pass a river near Parma (which, if I mistake not, is
called the Oglio), unless his majesty invaded the Duke of
Milan ; and the said proveditor and I took private tokens
and directions how we might correspond with each other, if
there should be any occasion, to make a treaty of peace ; for
I was unwilling to refuse any overture of that nature,
because I knew not how my master's affairs might succeed.
There was present at our conference one Monsieur Lewis
Marcel, who (as a kind of treasurer) had that year the command of the Mots Viere†, and had been sent by them to
escort me. There were besides in the company some of
the Marquis of Mantua's servants, who were carrying him
money ; but they were at a distance, and heard nothing of
our discourse. From these or others I procured for the
king a list of the confederate army, their horse, foot, and
Stradiots, and the chief officers that commanded them all ;
but few about the king believed what I told him.

After the king had halted two days at Siena to refresh his

* The king reached Sienna on Saturday, the 13th of June, 1495.
† It is so in all the French copies; but certainly it should be Mont
Vieil, in Italian Monte Vecchio, which is a certain treasure set apart by
the Venetians for the payment of interest due to the ancient creditors of
their republic, as appears by the book of Donato Gianotti.

troops, I earnestly pressed his majesty to march onward, for the enemy were not yet together, and I feared nothing till the Germans came up; for the King of the Romans was busily raising both men and money.   But, notwithstanding all I said to the contrary, the king would have two things first solemnly debated in council, which took up but a little time: one was, whether he should restore all the Florentine towns, and receive thirty thousand ducats (which was an arrear of a former gift), and seventy thousand more which they offered to lend him, besides a reinforcement of three hundred men-at-arms (under the command of Francisco Secco, an experienced and brave commander, and one in whom the king put great confidence), and two thousand foot, to secure his passage into his own kingdom.   It was my opinion (and several others agreed with me) that the king should restore all but Leghorn, which he should keep till he had reached Asti.   If he had followed our advice, he would have been able to have paid his army, and have had enough to have bribed the enemy, and then he might have fought them as he pleased; but we could not get a hearing; Monsieur de Ligny prevented it (who was a young gentleman, and cousin-german to the king); but he scarce knew why he did so, unless it were in compassion to the Pisans. The other point to be debated was set on foot by Monsieur de Ligny himself, and proposed in council by one Gaucher de Tinteville *, and by a party in Siena who wished to have Monsieur de Ligny for their governor; for that town is always divided into factions, and is governed the worst of any in Italy.   My judgment was demanded first, and I answered that I thought it would be better for the king to march forward than to amuse himself with things of so litle importance, which could not be of any service to him for a week; besides, that town belonged to the emperor, and to dispose of it in that manner was to set the whole empire against us. Everybody agreed with my opinion, and yet it was carried against us; and Monsieur de Ligny was made the governor of Siena, with large promise of a revenue, but he never received any.   This trifling debate detained us six or seven days, during which time the king diverted himself among

* Gaucher de Dinteville, Lord of Chenets, and Bailiff of Troyes.

the ladies; and he left in this town above three hundred of his choicest troops, to the great weakening of his army. He then advanced towards Pisa *, by the way of Poggibonzi, a castle belonging to the Florentines; but those who were left at Siena were driven out in a month.

Ch. III.—Of the memorable Preachings of Friar Jerome of Florence.— 1495.

I HAD almost forgotten to mention that while I was at Florence, on my way to join the king, I went to pay a visit to a certain friar called Friar Jerome †, who, by report, was a very holy man, and had lived in a reformed convent fifteen years. There went along with me one John Francis ‡, a very prudent person, and steward of the king's household. The occasion of my going to visit him was upon the account that he had always, both in the pulpit and elsewhere, spoken much in the king's favour, and his words had kept the Flo-

* He entered Pisa on Saturday, June 20. 1495.

† Girolamo Savonarola, a Dominican monk of Ferrara, arrived on foot at Florence in the year 1489, and lodged in the convent of St. Mark. He began immediately to preach there, from profound conviction on his own part, and with a talent equal to his energy, against the scandalous abuses which had been introduced into the Church of Rome, and against the criminal usurpations in the State, which had deprived the citizens of their just rights. On the expulsion of Piero de' Medici, in 1494, he became the leader of the democratic party, which was for a time successful. Savonarola's influence was now very great; for he was looked upon by his party as a kind of prophet and supreme judge. But the opposition were not idle; they represented him to the people as an impostor, and accused him of heresy at Rome. Pope Alexander VI. summoned him to appear before him, and, in default, excommunicated him. After a long contest, in the course of which Savonarola completely lost his credit with the populace, a party of his enemies entered the convent of St. Mark by force, and dragged him to prison. He was tried before a mixed lay and ecclesiastical commission appointed by Alexander VI. and condemned to death. On the 23rd of May, 1498, he was burnt alive in the public square of Florence.

‡ Jean François de Cardonne, councillor and Chief Steward to King Charles VIII.

rentines from confederating against us; for never any preacher had so much authority in a city. Whatever had been said or written to the contrary, he always affirmed that our king would come into Italy, saying that he was sent by God to chastise the tyranny of the princes, and that none would be able to oppose him. He foretold likewise that he would come to Pisa and enter it, and that the State of Florence should be dissolved on that day. And so it fell out; for Peter de Medicis was driven out that very day. Many other things he presaged long before they came to pass: as, for instance, the death of Laurence de Medicis; and he openly declared that he knew it by revelation; as likewise he predicted that the reformation of the Church should be owing to the sword. This is not yet accomplished; but it very nearly occurred, and he still maintains that it shall come to pass.

Many persons blamed him for pretending to receive divine revelations, but others believed him; for my part I think him a good man. I asked him whether our king would return safe into France, considering the great preparations of the Venetians against him, of which he gave a better account than I could, though I had lately come from Venice. He told me he would meet with some difficulties by the way, but he would overcome them all with honour, though he had but a hundred men in his company; for God, who had conducted him thither, would guard him back again. But because he had not applied himself as he ought to the reformation of the Church, and because he had permitted his soldiers to rob and plunder the poor people (as well those who had freely opened their gates to him as the enemy who had opposed him), therefore God had pronounced judgment against him, and in a short time he would receive chastisement. However, he bade me tell him that if he would have compassion upon the people, and command his army to do them no wrong, and punish them when they did, as it was his office to do, God would then mitigate, if not revoke, his sentence; but that it would not be sufficient for him to plead that he did them no wrong himself, and that he would meet the king when he came, and tell him so from his own mouth; and so he did, and pressed hard for the restitution of the Florentine towns. When he mentioned the sentence

of God against him, the death of the dauphin * came very
fresh into my mind; for I knew nothing else that could
touch the king so sensibly. This I have thought fit to record,
to make it the more manifest that this whole expedition was
a mystery conducted by God Himself.

CH. IV.—How the King retained Pisa and several other Florentine
Towns in his Hands, while the Duke of Orleans on the other Side entered Novara, in the Duchy of Milan.—1495.

WHILE the king (as I said before) was at Pisa, the people of
that town, both men and women, begged of us that for God's
sake we would intercede for them to the king, that they
might not again be subjected to the tyranny of the Florentines, who, indeed, treated them very barbarously; but they
fared as well as their neighbours, who are subject to other
States in Italy. Pisa and Florence had been at war for three
hundred years before the Florentines subdued them. These
supplications, being delivered with tears in their eyes,
wrought strangely upon our soldiers; so that, forgetting what
our king had promised and sworn before the altar of St.
John in Florence, they all unanimously (including even the
very archers and Swiss) interposed in their behalf, and
threatened all such as wished that the king should keep his
oath, and particularly the Cardinal of St. Malo †, who, in
other places, I have called the General of Languedoc; and
him I heard an archer threaten myself, and others talked as
boldly to the Marshal de Gié. The President Gannay, for
three nights together, durst not lie in his own quarters; and
the great promoter of all this was the Count de Ligny. The
Pisans daily made their sad complaints to the king, and
moved us all to compassion, though we had no reason to relieve them.

* Charles Orlando, born on the 10th of October, 1492, and died on
the 6th of December, 1495.
† Elsewhere called the General Brissonet.

One day after dinner, as the king was playing at tables
with the Lord de Piennes, and only two or three of the gentlemen of the bed-chamber waiting on him, forty or fifty
armed gentlemen of his household entered the room, and, in
the name of the rest, the son of Sallezard the elder * made a
speech to the king in favour of the Pisans, and charged some
of the persons above named of nothing less than betraying
him; but the king reprimanded them severely, and there
never was any such thing afterwards.

Six or seven days the king spent to no purpose at Pisa;
and, having altered the garrison, he put into the castle one
Entragues †, a servant to the Duke of Orleans, but an ill-
conditioned man. Monsieur de Ligny had recommended him
to the king, and by his interest a detachment of infantry from
Berry was left with him. This Entragues managed his
affairs so well (I suppose by means of his money), that he
got Pietrasanta into his hands, and another town not far off,
called Mortano; besides which, he had another government
at Librefacto, near Lucca. The castle of the town of Sarzana,
which was extremely well fortified by the interest of Monsieur
de Ligny, was put in the hands of the bastard of Roussi ‡, who
was the Count's servant. Another castle, called Sarzanello,
he put into the hands of one of his other servants; and the
king left great bodies of his forces in these places (though
he will never have so much need of them again), and rejected the assistance and offers of the Florentines, who, upon
his refusal, grew desperate. And yet, before he left Siena,
he had intelligence that the Duke of Orleans had taken the
city of Novara § from the Duke of Milan; and it was therefore certain that the Venetians would declare war against
him; for they had sent him word that if he invaded the
Duke of Milan, they should be obliged, by the alliance they
had lately made, to assist him; and their army, which was
numerous, was quite ready to take the field.

Now you must understand, that just upon the conclusion

* Louis de Salazar, Lord of Asnoi.
† Robert de Balsac, Lord of Entragues.
‡ Antoine de Luxembourg, Bastard of Brienne, son of Antoine de
Luxembourg, Count of Roussy, and nephew of the Count de Ligny.
§ Novara opened its gates to the Duke of Orleans on the 11th of
June, 1495.

of the league, the Duke of Milan had a design upon Asti, supposing he should have found no troops in it. But my letters prevented him, and hastened the supplies which the Duke of Bourbon sent thither; and first there arrived forty lances of the Marshal de Gié's troops, who had been left behind in France, all very well appointed; and after them five hundred foot from the Marquis di Saluzzo. The arrival of these forces diverted the Duke of Milan's army, commanded by Galeas di St. Severino, who was posted at Annone, a castle belonging to the said duke, within two miles of Asti. Some time after they were joined by three hundred and fifty men-at-arms, and gentlemen of Dauphiny, and all the Frank-Archers of that country, and about two thousand Swiss; so that they were in all fully seven thousand five hundred fighting men. It was a prodigious expense and trouble to assemble these forces, and when that was done, they did not answer the end for which they were designed; for they were sent for to have assisted the king, and instead of that he was forced to support them. The king had written to the Duke of Orleans and his chief officers that they should attempt nothing against the Duke of Milan, but only have a care to secure Asti, and come to meet his majesty as far as the river Tesino, where they were to assist and favour his passage, there being no other river where he could be stopped; for the Duke of Orleans had been left at Asti, and had gone no further with the king. However, notwithstanding the king's orders to the contrary, he was so pleased with the honour of having Novara delivered into his hands (which was but ten leagues from Milan) that he could not contain himself, but entered it in a triumphal manner; and the whole city, both Guelphs and Gibellines, received him with all imaginable demonstrations of joy; and the Marchioness of Montferrat was a great instrument in carrying out the plot. The castle held out two or three days; but if in the meanwhile he had gone or sent to Milan, where his party was strong, he would have been received with more joy (as I have been told by many great persons of that duchy) than ever greeted him at his own castle at Blois; and during the first three days he might have done it with ease, for the Duke of Milan's forces were at Annone, near Asti, when Novara was surprised, and came not up till four days after; but perhaps he durst not rely upon the information he received.

CH. V.—How King Charles crossed several dangerous Passages over the Mountains between Pisa and Sarzana; and how the Germans burned Pontremoli.—1495.

FROM Siena the king was come to Pisa, as you have already heard, and from Pisa he marched to Lucca, where he was well received by the townsfolk, and stayed with them two days; and from thence he went to Pietrasanta, where Monsieur Entragues was governor; and neither he himself, nor any that were about him, had the least fear or apprehension of the enemy. Yet he found great difficulty in his march over the mountains betwixt Lucca and that place, where there were several passes very easy to have been defended by small bodies of foot; but the confederates were not assembled as yet. Not far from Pietrasanta, on one side there is the pass of Seierre, or Salto della Cerva, and on the other that of Roctaillé, or Rotaio, with a deep marsh at the foot of it, over which we were forced to march upon a causeway, as if it had been through a standing pool. This was the pass of which I had heard so much, and which I dreaded more than all the rest between Pisa and Pontremoli; for a small body of troops, with a cart overturned in the midst of it, and two pieces of cannon, would have stopped our passage, and left our army helpless. From Pietrasanta the king marched to Sarzana, where the Cardinal of St. Peter ad Vincula met him, and offered (if he pleased to send some of his forces thither) to make Genoa revolt to him. This proposal was referred to a council of officers, of whom I was one, and it was concluded by all that it should not be attempted; for if the king got the victory, Genoa would surrender of course; and if he lost the battle, it would do him no good; and this was the first time we ever heard fighting mentioned. Our resolution was reported to the king; but for all that, he sent

thither the Lord de Bresse (since Duke of Savoy), the Lord
de Beaumont de Polignac*, my brother-in-law, and the Lord
d'Aubijoux†, of the house of Amboise, with six-score men-
at-arms, and five hundred archers, newly sent him by sea
out of France. I wondered that a prince of his age should
not have one minister of state about him that durst be plain
with him, and tell him the dangers to which he exposed his
person; but indeed he put no confidence in what I said.

We had a few forces at sea, which came from Naples,
under the command of Monsieur de Miolans, Governor of
Dauphiny, and one Stephen de Neves, of Montpelier; they
were in all about eight galleys, and were arrived at Spezzia and
Rapalo, where they were defeated at the time I speak of, and in
the same place where our men had beaten King Alphonso's
forces in the beginning of this expedition, and by the same
party who had been on our side at that battle (that is to say,
Signor John Lewis di Fieschi, and Signor John Adorno); and
everything was changed in Genoa. It had been better management to have had them on the king's side, though that would
have been little enough. Monsieur de Bresse and the Cardinal
advanced into the suburbs of Genoa, expecting their party
in the town would rise in their favour; but the Duke of Milan
had taken care to prevent any insurrection; and the Adorni
and Signor John Lewis di Fieschi had given such orders
about the affair that our forces were in great danger of being
handled as they had been at sea, considering the smallness
of their numbers; nor did anything prevent it but the fear
the prevailing party in Genoa had, that if they sallied out of
the town, the Fregosi would rise up in arms and shut the
gates upon them; however, our men met with difficulty
enough before they got to Asti; and they were not at the
battle, where they might have been more serviceable and
better employed.

From Sarzana the king marched on towards Pontremoli,
which he was forced to pass, it being the entrance into the

* John de Polignac, Lord of Beaumont and Randan. He married
Jeanne de Chambes, eldest sister of Helene de Chambes, wife of Philip
de Commines.

† Hugh d'Amboise, Baron of Aubijoux, brother to the famous Cardinal George d'Amboise. He was killed in the battle of Marignan, in
1515.

mountains. The town and castle were strong, and the country about them almost inaccessible; and had they been well garrisoned, they could never have been taken; but it seemed as if what Friar Jerome told me proved true, that God would lead him, as it were, by the hand, till he was out of all danger; for the enemy were blind and stupid, and had not put above three or four hundred men to defend that important pass. The king sent his vanguard to Pontremoli, under the command of the Marshal de Gié and Signor John James di Trivulce, whom he had entertained in his service ever since King Ferrand's flight out of Naples. This Trivulce was a gentleman of Milan, of a noble family, a good officer, a worthy man, and a great enemy to the Duke of Milan, for he had been banished by him; and by his means the place was presently delivered without an assault, and the garrison marched out. But a great inconvenience ensued upon this; for, as I have already mentioned, when the Duke of Milan was there last, there happened a dispute between the townsmen and some of the Germans (forty of whom were slain by the townsmen), so that the Swiss, in revenge, and contrary to their articles, now put all the men to the sword, plundered the town, set fire to it, and burned it and all the magazines, with about ten of their own men, who, being drunk, could not escape, and it was not in the Marshal de Gié's power to prevent it. After they had committed this outrage, they besieged the castle, in order to have used those who were in it after the same manner, though the garrison consisted of none but Signor John James di Trivulce's troops, who had been put into it when the enemy marched out; neither would they give over their attack till the king himself sent to command them to desist. The destruction of this place was a great inconvenience to the king, as much for the dishonour it brought on us as for the provisions that were spoiled, of which there was great plenty, and we were in extremity of want, though the people were not much against us, excepting only those about the town, who had suffered more particularly. But if the king had hearkened to the overtures made him by Signor John James di Trivulce, several places and persons of importance would have surrendered and allied themselves to him; for he advised him to set up the young duke's standard, who was son of John Galeas, the last

Duke of Milan, that lies buried at Pavia, as you have heard; which young duke was in the Lord Ludovic's power. But the king would not be persuaded to do it, out of kindness to the Duke of Orleans, who laid claim to the duchy. After this the king marched from Pontremoli, and encamped in a small valley, where there were not ten houses, and the name of which I have forgotten. He lay in that camp five days (I know not why), with his army in great distress, for provisions, and the main body thirty miles behind the vanguard, with high and steep rocks all around, where such great cannon had never been seen till then; for those with which Duke Galeas had passed that way were but four falconets, which perhaps weighed five hundred pounds a-piece, and yet the people regarded them with infinite wonder.

Ch. VI.—How the Duke of Orleans behaved himself in the City of Novara.—1495.

But to return now to the Duke of Orleans. As soon as he had taken the Castle of Novara, he lay still for some days, and then marched to Vigevano. Two little towns * hard by sent to him and offered to receive his troops; but he wisely refused the overtures they made him. The citizens of Pavia sent twice to him likewise, and certainly he was mightily to blame in refusing their offer. However, he drew up in battle array before the town of Vigevano, where the Duke of Milan's whole army was encamped, and commanded by the sons of Galeas St. Severino, whom I have so often mentioned before. The town is worth nothing, not a jot better than St. Martin de Cande. † I came thither not long after the Duke of Milan had been there, and the chief officers who were there showed me the places where their armies had been drawn up, both within and without the town; and if the Duke of Orleans had advanced but a

* Mortara and Correano.—Guazzo, 160.
† Candes, a small town in the Department of Indre-et-Loire.

hundred paces farther, the enemy must have retreated over
the river Tesino, where they had made a large bridge of boats,
and were drawn up on the bank; and I saw them demolish
an earthwork which they had made on the other side to secure their retreat; for they had resolved to quit both the
town and the castle, which would have been a great disadvantage to them. This is the place where the Duke of
Milan generally resides, and indeed it is the best seat for
hunting and hawking, and all kinds of sports, that I ever
yet saw.

But perhaps the Duke of Orleans thought the town
stronger than it really was, and that he had done enough
already, without attempting anything farther; and therefore
he marched off to a place called Trecate, the lord of which
place had a conference with me not long after, and had something in charge from the Duke of Milan. To this town of
Trecate the chief citizens of Milan sent to invite the Duke
thither, and tempt him into their town, offering their
children as hostages; and they could easily have put him
into possession of it, as I have been credibly informed since
by persons of great authority who were there at that time;
for the Duke of Milan would not have found men enough to
have defended the castle, and the nobility and commons both
desired the destruction of the house of Sforza. The Duke
of Orleans also, and his men, have told me the same, but
they durst not trust the citizens; and they wanted a person
that understood them and their ways better than they did;
besides, his great officers were not all of the same opinion
in relation to that affair.

A body of two thousand Germans sent by the King of the
Romans, and about a thousand German horse under the command of Monsieur Frederic Capelare, a native of the county
of Ferrette, now joined the Duke of Milan's army. With
this reinforcement Galeas and the rest of the officers were so
mightily encouraged that they marched directly to Trecate,
and offered the Duke of Orleans battle; but he was advised
not to fight, though his army was more numerous than
theirs. Perhaps his officers were unwilling to hazard their
army, lest the loss of a battle should be the ruin of the
king, of whom they could get no intelligence, because the
couriers were all stopped. Upon this the Duke of Orleans

retreated with his whole army to Novara, having with great indiscretion neglected the favourable opportunity of supplying the town with provisions, or preserving as they ought what was already in their magazines, though they might have got enough at that time in the country round about without money; but when they wanted it afterwards, the enemy was within half a league of the town.

————————

Ch. VII.—How the King passed the Apennine Mountains with his Train of Artillery, by the Assistance of the Swiss; and of the great Danger to which the Marshal de Gié and his whole Vanguard were exposed.—1495.

We left the king encamped in a valley on this side Pontremoli, in great want of provisions, and yet he stayed there five days without any manner of necessity for doing so. Our Swiss, who had committed the great fault at Pontremoli*, did us a singular piece of service at this time; they were fearful their crime would give the king a displeasure against them, and that his majesty would never endure them more; and therefore, to atone for what was past, they came to him of themselves, and offered to convey his great guns over those almost impassable mountains (and well I may call them so, for their height and steepness), where there was no track or path to direct them.   I have seen most of the chief mountains both in Italy and Spain, but none of them are to be compared to these; and this offer the Swiss made upon condition the king would forgive them, which he did.   Our train consisted of fourteen extraordinary great guns.   At the farther end of the valley we began to climb up a very steep path, where our mules could scarce get up; but these Swiss corded themselves two and two abreast, and drew a hundred and sometimes two hundred in a company, till they were weary, and then they were relieved by as many more; besides these, there were the horses belonging to the artillery, and every one of the courtiers who had any carriage,

* See Chapter V., p. 196.

lent a horse to hasten their passage; but had it not been
for these Swiss, the horses would never have done it; and
to speak truth, they helped over not only the artillery, but the
whole army; for had it not been for them, not a man could
have passed the mountains; wherefore they were well assisted; and besides, they had as great a desire to be over as
the rest of the army; they had committed many faults, but
this good action did more than sufficiently atone for all.
However, the greatest part of the difficulty was not to get
the artillery up; for as soon as our men were at the top, they
saw great deep valleys below them, to which there was no
way but what nature had prepared; so that our horses and
men were forced to draw backward, and the letting the guns
down was infinitely more trouble than the hauling them
up; and besides, the smiths and the carpenters were forced
to be constantly by; for if any of the guns slipped, they had
to be mended before they could go on.   Many advised the
king, for expedition's sake, to break up his great guns, but
he would by no means consent to it.

The Marshal de Gié was thirty miles before us, and
pressed the king to hasten his march; and yet it was three
days before we could reach him, and by that time the enemy
was come within sight.   Their army was encamped in a
large field about half a league from him; and if they had
attacked him, he would certainly have been defeated.   The
marshal afterward took up his quarters at Fornovo, a strong
town at the entrance into the plain, and this he did to keep
the enemy from assaulting us on the mountains; but we had
a better guardian than he to protect us, for God put other
thoughts into the heads of our enemies, and so blinded their
understandings with avarice that they were resolved to wait
for our coming into the plain, that nothing might escape
them; for they thought if they should attack us upon the
mountains we might retreat to Pisa, or some of the towns
we had in the territory of Florence; but they were mistaken, for those places were too remote; and if they had
beaten us, they might have pursued as fast as we could
have fled, and they would have had the advantage of knowing the country better than we.

Thus far on our side the war was not begun; but the
Marshal de Gié sent the king word that he had passed the

mountains, and that having sent out a party of forty horse to reconnoitre the enemy, they had been charged by the Estradiots, and one of them (called Lebeuf) being slain, the Estradiots cut off his head, put it upon the top of a lance, carried it to their proveditor, and demanded a ducat. These Estradiots are of the same nature with the Genetaires * ; they are horse and foot, and habited like Turks, only they wear no turbans upon their heads. They are hardy people, and lie abroad all the year round with their horses ; they were all Greeks, from the places which the Venetians possess in those parts, some of them from Naples and Romagna and the Morea, others from Albania and Durazzo. Their horses are all Turkish, and very good ; the Venetians employ them often in their wars, and put great confidence in them. I saw them all upon their first landing at Venice, and they mustered in the island where the abbey of St. Nicholas is built, and their number was near fifteen hundred ; they are stout, active fellows, and will plague an army terribly when they once undertake it.

These Estradiots, as I said before, having beaten our party, pursued them to the marshal's quarters, where the Swiss were posted, of whom they killed three or four, and carried away their heads according to their custom. For the Venetians, having been at war against the Turks formerly, in the time of Mahomet, the present Turk's father, Sultan Mahomet would not suffer his soldiers to give quarter, but allowed them a ducat for every head, and the Venetians did the same. My opinion is they did it on purpose to terrify us, and indeed so they did ; but the Estradiots themselves were no less affrighted with our artillery ; for a shot from a falconet having killed one of their horses, they retired with great precipitation ; but in their retreat they took one of our Swiss captains, who had gotten on horseback to watch their retreat, and, being unarmed, was run through the body with a lance. This captain was a wise man, and they carried him before the Marquis of Mantua (who was captain-general for the Venetians) and his uncle, the Lord Rodolph of Mantua, and the Count di Cajazzo, who commanded for the Duke of Milan, and who knew him extremely well.

---

* Spanish light horse, so called from the *jennets* which they rode.—See BRANTÔME, i. 213.

The enemy's army had taken the field (at least all of them that were joined, for some were still to come up) about eight days before, but lay still in expectation of their confederates; so that the king might have gone back into France without any impediment in the world, had he not squandered away his time to no purpose by the way, as you have heard; but God had ordered it otherwise.

CH. VIII.—How the Marshal de Gié withdrew with his Army to the Mountains, and waited until the King came up to him.—1495.

THE Marshal de Gié, fearing to be attacked, retired to the mountains. He had with him (as he told me) about eight score men-at-arms, and eight hundred Swiss, and no more, and from us he could not expect any assistance; for, by reason of our heavy cannon, we could not join him in less than a day and a half. The king, in his march, lay at the houses of two little marquises. Our vanguard, being posted upon the mountain, was awaiting an attack by the enemy, whom they saw drawn up in order of battle at a good distance in the plain; but God (who had always preserved our army) infatuated our adversaries' understanding. Our Swiss captain, being examined by the Count di Cajazzo, who commanded their army, and was then in their van, was asked what number of men-at-arms were with the marshal, though the count knew our strength as well as we did ourselves, for he had been with us during the whole campaign.

The Swiss magnified our forces, represented us to be much stronger than we were, and said the marshal had with him three hundred men-at-arms and fifteen hundred Swiss. The count told him plainly that he lied, for in the whole army we had not above three thousand Swiss, and it was improbable we would send half of them in our van; upon which the captain was sent prisoner to the Marquis of Mantua's tent, where a council of war was called, in order to consult how to attack us. The marquis believed what the Swiss captain had said, and urged that their infantry were not so good as the Swiss; that all their forces had not joined them; that it would be a great injury to the allies to engage without them; and that, if they should lose the battle, the Signory would have just reason to blame their conduct; that it would be better, therefore, to wait for our coming into the plain, where we must pass in front of them; and the two proveditors being of the same opinion, the rest durst not oppose. Others affirmed, that if they routed our vanguard, the King must of necessity be taken prisoner; but, for all that, it was concluded to await us in the plain, and they confidently believed that none of us could escape. This I have been informed of since by the very persons whom I have mentioned; for, afterwards, we discoursed together, and the Marshal de Gié and I had this relation from their own mouths. Upon this they retired into the plain, being assured that within a day or two the king must of necessity come to Fornovo; and in the meantime the rest of the confederate forces arrived in their camp, and the way was so narrow we were obliged to march close by them.

Upon our descending from the mountains, we had a prospect of the plain of Lombardy, which is the pleasantest and best country in the world, and most plentiful in everything; yet, though I call it a plain, it is scarce passable for horses, for it is as full of ditches as Flanders, or rather more, but much better, and more fruitful both in corn, wine, and fruit; and their ground never lies fallow. It pleased us exceedingly to see so fine a country after the famine and hardships which we had suffered since our departure from Lucca; but our train of artillery gave us great trouble, especially to let down, so steep and difficult was the pass. In the enemy's camp there were great numbers of tents and pavilions, which made it look very large, and indeed so it was. The Venetians made good their message by me to the king, when they promised that the Duke of Milan and they would bring forty thousand men into the field; and if they had not their full number, they wanted not much of it, for they were five and thirty thousand effective men, and of them four-fifths were in the Venetian pay. They had at least two thousand six hundred men-at-arms barded, every one attended by his bowman on horseback, or some other person in livery, making four horses to every man-at-arms. Their Estradiots and other light horse were about five thousand, and the rest were infantry, encamped in a very strong position, and furnished with a large train of artillery.

CH. IX.—How the King and his small Army arrived at Fornovo, near the Camp of his Enemies, who awaited him in very fine Order, and with a Determination to defeat and capture him.—1495.

THE king descended from the mountains about noon, and took up his quarters in Fornovo on the 5th of July, being Sunday, in the year 1495. We found good store of provision in the town both for our horses and ourselves. The people received us very kindly, for nobody did them the least injury; they brought us victuals and bread, but their bread was small and black, and they sold it very dear, and their wine was three parts water; they brought us likewise some of their fruits, and were exceedingly diligent in attending our army. I ordered them to bring me a little of everything, which I had tested in my presence; for we had great suspicion that this plenty of provisions had been left there on purpose to poison us, so that at first nobody touched them; and our suspicion was much increased by the death of two of our Swiss, who were found dead in a cellar, having killed themselves with excessive drinking, or else died of cold in the cellar; but before night our horses began to eat, and at last the soldiers followed their example, and we refreshed ourselves very well. I must say this in honour of the Italians, that we never found that they endeavoured to do us any mischief by poison; if they had, we could hardly have secured ourselves in this march. On the Sunday (as I said before) we arrived about noon at Fornovo; most of our people of quality ate nothing but a crust of bread at the place where the king alighted and drank; and, indeed, at that time there was little else to be got; for the provisions that were in the town nobody durst venture to taste.

Presently after this refreshment, the Estradiots sallied
out of their camp, and dashing up to our very army, gave
us a strong alarm. Our men, being unacquainted with their
way of fighting, drew out into the field, and put themselves
into order of battle, with a van, main body, and rear so exactly well distanced that they were not a bowl's cast one
from another, so that upon any disaster they might easily
have supported each other; but no action happened at that
time, and both parties retired to their camps. Our tents
were but few, and our camp extended so near to theirs that
twenty of their Estradiots were enough to give us an alarm at
any time; wherefore they lay constantly in our front, having
the benefit of a wood, through which they might march
close up to us before they were discovered. We lay betwixt
two little hills in a valley, divided by a small river called
Tarro, which is usually fordable on foot, unless it is swelled
by the waters from the mountains, which fall very suddenly,
and are as suddenly gone. The valley in which we lay
encamped, being full of gravel and great stones, was very
incommodious for our cavalry; it was about a quarter of a
league in width; and upon the hill on our right hand, within
half a league of us, the enemy were posted, so that we were
obliged to pass in sight of their whole army, with only that
river between us. On that side on which we were quartered,
beyond the hill on the left hand, there was another road
which we might have taken; but then we should have
seemed to have been afraid of them. About two days before,
it was proposed to me by some prudent persons in our army,
who now began to be apprehensive of their danger, that I
should go and desire a parley with the enemy, and should
take another along with me, to observe their numbers and
the situation of their camp. I had no great inclination to
undertake this duty (and without a safe-conduct there was
no going at all); wherefore I told them that, at my departure from Venice, and at Padua, I had taken my leave
very kindly of the proveditors, and that we had promised correspondence upon occasion, and therefore I did not question
but upon any overture of a treaty they would meet me half
way; whereas, if I should condescend to go to them, it
would but make them the more arrogant; besides, I feared
it was too late.

The same Sunday I wrote to the proveditors (one of them was called Luca Pisani, and the other Melchior Trivisano), desiring that, according to the agreement between ourselves at my departure from Padua, they would send me a passport, in order that I might have a conference with them. They sent me word they would have done it with all their hearts, had we not begun a war against the Duke of Milan; however, one of them (as they should agree) would meet me in some place midway between the two armies. I had their answer the same night, but none of those who had influence with the king attached any importance to it. I was fearful of going too far, lest they should have interpreted it as cowardice; so that I pressed it no farther that night, though I would willingly have done anything to have delivered the king and his army out of danger, had I been able.

About midnight the Cardinal of St. Malo left the king; and his tent being near mine, he came to me, and told me that the king would march the next morning, and that he was resolved to pass by them, and when he began to march, that he would fire some of his great guns into their army by way of defiance, and then march on in as good order as he could. I am of opinion this was the Cardinal's own advice, for he was ignorant in such cases, and knew not what counsel to give; and it had been much more prudent in the king to have called a council of his officers and all the grave men about him, to have consulted what measures it would be proper to take in that exigence of affairs; but the result would have been the same, for in this very march I had seen many things concerted in council with very great prudence, but managed quite contrary when they came to be executed. I told the Cardinal that if we came so near as to fire into their camp, they would certainly come out and skirmish with us, and that then it would be impossible to avoid a general battle; besides, it did not consist with the overture I had made, so that I was extremely concerned to hear the resolution the king had taken. However, such had been my condition from the beginning of this king's reign, that I durst not object, for fear I should disoblige his favourites, and make them my enemies; for they had, indeed, greater authority with him than they ought to have had.

That night we had two great alarms, and all through our

own negligence, in not having taken the same precautions
to secure ourselves against the incursions of the Estradiots,
as we used to do against the light horse; for twenty of our
men-at-arms, with their archers, would easily have stopped
two hundred of them; but they were new to us then. We
had great rains that night also, and such claps of thunder
and lightning, as if heaven and earth were coming together,
or that this was an omen of some impending mischief. But
we were at the foot of great mountains, in a hot country,
and in the height of the summer, so that the thing was
natural enough; however, it was very terrible, and our consternation was increased by our enemies being so numerous
before us, and our having no possibility to pass without
fighting them, which must be done to our great disadvantage; for our army was but small, not amounting to above
nine thousand men in the whole; and of these, I believe,
two thousand were servants, and such as followed the camp,
without reckoning pages and footmen belonging to the
officers.

CH. X.—The Arrangement of the two Armies for the Battle of Fornovo.—1495.

On Monday morning, the 6th of July, in the year 1495, by
seven o'clock, the noble king mounted on horseback, and
called for me several times: I came to him, and found him
completely armed, and mounted upon the best horse I ever
saw in my life. The horse was called Savoy, of the Bressian
breed, and had been given him, according to common report,
by Charles, Duke of Savoy. It was a black horse, with but
one eye, of no extraordinary stature, but tall enough for him
that was to ride him. This young prince seemed that day
quite another person than what one would take him to have
been by his nature, proportion, and complexion. He was
exceeding bashful, especially in speaking, and is so to this
day; and no wonder, for he had been brought up in great
awe, and in the company of inferior people; but now, being

mounted on his horse, his eyes sparkled with fire, his complexion was fresh and lively, and all his words showed wisdom and discretion,—so that I could not but believe the predictions of Friar Jerome (and I thought of them at that time) when he told me that God would conduct him, as it were, by the hand, and that he should meet with some difficulties in his return to his own dominions, but that he should overcome them all, and gain immortal honour by it. The king told me that if those people wished to treat, I might go treat with them; and the Cardinal being by, he nominated him to go along with me, and also the Marshal de Gié, who at that time was in a violent passion, occasioned by a dispute between the Counts of Narbonne and Guise, both of whom pretended to the command of the van that day. I replied, "Sire, I shall observe your commands; but I never saw two great armies so near without fighting before they parted."

Our whole army marched out of their camp in good order, the battalions being near one another, as on the day before; but yet methought they did not make so fine an appearance, as those I had formerly seen under Charles, Duke of Burgundy, and our king's father Louis XI., nor indeed were they half so numerous. The Cardinal and I withdrew a little, and dictated a letter to the two proveditors, which was written by one Monsieur Robertet *, one of the king's secretaries, in whom he had great confidence. The substance of the letter was, that it was the Cardinal's duty, by virtue of his quality and function, to procure peace, if it lay in his power, and mine also, as I had been ambassador lately at Venice; wherefore it would not be improper for me to be a mediator now. We signified to them that the king's resolution was only to march through the country in his way to France, without committing any hostilities; and therefore, if they desired a conference, as was proposed the day before, we were ready to meet them, and would employ all our interest to accommodate matters. By this time the fight was begun, and there was skirmishing on all sides. As we were marching on slowly, with the river between us, we came within a quarter of a league one of the other, they being also

* Florimont Robertet, a native of Montbrison, was Secretary of State under Kings Charles VIII., Louis XII., and Francis I.

drawn up in order of battle; for it is their custom to make their camp so large, that they can put themselves into battle array within it.

They sent out a party of their Estradiots and mounted bowmen, and some few men-at-arms, who marched directly, by private roads, to the village of Fornovo, which we had just left, with a design to pass the little river Tarro in that place, and fall upon our baggage-train, which was very numerous (in all, I believe, besides waggons, about six thousand sumpter-horses, mules, and asses). Their army was drawn up in as good order as possible, and had been so for several days before; and they relied much upon the superiority of their forces. They attacked the king's army on every side; so that, if we had been beaten, not a man of us could have escaped, considering the country we were in, and that those whom I mentioned before had fallen upon our baggage. On the left hand, there were the Marquis of Mantua and his uncle, the Lord Rodolph, with the Count Bernardino di Montone *, and the flower of their army, consisting of six hundred men-at-arms, as they told me afterwards; and these charged our rear. All the men-at-arms were well barded, with fine plumes of feathers, and bourdonnasses †; and with their cross-bow men on horseback, their Estradiots, and their infantry to support them. Against the Marshal de Gié and our vanguard, the Count di Cajazzo advanced with about four hundred men-at-arms well accoutred, and supported also by a good body of foot. There was also another brigade of about two hundred men-at-arms, commanded by the son ‡ of Signor John Bentivoglio, of Bologna, a young gentleman who had never been in battle before; and, to speak the truth, they wanted good officers as much as we did. These were to second the Count di Cajazzo, and fall upon our van; and there was also another squadron, in the nature of a reserve to the Marquis of Mantua's brigade, which was commanded by Anthony d'Urbino, a bastard of the late Duke of Urbino;

* Bernardino de Montone, a Venetian condottiere, and grandson of the celebrated Braccio de Montone.

† Bourdonnasses were hollow lances, curiously painted, and used in Italy by the men-at-arms, in tournaments.

‡ Annibale de Bentivoglio, who had been created Gonfalonier of Justice on the 1st of November, 1489.

and, besides all these, there were two great bodies left in their camp. This I understood afterwards from themselves, and the next day I saw it with my own eyes; for the Venetians would not venture all at one stake, nor leave their baggage unguarded; yet, in my judgment, they had done better to have put all to a push, since they were so far engaged.

I shall now acquaint you with what became of the letter which the Cardinal and I had sent by a trumpeter. It was received by the proveditors, and as soon as they had read it, our great guns began to fire, and they immediately answered us; but their artillery was not so good as ours.* The proveditors sent the trumpeter back, and the marquis sent another of his own with this message, that they would willingly treat, and if we would give over cannonading, they would do so too. I was then at a distance from the king, who was riding up and down from rank to rank: so I sent back the trumpeters to say, that our cannon should cease firing; and having given orders to that purpose to the master of the artillery, both sides ceased for a time; but on a sudden they fired a gun amongst us, and ours began to play more fiercely than before, with three fresh pieces which we had levelled against them. As soon as our two trumpeters were arrived in their camp, they were carried to the marquis's tent, where it was solemnly debated whether they should treat or engage. The Count di Cajazzo (as they told me, who were present) urged that we were half vanquished already, and that this was no time for a treaty; and one of the proveditors (who told me the story) was of

* "The French," says Mr. Prescott, " in artillery, were at this time in advance of the Italians, perhaps of every nation in Europe. The Italians, indeed, were so exceedingly defective in this department that their best field-pieces consisted of small copper tubes covered with wood and hides. They were mounted on unwieldy carriages drawn by oxen, and followed by waggons loaded with stone balls. These guns were worked so awkwardly, that the besieged, says Guicciardini, had time between the discharges to repair the mischief inflicted by them. . . . . The French, on the other hand, were provided with a beautiful train of ordnance, consisting of bronze cannon about eight feet in length, and many smaller pieces. They were lightly mounted, drawn by horses, and easily kept pace with the rapid movements of the army. They discharged iron balls, and were served with admirable skill, intimidating their enemies by the rapidity and accuracy of their fire, and easily demolishing their fortifications, which were constructed with little strength or science."—*History of Ferdinand and Isabella*, vol. ii. p. 259.

his judgment, but the other was not.   The marquis was of
that mind too, but his uncle was against it; and being an
honest and discreet man, strenuously opposed it, for he loved
us well, and served against us unwillingly.   At length they
were unanimous in their opinion for fighting.

CH. XI.—How Parleys were vainly attempted; and the Beginning of
the Battle of Fornovo.—1495.

YOU must know that the king had placed his greatest
strength in his van; for in it there were about three hundred and fifty men-at-arms, three thousand Swiss (the
hopes of the whole army *), three hundred archers, and
some of the two hundred mounted cross-bow men of his own
guard (which was a great loss to him, as he ordered them
to fight on foot).   Besides these we had very few foot; but
what we had were distributed among them.   There fought
on foot among the Swiss the Lord Englebert of Cleves†,
brother to the Duke of Cleves, the Lord of Lornay ‡, and the
bailiff of Dijon, who commanded them: and the artillery
was placed in their front.   The forces that had been left in

* The Swiss mercenaries were the finest infantry of that age, and, by
their defeat of the Burgundian chivalry at Granson and Morat, had fully
demonstrated the superiority of infantry in battle.   Their organisation
is thus described by Mr. Prescott: " The Swiss were formed into
battalions, varying from 3000 to 8000 men each.   They wore little
defensive armour, and their principal weapon was the pike, eighteen
feet long.   Formed into these solid battalions, which, bristling with
spears all around, received the technical appellation of the *hedgehog*,
they presented an invulnerable front on every quarter.   In the level
field, with free scope allowed for action, they bore down all opposition,
and received unshaken the most desperate charges of the steel-clad
cavalry on their terrible array of pikes.   They were too unwieldy, however, for rapid or complicated manœuvres; and they were easily discon-
certed by any unforeseen impediment or irregularity of the ground."—
History of Ferdinand and Isabella, vol. ii. p. 258.

† Engilbert de Cleves, Count of Auxerre, and afterwards Count of
Nevers and Eu, became a naturalised Frenchman in 1486, married
Charlotte de Bourbon, and died on the 21st of November, 1506.

‡ Louis de Menton, Lord of Lornay, captain of the king's hundred
Swiss guards, and Master of the Horse to the Queen.

the territories of Florence, and those which had been sent to
Genoa against the judgment of all people, would have been
of very great service to us on this occasion. Our vanguard
had by this time marched on as far as the enemy's camp,
and everybody expected they would have attacked us; but
our two other bodies were neither so near each other, nor so
well ordered as on the day before; and because the Marquis of Mantua (who had already passed the river, and entered the plain) was within a quarter of a league of our rear
ready to attack them, but marching slowly on, and in such
close order, that it was a very fine sight to behold, the king
was forced to turn his back upon his own vanguard, and
face about to his enemies at the rear. I was at that time
with the Cardinal, awaiting an answer; but I told him it
was no time to trifle any longer, and so I passed by the
Swiss squadron and went to find out the king. In my
passage I lost a page (who was my cousin-german), a valet-
de-chambre, and a foot-boy, who followed me at a little distance; and I did not see when they were slain.

I had not come a hundred paces, when I heard a great
noise in the place from whence I came, or a little behind it:
it was the Estradiots, who were gotten into the king's quarters, where there were not above three or four houses; and
they rifled his baggage, and killed or wounded four or five
men, but the rest escaped. They killed altogether about a
hundred footboys and servants belonging to our carriages, and
put our whole train in very great disorder. When I came
where the king was, I found him making knights. The enemy
being come very near him, he was obliged to give over;
and I heard Matthew the bastard of Bourbon * (who was in
great favour with the king), and one Philip du Moulin † (a
very brave gentleman), call to the king, and say, " On, sir,
on;" upon which he went to the head of the army, and placed
himself directly before his standard, so that there was not a
man that I saw nearer the enemy, unless it were the bastard
of Bourbon. I had not been with the king a quarter of an

* Matthew, surnamed the Great Bastard of Bourbon, was a natural
son of John II., Duke of Bourbon. On his return from Italy he was
created Admiral and Governor of Guienne and Picardy; and he died
in 1505.

† Philippe du Moulin, Knight, is mentioned as one of the members
of the king's council.

hour before the enemy were advanced within a hundred
paces of his majesty, who was as ill guarded and attended as
any prince or noble that I ever saw ; but he is well guarded
who is guarded by God : and it was true what the venerable Friar Jerome had presaged, who said, "That God would
lead him as it were by the hand." His rear was posted on the
right, a little behind him.   The next battalion to him on that
side was the Duke of Orleans' troop, consisting of about eighty
lances, commanded by Robinet de Framezelles *, about
forty more under the Sieur de la Trimouille, and the hundred
Scottish archers, who put themselves into as close order as
if they had been men-at-arms.   I was on the left among the
gentlemen of the Vingt-Escus †, the pensioners, and others
of the king's household : I will not mention their several
captains for brevity's sake ; but the rear was commanded
by the Count of Foix.

About a quarter of an hour after my arrival, the enemy,
being advanced so near the king (as you have heard), began
to couch their lances, advanced upon a gentle gallop, and
in two bodies charged our two squadrons on the right
of them, and the Scottish archers ; our men advanced towards them, and the king as bravely as any.   On the left,
where I was posted, we charged them on the flank much to
our advantage ; and, indeed, to say truth, never charge was
brisker on both sides.   The Estradiots, who were in the rear
of that division, seeing our mules and sumpter-horses making
with all speed to our vanguard, and that their comrades
were beginning to plunder, quitted their men-at-arms, and
ran to get their share of the booty ; but certainly, if fifteen
hundred light horse had but attacked us with their scimitars
in their hands (which is a terrible weapon), considering the
smallness of our number, we must certainly have been
beaten ; but God assisted us, for no sooner had they charged
us with their lances but their Italian men-at-arms fled, and
all their infantry, or the greatest part of them, gave ground
also.   At the same time that this squadron charged us the
Count di Cajazzo attacked our van ; but they came not so

* Robinet de Framezelles was lieutenant to the Duke of Orleans at
the capture of Novara in 1495.

† Part of the king's guard, who received *twenty crowns* a month,
whence the name.

close, for when they should have couched their lances their
hearts failed, and they fell into disorder; and the Swiss
took fifteen or twenty of them in a company, and put them
to the sword: the rest fled, and were but indifferently pursued; for the Marshal de Gié with much ado kept his
forces together, for he perceived another great body of them
not very far off. However, some followed the chase, and
the enemy fled over the ground where we had charged along
the highway, with their swords only in their hands; for
they had thrown away their lances.

But you must know that that brigade which charged the
king was warmly pursued; for all of us made after them:
some of them fled to the village from whence we were come,
others made at the top of their speed to their camp, and all
of us after them: only the king stayed behind with some of
his troops, and put himself in no little danger by doing so.
One of the first men of the enemy who was slain was the
Lord Rodolph of Mantua, the marquis's uncle (who was to
have sent orders to the Lord Anthony of Urbino, when it
was time for him to advance), for they thought the battle
would have lasted a long while, according to the custom of
Italy; and the Lord Anthony excused himself upon that
score, but I believe he saw nothing to encourage him to
advance. We had a great number of grooms and servants
with our waggons, who flocked about the Italian men-at-
arms, when they were dismounted, and knocked most of them
on the head. The greatest part of them had their hatchets
(which they cut their wood with) in their hands, and with
them they broke up their head-pieces, and then knocked out
their brains; otherwise they could not easily have killed
them, they were so very well armed; and to be sure there
were three or four of our men to attack one man-at-arms.
The long swords also which our archers and servants wore
did very good execution. The king continued on the
ground where he had been charged, declaring that he would
neither follow the chase nor retire to our vanguard, which
was at too far a distance. He had appointed seven or eight
young gentlemen to attend constantly about him. He had
escaped very well the first charge, considering how near he
was to the enemy; for within twenty paces of him the bastard of Bourbon was taken prisoner and carried off to their
camp.

CH. XII.—Consequences of the Victory gained by the French at Fornovo; and the Danger to which King Charles VIII. found himself
exposed.—1495.

THE king (as I said before) remained in the same place,
and so ill attended that of all his squadron he had none left
him but Anthony des Aubus, a gentleman of his bed-chamber, a little man, and but ill-armed; the others were all dispersed, as he told me himself at night before their faces, and
they ought to have been ashamed of themselves: but they
returned to his assistance very seasonably; for a small party
of the routed enemy coming along the road, and perceiving
it so thin of men, fell upon the king and the aforesaid gentleman of his bed-chamber; but the king, by the activity of his
horse (which was the best in the world), kept them at bay
till others of his men came up, who were not far off; and
then the Italians were all forced to fly. Upon this the king
took their counsel and retired to his van, which had never
stirred from its ground. Thus the king came off victoriously
with the main battle, and if the van had advanced but a
hundred paces, the enemy's whole army would have fled:
some said they ought to have advanced, and others that they
ought not.

Our troops, which had pursued, followed the enemy to
their very camp, which was extended towards Fornovo; and
I saw none of our men touched but one Julian Bourgneuf,
who fell down dead from a blow that was given him by an
Italian who passed by him; but he was very ill armed.
Upon that accident our men stopped, and cried, "Let us return to the king;" and at that very word the whole party
halted to give their horses breath, which had been very
hard ridden, and were tired with the length of the way,
which was full of sharp stones and gravel. Not far from us
we saw a party of about thirty of the enemy's men-at-arms
march along in retreat; but we were in disorder and suffered them to pass. When our horses had taken a little
breath we went in search of the king, not knowing where
he was: we set off at a good trot, but we had not gone far
before we perceived him at a great distance. We then

caused our servants to alight and gather up the lances, which lay very thick upon the field, and especially the bourdonnasses; but they were good for nothing, for they were hollow and light, and weighed no more than a javelin, yet they were finely painted; so that we were now better furnished with lances than on the day before, and marched directly towards the king. In our way we fell in with several bodies of the enemy's foot, who were of the marquis's division, and had hid themselves behind the hills when he made his charge upon the king. Several of them were slain; but others got over the river and escaped, and we did not trouble ourselves much about them.

Some of our men in the heat of the action cried out "Remember Guynegate," which was a battle * we had lost in King Louis' time in Picardy against the King of the Romans, because our people fell to plundering the waggons, though there our men had got nothing; but here their Estradiots took what they thought good, and pillaged as they pleased; but they carried off only five and fifty of our richest and best-covered sumpters, which belonged to the king and his chamberlains, and took one of the king's gentlemen of the bed-chamber called Gabriel †, to whose care were committed all the relics and curiosities which for a long time had belonged to the kings of France, and were then in the army, because the king was there in person. Many other of our sumpters and waggons were overturned, destroyed, and plundered by our own men; but the enemy had no more than I have already mentioned. We had, indeed, several pimps and wenches who followed the camp on foot, who stripped the dead and did a great deal of mischief.

To speak the truth (upon impartial information from both sides), we lost only Julian Bourgneuf, the captain of the king's gate, nine of the Scottish archers, one gentleman of the household, about twenty horse of the vanguard, and seventy or eighty servants belonging to our baggage. On their side they lost three hundred and fifty men-at-arms upon the field; for no prisoners were taken, which perhaps never happened before. Few of their Estradiots were slain, for they were busy in plundering when they should have

---

* See Book VI. Chap. 5. for an account of this battle.
† Gabriel de la Bondinière.—DUPONT, ii. 478.

been fighting. In the whole (as I have been informed by several of their nobility) they lost three thousand five hundred men (others say more), and among them were several persons of quality. I myself saw a list of eighteen, all of them considerable persons, and among the rest four or five of the Gonzagas, which is the name of the marquis's own family. The Marquis of Mantua in this battle lost sixty gentlemen of his own subjects, all mounted and not one on foot among them. It is strange that so many should have been killed with the sword, for our artillery killed not ten in both armies, and the battle lasted not a quarter of an hour; for as soon as the enemy had broken their lances they fled, and the chase lasted about three-quarters of an hour. Their battles in Italy used not to be managed at this rapid rate; their custom was to fight squadron after squadron, and the fight lasted sometimes a whole day together, without either side winning the victory.

The rout was great on their side: three hundred of their men-at-arms, and most of their Estradiots fled, some to Reggio*, and others to Parma, which was about eight leagues from the field of battle. When our army was first engaged in the morning, the Count de Petillane and the Lord Virgil Ursini fled from us: the Lord Virgil only retired to a gentleman's house hard by, and stayed there upon his parole; but the truth is, we had done him an injury. The Count de Petillane went over to the enemy; he was a person well known in their army, for he had always had a command under the Florentines or King Ferrand. As soon as he was got amongst them he began to cry out "A Petillane, a Petillane;" and he followed those who fled above three leagues, calling out to them, and assuring them that there was no danger, and that if they faced about, the day would still be their own: by which means he rallied a great part of them, and gave them good hopes; and if it had not been for him, it would have been a total defeat, for it was a great encouragement to them to have such an officer escape from us and come to their assistance.

He was eager for attacking us again that very night, but all the rest of the officers opposed it. He told me so him-

* This is not Reggio in Calabria, but another city of the same name in the dukedom of Modena, fifteen miles from Parma.

self afterwards, and the Marquis of Mantua confirmed it, and owned that advice to be his; and this is certain, had it not been for him, their army would not have kept together till morning.

As soon as we were got up to the king, we discovered a great body of men-at-arms drawn up in order of battle outside their camp, with some infantry; but we could only see their heads and the tops of their pikes and lances. They had stood there all day, but they were farther off than we imagined: before we could have come at them we must have passed the river, which was deep, and increased every hour, for it had thundered, lightened, and rained most prodigiously all that day, especially during the fight and while we were in the pursuit. The king immediately called a council of war, in which it was debated whether he should advance against this new body or not. There were then with him three Italian knights; one of them was Signor John James di Trivulce (who is yet living, and behaved himself very well that day); another was Signor Francisco Secco, a brave man of seventy-two years of age, who had been bred a soldier under the Florentines; the third was Signor Camillo Vitelli, who, with three of his brothers, was then in the king's service.. These came unsent for from Citta-de-Castello as far as Sarzana (which is a great way), to be present at this battle; and, finding that it was impossible to come in time enough with his troops, Camillo left them to march slowly after, and advanced with all speed to overtake the king. The last two were of opinion that we should attack the body that was still unbroken; but the French officers being consulted, gave their judgment against it, pretending that we had done enough, and that it grew late and was time to think of quarters.

Secco persisted, and pressed hard to have that body charged; he showed them that people were passing to and fro upon the great road that led to Parma (which was the next town they had to retreat to), and assured them that the enemy were either flying or rallying again; and, as we heard afterwards, he was in the right. His behaviour and counsel denoted him to be a brave and wise man, for all the officers told me afterwards, and some of them before the Duke of Milan's face, that, if we had but advanced against them, we had certainly obtained the greatest and most glorious victory that the French nation had won for ten years! and, had we known how to have improved it, and obliged the people by our civil treatment of them, in eight days' time the Duke of Milan would not have had anything left but the castle of Milan, so inclinable were his subjects to revolt from him. And the Venetians would have been much in the same condition, and there would have been no need to care about Naples; for the Venetians would have been able to have raised men only in Venice, Brescia and Cremona (which is but a small place), for all the rest of their territories in Italy would have been lost. But God had dealt by us as Jerome had foretold, and we had the honour of the day, though, to speak truth, our ill conduct did not deserve it, nor did we then know how to manage our victory; but now, in the year 1497, if such good fortune should happen to the king, I think he could order it better.

Whilst we were in this suspense the night drew on, and the enemy that had faced us marched off into their camp. We, on the other side, took up our quarters about a quarter of a league from the field of battle. The king lay in a farm-house or cottage (to judge by the meanness of the building), but the houses belonging to it were full of unthreshed corn, which served for provender for our horses. There were a few houses besides that in which the king lay, but they were even worse than it; so they were but little benefit to us, and every one was forced to quarter as he could. For my part, I remember I lay in a little pitiful vineyard, upon the ground without any shelter; for the king had borrowed my cloak in the morning, and my baggage was not to be found. He that had anything to eat kept himself from starving; but very few had any victuals more than a crust of bread or so, which they took from their servants. I saw the king in his chamber, where there were several wounded; amongst the rest, the seneschal of Lyons and others, whom he caused to be dressed. The king was very cheerful, and every one was pleased he had escaped so well; but we did not boast and swagger as we used to do, for the enemy was at hand. All our Swiss were that night upon the guard; the king gave them three hundred crowns, and they watched very diligently and their drums beat bravely during the whole night.

Ch. XIII.—How the Lord of Argenton went alone to parley with the
Enemy, upon the Refusal of those that were deputed to go along with
him, and of the King's safe Arrival with his whole Army at Asti.—
1495.

THE next morning I resolved with myself to pursue our
negotiations for peace, as I was still very solicitous about the
king's passage in safety; but I could scarce find a trumpeter
that would venture to the enemy's camp, because nine of
their trumpeters had been slain (unwittingly) in the battle,
and they had taken one of ours and killed another, whom (as
I mentioned before) the king had sent to them before the
fight began; but at last one of our trumpeters was prevailed upon to go, and went to the enemy with a passport
from the king, and brought me another to meet and confer
in the midway between the two armies. I judged it to be
dangerous; however, I resolved not to break with them, nor
pretend any difficulty. The king nominated the Cardinal of
St. Malo, the Lord de Gié, marshal of France, the Lord de
Piennes his chamberlain, and myself. The enemy appointed
the Marquis of Mantua captain-general of the Venetians,
the Count di Cajazzo general for the Duke of Milan, and
formerly of our side, and Signors Luca Pisani and Melchior
Trevisano the two proveditors. We approached so near that
we could plainly discern them, and that there were only
those four upon the bank and the river between us, which
was much swollen since the day before. Nobody but they
appeared out of their camp, and on our side there was nobody but we four and a sentinel that stood over against
them. We sent a herald to know whether they would pass
the river to us, which I thought a hard matter to persuade
them to, because I believed it was what both sides would
scruple to do. Their answer was, that by agreement the
conference was to be in the midway between the two armies;
that they had advanced already above half-way, and, being
the chief officers in their army, they could not pass over without danger, which they did not think it prudent to venture.
Our deputies were as careful of themselves, and made the
same difficulty on their side, but would needs have me go

and confer with them without further instructions. I told
them I could not in discretion go alone, and that I would at
least have one witness along with me.   Upon which there
went with me one of the king's secretaries called Robertet,
a servant of my own, and a herald, with whom I passed the
river, in confidence that, if I could not come to any accommodation, I should yet discharge my duty to them, since by
my means the conference had been accepted.   When I came
within hearing, I told them they were not come half-way as
they pretended, and that they ought at least to have come to
the river's side ; however, since they were so near, I did not
think it fit to let them return without being spoken with.
They replied that the river was broad, and the noise of the
waters so great, that they could not hear us from the other
side ; and I could use no argument powerful enough to persuade them to advance any farther ; but they asked me for my
proposals.   I answered, that I had no such commission, and
that alone I could say nothing to them ; but, if they pleased
to offer anything, I would acquaint the king with it.   While
we stood talking in this manner, a herald came to me to let
me know that our commissioners were going back, and I
might make what overtures I pleased ; but I refused to do
that, for they understood the king's pleasure better than I,
as being his confidants ; besides which, they had whispered
in his ear at their coming away ; but, as to the business then
in discussion, I knew as much as the best of them.

    The Marquis of Mantua began to discourse about the battle,
and asked me if the king would have put him to death if he
had taken him prisoner.   I told him "No," but he would
have treated him honourably ; for the king had reason to
esteem him, for the great honour he had gained by attacking him.   Then he spoke to me in behalf of the prisoners,
and particularly of his uncle the Lord Rodolph, whom he
thought to be alive, but I knew the contrary ; however, I
assured him they should all be civilly used ; and then I
recommended to him the bastard of Bourbon, who was
their prisoner.   It was no hard matter to use our prisoners
well ; for we had none, which perhaps had never been
known in any battle before ; and the marquis had lost
seven or eight of his near relations, and about sixscore of
his men-at-arms.   After which discourse I took my leave,

and promissed to return before night; until when we agreed
to a cessation of arms.

Upon my return to the king, with his secretary, he asked
me what news? and immediately called a council of war in
a pitiful poor chamber; but everybody's eye was fixed
upon his neighbour, and we came to no resolution. The
king whispered something in the Cardinal's ear, and then
told me I should go back, and see what they would say
(but, as the proposition of a conference had proceeded from
me, it was probable they would insist that I should make
some overtures first); however, the Cardinal told me I must
conclude nothing; but that was trifling, for it was not in
my power to conclude anything unless I had instructions
from them. However, I would neither say nor do anything
that might hinder my going, for I resolved to do no harm,
and I was in hopes to discover something by the enemy's
looks, who, without doubt, were more fearful than we;
and I thought perhaps something or other might fall from
them that might be improved to the benefit of both parties.
So I set out for their camp; but it was night before I
reached the banks of the river. One of their trumpeters
met me there, with a message from their four commissioners to desire I would advance no further that evening;
for their Estradiots were upon the guard, who knew nobody,
and therefore, in all probability, it would be dangerous for
me to venture; but, if I pleased, he told me he would stay
with me all night, and conduct me in the morning. However, I sent him back, and told him I would be there again
next morning by eight o'clock, and that he should await
me; or, if anything happened to prevent me, I would give
them notice by a herald; for I had no mind he should know
anything of our condition that night, nor could I tell what
resolution the king would take; for I saw people whispering
in his ear, which made me suspicious; and so I returned to
give his majesty an account of what I had done.

Every man supped on what he could get to eat, and took
up his lodging upon the ground. About midnight I went
to the king's quarters, where I found the gentlemen of his
bed-chamber booted and spurred, and ready to mount on
horseback. They acquainted me with the king's resolution
of retreating with all expedition towards Asti and the

territories of the Marchioness of Montferrat; and desired
me to stay behind and amuse the enemy with a treaty. I
heartily thanked them for their love, told them I took no
delight in being killed, and that I would be on horseback
as soon as the best. Awhile after the king awaked; and,
having heard mass, he mounted immediately. An hour
before day one of our trumpeters sounded the watch, but
when we marched off we made no use of our trumpets, nor,
indeed, was it proper to do so: however, this silent stealing
away in the night was enough to have discouraged the
whole army, especially those who knew what it meant; for
we turned our back upon the enemy, and consulted nothing
but our safety, which in an army is of dangerous consequence. Besides, at our first decampment we had very
difficult marching; for the ways were deep and woody, and,
having no guides, we lost ourselves several times. I heard
the soldiers call for guides to their ensigns; but the master
of the horse and all of them answered there were none:
but we had no need of any, for God had conducted us
thither, and (as Friar Jerome said) He would carry us back
again; otherwise it could not have been supposed that so
great a prince would have marched in the night without a
guide, where so many might have been had. Besides, God
gave us a greater evidence than this of His immediate protection; for the enemy perceived nothing of our decampment till noon the next day, as they still depended upon
the treaty which I had set on foot: and then the river was
so swollen, it was past four in the afternoon before any
durst venture over to pursue us. The first that passed was
the Count di Cajazzo, with two hundred Italian light horse,
but the current was so strong, they passed in a great deal
of danger, and, as I was told afterwards, one or two men
were drowned.

In the meantime, we marched on through woody and un-
even ways, where we could go but one abreast for near six
miles together; but at last we came into a fair plain, where
our van, artillery, and baggage were arrived already, and
were so numerous and great, that at first sight they frighted
us, when we saw the white colours chequered with red,
which belonged to Signor John James di Trivulce, and were
like those which were carried before the Marquis of Mantua

in the fight. Our van were in no less fear of our rear, seeing them at a distance along the road, and marching towards them as fast as they could; upon which both parties stood to their arms, and drew up in order of battle: but this fear was soon over, for our scouts met immediately, and recognised one another; so we marched to Borgo San-Donino, where we halted and refreshed our men, and where also a false alarm was given, on purpose to get our Swiss out of the town, lest they should have plundered it. From thence we marched, and took up our quarters that night at Firenzuola, and the second night near Piacenza, where we passed the Trebia, but left two hundred lances, our Swiss, and all our artillery, except six guns, on the other side of the river: and this the king did, that his army might encamp more commodiously; for the river is usually low, and especially at that time of the year. However, about ten o'clock at night it swelled so fast, that nobody could get over either on foot or on horseback; neither could one party have relieved the other, in case of necessity, which was a matter of great concern, considering how near the enemy were to us. All that night was spent on both sides in contriving a remedy; but nothing would do till the water fell of itself, which happened at about five in the morning. Then we threw over ropes to the other side, to help the passage of our foot, who were forced to wade up to the waist in water. When they were over, the horse and artillery followed; but with great difficulty and danger, not only from the garrison of Piacenza, but from the Count di Cajazzo, who was got into the town, upon intelligence that there were designs to betray it to the king, in trust for a young son of John Galeas, the last Duke of Milan, who had died not long before, as you have heard. If the king would have accepted such overtures as these, several other persons and towns would willingly have come over to him, by the interest of Signor John James di Trivulce; but he would not hearken to anything prejudicial to the pretensions of his cousin the Duke of Orleans, who was then in Novara; and yet, to speak impartially on the other hand, his majesty was not desirous to advance the grandeur and power of his cousin; but his chief design was to march on with his army, and leave these disputes to be adjusted as they might. The third day after the battle, the king dined at Castel San-Giovanni, and lay in a wood; the fourth he dined at Voghera, and lay at Ponte Curone; the next night he lay near Tortona, where he passed the river Scrivia, which Fracasse * was to have defended, for the garrison of Tortona supported the Duke of Milan, and were commanded by him: but when he was informed by our quarter-masters that the king intended not to remain, he retired into the town, and sent us word, that he would furnish us with what provisions we pleased; and he faithfully performed his promise; for when our whole army marched under the walls of the town, Fracasse came out (in his armour) to wait upon the king, but attended only by two persons; he excused himself as handsomely as he could for not quartering us in the town, sent us out more provisions, (so that our army was plentifully furnished,) and came again at night, to pay his respects to the king in his tent. But you must know he was of the house of St. Severino, brother to the Count di Cajazzo, and the Lord Galeas; and not long before had served the king in Romagna, as has been already observed. From thence our next march was to Nizza della Paglia †, which belongs to the Marquisate of Montferrat; and glad we were to reach that place; for then we were safe, and in the country of our friends. Before our arrival there, the enemy's light horse, under the command of the Count di Cajazzo, were perpetually at our heels, and gave us great disturbance; for few of our horse were willing to be in the rear, and the nearer we approached to a place of security, the more difficult it was to persuade them to fight. Some say this is the nature of the French, and Italian authors have written, that in their attacks they are more than men, but less than women in their retreats. The first part of their character I believe, for certainly upon a charge they are the fiercest nation in the world (I mean their cavalry); but at the end of an engagement, there is no nation in the world but is less daring and courageous than they were in the beginning of the action.

   * Gasparo, surnamed Fracasso de San Severino.
   † Generally known as Nice. Charles VIII. arrived there on Monday, July 13. 1495.

Ch. XIV.—How the Swiss secured the French army in its retreat.—
1495.

But to continue this discourse: Our rear was brought up
by three hundred Swiss, with several field-pieces, and a
strong body of hackbutters, who drove off the Estradiots,
who were not numerous.   However, the grand army which
had fought us was pursuing with all possible diligence, but
as they began their march a day after us, and were heavily
armed, they could not get up to us; so that we lost not a
man in our retreat, nor could they ever come within twenty
miles of our rear.   When they found they could not come
up with us, (and perhaps they never desired it,) they turned
off towards Novara, where, as we said before, the Duke of
Milan and the Venetians had another army; but if they
could have reached us, soon after we began our retreat, in
all probability they had succeeded better than in the valley
of Fornovo.

I have said in several places of these Memoirs, that I
have seen, and by experience found, that God the Creator
was our conductor in this expedition into Italy; yet it is
convenient for me to repeat it again, for though from the
time of the battle to our arrival at Nice, our quarters were
taken up without proper order, yet we bore the hardships and
inconveniences of the long march, without raising any mutiny
or murmuring in the least.   Our great want was of provisions, yet we were in some measure supplied by the country
people, who might easily have poisoned us if they had
pleased, not only in our victuals and wine, but in our water
too, and our wells, which might have been dried up in a
moment; for I do not remember I saw any but what were
very small.   If they had had a mind to have destroyed us
by poison, it was in their power to have done it, and therefore we may reasonably believe our Saviour and Redeemer
Jesus Christ prevented that desire in them.   I have seen
our men so thirsty, that our foot in great numbers have lain
down, and drank out of the ditches round about the little
villages through which we marched.   Our marches were
long, and our drink nothing but standing water that stank;
and yet our men were so greedy, they plunged in it up to

the waist to come at it ; for we had multitudes that followed
the camp, and were not soldiers, but attended to our mules.
The king always marched before day, but never took a
guide with him, nor baited till noon, and then he dined;
and those that attended him took what care they could of
themselves.   No man in the whole army, though of the
best quality, was excused from looking to his own horse,
but every one brought his own straw or hay in his arms.
Twice I did it myself, and was two days without eating any
thing but bread, and that none of the best; yet I suffered
not so much hardship as others did.   Our army was highly
to be commended for one thing, and that is, that I never
heard any of our soldiers complain ; and yet it was the most
painful and incommodious march I ever made, though I
have been through several that were bad enough, with
Charles Duke of Burgundy.   We marched no faster than
our artillery, and were often forced to halt, on purpose to
mend the guns, which, because of the want of horses to
draw them, incommoded us extremely ; but whenever we
were hard put to it, we were generously supplied by the
officers of the army ; so that we lost not one piece, nor one
pound of powder in our retreat; and yet I am of opinion
never any man saw guns of their size conveyed with such
expedition through such impassable places.   And if I have
mentioned any thing of disorder or inconvenience in our
quarters or elsewhere, it was not for want of good officers
and men of experience in our army ; but (as fortune would
have it), they had no authority with the king, who was
young and intractable, as I have said before ; so that to
conclude, our Saviour Jesus Christ did most manifestly
reserve all the glory of that journey to himself.

The seventh day after the battle, we marched from Nice,
and encamped all together in the field, not far from Alessandria.   We doubled our guards that night, and kept very
strict watch, and the next morning we marched to Asti,
that is to say, the king and those that attended on him, but
the army continued in the field.   We found the town of
Asti well furnished with provisions, which was a great refreshment to our wearied troops, who wanted them severely,
having endured much hunger, thirst, labour, heat, and
watching ; and after all had no clothes to their backs, but

what were ragged and worn out.   As soon as the king was
in Asti, about an hour before bedtime, I despatched a
gentleman named Philip de la Couldre (who had formerly
been in my service, but was then a servant to the Duke of
Orleans), to Novara, where the duke was besieged, though
not so closely but that people might get in and out; for
their design was only to starve them.   I sent him word by
this gentleman, that our king had several treaties on foot
with the Duke of Milan (one of which I managed by means
of the Duke of Ferrara), for which reason I thought it convenient he should immediately come to the king, after he
had assured his party in the town that he would return in a
short time, or send them relief.   They were no less than
7500 men in pay, and as fine a body of troops (for their
number) both French and Swiss, as ever were seen in the
field.   After the king had been a day at Asti, he had intelligence from the Duke of Orleans and from others, that the
enemies' two armies were joined before Novara; and the
duke pressed for supplies, for (by reason of their imprudence
at first) their provisions now began to fail; but had they
been so provident when they came into the town, as they
ought to have been, they need not have been in distress;
for there was plenty enough in the villages about it, especially of corn, which if they had brought in time into the
town, and carefully laid up in their magazines, they would
not have been forced to surrender: for had they held out
but one month longer, they would have come off honourably
themselves, and covered the enemy with shame and confusion.

———————————

CH. XV.—How the King fitted out a Fleet with an intention to have
    relieved the Castles of Naples ; and of the Miscarriage of that De-
    sign.—1495.

As soon as the king had refreshed himself for some few
days at Asti, he marched to Turin*; and at his departure

* Charles VIII. arrived at Turin, on Thursday, July 30. 1495.

from Asti he despatched Peron de Basche, the steward of his household, to equip a fleet at Nice with all speed for the relief of the castles of Naples, which held out for the king. Peron obeyed his majesty's orders, prepared a fleet, and gave the command of it to the Lord d'Arban *, who sailed with it as far as Pruce †, within sight of the enemy ; but the weather was bad, and would not suffer them to engage, so that the fleet did nothing ; for the Lord d'Arban returned to Leghorn, where most part of his men got on shore, and ran away from their ships; and the enemy came with their fleet into the port of Bengon ‡, not far from Piombino, where they continued two months; so that our men were able to send some small supplies into Naples, by reason that the nature of the port of Bengon is such, that unless it be by one single wind ships can hardly get out, and that wind blows seldom in winter.   The Lord d'Arban was valiant in person, but not a very skilful admiral.

During the king's stay at Turin many proposals of treaties passed between the king and the Duke of Milan ; and some were managed by the mediation of the Duchess of Savoy, who was the Marquis of Montferrat's daughter, a widow, and mother to the young duke § that was then living. Others were transacted by other people: I was also concerned therein : for the confederates (by whom I mean the commanders at that time before Novara), had a great desire to have me employed in the matter, and sent me a passport ; but (as there are always emulations at court) the Cardinal would not suffer it, but prevailed that the overture proposed by the Duchess of Savoy might be preferred, which was managed by the Cardinal's landlord, who was treasurer of Savoy, a wise man, and a good servant to his mistress: this

---

* Louis Aleman, Knight, Lord of Arbent and Mornay, was long in the service of Charles, Duke of Burgundy ; but having sold the Castle of Jou, of which he was governor, to Louis XI. for 14,000 crowns, he transferred his allegiance to the French King, from whom he received considerable preferment.   Guicciardini speaks of him as " uomo bellicoso ma non esperimentato."

† Ponza, a rocky island off the coast of Naples, 35 miles south-west of Gaeta.

‡ Porto-Longone, near Piombino.

§ Charles John Amadeus, born on the 24th of June, 1488, succeeded his father in 1489, and died on the 16th of April, 1496.

treaty took up a long time, and for this cause the Bailiff of
Dijon was sent ambassador into Switzerland, to raise five
thousand of their men.

I have already mentioned the equipment of our fleet at
Nice, and its setting sail for the relief of the castles of Naples,
which it was unable to effect for the above-mentioned reasons ; whereupon the Lord de Montpensier, and the rest of
the officers that were in the castles aforesaid (perceiving
their condition), resolved to march off by the help of the
army, which had been left in divers places for the defence of
that kingdom, and was then drawn as near the castle as possible ; but they left a number to defend the castles propor-
tionable to the quantity of provisions which remained ; for
they were insufficient to sustain them all. And having
given the command of the garrison to the Lord Ognas and
two other officers of conduct and experience, the Lord de
Montpensier, the Prince of Salerno, the Seneschal of Beaucaire and others, marched off with two thousand five hundred men, for Salerno.   King Ferrand pretended it was contrary to their treaty, and that the hostages which they had
given him a few days before (which were the Lord d'Alegre,
Monsieur de la Marche d'Ardain*, the Lord de la Chapelle
d'Anjou, Monsieur Roquebertin, a Catalonian, and one Monsieur Genly†), were at his mercy, and that he might lawfully put them to death.   You must understand that some
three months before, by intelligence with the enemy, and
our bad order, King Ferrand had got into the town of
Naples ‡, though our men had notice of all his designs.
I would enlarge upon this, but I can say nothing of it except by hearsay (yet I had it from very good hands) ; however, it is not my method to insist upon any thing that I was
not an eye-witness of myself.   But while King Ferrand was
in Naples, he received the news of our master's being killed

* Robert de la Marck, Duke of Bouillon, and Lord of Sedan.

† Jacques de Hangest, Lord of Genlis, and councillor and chamberlain to the king. After his deliverance from Naples, he went on a pilgrimage to Jerusalem, and on his return he was sent on an embassy to
Charles, Archduke of Austria, in 1514.

‡ Ferdinand re-entered Naples on the 7th of July, 1495. The story
of his recovery of his capital is thus told by Mr. Prescott :—" King Ferdinand, having gained new confidence from his experience of the favourable dispositions existing towards him in Calabria, and relying on a

in the battle of Fornovo; and our men in the castle had the same news, from several letters and stories forged by the Duke of Milan, which they believed as readily as the Colonne, who revolted from us immediately, as desiring to be always on the strongest side, though (as I said before) they were under great obligations to the king. Upon these reports, but chiefly because our men were confined in great numbers in the castle (where provisions were scarce), and had lost all their horses and household stuff in the town, they came to a treaty, on the 19th of October 1495, after they had been besieged three months and fourteen days); and

similar feeling of loyalty in his capital, determined to hazard a bold stroke for its recovery. He accordingly embarked at Messina, with a handful of troops only, on board the fleet of the Spanish admiral, Requesens. It amounted in all to eighty vessels, most of them of inconsiderable size. With this armament, which, notwithstanding its formidable show, carried little effective force for land operations, the adventurous young monarch appeared off the harbour of Naples before the end of June, 1495. The Duke of Montpensier at that time garrisoned Naples with 6000 French troops. On the appearance of the Spanish navy, he marched out to prevent Ferdinand's landing, leaving a few only of his soldiers to keep the city in awe. But he had scarcely quitted it before the inhabitants, who had waited with impatience an opportunity for throwing off the yoke, sounded the tocsin, and rising in arms through every part of the city, and massacring the feeble remains of the garrison, shut the gates against him; while Ferdinand, who had succeeded in drawing off the French commander in another direction, no sooner presented himself before the walls, than he was received with transports of joy by the enthusiastic people.

" The French, however, though excluded from the city, by making a circuit effected an entrance into the fortresses which commanded it. From these posts Montpensier sorely annoyed the town, making frequent attacks on it, day and night, at the head of his gendarmerie, until they were at length checked in every direction by barricades, which the citizens hastily constructed with waggons, casks of stones, bags of sand, and whatever came most readily to hand. At the same time the windows, balconies, and house-tops were crowded with combatants, who poured down such a deadly shower of missiles on the heads of the French as finally compelled them to take shelter in their defences. Montpensier was now closely besieged, till at length reduced by famine, he was compelled to capitulate. Before the time prescribed for his surrender had arrived, however, he effected his escape at night, by water, to Salerno, at the head of twenty-five hundred men. The remaining garrison, with the fortresses, submitted to the victorious Ferdinand, at the beginning of the following year."—*History of Ferdinand and Isabella*, vol. ii. pp. 288-290.

about three weeks after making the treaty, they marched away. They had promised, that if they were not relieved by a certain day, they would march off into Provence, and leave the castles without doing any farther act of hostility against that kingdom, either by sea or by land; for performance of which promise the said hostages were given. And King Ferrand alleged they had broken their promise by departing without leave; but our men affirmed the contrary; howbeit, the hostages were in no little danger, and not without cause. Whatever their articles were, I think our men did wisely to march away; but they had done better if they had delivered up the castles when they went, and taken their hostages along with them: for by reason of their want of provisions and their despair of relief, the remaining garrison was forced to surrender within twenty days after, and the loss of the castle of Naples was the loss of the whole kingdom.

Ch. XVI.— Of the great Famine and Misery to which the Duke of Orleans and his army were reduced at Novara: Of the Death of the Marchioness of Montferrat: Of the Death of the Duke of Vendôme; and the conclusion of a Peace for the preservation of the besieged after several negotiations.—1495.

THE king, during his stay at Turin, or at Quiers*, (whither he went sometimes for his diversion) grew impatient for the Swiss whom he had sent the Bailiff of Dijon to raise in Switzerland; for he was extremely desirous, if possible, to restore the young Duke of Milan, and paid but little attention to.the distress of his cousin the Duke of Orleans, who began to be straitened in provisions, and sent couriers to us every day to beg the king to relieve him. The enemy had advanced their approaches, and gotten nearer the town than ever: besides, they were reinforced with a thousand German horse, under the command of Monsieur Frederic Capelare,

* Chieri, a pleasant little Sardinian town, about eight miles south-east of Turin.

of the county of Ferrete, a brave soldier and an excellent officer, and trained in the wars of both Italy and France; they had a recruit likewise of eleven thousand Landsknechts, out of the territories of the King of the Romans, commanded by Monsieur George Dabecfin *, a native of Austria, a person of great valour, and the very same that took St. Omers for the King of the Romans.

The king, seeing the enemy's army daily reinforced, and that no honourable terms were to be expected, was persuaded to retire to Vercelli †, and there to concert measures how to relieve the Duke of Orleans, who (as I have said before) had taken no care to erect any magazines for the subsistence of his army upon his first entrance into Novara; and certainly it had been much better for the duke to have followed the advice which I gave him upon the king's return to Asti, to put all useless persons out of the town, and repair himself to the king: for his presence would have advanced his affairs, or at least the troops he had left behind would not have been reduced to such extremity of hunger, for he would have capitulated sooner, had he found there was no hope of relief. But the Archbishop of Rouen ‡, who was with him at the taking of Novara, and was then with the king, to solicit in his behalf, sent him word not to stir, and assured him of relief; grounding his confidence upon the promises of the Cardinal of St. Malo, who was all powerful with the king. The archbishop spoke as his affections prompted him; but I was assured of the contrary, for nobody had any inclination to return to the battle, unless the king went in person, and his Majesty had no inclination to do so, as the dispute was only about that town, which the Duke of Orleans desired to keep, and the Duke of Milan to recover; because as it is within ten leagues of Milan, he thought it necessary that they should be both under one

* Called by Molinet (iii. 438.) "George Obestain, a native of Trent, in Germany." It seems probable that he was a member of the Styrian family of Herberstein, one of whom greatly distinguished himself in the wars against the Turks, in 1509. The Landsknechts were the heavy German infantry.

† Vercelli is sixteen miles south-west of Novara.

‡ George d'Amboise, afterwards a cardinal, and chief minister of state to Louis XII. from 1498 to 1509. He died at Lyons, on the 25th of May, 1510.

jurisdiction, there being nine or ten great cities near one another, within a small compass, and all depending upon the said duchy. However, Ludovic Sforza offered fair terms, that if we would deliver up Novara, and not disturb him in Genoa, in other things he would serve the king to the utmost of his power.

Several great convoys of provision, both of corn and meal, were sent into Novara; but they always lost half by the way; and once a small force of sixty men-at-arms, under the command of Chastillon, a young gentleman belonging to the court, was quite routed; some were taken, some few entered, and others with great difficulty escaped; so that it is not possible to imagine the extremity the garrison was reduced to. Every day some were starved to death; two parts out of three were afflicted with distempers of which we had pitiful and continual accounts, both in cipher and otherwise, which came to us with very great difficulty. We constantly gave them fair promises, and as constantly deceived them; those who had the sole administration of affairs were very inclinable to fight, but they did not consider that nobody desired it beside themselves; for the great officers, as for instance the Prince of Orange (whom, upon his late arrival, the king often consulted in military affairs), and all the other officers of the army, desired things might be composed and adjusted by a peace, because winter was approaching, money wanting, the army but weak and sickly, and soldiers deserting daily, whilst others were dismissed by the king. Yet all the wise men in the camp were not able to persuade the Archbishop of Rouen from encouraging the Duke of Orleans not to leave Novara; by which advice they brought him into a great deal of danger; but this advice proceeded from an expectation of great recruits out of Switzerland, which the bailiff of Dijon had assured them he could raise. Some of our courtiers wrote to him to bring as many troops as he could assemble; thus our councils were divided, and every man wrote and said what he pleased.

Those who were averse to an accommodation, or to any meeting about it, pretended the enemy ought to make overtures first, and that it did not consist with the king's honour to begin; and the enemy being equally haughty on their side, the poor garrison in Novara suffered incredibly, and their letters were full of nothing but relations of their miseries, assuring us, first, that they could not hold out above ten days, then eight, and at last three; but they exceeded the time which they had mentioned. To be brief, such necessities had not been known in our time, nor did ever men suffer so great a famine in a hundred years before.

During this posture of affairs the Marchioness of Montferrat died, and left her country involved in some troubles in respect of the competition for its government. The Marquis of Saluzzo pretended to it on one side, and the Lord Constantine, uncle to the Marchioness, claimed it on the other. He was a Greek as well as his niece, who was the King of Servia's daughter; but both of them had been ruined by the Turks. This Lord Constantine had fortified the castle of Casale, where he kept in his hands the two sons (the eldest of whom was scarce nine years old) of the late marquis, and that beautiful and discreet lady his niece, who died in the twenty-ninth year of her age, and was a constant friend to the French. Other persons pretended likewise to the government, and there was great contest for it before the king by their respective agents. The king commanded me to proceed thither, with instructions to settle things for the advantage of the young children, and the general satisfaction of the people; fearing lest by these differences the Duke of Milan should be brought in, for the lord of that country was our very good ally.

I was extremely concerned at these orders, especially as I had to depart before I could set the treaty of peace on foot again; for I was sensible in what condition the town was. I saw winter approaching, and apprehended lest the prelates * should bring the king to a new battle, in which (unless mightily supplied from Switzerland) he would be probably too weak, and if the supplies were as numerous as they were reported to be, it would not be safe for the king to venture himself in their hands; besides, the enemy were powerful, strongly encamped, and very well fortified. Upon these considerations, I presumed to tell the king that, in my judgment, he was about to put himself and his kingdom in very great hazard, upon a small and trifling occasion; that the danger which he escaped at the battle of Fornovo ought

* The Cardinal of St. Malo, and the Archbishop of Rouen.

not to be forgotten, but that there he was under necessity, and here he was not. Wherefore I did humbly recommend him not to lose an honourable accommodation by stickling for the first overture; and if he pleased to authorise me, I questioned not but I could make a peace without the least dishonour to either side. He replied that he would have me speak to the Cardinal; and so I did, but he gave me strange unaccountable answers, expressing an inclination to fight, and making sure of the victory; and he told me the Duke of Orleans had promised, whenever he came to the duchy of Milan, to give him ten thousand ducats a year for one of his sons. The next morning I went to wait on the king, and take leave of his majesty, in order to begin my journey to Casale (which would take me about a day and a half). I there met the Lord de la Trimouille, and acquainted him with what had passed (he being related to the king*), and desired his judgment whether I ought to mention the affair to him again; he told me to do so by all means, for everybody was very desirous of peace. The king was at that time in the garden; so I revived the discourse before the Cardinal, who told me that it was most proper for him, being an ecclesiastic, to begin it. I answered, if he did not, I would; for I perceived the king was inclinable enough, and so were all that were about him. After which I took my leave; and at my departure I told the Prince of Orange (who commanded the army in chief), that if I began anything in that business, my addresses should be to him; and so I went to Casale, where I was well received by all that family, and found them nearly all in favour of the Lord Constantine, as a fitter person for the guardianship of the children; for he was incapable of the succession, to which the Marquis of Saluzzo pretended a right. For several days together, I assembled both the nobility, clergy, and townsmen, and, at the request of most of them, I declared that it was my master's pleasure that the Lord Constantine should be continued in the government; for, considering the king's forces on that side of the mountains, and the affection that country had always retained to the court of France, I presumed they would not contradict the king's desires.

* By his wife, Gabrielle de Bourbon, who was a daughter of the Count de Montpensier.

I had scarce been three days at Casale before there arrived a gentleman from the Marquis of Mantua, captain-general of the Venetians, with compliments of condolence upon the death of the late Marchioness; for he was related to the family of Montferrat. This gentleman was steward of the marquis's household, and he and I by degrees began to consult how we might prevent the battle that was likely to occur shortly; for all things tended to war, and the king was encamped not far from Vercelli; though, to speak the truth, he had only passed the river, and let his army encamp there, which was but ill-provided with tents and pavilions, for they had brought but few with them, and those few were lost; besides, the ground was moist, — for winter was coming on, and the country is but low.

The king lay but one night in the camp, and returned next morning to the town; but the Prince of Orange remained with the army, and with him the Counts of Foix and Vendôme*, the latter of whom fell into a dysentery and died, to the unspeakable sorrow of the whole army, for he was a young gentleman of great valour and conduct, and came thither post upon the report of a coming battle; but he was not with the king in his expedition into Italy. There were likewise the Marshal de Gié, and several other commanders, but their principal force was the Swiss, who had been in Italy with the king; for the French, being so near home, were very unwilling to stay any longer in the camp, and several had already left it, some with leave and others without it. From Vercelli to Novara was ten good Italian miles, that is six French leagues; the country was flat and dirty, with ditches on both sides the road, much deeper than those in Flanders: in winter the roads are full of mud, and in summer of dust. Between our army and Novara there was a little town called Borgo, which we had taken possession of; and the enemy had another about the same distance from their camp, called Cameri: but the waters being up, the passage was very difficult from one army to the other.

But as I was saying, the steward of the Marquis of Mantua's household and I continued our conferences. I gave him several reasons why his master ought to be cautious of com-

* François de Bourbon, Count of Vendôme, born in 1470, died on the 3rd of October, 1495.

ing to a battle. I put him in mind of the danger he had
lately escaped, and that he would expose himself for a people
who had never rewarded him for services he had done ; and
that, therefore, his wisest method would be to endeavour an
accommodation, and I promised to do all that lay in my
power to promote it. He replied that his master was well
enough inclined, but that it would be necessary (as I had
received intimation before) that we should make the first
overture, because they looked upon their alliance, which
consisted of the Pope, the King of the Romans, the King of
Spain, and the Duke of Milan, to be of greater dignity than
a single monarch. I answered that this punctilio was idle
and trifling, and that in justice our king was to be preferred,
because he was there in person, and the confederates were
represented only by their lieutenants. But I offered, if he
pleased, that he and I as mediators would set the treaty on
foot, provided I could be assured his master would continue
it, and observe it; and finally it was concluded that I
should send a trumpeter to their army the next morning, and
that I should write to Signor Luca Pisano and Signor Melchior Trevisano, the two Venetian proveditors, or commissioners appointed to advise their generals and superintend
the affairs of the army.

In pursuance of what we concluded, I wrote to the proveditors the substance of what I had mentioned before to the
Marquis of Mantua's steward : and I had a fair opportunity
to offer my mediation, upon account of the agreement made
between us at my departure from Venice. Besides, I knew the
king was desirous of peace, and I thought it necessary,—for
there are always enough persons to perplex and exasperate
an affair, but few that combine the good fortune and courage
necessary to compose so great a difference, or to endure so
many hard words as are said by the plenipotentiaries in
such negotiations; for in great armies there is sure to be a
variety of opinions. The proveditors were glad of the news,
and sent me word I should have an answer very suddenly,
for they sent post to Venice for instructions ; and having a
speedy answer from the Signory, a count belonging to the
Duke of Ferrara was sent to our camp. The Duke of Fer-
rarra had one son in the Duke of Milan's service, and
another in the king's. The count also was in the Duke of

Milan's service, his name was Albertini*; but his pretence of coming into our army was to visit Signor John James di Trivulce, and to inquire after one of his sons who was then in that captain's service. He made application to the Prince of Orange, according to the agreement between the steward and myself, and told him he had a commission from the Marquis of Mantua, and the proveditors and other captains, to desire a passport for the marquis and fifty horse, to meet and confer with such persons as the king should depute; and he acknowledged that in reason they ought to make the first overture to the king, or such as he should appoint, and that they would pay him that honour; and then he desired he might have a private conference with his majesty, which was granted him, and in which he advised him not to set any treaty on foot, assuring him that their army was in great consternation, and would break up in a very short time. By these words he seemed desirous to obstruct that peace which he was sent to promote, though his public commission was as you have heard. Signor John James di Trivulce was present when he gave the king this advice, and being a great enemy to the Duke of Milan, he had no mind to the peace; but, above all, no man was so averse to it as Count Albertini's master, the Duke of Ferrara, who desired the continuation of the war upon account of an old pique against the Venetians, who had taken from him several territories, as the Polesan and others; and this duke was therefore come himself into the army of the Duke of Milan, who had married his daughter.

As, soon as the king had heard what the count had to offer, his majesty sent for me, and it was warmly debated whether a passport should be granted or not. Those who were against the peace (as Signor John James di Trivulce and others, who thought themselves great favourers of the interest of the Duke of Orleans,) were for fighting by all means; but they were, most of them, churchmen, and not like to be in the battle, and they pretended to have certain intelligence that the enemy must suddenly raise the siege, or be starved to death. Others objected (and I was of that number) that we should be starved first; that the enemy were in their own country, and their power too great to be

---

* Albertino Boschetto.—GUAZZO, p. 218.

so easily destroyed; and that such counsel proceeded from persons who had a mind to engage us in their quarrels, and set us fighting purely to gratify their own revenge and ambition. Yet, for all this, the passport was granted and sent, signifying, that the next day at two o'clock in the afternoon, the Prince of Orange, the Marshal de Gié, the Lord de Piennes, and myself, with our retinue, should be between Borgo and Cameri, near a certain tower, in which they had a guard, and that there we should be ready to enter into a conference. At the appointed hour, we went to the place under a strong guard. The Marquis of Mantua and a Venetian who had the command of their Estradiots *, came to us, and in very civil language told us, that for their part they were desirous of peace. For better convenience of treating, it was agreed, that the next day some of their deputies should come into our camp, and that the day after some of ours should go into theirs, which was done. The next morning there came to us Signor Francisco Bernardino Visconti on behalf of the Duke of Milan, and a secretary from the Marquis of Mantua. On our side, besides the persons above mentioned, we had added to us the Cardinal of St. Malo, and we began to treat. They demanded Novara, in which the Duke of Orleans was besieged; and we insisted upon having Genoa, saying, it was feudatory to the king, and that the Duke of Milan had confiscated it. They excused themselves as to that, assuring us that their master had done nothing against the king except in his own defence; that the Duke of Orleans had taken Novara from them by force, and begun the war with our king's forces; and that therefore they thought their masters would be hardly persuaded to agree to these demands, but in any thing else would be ready to comply. Our conferences lasted two days, after which they returned to their camp, whither the Marshal de Gié, the Lord de Piennes, and myself, were sent after them to press for the restitution of Genoa. We would have been content that Novara should have been surrendered to the forces of the King of the Romans, which were commanded by Signor George di Pietraplanta †, the

* According to Guicciardini (i. 336.) his name was Bernardo Contarino.

† This is the Herberstein mentioned in a previous note, whose name is thus Italianised by Guicciardini also.

Lord Frederic Capellare, and another called Monsieur Hans;
for we found it could not be relieved without a battle, which
we had no great inclination to venture; and by this means
(as we pretended) we proposed to acquit ourselves very
honourably to the emperor, of whom the whole duchy of
Milan is held as a fief.   Several goings and comings there
were between our camp and theirs, but we came to no manner of conclusion.   I continued constantly with them by
the king's direction (who was unwilling the treaty should
be broken off); and, at last, our deputies came to them
again, and with us we had the President de Gannay, and
one Monsieur de Morvilliers, Bailiff of Amiens, to speak
with them in Latin, (for till then I had conducted the conferences in bad Italian,) and to draw up the articles.   Our
manner of treating was to go to the duke's quarters, and he,
in complaisance, used to meet us with his duchess at the
end of a gallery, and then sent us all before him into his
chamber, where there were two great rows of chairs ready
set, as close as was convenient, and opposite to each other.
They placed themselves on one side, and we sate on the other.
The first on their side was the commissioner for the King
of the Romans, then the Spanish ambassador, then the
Marquis of Mantua, after him the two proveditors, then
the Venetian ambassador, then the Duke and Duchess of
Milan, and last of all the ambassador of Ferrara.   On their
side none spoke but the Duke of Milan, and on our side
nobody but one.   It is not our method to discourse with
that sedateness of temper which they do, for sometimes two
or three of us were speaking at a time; but the duke always
interrupted us with, " Hold, gentlemen, one to one."   As we
were obliged to digest all into articles, whatever was agreed
upon was immediately put into writing by one of our secretaries for us, and by another of theirs for them; and this
was read aloud by the secretaries, one in Italian, and the
other in French; and this was done again at our next meeting, that we might see whether any thing had been changed;
and it is a good way to dispatch any affair of importance.
This treaty was in progress about a fortnight or longer;
but the first day of our conference it was concluded that the
Duke of Orleans might have liberty to come out of Novara,
to which end a cessation of arms was agreed upon for that

VOL. II.   B

day, and continued from day to day till the conclusion of
the peace; and for surety for the passage of the Duke of
Orleans, the Marquis of Mantua delivered himself as a
hostage into the hands of the Count de Foix; and he did it
voluntarily, and more to give us pleasure than from any
fear; yet first they made us swear that we were proceeding
with sincerity and *bona fides* in the treaty of peace, and
that we did not do it merely to deliver the duke out of
danger.

CH. XVII.—How the Duke of Orleans and his Army were delivered
upon Terms of Accommodation from the dire Misery they suffered
during their being besieged in Novara; and of the Arrival of the
Swiss that came to the Relief of the King and the said Duke of Orleans.—1495.

THE Marshal de Gié went into the town of Novara, with
other commissioners deputed by the Duke of Milan, and
dismissed the Duke of Orleans, and some few of his attendants, to their very great satisfaction. Those who were in the
place were so pressed with hunger and sickness, that the
marshal was forced to leave his nephew Monsieur de Romefort* as an hostage, promising they should all be at liberty to
depart within three days. You have heard how the Bailiff
of Dijon had been sent into Switzerland to raise five thousand men in all the cantons; but when the Duke of Orleans
marched out of Novara they were not arrived; and it was
well they were not, for had they joined our army, certainly
(at least in my judgment) we should have fought a battle;
but if we had been sure that their number would be far
greater than we expected, we could not have stayed till
their arrival, by reason of the extreme famine in the town,
where two thousand people were already dead, some with
hunger, some with disease, and the rest were so lean and
meagre they looked more like dead than living people; and,
truly, I believe never men endured more misery (unless,
perhaps, at the siege of Jerusalem). All which had been

* Louis de Rohan, Lord of Montauban and Remefort.

prevented, if they had been so prudent as to have brought in all the corn and provisions about the town upon their first coming into it: had they acted so wisely they had never plunged themselves into those exigencies, for the enemy would have been obliged to have abandoned the siege, and to have marched shamefully off.

Some three or four days after the Duke of Orleans had left the town, it was agreed on both sides that the whole garrison should march out; and the Marquis of Mantua, and the Lord Galeas di San Severino, (who commanded both the Venetians and the Duke of Milan's army,) had orders to see them safely conducted away; which was performed, and the town left in the hands of the inhabitants, under an oath not to deliver it either to the French or the Italians till the conclusion of a general peace. Only thirty men were put into the castle, who were supplied with provisions by the Duke of Milan, for money, and they were never to have more provision at a time than was sufficient for one single day. No man that did not see it, can conceive the poverty of the garrison that marched out. They had few or no horses left, for most of them were eaten; and of the five thousand men that marched out, scarcely six hundred were able to defend themselves; they fell down frequently in the road as they marched along, and the enemy were forced to help them up again. I know I saved fifty of them, at the cost of a crown, not far from the little castle called Cameri, which was in the enemy's possession, by lodging them in a garden, and giving them warm broth, so that but one of them died. Upon the way (it being ten miles between Novara and Vercelli) four more of them died. The king (as a token of his compassion) caused eight hundred francs to be distributed amongst those who came to Vercelli, as a benevolence in addition to their pay, which was paid to a farthing, both to the living and the dead, and particularly to the Swiss, of whom there were near four hundred dead; yet, notwithstanding all the care that could be taken of them, about thirty of them died in Vercelli, some with eating too much, others by diseases, and some on the dunghills of the town.

About the time that all of them had evacuated the town, except the thirty left in the castle (and of these one or other came away every day), the Swiss arrived, to the number of eight or ten thousand, in our camp, in which we had already about two thousand who had served in our expedition to Naples. There were also ten thousand more, but they were quartered at some distance from Vercelli; for the king was advised not to suffer the conjunction of two such treat bodies, which would have amounted together to wenty-two thousand men, the greatest number (I think) that ever came out of their country at one time; and I have been informed by those that were well acquainted with the affairs of Switzerland, that they scarce left any fighting men behind them; and those who did come, came for the most part, in spite of our teeth, and their wives and children would also have come along with them, had we not set guards upon the passes in Piedmont on purpose to stop them. It may be demanded whether this extraordinary alacrity proceeded from any extraordinary affection; for King Louis XI. had done them many good offices, and contributed much to make them a reputation in the world. Indeed there were some old soldiers who had a respect for the memory of King Louis; and some of their officers were above seventy-two years old, and had been captains in the wars against Charles Duke of Burgundy; but the chief motives that induced them to leave their own country were avarice and poverty. To speak truth, all their best men came to us; and such a number of brave fellows I had never seen before together in my life; and to me it seemed impossible to conquer them, unless by cold, famine, or some other distress.

But to return to the principal point of our treaty. The Duke of Orleans having lived eight or ten days at his ease and pleasure, and being attended by all sorts of people, was told that it had been stated, as some diminution to his honour, that such a numerous garrison as he had in Novara should have been reduced to such necessities; upon which he began to talk of fighting again, and one or two that were about him encouraged him to it. Monsieur de Ligny and the Archbishop of Rouen were highly for his interest; and some mean persons bribed thirty of the Swiss to come of themselves and offer the enemy battle; but without any reason, for the Duke of Orleans had only thirty men left in the castle, and there was no further occasion to fight, for the king pretended no quarrel of his own, but had come thither only to rescue the duke and his friends ; besides the enemy were very powerful, and it was impossible to attack them in their camp; for besides the natural strength of the place, they were strongly entrenched, all the ditches were full of water, and there were no forces but ours to give them any disturbance, as no sallies could be expected out of the town. Their army consisted of two thousand eight hundred men-at-arms barbed, five thousand light horse, and eleven thousand five hundred Germans commanded by good officers (as Signor George di Pietraplanta, Count Frederic Capellare, and Monsieur Hans), besides a great number of foot ; so that to talk of attacking them in their entrenchments, or beating them so easily, was but a rhodomontade, and spoken in flattery. Another great dread we had, and that was, lest the Swiss should join in one body, and seize upon the king and all the chief officers of his army (who were not able to resist their power), and carry them into their own country ; and of this there was some appearance, as you will see by the conclusion of the peace.

CH. XVIII.—How Peace was concluded between the King and the Duke of Orleans on the one Part, and the League on the other; and of the Conditions and Articles contained in that Treaty of Peace.— 1495.

THE debate about this affair grew at last so fierce amongst us, that, in the heat of argument, the Duke of Orleans gave the Prince of Orange the lie; but at last, the Marshal de Gié, the Lord de Piennes, the President Gannay, the Lord de Morvilliers, the Vidame of Chartres*, and I, re-turned to the enemy's camp, and concluded a peace†, though by several indications we judged it unlikely to continue long ; but we were under a necessity of doing it, both in re-spect of the season of the year, our want of money, and that

* Jacques de Vendôme, Prince of Chabanois, and Vidame of Chartres.
† Dated at Vercelli, on the 10th of October, 1495.

we might come off honourably in the business; to which end the peace was concluded and engrossed, so that it might be published throughout the world, which was done afterwards by the king's express order in council, and in the presence of the Duke of Orleans. The substance of it was, that the Duke of Milan should serve the king against all opposers; that, at his own proper charge, the Duke of Milan should fit out two ships for the relief of the castles of Naples, which still held out for the king; that the next year (in case the king made a new invasion upon that kingdom), he should furnish him with three ships, and assist him in person, and give free passage to his troops; that in case the Venetians did not accept the said peace within two months' time, but continued to assist the House of Aragon, the duke should then take part with the King of France against them, and employ his person and interest in his service, upon condition that whatever was taken from the enemy should be delivered to the duke, for which terms he was to remit to the king eighty thousand of the hundred and twenty-four thousand ducats which he had lent him in his voyage to Naples; that with regard to Genoa, he should put two hostages into the king's hands; that Castelleto should be committed to the Duke of Ferrara, as a neutral, for two years; that the Duke of Milan should pay one-half of the garrison of Castelleto, and the king the other; and that if it should happen that the duke should at any time attempt to do any thing against the king at Genoa, then the Duke of Ferrara was to deliver Castelleto to the king. He was likewise to give two hostages for Milan, which was performed; and he would have done as much for Genoa, had not the king been in such haste to be gone; but as soon as he went away, the duke made use of shifts and evasions to excuse himself from doing it.

Immediately upon our return from swearing the Duke of Milan to observe this peace, and bringing word that the Venetians had taken two months to accept or refuse (for to other terms we could not persuade them), the king swore likewise to observe the peace; and the next day he resolved to begin his march, as both he and his whole army had a great desire to return into France; but that very night the Swiss who were in our camp began to cabal, and hold private consultations among the men of their several cantons, beating their drums and standing to their arms (as their manner is when they call any councils); and this I was informed of by Monsieur de Lornay, who was then (and had been long before) one of their chief officers, and was well acquainted with their language, and he gave the king intelligence of it.

Some proposed to seize upon the king, and all the chief (that is to say, the rich) officers of the army; others went not so far, but moved that they should demand three months' pay, on the score of an old promise made them by the late king*, that such a sum should be paid them whenever they came out of their own country into his service with their colours displayed. Others were for securing the chief ministers about the king, without meddling with his person; and this they designed to put in execution, having already got a great number of their own troops into the town; but before they could come to an agreement among themselves, the king had left for Trino † (which is a town belonging to the Marquis of Montferrat). In this they were much in the wrong, for there was never but one month's pay promised them, and they had done nothing for that. At length, this troublesome affair was adjusted; but first, those Swiss who were with us in the expedition to Naples, had seized upon the Bailiff of Dijon and Monsieur de Lornay (who commanded them all along), and pressed hard for a fortnight's pay before they marched; but the rest insisted upon pay for three months, which in all amounted to five hundred thousand francs, for the raising of which they took hostages; and to this they were animated by the French themselves, who were averse to the peace; and of this the Prince of Orange was informed by one of their captains, and he immediately informed the king of it.

The king, upon his arrival at Trino, sent the Marshal de Gié, the President Gannay, and myself, to the Duke of Milan, to desire that he would come to him thither. We used several arguments to persuade him, and told him it would be a great confirmation of the peace; but he gave as many to the contrary, and excused himself upon a proposition which

* By a treaty made with them in 1474.—LENGLET, iii. 369.
† The king arrived at Trino on Sunday, the 11th of October, 1495.

Monsieur de Ligny had formerly made to have him seized
upon, when he was with the king at Pavia, and upon certain
expressions which the Cardinal of St. Malo had used, who,
at that time, was the only minister who had influence with
the king.   It is certain that several idle words had been
spoken by some about the court, but yet the king had a great
desire to cultivate a friendship with him.   The Duke of
Milan was at a place called Bolia*, and consented to a conference, provided it might be upon some river, with a barrier between them.†   As soon as the king had received his
answer, he removed to Quiers‡, where he staid but a night
or two, and then marched away to cross the mountains,
having despatched me to Venice, and others to Genoa, to see
the ships equipped which the Duke of Milan was to lend
him; but the duke put the king to great expense in preparations, and at last would not let them go; but instead of
keeping his promise, he sent two ships to the enemy.

CH. XIX.—How the King sent the Lord of Argenton to Venice again,
to invite the Venetians to accept the Terms of Peace that were
offered, which the Venetians refused; and of the Tricks and Jugglings of the Duke of Milan.—1495.

THE business of my embassy to Venice at this time was to
know whether they would accept the peace, and subscribe
to three articles.   The first was to restore Monopoli, which
they had lately taken from us; the second was to withdraw
the Marquis of Mantua and his forces out of the kingdom of
Naples, and from the service of King Ferrand; and the
third was to declare that King Ferrand was not comprehended in their recent league, in which mention was made
only of the Pope, the King of the Romans, the King of Spain,
and the Duke of Milan.   Upon my arrival at Venice they

* Bobbio, the chief town of the province of that name in the Sardinian territories.
† Charles VIII. refused to consent to this proposition, regarding such
precautions as an insult to his honour.—GUICCIARDINI, i. 350.
‡ The king arrived at Chieri on Sunday, the 18th of October, 1495.

received me very honourably, but not quite in the same manner as when I was there first,—for then we were at peace, but now at war with each other. I delivered my message to the Doge of Venice, who complimented me highly, and told me I was very welcome; and that he would consult with the Senate, and in a short time return me an answer.

For three days together they appointed solemn processions to be made, public alms to be given, and sermons to be preached all over the city, beseeching God of His grace to direct them in their consultations, which, as I was informed, was no more than what they frequently do upon extraordinary occasions. And truly, in religious affairs, and in the beautifying and adorning their churches, it is a city of the greatest reverence and decency that ever I saw; and in these things I esteem them equal to the Romans, and I question not but that their Signory derives much of its grandeur from this fact, and it is worthy rather to be augmented than lessened. But to the business of my embassy. I waited a fortnight before I had an answer, and then it was a refusal of all I had demanded. They told me they had no war with the king, and that what they had done was only to assist and support the Duke of Milan, who was their ally, and whom the king had a desire to destroy; yet they permitted their Doge to talk with me alone, and he offered very advantageous terms, which were, that King Ferrand should do homage to our king for the kingdom of Naples, by the Pope's consent; that King Ferrand should pay our king a yearly tribute of fifty thousand ducats, besides a sum of money down, which they would lend (intending to have the towns of Brindisi, Otranto, Trani, and others in Apulia, put into their hands for security for the said loan); and that King Ferrand should deliver up or leave the king in possession of some towns or places in Apulia for his security (and they meant Tarento, which our king has still in his hands *), and (if he pleased) two or three more, which they offered should be on that side, because it was farthest from them, though they pretended it was for the convenience of his designs against the Turk, of which our king had talked much at his first entrance into Italy, declaring he undertook that enterprise for

---

* Tarento surrendered to Frederic King of Naples, in 1496.

no other end but to be nearer and more ready to invade him; but it was an evil invention, a mere fraud, and we cannot conceal our thoughts from God. The Doge of Venice offered besides, that if our king would attempt any thing against the Turk, he should have free passage for his troops, through all those places; and all Italy should contribute: the King of the Romans would make a diversion on his side; and the king, in conjunction with them, would be able to govern all Italy, in such a manner as to compel any of the princes as should refuse, to comply with their orders; and that for their part they would assist his majesty, at their own charge, with a hundred galleys at sea, and five thousand horse on land.

When I had my audience of leave, I told the Doge and Signory I would report all faithfully to the king. I returned by Milan, and found the Duke of Milan at Vigevano, and the king's ambassador with him, who was one Rigault d'Oreilles*, steward to his household. The duke pretended to go a hunting, and came out to meet me (for they are very civil to ambassadors) and ordered me a very noble apartment in his castle. I begged that I might have the honour of a private conference with him, which at last he promised me, but with some signs of reluctancy. As the castle of Naples still held out for us, I was resolved to press for the ships with which he was bound to furnish us by the treaty at Vercelli. The ships were ready, and he was willing in appearance to send them out, but Peron de Basche and Stephen de Neves being at that time at Genoa on behalf of our king, and understanding I was at Vigevano, wrote to me immediately, complaining of the Duke of Milan's treacherous way of dealing, who pretended to furnish us with ships and had sent two against us; that the governor of Genoa had told them one day that he could not suffer the ships to be manned with French sailors, and another, that there could not be above five and twenty of them permitted to be in any one vessel, with many such trifling excuses to protract and gain time, till they had heard the news of the cap-

---

* Rigault Doreille, Knight, Lord of Villeneuve, was steward in ordinary to Louis XI. and Charles VIII. He was appointed Bailiff of Chartres in 1496, and died on the 15th of September, 1517.

ture of the castle of Naples, in which the Duke of Milan knew there was not provision enough for above a month, and that the king's forces in Provence would be unable to raise the siege without the assistance of those two ships, for the enemy had blocked up the castle by sea with a great fleet furnished by the Venetians and the King of Spain as well as by themselves.

I was three days with the duke; the first he spent most in conference with me, and seemed to be angry that I was not satisfied with his answer about the ships, to which he added that though at the treaty of Vercelli he had promised to serve the king with two ships, yet he had never promised that they should be manned with French. I replied, that in my judgment that excuse was but weak and trifling, for if he should lend me a good mule with which to pass the mountains, what favour would it be if he should oblige me to lead her by the hand? I should only have liberty to see her, but no advantage unless I had leave to mount her. After a long conference he conducted me into a gallery apart, where I took occasion to remonstrate the great pains which others and myself had taken about the treaty of Vercelli; and the danger he would bring upon us by acting so contrary, and causing the king to lose his castles in Naples, which would be the total loss of the kingdom, and an occasion of perpetual animosity between my master and him, and I offered him the principality of Tarento, and the duchy of Bari, which duchy was already his own. I represented to him the danger he brought upon himself and all Italy by consenting that the Venetians should hold those places in Apulia; and he confessed that what I had urged was true, especially in relation to the Venetians, but told me plainly at last he could repose no confidence in our king.

After this discourse I took my leave of the Duke of Milan, who conducted me a league on my way home, and even at my departure he invented a more cunning lie (if it be decent to use such an expression towards a prince) than any of his former falsehoods. Perceiving I was melancholy, he told me on a sudden (as a man who had quite changed his resolutions) that he would show himself my friend at the last, and do that which should make me acceptable to my master; and he promised me that the next day he would send the Lord Galeas (who was the fittest man for that purpose) to see his ships at Genoa equipped and sent away to join our fleet; that he would do the king that service so as to save his castle, and by consequence the whole kingdom of Naples (and if he had performed his promise, this would have been the result); and that when the ships had sailed he would give me an account of it by a letter under his own hand, that the king might have the first news of it from myself, and be sensible of the service which I had done him, adding also that his letters should overtake me before I got to Lyons. Big with these hopes I departed, and continued my journey over the mountains. I knew the man, and durst not be too confident; yet I never heard any courier behind me, but I fancied he was bringing me those letters. I passed on till I came to Chambery, where I found the Duke of Savoy, who received me very graciously, and obliged me to stay a whole day with him. From thence I proceeded to Lyons (but no letters overtook me) to give the king an account of my transactions; for he was there at that time, giving himself up wholly to feastings, jousts, and other gay entertainments, without the least regard to anything else.

Those who had been enemies to the peace of Vercelli were extremely pleased with the Duke of Milan's prevarication; and indeed they had reason, for their authority was increased by it, and I was traduced, which in the like cases is an ordinary thing in the courts of princes.

I was very melancholy and angry: I informed the king of all I had done, and showed him in writing the offers which the Venetians had made him; but he seemed not to value them much, and the Cardinal of St. Malo, who at that time had the sole administration of affairs, valued them still less. However, I pressed the king again, believing it better to accept that offer than lose all; for I saw nobody about him fit to manage such an important affair, and those who were most able were never consulted, or at least as seldom as possible. The king himself was inclinable enough to do it, but loth to displease those to whom he had committed his affairs, especially those who managed his treasury, namely, the Cardinal, his brothers and relations. This is a fine example for princes. It is necessary that they should take upon themselves the conduct of their own affairs, and not only call

others to council upon occasion, but give them equal authority and countenance in certain matters; for if any minister
of state be grown so great as to became terrible to the rest,
and to manage the whole affairs of a kingdom according to
his own will and pleasure (of which sort King Charles VIII.
was never without one) that minister is king in reality, and
his master is ill served, as King Charles was always by his
ministers, who did their own business well enough, but
neglected his, to his great prejudice and dishonour.

Ch. XX.—How the King forgot those that were left behind at Naples,
upon his Return into France; and of the Dauphin's Death, which
was a great Affliction to the King and Queen.—1495.

I ARRIVED at Lyons on the 12th of December, in the year
1495; and there I found the king and his whole army. The
king had been absent on his expedition about a year and two
months.*   The castles of Naples still held out for him, as
you have heard.   The Lord de Montpensier, his lieutenant
in that kingdom, was at Salerno with the prince of that
place; the Lord d'Aubigny was in Calabria, where he had
done signal service, though under a long fit of sickness; the
Lord Gracian des Guerres was in Abruzzo, Don Julian at
Mount St. Angelo, and George de Suilly at Tarento; but all
of them most miserably poor, and so far abandoned by our
court that they could seldom or never receive letters or news
out of France, and when they did, it was nothing but shams
and promises without effect; for (as I said before) the king
did nothing of himself. If they had been supplied with
money in time, even a sixth part of what was spent afterwards to no purpose would have saved that kingdom from
being lost; for at length when all was lost, they sent them
forty thousand crowns as part of a year's pay, and yet if
that had arrived but a month sooner, the calamities and dis-
graces which they endured had never befallen them, and

* The king started from Grenoble on the 13th of August, 1494, and
arrived in that town on his return, on the 27th of October, 1495.

their divisions had been prevented; all which was occasioned through the negligence of the king, who managed nothing himself, and would not so much as hear anybody that came from them, and those whom he employed were careless and inexperienced, and I think some of them held a correspondence with the Pope; so that in appearance God had forsaken our king, and taken away that grace with which He had hitherto conducted him.

The king had not been at Lyons above two months, or thereabouts, when he received news that his only son, the dauphin, lay dangerously ill; and three days after, letters came that gave an account of his death.* The king was extremely concerned at first, as he ought to have been out of paternal affection; yet his sorrow soon wore off. But the queen (who was Anne, Duchess of Bretagne) took it more to heart than perhaps any other woman would have done, and her sorrow remained longer upon her; and I am afraid, that besides the natural affliction of mothers upon the loss of their children, her mind misgave her, and she was apprehensive that some greater misfortune would soon happen to her. The king (as I said before) having got over his own grief, had a great desire to give the queen some diversion at a ball of young gentlemen, which the king had appointed; among the rest of the dancers, the Duke of Orleans was one, who was at that time about thirty-four years old †; but he behaved himself so, that it was visible to all the court he rejoiced at the dauphin's death, for he was (after him) next heir to the crown. Wherefore the king and he never spoke to one another for a long time after. The dauphin was about three years old when he died, yet a very handsome and precocious child, and not alarmed at those things wherewith children are usually frighted; for which reason his father was the sooner recovered from his sorrow, as being fearful already lest he should have grown too fast, and lest, if his courage increased with his years, he would have entrenched upon his father's power and authority; for the king was not commanding either in person or understanding, but of the mildest and best disposition in the world. By this example we may see to what

* He died on the 6th of December, 1495.
† He was born on the 27th of June, 1462.

miseries great kings and princes, who grow jealous of their own children, are subject. His father, Louis XI., though so wise and virtuous a prince, was yet fearful of Charles VIII., but he provided prudently against the worst, and left him the crown when he was but fourteen years old. Louis XI. had been no less terrible to his father Charles VII., for at the age of thirteen years he was in arms, and confederated against him with certain of the nobility, upon some court-quarrels * and complaints against the government, (and this King Louis has often told me himself,) yet these troubles lasted not long. But when he came to man's estate, he had great controversy with his father Charles VII., retired into Dauphiny, and from thence into Flanders, leaving Dauphiny to his father, as has been observed at the beginning of these Memoirs†, in relating the reign of Louis XI.

No creature is exempt from adversity ; every man eats his bread in pain and sorrow : God Almighty promised it to our first parents, and he has performed it very faithfully ever since to all people. Yet there are degrees and distinctions of sorrow, and the troubles and vexations of the mind are greater than those of the body ; the anxiety of the wise is of one sort, and that of the fool of another, but that of the fool is the greater of the two (though some are of a contrary opinion) because he is less capable of comfort.

The poor people, who labour, drudge and toil to maintain themselves and their children, and pay their taxes and subsidies to their princes, would have but little comfort in this world if princes and great lords were sensible of nothing but pleasure, and they of nothing but sorrow and misery. But the thing is quite otherwise ; for, should I endeavour to give an account of the sufferings and disorders which (for these thirty years) I have seen endured by persons of quality of both sexes, it would swell to a large volume. I do not mean such persons as Boccace mentions in his book‡, but such as raise the envy of all people, by their riches, health,

* The Praguerie. See Book VI. chap. 12.

† See Book I. chap. 10.

‡ The reference is here to Boccaccio's treatise, " De Casibus virorum et fœminarum illustrium," of which two French translations existed at the time when Commines wrote.

and prosperity. Those who have not conversed with them so much as I have done, believe the condition of great persons to be the happiest in the world; but I have seen their troubles and disquiets, aroused upon such trifling occasions, as persons at a distance could hardly believe; an idle apprehension or an extravagant report disturbs them extremely; and this is the secret distemper that reigns in the courts of great princes, from whence many mischiefs arise to the sovereign, his ministers and subjects; and it is so great a shortener of life, that there is scarce a king of France (since the time of Charlemagne) who lived to be sixty years old.

Upon this bare suspicion, when Louis XI. came to be about that age, being sick of that disease, he concluded himself already dead. His father Charles VII., who had done so many memorable things in France, took a fancy that his courtiers had a design to poison him, and upon that account he ate nothing. Charles VI. had his jealousies too, and became crazed in his understanding upon a mere report. Certainly, princes are guilty of great error in not examining, or causing other people to examine, such tales as concern them, though, perhaps, they may be of themselves of no great importance; but this would keep them from being so frequently current, especially if they confronted the accused with the informer; by that means nothing would be reported but what was true. But there are some princes so stupid as to promise and swear to the accusers they will never discover them; and these are they who are subject to those anguishes and torments of mind of which I speak and who many times hate and injure the best ministers they have, upon the bare reports and calumnies of evil-minded and designing people, by which means they occasion great mischiefs and sorrows to their subjects.

CH. XXI.—How the King received News of the Loss of the Castle of
Naples; of the selling of the Towns belonging to the Florentines to
several Persons; of the Treaty of Atella in Apulia, much to the
Prejudice of the French; and of the Death of Ferrand, King of
Naples.—1496.

THE death of the Dauphin (only son to Charles VIII.),
occurred about the beginning of the year 1496, and was
the greatest loss that happened or could possibly happen to
the king, for he had never any child afterwards that lived.
But this misfortune came not alone; for at the same time
he received advice that the castle of Naples had been surrendered by those whom the Lord de Montpensier had left
in it, under pressure of famine, and for the safety of the
hostages, who had been delivered into the enemy's hands by
the Lord de Montpensier. The names of the hostages were
Monsieur d'Alegre, one of the sons of the Lord de la Marche
d'Ardaine, one called the Lord de la Chapelle de Loudon-
nois, and John Roquebertin, a Catalonian.* Those who
had been in the castle were sent back again by sea. After
this, another disgraceful accident befel him, and that was,
that one Entragues, who was governor of the citadel of Pisa
(which was strong, and commanded the whole town), delivered it up to the Pisans; which was contrary to the king's
oath, for he had sworn twice to the Florentines to deliver
the said citadel to them, and other places, as Sarzana, Sarzanello, Pietrasanta, Librefatto, and Mortron, which the
Florentines had lent the king in his necessities, at his first
coming into Italy, and had given him six score thousand
ducats, of which there were not above thirty thousand in
arrear when he returned into France, as has been mentioned in another place.† In short, all these places were
sold; the Genoese bought Sarzana and Sarzanello, and they
were sold by the Bastard of St. Paul.‡ Monsieur Entragues

* See Book VIII. Chap. 15.
† See Book VII. Chap. 11.
‡ The Bastard of Roussi, one of the lieutenants of the Lord d'Entragues, sold Sarzana to the Luccese for 30,000 florins.—SISMONDI,
xii. 379.

sold Pietrasanta to the citizens of Lucca*, and Librefatto to the Venetians, to the great dishonour of the king
and his subjects, and to the detriment and I may say destruction of the kingdom of Naples. The first oath King
Charles VIII. took for the restitution of those places was at
Florence, upon the high altar in the great church of St.
John; the second was at Asti, on his return, where the
Florentines furnished him in his extremity with thirty
thousand ducats, upon condition that if Pisa were surrendered to them, the king should be discharged of the said
sum, and all his jewels and pawns should be restored; and
they were to lend him threescore thousand more, to be paid
down in the kingdom of Naples, to those whom his majesty
had appointed to manage his affairs there, and to maintain
at their charge three hundred horse for the service of our
king in the kingdom of Naples, which were to continue
there during the whole expedition; but upon the selling of
Pisa and the rest of the towns all was at an end, and the
king was obliged to repay the thirty thousand ducats which
the Florentines had lent him, and all this by the dis-
obedience and whisperings of some persons about the king,
who had given private encouragement to Entragues to act
thus in the business.

About the same time, in the beginning of the year 1496,
the Lord de Montpensier, the Lord Virgil Ursini, Signor
Camillo Vitelli, and the rest of the French officers, seeing
that all was lost, took the field, and made themselves masters
of several small towns; upon which King Ferrand, the son
of Alphonso (who was turned monk, as you have heard
before), with the Marquis of Mantua, brother to the Lord
Montpensier's wife†, and captain-general of the Venetians,
drew out against them, and found the Lord de Montpensier
in a town called Atella, situated very disadvantageously for
the supply of provisions. The enemy immediately encamped
on a hill, and fortified themselves as strongly as they could,
not daring to venture a battle, for King Ferrand and the
Marquis of Mantua had been beaten by us in every engagement they had fought. The Venetians had in pledge six

---

* For twenty-four thousand florins.—SISMONDI, xii. 379.
† Clara de Gonzaga.

towns* in Apulia, of very great importance, namely, Brindisi, Trani, Gallipoli, Crana, Otranto, Monopoli, and Tarento, which last they had taken from us. And they lent some money to King Ferrand, but they valued the service of their forces in that kingdom so high, that it was computed and charged upon the said towns at two hundred and fifty thousand ducats, besides what they demanded for the fortifications and other expenses in keeping them; so that I am persuaded they have no intention to restore them†; for it is not their custom to part with anything that is for their convenience, as those towns are, lying all upon the Gulf of Venice, and making them absolute lords of it, from Venice to Otranto, which is nine hundred miles complete. The Pope, indeed, has Ancona and some few other towns between them; but all must pay duties to the Venetians, or there is no passing through the Gulf; so that it was a great advantage to them to have those towns in their hands, and perhaps more than many people imagine, for they receive from them great quantities of corn and oil, which are two commodities very beneficial and necessary for them.

At the town of Atella† above-mentioned, our troops began to mutiny, not only for provisions (which were beginning to fail), but for their pay, for there was already an arrear due to them for above eighteen months, and they had suffered very great hardships. The Swiss, too, were largely in arrear, but not altogether so much, for all the money the Lord de Montpensier could raise in that kingdom went to the payment of them, and yet they had above a year due to them. They had, however, plundered several little villages, and got a considerable booty. If the forty thousand ducats which had been so often promised had been sent in time, or had they known they would receive them at Florence, this mutiny had never happened; but now all that was done

* The Venetians were forced to surrender all these towns to Ferdinand the Catholic in 1509, after the bloody battle of Agradel, which utterly broke their power.

† Atella, a town of the kingdom of Naples, lies intrenched among the Apennines, on the western border of the Basilicate. It is situated in a broad valley encompassed by a lofty amphitheatre of hills, through which flows a little river, tributary to the Ofanto, and watering the town.

proceeded merely from despair. Several of the commanders
have told me since, that if our men would have agreed to
have ventured a battle, in all likelihood the victory would
been theirs, or if they had lost it, it could not have been
with the destruction of half so many as they lost by their
base and dishonourable surrender. The Lords de Montpensier and Virgil Ursini would willingly have fought, and
they died in prison, and not one of the articles of their
treaty was observed to them. These two gentlemen accused
the Lord de Percy (a young gentleman of Auvergne), of
having been the occasion of their not fighting; and the
truth is, the Lord de Percy was an ill-conditioned and
mutinous knight.

There were two sorts of Germans in that army* ; one
was the Swiss, of whom we had about one thousand five
hundred, who had been with us from the beginning of our
expedition, and they served us faithfully and as well as men
could do to the very last. There was another commonly
called Lansquenets, which is as much as to say, Companions
of the Country, and these have a natural antipathy to the
Swiss; they are a collection from all the countries upon the
Rhine, Swabia, the Pays de Vaux in Sequania, and Guelderland; and they consisted of about seven or eight hundred
men lately sent thither, with two months' pay in advance,
which was spent by them before they arrived. Seeing
themselves in such danger and distress, they retained not
that affection to us which the Swiss did, but began to hold
parleys, and by degrees revolted to the enemy; upon which
and the division among our commanders, the soldiers made
a villanous and infamous agreement, which King Ferrand
swore to observe; for the Marquis of Mantua took great
care to secure the person of the Lord de Montpensier, his
brother-in-law.

By the said agreement they delivered themselves into the
hands of their enemies, gave them all the artillery which be-

---

* Du Bos similarly discriminates between the character of the German
Landsknechts and the Swiss. He says: " The Lansquenets were, generally speaking, much better made men, and much better looking in their
armour, than the Swiss infantry; but they were incapable of discipline.
Unlike the Swiss, they paid no obedience to their commanders, and had
no friendship for their comrades."—LIGUE DE CAMBRAY, vol. i. p. 66.

longed to our king, and promised to restore all the places which our. king possessed in that kingdom, as well in Calabria, where the Lord d'Aubigny commanded, as in Abruzzo, where the Lord Gracian des Guerres was chief; besides Gaeta and Tarento. Upon which terms King Ferrand undertook to send them into Provence by sea, and their baggage with them, which was worth little or nothing.* They were about five or six thousand men, and King Ferrand caused them to be conducted to Naples. So ignominious an agreement had not been made before in our times, nor did I ever read of any like it, unless it was that which (as Titus Livius reports †) was made by the two Roman consuls with the Samnites (who are now supposed to be the inhabitants of Beneventum) at a certain place upon the mountains, which was then called the Caudine Forks; but the Romans refused to ratify and confirm it, and sent the two consuls back prisoners to the enemy.

If our army had fought and been defeated, we had not lost so great a number of men as we did, for two-thirds of them died of famine and plague on ship-board, and in the Isle of Procida, whither they were sent afterwards by King Ferrand; among the rest, the Lord de Montpensier died there, some say of poison, others of a fever, (which I rather believe). And I think of their whole number there came not above one thousand five hundred back; for of the Swiss, who were one thousand three hundred, there returned not above three hundred and fifty, and those in a weak and miserable

* The capitulation was signed at Atella on the 21st of July, 1496. The terms were soon arranged with the King of Naples, who had no desire but to rid his country of the invaders. It was agreed that if the French commander did not receive assistance in thirty days, he should evacuate Atella, and cause every place holding under him in the kingdom of Naples, with all its artillery, to be surrendered to King Ferdinand, and that, on these conditions, his soldiers should be furnished with vessels to transport them back to France; that the foreign mercenaries should be permitted to return to their own homes; and that a general amnesty should be extended to such Neapolitans as returned to their allegiance in fifteen days. The reproach which Commines casts on the authors of this treaty is certainly unmerited, and comes with an ill grace from a court which was wasting in riotous indulgence the very resources indispensable to the brave and loyal subjects who were endeavouring to maintain its honour in a foreign land.

† In the eleventh book of his history.

condition. These Swiss were highly to be commended for their loyalty; for they would never bear arms under King Ferrand, but chose rather to die, as many of them did in the island of Procida, some of a calenture, some of other diseases, and some of very hunger; for it is not to be imagined in what want of food they were kept on ship-board, and how long. I saw some of those who returned, and particularly the Swiss, who brought back all their colours; but by their looks one might see what they had suffered; for all of them were so very sick, that when they came ashore to take a little air, they could not walk without being supported. The Lord Virgil Ursini by his articles was to have had liberty to return into his own country with his son *, and his whole regiment; but they detained him, and his lawful son with him (of which sort he had but one); yet he had a bastard who was a brave man, called Signor Carlo †; but he was killed by certain Italians who were in his company upon the road. Had this misfortune fallen upon any but those who had a hand in the treaty, it had been a very deplorable accident.‡

* Gian Giordano Orsini, Lord of Bracciano.
† Carlo Orsini, Count of Anguillara.
‡ The misfortunes of the French, after the surrender of Atella, are thus described by Mr. Prescott: "Unfortunately Montpensier was unable to enforce the full performance of his own treaty: as many of the French refused to deliver up the places entrusted to them, under the pretence that their authority was derived not from the viceroy but from the king himself. During the discussion of this point, the French troops were removed to Baiæ and Pozzuolo and the adjacent places on the coast. The unhealthiness of the situation, together with that of the autumnal season and an intemperate indulgence in fruit and wine, soon brought on an epidemic among the soldiers, which swept them off in great numbers. The gallant Montpensier was one of the first victims. He refused the earnest solicitations of his brother-in-law, the Marquis of Mantua, to quit his unfortunate companions, and retire to a place of safety in the interior. The shore was literally strewed with the bodies of the dying and the dead. Of the whole number of Frenchmen, amounting to not less than five thousand, who marched out of Atella, not more than five hundred ever reached their native country. The Swiss and other mercenaries were scarcely more fortunate. 'They made their way back as they could, through Italy,' says Giovio, 'in the most deplorable state of destitution and suffering; the gaze of all, and a sad example of the caprice of fortune.' Such was the miserable fate of that brilliant and formidable army which, scarcely two years before, had poured down

Not long after King Ferrand had gained this honour, and newly married the daughter of his grandfather King Ferrand, whom he had by the present King of Castile's sister (so that his queen was sister to his own father King Alphonso), and who was a young lady not above thirteen or fourteen years old, he fell into a hectic fever, and died in a few days.* He left the possession of his kingdom to King Frederic (now reigning) who was his uncle. I cannot think of this marriage without horror, though there were several of the same nature in that family within the memory of man, and that within the space of thirty years. He died not long after that infamous treaty of Atella in the year 1496. King Ferrand, when he was living, and Frederic since his accession to the throne, excused themselves, because the Lord de Montpensier had not surrendered the towns that were mentioned in the articles of agreement; but it was not in his power, for Gaeta and other places were not in his hands; and indeed though he was our king's lieutenant in that kingdom, yet the governors of the respective towns were not bound to surrender them at his command, though if they had, our king had been no great loser by the bargain; for they afterwards cost a great deal to repair and victual: and so they were lost at last. I was present myself when provisions were sent, once to the castles of Naples, and thrice to Gaeta; and I think I should not mistake if I said those four supplies cost the king above three hundred thousand francs; and yet all came to nothing.

on the fair fields of Italy in all the insolence of expected conquest."— *History of Ferdinand and Isabella,* vol. ii. p. 300.

* Ferdinand died on the 7th of September, 1496, in the twenty-eighth year of his age, and second of his reign. He was the fifth monarch who, in the brief compass of three years, had sat on the disastrous throne of Naples.

CH. XXII.—How several Plots were formed (in favour of our King) by
some of the Italian Princes, not only for the Recovery of Naples, but
for the Destruction of the Duke of Milan; how they miscarried for
want of Supplies; and how another Design against Genoa came to
the same ill End.—1496.

THE king, after his return from his expedition to Naples,
as we have already mentioned, continued a long time at
Lyons, entertaining himself with jousts and tournaments;
and though still desirous to regain the places he had lost in
the kingdom of Naples, whatever it cost him, he would take
no pains to manage his own affairs. He had very good
intelligence in Italy, and great designs were set on foot in
his favour; which could easily have been managed by the
kingdom of France, which is very populous, and plentiful in
corn, especially in Languedoc and Provence, and other countries, out of which it is no difficult task to raise money.
But if any other prince besides the King of France should
embrace the cause of the Italians, and undertake their assistance, it would impoverish and exhaust him to no purpose;
for they will do nothing without money; nor, indeed, are
they able to do anything, unless it be the Duke of Milan, or
some of the great States. But a private governor or general,
how well affected soever he may be to the House of France,
and its pretensions to the kingdom of Naples, or the duchy
of Milan, let him be as devoted as he will to its interest
(and from Italians you must expect nothing more than
partisanship), yet he cannot serve that house long after the
pay begins to fail; for the poor general would be deserted
by his own soldiers, and would himself be utterly undone;
because for the most part they have nothing wherewith to
raise men, but their reputation and credit; and the soldiers
are paid by the general, and the general by him who employs
him in his service.

But as to the designs which I have mentioned as being so
considerable, they began before the surrender of Gaeta, upon
the Duke of Milan's not keeping his promise, and continued
for two years after our king's return. As for the Duke of
Milan, he did not break his promise so much out of malice

and deceit, as through fear; for he was fearful that the king could not have so great an addition to his power, without some diminution of his own; besides, he did not think our king a prince of any firmness or resolution. At length it was concluded that the Duke of Orleans should march to Asti with a considerable body of forces; and I saw him and his troops ready to set out. We were secure of the Duke of Ferrara with five hundred men-at-arms and two thousand foot (though he was the Duke of Milan's father-in-law); for he joined with us to preserve himself against the danger he was in between the Duke and the Venetians, who not long previously (as I have said before*) had taken from him the the Polesan, and endeavoured all they could to ruin him: upon which account he preferred his own and his children's safety before the friendship of his son-in-law; and perhaps he was of opinion that his son-in-law would, by his mediation, come to some agreement with the king, when he found himself in danger. We had also engaged the Marquis of Mantua on our side, who had been, and was at that time general for the Venetians; but they were so jealous of him, and he so dissatisfied with them, that he remained with three hundred men-at-arms with his father-in-law the Duke of Ferrara, for his wife was sister to the Duchess of Milan, and the Duke of Ferrara's daughter. Signor John Bentivoglio (who was governor, and as it were Prince of Bologna,) was to have provided a hundred and fifty men-at-arms, besides the horse and foot which his two sons were to have brought with them, and his country was well situated for an attack on the Duke of Milan. The Florentines, who saw they were utterly undone, and were afraid they should be dispossessed of Pisa and the rest of their towns, unless they exerted themselves, and did something extraordinary in this critical juncture of affairs, agreed to assist us with eight hundred men-at-arms, and five thousand foot, and to maintain them at their own expense; and they had six months' pay ready in bank. The Ursini and the Prefect of Rome† (who was brother to the Cardinal of St. Peter ad Vincula, so often mentioned before), who were

* See Book VII. Chap. 3.
† Giovanni della Rovere, Duke of Sora. See Book VII. Chap. 16.

in the king's pay, would have brought a thousand men-at-arms, but you must know the retinue and equipage of their men-at-arms is not so great as ours; for they have no archers, but their pay is alike; for the pay of a man-at-arms (if he is well paid) is one hundred ducats a year, but if he be attended by archers it is double. These soldiers the king would have paid, but the Florentines were to have paid their own forces. The Duke of Ferrara, the Marquis of Mantua, and Signor Bentivoglio desired only their expenses; for they expected their reward out of the towns which they should take from the Duke of Milan, had he been suddenly invaded by the Duke of Orleans' forces. And of those who were his confederates, none would have been able to avoid siding with the king against the Venetians; and for less than eighty thousand crowns the king could have kept all these Italians together a long time; and if the Duke of Milan had been conquered, the kingdom of Naples would have fallen of course.

The miscarriage of this important design proceeded merely from the Duke of Orleans' inconstancy. He intended over-night to set out in the morning; he had sent all his equipage, baggage, and whatever else belonged to his person, before him; so that there was nothing to follow but himself. His army, consisting of eight hundred French men-at-arms and six thousand foot (among whom were four hundred Swiss), lay ready at Asti, and their pay in advance in their pockets; yet on a sudden he changed his mind, and made two several requests to the king, that the expedition might be once more debated before the council; and it was done twice. I was present on both occasions: the result was, *nemine contradicente* (though there were always ten or twelve in council), that he should proceed on the expedition; because they had given their above-mentioned friends in Italy repeated assurances of his coming; and they had raised men, and been at great expense in expectation of him. But the Duke of Orleans (either by the advice of some other person, or through his own unwillingness to go, on account of the king's illness, and his being the next heir to the crown,) plainly declared he would not undertake that enterprise upon any quarrel of his own; but as he was the king's lieutenant, if his majesty pleased to command it, he would go with all his heart; and so the council broke up. The next day, and several days after, the Florentine envoys, and the rest of the ambassadors, pressed the king, that he would command the duke to go; but the king's answer was, that he would never send him to make war against his inclinations. And thus was that enterprise quashed in a moment, to the king's great displeasure, who had been at vast charges, and had great hopes of revenging himself on the Duke of Milan, considering his own alliances at that time, and what he might have had by Signor John James de Trivulce, who was lieutenant-general for the king; and that the Duke of Orleans was born, and had great interest and alliance in the duchy of Milan, where many persons would have supported him.

But though this design miscarried, another revived, nay two or three at a time, in Genoa, which is a place ever prone to revolutions. One was contrived by Signor Baptista di Campoforgoso*, a great leader of faction in Genoa; but he was banished, and his party could do nothing; nor could the family of Doria, who were gentlemen, but the Campoforgosi were not. The Dorias are of the same party with the Campoforgosi, but cannot be Doges themselves, because they are gentlemen; for no gentleman is capable of being Doge by their laws. But this Baptista had been Doge not long before, but was supplanted by his uncle the Cardinal of Genoa, who put the government into the hands of the Duke of Milan, under whom the city was governed by the Adorni, who also are not gentlemen; yet they have been often Doges, and are supported by the house of the Spinoli, who are gentlemen. The nobility in Genoa make Doges, but cannot be made so themselves. This Signor Baptista expected his whole party (both in the city and country) would take arms in his favour, and that the king would obtain the sovereignty, but the government would fall into the hands of himself and his party; and they did not question but to drive out the rest.

* Baptista Fregosi was raised to the dignity of Doge of Genoa in 1478. Under the pretext that he was plotting the subjection of Genoa to the Emperor, his uncle, Cardinal Fregosi, in concert with Lazaro Doria, arrested him, and procured his banishment, in 1483.—SISMONDI, xi. 287.

The other design was set on foot by several persons in Savona, who addressed themselves to the Cardinal of St. Peter ad Vincula, assuring him they would deliver up the town, provided their liberties and privileges might be secured to them; for they were then under the jurisdiction of Genoa, and paid heavy duties. If he could have made himself master of this town, he would have reduced Genoa to great straits, considering Provence was our king's own country, and Savoy at his command. Upon this news, the king sent to Signor John James di Trivulce to assist the said Baptista di Campoforgoso with such supplies as might carry him to the very walls of Genoa, to see whether his party would rise. On the other side he was pressed hard by the Cardinal of St. Peter ad Vincula, who also obtained a letter to Trivulce from the king, commanding him to furnish the Cardinal with men enough to conduct him to Savona; and he received the same message by word of mouth from the Lord of Sernon in Provence, who was the Cardinal's friend, and a bold talker. The king also sent orders to Signor James di Trivulce to contrive matters so as to support both parties, and yet do nothing against the Duke of Milan, or contrary to the peace that had been made with him the year before; but these orders were downright contradictions.

And after this manner the affairs of great princes are managed, when they are not present themselves, or are too hasty in commanding letters and messengers to be despatched, without mature and requisite deliberation. In this case, if one considers what was required by Signor Baptista di Campoforgoso and the Cardinal, we shall find that it was impossible to supply them both at a time. For to approach the walls of Genoa without a considerable body of forces, was ridiculous and impracticable, by reason of the numbers and courage of the inhabitants; and to have supplied the Cardinal had been to have divided his own army into three bodies, for part must of necessity have remained with Signor John James; and, besides, the alarm was taken, and the Duke of Milan, the Venetians, Don Frederic, and the Pope, had all of them sent forces to Genoa and Savona, suspecting their intended revolt.

Besides these two, Signor John James Trivulce had a

third design of his own, and that was, to march directly with all his forces against the Duke of Milan, and lay those other enterprises aside ; and certainly if he had been permitted to pursue his own scheme, he would have performed some great action; for, under pretence that he could not otherwise protect such as were engaged in the designs upon Genoa and Savona, he posted himself upon the high road from Alessandria to Genoa (and indeed the Duke of Milan could send forces no other way to molest us), and possessed himself of two or three small towns, without any resistance, pretending that this was no violation of the peace with the duke, for he was forced to it of necessity ; and that the king could not be said to have made war upon the duke by endeavouring to recover Genoa and Savona, because they held of the king, and had forfeited their allegiance.   However, to satisfy the Cardinal, Signor John James di Trivulce sent part of his army to Savona; but he found the garrison reinforced and his designs defeated, and so he marched back. He sent other troops to Signor Baptista, to attempt something upon Genoa, and great matters were expected from thence; but before they had marched four leagues, both the French and Swiss who were in his company grew suspicious of him (though I think it was wrongfully), and it was well things happened so ; for their number being very inconsiderable, they would have exposed themselves to great danger if their party in the town had not risen.   Thus all these enterprises and designs miscarried, and the Duke of Milan became strong; but he had run great danger if Signor John James had not been countermanded.   Our army marched back, our foot were disbanded, the small towns restored, and the war was concluded, but with little advantage to the king, considering what expense he had been at in military preparations.

CH. XXIII.—Of certain Differences that arose between Charles King of France, and Ferrand King of Castile; and the Ambassadors who were sent by both of them to accommodate the Affair.—1497.

FROM the beginning of 1496, when the king had already been four months on this side of the mountains, till the year 1498, our forces lay still, and did nothing in Italy: I was present all that while with his majesty, and privy to most of his affairs. He went from Lyons to Moulins, and from Moulins to Tours, spending his time in nothing but jousts and tournaments wherever he came, without ever thinking of other affairs. Those who were in greatest reputation with him, were in great dissension among themselves, and it could hardly be greater. Some (as the Cardinal and seneschal) were for carrying on the war in Italy, because it was for their profit and advantage; the admiral* on the other side (who before that expedition had been the king's greatest favourite), opposed it in hopes to be restored to his former authority and to supplant his competitors; and in this posture things stood about a year and a half.

In the meantime our king sent ambassadors to the King and Queen of Castile, for his majesty desired to be at peace with them, because they were very powerful both at sea and land; and though at land they had done no extraordinary exploits, yet by sea they had given Kings Ferrand and Frederic very considerable assistance; for the island of Sicily is distant from Rhegio in Calabria only a league and a half. Some are of opinion it was formerly joined to the continent †, and in process of time separated from it by the sea. The opening is now ca"ed the Straits of Messina. From this island of Sicily, which belonged to the King and Queen of Castile, large supplies were sent to Naples, as well in caravels from Spain, as in men from the island, out of which several men-at-arms passed the sea into Calabria, with a good number of Spanish Genetaires, and made war against those

---

* Louis Malet. See Book VII. Chap. 1.
† Virgil was of this opinion, as appears by the following lines:—

"Ast, ubi digressum Siculæ te admoverit oræ
Ventus, et angusti rarescent lustra pelori;
Læva tibi tellus, et longo læva petantur
Æquora circuitu: dextrum fuge littus et undas
Hæc loca, vi quondam et vasta convulsa ruina
(Tantum ævi longinqua valet mutare vetustas)
Dissiluisse ferunt: cum protinus utraque tellus
Una foret, venit medio vi pontus, et undis
Hesperium Siculo latus abscidit: arvaque et urbes
Littore diductas, angusto interluit æstu."
                              VIRG. Æneid. III. 410—419.

who appeared for our king.   Their fleet was continually
joined with the confederates, and when they were united,
our king was too weak to meet them at sea; otherwise the
King of Castile had not done him much mischief.   It is true
a good body of his horse made an inroad into Languedoc,
plundered some few towns, and quartered up and down that
country for three or four days; but that was all, and no considerable damage done.   Monsieur de St. André * (of Bourbonnois) being then upon the frontier with some troops
belonging to the Duke of Bourbon, who was governor of
Languedoc, attempted to take Sausses †, a small town in Roussillon, from whence the enemy made all his incursions; for
the king had restored the said Roussillon to them about two
years before, in which province there is the territory of Perpignan, and this Sausses is in the middle of it.   The design
was great, because the town was strongly garrisoned with a
detachment of the King of Castile's own guards, and within
a league lay their whole army, which was more numerous
than ours, and ready to engage us.   However, Monsieur de
St. André managed his affairs so prudently, and with so
much secrecy, that in ten hours' time he took the town
(which I have seen) by assault ‡, and in it there were thirty
or forty Spanish gentlemen of good quality slain, and among
them the son of the Archbishop of St. James's §, besides
three or four hundred more.   They did not suppose we
should have been masters of it so soon, because they knew
not the goodness of our cannon, which certainly are the
finest and best in Europe.

No other but this action happened between these two
kings, and this was much to the dishonour of the King of
Castile, who had such a numerous army in the field.   But
when God Almighty is pleased to chastise a nation for its

* Guichard d'Albon, Lord of Saint-André and Oulches, was lieutenant-general for the king in Languedoc in the year 1496, and became
Bailiff of Montferrand in 1498.

† Salces, a village in the department of the Pyrénées Orientales, and
formerly the key of Roussillon.   The strong castle of Salces was garrisoned by the Spaniards in July, 1495, and from it they made frequent
incursions upon the territories of Narbonne and Carcassonne during
the ensuing winter.

‡ On Friday, the 8th of October, 1496.

§ Don Diego de Azevedo.

sins, He begins with such small and supportable afflictions ;
for the King and Queen of Castile were visited afterwards
with greater afflictions, and so were we too. The King and
Queen of Castile acted very imprudently, and were ill-
advised to forswear themselves to our master, especially after
he had been so friendly as. to restore Roussillon, which had
cost his father so much to fortify and defend, and which had
been mortgaged to him for 300,000 crowns; all which was
remitted to hinder him from disturbing our king in his intended conquest of Naples. Besides which, they renewed
the ancient alliances with 'not only king and king, kingdom
and kingdom, but the individual subjects on both sides were
mutually bound ; and they promised not to interrupt us in
our conquest, nor to marry any of their daughters with the
houses of either Naples, England, or Flanders; which offer
came first from themselves, and was made by one Friar
John de Mauleon, on the part of the Queen of Castile. Yet
as soon as they saw the war begun, and the king at Rome,
they sent their ambassadors to all the neighbouring states
to make an alliance against our king; and particularly to
Venice, where I was resident at that time; and there the
league (which I have spoken of so much) was made between
the Pope, the King of the Romans, the Signory of Venice,
the Spaniards, and the Duke of Milan; and immediately they
began to act offensively against our king, and to declare that
their former obligation had become void, and they were no
longer bound to observe it, especially that article about the
marriage of their daughters (of whom they had four, and
but one son), though they first made that offer of themselves,
as you have already heard.

But to proceed in my history. After the wars in Italy
were over, and the king had nothing left in the kingdom of
Naples but Gaeta, which he lost afterwards,—after the rival
pretensions to Roussillon were adjusted, and each prince was
in possession of what was his own, they sent a gentleman
to King Charles, and with him certain monks of Montferrat,
it being the custom of Spain to manage all their negotiations
by such people, either out of hypocrisy and pretence of religion, or to save expense; for, as I said before, the treaty
about Roussillon was managed by Friar John de Mauleon.
These ambassadors, at their first audience, besought the

king that he would forget the injury that had been done
him by the King and Queen of Castile (which king and queen
are always mentioned together, because Castile came by
her, and she had in that country the principal authority,
and it was a marriage of more than ordinary honour). Then
they began to propose a truce, in which their whole league
was to be comprehended, and our king was to keep Gaeta
in his possession, and what other places were then in his
hands in the kingdom of Naples ; that during the truce his
majesty might victual them as he pleased ; and that a time
and place should be appointed, at which ambassadors from
all the parties to the league (or as many as desired it) should
meet to conclude a final peace; after which the King and
Queen of Spain intended to pursue the conquest of the
Moors, and, having finished that, to pass over from Granada
into Africa against the King of Fez, whose kingdom reaches
to the coast on the other side of that sea. However, some
say they never designed to do this, but were resolved to be
satisfied with the conquest of the kingdom of Granada,
which indeed was a glorious action, and the fairest acquisition which had been gained, not only in our times, but by
all their predecessors ; and I wish for their own sakes they
had rested there, and kept their promise to our king.

With these ambassadors of theirs our king sent back the
Lord of Clerieux *, in Dauphiny, and endeavoured to conclude either a separate peace or a truce with them, without
comprehending any of the rest of the confederates ; but if
the king had accepted their overture, he had preserved
Gaeta, which might have been sufficient for the recovery of
the whole kingdom, considering what friends his majesty had
in it. When the Lord of Clerieux returned, he brought new
propositions, for Gaeta was lost before he got to Castile.
These propositions were, that the ancient alliance between the
two crowns should be renewed, and that by common consent
and expense they should endeavour the conquest of Italy,
and that both the kings should be personally present in that
expedition.† But first they insisted that a general truce

* Guillaume de Poitiers, Lord of Clerieu, and titular Marquis of
Cotron in Calabria.

† "The Spanish writers," says Mr. Prescott, "impute the first sug-
gestion of this project for the conquest and division of the kingdom of

might be concluded, wherein the whole league should be comprehended, and a day and place appointed in Piedmont, to which each of them might send their ambassadors; for they were desirous to acquit themselves honourably towards their confederates. But all this overture, in my opinion, (and I have understood as much since), was but an artifice to gain time, and suffer King Ferrand and his successor King Frederic to breathe a little. However, they would have been contented to have had that kingdom to themselves, and their title was better than that of those who possessed it; but our king's title (which was the house of Anjou's) was better than either; yet, considering the nature of the country, and the people who inhabit it, I think he has best right to it that can keep possession of it, so strangely are they inclined to revolutions.

After this, the king sent Clerieux back again into Spain, and with him one Michel de Grammont, with certain new proposals. This Lord de Clerieux had some little affection for the house of Arragon, and hoped to have the marquisate of Cotron in Calabria, which the King of Spain obtained among the last conquests which he made in that province. Clerieux pretended it was his, for he is an honest man, but something too credulous, especially of such great persons. The second time he returned, he brought back with him another ambassador from them, and the Lord de Clerieux reported that the King and Queen of Castile would be contented to take Calabria (which is the part of Italy that lies next Sicily) for their whole interest in that kingdom, and that our king should have the rest; he offered likewise that the King of Castile should be present in person in this in-

Naples by the combined powers of France and Spain, to the French, who, they say, went so far as to specify the details of the partition subsequently adopted; according to which the two Calabrias were assigned to Spain. However this may be, there is little doubt that Ferdinand had long entertained the idea of asserting his claim at some time or other to the crown of Naples. The accession of Frederic, in particular, had given great umbrage to the Spanish monarch; and the Castilian envoy, Garcilasso de la Vega, agreeably to the instructions of his court, urged Alexander the Sixth to withhold the investiture of the kingdom from Frederic, but unavailingly, as the Pope's interests were too closely connected by marriage with those of the royal family of Naples."— *History of Ferdinand and Isabella*, vol. ii. p. 311.

tended expedition, and contribute as much towards paying
the army as our king; and, indeed, he was at that time master of four or five fortified towns in Calabria, and among the
rest was Cotron, which is not only a strong, but a beautiful
city.   I was present when the ambassador made his report,
and most were of opinion he had been imposed upon, and
that it would be necessary to send another ambassador of
greater sagacity, to search more narrowly into the affair.
Upon which the Lord du Bouchage was joined with him in
the embassy.   He was a person of great wisdom and penetration in state affairs, and had enjoyed places of great trust
and honour in the late king's reign, and was still highly
valued and esteemed by his son.   The Spanish ambassador,
who came along with the Lord de Clerieux, would never
confirm what he had said; only he told us, that he believed
Monsieur de Clerieux would not have made that report, if
the King and Queen of Castile had not said it; which gave
us the more suspicion it was a trick; and, besides, nobody
could believe the King of Spain would go thither in person,
or that he would, or indeed could, bear an equal share of the
expense with our master.

As soon as the Lord du Bouchage, Monsieur de Clerieux,
Michel de Grammont, and the rest of our ambassadors, were
arrived at the court of the King and Queen of Castile, they
ordered them to be lodged in apartments where none could
converse with them, and appointed persons to have an eye
over them, and they were admitted to three private audiences
of the king and queen.   When the Lord du Bouchage had acquainted them with what the Lord de Clerieux had reported
to his master, and Michel de Grammont had confirmed it,
they answered, that they might have said some such thing by
way of discourse, but not otherwise, yet they would readily
engage themselves in any peace that should be for our
master's honour and advantage.   The Lord de Clerieux was
very uneasy at their answer (and with reason), and justified
to their faces, in the presence of the Lord du Bouchage, that
they had made him this offer.   However, the Lord du Bouchage and the other ambassadors concluded a truce for two
months *, without comprehending the league in it; but in-

* This truce was signed on the 5th of March, 1497, and was to last
until the end of October in that year.—SISMONDI, xii. 444.

cluding the princes who had married their daughters, and the fathers of their sons-in-law (namely, the King of the Romans, and the King of England), for the Prince of Wales* was but very young at that time. The King and Queen of Castile had four daughters; the eldest was a widow, and married to the son of the King of Portugal†, who died lately, having broken his neck in her sight as he was passing a career upon a jennet before her, three months after their marriage; and they had one daughter‡ unmarried.

As soon as the Lord du Bouchage was arrived, and had informed the king of his reception at the Spanish court, his majesty was sensible he had acted wisely in sending him, for now he was assured of what he but suspected before, and that was, the credulity of the Lord de Clerieux. The Lord du Bouchage told him, moreover, that all he could obtain was that truce, which, however, his majesty had liberty either to accept or reject. The king confirmed it, and therein he did wisely, for it broke up that confederacy which had given so much disturbance to his affairs, and which hitherto he had been unable to dissolve, though he had tried all possible means to do it. The Lord du Bouchage also acquainted his majesty, that they would send ambassadors to him with power to conclude a peace; and of this the King and Queen of Castile had assured him when he had his audience of leave. He told our king also, that at his coming away he left their only son, the Prince of Castile, very dangerously ill.

---

* Arthur, son of King Henry VII. of England, was born on the 20th of September, 1486, and married to Catherine of Arragon on the 12th of November, 1501. But a few months after his marriage the young prince sickened and died, and his widow was contracted to his brother Henry, afterwards Henry VIII.

† Alphonso, son of John II., King of Portugal, was born on the 18th of May, 1475, and married to Isabella of Castile in 1490. He died of a fall from his horse in the following year, and his widow married Emanuel, his successor on the throne.

‡ This was the Infanta Maria, who married her brother-in-law, Emanuel of Portugal, after the death of her sister Isabella. The fourth daughter of Ferdinand and Isabella was named Juana, and married Philip, Archduke of Austria, in 1496.

Ch. XXIV.—A Digression concerning the Fortunes and Misfortunes which happened to the House of Castile in the Author's Time.—1497.

THE Lord du Bouchage, ten or twelve days after his return into France, received letters from a herald, whom he had left behind to wait on the ambassadors that were to come from thence. The letters were to this purpose, that he must not wonder at their deferring the embassy, because of the death of the Prince of Castile * (as they called him), to the unspeakable grief of the king and queen, but especially of the queen, who was more like to die than to live; and certainly I never heard of so solemn and so universal a mourning for any prince in Europe. I have since been informed by ambassadors, that all the tradesmen put themselves into black clothes, and shut up their shops for forty days together; the nobility and gentry covered their mules with black cloth down to their very knees, so that there was nothing of them to be seen but their eyes; and set up black banners upon all the gates of the cities. When the Lady Margaret (daughter to the King of the Romans †, sister to the Archduke of Austria ‡, and wife to the said Prince of Castile) was informed of the news of his death, she miscarried of a daughter (being six months gone with child), which was born dead. What a terrible blow must this have been to a family which had known nothing before but felicity and renown, and had a larger territory (I mean by succession) than any other prince in Christendom! And, besides the late acquisition of Granada, they had forced the greatest monarch in Europe out of Italy, and defeated his enterprise, which was looked upon to be such a mighty action even by the Pope § himself, that he would have taken away the title of "Most Christian" from the King of France, and conferred it on the King of Castile, to whom several briefs were addressed with that title superscribed; but, because some of the Cardinals

* On the 4th of October, 1497, in the twentieth year of his age.
† Maximilian I., afterwards emperor.
‡ Philip I., Archduke of Austria.
§ Alexander VI.

opposed it, he gave him another title, which was, "The Most Catholic," by which title he is called now, and I suppose he will be styled so for ever at Rome. What a sad and surprising turn of fortune must this accident have been! at a time when they had reduced their kingdom to obedience, regulated the laws, settled the administration of justice, and were so well and happy in their own persons, as if God and man had conspired to advance their power and honour above all the rest of the princes in Europe.

Nor was this their only affliction, for their eldest daughter (the dearest thing to them in the world after the death of her brother) was forced to leave them, having some few days before been married to Emanuel*, the young King of Portugal. He was then indeed but Prince of Portugal; but the crown of Portugal fell to him by the death of the last King of Portugal, who had most barbarously caused the head of his father-in-law † to be cut off, and killed his wife's brother‡ with his own hand (who was elder brother to the king that now reigns in Portugal), and kept this present king in perpetual fear, and killed his own brother before his wife's face, as they were sitting at dinner, to make way for one of his bastards§ to be king. After which cruelties he lived in continual fear and suspicion, and not long after his only son broke his neck by falling off his mule, as you have heard; and he was the first husband to the lady of whom I am now speaking, and who is Queen of Portugal at present, into which kingdom she has been twice married; and by report she is one of the wisest and most honourable persons in the world.

---

* Emanuel, surnamed the Fortunate, was the son of Ferdinand, Duke of Viseo. He succeeded his cousin, John II., on the throne of Portugal in 1495, and died on the 13th of December, 1521.

† This is a mistake. Eleanor of Portugal was the daughter of Ferdinand, Duke of Viseo; but it was Ferdinand, Duke of Braganza, who was beheaded by order of John II. in 1483, on the charge of having revealed secrets of state.

‡ James of Portugal, Duke of Viseo, having conspired against John II. was stabbed by him on the 23rd of August, 1484.

§ George, son of John II. and Anne de Mendoza. His father wished to legitimate him in order to leave him the crown; but the Pope interposed, at the request of Queen Eleanor, and George was made Duke of Aveiro.—ANSELME, i. 668.

But, to continue our relation of the miserable accidents which in a short space befel the King and Queen of Castile, who had lived in so much glory and felicity to the fiftieth year of their age or more, you must know they had married their eldest daughter to the King of Portugal, first that all Spain might be in peace; for they were entirely possessed of all its provinces, except the kingdom of Navarre, which they governed as they pleased, and in which they had also four of the strongest towns. Secondly, to adjust and compose the difference about her dower and marriage-portion: and, thirdly, for the benefit and advantage of some of the grandees of Portugal, who were in the King of Castile's interest; for by this match those lords who were banished that country upon the death of the two princes above-mentioned, and had had their estates confiscated (which continues to this day, though the crime of which they were accused was only endeavouring to set this king up who now reigns), had estates given them in Castile; and their lands in Portugal, which were forfeited by the attainder, were assigned to the queen's use. And yet, notwithstanding all these considerations, the King and Queen of Castile were extremely troubled at this match; for you must understand there is no nation in Europe that the Spaniards abhor and deride so much as they do the Portuguese. So that it was no small mortification to them that they had married their daughter to a person that was not pleasing to the Castilians and the rest of their subjects, and had it been to be done again, it would never have been done; which must needs have been a great affliction to them, and the greater, because she had to leave them. But, having mastered their sorrow as well as they could, they conducted them through all the chief cities in their kingdoms, caused the King of Portugal to be received as their prince, his queen as princess, and declared them their successors after their decease. And now a little comfort came to them; for their daughter, Princess of Castile and Queen of Portugal, was pregnant of a child. But then followed the consummation of their sorrows, this young lady, whom they loved and valued so highly, died in childbed of a son about a month since, and it is now October 1498. Though the queen died, yet her son lived, and is

T 4

called Emanuel* after his father; yet I am informed their affliction is so great, they would have given God thanks to have taken them with their daughter.

All these great misfortunes happened to them in three months' space; nor were we without our share of afflictions; for, before the death of the above-mentioned princess, we in this kingdom were chastised and afflicted by the death of King Charles VIII., of whom I have spoken so much, and who died as you shall hear hereafter; and it seemed as if God had been offended with both these illustrious families, and would not suffer the one to triumph over the other. No such revolution happens in a kingdom, but it is generally attended with very sad consequences, and though possibly some may be gainers, yet there will be a hundred losers to one who profits, besides the changing of a man's whole life and conversation; for that which pleases one king will hardly be agreeable to another. And (as I have said in another place) he that reflects upon the sudden and severe chastisements which God has inflicted on the great princes of Europe within these thirty years, shall find them more and greater than in two hundred years before, including France, Castile, Portugal, England, the Kingdom of Naples, Flanders, and Bretagne; and if any should attempt to give a particular account of all the misfortunes which I have seen, (and perhaps most of the persons, both men and women, on whom they fell), it would swell into a vast volume, and astonish the whole world, though it contained no more than the occurrences of ten years past. By these afflictions the power of God ought to be acknowledged and remembered; for the troubles which he lays upon princes are heavier, more grievous, and more lasting than those he lays upon inferior persons. So that, in short (upon a full and just consideration of all circumstances), I think the lives of princes are as much subject to afflictions and anxiety of mind as other men's, at least if they regard their own affairs themselves, and endeavour to prevent such miseries from falling upon them as they see have ruined their neighbours.

* This child, whose birth had cost so dear, was born on the 23rd of August, 1498, and received the name of Miguel, in honour of the saint on whose day he first saw the light. He died on the 19th of July, 1500. —ANSELME, i. 602.

It is true they punish their subjects at their pleasure, and God does the same by them; for, besides Him, there is none above them.   But that kingdom is most happy whose king is wise, and fears God and his commandments.

Thus have you seen, in few words, the misfortunes which within the space of three months befel these two great and potent kingdoms, which not long before were so incensed one against the other, so busy to subvert one another, and so intent upon their own interest and advancement, that nothing which they enjoyed was sufficient to satisfy their boundless ambition.   I confess (as I said before) no change happens in any government but some people are the better for it; yet when a prince dies suddenly his death is at first terrible to all.

———————

CH. XXV.—Of the magnificent Building which King Charles began not long before his Death; his good Inclination to reform the Church, the Laws, the Treasury, and himself; and how he died suddenly in this Resolution in his Castle at Amboise.—1498.

I HAVE now done with the affairs of Italy and Spain, and shall return to speak of our own misfortunes and losses in France (at which some people might possibly rejoice, especially if they gained anything by them), and give you an account of the death of Charles VIII., our king, who died suddenly at his castle of Amboise, where he had begun the most august and magnificent building that any prince had undertaken for one hundred years before, both in the town and the castle; and this appears by the towers, to the top of which one may ride on horseback.   As to his building in the town, the design was admirable, the model lofty, and the erection would have required a great deal of time.   He had brought his artificers (as his carvers, painters, and such like) from Italy, so that the whole fabric seemed the enterprise of a young prince who had no thought of dying so soon; for he collected whatever was commended to him either in France, Italy, or Flanders.   Besides this great work, his mind was bent upon another expedition into Italy, for he was sensible he had committed many great errors in his first; he spoke often of them, and resolved, if ever he recovered what he had lost in that country, he would keep it better than he had done; and, having partisans and intelligence in all places, he thought it not impossible but he might return and recover the kingdom of Naples; to which purpose he resolved to send thither a body of fifteen hundred Italian men-at-arms under the command of the Marquis of Mantua, the Ursini, the Vitelli, and the Prefect of Rome, who was brother to the Cardinal of St. Peter ad Vincula; and the Lord d'Aubigny, who had done such good service in Calabria, was to march into the territories of the Florentines, who were to bear half the charges for six months. His first attempt was to have been upon Pisa, or the adjacent small towns; and then, joining all his forces, to march in one body into the kingdom of Naples, from whence messengers were sent to him continually. Pope Alexander VI., who now reigns, being offended with the Venetians, endeavoured to come into the alliance, and carried on private intrigues for the purpose by means of an agent that lay incognito, whom I privately conveyed into the king's chamber not long before his death. The Venetians were ready to join with us against the Duke of Milan, and our negociations with Spain were as you have heard; the King of the Romans desired nothing so earnestly as the friendship of our king, and that they two might manage their own affairs in Italy by themselves. This King of the Romans was called Maximilian, and he was a mortal enemy to the Venetians, because they had taken and kept several places belonging to the house of Austria, of which he was next heir, and heir to the empire besides.

The king had also resolved within himself to live a more strict and religious life than he had formerly done, to regulate the laws, to reform the Church, and so to rectify his finances that he would not raise above one million two hundred thousand francs upon his subjects by way of annual tax, which was the sum given him by the three Estates at their convention at Tours, upon his accession to the throne. He intended the said sum should be employed in the defence of the kingdom, and for himself he would live upon his crown lands, as his predecessors had done before him; which he might easily

have done if it had been well managed, for his private revenue (comprehending his duties and customs) came to above
a million a year. Had he done as he resolved, it would have
been a great ease to the people, who pay now above two
millions and a half. He was very earnest likewise to have
reformed the abuses in the order of St. Benedict and others.
He got good preachers about him, and was a constant
hearer of them. He would fain have ordered it so that a
bishop should have enjoyed but one bishopric, a cardinal
two, and that all should have been obliged to be resident
upon their benefices; but he would have found it a difficult
task to have persuaded the clergy to it. He gave alms
liberally to the poor not many days before his death, as I
was since informed by his confessor the Bishop of Angers*,
who is a very eminent prelate. He had erected also a place
for public audience†, where he heard and dispatched causes,
especially for the benefit of the poor; in which place I saw
him for two hours together, not above a week before he
died; after which time I never saw him again. Matters of
great moment were not dispatched at these audiences, but
he had set up that court to keep people in awe, and especially his officers, some of whom he suspended for bribery and
corruption.

The king being in such great glory in relation to this
world, and in such a good mind as to God, on the 7th of
April, 1498, being the eve of Palm Sunday, took his queen
(Anne of Bretagne) by the hand, and led her out of her
chamber to a place where she had never been before, to see
them play at tennis in the castle-ditch. They entered
together into a gallery called the Haquelebac Gallery, upon
the account of its having been formerly guarded by one
Haquelebac. It was the nastiest place about the castle,
broken down at the entrance, and everybody committed a
nuisance in it that would. The king was not a tall man,
yet he knocked his head as he went in. He spent some
time in looking upon the players, and talked freely with
everybody. I was not there myself (for I had gone to my

* Jean de Rely, a native of Arras, was made Bishop of Angers on
the 1st of December, 1491, and died at Saumur on the 27th of March,
1498.
† By letters dated on the 30th of December, 1497.

country-house about a week before) but his confessor the
Bishop of Angers, and the gentlemen of his bed-chamber,
who were then about him, told me what I write.   The
last expression he used whilst he was in health was, that he
hoped never to commit a mortal sin again, nor a venial sin
if he could help it; and with those words in his mouth he
fell down backwards, and lost his speech. It was about two in
in the afternoon when he fell, and he lay motionless till eleven
o'clock at night. Thrice he recovered his speech, but he quickly
lost it again, as his confessor told me, who had confessed
him twice that week, once of course, and a second time upon
occasion of his touching for the king's evil. Every one
went into the gallery that pleased, where the king was laid
upon a coarse bed; and he never left it till he died, which
was nine hours after. The confessor told me that every
time he recovered his speech he called out upon God, the
glorious Virgin Mary, St. Claude, and St. Blaise, to assist
him. And thus died that great and powerful monarch in a
sordid and filthy place, though he had so many magnificent
palaces of his own, and was building another more stately
than any of them, yet he died in this poor chamber. How
plain, then, and natural is it, from these two examples, for us
to acknowledge the power and omnipotence of God, and
that our life is but a span and a trifle, though we are so
greedy and ambitious after the riches of this world; and
that princes no more than peasants are able to resist the
Almighty.

CH. XXVL—How holy Friar Jerome was burned at Florence by the
Malice and Solicitation of the Pope, and several Venetians and Florentines who were his Enemies.—1498.

IN my relation of the affairs of Italy *, I have mentioned a
Jacobite friar who lived at Florence for the space of fifteen
years, in great reputation for the sanctity of his life, and
whom I saw and conversed with in the year 1495. His

* See Book VIII. Chap. 3.

name was Jerome, and he had foretold several things which afterwards came to pass. He had always affirmed that the king would make a voyage into Italy, declaring it publicly in his sermons, and asserting he had both that and other things by revelation from God, by whom he pronounced our king to have been chosen to reform the Church by the sword, and chastise the insolence of tyrants. But his pretending to revelation created him many enemies, made him incur the displeasure of the Pope, and gained him ill-will from several in Florence. His life and discourses (as far as could be discovered) were the severest and most holy in the world, for he was declaiming perpetually against sin, and making many proselytes in that city.

In the same year 1498, and within four or five days after the death of King Charles VIII., died Friar Jerome also *; which I mention the rather, because he had always publicly asserted that the king should return again into Italy, to accomplish the commission which God had given him for the reforming of the Church by the sword, and the expulsion of tyrants out of Italy; and that in case the king refused or neglected it, God would punish him severely; all which former sermons and those which he preached at this time, he caused to be printed, and they are to be purchased at this day. His threats to the king of God's severe anger if he returned not into Italy, he wrote several times to his majesty a little before his death; and he told me as much at my return from Italy, assuring me that sentence was pronounced in heaven against the king, provided he refused to observe what God had commanded, and did not keep his soldiers from plundering.

About the time of the king's death there were great divisions among the Florentines. Some expected the king's return, and very earnestly desired it, upon confidence in Friar Jerome's assurance; and in that confidence they exhausted and ruined themselves in their expenses to promote the recovery of Pisa and the rest of the towns which they had delivered to the king; but Pisa remained in possession of the Venetians. Some of the citizens were for siding

* Charles VIII. died on the 7th of April, and Savonarola on the 23rd of May.

with the league and deserting our king; and these alleged that all was but folly and delusion, and that Friar Jerome was a heretic and a hypocrite, and that he ought to be put into a sack and thrown into the river; but he had friends in the town who protected him against that fate. The Pope and the Duke of Milan wrote often against him, assuring the Florentines that Pisa and the rest of their towns should be restored, if they would abandon our king and punish Friar Jerome. It accidentally happened, that at the time of the king's death the Signory consisted chiefly of Friar Jerome's enemies (for the Signory in that city is changed every two months), who suborned a Cordelier* to quarrel with him, and to proclaim him a heretic and an abuser of the people, in pretending to revelation, and to declare publicly that he had no such gift; and, to prove what he said, he challenged him to the ordeal of fire before the Signory. Friar Jerome had more wit than to accept this challenge; but one of his brethren† offered to do it for him, and another of the Cordeliers‡ volunteered to do as much on the other side; so that a day§ was appointed when they were to come to their trial, and both of them presented themselves to enter the fire accompanied by all the friars of their orders. The Jacobite brought the Host in his hand, which the Signory and Cordeliers insisted he should lay by; but the Jacobite, being obstinate to the contrary, and resolved not to part with it, they returned all to their convents. Whereupon the people, encouraged by Friar Jerome's enemies, and authorised by the Signory, went to his convent and fetched him and two more of his brethren‖ out, and tortured them most cruelly, killing the chief man

---

* Friar Francis of Apulia, of the Order of Minor Observantines. His challenge to Savonarola was in these terms: "I know," he said, "I am a sinner; I have not the presumption to perform miracles: nevertheless, let a fire be lighted, and I am ready to enter it with him. I am certain of perishing, but Christian charity teaches me not to withhold my life if, in sacrificing it, I might precipitate into hell an heresiarch, who has already drawn down into it so many souls."—SISMONDI, xii. 461.

† Friar Domenico Buonvicino.

‡ Friar Andrea Rondinelli.

§ On the 17th of April, in the public square of Florence.

‖ These were Domenico Buonvicino and Silvestro Maruffi.

in the city (called Francisco Vallori*), only for being his friend. The Pope sent them power and commission to make out process against him, and at last he and his two brethren were burnt.† The charge against him consisted only of two articles; that he created disorder in the city, and that he was an impostor; and that what he pretended to know by revelation he was told by his friends in the council. For my own part I will neither condemn nor excuse him, nor will I say they did ill or well in putting him to death; but I am sure he foretold several things which afterwards came to pass, and which all his friends in Florence could never have suggested. And as to our master and the evils with which he threatened him, they happened exactly as you have heard, first the death of the Dauphin, and then his own death; predictions of which I have seen in letters under his own hand to the king.

Ch. XXVII.—Of the Obsequies and Funeral of King Charles VIII., and the Coronation of his Successor Louis XII.; with the Genealogies of the Kings of France to King Louis XII.—1498.

THE distemper of which the king died was an apoplexy, or a catarrh, which the physicians hoped would have fallen down into one of his arms, and, though it might have taken away the use of that member, they were in no fear of his death. His majesty had four physicians about him, but his greatest confidence was in him that had the least knowledge and experience in physic; and by his directions he was so entirely governed, that the other three durst not give their judgments, though they saw the indications of death, and would gladly have ordered him a purge three or four days before. All people addressed themselves to the Duke of Orleans immediately, as next heir to the crown; but the

* Francesco Valori had been chief gonfalonier of the city during the preceding year.
† On the 23rd of May, 1498.

gentlemen of King Charles's bed-chamber buried him in great pomp and solemnity. As soon as he was dead, service was begun for his soul, which continued day and night; for when the Canons had done the Cordeliers began; and when they had ended, the Bons-hommes or Minims took it up, for they were an order of his own foundation. He lay eight days at Amboise, part of the time in a chamber very richly hung, and part in the church. In short, he lay in great state, and the whole solemnity was more costly than the funeral of any of his predecessors had been. The gentlemen of his bed-chamber, all that had waited on his person, and all the officers of his court, never stirred from his corpse, but watched it constantly; and the service continued till his body was interred, which was about a month after*; and, as I have been told by some of the officers of his exchequer, this ceremony cost forty-five thousand francs. I came to Amboise two days after his death, went to pay my devotions upon his bier, and stayed there five or six hours. To speak impartially, I never saw so solemn a mourning for any prince, nor one that continued so long; and no wonder, for he had been more bountiful to his favourites, to the gentlemen of his bed-chamber, and to ten or twelve gentlemen of his privy-chamber, had treated them better, and given them greater estates than any king had ever done before; and indeed he gave them too much. Besides, he was the most affable and sweetest natured prince in the world. I verily believe he never said a word to any man that could in reason displease him; so that he could never have died in a better hour to make himself memorable in history, and lamented by all who had served him. I do really think I was the only person in the whole world to whom he was unkind; but, being sensible that he was in his youth, and my treatment not at all his own doing, I could not resent it.

Having lain one night at Amboise, I went and paid my respects to the new king, with whom I had been formerly as intimate as any other person about the court, and much of my troubles and losses were incurred for his sake; but now all our former acquaintance and the service I had done him were forgotten. However, he entered upon his government

---

* The corpse was conveyed from Amboise on the 17th of April.

with great wisdom.   He altered not any pensions for that
year, though they were still to last for six months.   He retrenched nothing of his salaries, but declared that every
officer in his kingdom should continue in the post in which
he found him; which was very honourable and discreet.
As soon as all things were made ready, he proceeded to his
coronation *, and I was there among the rest.   The peers of
France (according to ancient custom) were represented by
these following : The Duke of Alençon represented the
Duke of Burgundy ; the Duke of Bourbon the Duke of Normandy ;. and the Duke of Lorraine the Duke of Guienne.
The first of the Counts was Monsieur de Ravestain, who
represented the Count of Flanders.   The second was Engilbert of Cleves, who represented the Count of Champagne,
and the third was Monsieur de Foix, who represented the
Count of Toulouse.   The said coronation was at Rheims on
the 27th of May, 1498, and Louis XII. was the fourth king
who came collaterally to the crown.   The two first were
Charles Martel, or Pepin his son, and Hugh Capet, both of
them mayors of the palace, or governors of their kings, who
afterwards turned usurpers, deposed their masters, and took
the government upon themselves.   The third king was
Philip of Valois, and the fourth King Louis, who now reigns.
But the two last came by a just and indisputable title to the
crown.   The first race of the Kings of France is deduced
from Meroveus: there had been two kings before this Meroveus, that is to say, Pharamond, (who was the first that
was elected King of France ; for, before his time they were
called Dukes or Kings of Gaul,) and after him one of his
sons called Clodion.   Pharamond was chosen king in the
year 420, and reigned ten years ; his son Clodion reigned
eighteen, so that Pharamond and his son reigned twenty-
eight years.   Meroveus, who succeeded, was not Clodion's
son, but his kinsman; so that there seem to have been five
interruptions -in the royal line.   However, as I said before,
the genealogy of the Kings of France begins generally at
Meroveus, who was made King in the year 448; so that the
right line is derived from thence, and runs down to Louis
XII., who was crowned one thousand and fifty years after

* He was consecrated and crowned at Rheims by Cardinal Briçonnet,
on the 27th of May, 1498.—ANSELME, i. 127.

the pedigree of the said kings began. They who would derive it from King Pharamond need only add twenty-eight more, and the number will amount to one thousand and seventy-eight years since there were kings called kings of France. From Meroveus to King Pepin there were three hundred and thirty-three years, during which time the line of Meroveus lasted. From King Pepin to Hugh Capet there were two hundred and thirty-seven years; and during that time the line of King Pepin and his son Charlemagne continued. Hugh Capet's line lasted three hundred and thirty-nine years, and expired at the accession of Philip de Valois; and the line of the said Philip de Valois became extinguished in Charles VIII., who (as is said before) died in the year 1498, and was the last of that family, which had continued to possess the kingdom one hundred and sixty-nine years, during which time seven kings had succeeded of that line, that is to say, Philip de Valois, King John, King Charles V., King Charles VI., King Charles VII., King Louis XI., and King Charles VIII., who was the last of the right line of Philip de Valois.

END OF THE MEMOIRS OF PHILIP DE COMMINES.

HISTORY

OF

LOUIS XI. KING OF FRANCE,

AND OF THE MEMORABLE OCCURRENCES OF HIS REIGN,

FROM THE YEAR 1460 TO 1483;

OTHERWISE CALLED

THE SCANDALOUS CHRONICLE,

WRITTEN BY A

CLERK IN THE HOTEL DE VILLE OF PARIS.

EDITOR'S PREFACE.

THE Scandalous Chronicle forms so valuable a supplement
to the Memoirs of Commines, that I have determined to
follow the example of previous editors, and insert it in this
place. In reliance on the opinion of Petitot, I have ascribed
its authorship to Jean de Troyes.

The literary history of this work is somewhat singular.
The first known edition was published under the following
title, — *The Chronicle of the very Christian and very victorious Louis of Valois (whom God absolve!), eleventh of the
name ; with various other adventures which occurred in the
kingdom of France, as well as in neighbouring countries, from
the year 1460 to the year 1483 inclusive.* It is a small folio
volume, printed in Gothic characters, and was probably published about the end of the fifteenth century, though the
title-page bears no date, and mentions neither the author's
nor the printer's name. The three following editions are
equally silent as to the authorship of the work ; but the
fifth edition, published in 1529, ascribes it to a clerk in the
Hotel de Ville of Paris. In 1583, Gilles Corrozet, in his
Trésor des Histoires de France, quotes it as " The Chronicle
of King Louis XI. otherwise called the Scandalous Chronicle,
by Jean de Troyes ; " and in the following year, La Croix
du Maine, in his *Bibliothèque Française,* makes this statement : " Jean de Troyes was a French historian of the time

U 3

of Louis XI., king of France; he wrote a chronicle of the said king, which is vulgarly called the Scandalous Chronicle, because it makes mention of everything done by the said king, and relates matters which are not greatly to his advantage, but rather to his dishonour and scandal."

Such is the authority for the name and authorship of the work; and though slight, it has been deemed sufficient by most bibliographers, notwithstanding the controversies raised by some eminent writers on the subject. The Chronicle was first appended to the Memoirs of Commines, in Jean Godefroy's edition, published at Brussels in 1713. It will also be found in Lenglet du Fresnoy's edition, published in 1747.

The present translation is from the text in Petitot's great collection of memoirs relating to the history of France.

But although it has been agreed to attribute this Chronicle to Jean de Troyes, no researches have succeeded in discovering any particulars in relation to the author himself. It has not even been positively established whether he can be identified with the clerk in the Hotel de Ville of Paris, mentioned on the title-page of some of the earlier editions. In fact, all is speculation regarding him: but it is conjectured reasonably enough by Grosley that he was a son of a certain Jean de Troyes mentioned by Juvenal des Ursins as having distinguished himself in the disturbances at Paris during the reign of Charles VI., and who was appointed Grand Master of the Artillery by Charles VII., in reward for his services.

It is hard to understand why this should have been called the Scandalous Chronicle; unless, as Sorel suggests, the name was given to it by some bookseller in order to pique the curiosity of the public. Far from seeking to defame Louis XI., the author omits all mention of a vast number of the actions most discreditable to his memory; and in regard to his gallantries, he is almost as silent as Commines. The chief characteristic of the work is its straightforward simplicity: it is full of curious remarks on passing events, such as might be made by a superficial observer, who took no pains to penetrate into the causes and consequences of the occurrences he describes. It is this quality which renders the perusal of the memoirs of Jean de Troyes most interesting, after reading those of Commines. The latter unmasks the policy of his sovereign, reveals all his intrigues, and indicates the secret springs of his conduct; the former attempts nothing of the kind, but merely portrays events in the light in which Louis XL. desired that they should be seen by his subjects. Take, for instance, the narrative of the king's visit to Peronne, in 1468. No one would suppose, from the account given by Jean de Troyes, that Louis, a dupe to his own artifices, had imprudently placed himself in the power of the Duke of Burgundy, and been detained a prisoner by him; the treaties concluded in the town appear to have been signed freely by the French monarch, who thereupon voluntarily consented to join Duke Charles in his expedition against the Liegeois. After reading the true history of the whole affair in Commines, it is curious to notice the colour which the king gave to it in the eyes of his subjects, in order to keep them in ignorance of the dangers he had incurred by his own fault, and of the excess of humiliation to which he had been subjected by his less wily rival.

In many other respects, this Chronicle is no less valuable and instructive. It is not only remarkable for many curious traits characteristic of its individual author; but it contains interesting details of the manners and customs, of the habits and domestic life, of the Parisians, and of the view they took of contemporary events. Indeed, no existing work supplies us with a better picture of Paris as it was towards the end of the fifteenth century.

As Jean de Troyes for the most part relates only what he

heard, and was seldom an eyewitness of the occurrences which he chronicles, there are many errors in his memoirs ; but these may easily be rectified by reference to the parallel passages in Commines, where they have not been expressly corrected in the notes.

A. R. SCOBLE.

𝕿𝖍𝖊 𝕾𝖈𝖆𝖓𝖉𝖆𝖑𝖔𝖚𝖘 𝕮𝖍𝖗𝖔𝖓𝖎𝖈𝖑𝖊.

THE CHRONICLES

OF THE

VERY CHRISTIAN AND VERY VICTORIOUS

LOUIS OF VALOIS,

LATE KING OF FRANCE (WHOM

GOD ABSOLVE),

WITH

VARIOUS OTHER ADVENTURES WHICH OCCURRED BOTH IN THE REALM
OF FRANCE AND IN NEIGHBOURING COUNTRIES, FROM THE
YEAR 1460 UNTIL 1483, INCLUSIVELY,

To the honour and praise of God, our sweet Saviour and
Redeemer, and the blessed glorious Virgin Mary, without
whose assistance no good works can be performed. Knowing
that several kings, princes, counts, barons, prelates, noblemen, ecclesiastics, and abundance of the common people, are
often pleased and delighted in hearing and reading the surprising histories of wonderful things that have happened in
divers places both of this and other Christian states and
kingdoms, I have applied myself with abundance of pleasure,
from the 35th year of my age, instead of spending my time
in sloth and idleness, to writing a history of several remarkable accidents and adventures that happened in France, and
in other neighbouring kingdoms, as far as my memory would
permit me; but especially from the year 1460, in the reign
of Charles VII., to the death of Louis XI., his son, who
died on the 30th of August, in the year 1483. However,
I neither design nor expect that this historical essay of mine

should be called a Chronicle, being wholly unfit for so bold an undertaking; neither indeed was I ever employed or permitted to write one; but what I have here ventured to record, is purely by way of amusement to please and divert those who will give themselves the trouble of reading it or hearing it read; whom I also humbly entreat to excuse, and supply my ignorance, by correcting and altering whatever they find amiss; for abundance of these remarkable accidents have happened after so very different and so strange a manner, that it would have been a very difficult task, either for me or any other writer, to have given an exact and particular account of every thing that happened during so long a period of time.

1460.

And first of all, then, I must speak concerning the goodness and fertility of the earth in the year 1460, which was so prodigiously fruitful throughout the whole kingdom of France, and bore such plenteous crops of corn, that at the very dearest time a quarter of wheat was sold for only twenty-four Parisian sols; but there was a great scarcity of fruit, and as for the vines, there was but little wine, especially in the Isle of France, so that they had scarce an hogshead to every acre of ground, but the wine was extraordinarily good, and that which grew in the fat vineyards round Paris was sold very dear, and bore the price of ten or eleven crowns a hogshead.

About that time several poor indigent wretches that were guilty of thieving, sacrilege, house-breaking, and other enormous crimes, were made an example of, and severely punished at Paris; amongst whom some were only whipped at the cart's tail, and afterwards pardoned, as being their first offence; and others, who were old offenders, and had been often guilty of crimes of the like nature, were condemned to be hanged, and executed accordingly.

Much about that time also a certain woman, named Perrette Mauger, was condemned to be burnt alive for having committed several robberies, and for harbouring and concealing several notorious thieves and house-breakers, who had committed divers robberies in and about Paris; as also for having sold and disposed of the said goods that were stolen by these thieves, and sharing with them the money that arose from the sale thereof: for which crimes, and several others besides, which she confessed at last, she was condemned by M. Robert Destouteville, mayor of Paris, to be burnt alive at the stake before the gallows, and all her goods and chattels to be forfeited to the king. From which sentence she formally appealed to the court of parliament, upon the account of which appeal her execution was deferred for some time; but after the parliament had examined into her trial, they confirmed the above-mentioned sentence, and having declared that the said Perrette Mauger had no manner of grounds for her appeal, ordered it immediately to be executed; upon which she declared herself to be with child, which deferred the execution a little longer; and presently a jury of midwives and matrons was impannelled, and ordered to search her, who, upon a strict examination, reported to the judges that she was not breeding, upon which report she was immediately ordered to be burnt before the gallows by Henry Cousin, hangman of Paris.

Strange Adventures that happened in England in the same Year, 1460.

In this year the Pope sent a legate into England, who preached to the people of that country, but especially in London, the chief city of that kingdom; where he made several remonstrances to the inhabitants of that and the adjacent parts, much to the prejudice, and contrary to the interest of, Henry VI., king of England; which remonstrances the Cardinal of York, who accompanied the legate, explained in their own language, with a long exposition on the same. Upon which the common people, who were wavering and fickle enough at the best, began to rise up in rebellion against King Henry, and his queen, daughter of René, King of Sicily and Jerusalem, and their son the Prince of Wales. The common people chose the Earl of Warwick for their head, who was governor of Calais, in the room of Richard, Duke of York, who pretended to be king, and boldly maintained the kingdom of England belonged to him, as being the next heir of the family of King Richard II. A little time afterwards the Duke of York, who had assembled a great number of the populace in arms, took the field, and marched directly to a park where Henry VI. was attended by several dukes, princes, and other lords, all in arms also.   There were eight avenues that led to this park, and these were guarded by eight barons of the kingdom, all of them traitors and rebels to King Henry ; who, as soon as they were informed of the Duke of York's arrival, immediately gave him admittance into the park, with the Earl of Warwick, and several others, who went directly to the place where the King was, whom without any farther ceremony * they seized upon.   Immediately after this action, they slew several princes and great lords of the blood royal that were with him.   When the Earl of Warwick had so done, he took King Henry and brought him directly to London, carrying the naked sword before him, as if he had been his constable; and, upon his arrival at London, he led him straight to the Tower, in which there were four barons of the kingdom of King Henry's party, that were kept prisoners there ; to whom King Henry some time after, and the Earl of Warwick, gave very fair words, and released them out of the Tower, after they had solemnly promised them that their persons should be protected from all manner of danger whatsoever, and in confidence of these fair promises they consented to go out of the Tower.   But as they were leading these four barons after King Henry and the Earl of Warwick, there happened to be an insurrection of the mob, and some of them came and killed one of the barons, and gave him several blows and contusions; and the next day, notwithstanding all the fine promises that were made them, the three other barons were executed on Tower-hill.

At the same time there arose a great quarrel between the king's officers belonging to the Court of Aids, and one of the beadles of the University of Paris, for some affront the said beadle had given to two counsellors of the same court; for

* Thomas, the son of Edward Talbot of Lancashire, apprehended King Henry VI. as he sat at dinner at Waddington Hall in Cleatherwood, in Lancashire ; and, forgetting all respect due to so great a prince, like a common malefactor, with his legs tied under his horse's belly, guarded him up towards London. By the way the earl of Warwick met him, who arrested him, and taking off his gilt spurs, led him prisoner to the Tower. — *Old note.*

which misdemeanor the said beadle was put into the common gaol of Paris ; which method of proceeding the whole University highly resented, and were so extremely displeased with it, that, till the affair was accommodated, and the beadle restored to his liberty, they refused either to preach, pray, or read to the people ; but, upon his enlargement, they were well satisfied, and performed their usual duty.

About this time a certain person, called Anthony the Bastard of Burgundy, came into Paris in a disguise, and staid there only one day and a night ; and when the inhabitants of the city were informed of his coming in that manner, several officers and men of note could not imagine what should be the meaning of it, and immediately despatched certain persons to carry the news of it to the king, who spoke very favourably of the citizens, and declared they were not in the least privy to his coming in that clandestine way. Upon which the king in all haste sent the Marshal de Loheac, and M. John Bureau, Treasurer of France, to inquire into the truth of the relation that was brought him, and to take all the care imaginable to prevent whatever designs this emissary of the house of Burgundy might have formed in the city. At the same time also the citizens of Paris, (to free themselves from all manner of suspicion of their consenting to his coming *incognito*,) deputed some of the chief of their citizens, among whom were M. John de Lolive, Doctor of Divinity, and the Chancellors of the Church of Paris, Nicholas de Louviers, M. John Clerebourg, Master of the Mint ; M. John Lullier, Town Clerk ; James Rebours, Attorney ; John Volant, Merchant, and several others, to represent the matter fairly to the king. His majesty received them very graciously ; and, after they had ended their speech, which was made to clear their innocence, he was extremely well satisfied with them, and having given them a very mild and gracious answer, they returned to Paris with great joy and gladness of heart.

At that time M. Robert Destouteville, who was mayor of Paris, was committed prisoner to the Bastille, and afterwards to the Louvre, by the command of the Marshal de Loheac and M. John Bureau ; for some injustice and abuses he had committed in the exercise of his office, though it was never fairly proved upon him. About that time also several rude and uncivil actions were committed by M. John Advin, counsellor of the parliament of Paris, in the house of the said Destouteville, such as searching of boxes, trunks, and other places for letters; not to mention the several incivilities he offered to the Lady Ambroise de Lore, his wife, who was a woman of great virtue, honour, and wisdom.

In this year the rivers Seine and Marne were swollen so prodigiously, that in one night's time the Marne rose above six feet high about St. Maur des-Fossez, and did a great deal of damage in several places; but among the rest, the river came up so high in a village called Claye, in which there was a palace belonging to the Bishop of Meaux, that it washed away all the brick-work of the front of it, where there were two stately towers newly erected, in which there were fine and large apartments richly furnished and adorned with tapestry, pictures, &c., but the river swept all away.

About that time also it happened, that the body of the church of Fecamp in Normandy was burnt down to the ground by a fiery exhalation that came from the sea towards the Marches of Cornwall; and caught hold of the steeple of the said abbey which was quite consumed, and all the bells melted down, to the great loss and detriment of the abbot and his whole fraternity.

At the same time there was a great noise and discourse all over the kingdom of France, and other places, of a young girl of about eighteen years of age, who lived in the city of Mans, and played several ridiculous pranks and follies; such as foaming at the mouth, leaping into the air, screaming out aloud, putting her body into a thousand convulsive motions, and pretending to be tormented by the devil; by which antic tricks, and several others too tedious to mention here, she imposed upon and cheated abundance of people that came to see her. But at last she was discovered to be an idle hussy, and that she played all her devilish pranks by the instigation and contrivance of some of the officers belonging to the Bishop of Mans, who maintained her for that purpose; and had so far brought her to their beck, that she would do anything they bid her, and they had trained her up from her infancy to play these pranks.

About the same time it happened in England, some time

after the Earl of Warwick's seizing upon the person of King Henry, that the Duke of Somerset the king's cousin, in conjunction with several young noblemen, relations and heirs to those who were slain at the taking of King Henry, having got together a considerable body of men, took the field, and marched directly against the Duke of York, found him encamped in the plains of St. Albans *, where they gave him battle, and cut him and his whole army to pieces. In this battle the Duke of York was slain himself, and when his body was found they cut off his head, and by way of derision, because he pretended to the crown of England, they fixed it upon the point of a lance, and put a crown of straw in the form of a royal crown upon it. With him there fell in the battle six and twenty barons, knights, esquires, and persons of note in the kingdom; besides a great number of common soldiers, amounting in all to above eight or nine thousand men.

And on Wednesday the third of February in the same year 1460, were read and published at Rouen, and in several other places in the duchy of Normandy, in the public market-places by sound of trumpet, the king's letters patent; by which he declared it was his royal will and pleasure that the whole country of Normandy, together with its seaports, should be free and open to all English men and women, of what rank or condition soever; and in what habit soever they shall think fit to wear, (provided they were of King Henry's party,) and without having any passport, to have free liberty of trade and commerce throughout his whole kingdom.

---

* The battle was not fought at St. Albans, but at Wakefield in Yorkshire, on the 30th of December, 1460, in which the Duke of York was killed, and afterwards had his head cut off, and by way of derision a crown of paper, not of straw, as our author writes, set upon it, and presented to Queen Margaret, who not long after sent it with the heads of other lords to be fixed upon poles over the gate of the city of York. The person that committed this ungenerous action was the Lord Clifford, who, after the battle of Wakefield, in cold blood murdered the young Earl of Rutland, the Duke of York's third son. — *Old note.*

1461.

In the year 1461, in the month of July, it happened that King Charles VII. fell sick at the castle of Meun upon the Yevre, of a distemper that was incurable, and of which he died on Wednesday the 22nd of July, between one and two o'clock, in the afternoon, much lamented by the whole kingdom; as being a very wise and valiant prince, and leaving his kingdom in a very peaceful and flourishing condition.

Immediately after the death of the king was publicly known, the greatest part of the officers of Paris, and several others of the kingdom, went to pay their respects to the Dauphin, who resided at the Duke of Burgundy's court at Hainault; and who by the decease of his father came to the crown of France. The occasion of their waiting on him there, was, to know his royal will and pleasure; and whether they should be continued in the same posts and employments they enjoyed under his father: At which place after his death he made a promotion of several officers in the chamber of accounts or exchequer, at Paris: Amongst the rest, he made M. Peter l'Orfevre Lord of Ermenonville and Nicholas de Louviers counsellors of the same exchequer, and M. John Baillet master of the requests and reporter of the court of chancery: He also confirmed M. Simon Charles, who was carried in a litter into Hainault, in the place he was possessed of in the exchequer: and the rest of the officers that came thither to beg the favour of being continued in their respective posts and employments, were ordered back to Paris to wait for the king's coming thither.

And upon the 24th of July, 1461, M. Etienne Chevalier, who was treasurer or chief director of the finances in the reign of the late King Charles, and whom he appointed to be one of the executors of his last will and testament, and also M. Dreux Budé, the grand audiencier * of France, went from Paris to see the king's corpse that lay in state at Meun; but the Lord d'Aigreville, captain of Montargis, at the earnest solicitation of a certain gentleman named Vuaste de Morpedon, caused them both to be seized at Montargis; where they remained prisoners for some time, till the king

* One of the chief officers of the Chancery of France, who examines all letters-patent, &c., before they pass the seals.

sent orders for their release, and continued them both in their respective employments of treasurer and audiencier.

But it was very observable, that on the 23rd of July, in 1461, which was the next day after the king's death, a large blazing star was seen in the sky about seven o'clock at night, which cast such a glaring and resplendent light through the air, that all Paris seemed to be in a flame; but Heaven in its mercy has been still pleased to preserve that good city.

On Thursday the 6th of August, 1461, the body of the late King Charles VII. was brought from Meun with great solemnity, to the Church of Notre-Dame in the Fields, without the gates of Paris; and the next day the clergy, nobility, officers, citizens, and abundance of the populace repaired thither, and conducted it from thence to Paris, with a great deal of pomp, ceremony, and respect, as is usual upon such occasions. The funeral procession was thus regulated. Before the corpse were borne two hundred wax-candles of four pounds each, adorned and painted with the arms of France, and carried by two hundred inferior persons dressed in long mourning robes and black caps. The body was borne in a litter by the salt-porters of Paris, and it was lined and covered with a rich cloth of gold, valued at one thousand two hundred crowns of gold; and upon the top of it was placed the effigies of the late king Charles dressed in his royal robes, with a crown on his head, holding in one hand a sceptre, and in the other a regal truncheon. And in this state it was carried to the great Church of Notre-Dame in Paris; all the bellmen of the city clothed also in black, and bearing on each side of their gowns the arms of France, marching before it; and after them came those that bore the candles, adorned and painted with the same arms, before the litter. After the litter came the Duke of Orleans and the Count d'Angouleme as chief mourners, accompanied by the Counts d'Eu, and Dunois; M. John Jouvenelle des Ursins, knight and chancellor of France, and the master of the horse; all clothed in deep mourning, and mounted on horseback. Next to them marched all the officers of the household to the late king, on foot, by two and two, dressed in deep mourning also; and close to the litter rode six pages in black upon six fine horses covered all over with black velvet, which was a very dismal and melancholy sight to behold. And there was such an universal concern and lamentation for his death, that scarce a dry eye was left in the whole city; nay, it is reported, that one of his pages took his master's death so to heart, that for four whole days together he neither ate nor drank anything. The next day, which was the 9th of August, his body was removed from the Church of Notre-Dame, in Paris, about three in the afternoon, and carried with the above-mentioned pomp and ceremony to St. Denis, where it was deposited, and now lies.

Towards the end of this month our most gracious sovereign Louis XI., then only dauphin and eldest son of Charles VII. lately deceased, was crowned King of France at Rheims by the Archbishop Jouvenal, where he was attended by the greatest part of the nobility of his kingdom.

Upon the last day of this month of August, the king set out from an hotel named Les Porcherons, which was in the suburbs near the gate of St. Honoré, belonging to M. John Bureau, who was knighted at his coronation at Rheims, in order to make his public entry into Paris; upon which the whole body of the nobility, clergy, and gentry came out to pay their homage to him, and welcome him to their city; amongst whom were the Bishop of Paris named William Chartier, the whole University, the Court of Parliament, the Mayor of Paris, all the officers of the Exchequer, and the provost of the merchants, with the aldermen in their damask robes lined with sables. And the mayor and aldermen, after they had saluted and paid their respects to the king, presented him with the keys of the city gates, through which he was to make his entry, which he very graciously returned; and then the way was ordered to be cleared, to make room for others to approach his majesty, and make their compliment to him, of which number he made a great many knights on the spot. As the king passed through the gate of St. Denis, he found near the Church of St. Ladre a herald mounted on horseback, and clothed in the city livery, who presented to him five ladies on the part of the city, richly dressed, and mounted on five fine horses sumptuously accoutred with rich furniture, on which were embroidered the city arms; and these five ladies were habited after a sort of manner representing the five letters of Paris, and every one of them made a speech to the king, which was prepared for them beforehand.

There was a very great appearance at the king's public entry into Paris, both of his own nobility, and of foreign princes and noblemen, amongst whom were the Dukes of Orleans, Burgundy, Bourbon, and Cleves, the Count de Charolois, the Duke of Burgundy's eldest son, the Counts d'Angouleme, St. Paul, and Dunois, besides several other earls, barons, knights, captains, and a great number of persons of note and distinction, who, in honour of the day, and to augment the splendour and magnificence of the triumphal entry, had bestowed vast sums in rich and costly furniture, with which their horses were caparisoned: some of their housings were of the richest cloth of gold, made after different fashions, and lined with sables; others were of crimson velvet, lined with ermine or rich damask, embroidered with gold and silver, and hung round with great silver bells, which were of a considerable value; and upon the horses rode fine young pages, the very flower of youth and beauty, richly dressed, and wearing embroidered scarfs over their shoulders, that hung down to the crupper, which made a very noble and gallant show.

The Parisians on this occasion caused a very fine ship to be cast in silver, which was borne aloft upon men's shoulders, and just as the king made his entry through the gate of St. Denis, it was placed upon the drawbridge near the said gate, to represent the city arms. In it were placed three persons representing the three estates of the kingdom; and in the stern and the poop sat two more personating justice and equity; and out of the scuttle, which was formed in the shape of a fleur-de-lis, issued a king dressed in royal robes, and attended by two angels. A little farther, at the fountain du Ponceau, there were wild men that played the parts of gladiators, and near them were placed three handsome wenches, representing mermaids, sporting and singing gay enlivening airs, which were humoured and accompanied with the melodious harmony of soft music. And to comfort and refresh the people, there were several pipes in the said fountain that ran milk, wine, and hippocras, of which every one drank what he pleased; and a little below the fountain, the passion of our Saviour was represented as he was crucified

x 2

between two thieves.   At a little distance from this crucifix
there were posted a band of men richly dressed, representing
hunters that had just run down a stag, whose death was
accompanied with the melodious noise of dogs and horns;
and in the Rue de la Boucherie there were large scaffolds
erected in the form of the Bastile at Dieppe.   And when
the king had passed by them, the English who were within
the Bastile were furiously attacked by the king's soldiers,
taken prisoners, and had all their throats cut.   Opposite to
the gate of the Chastellet there was a fine appearance of
persons of quality; all the windows were hung with rich
tapestry, and the streets through which the king passed were
crowded with a prodigious number of people.   In this pompous manner he proceeded to the Church of Notre-Dame;
and having performed his devotions to the blessed Virgin, he
returned to his royal palace, where he had a splendid and magnificent entertainment, and lay there that night.   The next
morning, which was the first of September in the year 1461,
he removed from thence into his Hotel des Tournelles, near
the Bastile de St. Antoine, where he staid some time, during
which he made several acts and ordinances, and turned
several of the officers of his kingdom out of their posts and employments, amongst the rest the Chancellor Juvenal des
Ursins, the marshal, the admiral, the first president of the
Court of Parliament, and the provost of Paris, and put new
ones in their places.

He also made a new regulation in all his courts of justice
and offices belonging to the crown, especially in the Exchequer, Treasury, and the Mint, turning out abundance
of counsellors, secretaries, receivers-general, clerks, and
other officers of an inferior nature, and putting others in
their room.

The 3rd of September, 1461, the king, attended by some
of the lords and gentlemen of his court, was entertained at
supper in the house of one M. William de Corbie, a counsellor of the court of Parliament, whom he made President
of Dauphiny that very night.   There were abundance of
fine ladies and honest citizens' wives to see the king at
supper; and during his stay at Paris he ordered several
feasts and entertainments to be made in divers places of the
city on purpose to treat and divert them.

About this time it happened, that a beautiful young

woman named Joan du Bois, wife to a certain officer belonging to the Chastellet of Paris, made an elopement from her husband, but afterwards, by the counsel and advice of his intimate friends, he took her home again. She became a very good woman, and lived a sober and virtuous life with her husband afterwards.

1462–3.

In the years 1462 and 1463 nothing material or worth recording happened, and therefore I have passed them over in silence. And as for the year 1463, as I have already observed, there was nothing happened in it worth taking notice of, unless it was the shortness of the winter and the length of the summer, which was extremely pleasant, and very favourable to the vines, so that we had plenty of good wine that year, but a great scarcity of all other fruits of the earth.

1464.

In the year 1464, upon Tuesday the 15th of May, the king came from Nogent le Roy, where the queen was brought to bed of a young princess; and on the same day in the evening supped at the house of M. Charles d'Orgemont Lord of Mery, and from thence he set out for the frontiers of Picardy, where he expected to have found the ambassadors whom Edward King of England had promised to send thither to him, but they never came; whereupon the king left Picardy and made a progress to Rouen, and several other places in Normandy. About that time it happened that a small vessel of Dieppe was seized upon the coast of Holland by some of the Duke of Burgundy's ships, in which there was a person named the Bastard of Rubempre, who, with the rest of the ship's crew, was immediately clapped into prison, upon pretence that their design of hovering about those parts was purely to seize upon the person of the Count de Charolois: and this report the Flemings spread abroad everywhere, but there was nothing in it.

About that time the king set out from Normandy in his return to Nogent, from whence he went to visit Tours, Chinon, and Poitiers, at which place arrived the deputies that were sent by the city of Paris to desire his majesty to grant them farther privileges; but all they were able to obtain of him was, only to be exempted from a small tax called the Foreign Impost, which was no great matter; and even that small gift they did not enjoy, for the clerks of the Exchequer, to whom their letters patent were directed, were negligent, and would not despatch their business in time.   The ambassadors of the Duke of Bretagne were likewise to wait on him there, whom he heard upon several articles that were brought him in relation to the affair between the duke and him; which articles, or at least the greatest part of them, were granted and allowed by his majesty; and by those articles of agreement the said ambassadors did promise and engage that their master the Duke of Bretagne should wait on his majesty, either at Poitiers or elsewhere, to confirm and ratify the said articles.   After which, the ambassadors took their leave of the king, pretending to return into Bretagne; but they did quite the contrary, as you will find hereafter.   The day they set out from Poitiers, which was Saturday, they went but four leagues, where they stayed till the Monday following; and upon Sunday the Duke of Berry, the king's own brother, departed from Poitiers also, and lay that night with the ambassadors, who received him with abundance of kindness and civility, and the next morning early in great haste they all set out together for Bretagne, fearing lest the king should be informed of his brother's going with them, and upon that account follow them: besides the Count de Dunois was already arrived at the Duke of Bretagne's court, which would be apt to give the king a suspicion of some secret designs on foot against him.

Soon after the departure of these ambassadors, the Duke of Bourbon declares war against the king, and invades his dominions, seizing upon whatever belonged to the king, in his territories, and putting the Lord de Croussol, a great favourite of the king's, under an arrest.   This Lord de Croussol was only passing through his country with his lady and the rest of his family; however, they were all of them arrested and confined in the city of Cosne in Bourbonnois.

After this, William Juvenal des Ursins Lord of Traynel, formerly chancellor of France, and M. Peter Doriolle the late treasurer, were also arrested in the city of Moulins, where they endured a long imprisonment; but at last the Duke of Bourbon released them, and gave them liberty to go back to the king.

On Sunday the 12th of March, in the year 1464, after the Duke of Berry's departure from Poitiers, Anthony Chabannes Count de Dammartin, who was a prisoner in the Bastile de St. Antoine, made his escape and fled into Berry and Bourbonnois, where he was kindly received. But several who were suspected to have been accessary to his escape, were immediately committed to prison.

On Wednesday the 15th of March, M. Charles de Melun the king's lieutenant, M. John Balue Bishop of Evreux, and M. John le Prevost, with the king's secretary, met together in the Hotel de Ville, where they caused several articles, that the king had given them in charge, to be read; and after the reading was over, they made several acts and ordinances for the better defence and security of the city. Amongst the rest, there was a particular order to appoint a strong watch to guard the city gates by night, to shut them at a fixed hour, to have iron chains fastened at the end of every street, to bar them up upon any occasion; and several others, which being too long to be inserted here, I shall for brevity's sake omit them.

But after the escape of the Count de Dammartin, the king found out a stratagem to surprise the two strong places of Fourgeau and Morue, which were defended by Jeffery Cœur, son of the late Jacques Cœur, whom he made prisoner, and seized upon all the riches he found in them.

As soon as this business was over, the king, attended by the King of Sicily and the Lord du Maine, marched towards Angers and Pont de Ce, to demand of those who had so basely deserted him what reasons induced them to retire and withdraw themselves into Bretagne. He ordered his army, which was chiefly composed of the standing forces of the kingdom, and amounted to twenty or thirty thousand men, immediately to follow him; but after he had been there for some time, and found he could not possibly finish the war on that side so soon as he expected, he marched with a strong detachment and some cannon into the duchy of Berry, towards Yssoudun, Viarzon, Dreux, and other neighbouring towns, leaving the King of Sicily and the

Count du Maine with a good body of troops to defend and guard the passes, and to hinder the Bretons from penetrating either into Normandy, or into any other part of his kingdom.

The king made but a short stay in the Duchy of Berry, and from thence he marched into Bourbonnois, leaving the city of Bourges behind him, in which there was a strong garrison commanded by Monsieur the Duke of Bourbon's bastard, who held it for the Duke of Berry. He marched into Bourbonnois, where the town and castle of St. Amant Lalier were taken by storm on the day of our Lord's ascension, and a little after the town and castle of Molucon surrendered upon articles of capitulation, in which were James de Bourbon with about thirty-five lances, who took an oath never to bear arms against the king again, upon which they were suffered to march out without being plundered, and had the liberty of going where they pleased.

Upon Ascension-eve the Chancellor Traynel, M. Estienne Chevalier, Nicholas de Louviers, and M. John de Molins arrived at Paris, by whom the king wrote to his good people and citizens of that place, thanking them for their good inclinations and loyalty to him, exhorting them to continue firm and steadfast in their allegiance, and commanding them to conduct the queen safe to Paris, where he would have her lie in, as he loved that city above any in his kingdom.

1465.

On Thursday the 30th of May, in 1465, it happened that one John de Hure, merchant of the city of Sens, came with his nephew and some other company to lodge in a mill, which was called the Little Mill, on the other side of Moret in Gastinois; and about midnight thirty or forty horse, well armed, came and beat up their quarters, plundered them of all they had, and carried away the merchant and his whole company prisoners. At the same time the king ordered the bridges of Chamois and Beaumont on the Oise, with several others, to be broken down.

About that time the Bastard of Burgundy and the Marshal of Burgundy, with a considerable body of the Count de Charolois's forces, invaded the king's dominions, and took

from him the towns of Roye and Montdidier.   Upon which
the Count de Nevers and Joachim Rouault Marshal of France,
who were in Peronne with a garrison of about four thousand
men, retired with part of them to Noyon and Compiegne,
leaving some of the nobility with about five hundred Frank
archers in Peronne for its defence.

At the same time the king, who was then in Bourbonnois,
left that country and retired to St. Poursain, whither his
sister the Duchess of Bourbon and Auvergne came also to
wait on him, being extremely concerned at the difference
that there was between the king her brother and her husband
the Duke of Bourbon, and she hoped by that means to have accommodated matters between them; but it was not in her
power to do it.   In the mean time, however, the Duke of
Bourbon evacuated Moulins, and retired to Riom.

About this time came orders for the besieging of St.
Maurice, which the Count de Dammartin obstinately held
against the king.   M. Charles de Melun, Bailiff of Sens,
with several others of the same corporation, had the direction of that siege, but finding the body of men that were
under their command too weak for such an undertaking, M.
Anthony Bailiff of Melun was ordered thither with a
strong reinforcement of archers and cross-bow-men from
Paris, and upon the arrival of these forces, the count beat
a retreat, and surrendered the town upon articles of capitulation.

On the 25th of June, it was ordered by the magistrates of
Paris assembled in the Hotel de Ville, that the streets should
be unchained, but that the iron chains should still remain
hanging at the corner of every street to which they belonged, in order to have them in a readiness upon any occasion; that persons should be deputed to examine what condition they were in, and if they wanted mending to get
them instantly repaired, and keep them always fit for service; which was accordingly done.   There was also another
order issued out, by which every citizen was obliged to take
arms, and to lay in a stock of provision and ammunition for
the defence of the city in case of need; and this order
was sent in writing to every particular housekeeper in
Paris.

It was much about this time that a great body of Burgundians, Picardians, and of other nations subject to the Count de Charolois, marched into France as far as Pont St. Maxence, which one Madre, who was the governor of it, delivered up to the Count de Charolois for a certain sum of money : upon which he advanced with his army into the Isle of France, where he committed great ravages and devastations, notwithstanding he pretended this war was undertaken purely for the public good, and to free the subjects of France from the tyranny of their king.

Soon after this business of Pont St. Maxence, the Burgundians took Beaulieu, which a party of the Marshal Joachim's own regiment had a long time defended, and held out against them; who at last surrendered upon articles, and marched out with bag and baggage, and the usual marks of honour.

And as soon as the Burgundians had entered the Isle of France, they dispersed themselves in small bodies all over the county, and took Dammartin, Nantouillet, Villemonble, and several other inconsiderable places, and afterwards at Laigny they committed great disorders and outrages, tearing and burning all the papers relating to the public accounts of the province, ordering that all commodities should be free from taxes in the town, and commanding the salt which was stored up in the public granaries for the king's use, to be given to whomsoever had occasion for it, upon paying custom for it.

About this time the king, who was in Bourbonnois, laid siege to Riom, in Auvergne, in which were the Duke of Bourbon and Nemours, the Count d'Armagnac, the Lord Albret, and several other persons of note. The king had, at that time when he invested the town, the finest army that ever was seen ; having, in all, including the nobility and persons of note and distinction, above 24,000 effective men of regular troops.

And, on Wednesday, the 4th of July, in the same year, the king, who was still before Riom, wrote letters to M. Charles Melun, his lieutenant in Paris, the Marshal Joachim, and the citizens of Paris, which he sent by M. Charles de Charlay, the captain of the watch; and in these letters he heartily thanked his good citizens of Paris for their steadfastness and loyalty to his person, desiring and exhorting them to continue in their duty and allegiance, and assuring them that within fifteen days he would be at Paris, with his whole army. He also ordered the said Charles de Charlay to acquaint them by word of mouth of certain terms and articles of agreement that he had made with the Dukes of Bourbon and Nemours, and the Lords d'Armagnac and Albret, and how by the compact all and every of them had solemnly and sincerely promised henceforth never to bear arms against him, but to live and die in his service ; and that the said dukes and lords above-mentioned had faithfully promised to do their duty, in endeavouring to persuade the other lords that were engaged in the confederacy to accept of the same terms of accommodation ; and that the four above-mentioned lords had agreed to send, before the feast of August, their ambassadors to the king at Paris, in order to treat of peace ; and that if they could not induce the other lords engaged in the same confederacy to hearken to a peace, they had solemnly vowed and sworn to keep the promise they had made of never bearing arms against the king, but to live and die in defence of him and his kingdom. And, that, as a farther confirmation of this promise, the above-mentioned lords had caused it to be registered by two public notaries at Mossiat, near Riom, agreeing and consenting to be excommunicated, provided they, or either of them, should act to the contrary.

On the Friday following, a large body of the Count de Charolois's forces, the greatest part of them Burgundians, arrived at St. Denis, from whence they sent a detachment to Point St. Cloud, in hopes of making themselves masters of it, but not being able to effect their project, they marched back to St. Denis.

On Sunday, the 12th of July, 1465, the Burgundians appeared before Paris, but finding they could not carry their point, they retired to St. Denis with the loss of a few men, who were endeavouring to scale the walls.

On Monday, the 8th of August, the Burgundians came a second time before Paris, with all their artillery and heavy cannon; but before their army appeared in sight of the town, they sent four heralds to the Gate of St. Denis, at which M. Peter l'Orfevre, Lord of Ermenonville, and M. John de Pompaincourt, Lord of Cercelles, commanded as captains of the guards that day. Their pretended message was to demand provision for their army, and a free admittance into Paris in a peaceful and friendly manner; and to let the citizens know, that if they refused to grant their demands, they would enter the town by force, and give it up to be plundered by their soldiers.

Scarce had the four heralds delivered their message, when the Burgundians (who thought to have surprised the town, and cut in pieces the guard that defended the gate of St. Denis, without giving the citizens time to return an answer) appeared with a considerable body of forces, and penetrating as far as St. Ladre, were in hopes of getting within the barriers that led to that gate, which they designed to have forced with their cannon and other warlike engines: but the citizens made a vigorous resistance, and the Marshal Joachim with his own regiment gave them a very warm reception; so that the Burgundians finding that they could not succeed in their design, retired to their camp, with the loss of abundance of men killed and wounded. Immediately their whole army invested the town, in which they did great execution with their cannon, culverins, and other warlike engines, and killed and wounded a great many men. During this bombardment, there was a cowardly rascal of a bailiff named Casin Chollet, that ran up and down the streets, like one frightened out of his wits, crying out, "Get you into your houses, O Parisians, and shut the doors, for the Burgundians are entered the town;" which put the inhabitants into so dreadful a consternation, that several women with child miscarried, and others died of the fright.

No action happened before Paris on the Tuesday following, only the Count de St. Paul, who was at St. Denis, with the Count de Charolois, marched from thence with a detachment of Picardians and Burgundians, in order to possess himself of Point St. Cloud; but the project failed at that time. And on the Wednesday following, there arrived in his camp a fine train of artillery, consisting of about fifty or sixty pieces of cannon, which the Count de Charolois had ordered to be sent him; and on the same day, a brigade of M. Peter de Brezé's regiment marched out of Paris, to intercept the Burgundians in their march to St. Cloud, two of whom they killed, and took five prisoners; one of whom received so

terrible a blow as clove his head asunder, and the fore part
of it hung down by a bit of skin upon his breast.   The
Burgundians also took an archer, servant to M. John Noyer,
of the same regiment; and in the evening they made a
vigorous attack upon St. Cloud, and storming the outworks,
put the garrison, who held it for the king, into such a consternation, that they agreed to capitulate, and surrendered
the town immediately upon condition to be safely conducted
to Paris, and to deliver up the five Burgundians they had
taken that day; and for performance of these articles, hostages were exchanged on both sides.

On the Friday following, the magistrates of Paris held a
great council in the Hotel de Ville, to advise and consider what
answer they should return to the Burgundians, who required of them to send some commissioners to treat with
the Count de Charolois, who would privately inform them,
by word of mouth, of the reasons that had induced him to
take up arms against the king.   At last, after some debate,
they resolved to acquaint the Count de Charolois with their
resolution of sending some commissioners (provided he
would send them a passport to Paris), to treat with him,
and to hear what propositions he had to make; letting him
know, at the same time, that they would communicate whatever he had to offer, either to the king, who was at Orleans,
or to his privy council at Paris; who might return what
answer they thought most proper in the present posture of
affairs.   The same day, about six in the evening, two heralds
from the Count de Charolois came to the gate of St. Honoré
for the answer you have already heard; who were told, that
if the Count de Charolois would be pleased to come any-
where near Paris, and send a passport, commissioners
should be sent to wait on him, but nothing farther could be
granted.   After this, they desired leave to buy some paper
and parchment, which was granted them, but were denied
sugar and other things that they wanted in their camp for
their sick and wounded; so that they were forced to return
without these commodities, which they took very ill of the
Parisians.

On Sunday, the 14th of July, 1465, early in the morning,
arrived at Paris the Count de la Borde and M. Cousinot,
who brought letters from the king to his good citizens of

Paris; in which the king, as he had done before, thanked them for their zeal and affection to his person, and for their brave resistance and defence of his capital against the Burgundians, desiring them withal to depend upon whatever the said De la Borde and Cousinot should tell them in his name; the substance of which was, that the king thanked them heartily for their loyalty and good affection towards him, desired them to continue firm and steadfast in it, and that they might depend on his being at Paris (as a place he desired the most to be in) on the Tuesday following; and that he had rather lose half his kingdom than any misfortune or inconveniency, that was in his power to prevent, should happen to his good citizens of Paris; whom he desired by the said Cousinot to provide lodgings and quarters for his men at arms, and the retinue that he should bring with him, and to set a reasonable price on all manner of provision; to which M. Henry de Livre, the mayor of Paris, immediately consented, and took all the care imaginable to see it done.

On the Monday following, the Burgundians broke up from St. Cloud, and marched with all their artillery and heavy cannon to Mont l'Hery, where they encamped, in order to join the Dukes of Berry and Bretagne, the Count de Dunois, and several others that were coming in to the Count de Charolois. The news of this movement was immediately despatched to the king, who was on this side Orleans on his march towards Paris, and who in all haste, by long and tedious marches, on Tuesday morning, the 6th of July, arrived at Chartres, near Mont l'Hery; from whence, without staying so much as to refresh himself, or to wait for the coming up of his whole army, which was composed of the finest horse (considering their number) that ever were seen, he marched directly towards the Burgundians, whom he attacked with so much vigour and intrepidity (though but with a handful of men), that at the first charge he broke and entirely defeated their vanguard, of which a great number were killed and taken prisoners. As soon as the news of this defeat had reached Paris, above thirty thousand sallied out of the gates, some of whom being horse, scoured the country round, defeating and taking several small bodies of the flying Burgundians, as did also the inhabitants of the

neighbouring towns round Paris. The Burgundians lost in
this action great part of their bag and baggage; and the
whole damage they sustained, reckoning everything, was
computed to amount to two hundred thousand crowns of
gold.   The king, not being content with defeating the
enemy's vanguard, and hoping to gain a complete victory
over them, without refreshing either himself or his troops,
once more attacked, with only his own guards and four hundred lances, a strong party of Burgundians, who had rallied
under the command of the Count de St. Paul, who did the
Count de Charolois good service that day. The Burgundians gave the king's troops a warm reception, and being
drawn up in order of battle, with their cannon playing upon
them, sorely galled them, and killed abundance of them,
among whom were several officers of the king's own guard,
who behaved themselves handsomely during the whole action, and stood firmly by the king, who was hard put to it
that day, and several times in danger of his own person; for
he had but a handful of men, and no cannon. The king
was pressed so hard by the Burgundians, that he knew not
which way to turn himself, and was forced to charge at the
head of his troops during this engagement; and though he
had but a small body with him, yet he still maintained his
ground; and if he had had a reinforcement but of five
hundred Frank archers to have pushed the Burgundians
when they began to give way, he would have gained the
completest victory over them that ever was known in the
memory of man. The Count de Charolois lost all his guards,
and the king a great part of his; the Count de Charolois
was twice taken prisoner by Jeffery de St. Belin and Gilbert
de Grassay, but was afterwards rescued. Abundance of
men and horses were killed that day, the greatest part of
which were killed by the rascally Burgundian foot, with
their pikes and other weapons tipped with iron, and not
a few men of note fell on both sides. And after the battle
was over, the number of the slain was computed at three
thousand six hundred men; and towards night, the Scotch
guards, considering the danger the king was in, and the
great loss they had sustained, and finding that the Burgundians were still pursuing those squadrons they had already
broken, took his majesty, who had been in arms all day

without eating and drinking, and was much fatigued and dispirited, and conducted him safe to the castle of Mont l'Hery; which was the reason that several in the army, who knew nothing of the king's removing thither, and not knowing where to find him, reported he was either killed or taken prisoner. Upon the news of which the greatest part of his army ran away, and among the rest the Count du Maine, the Admiral de Montauban, the Lord de la Borde, and several other officers, with about eight hundred lances, without ever being engaged at all that day; by which means the Burgundians remained masters of the field of battle, on which were found amongst the slain several persons of quality and distinction on the king's side, to wit, M. Peter de Brezé, knight and seneschal of Normandy; Jeffery de St. Belin, bailiff of Chaumont; Floquet, bailiff of Evreux, besides several other knights and esquires. The Burgundians also lost abundance of men, and had more taken prisoners than they took of the king's army. After the king had refreshed himself a little at the castle of Mont l'Hery, he marched with a strong detachment of his forces to Corbeil, where he stayed till the Thursday following, on which he arrived very late in the evening at Paris, and supped that night at M. Charles de Melun's, his lieutenant-general, with several lords and ladies of his court, besides several of the chief citizens and their wives, to whom his majesty related the particulars of the action at Mont l'Hery in such moving and pathetic terms, as drew tears from the eyes of the whole company; adding withal, that he designed by the blessing of God to attack the enemy once more on the Monday following, and either die on the spot, or drive them out of his dominions; but he was advised not to hazard another battle, considering the cowardice and desertion of his troops, that would not stand by him in the late engagement. However, it was to no purpose, for he was a prince of an undaunted courage and resolution.

On Friday, the 19th of July, 1465, M. William Chartier Bishop of Paris, with several counsellors and clergymen, went to wait on the king at his Hotel des Tournelles, and humbly besought his majesty that he would be pleased to make choice of some wise and prudent council to aid and assist him in the administration of public affairs for the

future, to which he graciously consented; and immediately
it was ordered that six city counsellors, six counsellors of
the court of parliament, and six doctors of the University
of Paris, should be added to the king's ordinary council.
And because the king found he had many enemies in his
kingdom, they went upon ways and means to raise more
forces, and recruit those regiments that had suffered most in
the late action of Mont l'Hery. In order to try how many
men they could raise in Paris, it was proposed that the
number of the inhabitants of every ward should be taken in
writing, and that each ward should furnish ten men; but
there was nothing done in it.

Upon the king's arrival at Paris, abundance of his troops
were forced to be quartered in the villages round that city,
Brie, and other neighbouring places, where they committed
great disorders, not being content with eating and drinking
on free cost, but also plundering the inhabitants of all they
had, and seizing upon whatever they could find, though belonging to some of the citizens of Paris. Nay, the king
himself was under some difficulties of raising a sufficient
sum of money to pay those forces he had in Paris, for some
of the princes that had taken up arms against him were in
possession of those very towns on which the taxes assigned
for that use were to be levied, and they refusing to let any
be raised in their dominions, he was forced to borrow money
of his officers and wealthy citizens of Paris, some of whom,
upon their refusal to lend him as much as he proposed, were
immediately put out of all their posts and employments, both
military and civil: among the rest, M. John Cheneteau,
clerk in parliament, M. Martin Picard, counsellor of the
exchequer, and several others.

On Wednesday, the 24th of July, 1465, the king ordered
the bridge of St. Maxence to be broken down, upon intelligence that the Lord de Saveuses was marching with a great
body of forces in order to beat out the king's troops, and put
a garrison of his own into it. On the same day his majesty
gave the command of it to John l'Orfevre, who was the
governor of it, and charged him to defend it to the last extremity, which he did with so much bravery and resolution,
that there was no occasion to break down the said bridge;
and on the Friday following the king ordered that two hun-

dred lances, under the command of the Bastard d'Armagnac, Count de Comminges, the Sieur Giles de Symon, bailiff of Senlis, the Sieur de la Barde, and Charles des Mares, should stay at Paris; and on the same day, at the desire and request of the Mayor of Paris and some churchmen, his majesty continued M. Charles de Melun in his former post of lieutenant of the city.

After the battle of Mont l'Hery, the lords and princes that were engaged in the confederacy against the king retired to Etampes, where they stayed for the space of fifteen days, and upon their breaking up from thence, they marched towards St. Mathurin de l'Archant, Moret in Gastinois, Provins, and the neighbourhood of those countries; upon which the king, having intelligence of their motions, throws small bodies of forces with some cannon into Melun, Montereau, Sens, and other neighbouring towns, to reinforce the garrisons, and make frequent sallies whenever they had an opportunity of falling upon the enemy.

On Saturday, the 3rd of August, 1465, the king, being willing to oblige his good city of Paris by some singular act of grace and favour, changed the tax of the fourth penny on retailed wines to that of the eighth, and granted to all the inhabitants the same privileges they enjoyed in the reign of his father Charles VII. He also took off all the taxes that had formerly been levied in the city, except those on wood, cattle, and cloth, sold by wholesale, which were let out to the farmers of the revenue; and on the same day it was proclaimed by sound of trumpet in all the public streets of Paris, by Denis Hesselin, chief collector of the subsidies; upon the news of which the common people were so overjoyed, that they flocked together from all parts of the city, and filled the streets with bonfires and acclamations of joy.

About this time the Bretons and Burgundians passed the Seine and the Yonne upon a bridge of boats, which were brought from Moret in Gastinois and other places. M. Salezart, with a brigade of Marshal Joachim's regiment, had posted himself on the other side to dispute the passage with them; but finding himself too weak, and having no cannon (of which the enemy had great store), he thought fit to retire upon their approach. The Burgundians, to favour the passage of their troops, cannonaded the enemy all the while, and killed abundance of the king's men; at last a random shot took off a page's arm, struck a gentleman named Pamabel, a relation of Marshal Joachim's, in the belly, and killed three soldiers afterwards.

On Thursday, the 8th of August, the Lord de Pretigny, one of the king's counsellors, and president of the exchequer, and Chrisstofle Paillart, a counsellor, also of the same court, arrived at Paris with an answer to some letters that the king had sent by them to the Duke of Calabria, who was then in Auxerrois; and on Saturday the 10th of the same month, the king set out from Paris in order to visit Rouen, Evreux, and several other places in Normandy, and lay that night at Pontoise; but before he left Paris, he ordered several companies of Frank archers that were newly arrived from Normandy, and about four hundred lances drawn out of the regiments of the late Floquet, of the Boulonnois, of the late Jeffery de St. Belin, of the Lord de Craon, and the Lord de la Barde, to remain in garrison for the defence of the city.

About this time M. John Berard, counsellor of the court of Parliament, went over to the Duke of Berry, who was then in Bretagne, being highly disgusted at his wife's being committed to prison, and afterwards banished the city for holding correspondence with the said duke and the rest of the princes, who were the king's open and professed enemies.

About this time M. Charles de Melun, who had hitherto been the king's lieutenant in Paris, resigned his place, which was immediately given to the Count d'Eu; but the king, in consideration of the many services M. Charles de Melun had done, made him steward of his household, and gave him the government of the bailiwick and towns of Evreux and Honfleur.

About this time also a party of Burgundians and Bretons, who had been refreshing themselves in the town of Provins, returned to Laigny upon the Marne, and the Friday following they came and took up their quarters at Creteil, a house upon the Seine, Sheelle, Saincte, Bapteur, and several other places in that neighbourhood. And because the Parisians were fearful that the Burgundians would once more invest Paris, there being a report that M. Gerauld, their chief engineer, had given out that he designed to erect a battery in the lay-

stall before the gates of St. Denis and St. Anthony, in order
to bombard the town, and at the same time to make a breach
in the walls, they caused an order to be immediately published, by which every one was obliged to repair the next
morning to the lay-stall with a pick-axe and shovel, to break
it up, and render it unfit to erect a battery on, and accordingly the order was put in execution; but what they did
signified little or nothing, so that they were forced to build
a great many sheds, erect bulwarks, and throw up trenches
to cover and defend the city, as also the soldiers employed
in its defence.

On the Monday following, the same party of Burgundians
and Bretons that were quartered at Creteil and thereabouts,
being joined by some more forces of their own country,
came to Pont de Charenton, where they erected a battery;
and began to play upon the tower that defended it, upon
which the garrison, without making the least opposition,
retired to Paris, and the Burgundians and Bretons took
possession of it, and in the evening of the same day they
appeared before Paris, in which several of them were taken
prisoners, and two of the Frank archers of Caen killed. And
that night a body of Burgundians and Bretons, amounting
to about four thousand men, came and encamped in a park
belonging to the Bois de Vincennes. The Tuesday following,
the Count d'Eu sent one M. de Rambures to the princes to
know their intentions, and the next day he returned to
Paris, but the answer they made him was kept very secret;
and the same day the Burgundians came before Paris, upon
which the Parisians made a sally, but scarce any action
happened between them, only one of the Frank archers of
Alençon happened to be killed by a random shot.

On Thursday, the 22d of August, the Duke of Berry, who
had taken up his head quarters at Beaulcé, with several
other princes near allied to him, sent his heralds with four
letters to Paris, one to the citizens, one to the university,
and one to the ecclesiastics, and one to the court of parliament. The contents of which were, in short, that he and
the rest of the princes engaged in the same confederacy had
taken up arms for the public good of the kingdom, and that
if they would make choice of five or six able men in the
character of commissioners to treat and confer with them,

he would let them know the reasons that had induced him and the rest of the princes to appear in this open and hostile manner. Accordingly, in pursuance of these letters, the following commissioners were deputed to wait on the princes to hear what they had to propose. On the part of the city were chosen M. John Choart, the civil lieutenant of the Chastellet of Paris, M. Francis Hasle, advocate in parliament, and Arnold Lullier, banker at Paris. The church of Paris made choice of M. Thomas de Courcelles, Dean of Paris, M. John de Lolive, doctor of divinity, and M. Eustace Lullier, advocate in parliament. For the court of parliament were chosen M. John de Boulenger, M. John de Sellier, Archdeacon of Brie, and M. James Fournier. And by the university for the sciences in general were chosen M. James Minglisant, for divinity, M. John Lullier, for the law, M. John Montigny, and for physic, M. Auerant de Parenti; and all these commissioners were introduced and presented to the princes by William Chartier, Bishop of Paris.

On Saturday following, all the above-mentioned commissioners sat in the Hotel de Ville, where several persons of quality and distinction were assembled on purpose to hear what proposals the princes had made them, but they came to no manner of conclusion that morning; however, it was agreed that in the afternoon the whole body of the university, church, court of parliament, and the chief magistrates, should meet together, to take into consideration what the princes had proposed to the commissioners. At this meeting, after some debate, they unanimously agreed, that the calling an assembly of the three estates of the kingdom, which was the chief thing the princes insisted on, was highly just and reasonable; that they would consent to supply their army with provisions for money, and that they should have free admittance into Paris, provided they could give them security that neither they nor their soldiers would commit any act of hostility within the town to the prejudice of the inhabitants; and the king consented to it. After which the commissioners went a second time to wait on the princes, and acquaint them with their final resolution. During the whole time that this assembly were sitting in council, all the cross-bow men and archers were drawn up before the Hotel de Ville, to hinder the mob from crowding and disturbing them, as they would certainly have done, had they not been prevented by this means.

On the same day there was a review made of all the king's forces in Paris, which made a very fine appearance. First of all marched the archers of Normandy on foot; these were followed by the archers on horseback; and last of all came the men-at-arms belonging to the companies of the Count d'Eu, the Lord de Craon, the Lord de la Barde, and the Bastard of Maine, which might make in all about five hundred men, well armed and mounted, without reckoning the foot, which were about one thousand five hundred, or more. And on the same day the king wrote letters to Paris, by which he acquainted the inhabitants of his being at Chartres with his uncle the Duke du Maine, and abundance of soldiers with him, and of his resolution of coming to Paris on the Tuesday following. In the afternoon the Admiral de Montauban arrived at Paris with a good body of troops, and towards the evening the Duke of Berry broke up from Beaulcé, and marched towards St. Denis; but being told by some of his officers that were with him that Beaulcé was a much safer place for him to be in than St. Denis, which lay too near the enemy, and upon hearing the news of the king's coming to Paris, he marched back to his old quarters.

On the Wednesday following the king came to Paris, attended by his uncle the Duke du Maine, the Lord de Pantheure, and several other officers of note; he also brought back the fine train of artillery he carried with him, and a great number of pioneers from Normandy, who were all quartered in his Hôtel de St. Paul. And when the king made his entry into Paris, he was received with the universal shouts and acclamations of the people; and the next day, very early in the morning, the Burgundians and the Bretons, planting themselves over against the tower of Billy, saluted him with a triple discharge of their cannon, accompanied with drums, trumpets, clarions, and other warlike instruments of music. The same thing they did also over against the bastille St. Anthoine, shouting and huzzaing, and crying out, "To arms, to arms!" which put the whole city into a dreadful consternation, and immediately they mounted the walls, and prepared all things for a vigorous defence. In the afternoon the Burgundians and Bretons appeared again before Paris, upon which a considerable body of the king's regular forces, with some cannon and field-pieces, were immediately ordered to march out of Paris to beat off the enemy, who, falling in with a party of them, killed and took several prisoners that day.

On Saturday, the last of August, the king went with a strong guard as far as the tower of Billy, to take a view of the enemy, and commanded the four hundred pioneers that came from Normandy to cross the Seine, and throw up a trench over against the English port, and before the Hôtel de Conflans, which was directly opposite to the place where the Burgundians were posted, quite down to the river Seine. And because the Burgundians had given out that they designed to pass that river, the king ordered a good body of troops to be posted there, to hinder them from laying a bridge over it, and to dispute the passage with them; and as soon as the pioneers had passed the river, the king passed it also in a ferry-boat without alighting from his horse.

On Sunday, the first of September, the Burgundians laid a bridge over the Seine at the English port; and just as they were preparing to pass it, a great number of Frank archers, and other soldiers of the king's party, arrived there, who, immediately planting some cannon and field-pieces at the end of the bridge, fired briskly on the Burgundians, and obliged them to retire, with the loss of several men killed and wounded; and a certain Norman swam across the river, and cutting the ropes with which the bridge was fastened, it went cleverly down the stream. Abundance of cannon was fired that day from several batteries that the Burgundians had erected, but from one especially, which played so briskly on the king's troops that were posted at the English port, that they were forced to retire.

And on the Tuesday following, ambassadors were chosen by the king and the Burgundians, in order to adjust the difference between them. On the king's side were chosen the Duke du Maine, M. de Pretigny, president of the exchequer, and M. John Dauvet, president of the parliament of Toulouse; and the Burgundians chose the Duke of Calabria, the Count de St. Paul, and the Count de Dunois. And

as soon as they were nominated, and had received their instructions, they went immediately upon the business of accommodation; and there was a truce granted till the Thursday
following, during which no acts of hostility were committed
on either side; but both parties took care, in the mean time,
to fortify themselves, and make what preparations they could,
not knowing how matters might happen.

On Monday, the ninth of September, the Bretons and
Burgundians marched into the territories of Clignancourt,
Montmartre, La Courtille, and other vineyards about Paris,
where they spoiled and destroyed the whole vintage, cutting
down all the grapes, green as they were, to make wine for
present drinking; upon which the Parisians were forced
to do the same with all their vineyards round Paris that
had escaped their fury, though the grapes were scarce half
ripe, and it was not the usual season for their vintage;
besides, it was the worst year for vines that had been known
in France for many years; so that they called the wine of
this year's growth by the name of Burgundy.

About this time several of the nobility of Normandy
arrived at Paris to serve the king in his wars, all which
had their quarters assigned them in the Faubourg de St.
Marcel, amongst whose retinue there were some particular
persons that committed great thefts and disorders, two of
whom were seized by some of the citizens as they were
forcing their way into the city; and upon the citizens stop-
ping them, the Normans began to abuse and rail at the citizens, calling them traitors and rebellious Burgundians,
vowing to be revenged of them, and telling them that they
came from Normandy with no other design but to plunder
and destroy the whole city. Of which words a complaint
being made, and an information given by the said citizens
to the mayor of Paris, the principal offender, who spoke
these dangerous words, was condemned to the ignominious
punishment of walking barefoot and bareheaded, with a
lighted torch in his hand, through the streets, and in the
public market-place before the Hotel de Ville, in this shameful
condition, to acknowledge his offence before the town-clerk,
and to ask the good citizens of Paris pardon and forgiveness
for what he had falsely and maliciously spoken, and afterwards to be bored through the tongue, and banished the city.

On the Monday following, the Burgundians came and showed themselves before Paris, amongst whom was the Count de St. Paul, to meet whom the king went out of Paris, and they had a conference together, which lasted two hours; and as a surety for the Count's safe return, the king delivered up the Count du Maine, who staid in the Burgundians' army till the return of the said Count de St. Paul.

And on the same day a great council was held in the exchequer-chamber, at which, amongst the other officers and magistrates of that court, the sixteen quarteniers *, the cinquanteniers †, and some of the councillors belonging to the court of parliament, were present; to whom, by the king's order, Morvillier, chancellor of France, made a speech, in which he acquainted them how honourably his majesty had acquitted himself towards the princes, and what generous offers he had made them upon their demanding the duchy of Guienne, Poitou, with the country of Saintonge, or the duchy of Normandy, as an appanage for the Duke of Berry. He farther told them that the king's council, who were there present, had informed the princes that it was not in his majesty's power to give away or dismember anything belonging to the crown; and that since he was pleased to offer the countries of Champagne and Brie, reserving only to himself Meaux, Montereau, and Melun, in lieu of the said appanage, they were of opinion that the Duke of Berry ought not in reason and honour to refuse it. After this the assembly broke up, and (all hopes of an accommodation being vanished) the young seneschal of Normandy was ordered out with six hundred horse to skirmish with the Bretons and Burgundians, who were drawn up in order of battle on the other side of the Seine, and, firing upon them, killed a gentleman of Poitou belonging to M. Panthieu's regiment, called John Canreau, Lord de Pampelie.

On the Saturday following, at break of day, one Lewis Sorbier, whom Marshal Joachim Rouault had left in Pontoise as his lieutenant, basely and treacherously betrayed his trust, and suffered the Bretons and other troops belong-

* Civil officers, having the same power and authority in Paris as an alderman has in London, there being one to every ward.

† Certain officers or magistrates in Paris, somewhat like our aldermen's deputies in London.

ing to the enemy to possess themselves of the town, having
agreed with them beforehand, that whoever of the Marshal
Joachim's regiment refused to enter into their service, should
have the liberty of marching out with their bag and baggage, without being examined or molested.   And as soon as
he had delivered up Pontoise into the enemy's hands, he
marched with some of his confederates to Meulan, where,
not believing that his treason was already known, he thought
that, by showing Marshal Joachim's colours, he would get an
easy admittance ; but upon his arrival at the gates, the inhabitants of Meulan, who had been informed of his treachery, and were in arms upon the walls, cried out, "Get you
gone, vile and despicable traitor," and fired their cannon
upon him and his party, which obliged him to retire with
the utmost shame and confusion to Pontoise ; and on Sunday, by break of day, the enemy came and gave the city an
alarm on the side of St. Anthony's gate, and a great body of
them penetrated as far as St. Anthoine des Champs ; and
in order to dislodge them, several cannon, field-pieces, and
culverins were fired, but there were no sallies made.

About this time the Bretons and Burgundians who lay
before Paris made songs, ballads, lampoons, and other scandalous verses, on some of the chief officers of the court, which
set the king so against them, that he turned them out of
their places.   Neither did the king's own soldiers, who were
quartered in Paris, behave themselves much better, but
spent their time in all manner of lewdness, debauching and
seducing the hearts of several wives, maids, and widows,
who left their children, husbands, and places to follow and
live with them.

In the evening, M. Balue, Bishop of Evreux, was set
upon by some people that owed him a spite, in the Rue de
la Barre du Bec, who at the first stroke beat the two torches
that were carried before him out of the servants' hands, and
afterwards they came up to the bishop, who, being mounted
on a stout mule, carried him off cleverly to his own hotel in
the cloister of Nostre-Dame ; by which means he saved his
life, for his servants, who were afraid of being knocked down,
had quite forsaken him ; however, before he made his escape
he received two wounds, one in his hand, and another in one
of his fingers.   The king was extremely concerned at this

accident, and ordered a strict inquiry to be made after the assassins; but they were never discovered.

On the Thursday following, there was a great complaint made in the Hotel de Ville by some of the citizens against the soldiers for having spoken and published certain words and speeches of a dangerous consequence to the inhabitants. Among other things, they boldly affirmed that neither the city of Paris nor anything in it belonged to the inhabitants, but to them who were quartered in it; that they would have the citizens know that the keys of their houses were at the soldiers' disposal; that they would turn out the present possessors, and live in them themselves; and, in short, if the citizens pretended to make resistance, they should find, to their sorrow, they were able to conquer them. And the very same day a foolish Norman said openly at St. Denis's gate that the Parisians were very weak to think that chaining up their streets would signify anything against the forces of their country. A report of these dangerous and insolent words being made to some of the officers of the Hotel de Ville, they immediately issued out an order commanding several streets to be chained up, and that every quartenier of Paris should cause great fires to be made in every ward under his jurisdiction, and that one of them should be in arms upon the watch before the Hotel de Ville all night, which was accordingly done. And that very night there was a hot report that the gate of the Bastille St. Anthoine was left open on purpose to let the Bretons and the Burgundians into the town; and, to confirm it the more, several cannon were found nailed up, and rendered unfit for service.

On the Friday following, two pursuivants-at-arms arrived at Paris; one was despatched from Gisors to acquaint the king of the weak condition of that place, which was wholly unprovided with everything necessary for its defence, and to let his majesty know that if he did not send them a speedy supply of men, arms, ammunition, and provision, they must be forced to surrender to a body of six hundred horse that lay before the town. The other pursuivant was sent by one Hugh des Vignes, a man-at-arms belonging to M. de la Barde's regiment, and who at that time was at Meulan, to inform the king that he was assured from very good hands that the Bretons had a design of surprising Rouen as they did Pontoise, if they were not prevented. And on the same day the ambassadors that were chosen on both sides dined together at St. Anthoine des Champs without Paris; and on the next day the same ambassadors on both sides were assembled again, but in two distinct parties, that is to say, the Duke du Maine and those of his party, who were for the king, with the rest of the lords and princes, were all of them together at the Grange-aux-Merciers. There were also several others nominated by the king, who were at St. Anthoine des Champs; but notwithstanding this meeting, very little business was despatched this day.

In the afternoon the king received letters from the widow of the late Peter de Brezé, by which she informed his majesty of her having caused the Lord Broquemont, captain of the palace at Rouen, to be apprehended upon suspicion of not being well affected to his government, and having a design to deliver it up to the Bretons; but that he need not give himself the least pain about Rouen, for he would certainly find all the citizens hearty and true to his interest. The same day, in the afternoon, arrived the unwelcome news of the taking of Rouen by the Duke of Bourbon, who entered the town by the castle of Rouen, which was the weakest side, and lay towards the fields.

As soon as the princes that lay before Paris heard of the taking of Rouen, they sent to acquaint the king that his brother, the Duke of Berry, who was before contented with Champagne and Brie, would accept of no other appanage than the duchy of Normandy; so that the king was forced, notwithstanding the former agreement, to give the Duke of Berry the duchy of Normandy, and reserve for himself that of Berry. The Count de Charolois had for his share the towns of Feronne, Roye, and Mondidier, for him and his heirs for ever; besides, the king gave him during his life all the lands and towns that were lately redeemed for four hundred thousand crowns, and had been pawned to his father Philip, Duke of Burgundy, to which he added the countries of Guynes and Boulogne, to be enjoyed by him and his heirs for ever. He also gave to the Duke of Calabria a great sum of money, and lent him a certain number of troops, which were to be paid by the king, and to be employed wherever the Duke of Calabria thought fit.   The

Duke of Bourbon was to have the same pension, and the same quota of troops allowed him that he formerly had in the reign of the late King Charles, besides the remainder of his wife's marriage dower, which was left unpaid; and this was all he demanded.   The Count de St. Paul was restored to all his places that had been taken from him during this unhappy rupture between the king and the princes, and a considerable pension settled upon him for life.   The Count de Dammartin was also restored to all his lands and possessions that were confiscated by a decree in Parliament, and had considerable presents made him by the king.   As for the other lords, they had every one of them a large share, and departed well satisfied with what they had got.

And on Tuesday, the 1st of October, a peace was proclaimed between the king and the princes, and that day the Count de St. Paul came to Paris, and, having dined with the king, was conducted into the Hotel de Ville, where he was created Constable of France, and took the oaths accordingly. And on the same day the king ordered a proclamation to be issued out, by which free leave was granted to all the inhabitants to supply and furnish the Bretons and Burgundians with whatever necessaries they wanted; upon which proclamation several merchants of Paris immediately sent a great quantity of all sorts of provision into the fields before St. Anthony's gate, which was quickly bought up, especially the wine and the bread, by the whole army, who instantly repaired thither half starved, and in a miserable condition, with their thin, lank cheeks over-grown with hair, and full of lice and nastiness, and the greatest part of them without stockings or shoes.   But every one will be amazed at the inconceivable strength and richness of Paris, which was able to maintain four hundred thousand horse, including the Burgundians, Bretons, Calabrians, Picardians, and the rest of the enemy's forces for a long time, and plentifully to supply them, without ever raising the price of any manner of provision; nay, immediately after the enemy had left it, things were sold cheaper than they were before; and the whole Thursday following was spent in victualling the Burgundian camp.   The same day the king went to make a private visit to the Count de Charolois near Conflans, which was looked upon by all persons that had a respect

and concern for his majesty, as a very indiscreet action;
nay, the very Picardians themselves and the rest of the
army could not forbear reflecting upon him, and breaking
their jests upon the Parisians after this manner: " Here, take
your king, who has at last submitted to the Count de Charolois, and meanly condescended to visit him in private; in
a little time we shall have him at our command."

On Friday, the fourth of the same month, the king gave
orders for the admittance of the Burgundians into the city
through St. Anthony's gate, who, upon that permission,
came in large bodies, and committed several riots and
disorders, which certainly they would never have done
had they not been encouraged by the king's late condescen-
sion in visiting the Count de Charolois in so private a
manner.

On the Sunday following several men of quality and
officers of the army came and supped with the king at Paris
in an hotel belonging to M. John Lullier, the town-clerk, at
which entertainment several ladies of quality and distinction
were also present.

And in this month of October a detachment of the Count
de Charolois's troops came before Beauvais, and summoned
the town to surrender; upon which the inhabitants set
down the summons in writing, and sent it to the king, who
immediately sent it to the Count de Charolois, with whom
he had lately concluded a peace. The Count de Charolois
sent back word to the king that he knew nothing of the
summons; and that whosoever had done it, did it without
his knowledge or order. The king returned a very civil
answer to the Count de Charolois, and told him it was not
a fair way of proceeding; that for the future, in pursuance
of the articles of peace that had been lately concluded between
them, he must forbear committing such acts of hostility;
and that if he had a mind to Beauvais, he should have it.

On the Thursday following, several waggon-loads of gold
and silver, for the payment of the Count de Charolois's
troops, arrived in the Burgundian camp, under a strong
convoy both of horse and foot, commanded by the Lord de
Saveuses; and on the same day the Duke of Bretagne and
the king came to an agreement in relation to the affair that
was between them, by which compact the king was obliged

to restore the county of Montfort and several others; besides a vast sum of money to pay that very army which he, in conjunction with the rest of the princes, had raised to invade the king's dominions. The next day M. John le Boulenger, president of the court of parliament, was sent by the king's order to the Hotel de Ville to acquaint the mayor and aldermen of Paris that the Burgundians had a design to review their army that day before the city gates, and to desire them to acquaint the common people with it, lest they should be surprised and astonished to see them thus drawn up against the town. But after all, the review was not made in sight of Paris that day, but from the Pont de Charenton to the Bois de Vincennes, whither the king, attended only by the Count de Charolois, the Duke of Calabria, and the Count de St. Paul, very imprudently went to see the review. As soon as the review was over, the king came back by water to Paris; and the Count de Charolois, upon his taking leave of his majesty, in the presence of those lords that attended the king thither, made the following acknowledgment in these words:— "My lords, you and I are subjects to the king here present, our lord and sovereign, and ought to serve him whenever he pleases to command us."

Not long before this, the king had received a private information of a design formed by some of his enemies either to kill him or seize upon his person; upon which he immediately ordered his guards to be doubled, great fires to be made every night in the streets, the number of the watch to be augmented, as well upon the walls as in the streets, and took all the care imaginable to prevent their designs and secure his own person; and upon hearing of the surrender of Caen and several other towns in Normandy, he immediately reinforced the garrison of Mantes with a considerable body of men-at-arms and Frank archers.

On Tuesday, the 22d of October, the king made a private visit to the princes at the Grange-aux-Merciers, where all but the Duke of Berry were met together; and the next day the Duke of Bourbon had a long conference with the king in a place without the gates of Paris, on this side of the ditch of the Grange de Ruilly.

On the Saturday following, the Count de Charolois, with a small detachment, left the army, having first caused an order to be published in his camp, by which all soldiers were obliged, under pain of death, to hold themselves in readiness to march against the Liegeois, who with fire and sword had invaded his territories. Sunday, Monday, and Tuesday the Duke de Berry lay ill of a fever at St. Maur des Fossez; but being pretty well recovered of his illness by Wednesday, the 30th of October, and able to go abroad, he went to wait upon the king at the Bois de Vincennes, where he did homage to him for the Duchy of Normandy, which the king gave him for his appanage; and on the same day the articles of peace between the king and the princes were read and published in the court of parliament, and ordered to be registered in the same court.

And on the Thursday following, the Duke of Berry, the Count de Charolois, and the rest of the princes, separated, and went different ways. The Duke of Berry, whom the king waited on some part of the way to Pontoise, went into Normandy; and afterwards the king and the Count de Charolois retired to Villiers le Bel, where they stayed two or three days, and from thence the count marched with all speed through Picardy to make war upon the Liegeois.

On the Monday following, M. Robert Destouteville, Lord of Beine, who was mayor of Paris in the reign of the late King Charles, and had been displaced by the king upon his accession to the crown, was restored to his former office, which had been given to James de Villiers, Lord of Lisle Adam, and that day he sat in the Hotel de Ville as mayor, and despatched a great deal of the king's business.

On Thursday, the 7th of November, 1465, M. Robert Destouteville was conducted to the Chastellet of Paris by M. Charles de Melun and M. John Dauvet, first president of the parliament of Toulouse, whom the king had acquainted with the said Robert Destouteville's having taken the oaths already as mayor of Paris in the room of James de Villiers, whom, upon his first accession to the crown, he had advanced to that office. And after the letters patent, by which the king appointed and constituted the said Robert Destouteville mayor of Paris, were read, he was immediately. put into possession of his office, without giving the said Villiers any time to lodge an appeal against him.

On Saturday, the 9th of November, M. Peter Morvillier,

Chancellor of France, resigned the seals, and was succeeded in the chancellorship by Juvenal des Ursins, who was in the same post at the death of the late King Charles VII.

About this time also the king made several alterations and promotions in his court; amongst the rest, he turned M. Peter Puy out of his office of Master of the Requests, and gave it to M. Regnault des Dormans.

After the settling of this affair the king went to Orleans and took with him Arnold Lullier, banker and citizen of Paris, whom he commanded to attend him during his stay there; he also carried along with him M. John Longuejoye the younger, who was newly married to Madame Genevieve, daughter of M. John Baillet, and made him one of his counsellors of state. Before he left Paris, he made M. Charles d'Orgemont, Lord of Mery, Treasurer of France, Arnold Lullier Treasurer of Carcassonne, and M. Peter Ferteil Comptroller of his Household.

The king during his stay at Orleans, made several acts, laws, and ordinances, turned out several officers of the army, and gave their commissions to others; amongst the rest he took away the command of a hundred lances from Poncet de Riviere, and made him Bailiff of Mont Ferrant, upon which, in disgust, he went beyond sea, and visited Jerusalem, and the Holy Hill of St. Catharine. Several other officers had their commissions taken from them, and given to others that did not so well deserve them. The king also restored Monsieur de Loheac, Marshal of France, to all his former places in the government, some of which had been given to the Count de Comminges, Bastard of Armagnac; and after he had settled these regulations, he left Orleans, and marched with his whole army and artillery directly into Normandy towards Argentan, Exmes, Falaise, Caen, and other places, in order to reduce them to his obedience, where he found the Duke of Bretagne, who stayed there some time with his majesty.

A little after this, the Duke of Berry went from Rouen to Louviers, thinking to find the Duke of Bourbon there, but being disappointed of meeting him, he immediately came back again. Upon his return to Rouen, he was with great pomp and ceremony conducted into the town-hall by the magistrates of the city, who, according to the usual custom of the place, acknowledged him for their duke by putting a ring on his finger; afterwards he took an oath to maintain and support them in their privileges and franchises, and immediately remitted to them half the taxes they were formerly used to pay.   This act of generosity won the hearts of the whole city, and so firmly united them to his interest, that the nobility, gentry, clergy, and the common people, vowed to sacrifice their lives and fortunes in his service, and to remain his faithful and loyal subjects for ever.   And afterwards they presented him an old book of records that was in the town-hall, and made him read an article in it aloud before all the people, which gave an account of a king of France heretofore who at his death left two sons, the eldest of whom succeeded his father, and the youngest had the duchy of Normandy for his appanage: how that the elder brother, as soon as he was settled in his kingdom, demanded a restitution of the said duchy, and being denied, how he made war upon his younger brother, and thought to have taken it from him by force, but his subjects unanimously joining with him, they dethroned his brother the King of France, and set up their duke for king.   After he had done reading, they boldly told him they feared nothing; that their fortifications were strong and in good repair; that they had great store of cannon, arms, ammunition, and provision, and could upon occasion make a brave defence, assuring him they would one and all to a man stand by him, and defend him, themselves, and the town, against any opposers whatsoever.

On the 30th of December of the same year the king in his return from Lower Normandy arrived at Pont Audemer, and from thence marched into the county of Neufbourg, from whence he detached the Duke of Bourbon with a body of forces to summon Louviers, which surrendered on the Wednesday following, and the Duke of Bourbon took possession of it for the king, into which his majesty made a public entry the same day after dinner.   From Louviers the king marched to a town called Pont des Arches, about four leagues from Rouen, which he formally besieged.

On Monday, the 6th of January, 1466, a proclamation was issued at Paris, commanding all the sutlers that were used to supply the army with provisions, to repair immediately to the camp before Pont des Arches, and all the prisoners were ordered to be ready by the next morning, to set out for the same place, under the command of M. Denis, one of the four aldermen of the city, who was appointed to take care of them.

On the Wednesday following the king entered Pont des Arches, and M. John Hebert with several others who were in the town retired to the castle, which three days after was also surrendered to the king. After the surrender of the town and castle, the citizens of Rouen sent deputies to treat of an accommodation, who highly complained of the Dukes of Bourbon and Bretagne. And amongst other requests and remonstrances that the said deputies were ordered to make to the king, one was, that his majesty would be pleased to be reconciled to them, notwithstanding what they had done; that he would openly declare that they had not been wanting in their duty, nor acted contrary to his interest; and that he would grant them the same privileges and immunities he had granted his good city of Paris; to which his majesty answered, he would consult his council about it.

Whilst this affair was in agitation, several of the king's party had free admittance into Rouen, and conversed familiarly with the citizens; in the mean time, the Duke of Berry and several of his adherents retired to Honfleur and Caen, where they stayed for some time. During these transactions, M. John de Lorrain thought to have made his escape into Flanders, but was taken and brought before the king, who disposed of most of the officers belonging to the duchy of Normandy, putting in new officers, and turning out the old ones. And after the Duke of Berry's leaving Rouen, the city was reduced to the king's obedience, upon which the king dismissed all his Frank archers from his service till the 1st of March following, sent all his artillery to Paris, and retired to Mount St. Michael in Lower Normandy. About that time the king gave the command of one hundred lances which belonged to M. Charles de Melun to the Count de Dammartin, who was with him, and not long after deprived him of his office of high steward of his household, and gave it to M. de Craon; however, several people were of opinion that M. de Melun had done the king signal services, and been very faithful to him, especially in his great care and defence of Paris in the king's absence in Bourbonnois, which he managed and regulated so well, that many sincerely believe that the preservation of that city and the whole kingdom is in some measure owing' to his conduct and vigilance in that affair.

About that time the king commanded Chaumont upon the Loire (belonging to M. Peter of Amboise, lord of the same place) to be burnt; and it was accordingly done.

On Monday, the 3rd of February, one Gauvain Manniel lieutenant-general of the bailiwick of Rouen, was taken in the city and carried prisoner to Pont de l'Arche, and there, upon a scaffold erected near the town bridge, was beheaded by the provost-marshal for high treason, his head fixed on a lance on the same bridge, and his body thrown into the river Seine. Just after this the Dean of Rouen and six canons were banished the city, and expelled the duchy of Normandy.

After this the king went to Orleans, where he stayed a considerable time with the queen, and then retired to Jargeau and the neighbourhood of that place, where ambassadors from several potentates upon different affairs came to wait upon his majesty. And about that time he resolved to send an embassy to the King of England; and accordingly the Count de Roussillon Bastard of Bourbon and Admiral of France, the Lord de la Barde, the Bishop and Duke of Langres, M. John de Pompaincourt, and M. Oliver le Roye one of the counsellors of the exchequer, were chosen to go in that embassy, and they set out for England in April, 1466.

On Saturday, Whitsun Eve, an order was published by sound of trumpet in all the public streets of Paris, by the command of the Constable of France, in which order was inserted the royal mandate he had newly received from the king, the substance of which was, that the king (having received certain advice that the English, his ancient enemies, had a design to invade the kingdom of France with a powerful army, and for that descent were fitting out a strong squadron of men-of-war,) was resolved to make what preparations he could to oppose and defeat their designs, and therefore had given full power and command to his Constable of France to make proclamation of it in all the cities, towns, villages, and hamlets of the kingdom, in order that all the nobility and gentry holding any lands by homage or fealty of the crown, not excepting the Frank archers, should be ready in arms by the 15th of June following, under pain of imprisonment and confiscation of goods.

At the same time a peace was concluded with the English both by sea and land, which was publicly proclaimed; and about that time also, the Duke du Maine was for some secret reason turned out of his government of Languedoc by the king, which was given to the Duke of Bourbon.

After the consummation of marriage between the Admiral of France and the king's natural daughter, the king gave the said admiral the castle of Usson in Auvergne, which was looked upon to be the strongest place in the whole kingdom, with the government of Honfleur, and several other places in Normandy.

In July, several prelates, lords, churchmen, and counsellors, that the king had sent for to make some new regulations in all the courts of justice, and to reform some abuses, arrived at Paris, to whom the king gave full power. and authority; and by virtue of the same, he nominated and appointed twenty-one commissioners, of which M. Charles d'Orleans, and the Counts of Dunois and Longueville were chief commissioners; and even these commissioners had no powers of acting, unless thirteen of them, besides their presidents the Counts de Dunois and Longueville, were assembled together; and in pursuance of the commission that had been granted them, they began their sittings on Tuesday the 16th, and were called by the people the reformers of the nation. This was just a year since the battle between the king and the Count de Charolois at Mont l'Hery.

About this time a war broke out between the Liegeois and the Duke of Burgundy, upon which he immediately took the field with his whole army, and being a little indisposed, was carried in a litter, commanding his son the Count de Charolois, with all the nobles and officers that were with him, to march forward with a strong detachment to invest Dinant, and leave him to come up with the rest of the army. Upon his arrival the town was formally besieged, which occasioned several sallies and bloody actions on both sides, much to the disadvantage of the Burgundians in the beginning of the siege, but at last, whether by force of arms or treason, the town was taken by the Burgundians, who, only reserving a few of the chief citizens, whom they made prisoners of war, turned out men, women, and children, and gave the town up to be plundered by their soldiers. Nor were they contented with this; they set fire to the churches and the houses, and having burnt and consumed everything they could lay their hands on, they ordered the walls to be demolished, and the fortifications to be blown up, by which means the poor inhabitants were reduced to extreme want and necessity, and abundance of young women were forced to betake themselves to a vile and shameful way of living.

In August and September in the same year, the heats were so violent as to breed the plague and several other contagious distempers in France, which swept away, in a little space of time, above forty thousand people in Paris and the neighbouring towns. Some persons of note and learning died also of it, amongst whom we may reckon M. Arnoul, the king's astrologer, a very worthy, learned, and facetious person, several eminent physicians, and abundance of officers belonging to the city.

During the plague, the king and his council stayed at Orleans, Chartres, Bourges, Meun, and Amboise, and during his abode in that neighbourhood he received several embassies from foreign princes and states, especially from England and Burgundy; and it was there he declared in council his resolution of making war upon the Duke of Burgundy, and his son, the Count de Charolois, upon which the ban and arriere-ban were ordered to be raised, and a considerable augmentation to be made to the body of Frank archers.

After this affair was despatched, the king made several new ordinances and establishments for the better defence of his kingdom, and the garrisoned towns in it, and accordingly he made the Marshal de Loheac his lieutenant of Paris and the Isle of France, M. de Geilon had the government of Champagne, and the government of Normandy was given to the Count de St. Paul, Constable of France, who formerly was the king's enemy, and had joined with the Duke of Burgundy and the Count de Charolois.

Some time after this, in February 1467, an ambassador from Bretagne arrived at Paris, who, after he had had audience of the king, set out for Flanders, to wait on the Duke of Burgundy and the Count de Charolois his son. The many civilities that the king showed this ambassador made some persons of note imagine that the affair between the king and his brother was amicably adjusted, at which they were extremely glad.

Immediately after this, the king set out from Paris, in order to visit Rouen and several other places in Normandy, and during his stay at Rouen he sent for the Earl of Warwick out of England, and went by water, attended by several of his nobility, as far as Bouillé, to meet him, which was situated on the Seine, about four leagues from Rouen. He arrived there on the 7th of June, 1467, about dinner-time, where he found a magnificent entertainment ready prepared for him and his nobility, and after dinner the Earl of War- wick came to pay his compliments to the king, after which he went to Rouen by water, and the king and his nobility by land. The magistrates of Rouen, in their formalities, were ordered to go out to meet the Earl of Warwick, and receive him, upon his landing, at the Key-Gate of St. Eloy, with abundance of pomp and ceremony, bearing before him crosses, banners, holy-water bottles, and the relics of several saints, attended by the priests in their copes; and after this manner he was conducted to the church of Notre Dame, where he made his offering, and from thence to a magnificent apartment prepared for him in one of the religious houses. Soon after this, the queen and the young princesses came to Rouen, and the king stayed there with the Earl of Warwick about a fortnight; after which the earl took leave of his majesty, and returned to England, accompanied by the Admiral of France, the Bishop of Laon, M. John de Pom- paincourt, M. Olivier le Roux, and several others, whom the king had ordered to wait on him thither.

The king presented the Earl of Warwick, during his stay at Rouen, with several valuable and rich presents, amongst the rest a piece of gold-plate, and a large gold cup set with precious stones. The Duke of Bourbon also presented him with a fine diamond, and several other things of value; besides which, he and his whole retinue had all their expenses borne by the king from their first landing in France to their embarking for England. After the earl's departure

the king returned from Rouen to Chartres, where he stayed
some time; and in this month died Philip, Duke of Burgundy, and his body was carried with great solemnity to
Dijon, and interred in the church of the Carthusians.

Immediately after this, the king ordered a proclamation
to be published, by which (in order to repeople his good city
of Paris, that had been greatly diminished by war, sickness,
and other misfortunes) his majesty gave leave to 'strangers
of all nations, of what crimes soever they had been guilty,
except high-treason, to come and settle in the city, suburbs,
or precincts thereof, promising to grant them the same privileges as his own subjects, and to defend and protect them,
even not excepting those that had been banished to St.
Maloes and Valenciennes. At the same time, also, by sound
of trumpet, was published an order, commanding all the
nobles and gentry holding any lands or tenures by homage
or fealty, even not excepting those in the Isle of France, as
well in Paris as elsewhere, to be ready in arms by the 15th
of August.

About this time, the Admiral of France, and those that
were ordered by the king to wait on the Earl of Warwick
into England, returned, where they had stayed a long while
without doing any thing, and brought with them some
hunting-horns and leathern bottles, as a present from the
King of England to the King of France, in return for all the
valuable gifts his majesty and the Duke of Bourbon had
made the Earl of Warwick at his departure from Rouen.
And on Friday, the 18th of August, the king arrived at
Paris, about nine at night, attended by the Duke of Bourbon
and several of the nobility.

On Tuesday, the 1st of September, the queen also came
from Rouen to Paris by water, and landed at Notre Dame,
where her majesty was received by all the presidents and
counsellors of the court of parliament, the Bishop of Paris,
and several persons of quality in their robes and formalities.
There was also a certain number of persons richly dressed
to compliment her on the part of the city, and abundance of
the chief citizens and counsellors of Paris went by water to
meet her majesty in fine gilded boats covered with tapestry
and rich silks, in which were placed the choristers of the
Holy Chapel, who sang psalms and anthems after a most

heavenly and melodious manner. There was also a great number of trumpets, clarions, and other softer instruments of music, which altogether made a most harmonious concert, and began playing when the queen and her maids of honour entered the boat; in which the citizens of Paris presented her majesty with a large stag made of sweetmeats, besides a vast quantity of salvers heaped up with spices and all sorts of delicious fruits, roses, violets, and other perfumes being strewed in the boat, and as much wine as every body would drink. After the queen had performed her devotions to the blessed Virgin she came back to her boat, and went by water to the Celestines' church-gate, where she found abundance of persons of quality ready to receive her majesty, who, immediately upon her landing, with her maids of honour, mounted upon fine easy palfreys, and rode to the Hotel des Tournelles, where the king was at that time, and where she was received with great joy and satisfaction by his majesty and the whole court; and that night there were public rejoicings and bonfires in Paris for her majesty's safe arrival.

On the 14th of September, the king, who had ordered the Parisians to make standards, published a proclamation, commanding all the inhabitants, from sixteen to sixty, of what rank or condition soever, to be ready to appear in arms that very day in the fields, and that those that were not able to provide themselves with helmets, brigandines, &c., should come armed with great clubs, under pain of death; which orders were punctually obeyed, and the greatest part of the populace appeared in arms, ranged under their proper standard or banner, in good order and discipline, amounting to eighty thousand men, thirty thousand of whom were armed with coats of mail, helmets, and brigandines, and made a very fine appearance. Never did any city in the world furnish such a vast number of men, for it was computed there were sixty-seven banners or standards of tradesmen, without reckoning those of the court of parliament, exchequer, treasury, mint, and chastellet of Paris, which had under them as many or more soldiers than what belonged to the tradesmen's banners. A prodigious quantity of wine was ordered out of Paris, to comfort and refresh this vast body of men, which took up a vast tract of ground, extending themselves from the end of the Lay Stall, between

St. Anthony's gate and that of the Temple, as far as the Town-ditch upwards to the Winepress, and from thence along the walls of St. Antoine des Champs, to the Grange de Ruilly, and from thence to Conflans, and from Conflans back again by the Grange-aux-Merciers, all along the river Seine, quite to the Royal Bulwark over against the tower of Billy, and from thence all along the Town-ditch on the outside to the Bastile and St. Anthony's gate. In short, it was almost incredible to tell what a vast number of people there were in arms before Paris; yet the number of those within was pretty nearly as great.

About this time a terrible war broke out between the Liegeois, and the Duke of Burgundy, and their bishop, cousin to the Duke of Burgundy, and brother to the Duke of Bourbon, whom they besieged in Huye, and after a long siege took the town, but the bishop made his escape; and towards the latter end of it the king sent four hundred lances under the command of the Count de Dammartin, Sallezart, Robert de Conychan, and Stevenot de Vignolles, with six thousand Frank archers, picked and chosen out of Champagne, Soissonnois, and several places in the Isle of France. As soon as the Burgundians heard that the Leigeois had taken Huye, they resolved immediately to take the field with their whole army, and to march against them and destroy them with fire and sword, to be revenged of them, for the Burgundians they had slain upon their taking the town. Accordingly they declared war against them throughout all their dominions by the ceremony of a naked sword in one hand, and a burning torch in the other, signifying that this was a war of blood and fire.

About the same time the king sent the Bishop of Evreux, who was lately made a cardinal at Rome, M. John de Ladriesme, treasurer of France, and several others, on an embassy to the Count de Charolois, to negotiate some secret affair with that prince.

On Sunday night about nine, there was such terrible thunder and lightning as had scarce been known in the memory of man; and during the whole month there were such prodigious heats as surprised every body, which was looked upon to be very strange and unnatural.

On Thursday the fifteenth of the same month, the king received advice that a great detachment of Bretons had possessed themselves of the town and castle of Caen, in Normandy, and from thence marched to Bayeux, which they also surprised, and turning out the garrison, put some of their own troops in it. The king was extremely concerned at this news, and immediately sent the Marshal de Loheac, who had the command of one hundred lances of Bretagne, into Normandy, to see how affairs stood there.

About this time, M. Anthony de Chasteauneuf (Lord of Lau, great butler of France, and seneschal of Guienne, great chamberlain to the king, and the most beloved and rewarded of any favourite the king ever had) was, by his majesty's order, moved from the castle of Sully upon the Loire, where he had been long a prisoner, to the castle of Usson in Avergne, by M. Tristan l'Ermite the king's provost-marshal, and William Serisay, newly chosen register in parliament; and upon this removal there was a discourse, which lasted some time, that he was executed, but it was a false report.

On Tuesday, the 20th of October, the king set out from Paris for Normandy, and lay that night at Villepereux, and the next at Mantes. Before he left Paris he sent for several of his captains and officers of his army, and ordered them to get the troops that were under their command in readiness to follow him into Normandy, or wherever there should be most occasion for them; and on the same day he published certain letters and ordinances, by which he declared that it was his royal will and pleasure that for the future all the officers of his kingdom, both civil and military, should continue in their places, and that no place should become vacant but by death, resignation, or forfeiture, resolving to dispose of no places but what became vacant by one of the three before-mentioned ways, and therefore it would be in vain for any one to expect or solicit for a post upon any other terms, since he designed to do justice to every one. After this declaration, he set out from Mantes for Vernon on the Seine, where he stayed some time, during which the Constable of France, who came thither to pay his respects to the king, found out an expedient how to conclude a peace between his majesty and the Duke of Burgundy, for six months from the date of the articles, without including the Liegeois,

who were actually in arms against the Duke of Burgundy, in hopes of being assisted by the king, as they were
promised; but by this treaty they were balked in their ex-
pectations, and left in the lurch. As soon as the treaty was
signed and sealed by the king, the Constable of France went
to wait on the Duke of Burgundy to acquaint him with it.

Soon after this M. John de Balue, Bishop of Evreux, M.
John Ladrische, and the rest that had been sent into
Flanders to negotiate an affair at the Duke of Burgundy's
court, came to Vernon, to give the king an account of their
embassy; immediately after which the king left Vernon, and
came to Chartres, where he stayed till the arrival of the
greatest part of his artillery from Orleans, which was to be
employed in the reduction of Alençon, and several other
towns in the same province. And afterwards the king sent
M. John Prevost into Flanders with the articles of peace to
the Duke of Burgundy.

On the 16th the Bishop of Evreux, the Treasurer de
Ladrische, M. John Berart, and M. Jeffery Alnequin, arrived
at Paris, in order to review the banners, and to inspect
several other things that the king had given them in charge.
After that the king went from Chartres to Orleans, Clery,
and other towns in that neighbourhood, and afterwards to
Vendome, from whence he marched with great part of his
artillery and a considerable body of troops to Mount St.
Michael. In the mean time the Bretons with a strong army
left their own country, and penetrated into Normandy as far
as the city of Orange, and other towns of that province, and
also dispersed themselves in small bodies all over Normandy,
as far as Caen, Bayeux, Coutances, and other places.
About the same time the Duke of Burgundy, taking advantage of the peace that was concluded between him and the
king, in which the Liegeois were excluded, marches against
them with his whole army, and lays siege to their capital city;
and they being balked in the expectation of those succours
that the king promised to send them, and seeing their ruin
near at hand, were at last forced to surrender all their towns
to the Count de Charolois, besides giving him a vast sum of
money, and consenting to have their gates pulled down, and
part of their walls demolished.

On Saturday, the 22nd of November, the Bishop of

Evreux, and the rest of the commissioners appointed for that purpose, reviewed the bands of the tradesmen as they were drawn up and ranged under their respective banners in several places in the city. And the very same day the king commanded a proclamation to be issued out, commanding all persons that were used to serve in the wars to repair forthwith to certain commissaries appointed to receive and give them pay. And the next day M. John Prevost returned from the Duke of Burgundy's court, whither the king had sent him with the articles of peace, and brought his majesty back the answer the Count de Charolois had given him in relation to that affair. On Thursday the 16th of November, there was another review made of all the banners without the gates of Paris. As soon as the review was over, the Bishop of Evreux, and the rest of the commissioners, with M. John de Ladrische, Treasurer of France, M. Peter l'Orfevre, Lord of Ermenonville, and several other of the king's officers, set out from Paris to wait upon the king, who was between Mans and Alençon with a prodigious army consisting of one hundred thousand horse, and twenty thousand foot, in order to oppose the Bretons; upon which his majesty ordered the greatest part of his artillery to be brought up, to be employed in the siege of Alençon.

During these transactions there were some overtures of peace which hindered the king from entering upon action; and so by consequence his army was forced to destroy and eat up all the flat country for twenty or thirty leagues round Mans and Alençon. In the mean time the Count de Charolois, who had already destroyed the Liegeois, and overrun the country, retired to St. Quentin; and ordered a proclamation to be issued out through his whole dominions, commanding all his subjects that were able to bear arms, and those forces that were already raised, to repair to St. Quentin by a certain day upon pain of imprisonment, in order to be reviewed by certain commissaries appointed for that purpose. The same proclamation he caused to be published in Burgundy, commanding all his subjects of that duchy to repair to Montsavion by the 22nd of December, as a place of general rendezvous, where several commissaries were also appointed to enlist and enter them in his service; from whence they were ordered to march and join the forces at St. Quentin, which were to act in conjunction with those of the Dukes of Berry and Bretagne, against the king of France. Upon publishing of this proclamation, several merchants of Paris that were gone into Burgundy to buy up some commodities, made a quick return, without doing any business; and the Count de Charolois ordered all his forces to rendezvous at St. Quentin on the 4th of January following.

On Innocents' day, which was the 28th of December, the Duke of Bourbon, who came by the king's order to put strong garrisons into his frontier-towns, and to cover his country, that the Burgundians might not penetrate into it, arrived at Paris, and with him the Marshal de Loheac, who, according to common report, was to be lieutenant of the city. The Duke of Bourbon made some stay at Paris; but the Marshal de Loheac set out two days after for Rouen, and several other towns in Normandy, to put them in a posture of defence, according to the king's orders; where he stayed a considerable time. The Parisians were extremely civil to the Duke of Bourbon, and during his stay there he was caressed by several of the chief citizens, who made feasts and entertainments on purpose for him. In the mean time the city of Alençon, which was in the hands of the Bretons, was surrendered to the king by the Count du Perche, son to the Duke of Alençon, who commanded in the castle at the same time that the Bretons were masters of the town. All this time the king did not stir from Mans; and during his stay there, he sent the Pope's legate, whom we have already mentioned, Anthony de Chabannes, Count de Dammartin, the Treasurer Ladriesche, and several others, on an embassy to the Duke of Berry, to offer terms of accommodation; and at last the king consented to the calling the three Estates of the kingdom. Tours was the place appointed for their meeting, where, according to order, they were assembled on the first of April, 1467, upon which the king left Mans, and came to Montils near Tours, Amboise, and thereabouts.

As soon as the three Estates of the kingdom were assembled, the king came and acquainted them with the occasion of their meeting; and had, from time to time, several debates and conferences with them concerning the affair between him and his brother the Duke of Berry, till the time of their breaking up, which was on Easter Day, 1468. There were present at this assembly, the king, the King of Sicily, the Duke of Bourbon, the Count du Perche, the Patriarch of Jerusalem, the Cardinal of Angers, several other lords, barons, archbishops, bishops, abbots, and abundance of other persons of quality and condition, besides several ambassadors from all parts of France. And by this august assembly it was agreed and resolved (after a long and mature deliberation, in order to end the dispute between the king and his brother Charles concerning his appanage), that his majesty should allow him twelve thousand livres a-year in land, with the title of count or duke; and that he should be obliged to give and allow him besides, an annual pension in money of sixty thousand livres more, without any prejudice to the rest of his majesty's children, who hereafter might come to the crown, and be required to give the same appanage. To which the king (being extremely desirous to live in perfect peace and union with his brother) at last consented, and willingly gave him the annual allowance of sixty thousand livres, seeing he generously relinquished the duchy of Normandy, saying it was not in the king's power to dismember or give away any thing that belonged to the crown. And as for the Duke of Bretagne, who had sided with Lord Charles, and had taken several towns in Normandy, being suspected to hold a correspondence with the English, the ancient enemies of France, it was agreed by the said assembly, that he should be summoned to surrender the towns he was possessed of, and that, upon refusal, and the king's having certain advice of his having made an alliance with the English, his majesty should immediately endeavour to recover them by force of arms, and the three Estates of the kingdom promised to stand by and support him; the clergy, with their prayers and estates; and the nobility, gentry, and commonalty, with their estates and persons. And, moreover, the king was extremely desirous that justice should be fairly and impartially administered through the whole kingdom; and therefore he proposed to this assembly the choosing some persons of honour and quality out of the three Estates, to regulate and take care of that matter; and the whole assembly were of opinion that nobody was so fit to be employed in that office as the Count de Charolois, who was a peer of France, and nearly allied to the crown. After this debate was over, the king left Tours, and went to Amboise; and a little after he sent to the assembly, then sitting at Cambray, to know how they approved of the resolution that had been taken by the three Estates of the kingdom that were convened at Tours, as you have already heard.

After the king had despatched this affair, he went to Meaux, in Brie, where he ordered a certain person, born in Bourbonnois, to be beheaded for some crimes he had committed, and amongst the rest for discovering the king's secrets to the English, the ancient enemies of France. Just before this, the king was graciously pleased to grant an act of grace and indemnity; and the Prince of Piedmont, the Duke of Savoy's son, was sent to Paris with full power and authority to release all the prisoners out of jail.

About the same time, the Burgundians or the Bretons, who had invaded Normandy, surprised the Lord de Merville between St. Sauveur de Dive and Caen, and made him deliver up his castle into their hands, in which there was a small number of Frank archers. As soon as they had surrendered it, they hanged the Lord de Merville, plundered the castle, and afterwards set fire to it. After this the king left Creil, and went to Compeigne, where he stayed some time, and then returned to Senlis, and from thence the Duke of Bourbon went to Paris, where he arrived on the Assumption of Our Lady. Some time before this, the king had sent M. de Lyon, the Constable of France, and several other lords, on an embassy to the Duke of Burgundy, to endeavour to adjust the difference between them, without coming to an open war, notwithstanding he had already sent an army into Normandy under the command of the Admiral of France, who had been so successful as in a month's time to drive the Bretons out of Bayeux. On Saturday, the 20th of August, 1468, M. Charles de Melun, Lord of Normanville (who had formerly been steward of the king's household), was brought out of the castle of Gaillart, where he had been newly committed prisoner, under the command of the Count de Dammartin, and publicly beheaded in the market-place of Andely, according to the sentence that had been pronounced against him by the provost-

marshal. After this, the king staid some time at Noyon,
Compiegne, Chavay, and other places thereabouts, till the
15th of September, where he received the agreeable news
of the Duke of Bretagne and his brother Charles's readiness
to consent to the terms of accommodation that his majesty had
proposed to them, and that his brother Charles was ready
to accept of his annual pension of sixty thousand livres tournois, till his appanage could be fully settled by the Duke
of Calabria and the Constable of France, who were the persons he had chosen to settle and manage that affair. The
Duke of Bretagne, on his part, offered to surrender all the
towns he had taken from the king in Normandy, provided
his majesty would restore all those that his troops were in
possession of in Bretagne, to which the king readily consented.

The king immediately sent an express to the Duke of
Burgundy, who lay encamped between Esclusiers and Cappy,
to acquaint him with this accommodation, but he would give
no credit to it till it was farther confirmed by certain ad-
vices from the Duke of Bretagne and Lord Charles; however,
he would not retire with his army, but still continued in the
same post between Esclusiers and Cappy, behind the river
Somme. During his encampment there, several persons of
quality were deputed to wait on the Duke of Burgundy,
amongst whom were the Constable of France, the Cardinal
of Angers, and M. Peter Doriolle, in hopes of accommodating
matters amicably between him and the king, which his majesty was extremely desirous of; but the officers of his army
were of another mind, and begged the king that he would
give them leave to attack the Duke of Burgundy in his
camp, not questioning but that they should defeat him, and
oblige him to accept of what terms his majesty should propose; but the king would not hear of it, and upon pain of
death forbade them to attempt anything against him. And
from that time to the 12th of October there was a great discourse of the king's having made a truce with the Duke of
Burgundy till the April following; and upon the hopes of
that truce the king resolved to return from Compiégne to
Creil and Pontoise; wherefore he sent harbingers before
to prepare his lodgings, but afterwards he altered his
resolution, and went in great haste from Compiegne to

Noyon, where he had been but a little time before. In the meantime Philip of Savoy, Poncet de Riviere, the Lord du Lau, and several others that were confederate with them, did abundance of mischief. And on Saturday, the 8th of October, a proclamation was issued out, commanding all the nobility and gentry within the precincts of Paris, that held any lands or tenures by homage or fealty of the crown, to be ready in arms at Gonesse, and to march from thence, on the Monday following, wherever they should be commanded; at which several persons at Paris were astonished, believing, by this preparation, that no truce had been made. After this, the king left Noyon, and the Duke of Burgundy set out from the army for Peronne, whither the king, attended only by the Duke of Bourbon, the Cardinal of Angers, and a few of the officers of his household, went immediately to pay the Duke of Burgundy a visit, who received him with all the respect and honour imaginable, as in duty he was obliged to do; and after a long conference together, the difference that was between them was amicably adjusted. The Duke of Burgundy, on his part, swore homage to the king, and vowed never to attempt anything against his majesty for the future; and the king confirmed and ratified the treaty of Arras, and several other things; upon which a courier was immediately despatched to acquaint the nobility, gentry, and commonalty with the news of this accommodation, and to order the Bishop of Paris to cause a general procession to be made, and *Te Deum* to be sung in the church of Notre Dame, which was accordingly performed; and the night concluded with bonfires, fountains running with wine, and the usual solemnities on such occasions. In the meantime news came that the Liegeois had taken and killed their bishop and all his officers; at which the king, the Duke of Burgundy, and the Duke of Bourbon, were extremely concerned, and there was great talk that the king and the Duke of Burgundy would go in person to destroy the Liegeois, and ruin their country, to be revenged on them for their late barbarous action of murdering their bishop. But, immediately, the news of the bishop's death was contradicted; however, the Liegeois obliged him to say mass, and afterwards humbly submitted to him, and acknowledged him for their sovereign lord, being willing to put an end to those calamities and misfortunes they had already brought upon themselves.

About this time the king went to Halle, in Germany, where he made but a short stay; during which, at the Duke of Burgundy's intercession, he pardoned Philip of Savoy and the rest of his confederates, and received them into his favour again. From Halle his majesty went to Namur to visit the Duke of Burgundy, whom he resolved to accompany to the siege of Liege, and had his quarters assigned him in the suburbs of that city during the whole siege, which lasted some time, and he was attended by the Duke of Bourbon, M. de Lyon, M. de Beaujeu, and the Bishop of Liege, who were all brothers. It seems the Bishop of Liege was sent out of the town to wait on the Duke of Burgundy, in order to make terms of capitulation with him in behalf of the Liegeois, who offered to surrender the town and all that was in it, provided he would spare the lives of the inhabitants; but he would not grant them those conditions, vowing to sacrifice his whole army rather than not force them to surrender at discretion, and he ordered the Bishop of Liege to be detained, notwithstanding he told him he had solemnly promised the Liegeois to return into the city, and live and die with them, if he could not obtain any honourable conditions for them. As soon as the Liegeois were informed that the Duke of Burgundy had detained their bishop against his will, they made several sallies upon the Burgundians and the king's forces, and all they took prisoners they put to death. However, notwithstanding all this, on Sunday, the 30th of October, the Duke of Burgundy ordered his men to prepare for storming the town, which was done the same day, and after little or no resistance the king, the Dukes of Burgundy and Bourbon, with the Lords de Lyon, de Liege, and de Beaujeu, entered it, out of which the greatest part of the inhabitants that were in health had retired just before the last attack, leaving only a few old men, women, children, priests, and nuns, whose throats were all cut by the soldiers, who committed a thousand other barbarous and inhuman actions, such as ravishing the women, and killing them afterwards, defiling of nuns even in the very churches, and murdering the priests while they were consecrating the host at the altar. And not being satisfied with this scene of blood and horror, they plundered the town, set fire to it, and demolished the walls.

After this action was over, the king returned to Senlis and Compiegne, where he ordered the court of parliament, the exchequer treasurers, and the rest of the civil officers of his kingdom to attend him, and upon their arrival he made several laws and ordinances; and having no design of staying there long, he ordered the Cardinal of Angers to acquaint them with the terms of accommodation between him and the Duke of Burgundy, which were specified and contained in forty-two articles, which were openly read to them by the said Cardinal, who told them that it was the king's royal will and pleasure that these articles of peace should immediately be ratified and confirmed in parliament under such penalties as he declared to them. The king, having despatched this affair, drew nearer to Paris, but would not enter the city; however, the Duke of Bourbon, M. de Lyon, M. de Beaujeu, the Marquis du Pont, and several other great lords, came and staid there some time.

On Saturday, the 19th of November, the peace between the king and the Duke of Burgundy was proclaimed by sound of trumpet in all the public streets in Paris. At the same time there was another proclamation issued out by the king's order, commanding everybody for the future not to speak against or reflect upon the Duke of Burgundy, either by speeches, signs, pictures, libels, or scandalous verses, under very severe penalties, which were explained and specified in the said edict.

In February the Duke of Burgundy's ambassadors arrived at Paris, to hasten the signing the articles of peace that had been concluded between the king and him, upon which the king wrote expressly to the mayor and the rest of the civil magistrates of Paris to treat and entertain them handsomely; and his majesty's orders were punctually obeyed, and the ambassadors were nobly entertained and feasted. In the meantime the articles of peace we have already mentioned were registered in all the courts of Paris.

In April 1469, M. John Balue, Cardinal of Angers (on whom the king had in a short time conferred vast riches and honours, doing more for him than for any prince of the blood, and whom the Pope, by his majesty's recommendation, had advanced to a cardinal's hat), most shamefully betrayed the confidence the king had reposed in him ; and having neither God in his thoughts, nor the honour nor interest of the kingdom before his eyes, basely betrayed his majesty into the Duke of Burgundy's hands at Peronne, where he advised him to that ignominious peace which was there concluded between them, and then persuaded him to accompany the Duke of Burgundy to the siege of Liege, who had taken up arms against him purely upon the king's account ; so that, in short, his majesty's going thither was the chief occasion of the ruin and desolation of the poor Liegeois. But to aggravate the matter, the king, the Duke of Bourbon, and the rest of the nobility that attended his majesty, were very near being all killed or taken, which would have been the greatest blow the kingdom of France had ever received since its first establishment. The Cardinal, not being contented with this piece of villany, immediately contrived how to do a greater ; and therefore, upon the king's return to Paris, in his way to Tours, he used his utmost endeavours to induce his majesty to fall out with his good citizens of Paris, who had hitherto expressed so much zeal and loyalty for his person. After this he employed all his cunning arts and stratagems to foment and inflame the difference that was between the king and his brother Charles. But finding himself disappointed there, and having certain advice that all matters were amicably adjusted in the late journey the king made to Tours and Angers, and that they were perfectly reconciled to each other, he tried to raise jealousy and misunderstanding between the king and the rest of the nobility, as he had formerly done. And, in order to create as much trouble and confusion as he possibly could in the kingdom, he despatched a certain emissary of his with letters to the Duke of Burgundy, to acquaint him that the peace or agreement that was lately concluded between the king and his brother Charles was directly contrary to his interest and advantage, and made on purpose to turn their arms jointly against him, wherefore he advised him to stand upon his guard, and immediately take the field, to prevent their designs. Several other arguments he made use of to induce the Duke of Burgundy to invade the kingdom of France with a powerful army ; but by good fortune his letters were seized and carried to the king, who, upon the discovery of his treacherous designs, immediately ordered him to be sent prisoner to Montbason, where he was committed to the charge and custody of M. de Torcy and several other officers. After this, the king seized upon all his goods, lands, and chattels, of which he ordered an inventory to be made, and also appointed M. Tanneguy du Chastel governor of Roussillon, M. William Cousinot, M. de Torcy, and M. Peter Doriolle as commissioners to examine him. The king some time afterwards disposed of the Cardinal's goods as his majesty thought fit; his set of plate was sold, and the money carried into the treasury for the king's use; the fine hangings of his palace were given to the governor of Roussillon; his library to M. Peter Doriolle; a fine piece of cloth of gold, valued at one thousand two hundred crowns, with a great quantity of sables, and a large piece of scarlet embroidered with gold, was given to M. de Crussol; and his robes, with a little more of his furniture, were sold to pay the clerks and other officers that were employed to take the inventory.

In the meantime the King and Queen of Sicily came to pay a visit to the king at Tours and Amboise, and were nobly and kindly entertained by his majesty. After which, attended by the Duke of Bourbon and several other lords of his kingdom, he made a tour to Niort, Rochelle, and several other places in that neighbourhood, where he met his brother the Duke of Guienne, and, by the grace of God and the assistance of the blessed Virgin, a firm union and friendship was settled between them, to the great joy and satisfaction of the kingdom; upon which *Te Deum* was ordered to be sung in the church of Notre Dame in Paris, and bonfires and rejoicings were made in all the cities and towns in France, and after that the king came back to Amboise, where he had left the queen, who had been very instrumental in his late reconciliation. Some time afterwards the king resolved in council to attempt the reduction of the earldom of Armagnac, and if the enterprise succeeded, promised to give it to his brother the Duke of Guienne; and in order to reduce it to his obedience, he sent a considerable body of forces with some cannon, which were to be followed, in case of need, by the whole army. After the king had finished his preparations for this expedition, he went to Orleans, where he stayed five or six days, and then returned to Amboise again.

On Saturday, the 4th of November 1469, was published, by sound of trumpet in all the streets of Paris, the league, offensive and defensive, that had been lately concluded between France and Spain, in the presence of both the criminal and civil lieutenants of that city, and the greatest part of the examiners of the Chastellet. And from that time the king, the Duke of Bourbon, and the rest of the nobility that attended on his majesty, stayed at Amboise and in that neighbourhood till Saturday the 23rd of December, upon which day the Duke of Guienne, attended by all the nobility of his duchy, came to wait on the king at his Chateau de Montils, near Tours, where his majesty was extremely glad to see him. And as soon as the queen was informed of the Duke of Guienne's being there, her majesty immediately left Amboise; and being attended by the Duchess of Bourbon, her maids of honour, and several other ladies of the court, came to pay him a visit, and to feast and entertain him. In the meantime the country of Armagnac was delivered up into the king's hands without any manner of bloodshed, and the king, queen, Duke of Guienne, and Duchess of Bourbon, spent their time at the Chateau de Montils in feastings and diversions till Christmas. And after the Duke of Guienne had taken his leave of the king and queen and the whole court, and was set out for his dukedom, the king went back to Rochelle, St. Jean d'Angele, and other neighbouring countries, where he called an assembly of the three Estates of the kingdom to consult about some important affair, and to appoint new officers in the duchy of Guienne, who might fairly and impartially administer justice to his subjects. And after the king had settled that affair, he returned to Amboise, where he stayed some time, during which he sent his ambassadors to the Duke of Bretagne with the order of St. Michael, which he had lately instituted, as he had done to several other lords of his kingdom; but the Duke of Bretagne at first refused the honour his majesty designed him, and would not wear it, pretending he could not take the oath belonging to that order, as he had already accepted of that of the Golden Fleece from the Duke of Burgundy, and was become his friend and confederate in arms; at which the king, being highly incensed, and not without cause, immediately ordered a considerable body of his men-at-arms and archers, with some cannon and field-pieces, to be ready to march into Bretagne, and lay the country under contribution; but before those forces were ordered to march, the king gave the Duke of Bretagne ten days' time to consider of it, and to acquaint his majesty with his resolutions.

On Wednesday, the 13th of February, 1470, was published in all the public streets of Paris the king's mandate, by which his majesty acquainted the mayor of Paris that he had received certain advice from England that King Edward IV., and the nobility, gentry, and commonalty, with whom that king had been at war for some time, were reconciled to each other, and that they had unanimously agreed in Parliament to invade the kingdom of France with a powerful army; wherefore the king (in order to oppose and prevent their designs) had commanded the ban and the arriere-ban to be raised, and ordered the mayor of Paris forthwith to summon all nobles and not nobles, all the privileged persons and not privileged persons, within the precincts of that city, holding any lands by homage or fealty of the crown, to be ready in arms on the first of March following, on pain of imprisonment and confiscation of goods. By the same letters patent, the mayor of Paris and all other officers belonging to the king were forbidden, under the same severe penalties, to admit of any excuse or certificate from any persons whatsoever holding lands or tenures by homage or fealty of the crown; and that whosoever should refuse to obey the summons should be looked upon as enemies to the king and government, and be punished as rebels and traitors to their country. On the same day news was brought to Paris that the Duke of Burgundy had been seen in Ghent with a red cross and garter upon one of his legs, which was the order of Edward IV., King of England; upon which the Duke of Burgundy was immediately declared an enemy to the kingdom, and looked upon as an Englishman.

In May, 1470, the Earl of Warwick and the Duke of Clarence, with their ladies, who had been driven out of England by Edward IV., with a slender retinue, and some ships, landed at Honfleur and Harfleur in Normandy, where they were kindly received and entertained by the admiral of France, who lodged the Earl of Warwick, the Duke of Clarence, with their ladies, and some of the chief of their retinue, in his own palace, and took care to have their ships laid up safely in the harbours of Honfleur and Harfleur. A little after the ladies and their attendants removed to Valognes, where fine apartments were prepared for them.

As soon as the Duke of Burgundy had advice of the Earl of Warwick's arrival in France, he immediately sent letters to the parliament to let them know he was informed that the king had favourably received and entertained the Earl of Warwick in some of his towns in Normandy, which was acting directly contrary to the treaty that was concluded at Peronne between his majesty and him; and humbly desired the court of parliament that they would make the king sensible of this infringement, and persuade him not to countenance the Earl of Warwick and his party, whom he had declared were enemies to the kingdom; otherwise he should be obliged to seize upon his person wherever he found him, though it was in the very heart of France; however, the Earl of Warwick stayed at Honfleur till the latter end of June. In the meantime the king drew his forces out of several garrisons, and ordered them to march into Normandy and Picardy, where they ruined and destroyed all the flat country thereabouts. In the meantime the king still kept about Tours, Amboise, Vendome, and other places thereabouts, whither the Queen of England and her son the Prince of Wales, with several of the English nobility, came to wait upon the king; and after a long conference with his majesty, the English returned to Honfleur, Valognes, St. Lo, and other places in Normandy. During these affairs, the Duke of Burgundy ordered all the effects belonging to the merchants of France, that were in his dominions, to be seized, till some restitution was made to the merchants of his country, from whom the English had taken several ships.

On Saturday, the last of June, 1470, between two and three in the morning, the queen was brought to bed, at the castle of Amboise, of a prince, who was christened Charles by the Archbishop of Lyons; the Prince of Wales, son to the late King of England, Henry VI., standing godfather, and the Duchess of Bourbon godmother. The birth of this prince occasioned great joy at court, *Te Deum* was ordered to be sung at Paris, and bonfires and rejoicings were made in all the cities and towns in France. And soon after this the King of Sicily, the Duke of Guienne, the Duke of Bourbon, the Lords de Lyon and Beaujeu, and several others, were sent to Angers, Saumur, and other places thereabouts, to endeavour to accommodate matters between the king and the Duke of Bretagne, where they stayed some time before they could settle the point; but, at last, the business was determined to the satisfaction of both of them; upon which the Duke of Bretagne sent his ambassadors to the Duke of Burgundy to deliver up the treaty of alliance that had been lately made between them; and when they informed him of the Duke of Bretagne's reconciliation with the king, he seemed highly displeased and out of patience. In the meantime, while the Earl of Warwick (whom we mentioned before,) was making all the preparations imaginable in Normandy, to return to England, the Duke of Burgundy fitted out a great fleet, and having well victualled and manned it with English, Burgundians, Picardians, and seamen of other nations, he put to sea, and sailing round by the coast of Normandy, thought to fall in with the Earl of Warwick's squadron near Havre, and fight them; but not finding them there, he dropped anchor, and waited in expectation of them, during which time the king left Amboise, and went a pilgrimage to Mount St. Michael; and after he had performed his devotions there, he returned by Orange, Granville, Coutances, Caen, Honfleur, and several other places on the coast of Normandy, where the Admiral of France put in to victual his fleet; on which the Earl of Warwick, the Duke of Clarence, and their whole retinue, went on board, together with a few archers and other soldiers that the king had ordered for the safety and defence of their persons. As soon as they were ready to set sail, the poor English, Burgundians, and Picardians, who had lain all this time in expectation of the Earl of Warwick's squadron, and had spent all their provision, weighed anchor, and sailed home to their duke with hungry stomachs, without doing anything; at which his highness laughed heartily, though he had no reason for it, having spent a great deal of time and money to no purpose. No sooner was the Burgundian fleet out of sight, but the

' Earl of Warwick, attended as you have already heard, set
sail, and, the wind serving, in a little time arrived on the
coast of England, and landed in the night at Dartmouth or
Plymouth; and immediately upon his landing, he sent a
party of his men ten miles up into the country, to seize upon
a baron of the kingdom, who little dreamed of that descent,
and was sleeping quietly in his bed; but they soon roused
him, and giving him but just time to put on his clothes, hur-
ried him away to the Earl of Warwick, who ordered him to be
beheaded the next morning. After this he marched from Dartmouth to a neighbouring town, where he was well received,
and where he had left his artillery and heavy baggage when
he escaped to Normandy.   He had scarce been landed three
days, and put what forces he had with him into a little order,
when sixty thousand men in arms, came voluntarily to him,
offering to venture their lives and fortunes in his service;
whereupon he immediately took the field, and marched directly in search of King Edward, so that it was above a fortnight from the day of his landing before we could hear any
news of him in France.   And then the king received certain
advice that the Earl of Warwick and the Duke of Clarence
were in full march with a powerful army in search of King
Edward, and that their affairs were in such a prosperous
condition that all the nobility, gentry, clergy, and commonalty of England (but especially the people of London) had
forsaken King Edward, and were come in to the Earl of
Warwick, who had delivered King Henry VI. out of the
Tower, where he had been long a prisoner, and reinstated
him in the possession of his kingdom.   Upon which the Earl
of Warwick was made governor and protector of England
under Henry VI., and immediately marched into the city of
London, where the citizens feasted and entertained him nobly.
After which he released all the French prisoners that were
in England, and sent them home without any ransom, but
seized upon all the effects belonging to the Duke of Burgundy's subjects.   At last King Edward, finding himself
abandoned and forsaken by all his subjects, left his queen
in England, and went over to his brother-in-law, the Duke of
Burgundy, with a very slender retinue, to solicit troops and
money to recover his kingdom.

After this the king wrote letters to Paris to acquaint them

that the Queen of England, wife to Henry VI., the Prince of Wales and his princess, daughter to the Earl of Warwick, the Countess of Warwick her mother, the Lady Wiltshire, and several other ladies of the English court, were coming to Paris, attended by the Counts D'Eu, De Vendome, De Dunois, Monsieur De Chastillon, and several other noblemen and persons of quality; and that it was his Majesty's command that the bishop, university, court of parliament, and the mayor and aldermen of Paris, in their robes and formalities, should go out and meet them, and compliment the Queen of England in his name.

Soon after this the Queen, the Duchess of Bourbon, the maids of honour, and several other ladies of the court, came along with his majesty to Paris, where they all stayed till the 26th, and then his majesty set out from thence for Senlis, Compiegne, and the neighbourhood of those places where the greatest part of his army that was to act against the Duke of Burgundy lay.

He ordered a large train of artillery to be brought from Compiegne, Noyon, and elsewhere, both by sea and land, into Picardy and Flanders; and published a proclamation by sound of trumpet in Paris, commanding all the nobility and Frank archers of the Isle of France to be ready in arms to follow him, and join the rest of the army. During this time great preparations were making at Paris, and a great quantity of cannon, ammunition, and provision were getting ready for the army.

About this time all the handicraftsmen in Paris, such as masons, carpenters, joiners, and the like, were pressed by the king's orders; not excepting those belonging to the towns and cities that had lately surrendered to his majesty. The command of this body of workmen was given to M. Henry de la Cloche, the king's attorney in the Chastellet at Paris, who was a loyal subject, and was to lead them to the town of Roye, where they were to be employed in repairing the old fortifications, and in making new ones; and when they had finished their work there, they were employed in doing the same in other towns that had lately submitted to the king, which took up a great deal of time, and kept them employed till Easter Day, at which time the king made a truce for a little while with the Duke of Burgundy, who was

closely besieged in his camp between Bapaume and the city of
Amiens by the king's army, and was reduced to so miserable
a condition that had it not been for the truce, both he and his
whole army must certainly have perished, or surrendered themselves prisoners at discretion. Since the beginning of the war,
to the day the truce was agreed on, the king's army defeated
the Burgundians and the Picardians in several smart engage-
ments, and took a considerable booty from them in the
duchy of Burgundy, not to mention their incursions
into the countries of Charolois and Maconnois, where they
enriched themselves by the plunder they got, and took a vast
number of prisoners, amongst whom were several persons of
quality, who paid handsomely for their enlargement, besides
a greater number killed in several actions that happened
between them. Some persons of quality on the king's side
would have been prodigious gainers by this war, had not his
majesty obliged them, upon the treaty, to deliver up all they
had taken from the enemy; at which, abundance of the nobility that had a great respect for the king were highly displeased. During this cessation of arms, the king, the Duke
of Guienne, and several other lords and men of quality went
to Ham, and stayed there with the Constable of France, who
was extermely proud of the honour his majesty did him.
During the king's abode at Ham, several ambassadors arrived
from the Duke of Burgundy, and as many were sent by the
king to the Duke of Burgundy's camp; but notwithstanding
all their embassies forward and backward, it was a long time
before they came to any resolution. At last, a truce for one
year only was agreed upon between the king and the Duke
of Burgundy, and commissioners were chosen on both sides
to accommodate the difference between them, and to terminate the dispute between the soldiers of each side. As
soon as this affair was settled, every one retired to his own
house, and the towns that had been taken before the treaty
were garrisoned by the king's soldiers.

About that time great quarrels and contests arose in
England between Henry of Lancaster, King of England,
the Prince of Wales his son, the Earl of Warwick, and the
rest of the lords of the kingdom who were of King Henry's
side, against Edward de la Marche, who had usurped the
crown from Henry. This civil war had occasioned already

abundance of murder and bloodshed, and was not like to be at an end yet; for in June, 1471, the king received certain advice from England that Edward de la Marche, with a puissant army of English, Easterlings, Picardians, Flemings, and other nations that the Duke of Burgundy had sent him, had taken the field, and was going to oppose King Henry's forces, which were commanded by the Earl of Warwick, the Prince of Wales, and several other lords of that party. In short, the battle was bravely fought, and a vast number of men were killed and wounded on both sides; but at last Edward de la Marche gained the victory, and King Henry's army, partly by the treachery of the Duke of Clarence, and partly for want of conduct, was entirely defeated. The poor young Prince of Wales, who was a lovely youth, was barbarously murdered after the action was over; and the valiant Earl of Warwick, finding himself betrayed, and scorning to fly, rushed violently into the thickest of his enemies, and was killed upon the spot. Thus died this great man, who was so desirous of serving his king and country, and who had cost King Henry so much money to bring him over and fix him in his interest.

In July, 1471, died the Count d'Eu, a person of great wisdom, honour, and probity, heartily devoted to the interest of his country, and one that faithfully served the king to the utmost of his power. Upon his death the king took possession of the earldom of Eu, which he gave to the Constable of France, which was highly displeasing to his brother the Count de Nevers, who thought to have enjoyed that earldom, with the rest of his estate, after his brother's decease, as being his right and lawful heir.

From this month of July to Christmas nothing of importance happened in the kingdom of France; several conferences, indeed, there were in the mean time between the commissioners chosen on both sides to adjust the difference and dispute that were between the king and the Duke of Burgundy, in order to settle a firm and lasting peace.

In the same year the Duke of Guienne, after his return from Amiens, began to grow a little dissatisfied with the king, and sent for the Count d'Armagnac, whom the king had banished the kingdom at the same time that he deprived him of his earldom. The count, immediately upon that summons, waited upon the Duke of Guienne, who gave him the greatest part of his earldom, against the king's consent and positive commands to the contrary.

In May, the Duke of Calabria, nephew to the King of Sicily and Jerusalem, and to whom the king had offered his eldest daughter in marriage, left his duchy of Lorraine, and went in person to the Duke of Burgundy's court, to treat of a marriage with his daughter, which was very strangely and unaccountably done by him (after the honour which the king, who was his sovereign lord, had designed him) to think of marrying the Duke of Burgundy's daughter, who was only a subject and a vassal to the king. But before this the Duke of Burgundy had often made war in France in favour of the Duke of Guienne, pretending his design was to give him his daughter in marriage; but he never intended it, and did quite the contrary, deluding him, as he had done several other lords, with fair promises and hopes of that match.

On Thursday, the 14th of May, 1472, the king received certain advice from M. Malicorne, a great favourite of the Duke of Guienne, that his master was dead at Bordeaux. And immediately after M. de Craon, M. Peter Doriolle, general of the finances, M. Oliver le Roux, and the rest of the ambassadors that were sent to the Duke of Burgundy, returned, and gave the king an account of their negotiation, and the truce which was prolonged till the 15th of June following. However, the Duke of Burgundy, notwithstanding the truce, took the field with his army, and fortified his old post between Arras and Bapaume, in a place called Hubuterne, in Artois.

After this the Duke of Burgundy still continued to play his mad pranks, and went on in his old obstinate ways, as he had formerly done. On Tuesday, the 11th of June, 1472, he sent a great detachment of his forces to summon Nesle, in which there was one named Le Petit Picart, that commanded five hundred Frank archers of the Isle of France, who refused to obey his summons, and sent him word that he would defend the town and castle to the last extremity; upon which the Burgundians made several attacks, but were always repulsed by Captain Picart and his garrison. The next day, about five in the morning, the Countess of

Nesle, attended by Captain Picart and the chief of the town, went out to wait on the Bastard of Burgundy, who commanded that detachment, in order to capitulate and make some honourable terms for the garrison. At last the Bastard of Burgundy agreed to spare their lives, provided they would immediately surrender the town, and march out, leaving their arms, horses, bag, and baggage behind, to which they were forced to submit. Upon their return they acquainted the garrison with what hard terms they must submit to; and accordingly Captain Picart, having drawn up his men in a body in the market-place, commanded them to dismount and lay down their arms, and imprudently delivered up the town to the Burgundians before the articles of capitulation were signed. No sooner were the Burgundians masters of the town but they immediately fell upon the garrison, who were naked and unarmed, and killed several of them, not sparing even those that fled to the churches for protection, without any manner of regard to the promise they had made them to spare their lives. Towards the latter end of this barbarous and inhuman action the Bastard of Burgundy entered the church on horseback, which swam in blood; and when he beheld the pavement all strewed with the dead bodies of these poor wretches, he said it was a glorious sight, and was pleased to find he had such good butchers in his company. Neither did his thirst of blood and vengeance cease here, for the next day he ordered the captain to be hanged, and the town to be set on fire. After this glorious expedition they marched the next day, which was Sunday, to Roye, in which there was a strong garrison, consisting of one thousand four hundred archers, commanded by Peter Aubert, bailiff of Melun and Nugon. Besides these forces, there were several volunteers and captains of the army, and amongst the rest Loisel de Balagny, governor of Beauvais, M. de Mouy, the Lord de Rubempre, and several others, who had with them about two hundred lances well armed and mounted. However, the king had just before caused the old fortifications of the town to be repaired, and new ones to be made, which had added considerable strength to the place, and had provided it with everything necessary for a long defence; yet they surrendered the town on the 16th of May, to the Burgundians, and marched shamefully out, leaving their cannon, horses, arms, bag and baggage behind them, after the king had been at the expense of one hundred thousand crowns of gold in erecting magazines, and putting it into a posture of defence. After the Duke of Burgundy had turned out the king's garrison in this naked and miserable condition, he took possession of the town, and after some stay there he came before Beauvais, which he likewise summoned, and upon their refusing to surrender, he resolved to besiege it; and immediately upon his arrival, which was on Saturday the 27th of June, 1472, he commanded his soldiers to storm it on every side, but they were bravely repulsed by the inhabitants of the same place. The very same night William de Valce, the Seneschal of Normandy's lieutenant, came to their relief with a reinforcement of two hundred lances, just as the Burgundians were going to make a vigorous attack, upon which they mounted the walls, and repulsed the Burgundians, who little expected so warm a reception. The next day, M. de Crussol, Joachim Rouault, Marshal of France, M. de Bueil, Guerin le Groing, M. de Torcy, and several other noblemen of Normandy, with a strong detachment, arrived there also, who behaved themselves handsomely during the whole siege, and gave signal marks of their courage and conduct. The Parisians were serviceable also to the besieged, and constantly supplied them with ammunition and provision; and during the siege several warm disputes and bloody actions happened between the Burgundians and the king's troops, in which several of the former were killed and wounded.

On Thursday, the 2nd of July, the Lord de Rubempré arrived at Paris from Beauvais and brought letters from the governor of that place directed to M. Gaucourt, the king's lieutenant in Paris, and to the mayor and aldermen, in which he acquainted them with the miserable condition that the Duke of Burgundy and his whole army were reduced to, that a halfpenny loaf was sold for threepence in their camp, that the Duke of Burgundy himself was grown desperate, and was resolved to have the town though with the loss and ruin of his whole army, and therefore begged of them that they would immediately send him some of their field-pieces, a body of their cross-bow men, and a supply of provision and ammunition, which were accordingly sent him under a

guard of sixty cross-bow men of Paris, commanded by the
bastard Rochechouart, Lord of Meru. And on Thursday, the
9th of July, about seven in the morning, the Duke of Burgundy began to batter the town wall over against the gate
of the Hotel Dieu with all his great and small cannon ;
and having made a breach, ordered his men to fill up the
ditch with fascines, timber, and hurdles, and to be ready with
their scaling-ladders ; which orders were instantly performed,
and a party of Burgundians came with great boldness and
resolution, and furiously attacked that part of the wall that
was opposite to the Hotel Dieu, but they were warmly
received and repulsed by M. Robert Destouteville, lord of
Beyne and mayor of Paris, who was posted there with some
of the king's troops. This attack lasted from seven in the
morning till eleven, during which action the Burgundians
had fifteen or sixteen hundred men killed and wounded; and
the number would have been greater, and their loss more
considerable, had not all the gates facing the Burgundian
army been so strongly barricadoed, that in the hurry and
confusion of storming the town they could not get them open
to make a sally and fall upon the enemy at the same time ;
at which all the noblemen and officers were extremely concerned, for if they could have come handsomely to have
engaged them, they would certainly have made a terrible
slaughter among them, for at that time the garrison consisted
of fourteen or fifteen thousand men, commanded by the
Count de Dammartin, Joachim Rouault, marshal of France,
Sallazart, William de Valce, Mery de Coue, Guerin le
Groing, the Lords de Beyne and Torcy, and several other
experienced officers of note and quality. During the whole
action the besieged lost but four men, and that through their
own rashness, as the report goes ; neither did the Burgundians, from their first investing the town to the 9th of July,
kill any more than four soldiers with their cannon, notwithstanding their constant firing from their batteries. The
next day after the attack, M. Denis Hesselin, mayor of
Paris, sent another body of cross-bow men to Beauvais with
arms, ammunition, provision, and some surgeons to dress
and take care of the sick and wounded.

On Friday, the 10th of July, which was the next day
after the attack, Sallazart, with a brigade of his own re-

giment, sallied out of Beauvais, and by break of day got into the Burgundian camp, where they killed all they met with, and burnt three fine tents with all that was in them, in one of which there were two men of quality killed, that offered a vast sum of money to save their lives. At last the whole camp took the alarm, and his soldiers shouting out, " A Sallazart, a Sallazart," made the Burgundians immediately run to their arms, and in a moment's time they were ready with a considerable body to oppose him ; upon which Sallazart thought fit to retire, which he did in very good order, and brought with him to Beauvais two pieces of cannon, one of which was a fine brass cannon, named one of the twelve peers, that the king lost at the battle of Mont l'Hery, and the rest that they could not bring off, they flung into a ditch by the way. Sallazart was closely pursued, and received several wounds : his horse was also wounded in several places of the body ; however he made a shift to carry him to Beauvais, where he dropt down dead immediately upon arriving there. From that sally to the 21st of July, no great action happened on either side.

On Wednesday, the feast of St. Magdalen, the Duke of Burgundy shamefully raised the siege of Beauvais, after having lain twenty days before it, and bombarded it night and day, without doing any considerable damage to the town, or killing many men. Twice in that time, indeed, he attempted to storm the place, but was as often repulsed, and in both actions lost a considerable number of men ; amongst the rest, several persons of note and distinction. In his retreat he lost the greatest part of his artillery, which the garrison of Amiens, who fell upon his rear, took from him. The Duke of Burgundy, being disappointed in his design of taking Beauvais, grew desperate, and commanded his army to burn the standing corn, and to destroy and set on fire all the towns and villages through which they marched in their way to St. Valery near Crotoy, which was immediately surrendered to him, there being but a small garrison in it, and the place itself not being capable of making a long defence against such a powerful army. From thence they marched to Eu, which was also surrendered to him on the same account. On Wednesday, the 29th of July, the Constable of France, with several other officers of the garrison of Beauvais, marched out with eight hundred lances, and took the route towards Arques and Monstiervillier, in the county of Caux, to intercept the Burgundians, who, it was believed, would march that way; and so they did, and encamped between that place, Eu, and Dieppe, near a village called Ferriers, where they lay a long time without doing anything, except taking the new castle of Nicourt, which made no resistance. After staying there three days, and upon their retreat, they set fire to the town and castle, which was a thousand pities, for it was a fine town and castle, and capable of being made a place of great strength. After this the Duke of Burgundy set fire to Longueville, Fahy, and several other towns and villages in the bailiwick of Caux; and all the mighty actions his army performed from their raising the siege of Beauvais, to the 1st of December, 1472, was only burning and destroying wherever they came. In the meantime, the king, who was in Bretagne, with an army of fifty thousand men, lay still and did nothing, being wheedled and cajoled by the smooth words and fair promises of the Duke of Burgundy's ambassadors, who still flattered him with the hopes of peace; besides, his majesty [was tender of the lives of his subjects, and was willing, on any reasonable terms, to prevent the effusion of Christian blood, not delighting in war and slaughter, as the Duke of Burgundy did, who had already given a sufficient demonstration of his bloody and revengeful temper, by the many cruel and inhuman actions he had committed, and the barbarities he was daily guilty of. After the Duke of Burgundy was returned from Caux, where he had burnt and destroyed everything, as you have already heard, and had been vigorously repulsed before Arques and Dieppe, he broke up from that country and marched to Rouen, where he met with a warmer reception than he had hitherto found before any town he had already besieged; so that after some time spent in vain, and a great number of his men being killed and wounded by frequent sallies, he was at last forced to abandon the siege, and shamefully march off towards Abbeville; upon which there was a report that he designed to form the siege of Noyon, whereupon the Lord de Crussol and several others of the king's officers were immediately sent thither with a good body of troops to garrison the town, who ordered some new works to be thrown up, on which they planted a fine train of artillery and supplied it with ammunition, provision, and whatever else was necessary for putting the place in a good posture of defence. But after all these preparations, the Burgundians never invested the town; however it suffered considerably on their account, for the officers were obliged to burn down the suburbs to hinder them from making a lodgment there.

About this time there was a report that the Burgundians were marching towards Lorraine and Barrois, upon which the king sent a detachment of five hundred lances, with all the nobles of the Isle of France and Normandy, besides a great number of Frank archers under the command of M. de Craon, his lieutenant-general, which were quartered in several towns in Champagne, where they lay above two months, and then marched back without doing anything.

In the meantime the Duke of Burgundy prevailed with the Emperor of Germany to go as far as Luxembourg, and from thence to the City of Metz, to persuade the inhabitants to admit a Burgundian garrison; but his imperial majesty, finding them utterly averse to it, returned to Luxembourg, and from thence to Germany.

About the same time, the Duke of Burgundy sent an agent to Venice to borrow money of the Venetians to pay the six hundred lances belonging to that state, which he had agreed to take into his service for three months. They were forced to march through the Duchy of Milan, and from thence to Upper Burgundy, being too weak to engage the king's army, which was posted on the frontiers of Burgundy, and hindered them from joining the Duke of Burgundy's forces any other way.

At the same time, the king married his eldest daughter, Anne of France, who was offered to the late Duke of Calabria, to M. de Beaujeu, the Duke of Bourbon's brother.

About this time, the Duke of Burgundy, partly by treason, and partly by surprise, entered Nivernois, where he took several places from the Duke of Nevers, as Roche, Chastillon, &c. At that time also the king's ambassadors that had been assembled before at Senlis, met together at Compiegne in hopes of finding the Duke of Burgundy's ambassadors there according to their appointment, but they did not come; so that after a long stay there to no purpose, the king's ambassadors returned to Paris; afterwards they went back again to Compiegne in January, and stayed there till the 5th of that month.

About the 20th of January, 1473, the Constable of France, who had turned the Lord de Creton and the whole garrison out of St. Quentin, and taken possession of it for himself, made his peace with the king, and his majesty was very well reconciled to him; and by the agreement that was concluded between them, the constable was to remain in St. Quentin, and to have Meaux and several other places that the king had taken from him, restored again; commissioners were likewise appointed by the king's order to inquire after those persons that had spoken reflectingly of the Constable concerning the seizure of St. Quentin, in order to have them severely punished; he had also a great sum of money remitted for the payment of his troops, which had been stopped immediately after the taking of St. Quentin. About this time the king came from Amboise to Senlis, and stayed some time in that neighbourhood; during which, the king's ambassadors and those of the Duke of Burgundy held several conferences, and at last a truce was agreed upon till the middle of May, in hopes that matters might be so ordered in that time, as to have a firm and lasting peace concluded between their two masters.

On Wednesday the 20th of April, 1474, the king ordered all the officers, citizens, and inhabitants of Paris to be reviewed; which was accordingly done; and they were all in arms, and drawn up in order without the gates of Paris, from the Bastille St. Antoine all along the town-ditch as far as the Tower of Billy, and from thence to the Grange-aux-Merciers. On the other side also they were drawn up in the same order of battle, and made a gallant appearance in their red coats with white crosses, and were computed to be in all about eighty thousand men, including those that belonged to the train of artillery, of which there was a great store brought out into the field that day. The king, attended by the Count de Dammartin (who made a great figure that day), Philip de Savoy, M. du Perche, Sallazart, and several other general officers of the army, with all his guards, was at the review. The King of Arragon's ambassadors were also there to wait upon his majesty; and were extremely surprised to see one city produce such a vast number of men in arms. After the review was over, the king went to the Bois de Vincennes to supper, and took the ambassadors along with him; and some time after presented the two chief ones with two gold cups richly embossed, that weighed forty marks of gold, and cost three thousand two hundred crowns, and after that his majesty returned to Senlis, where he stayed some time; during which he received two embassies, one from the Duke of Bretagne, and the other from the Emperor of Germany. The chief ambassador of the last embassy was the Duke of Bavaria, and the chief of the first was Philip des Essars, Lord of Thieux, the Duke of Bretagne's steward of his household, who had formerly declared himself against the king; however, his majesty, laying aside all animosities, received him very kindly, gave him a present of ten thousand crowns, and made him inquisitor-general and justice in eyre of Brie and Champagne, turning M. de Chastillon out of that post on purpose to oblige the said Philip des Essars.

About the same time of the king's being at Senlis, Ermenonville, and thereabouts, the Duke of Burgundy sent his ambassadors to wait on his majesty, who stayed there a great while, but did nothing; and presently afterwards the king went to Compiegne, Noyon, and several other places in that neighbourhood, where the Constable of France came to wait on the king, in order to adjust some difference that was between them. The king and he had an interview in the open field near a certain village thereabouts, and both were attended by a strong guard for the security of their persons. The Constable of France having thus made his peace with the king, who generously forgave and pardoned all his rebellious actions, solemnly swore never to be guilty of the like for the future, but henceforward to obey and serve the king, as a loyal and dutiful subject ought to do, against all invaders and opposers whatsoever.

About this time, the king, who had a singular love for his people, and was willing to prevent the effusion of Christian blood, prolonged the truce with the Duke of Burgundy, his mortal enemy, for another year, and in April 1475, though he had received several embassies from the Emperor of

Germany, humbly to intreat his majesty not to make any longer truce with him, but that he would give him leave to enter his territories by force of arms, and make him submit to what terms his majesty should offer; promising, moreover, that whatever conquests or acquisitions he should make in any of the Duke of Burgundy's dominions, should be made over to the king, without putting him to the expense of either men or money. But notwithstanding all these advantageous offers, a truce was concluded between the king and the Duke of Burgundy, who immediately broke it, and committed several acts of hostility, ruining and destroying abundance of the king's subjects living in those countries that bordered upon his dominions, for which he never made any reparation, and which was looked upon to be a base and audacious action for a vassal thus to ruin the countries and subjects of his sovereign lord and master.

About this time the Duke of Burgundy (whose restless ambition would not suffer him to sit still), had invaded some part of Germany, and besieged Nuz, a large and strong town, situated upon the Rhine, near Cologne, before which place he lay a considerable time with his whole army, and all his artillery. Not long after this the Burgundians surprised a town in Gastinois called Molins Engelbert, whither his majesty sent also another body of forces with some cannon, in order to retake it. In short, the Duke of Burgundy and his allies (notwithstanding the truce), still continued to make incursions into the king's dominions, to seize his towns whenever they had an opportunity, and to ruin and destroy his subjects.

About this time Edward IV., King of England, sent his heralds to the king, to demand the duchies of Guienne and Normandy, which he claimed as his lawful right, and upon refusal, to declare war against him. The king returned a very civil answer by the heralds, and also sent King Edward the finest horse he had in his stable as a present.

In February following, the Germans who were besieged in Nuz, by the assistance of the inhabitants of Cologne, and some other Germans of the circle of Austria, found out a way to throw some provisions into the town in spite of the Duke of Burgundy, who kept it closely besieged, and had caused several large vessels well manned to come up the

Rhine, in order to intercept the convoy, but to no purpose, for it safely arrived in the town, and all his ships (in which were about six or seven thousand Burgundians, who were all drowned), were sunk or split in pieces, and besides those a vast number of them had already been killed before Nuz.

About the same time the city of Perpignan was surrendered to the king, on condition that the garrison should march out with their arms, horses, bag and baggage, leaving only their artillery, of which they had a very fine train, for the king's use.

On the 7th of April, 1475, the league that had been lately concluded between the emperor and the king was published in Paris, but first of all the king ordered it to be proclaimed before the lodgings of M. du Maine, the Duke of Calabria, and the Duke of Bretagne's ambassadors. In the same month the king received two embassies, one from the Duke of Tuscany, and the other from the Emperor of Germany, and the ambassadors were nobly treated and entertained not only by the king, but by all the nobility of the court. In the beginning of May the king, attended by the Admiral of France, and the other officers of the kingdom, set out from Paris for Vernon on the Seine, whither his majesty went to consult about the military operations of the ensuing campaign, the truce being expired on the last day of April, and from whence he returned to Paris on the 14th of the same month.

On the feast of the Holy Cross the king's army invested Montdidier, which had also refused to surrender upon the summons, but afterwards they considered better of it, and finding the king's forces were actually preparing to storm the town, on Friday the 5th of April, they beat the chamade, and offered to surrender, provided they might march out, and be safely conducted to the next garrison town belonging to the Duke of Burgundy, which was granted on condition of leaving their horses, arms, bag and baggage behind them; so the king's troops immediately took possession of the town, which they afterwards demolished, as they did Tronquoy.

On Saturday the 6th of May, the town of Roye and the castle of Moreul was surrendered to the king upon the same terms. The taking of these towns in so short a time by the king's army struck such a terror into the Duke of Burgundy's subjects, that they either fled before it, or else came

in and joined it; so that the king's army being daily augmented by the Burgundian troops that came over to them,
all the cities and towns in Burgundy, Flanders, and Picardy,
were soon reduced to the king's obedience.

In July, notwithstanding the news that the Constable of
France had written to the king, his majesty received advice
from the emperor, that he had thrown a fresh supply of
troops into Nuz, had taken out all the sick and wounded,
and provided the town with provisions and all other necessaries for a year longer, and that some action had happened
between his forces and the Duke of Burgundy's, in which the
latter had lost great part of his artillery, plate and money,
which was sent to pay his army.   On Tuesday the 27th of
June, the Admiral of France, whom the king ordered to
march with a body of men into Flanders and Picardy to
plunder and destroy the countries with fire and sword, drew
near Arras, and having placed his men in an ambuscade, he
ordered forty men at arms to advance towards the city gates,
upon which part of the garrison of Arras immediately sallied
out and attacked them, who according to their orders retired
to the place where the rest of their detachment lay in ambush,
who all on a sudden fell so furiously upon the Burgundians,
that they entirely broke and defeated them, several of whom
were killed, and abundance taken prisoners, and among the
latter M. James de St. Paul, Governor of Arras, and several
other persons of note and distinction, whom the Admiral of
France carried with him when he went to summon the city,
and told the inhabitants, that if they would not instantly
surrender the town to the king, who was their lawful sovereign, he would certainly behead their governor and the
rest of the men of quality he had taken prisoners.

On Tuesday the 29th of August the king, attended by the
Duke of Bourbon, M. de Lyon, and several other persons of
quality, besides a vast number of officers of the army, consisting of one hundred thousand horse, marched from Amiens
to Picquigny, which was the place that had been appointed
for the interview between his majesty and Edward IV. King
of England, who had brought with him his vanguard and his
rear, which were drawn up in order of battle near Picquigny.
Upon Picquigny bridge, the king had ordered two large
pent-houses to be erected opposite to each other, one for him-

self, and the other for the King of England. In the middle between these two pent-houses was built a large wooden grate somewhat like a lion's cage, about breast high, so that the two kings might lean over it, and discourse together. The King of France came first to the grate, upon which an English baron, whom King Edward had commanded to wait there for his majesty's arrival, was despatched in all haste to acquaint King Edward with it, who lay strongly encamped with twenty thousand English at a place about a league from Picquigny, and who came attended only by twenty men at arms of his guards, who were ordered to stay on the other side of the river at the foot of the bridge during the whole conference between the two kings. In the mean time it fell a raining prodigiously, which did a considerable damage to the housings and furniture that the nobility and officers of the French court had prepared on purpose for this interview, and which were rich and magnificent. As soon as the King of England came within sight of the king, he threw himself upon one knee, and so he did twice before he came up and saluted his majesty, who received him with all the marks of honour and respect imaginable. After some compliments had passed between them, they began to discourse about the affair for which this interview was appointed, in the presence of above one hundred persons, among whom were the Duke of Bourbon, M. de Lyon, several other lords, and all the chief officers of the finances. After they had talked together for about a quarter of an hour, the king ordered every one to withdraw, and the two kings had a private conference, which lasted a considerable time, and when it was over, the king openly declared that there was a truce concluded between them for seven years, which was to begin from this day the 29th of August, 1475, and end on the same day in 1482. This truce, which was soon after proclaimed in Paris, and all other cities and towns of the kingdom, related chiefly to trade and commerce; and by this treaty the English, whether armed or unarmed, provided they were not more than one hundred in one company, were permitted to go and come when and where they pleased all over the kingdom of France. As soon as this affair was concluded, the king ordered seventy-five thousand crowns to be remitted to King Edward, made considerable presents to some of the lords that attended on him, and ordered money to be given and distributed among his trumpets and heralds, who highly extolled the bounty and generosity of the king.   The King of France besides all this promised King Edward to pay him fifty thousand crowns of gold yearly, and nobly entertained the Duke of Gloucester, the King of England's brother, to whom he also made considerable presents.   King Edward immediately ordered all the English that he had sent to reinforce the garrisons of Abbeville, Peronne, and other towns in the Duke of Burgundy's possessions, tó evacuate those places, and join the army, with which he marched back to Calais, where he embarked for England.   M. Herberge the Bishop of Evreux waited on King Edward as far as Calais, where he left two English barons till he had sent the king something out of England that he had promised him.   The Lord Howard was one of these barons that were left as pledges for performance of King Edward's promise, and the Master of the Horse to the king was the other; they were both of them highly valued and esteemed by the King of England, and were very instrumental in concluding the late treaty between the two kings. When the English barons took their leave of the king, his majesty presented them with a set of gold and silver plate, and sent an order to Paris to let them have what quantity of wine they pleased to carry over with them into England, provided they paid for it.

On Monday the 16th of October 1475, the truce in relation to trade and commerce that had been concluded for nine years between the king and the Duke of Burgundy, was solemnly proclaimed by sound of trumpet in all the public streets of Paris, and it was to commence on the 14th of September 1475, and to end on the same day of the month in 1484.   By this treaty all the subjects of Burgundy were to have full liberty of trading in any part of France, and during the term of nine years to settle and live there if they pleased.

The Duke of Burgundy having promised by his ambassadors in October last, when the truce was concluded between him and the king for nine years, to deliver up the Constable of France to his majesty, was now forced, much against his inclinations, to do it, and he was accordingly delivered up into the hands of the Admiral of France, M. de Bouchage, M. William de Cerisay, and several others, who brought him to Paris, where he was afterwards beheaded on Tuesday the 19th of December, 1475, and his goods confiscated to the king.

After the Constable of France's death, it plainly appeared that he had been guilty of several notorious crimes, and the whole course of his villanous and treasonable practices were openly declared in parliament, and all his underhand dealings and correspondence with the Duke of Burgundy were fully discovered. Then we perfectly knew the whole mystery of that affair, and how the Duke of Burgundy and he had often endeavoured to corrupt and debauch the Duke of Bourbon's principles, and draw him over to their party, and that at last, after many fruitless attempts, how he despatched a subtle agent of his named Hector de l'Ecluse to the Duke of Bourbon, to acquaint him that the English had a design to invade France, and that if he would join with them and the Duke of Burgundy, he questioned not but to conquer the whole kingdom, and that a great part of it should be annexed to his territories as a reward for his assistance. This was the master-piece of his villany and treason: but it seems the Duke of Bourbon had too much honour to hearken to such proposals, and told the said Hector de l'Ecluse that he would have no hand in it, and that he had rather be reduced to beggary, than ever consent to the ruin of either the king or kingdom.

In February, 1476, the king, who was at Tours or Amboise, set out from thence for Bourbonnois and Auvergne, from whence he went to Notre Dame de Puy to perform his devotions, and afterwards into Lionnois and Dauphiny. While the king was at Notre Dame de Puy he received an express that brought him the news of the defeat of the Duke of Burgundy's army by the Swiss, as he was endeavouring to penetrate into Switzerland, which happened after the following manner. After the taking of Granson the Duke of Burgundy marched with his army along the lake of Verdun towards Friburg, and by the way took two small castles situated upon the mountains, just at the entrance of them; but the Swiss, who had intelligence of his approach, and were also informed of his taking Granson, marched towards him; and on Friday the first of March, towards night, they arrived at the two above-mentioned castles, which they im-

mediately invested after such a manner as to prevent the
garrisons from making any sallies, and placed about 6000
men with fire-arms in a little copse between the two castles
near the place where the Duke of Burgundy lay encamped
with his whole army. The next day very early in the
morning, as the Duke of Burgundy was marching forward
with all his artillery, bag and baggage, this body of Swiss,
upon a signal given them, started out of the ambush where
they had lain all night, and all on a sudden made so terrible
a fire with their small arms upon most of the Burgundian
vanguard, as killed most of the chief officers, and entirely
broke and dispersed them; and notwithstanding the Duke
of Burgundy did all he could to rally his men, and make
them face the enemy once more, their consternation was so
great, that he could not bring them up to stand a second
charge; and the Swiss being animated by this success, and
eager to improve the advantage they had gained over the
enemy, as soon as they had discharged their muskets, fell on,
sword in hand, and entirely routed the whole army. At
last, the Duke of Burgundy finding the battle was lost, and
that he was in danger of being taken prisoner, in great
agony and confusion mounted his horse, and being attended
by only four officers of his army, made his escape to Joigny,
which was sixteen French leagues from the place where
this defeat happened. In this action, which happened on
Saturday the 2nd of March, 1476, the Duke of Burgundy
lost the greatest part of the chief officers and men of quality
of his army, besides all his artillery, bag and baggage. The
Swiss also retook both the castles, and hung up all the
Burgundians they found in them. Afterwards they retook
the town and castle of Granson, and ordered the Germans
to the number of 512, that the Burgundians had hanged,
to be cut down, and so many of the Burgundians that
were in Granson to be hanged up in the same halters.

In May, 1476, the Duke of Burgundy, notwithstanding
his defeat near Granson, was resolved still to push on the
war against the Germans, and to besiege Strasbourg, but
not being in a condition to do it without a fresh supply of
men and money, he sent M. William Hugonet and twelve
other deputies into his own dominions to acquaint his subjects, that though he had been defeated by the Swiss, yet he

was resolved to be revenged on them, and to push on the war with greater vigour ; and therefore, being unable to do it without a great supply of men and money, he commanded all his subjects by these deputies of Ghent, Bruges, Brussels, and other towns in Flanders, to exert themselves upon this occasion, and give him the sixth part of their estates, and such a number of men as he should demand. And in order to prevail with them to consent to his demands, he bid the deputies tell them that the Germans were got between him and home, and that without a fresh supply of forces he could not return into his own dominions. To which remonstrance the inhabitants of the above-mentioned towns made answer, that they were resolved to grant no more supplies of either men or money to carry on the war, but that if the German army was too strong for him, and hindered him from coming home, they would venture their lives and all they were worth to bring him safely into his own dominions.

In the mean time the king stayed at Lyons feasting and enjoying himself, where the King of Sicily his uncle came to wait on him, whom his majesty entertained very nobly, showed the diversions of the fair that was kept in that city, and gave several balls and entertainments, to which the handsomest ladies of Lyons were always invited on purpose to divert and entertain him.

Some time after this, the king, who was at Lyons, and had great part of his army with him, received advice that the Duke of Lorraine, in conjunction with the Swiss and Germans, besides a good body of Lorrainers, were in motion to oppose the Duke of Burgundy, who had rashly and imprudently penetrated into Switzerland, and with his whole army was set down before a little town in that country named Morat. And on Saturday, the 22nd of June 1476, between ten and eleven in the morning, the Duke of Lorraine at the head of all those forces we have already mentioned, attacked the Duke of Burgundy, and at the first charge entirely broke and defeated his vanguard, which consisted of twelve thousand men, and the slaughter and confusion was so very great, that the Count de Romont who commanded them had much ado to make his escape. After this defeat the garrison of Morat joined the Duke of Lorraine's army, which forced the Duke of Burgundy's entrenchments, where they gave no quarter, but killed all they found in them, so that the Duke of Burgundy was at last forced to retire with the remains of his broken army that had saved themselves by flight; nay, he himself fled as far as Joigny, which was sixteen French leagues from the field of battle, and in this action he lost all his artillery, plate, money, jewels, tents, pavilions, and in short, every thing of value that was in the camp. As soon as the battle was over, the Germans and Swiss returned the Duke of Lorraine many thanks for his care and conduct in the action, and in consideration of the great services he had done them, they presented him with all the Duke of Burgundy's artillery to make him amends for what he lost at Nancy, when the Duke of Burgundy by force of arms sacked that town, and carried away all the cannon that he found in it. The heralds that were appointed to take an account of the slain, reported that there were twenty-two thousand five hundred Burgundians killed on the spot, besides a vast number in the rout, for the Duke of Lorraine's army pursued them as far as Joigny, and afterwards burnt and destroyed the whole earldom of Romont in Savoy, putting all to the sword they could meet with, without any distinction of age or sex.

After this the Duke of Lorraine marched to Strasbourg, and from thence with a body of four thousand men detached from the grand army, went and besieged Nancy, in which there was a garrison of one thousand two hundred Burgundians, and after he had given some directions to the officer that commanded a body of troops under him, he returned to Strasbourg again, from whence he sent several convoys of provision and ammunition, and afterwards set out himself for the camp before Nancy, to command at the siege of that place in person.

After the Duke of Burgundy's defeat at Morat, and the besieging of Nancy, the town was surrendered to the Duke of Lorraine, on condition that the garrison (who were all Burgundians) should march out with bag and baggage, and the usual marks of honour, which was granted them; and as soon as the Duke of Lorraine was master of it, he immediately put a strong garrison of his own troops in it, and provided it with ammunition, provision, and all things necessary for a long defence; and it was well he acted so prudently, for

scarce had he been a month in possession of the town, when
the Duke of Burgundy, who was retired to Riviere, a town
near Salins in Burgundy, with what forces he could raise,
came and besieged it again, upon which the Duke of Lorraine
marched into Switzerland to solicit more troops, in order to
relieve the garrison, and raise the siege of Nancy.

After this, the King of Portugal, who laid claim to the
kingdom of Castile, and, in short, to all Spain, in right of his
queen, left his kingdom and came to the frontiers of France,
and from thence to Tours to visit the king ; and to desire
his majesty to assist him with some troops to recover those
kingdoms.   He was received by the king with all the marks
of honour and respect imaginable, and during his stay at
Tours, he was nobly treated and entertained by the king
and several of the nobility of the court.

In the mean time the Duke of Burgundy, who, as you
have already been informed, had besieged Nancy in Lorraine,
put the garrison to such great straits and necessities, that
for want of provision they were forced to capitulate, and
surrender the town upon articles.   And on Sunday the 5th
of January, the Duke of Lorraine arrived with an army of
twelve or fourteen thousand Swiss and Germans, in order
to raise the siege of Nancy, and fight the Duke of Burgundy.
On Saturday the 4th of January, the Duke of Lorraine arrived with an army of ten thousand Swiss, besides Germans
and Lorrainers at St. Nicholas de Varengeville.

On the Sunday following, the Lords of Switzerland and
Lorraine marched from thence to Neufville, and a little
beyond that place they halted some time, to consider how
they might draw up their forces to the best advantage ; and
accordingly they divided their army into two bodies, one of
which was commanded by the Count d'Abstain, and the
governors of Fribourg and Zurich ; and the other by the
chief magistrates of Berne.   About noon, the two bodies
began to march at once ; one towards the river, and the
other along the high road leading to Nancy.   The Duke of
Burgundy, who had intelligence of their coming, had quitted
his intrenchments, and drawn up his army in order of
battle ready to receive them.   In the front between him
and one of the enemies' bodies there was a little brook
and two strong hedges ; and on the high road, along

which the other was marching to engage him, he had
planted all his cannon and field-pieces; and as soon as
ever the Swiss came within bow-shot, the Burgundians
discharged a whole volley of arrows, which did no execution, upon which that body quitted the high road, and
marched higher towards the wood, till they had gained an
eminence opposite to the Duke of Burgundy's army. In
the mean time, the Duke of Burgundy commanded his
archers (who were all on foot) to face about; and at the
same time ordered two squadrons of his men-at-arms, commanded by James Galiot and M. de Lallain, to attack the
enemy. As soon as the Swiss had gained the rising ground
opposite to the Duke of Burgundy's army, they immediately
faced about; and marching up to him with all the fury
and intrepidity imaginable, made such a terrible fire upon
the body of foot that he commanded, that they entirely broke
and defeated them. The other body of Swiss marched at
the same time to engage the two squadrons commanded by
James Galiot and M. de Lallain, whom they entirely routed
at the first charge. Upon this, the right wing of the Burgundians, who had not yet been engaged, attacked the Swiss,
by whom they were repulsed, and, at last entirely defeated;
so that when the foot began to give ground and run away, the
horse presently followed them, and endeavoured to make their
escape by the bridge of Bridores, which was about a league
from Nancy, in the way to Thionville and Luxembourg.
But the Count di Campobasso having secured that pass by a
good body of troops, and the Duke of Lorraine and his men
following them close at the heels, vast numbers of them threw
themselves or were driven into the river, where they were
drowned; and the rest were either killed or taken, very few
or none making their escape; so that there was a greater
number killed in the rout than on the field of battle.
Some of the Burgundians, finding they could not get over
the bridge, retired to the woods in hopes of saving themselves; but they were pursued thither by the peasants of
the country, who killed them as fast as they could find
them, so that for four leagues round, the fields and high-
ways were strewed with the bodies of dead men. The
pursuit lasted till two hours after night, and then the
Duke of Lorraine began to inquire what was become of

the Duke of Burgundy, whether he had made his escape or was taken prisoner; but nobody could give any account of him, and immediately the Duke of Lorraine despatched a certain person to one John Dias of the city of Metz, to know if he had passed through that place in his retreat, who sent his highness word the next morning that he had not; that he was not at Luxembourg; neither could any body tell what was become of him. On Monday, which was Twelfth-day, the Count di Campobasso met with a page that was taken prisoner, belonging to the Count de Chalon, who was with the Duke of Burgundy in the battle. This lad, upon examination, confessed the Duke of Burgundy was killed; and the next day, upon diligent searching after him, they found him stripped stark naked, and the bodies of fourteen men more in the same condition, at some distance from each other. The duke was wounded in three places, and his body was known and distinguished from the rest by six particular marks; the chiefest of which was, the want of his upper teeth before, which had been beaten out with a fall; the second was a scar in his throat occasioned by the wound he received at the battle of Mont l'Hery; the third was his great nails, which he always wore longer than any of his courtiers; the fourth was another scar upon his left shoulder; the fifth was a fistula on his right groin, and the last was a nail that grew into his little toe. And upon seeing all these above-mentioned marks upon the body, his physician, the gentleman of the bed-chamber, the Bastard of Burgundy, M. Oliver de la Marche, his chaplain, and several other officers that were taken prisoners by the Duke of Lorraine, unanimously agreed it was the body of their lord and master the Duke of Burgundy.

Immediately after the defeat and death of the Duke of Burgundy, the Duke of Lorraine and the rest of the generals of the army called a council of war, the result of which was, that a considerable body of forces should immediately be sent into the Duchy of Burgundy and other provinces, to reduce the towns that were garrisoned by Burgundian troops, to the king's obedience; which was put in execution, and most of the towns surrendered without any opposition, as did likewise the country of Auxerre, the subjects of which took the oath of allegiance to the king.

In June, the Prince of Orange, who had been highly affronted by M. de Craon, lieutenant-general of the king's army in Burgundy, was resolved to be revenged on him and the king also, who, it seems, had taken the government of a province from him, and given it to M. de Craon; and therefore, he persuaded all the countries, cities, towns, and other places, which before had submitted to the king at his request, to revolt and rise up in rebellion against him. There was a Burgundian knight named M. Claude de Vaudray, that joined with the prince in this undertaking, and managed the war with tolerable success against M. de Craon. But at last, M. de Craon having intelligence that the Prince of Orange was in a little town called Guy, marched immediately and besieged it, and about two days after he had invested it, he received advice that M. Chasteauguyon was marching to relieve it, upon which he left a few troops before the town, to hinder the garrison from making any sally, and with the rest of the army, advanced to meet M. Chasteauguyon, the Prince of Orange's brother, whom he entirely routed and defeated; and in this action, there were above one thousand four hundred persons of note and distinction killed on both sides; and for this victory, the king ordered general processions to be made in the church of St. Martin in Paris.

In July, 1477, the Duke of Guelders, with about fourteen or fifteen hundred Germans, came and encamped at Pont d'Epierre near Tournay, with a design to burn the suburbs of that place, upon which, the garrison of Tournay made two sallies; in the first, the duke himself was slain, and in the last, the whole body of Germans and Flemings were entirely defeated, two thousand of them killed upon the spot, and seven hundred taken prisoners, for which, the king ordered *Te Deum* to be sung, and bonfires to be made in the streets of Paris.

About the same time, the king, who was in Picardy, left that country; having first made the Bastard of Bourbon, (who was Admiral of France,) his lieutenant-general, with whom he left a good body of forces to secure the country, and cover the frontiers of his kingdom. The king's troops under the Bastard of Bourbon's command were quartered in Arras, Tournay, la Bassee, and in several other towns upon

the frontiers of Flanders, and in those countries that still
held out for the Lady of Flanders, daughter to the late Duke
of Burgundy.

May, 1478. — All that the king did during this whole
month in Picardy, was only taking a little town called Condé,
which was still in the hands of the Burgundians, and which
stood very incommodiously for the garrison of Tournay;
for all the convoys both of provisions and ammunition must
of course pass by it. There happened to be some German
troops belonging to the Duke of Austria in it, who at first
seemed resolved to stand a siege, but when they saw the
prodigious army with which the king had invested it, they
immediately surrendered the town upon honourable terms,
as they did also the castle some time after.

About this time the king, who was gone into Picardy
with a design to reduce all the countries, towns, and places
that were in the possession of the late Duke of Burgundy at
his decease, and which belonged to his majesty, had assembled the greatest army, and provided the largest train of
artillery that ever was seen in France. He forebore entering
upon any action for a long time, in hopes of accommodating
matters between him, the Flemings, and the Duke Maximilian of Austria, whom they acknowledged for their sovereign,
to facilitate which the Duke of Austria sent ambassadors to
Cambray and Arras to treat with the king about it, who
talked mightily of surrendering up to the king the countries
of Artois, Boulogne, Douay, Orchies, St. Omers, and other
towns, besides the whole Duchy of Burgundy; and upon the
bare promises only of these ambassadors the king imprudently
delivered up Cambray, Quesnoy, Bouchain, and several other
towns. The Duke of Austria, upon the pretence of being
near the king, and having the conveniency of frequent conferences, came and encamped with an army of twenty thousand men between Douay and Arras, where he amused the
king with specious words and fair promises till the end of
June; and then, notwithstanding the king had so generously
given up those towns to him, he openly declared he would
not stand to the promises his ambassadors had made in his
name, neither was that affair brought to any conclusion.

In this month the king had better success in Upper Burgundy; whither his majesty had sent a considerable body

of forces under the command of M. d'Amboise, governor of Champagne, to recover some troops that had revolted from him. M. d'Amboise was so fortunate, that in three weeks he retook Verdun, Monsauion, and Semur in Auxois, partly by storm and partly by composition. Afterwards he besieged Beaune, which also was surrendered to him upon certain articles, the chief of which were, that the inhabitants should pay forty thousand livres to preserve the town from being plundered; that they should discharge all their debts that were owing to the merchants of Paris, and of other cities in the kingdom, and that the garrison should be allowed to march out with their bag and baggage, and be conducted to such a place mentioned in the articles.

In July the king, who was at Arras, received two extraordinary embassies, one from Maximilian, Duke of Austria, and another from the Flemings; and when the ambassadors had been heard by the king and his council, a cessation of arms was agreed upon between the king, Duke Maximilian, and the Flemings, for one year, during which time there was to be a free intercourse of trade between the subjects of both princes.

In April 1479, the king, who was in the county of Touraine, began to make preparations for the ensuing campaign, being resolved to push on the war with vigour as soon as the cessation of arms between him and the Duke of Austria, which was almost expired, was ended. Besides, the Duke of Austria had sent no ambassadors to him to treat of a prolongation of the truce, and therefore his majesty might reasonably conclude that his intentions were to renew the war as soon as the treaty was expired.

In May following (notwithstanding the truce was not expired) the inhabitants of Cambray treacherously admitted the Flemings, Picardians, and other soldiers belonging to the Duke of Austria's army, into their city, which his majesty thought had been safe enough in the hands of so vigilant and loyal a governor as the Lord de Piennes. As soon as the Duke of Austria's forces were masters of the town, they drove the king's garrison out of the castle, and immediately after a detachment of three or four hundred Flemings and Picardians presented themselves before the town and castle of Bouchain, upon intelligence that the inhabitants would murder the king's garrison, and open their gates to them, which accordingly they did upon their first approach, and killed all the king's soldiers except one archer, who had the good luck to escape. The king was extremely incensed and provoked at this unfair and treacherous manner of proceeding, seeing his troops had not committed the least act of hostility, nor given them any occasion or pretence for violating the truce, and therefore he immediately sent a considerable body of the nobles and Frank archers of the kingdom, with a large train of artillery, under the command of the governor of Champagne, to reduce the towns and places in the duchy of Burgundy and Franche-Compté that had lately revolted from him, who was so very fortunate as to retake the strong castle of Rochefort by storm, which he plundered, and put all the garrison to the sword. From thence the governor of Champagne, who was also the king's lieutenant-general, marched with his army to Dole, which, upon their refusing to surrender, he immediately attacked, carried it by storm, plundered it, put all the inhabitants to the sword, and razed the city to the ground.

On Saturday the third of July, 1479, the Bishop of Lombes, abbot of St. Denis in France, arrived at Paris as ambassador extraordinary from the King of Spain, and was met and complimented without the city gates by the mayor and aldermen, and all the persons of quality of that city, whom he afterwards nobly entertained at St. Denis. About the same time a young prince of the kingdom of Scotland, named the Duke of Albany, who had been driven out of the kingdom by the king his brother, arrived at Paris, where he was received with all the marks of honour and civility imaginable, and treated and entertained at the king's expense during his stay in France.

In the year 1480, the Lord Howard, and several other ambassadors from England, arrived in France, to treat with the king about prolonging the truce that was concluded between him and the King of England. The king received the ambassadors very kindly, feasted and entertained them nobly, and made them considerable presents when they left France in order to return to England.

During winter, and even till April (at which time the truce between the king and the Flemings was to expire) nothing was attempted on either side; for the Flemings had sent ambassadors to the king at Tours to desire the cessation of arms might be continued a year longer, to which his majesty readily consented, in hopes some expedient or another might be found in all that time to settle an honourable and lasting peace between him and them, which would put an end to a war that had already been the occasion of spilling so much Christian blood.

About the same time ambassadors from Edward IV., King of England, arrived in France, to treat with the king about the prolongation of the truce, and his majesty did them the favour to meet them at Chateau Regnault; and, as soon as they had despatched the affair which they were sent to negotiate with the king, they returned into England, and afterwards the prolongation of the truce between the two kings was proclaimed by sound of trumpet at Paris. Some time after this the king fell very ill at Plessis du Parc, near Tours, and his physicians were of opinion that his majesty was in a dangerous condition, but in a little time he grew better, and in less than a month was perfectly recovered of his illness.

In the year 1481, notwithstanding the cessation of arms, the king's troops in the garrison towns upon the frontiers of Picardy committed several hostilities, and had frequent skirmishes with the Duke of Austria's men, and all the prisoners that were taken on both sides were immediately hanged, without permitting any, of what degree or rank soever, to be ransomed.

About the same time the king, who had been very ill at Tours, removed to Thouars, where his majesty grew worse, and his physicians were of opinion he was in a dangerous condition, whereupon he made several large offerings and gifts to abundance of churches in the kingdom, in hopes to recover his health by these pious acts of charity and devotion. In his sickness he made a vow to go a pilgrimage to St. Claude, which he accordingly performed as soon as he recovered strength enough to undertake the journey. Before he left the county of Touraine, he went to see the dauphin, whom he had scarce ever seen before, and when he took his leave of him he gave him his blessing, and having committed him to the care and tuition of the Lord

Peter de Bourbon, whom he had made his lieutenant-general, he commanded him to obey that lord, and be ruled by him in everything till his return.

In the year 1482, on Thursday, the 4th of May, between four and five in the morning,, died the most noble and illustrious Princess Joan of France, wife to John Duke of Bourbon and Auvergne, in the castle of Moulins, in Bourbonnois, of a violent fever, and was buried at the church of Notre Dame, at Moulins. She was a lady of great wisdom and piety, and was extremely lamented by the duke, her husband, her servants, and all the people of France, upon account of the many extraordinary virtues and amiable perfections she was endowed with.

In the same year, about October, the king fell violently ill, and thought he should have died at Plessis du Parc, near Tours; and, therefore, as soon as his majesty had recovered a little strength, he went to Amboise, where he made several long remonstrances to the dauphin in behalf of his servants and officers of his household and kingdom, exhorting and desiring him to be kind to all of them, but especially to Monsieur Oliver, his barber, and M. John de Doyac, governor of Auvergne, who had done him many considerable services, and always been very loyal and faithful subjects. He also recommended the Lord de Bouchage and the Lord Guyotpot, bailiff of Vermandois, as being very wise and able counsellors, and desired the dauphin to make use of their advice in all state affairs. Moreover, he entreated him to continue all the officers in their posts and employments, and to have a tender regard to his people, whom he had already too much harassed and oppressed. Lastly, he recommended the Lord des Querdes for military affairs, as being an officer of great valour and conduct, and the fittest person to make a general of any in the kingdom of France. After this, the king returned to Montils, near Tours.

In October and November several ambassadors arrived from Flanders to treat of a peace between his majesty and the Flemings, which at last was concluded to the great joy and satisfaction of both parties, by a marriage between the dauphin of France and the Duke of Austria's daughter, upon which the king immediately ordered *Te Deum* to be sung, and bonfires to be made in the public streets of Tours.

In January, 1483, the ambassadors that had concluded the peace between the king and the Flemings upon the marriage between the dauphin and the Countess of Flanders, daughter to the Duke of Austria, arrived at Paris, and were met and complimented in the king's name by the Bishop of Marseilles, the mayor and aldermen of the city, and several other persons of quality, who nobly feasted and entertained them, and the next day they set out from thence to wait on the king at Amboise, who received them very kindly, as did also the dauphin; and upon their taking leave of the king, his majesty presented them with thirty thousand crowns, and afterwards they returned to Paris, where the articles of peace were ratified and confirmed in the court of parliament, and afterwards read, and published by sound of trumpet in all the public streets of that city; and as soon as the publication was over, Monsieur le Picard, bailiff of Rouen, treated the ambassadors and all the king's officers with a splendid and magnificent dinner.

On Saturday, the 19th of April, 1483, the Lord de Beaujeu and his lady came to Paris, in order to go into Picardy to meet and compliment the dauphiness, whom, by the treaty of peace, the Flemings were to deliver to the Lord de Beaujeu, who was to conduct her to Paris.

In April, Edward IV., King of England, died of an apoplexy, though some say it was of a surfeit, occasioned by drinking too much of some rich wines that the king had made him a present of; however, he lived long enough to settle the affairs of his kingdom, and to leave the succession of the crown to his eldest son, Edward V.

On Monday, the 2d of June, the dauphiness, accompanied by Madame de Beaujeu, the Admiral of France's lady, and several other ladies of quality, made her public entry into Paris about five in the afternoon, and all the streets through which the dauphiness passed were lined with soldiers, hung with tapestry, and crowded with persons of quality, richly dressed, who came thither on purpose to compliment and pay their respects to her; and in honour to the day of her arrival, all the prisoners in Paris were immediately set at liberty.

In July, the nuptial ceremony between the dauphin and the Lady Margaret of Austria was performed with great pomp and solemnity at Amboise, at which all the nobility and chief persons of the kingdom were present.

On Monday, the 25th of August, the king fell very ill at Montils, near Tours, and in two hours' time lost his speech and his senses, and the news of his death came to Paris on Wednesday, the 27th of the same month; upon which the mayor and aldermen ordered the city gates to be shut up, and a strong guard to be placed at each of them, that none might go out or in without being examined, which made the common people cry out that the king was dead; but it was a false alarm, for his majesty was only in a fit, out of which he presently recovered, and lived till Saturday, the 30th of August, and then died about six or seven in the evening of the same day.

As soon as he was dead his body was embalmed, and buried in the church of Notre Dame de Clery, near Montils, having, in his life-time, ordered it should be so, and positively commanded the dauphin not to bury him in the church of St. Denis, where three kings of France (his illustrious predecessors) were interred. He never gave any reason for it, but some people were of opinion it was for the sake of the church, which he had liberally endowed, and out of a singular veneration for the blessed Virgin, who was worshipped there after a more solemn manner than in any other place in the kingdom. The king had during his whole reign, by the evil advice of M. Oliver, his barber, M. John de Doyac, and several other wicked counsellors that were about his person, committed great injustice in his kingdom, and so miserably oppressed and harassed his people, that the very reflection of his tyrannical usage of them stung him to the heart, and almost drove him to despair; so that when he lay upon his death-bed he sincerely repented of all his sins, and gave prodigious sums of money to the clergy to pray for his soul, and rewarded them for their prayers with what he had by violence and extortion gotten of his subjects. It must be owned that his was a very busy reign, and full of many great and important actions, yet he managed his affairs so well, that he forced all his enemies to submit to his mercy, and was equally dreaded both abroad and at home.   He lay for a long time before his death under very sharp and severe illnesses, which forced his physicians to make use of violent and painful applications, which though they were not so successful as to recover his health and save his life, yet, doubtless, they were very beneficial to his soul, and, perhaps, the chief means of saving it from eternal damnation, and fixing it in paradise, through His tender mercy who liveth and reigneth world without end.   Amen.

END OF THE SCANDALOUS CHRONICLE.

INDEX.

Abbeville ceded to the duke of Burgundy, i. 74 ; submits to Louis XI., 346.

Abrigan, Sir Thomas, ii. 32.

Abruzzi, revolt of the, ii. 162.

Abstain, count d', ii. 385.

Acri, count d', ii. 162.

Adorni, lord John, ii. 126.

Advin, John, ii. 302.

Africa, slavery in, i. 381.

Agincourt, battle of, ii. 2. et n.

Agnes of Burgundy, notices of, i. 9.

Aigreville, lord d', ii. 304.

Ailly, Jean d', baron of Picquigny, i. 272.

Aimeries, Antoine Rolin, lord of, i. 161. 293.

Aire, town of, ii. 32 ; delivered up to the lord des Cordes, 59.

Albania, submission of, to the Turks, ii. 166.

Albany, duke of, ii. 391.

Albourg, duke of, i. 123.

Albret, Alain, lord d', ii. 61.

Albret, Charles II., lord of, i. 16.

Alegre, Monsieur d', ii. 257.

Alençon, René, duke of, his danger, i. 154.

Alenson, city of, ii. 350.

Alexander VI. pope of Rome, ii. 123 ; quarrels with his cardinals, 158 ; settlement of their differences, 159 ; enters into a league with the Venetians, 179 ; flies to Orvietto, 187 ; his intrigues against the Venetians, 282.

Allegre, Yves, baron of, ii. 147.

Alliance, treaties of. (See Treaties.)

Allies of the duke of Burgundy, i. 9. et seq., 42. et seq.

Alonzo Cariello, archbishop of Toledo, i. 122.

Alphonso the Great, king of Arragon, surnamed the Wise, ii. 123. 154. et n.; his armies in the field, 125.

Alphonso, king of Naples, abdicates, and causes his son Ferrand to be crowned, ii. 150. 155 ; his atrocities, 150, 151 ; his father's capricious cruelties, 151 ; flies into Castile, and does penance, 156.

Alphonzo V., king of Portugal, i. 321., ii. 176. et n.; designs of, i. 331 ; his escape, 333 ; visits Louis XI., ii. 385.

Amadeus, duke Charles John, ii. 229.

Ambassadors, the going and coming of, sometimes very dangerous, i. 204, 205 ; league formed at Venice by, ii. 179 ; grand procession of, 181.

Ambition, public dissertation on, i. 47. et seq.

Amboise, magnificent building at, ii. 281 ; the obsequies of Charles VIII. at, 288 ; the residence of Louis XI., 309.

Amboise, the illustrious family of, xix.; their family contests, xix

—xxi. xxvii. *et seq.*; property of, restored, xxxiii.

Amboise, Charles, lord of Chaumont, i. 34., ii. 38 ; appointed lieutenant of Burgundy, ii. 21 ; recovers many towns in Burgundy, 21. *et seq.*

Amboise, George d', archbishop of Rome, ii. 233, 234.

Amboise, Louis d', bishop of Alby, ii. 38.

Amboise, M. d', his military successes, ii. 390.

Amboise, Peter, lord of Chaumont, i. 34.

Amiens ceded to the duke of Burgundy, i. 74; delivered up to the king, 172; besieged by the duke of Burgundy, 177; conceded to the duke of Burgundy, 216; taken by the king, 233, 234; the English entertained at, 268; disturbances in, 269.

Amurath II., Sultan of Turkey, ii. 90.

Ancenis, castle of, captured, i. 110; treaty of, 111.

Angers, bishop of, imprisoned, i. 165.

Angoulesme, Charles, count of, ii. 11.

Anjou, king Charles of, ii. 95.

Anne, duchess of Bretagne, married to Charles VIII., ii. 110; death of all her children, 112.

Anne of France, marriage of, ii. 273.

Anthony, lord, bastard of Burgundy, i. 11. 20; comes to Paris in disguise, ii. 301.

Anthony le Breton, M., brings information to Charles of Burgundy, i. 26.

Antoine du Bec Crespin, archbishop of Narbonne, i. 2. *n.*

Apennines passed by Charles VIII. and his army, ii. 199; the great cannon transported over, 199, 200.

Apulia, revolt of, ii. 162.

Aquapendende delivered up to Charles VIII., ii. 144.

Aquila, revolt of, ii. 162.

Arban, Louis, lord of, admiral of the French fleet, ii. 229.

Archambambault, Peter, governor of Ferrette, captured and executed, i. 243; his extortions, 302.

Archers of the French army, ii. 211.

Argenton, lordship of, xxii; lord of, xxxiv; chateau of, xxxvi. (See Commines.)

Arleux ceded to the duke of Burgundy, i. 74.

Armagnac, John V., count of, i. 16.

Armuyden, Marguerite de, mother of Commines XII., death of, i. 16.

Army of the duke of Burgundy and the allies, i. 43, 44, 45.

Arragon, house of, in Naples, disliked by the Venetians, ii. 120, 121; revolt against the, 162, 163.

Arras, treaty of, i. 5. *n.*; the great personages assembled at the treaty of, 107; the commissioners from England at, *ib. n.*; arrival of the duke of Burgundy at, 172; treaty of, confirmed at the castle of Crotoy, 216; besieged by Louis XI., 245; the sally from, defeated, *ib.*; answer of the inhabitants to the king, 346; city and town of, surrendered, 361. 363; treaty of, between Louis XI. and duke Maximilian, ii. 45. *et seq.*; captured by the Burgundians, 111; attack on, 378.

Arthur, prince of Wales, ii. 64. *n.*, 276. *et n.*

Artillery, state of, at the end of the 15th century among the French and Italians, 210. *et n.*

Artois, the whole country of, lost, i. 16; country of, to be ceded as a dowry to the dauphin of

France, ii. 46. *et seq.* ; freed from the ordinary aid taxes, 51.

Ascanio, Sforza, cardinal, ii. 146. *et n.*

Asto, town of, visited by Charles VIII., ii. 124, 125 ; defence of, 178, 179 ; the king's retreat to, after the battle of Fornova, 223 ; his arrival there, 227.

Astoly, duke of, i. 314.

Atella, meeting at, ii. 259 ; treaty of, to the prejudice of the French, 260, 261, *et n.* ; misfortunes of the French after the surrender of, 261, 262. *n.*

Aubert, Peter, commander of Roye, ii. 368.

Aubigny, Beraut, lord of, ii. 125. 133.

Aubijoux, Hugh, lord d', ii. 195.

Aubus, Anthony des, ii. 215.

Ausonne, capture of, ii. 22.

Austria, the duke of, deceives Louis XI., ii. 389.

Austria and Bavaria, animosities between the houses of, i. 380.

Auxerre, village of, i. 136.

Azevedo, don Diego de, ii. 271. *n.*

B.

Bajazet II., the sultan of Turkey, ii. 67. *n.,* 130. *n.*

Balance of power, i. 379.

Ballaigny, Louis, lord of, governor of Beauvais, i. 218.

Ballasut, lord de, plunders the palace of Peter de Medicis, ii. 143.

Balue, Cardinal, bishop of Angiers, i. 94 ; appointed king's ambassador, 111 ; imprisoned, 165 ; his release, ii. 39 ; assault on, 330 ; persuades Louis XI. to an ignominious peace, 356, 357 ;

his treason discovered, and his property confiscated, 358.

Bar, duchy of, claimed by René II., ii. 94, 95.

Bar-sur-Seine, village of, i. 136.

Barberigo, Agostino, doge of Venice, ii. 170.

Barnet, battle of, i. 201.

Bashe, Peron de, ii. 109.

Bashe, Peter de, ii. 146, 147.

Bastard of Rubempré, seizure of, i. 2 ; his release demanded, 3.

Bastard of Burgundy, i. 28.

Battle, miseries of those who are defeated in, i. 159.

Battles, of Montlhery, i. 21 ; of the civil wars in England, 181 ; and their evil consequences, 182 ; of Barnet, 201 ; of Tewkesbury, 202.

Baudouin, bastard of Burgundy, his revolt, 171, 172.

Baudricourt, John, lord of, i. 44.

Bavaria, divisions in the house of, i. 380.

Bear, story of the, i. 246.

Beatrice d'Este, daughter of the duke of Ferrara, ii. 106.

Beaujeu, Madame de, xxxiii. xxxiv., i. 394.

Beaujeu, lord of, i. 16, ii. 69. 394. (See Bourbon.)

Beaulne, rebellion of, ii. 23 ; captured, 24 ; surrender of, 390 ;

Beauvais, Louis XI. at, i. 177, 178 ; attacked by the Burgundian forces, 218 ; siege of, 219 ; the besiegers repulsed, 221 ; the siege raised, *ib.* ; its successful defence against Charles of Burgundy, ii. 369—371.

Beauvoises, provostship of, i. 132.

Becchi, Gentile, bishop of Arezzo, ii. 127.

Bedford, John of Lancaster, duke of, account of, i. 47.

Begar, Abbé de, i. 207.

Belgrade, defeat of the Turks at, ii. 88. *n.*

Bellejoyeuse, count Charles de, ii. 108; meets Charles VIII. at Lyons, 122.

Bengon, port of, ii. 229.

Bentivoglio, Annibal de, ii. 209. et n.

Bentivoglio, Prince John, his handsome treatment of Commines, ii. 182.

Berard, Charles de, ii. 323.

Berghes, Sir John de, ii. 60.

Berry, Charles, duke of, i. xx., 15. 19. 34; joins the duke of Burgundy with his forces, 6; his offensive remarks in the council of war, 36, 37; suspicions of him excited, 37; crosses the Seine with Charles's army, 43; president of the council at the conference with the Parisians, 51; in a conference with the king he demands all Normandy, 65; the province ceded to him, 69; the inhabitants swear fidelity to, 70; sends heralds to Paris to negotiate, ii. 324; obtains the duchy of Normandy, 332; received as duke of Roan, 337; obliged to leave the city, 339.

Bertrand de la Cueva, grand master of the order of Santiago, i. 122.

Besançon, city of, captured, ii. 23; historical notices of, 23. n.

Besignano, Girolamo, prince de, ii. 100; the sons of, fly to Venice, ib.

Bessey, Antoine de, bailiff of Dijon, ii. 126.

Beurs, Philip, lord de, ii. 60.

Bianca Maria, daughter of Galeas, duke of Milan, ii. 112; duchess of Savoy, 112. n; married to the king of the Romans, ib.

Bianca de Montferrat, duchess of Savoy, ii. 124.

Bidant, Denis, ii. 148.

Bievres, Jean, lord of, i. 322. 324.

Billy, tower of, ii. 327.

Bisches, William, account of, i. 67; surrenders Peronne to the king, 359.

Bisignano, prince of, ii. 163.

Blasmond, town of, captured, i. 243.

Blazing star over Paris, ii. 305.

Boccaccio, treatise of, ii. 255. et n.

Bohain delivered up to the king, i. 350.

Bolia, town of, ii. 248.

Bomacourt, castle of, i. 304. n.

Bona of Savoy, duchess of Milan, i. 308. n., ii. 101; regent of Milan, ib.; deprived of the guardianship of her children, 102, 103.

Books, on the reading of, i. 117.

Booty taken by the Swiss from the Burgundians, i. 312.

Borde, de la, ii. 317, 318.

Borgia, Cæsar, cardinal of Valentia, ii. 159.

Borgia, Roderic, elected pope, ii. 123. n.

Boschetto, count Albertino, ii. 238, 239. n.

Bosuse, John, butler to the duke of Burgundy, i. 112.

Bosworth Field, battle of, i. 397.

Bouchage, lord de, i. 265; sent ambassador to Castile, ii. 275.

Bouchain, possessed by the king, i. 355; restored to the duchess of Burgundy, ii. 17.

Boudinière, Gabriel, ii. 216. et n.

Boulenger, John le, ii. 335.

Boulogne delivered up to the king, i. 363.

Bourbon, Charles II., duke of, i. 16.

Bourbon, Louis, bastard of admiral of France, i. 187; besieges Arras, 245.

Bourbon, John, duke of, lord de Beaujeu, ii. 69. 95. 99; takes possession of the castle of Rouen for the duke of Berry, i. 69; declares war against Louis XI., ii.

310; captures Roan, 332; concessions made to, 333.

Bourbon, duchess of, ii. 95.

Bourbon, Matthew, the bastard of, ii. 212. *et n.*

Bourbon, Monsieur et Madame de, ii. 61.

Bourbonnois, the king's march into, i. 15; Louis XI.'s operations in, ii. 312. 314.

Bourbons, family of the, i. 9. (See John, Philip, &c.)

Bourdonasses described, ii. 209.

Bourgneuf, Julian, slain, ii. 215, 216.

Boussiere, Guynot de, steward of the king's household, ii. 55.

Boutefeu, John, story of his squibs, i. 36.

Boutilhac, Jean, i. 141.

Bouvines, ill treatment of the inhabitants by the people of Dinant, i. 88, 89; their revenge, 90; meeting of the royal commissioners, at, 227; agreement signed against the constable of France at, 291.

Brabant to be taken possession of by the king, i. 351.

Bracci, the partisans of Braccio de Montone, ii. 151.

Bracciano, castle of, ii. 145.

Bresse, Philip of Savoy, lord of, i. 113; imprisoned by Louis XI., 114; becomes duke of Savoy, ii. 136.

Bressure, Jacques, lord of, i. 269.

Bretagne, Louis's design against the province of, i. 93; protected by the duke of Burgundy, 94; the king of France makes war in, on the duke of Burgundy's allies, i. 110. *et seq.*

Bretagne, duke and duchess of, xx; their family contests, xxi.

Bretagne, Francis, duke of, i. 3. *et n.* 5. 14. 19; treaty of alliance between him and Charles of Burgundy, 6; arrivals from his army,

32; joins the duke of Burgundy with his forces, 34; renews a treaty of alliance with Charles of Burgundy, 38; crosses the Seine with Charles's army, 43; his quarrel with the duke of Normandy, 83; concludes a treaty with the king at Caen, 84; enters into a treaty of alliance with the duke of Normandy, 85; signs the treaty of Ancenis, 111; his menacing communications to the duke of Burgundy, 174—176; the war between Louis XI. and the duke of Burgundy renewed through his solicitations, 200. *et seq.*; the king concludes a peace with him, 222—224: a faithful friend to Louis XI., 277; his ambassadors sent to Louis, ii. 319.

Bretagne, Anne, duchess of, queen of Charles VIII., ii. 254; her grief at the death of the dauphin, *ib.*

Breteilles, Louis de, i. 279.

Bretons in the army of Charles of Burgundy, i. 35; ravage the country near Paris, 54; the protectors of the malcontents of France, 93; protected by the duke of Burgundy, 94; their desire for peace, 223; their retreat from Paris, ii. 322; their military operations, 323, 324. *et seq.*; make peace with Louis XI., 333; their hostile spirit in Normandy, 347.

Brézé, Jaques de, grand seneschal of Normandy, i. 70.

Brezey, Pierre de, lord of Varenne, i. 19.

Bridge of boats built over the Seine, i. 43.

Brindisi, castle of, ii. 162.

Briquebec, Jean, lord of, i. 269.

Brissonet, Guillaume, lord of Varennes, ii. 93; appointed cardinal, and archbishop of Rheims,

93. *n.*, 94; ii. 159; disheartened at the prospect of the expedition against Naples, 123, 124; the seneschal, 129, 130.

Bruges, a place of trade, and of great resort for foreigners, i. 378, 379.

Bruges, Jean de, lord of Grutuse, ii. 75. *n.*

Brustan, village of, i. 96.

Buckingham, Henry, duke of, executed, i. 396. *n.*; ii. 64.

Budé, M. Dreux, ii. 304.

Bueil, John V., lord of, i. 18.

Burgundians, fight the battle of Montlhery, i. 23. *et seq.*; repulse of the, 26; the battle a drawn one, 29; number slain, 30; cross the Seine, 43; chief officers of the, 45; offices and employments among the, 46; their military operations, 61; always in amity with the Savoyards, 114; their attack on Beauvais, 218; their siege, 219; their repulse, 221; their military manœuvering, 272. *et seq.*; invade France, 312; enter the Isle of Man, 314; appear before Paris, 315; their military operations, 316. *et seq.*; capture St. Cloud, 317; defeated by Louis XI., 318; their retreat over the Seine, 322; their military operations, 323. *et seq.*, 327. *et seq.*; send heralds to Paris, 324; their negotiations, 325; make peace with Louis XI., 333; at war with the Liegeois, 341. 346; effect their destruction, 349; surprise and hang the lord de Merville, 352; their massacre of the inhabitants of Nesle, 360; their defeats and great slaughters by the Swiss and Germans, 382—386.

BURGUNDY, its great prosperity under Philip the Good, i. 12; its decline, 13; cessions made to the dukedom of, 74. 76. 78; the three

estates of, assembled at Abbeville, 179; the prosperous condition of, for about 100 years, 297; the four great sovereigns of—Philip the Bold, John, Philip the Good, and Charles the Bold, 298; ancient prosperity of the house of, 337; ambassadors, in the name of the three estates of, visit the king, 366. *et n.*; wealthiness of, ii. 14; continuation of the wars in, 20; entire subjugation of, by Louis XI., 23; treaty between Louis XI. and duke Maximilian respecting, 45. *et seq.*; factions of, 86; affairs of, settled at the treaty of Senlis, 113. *et seq.*; the territories of, ravaged by the French troops, 391.

Burgundy, duke of. (See PHILIP, and CHARLES the BOLD.)

Burgundy, duchess dowager of, Margaret of York, i. 368; letter written by, *ib.*

Burgundy, Mary, duchess of, daughter of Charles the Bold, and afterwards duchess of Austria, i. 173; sends an embassy to the king of France, 359; the Gantois rebel against her, 366; her letter to the king of France produced against her, 371; her entreaties for the lives of her ministers, 374; divested of all powers by the Gantois, 375; visible decay of her affairs, ii. 9; marriage of, contemplated, 10. *et seq.*; married to duke Maximilian, 15; her children, 16, 17; her death and character, 17. 41.

Burgundy, young princess of, daughter of the duchess Mary, forsaken by Charles VIII. of France, ii. 110. 113. (See Margaret of Austria.)

Burgundy, marshal of, no friend of the king's, i. 78.

Butler, Eleanor, her marriage to Edward IV., i. 396. *n.*

C.

Cadet, John, bravery of, i. 27.

Caen, treaty concluded at, between Louis XI. and the duke of Bretagne, i. 84; the town conferred on the lord de Lescut, *ib.*

Calabria, in Italy, ii. 274.

Cajazzo, Francisco count of, ii. 103. 133. 201; commands a troop of Italians, 126; examines the Swiss captain taken prisoner, 202.

Calabria, John, duke of, account of, i. 43. *et n.*; his forces which join the duke of Burgundy, 44, 45; his military qualities, 63, 64. 177; concessions made to, ii. 332.

Calabria, Nicholas, duke of, i. 177. 206; proposes to marry the duke of Burgundy's daughter, ii. 367.

Calabria, Alphonso II., duke of, ii. 31.

Calabria, Friar Robert, the holy man of, ii. 54.

Calais, the earl of Warwick repelled from, i. 84; the richest treasure belonging to him, and the best captaincy in Christendom, 85; affairs at, under lord Wenlock, 195, 196; wool the staple mart, 198; letter of Louis XI. respecting, ii. 40.

Caldoresques, the members of the Caldora family, ii. 163.

Cambray, John, bishop of, i. 10.

Cambray possessed by the king, i. 355; restored to the duchess of Burgundy, ii. 18; treachery of the inhabitants, 390.

Campobache, Nicolas, count of i. 44.

Campobasso, count of, i. 237. 299; ii. 386. 387; his treachery, i. 299, 300. 325. *et seq.*, 334—336.

Campoforgoso, Signor Baptista di, doge of Genoa, ii. 109. 267.

Candes, town of, ii. 197.

Cannon of unusual size, ii. 197; transported across the Apennines, 199.

Cannonading between the armies of Louis XI. and the duke of Burgundy before Paris, i. 55.

Canons of the church murdered at Liege, i. 119.

Canreau, John, lord de Pampelie, killed, ii. 329.

Capponi, Pietro, his enmity to the Medici, ii. 129; his spirited conduct, 143.

Capua entered by Charles VIII., ii. 161.

Caraffi, family of, their acquisitions, ii. 162.

Caramania overthrown by the Turks, ii. 91.

Caravels, light vessels used in the Mediterranean, ii. 183.

Cardinals of Rome, their quarrels with the pope, ii. 158. 160.

Cardonne, John Francis de, ii. 189.

Carency, Pierre, lord of, i. 245.

Casale, town of, ii. 236, 237.; visited by Charles VIII., ii. 125.

Castel del Ovo taken by storm, ii. 165.

Castellina besieged by the Florentines, ii. 29.

Castile, historical review of the fortunes and misfortunes which happened to the house of Castile, in the author's lifetime, ii. 277—281.

Castile, prince of, great lamentations and misfortunes attendant on the death of the, ii. 277.

Castile, Ferrand, king of, ii. 269, 270.

Castile, Ferdinand V., king of, i. 331.

Castile, John, prince of, married to Margaret of Austria, ii. 112.

Catherine, duchess of Guelders, i 9. *n.*

Catherine, daughter of Charles, duke of Bourbon, i. 232.

Cato, Angelo, archbishop of Vienne, biographical notices of, i. xlv. *n.*

Caux, the country of, ravaged by the Burgundians, i. 222; bailiwick of, ii. 372.

Cerisay, William de, i. 364.

Cesenna, town of, ii. 133.

Chabannes, Anthony, count de, his honours and territories restored to him, i. 82; escapes from the Bastile, ii. 311.

Chalanger, Thomas St. Leger, i. 262.

Chalon, Louis de, lord of Chasteaugnion, i. 57.

Chambes, Helen de, death of, i. xxxviii.

Chambre, the lords de la, ii. 41.

Chambre, lord de la, arrested, ii. 41.

Chambocé, castle of, captured, i. 110.

Champ des Plours, i. 33.

CHARLES the BOLD, Count CHAROLOIS, and duke of BURGUNDY, the son of Philip the Good, i. xii.; receives Commines into his service, *ib.*; fights the battle of Montlhery, *ib.*; his marriage, *ib.*; detains Louis in captivity, xiv.; captures and destroys Liege, xv.; his defeat and death, xxiii.; causes of the war between him and Louis XI., 1. *et seq.*; biographical notices of, 1. *n.*; meets the ambassadors of the French king at Lisle, 2. *et seq.*; his defence of the bastard of Rubempré, 4; treaty of alliance between him and Francis, duke of Bretagne, 6; raises an army against Louis XI. under pretence of the public good, 9; his declaration against the lords of Croy, 10; the amount of his forces, 11; his advance upon Paris, 13, 14; styled by Commines

" the greatest monarch in the world," 25; encamps near Montlhery, and gives battle to the French, 17. *et seq.*; his dangerous position and rescue, 26. *et seq.*; joined by the dukes of Berry and Bretagne, 33. *et seq.*; his exultation after the battle of Montlhery, 33; his valour and intrepidity, *ib.*; passes the Seine on a bridge of boats, and invests Paris, 42. *et seq.*; his cannonading with the king of France near Charenton, 54. *et seq.*; lays a second bridge of boats over the Seine, 57; his troops mistake some high thistles for a body of French lances, 61. 64; visited by the king of France, who discusses with him the causes of the quarrel, 65. *et seq.*; his extravagant demands on the king, 65; concludes a peace by signing the treaty of Conflans, 73; exclusive concessions made to, by Louis XI., 74. 76. 78; concludes a treaty of peace at St. Maur-des-fosses between his allies and the king of France, 80; becomes duke of Burgundy on the death of his father, i. 88. 92; his wars with the Liegeois, 88. *et seq.*; captures and destroys the town of Dinant, 89, 90; defeats the Liegeois in a set battle, 97; his triumphant entry into the city of Liege, 105; submission of the Gantois to him, 109; the king of France makes war on his allies, 110; their interview at Peronne, 118; he seizes the king, and confines him in the castle of Peronne, 118, 119; his interview with the emperor Frederic and other great princes, 124—126; vast concessions made to, by the treaty of Peronne, 132. *et seq.*;

compels the king to renounce his league with the Liegeois, and to sign a treaty of peace, 127. 130. *et seq.*; undertakes an expedition against the Liegeois, accompanied by the king, 145. *et seq.*; beleaguers the city of Liege, 149; great distress of his van guard, *ib.*; is in great danger from a sally of the Liegeois, 153; captures and devastates the city of Liege, 157; permits the king of France to return home, 161; his treatment of the Liegeois, and of the people of Franchemont, 161, 162; Louis acts in opposition to him, 165; and takes the occasion of making a fresh war, 167. *et seq.*; cited by the king of France to appear before the Parliament at Paris, 170; his territories invaded, 171. *et seq.*; designs against, 174; he takes the field and captures Picquigny, 175, 176; besieges Amiens, 177; enters into a truce with the king, 178; assembles the estates, 179; his opposition to the Earl of Warwick, 185. 187; his naval strength, 187; his difficulties with regard to Edward IV. and the Earl of Warwick, 195; his conference with Edward IV. at St. Rol, 198; his liberal assistance to him, 199; the war between him and King Louis renewed, 203. *et seq.*; negociations for peace broken off by the Duke of Guienne's death, 210; he captures and sacks the town of Nesle, 211; his attempt to outwit the King, 215; concludes a treaty at the Castle of Crotoy, 216; Amiens, St. Quentin, and various towns, castles, and fortresses, ceded to, 216; besieges Beauvais, 219; raises the siege

and marches against Rouen, 221; concludes a truce with the King, 224; his restless ambition, 235; seizes the Duchy of Guelders, and besieges Nuz, 236. *et seq.*; his military force, 237; the town relieved by the King of France, and others whom he had stirred up against the duke, 239. *et seq.*; his obstinacy, 241; loses the castle of Trouquoy, and several towns, 244; suspects the constable of France, 247; assisted by his ally the king of England, 251. *et seq.*; his visit to Edward, 267; concludes the treaty of Vervins with Louis, 287; delivers up the constable of France, who is publicly executed, 291—297; digression concerning his error in delivering up the constable contrary to the safe conduct, and what happened to him afterwards, 297—300; the last sovereign of Burgundy, 298; at his father's death one of the richest and most powerful sovereigns in Christendom, *ib.*; his delivering up the constable base and dishonourable, 298, 299; had grown distrustful of his best subjects, 299; makes war upon the Swiss, and is disgracefully defeated near Granson, 301—306; his honour and his wealth lost in one day, 305; abandoned by his allies, 309; again defeated by the Swiss near Morat with great loss, 315; seizes the duchess of Savoy who is rescued by the king of France, 317. 319; lives in melancholy retirement at La Riviere, 321; and loses the town of Nancy, 324; his impolitic rejection of advice, 326, 327; visited by the king of Portugal, while besieging Nancy, 332; rejects the advice of his officers, and is defeated and slain in a battle with the duke of Lorraine 335—7; Latin epitaph on, 337; reflections on his character, and on the ancient prosperity of the house of Burgundy, 340; state of affairs after his death, 344. *et seq.*; Louis XI. contemplates the destruction of his family, and the distribution of his territories 351; various cities and plains of Burgundy delivered up to the king, 350—364.

CHARLES the BOLD (*continued from Jean de Troyes' Chronicle*). His military operations against France and the Parisians, ii. 312. *et seq.*; concessions made to, by Louis XI., 332; concludes a peace, 333; at war with the Liegeois, 341; his conference with Louis XI. at Peronne, 354; receives intelligence of the massacres of the Liegeois, *ib.*; besieges and captures Liege, in company with Louis XI., 355; concludes a peace with Louis XI., 356; declared an enemy to France, 360; threatens to arrest the earl of Warwick, 361; enters into a truce with Louis XI., 365; renews his mad pranks, 367; captures Nesle and various French towns, 368. *et seq.*; his siege of Beauvais, and his great losses, 369; is compelled to retreat, 371; devastates the country, 372; agrees to a truce, 374, 375; besieges Nuz, 376; defeated by the Swiss, 381; his flight, 382; refused further supplies, 383; defeated by the Duke of Lorraine, *ib.*; his signal defeat and death near Nancy, 386, 387; recognition of his dead body, 387. (See BURGUNDIANS.)

Charles d'Amboise, lord of Chaumont, xxv.

Charles of Artois, Count d'Eu, notices of, i. 1. *et n.*

Charles, lord of France, receives the Duchy of Normandy from Louis XI., i. 78; requires the king to fulfil the terms of the treaty of Peronne, and grant him the investiture of Normandy, 164; the king offers him Guienne and Rochelle, in lieu of Brie and Champagne, in opposition to the duke of Burgundy, 165; he accepts the proposal, and is created duke of Guienne, 166. (See GUIENNE.)

Charles Martel, the first king of France who came collaterally to the throne, ii. 289.

Charles I. king of Naples, ii. 96.

Charles II. king of Sicily, ii. 96.

Charles V. king of France, i. 386.

Charles VI. of France, the wars of his reign, i. 47; insanity of, 273; his family jealousies, ii. 256.

Charles VII. king of France, i. 5. *n.* 273. 387; ii. 2; his power of levying taxes, 43; suppresses the rebellion of the Praguerie, 69; at war with his son, 82; his opinion of his son, 83. *n.*; his death, 304; his obsequies, 305.

CHARLES VIII., son of Louis XI., ascends the throne of France, xxxiii.; his patronage of Commines, xxxiv.; undertakes an expedition to Italy, xxxiv.—v.; notices of, i. 209. *n.*; birth of, ii. 8. *n.*; born at Amboise, 361; receives his father's last injunctions, 69; the commencement of his reign, 93. *et seq.*; account of his expedition into Italy, 93; crowned at fourteen years of age, 94; the Duke of Lorraine demands from him the duchy of Bar, *ib.*; restores the duchy, 95; his claim to the kingdom of Naples, 96—99: receives an embassy from Milan, 109;

makes peace with the King
of the Romans and the Archduke of Austria, 110; forsakes
the young princess of Burgundy, and marries the daughter
of the duke of Bretagne, 110;
death of all his children, 112;
signs the treaty at Senlis, 113;
his allies, 117; his endeavours
to obtain the alliance of the
Venetians before undertaking his
expedition to Naples, 119. *et
seq.*; his advance to Lyons, 121;
his great preparations for invading Naples, 122. 125. *et seq.*;
borrows jewels and large sums
of money from his friends, 124,
125; his military successes in
Piedmont, 126, 127; his visit to
Pavia, 131; marches to Placentia, 132; restores Pisa to its
ancient liberty, 138; the Pisans
raise his statue in the place of the
Marzocchi, 139; enters into a
treaty with the Florentines, 143.
et n.; enters Florence, 143; and
passes through various towns in
his march to Rome, 144. *et seq.*;
his entry into Rome, 149; his
agreement with the Pope during
his stay at Rome, 153; his departure from Rome to Naples,
159; account of his journey,
160; his entry into Capua, 161;
into Naples, 161; his enthusiastic reception, 161, 162; is
crowned king of Naples, 163;
the errors committed by him
165; designs in his favour against
the Turks by the Venetians,
165. *et seq.*; political intrigues
against, 174. *et seq.*; the Venetians enter into a league with
the Pope against, 179; his military preparations against the
league, 183. *et seq.*; his departure from Naples, 186; returns
to Rome, 186. 187; arrives at
Siena, 187; his deliberations

respecting the restitution of the
Florentine towns, 188; enters
Pisa, 189; retains Pisa and several
Florentine towns, 191; his dangerous passage over the mountains between Pisa and Sarzana,
194, 195; his naval forces defeated, 195; crosses the Apennines with great difficulty, 199;
enters Lombardy, 203; arrives
at Fornovo, near the camp of his
enemies, where they are waiting
to encounter and capture him,
204, 205; prepares for the
battle, 207. *et seq.*; gains the
victory, 211—214; the danger
to which he was exposed, 218;
his retreat to Asti, 223; his
arrival at Nice, 225; and also
at Asti, 227; fits out a fleet for
relieving the castles at Naples,
229; defeated in his object,
232; enters into and concludes
negociations for peace, 238. *et
seq.*; concludes a peace with the
League, 245. *et seq.*; arrives at
Trino, 247; sends to Venice to
invite the Venetians to accept
the terms of peace, 248. *et seq.*;
his stay at Lyons, 252, 253;
his feastings and pleasure, 252;
he forgets those who were left at
Naples, 253; receives intelligence of the death of his son, the
dauphin, 254; his family disputes and jealousies, 255, 256;
receives intelligence of the loss
of the castle of Naples, the
selling of the Florentine towns,
the treaty of Atilla, &c., 257.
et seq.; misfortunes of his troops
after the treaty of Atella, and
the surrender of Naples, 261—
263; several abortive plots
formed in his favour by the
Italian princes for the recovery
of Naples and Genoa, and the
destruction of the duke of Milan,
264—269; differences between

him and Ferrand king of Castile, 269; sends ambassadors to
accommodate the affair, 270. 273;
who sign a truce, 275; account
of his death, and of the magnificent building which he began a
while before he died, 281—284;
a short retrospect of his life, 281;
plans another expedition to Italy,
282; resolves to live a more
strictly religious life, *ib.*; his
good inclination to reform the
Church, the laws, the treasury,
and himself, 283, 284; his piety,
and dying moments, 284; his
obsequies and funeral, 287, 288;
the last of the direct line of
Philip de Valois, 290.

Charlotte, daughter of Louis, duke
of Savoy, ii. 82. *n.*

Charolois, Charles, count of, afterwards duke of Burgundy. (See
Charles the Bold.)

Chartier, William, bishop of Paris,
i. 50; ii. 320.

Chartreux at Pavia, ii. 137.

Chassa, Jean de, revolt of, i. 171.

Chasteau-Guyon, Louis and Hugh,
lords of, i. 376.

Chasteau-Guyon, Hugh, lord of, i.
309, ii. 20, 21; his defeat, ii.
388.

Chasteauneuf, Anthony de, ii. 347.

Chastel-Chinon, revenue of, i. 141.

Chastillon, M. de, an officer of the
king, i. 139; his illegal measures, 140.

Chaumont burnt, ii. 340.

Chaumont, Charles, lord of, i. 319,
ii. 21. 23. (See Amboise.)

Chaumont, Peter, lord of, i. 34;
death of, *ib. n.*

Chené, Sir John, i. 267.

Cheney, lord, ii. 4.

Chevalier, M. Etienne, ii. 304.

Childermas-day, sanctity of, i.
270.

Chimay, John, count of, i. 6. *n.*

Chimay, Philip, count of, i. 10;

his prudent advice rejected by
the duke of Burgundy, 335. *n.*

Chinon, town of, i. xviii.

Chollet, Casin, ii. 316.

Chronicles of Louis XI. from
1460 to 1483, containing various
adventures which occurred both
in France and in the neighbouring countries, ii. 297. *et seq.*

Church, reform of, attempted by
Charles VIII., ii. 282.

Churches of Liege protected from
spoliation, i. 158.

Cibo, cardinal Gian Battista, becomes pope of Rome, ii. 98.

Cico, Francisco, secretary to the
regent of Milan, ii. 101; arrested and executed, 101. *n.*, 102.

Cifron, treacherous execution of, i.
327.

Cinquanteniers of Paris, ii. 329.

Citizens of Paris, their conference
with the lords of France, i. 50.

Civil Wars in England, i. 48, 49.
93; during the contests between
Louis XI. and Charles of Burgundy, 181—6.

Clairet, Peter, steward of the
French king's household, ii. 5.

Clarence, George, duke of, death
of, i. 49.

Clarence, duke of, brother of Edward IV., i. 188, 189, 275; goes
over to his brother at the battle
of Barnet, 200; flies to Normandy, ii. 360; his return to
England, 363.

Clarence, duchess of, prematurely
brought to bed, i. 185.

Claude, Master, physician to Louis
XI., ii. 37.

Clerieux, Guillaume, lord of, sent as
ambassador to Castile, ii. 273, 274.

Cleves, John, duke of, i. 11. 233.
368, 369, 370; his quarrels and
dissatisfaction, 372; his attempts
to negociate a marriage between
his son and the young duchess of
Burgundy, ii. 11—13.

Clodion, the second king of France, ii. 289.

Clugny, William de, bishop of Therouenne, arrest of, i. 372.

Cluny, William of, account of, i. 37. et n.

Clutin, Master Pierre, i. xvii.

Coctier, James, physician of Louis XI., ii. 71. 74; predicts the king's death, 75.

Cohé, Mery de, i. 220.

Cold, fatal effects of, in the duke of Burgundy's army, i. 163.

Cologne, two pretenders to the bishopric of, i. 235; great expenses incurred to secure themselves against the duke of Burgundy, 239.

Colonna, Prospero, cardinal, ii. 147. 158.

Colonne, family of the, in possession of Ostia, ii. 145; opposed to the Ursini, 146; enemies of the French, ib.; their hostilities against Don Ferrand, 147; rewarded by Charles VIII., 185; their cabals and revolt, 185, 186.

Colpin, a brave English soldier, i. 322; is killed at Nancy, 323.

Commerce, treaty of, made at Vervins, i. 287.

Commines, town of, i. xi.; importance of the family name, ib.; the castle of, the birthplace of Philip de Commines, xi.; Jean de Clite, the lord of, xii.

COMMINES, PHILIP de, lord of ARGENTON, called the "Father of Modern History," i. v.; his memoirs relate to one of the most interesting periods of history, ib.; they terminate about twenty years before the Reformation, vi.; his tendency to praise the princes who enjoyed his allegiance, viii.; the composition of his memoirs the occupation of the last years of his life, ix.; the various editions of his memoirs, ib.; the present translation made from the text of Madlle. Dupont, x.; he was born in the castle of Commines in the year 1447, xi.; the son of the sovereign-bailiff of Flanders, ib.; Philip the Good, his godfather, ib.; left an orphan with a small patrimony, xii.; Philip the Good becomes his royal patron, ib.; appointed chamberlain and councillor of the duke of Burgundy, xiii.; engaged in various important missions, xvi.; receives tempting offers from Louis XI. to enter into his service, xvii.; abandons the duke of Burgundy, and enters the service of Louis, ib. 222.; confiscation of his property, xviii.; enriched by the munificence of Louis, xix.; becomes the prince de Talmont on his marriage to the wealthy heiress, Helene de Chambes, xxii.; receives the full confidence of Louis, ib. et seq.; his mission to Florence, xxvi.; details his personal history, xxvii. et seq.; compelled to restore the estates of the La Tremoille family after the death of Louis XI., xxxiii.; his political difficulties, xxxiv.; is thrown into prison, and condemned to banishment, ib.; recalled to the council of Charles VIII., ib.; accompanies the king in his campaign against Naples, xxxv.; sent on political missions to Venice and Milan, xxxv., xxxvi.; on the death of the king he retires into private life, xxxvi.; his last years embittered by vexatious law-suits, ib.; his death, ib.; interred in the Convent des Grands Augustins at Paris, xxxvii.; his personal and intellectual qualifications, ib.; his memoirs dedicated to Angelo Cato, the archbishop of

Vienne, xlv.—His first presentation to Charles, duke of Burgundy, and his own account of his early life and subsequent career, 1. *et seq. passim;* at the battle of Montlhery, 21—32; his mission to lord Wenlock at Calais, 185. 188; hospitably treated, at Calais, by lord Wenlock, 196, 197; acquits himself like a loyal and faithful subject, 224; the displeasure of the king with, 351; his embassy, 353; sent to Florence during the wars in Burgundy, ii. 25. *et seq.;* receives homage for the duchy of Genoa in the name of the king, 31; nobly treated at Florence, *ib.;* his return to France, 32; appointed one of the council of Charles VIII., 95; ambassador at Venice, 155; sent ambassador to Venice, 168; his opinions of her government, and his general description of, 169. *et seq.;* the subjects of his embassy, ii. 173. *et seq.;* leaves Venice, 182; handsomely treated, *ib.;* his interview with the king at Siena, 187; his difficulties with Charles VIII., 206; at the battle of Fornovo, 211. *et seq.;* sent to parley with the enemy, 220, 221; appointed to conduct negotiations for peace, 238. *et seq.;* sent to Venice to invite the Venetians to accept the terms of peace, 248.

Commines, Jeanne de, marriage of, xxxvi.; death of, xxxvii.

Comminges, John, count de, i. 165, ii. 83.

Commissioners appointed by Louis XI. to reform abuses, ii. 341.

Condé, town of, surrendered, ii. 389.

Conflans, the duke of Burgundy's army encamps at, i. 46; treaty of, 52; treaty of, between Louis XI.

and Charles of Burgundy, 173. *et seq.;* great concessions made to the latter, 74. 76. 78.; treaty of, confirmed at the castle of Crotoy, 216.

Constable of France. (See Louis de Luxembourg, and St. Paul.)

Constantine Aranito, ii. 164; his enterprise against the Turks, 167.

Constantine Palæologus, emperor of Constantinople, slain, ii. 90.

Constantinople, captured by Mahomet II., ii. 90.

Contay, William, lord of, i. 12; brings information to Charles of Burgundy, 26; his advice after the battle of Montlhery, 31; advises the death of the hostages of Liege, 95; his death predicted and verified, 96. 98.

Contay, Louis, lord of, surrenders the town of Corbie, i. 244; a servant of the duke of Burgundy, 265; discovers the duplicity of the constable of France, 266; sent on an embassy to the king, 307.

Copelare, M. Frederic, ii. 198.

Coppenolle, John, town-clerk of Ghent, ii. 42.

Corbeil, the king's retreat to, i. 29.

Corbie, town of, captured, i. 244.

Corbie, William de, entertains Louis XI., ii. 308.

Corbin ceded to the duke of Burgundy, i. 74.

Cordes, Philip, lord des, i. 21. 161; attacks the suburbs of Beauvais, 218, 219; surrenders the city of Arras, 360; under the service of the king, 361; his various officers, *ib.;* the king's lieutenant in Picardy, ii. 32.; his contests with the Flemings, 32, 33.

Cornaro, Catherine, married to the king of Cyprus, ii. 121. *n.;* her rights claimed by the Venetians, *ib.*

Correano, town of, ii. 197.

Corroget, Gilles, ii. 293.

Cossé, John, lord of, his speech to Louis XI., i. 310.

Cotereau, Robert, bravery of, i. 27.

Coulches, Claude de Montagu, lord of, i. 16.

Couldre, Philip de la, ii. 228.

Courtiers should conduct themselves with modesty and forbearance, i. 230, 231.

Cousinot, M., ii. 317, 318.

Craon, George, lord of, i. xxv. xxvi. 211. 332. ; his danger, 154 ; the king's lieutenant in Burgundy, 376 ; ii. 20 ; withholds the captured places from the Prince of Orange, 377 ; besieges Dole, 20 ; is defeated, and deposed, 20, 21 ; his successes over the Prince of Orange, 388.

Crespin, Jeanne, of Normandy, i. 69. n.

Crevecœur ceded to the duke of Burgundy, i. 74.

Crevecœur, Antony, lord of, i. 21.

Crevecœur, Philip de, i. 97.

Creville, Louis de, a servant of the constable's, i. 265.

Criminals, punishment of in 1490, ii. 298.

Croia, in Albania, surrender of, ii. 166.

Cross-bow-men of the French army, ii. 211.

Crotoy ceded to the duke of Burgundy, i. 74 ; treaty concluded at the castle of, between Louis XI. and the duke of Burgundy, 216.

Croussol, Lord de, arrested, ii. 310.

Croy, the lords of, expelled from the palace of the duke of Burgundy, i. 6; the duke of Burgundy's declaration against, 10.

Croy, Antony, lord of, i. 6. n.

Croy, John of, count of Chimay, i. 6. n.

Croy, Philip of, i. 10. n.

Cueur, Jeffery, ii. 3.

Crussol, Louis, lord of, i. 220.

Curton, Gilbert, lord of, i. 213.

Cyprus, title of the Venetians to, ii. 121.

D.

Dabecfin, Geo., ii. 232.

Dammartin, count of, is reconciled to the constable of France, i. 228; strange story about his intended assassination, 248; restored to his possessions, ii. 333.

Dauphin of France (son of Louis XI.), treaty respecting his projected marriage with Margaret of Flanders, ii. 45. et seq.; his marriage to the countess of Flanders, 58. 393, 394 ; receives his father's last injunctions, 69. (See CHARLES VIII.).

Dauphin (son of Charles VIII.), death of, ii. 254; loss sustained thereby, 257.

Davison, Jean, revolt of, i. 171 n.

Death divides all things, and defeats the counsels of mankind, i. 215.

De Croy, Sieux, i. 76.

D'Eu, count, i. 1. 5.

Denmark, king of, quartered at Unterbilk, i. 242.

Despiris, lord, i. 221 ; crushed to death at the siege of Beauvais, 222.

Destouteville, Robert, mayor of Paris, committed to the Bastille, ii. 301 ; restored to the mayoralty of Paris, 336.

De Ville, William de, i. 119.

Diamonds taken by the Swiss from the Burgundians, i. 311.

Digonne, Jean de, i. 141.

Dijon surrenders to the king, i. 376.

Dinant, town of, captured by the

duke of Burgundy, i. 88. *et seq.*; caused by its cruel treatment to the people of Bouvines, 88, 89.

Divine chastisements, i. 339.

Divisions, mischiefs of among princes, i. 85; among citizens, 89; result of among the Liegeois, 101; permitted by God for the punishment of wickedness, 378. *et seq.*

Doge of Venice, Commines' visit to the, ii. 170; his palace, *ib.*; his friendly assurances towards Charles VIII. 176—178; his conferences with Commines, 250.

Doges of Venice, ii. 267.

Dogs, &c., strange fancy of Louis XI. for, ii. 57.

Dole, the capital of Manche-Comté, besieged by the lord of Craon, ii. 20; historical notice of, 20. *n.*; taken by storm, 22; destruction of, 391.

Domjulien, Antoine lord of, ii. 184. *et n.*

Doreille, Rigault de, ii. 250.

Doriolle, Peter, Chancellor of France, i. 212; arrested, ii. 310.

Dormans, Regnault, ii. 337.

Dorset, Thomas Gray, Marquis of, ii. 4.

Douay, sally from, defeated, i. 363.

Doullens, or Dourlens, ceded to the duke of Burgundy, i. 74; the duke of Burgundy's arrival at, 171, 233.

Duisie, Guillot, notice of, i. 67.

Dunois, John, count of, i. 18; crosses the Seine, 42; his lands and lordships recovered from the count of Maine, 82; appointed royal commissioner, ii. 341.

Dunois, Francis, count of, ii. 74.

Du Pont, Marquis, i. 112. *n.*

Du Pont des Archers, town of, ii. 238; surrendered, 339.

Duras, Galhard, lord, 186.

Durazzo, Paolo, Archbishop of, ii. 166; his capture, 167.

Duties, regulations for the levying of, i. 133, 134.

E.

Easterlings, at war with England, i. 192; danger of Edward IV. being captured by the, 193; their opposition to the kings of Denmark, 380.

Edward, the black prince, his capture of king John at the battle of Poictiers, i. 390; his exalted character, 390. *n.*

EDWARD IV., king of England, i. 22; notices of, 37; his interview with Charles of Burgundy, 124; with Louis XI., 126; contemporary with Louis XI. and the duke of Burgundy, 181; his sister married to the latter, *ib.*; supported by the earl of Warwick, 183; imprisoned by the earl of Warwick, *ib.*; escapes and defeats the earl in various battles, 184; his character and person, 187; is driven out of England by the earl of Warwick, assisted by Louis XI., 190—194; dangers to which he was exposed, 191—193; his conference with the duke of Burgundy at St. Pol, 198; liberally assisted by the duke, 199; he returns to England, *ib.*; and defeats the earl of Warwick, who is slain, 201; defeats the prince of Wales at Tewksbury, 202; his executions, 203; his reign no longer disturbed, *ib.*; opposes the contemplated marriage of the duke of Burgundy's daughter, 208, 209; invades France, 251. *et seq.*; his great army, *ib.*; sends a letter of defiance to the king of France, 252; the courteous reception of his herald, 253, his landing at Calais, 255; the bad reception of his troops, 257; receives a herald from Louis XI., 251; receives overtures of peace from Louis, 261; enters into a truce for nine years, 263. *et seq.*; visited by the duke of Burgundy, 267; his troops entertained by Louis, 269; his answer to the constable of France, 270; disorderly conduct of his troops, 271; interview between him and Louis, 275. *et seq.*; the treaty signed, 276; his private conversation with Louis, 277; his return to England, 283; the vicissitudes of his life, 393. *et seq.*; his death, 394. *n.*; his amours, 395, 396; ii. 63; a voluptuous prince, ii. 7; offers made to, by Louis XI., 8, 9; his displeasure at the marriage of the dauphin of France and Margaret of Flanders, 62; remarks on his death and character, 62. *et seq.*; murder of his two sons, 63. *n.*; his life a continued scene of trouble, 85; his love of pleasure, 87; died of apoplexy, *ib.*

EDWARD IV. (*continued from Jean de Troyes' Chronicle*). He seizes the crown of England, ii. 300; his preparations for invading France, 360; expels the Earl of Warwick, *ib.*; flies to his brother-in-law the Duke of Burgundy, 363; demands the duchies of Guienne and Normandy, 376; his intercourse with Louis XI. at Picquigny, 378, 379; concludes a truce, 380; death of, 394.

Edward V., of England, birth of, i. 195.

Elizabeth, Princess, daughter of

Edward IV. of England, i. 263. 395. ii. 7; married to Henry VII., 8. *n.*

Embassies sent to Venice, ii. 173,174.

Emmanuel, King of Portugal, ii. 278.

ENGLAND, gradually loses her power in France, i. 48; civil wars in, 48. 93. 363, 364. *et seq.*; civil wars during the contests between Louis XI. and the duke of Burgundy, 181—186; the various battles fought, 181. *n.*; a check to France, 379; Scotland a check to, *ib.*; the excellence of her government, 385; the royal families of, and their misfortunes, 393. *et seq.*; revolutions in, 395—397; strange adventures that happened in, in 1460, ii. 299; Louis XI. sends an embassy to, 340.

Englebert, lord of Cleves, 211. *et n.*

English, in the service of the duke of Burgundy, i. 237; France invaded by the, 238. 251 (see EDWARD IV.); entertained by Louis XI., 269; their disorderly conduct, 271; anxiety of Louis concerning the, 279; cajoled by Louis XI., after the duke of Burgundy's death, from fear of being interrupted in his conquests, ii. 1. *et seq.*; how they became masters of the duchy of Guienne, 2. *et n.*; the French king's liberality to the, 3—5; and his policy, 7.

Entragues, Robert lord of, ii. 192; governor of Pietrasanda, 194; sells the Florentine towns, 257., ii. 255.

Envy, passion of, in high stations, ii. 255.

Espinal, in Lorraine, taken from the marshal of Burgundy, and, given to the duke of Calabria, i. 78.

Essais, Philip des, lord of Thieux, i. 222 ; pensions granted to, 224.

Estampes, Charles of Burgundy's army quartered at, i. 34; the united forces at, *ib.*; treaty of alliance at, between the dukes of Bretagne and Burgundy, i. 1. 3.

Estates, meeting of the Three, at Tours, 386.

Estiac, Jean, baron of, i. 207.

Estradiots, their skirmishes with the French and Swiss, ii. 201; description of them, *ib.*; number of, in the Venetian service, 204; attack the French, 205; their onslaught on the king's camp, 212; their flight, 213; their plunder, 216.

Eu, town of, captured by the Burgundians, i. 221, 222; retaken, 222; capture of, ii. 371.

Eu, Charles d'Artois, Count d', his complaint against the Duke of Burgundy, i. 169; death of, ii. 366.

Eugenius IV., Pope, i. 47.

Eustachio, Philippo, of Pavia, captor of the castle of Milan, ii. 102; seized and imprisoned, 105.

Exeter, Henry Holland, Duke of, reduced to beggary, i. 182.

F.

Factions, danger of, ii. 86; historical notices of, 146; appear as if necessary for the world, i. 381.

Faith in God, on the want of, i. 389.

Favre, Jourdain, the friar, i. 211. *n.*; 223. *n.*

Fay, lord of, i. 323. *n.*

Febvre, Gerard le, i. 141.

Fecamp church, in Normandy, burnt by a fiery exhalation, ii. 302.

Female diplomacy, i. 189.

Ferdinand, duke of Braganza, ii. 278. *n.*

Ferdinand I. (or Ferrand), King of Naples, i. 313; ii. 26; the conspiracy of the Pazzi at Florence promoted by, 26—28; besieges Florence, 29; rebellion against, 97; his treachery and cruelty, 99; his atrocities, 151; his tyrannical measures, 152; his death, 155.

Ferdinand II. (Don Ferrand), son of Alfonso, King of Naples, ii. 123. 133; hostilities against, 147; crowned king by his father Alfonso, 149; received as king of Naples, 157; prepares to oppose Charles VIII. at St. Germains, *ib.*; his flight and dispersion of his army, 160, 161. 163; retakes Naples from the French, 230, 231. *et n.*; conditions by which he was to abide for peace, 249; the advantages gained by him after the treaty of Atilla, 261; his marriage and death, 263.

Ferdinand II., of Castile (or Ferrand), cedes different towns to the Venetians, ii. 121. 172. *n.*; differences between him and Charles VIII., 269; ambassadors sent to, 270. 273; and a truce signed, 275.

Ferdinand V., King of Spain, i. 331. *et n.*

Ferrara, duke of, his handsome treatment of Commines, ii. 182.

Ferrand, king of Naples (See Ferdinand).

Ferrette, county of, i. 236; captured and restored to the duke of Austria, 243; the Swiss gain right of passage through, *ib.*

Ferriers, village of, ii. 372.

Fiennes, Jacques, lord of, i. 248.

Flanders, countess of, married to

the Dauphin, ii. 393. 397.; her public entry into Paris, 394.

Flemings, rebellion of the, i. 358; conclude a peace with Louis XI., ii. 393, 394.

Flisco, Breto di, of Genoa, ii. 126.

Flisco, Lord John Lewis di, ii. 126.

Flocquet, Captain Robert de Hain, i. 30.

Florence, Commines sent on a mission to, i. xxvi., ii. 25. et seq.; conspiracy of the Pazzi at, ii. 26, 27; besieged by Pope Sixtus IV., 29; governed by the Medici, 127; affairs of, 129. 135.; Peter de Medicis banished from, 141; entered by Charles VIII., 143; preachings of Friar Jerome at, ii. 189. et n.

Florentine towns, Charles VIII.'s deliberations respecting their restitution, ii. 188; several retained by him, 191.

Florentines send ambassadors to Charles VIII., ii. 127; cruelly treat the Pisans, 138; enter into a treaty with Charles VIII., 143. et n.; capture and sale of their towns, 257, 258; great divisions among them at the death of Charles VIII., 285.

Foix, count of, ii. 213.

Forgosa, Signor John, taken prisoner, ii. 127.

Forli, town of, ii. 133.

Fornovo, village of, xxxv.; arrival of Charles VIII. at, ii. 204; preparation for the battle of, 207; battle of, gained by the French, 211—214; consequences of the victory, 215. et seq.; losses at, 217; a grand parley takes place after the battle of, 220; retreat of the French from, 223.

Fortune nothing but a poetical fiction, i. 293; changes of, 294.

Fou, John du, i. 363.

Foucart, Captain Patris, i. 213.

Framezelles, Robinet de, ii. 212. et n.

Francasse, Gasparo, de Sanseverino, ii. 148.

FRANCE throws off the power of England, i. 48; plundered for many years by the nobility of England, 182; invaded by the English, 238. 251 (see Edward IV.); England a check to, 379; taxation of, in the fifteenth century, 386, 387.; women excluded from the throne of, ii. 14. 16; the founders of their different dynasties, 289; its fertility in 1460, 298; invaded by the Burgundians, 312; Edward IV. makes preparations for invading, 360.

France and Spain, league between, ii. 359.

Franhemont, the country of, i. 153; desperate attack of, on the duke of Burgundy's troops, 153—15; the hilly country of, 162; the dwellings burnt down, and the country devastated, 163; extreme cold in, ib.

Francis, duke, i. 397.

Francis, friar, of Apulia, ii, 286. et n.

Francisco de Puzzi, his conspiracy and death, ii. 28.

Frederic I., the count palatine, troops of, i. 44.

Frederic III., the emperor of Germany, his interview with Charles of Burgundy, i. 124; embassy sent by Louis XI. to, 245; his story and its moral, 246; declines the king's proposals, 247; sends an embassy to Charles VIII. ii. 110.

Frederic, Don, son of Alphonso king of Naples, ii. 123. 157; a military commander, 126; naval defeat of, 129; succeeds

Ferdinand II. as king of Na-Naples, ii. 263.

French, on the character of the, and the government of their kings, i. 385. *et seq.*; their affection towards their princes, 386.; their obedience, 387. : their difficulties in marching from Pisa, ii. 194. *et seq.*; their skirmishes with the Estradiots, 201. 205; gain the battle of Fornovo, 207 —214.; superiority of their artillery, 210.; their retreat from Fornovo, 223.; more than men in their attacks, and less than women in their retreats, 225; their sufferings, 226, 227; their retreat secured by the Swiss, 226.

French army, two sorts of Germans in the, ii. 260.

Friar, Robert, the holy man of Calabria, ii. 54.; sent for by Louis XI., 55.; biographical notices of, 56, 58.

Fumée, Adam, physician to louis XI., ii. 27.

G.

Gaeta, castle of, ii. 263.

Galeas, John Visconti, lord of Milan in 1378, ii. 100.

Galeas, Maria Sforza, Duke of Milan in 1466, ii. 101; banishment of his brothers, *ib. n.*

Galeas, John Sforza, duke of Milan, ii. 31, 100; pays homage to Louis XI. for the duchy of Genoa, 31; his duchess, 131; his illness, *ib.*

Galeas, Ludovic the Moor, (afterwards duke of Milan) ii. 101, 102; his dispute with St. Severino, 103.; seizes the castle of Milan, and assumes the reins of government, ii. 105; aspires to the ducal power, 106. *et seq.*;

sends an embassy to Charles soliciting an expedition to Naples, 108.

Galeazzo, Maria Giovanni, duke of Milan, 27.

Galee, Jacques de la, i. 141.

Galeot, James, notices of, i. 44. 237.

Galeot, lord de la Mirandola, ii. 148.

Gallipoli, town of, ii. 162.

Gannay, Jean, lord of Persan, ii. 147; president of Pisa, 191.

Gantois, their rebellion and submission to the duke of Burgundy, i. 106. *et seq.*; their character and customs, 108; their charters, 109; rebellion of the, 366; embassy from the, to Louis XI., 367; on the return of their ambassadors they put the chancellor Hugonet and the lord of Humbercourt to death, 375.; assume the sole authority of the duchess, and the management of government, 375. 377.; persecute the Burgundians, 377.; are defeated before Tournay, 378.; their negociations with Louis on the death of their duchess, ii. 42; their seditious spirit, ii. 60. See Ghent.

Garigliano, the river, ii. 157.

Garrison, a strong one cannot be attacked with safety, i. 220.

Gascony, the English merchant of, i. 280.

Gelders, duke de, slain, ii. 388.

Genetaires, a Spanish light horse, ii. 201.

Genly, Jaques, lord of, ii. 230.

Genoa, the duke of Milan pays homage to Louis XI. for the duchy of, ii. 31.; revolt of, 109. *et n.*; great military preparations at, 122.; the French at, 127.; defeat of the French forces at, 195.; plots of the Italian princes for the recovery of, ii. 267 ; the plan against, proves abortive, 268, 269.

Gens, bailiff of, i. 142.

Gens du Camp, pioneers so called, ii. 40.

George le Grec, i. 333.

George, prince of Scutari, ii. 166.

George, son of John II., ii. 278.

Gerault, M., the military engineer, i. 43.

Germans, inroads made upon the, by the duke of Burgundy, i. 223. et seq. ; the town of Nuz relieved by the, 240. et seq. ; Charles defeated and slain by the, 336., ii. 383—386. (see Swiss); boorish manners of the, 14 ; secretly assist the Burgundians, 18 ; liberal offers made to the, 210 ; their contests with the French in Florence, 135 ; capitulate to Charles VIII., 165 ; two sorts of, in the French army, 260.

Germany, several towns of, abandon their alliance with the duke of Burgundy, i. 311 ; confederacy of, defeat the duke of Burgundy, 315 ; factions and divisions in, 380.

Ghent, the duke of Burgundy's triumphal entry into, i. 106 ; riotous assemblies in, 107 ; their customs, 108, 109 ; submission of the Gantois, 109 ; fines imposed upon, ib. ; the duke of Burgundy retires to, 110 ; Master Oliver's designs upon defeated, 356 ; the citizens of, rebel against the duchy of Burgundy, and put their magistrates to death, 365. et n. (see Gantois); disquisition on its political and commercial position, 378. et seq. (see Gantois.)

Gié, Pierre de Rohan, lord of, i. 271 ; marshal of France, ii. 38 ; leads the French across the Apennines, 200 ; retires to the

mountains for fear of attack, 202 ; commands at the battle of Fornovo, 209. et seq.

Girault, the engineer. 56.

Girl, in the city of Mans, trained to certain impostures, ii. 302.

Gisors, weak condition of, ii. 331.

Gloucester, Richard, of York, duke of, afterwards Richard III. of England, i. 194. 201. 277 ; historical notices of, 395 ; his atrocities, 396, 397, ii. 63 ; declares himself king of England, ii. 63 ; his death, i. 49. n., 397 ; ii. 64, 65.

God, inscrutable ordinances of, i. 327 ; the sole governor of human affairs, 328 ; gives princes as He in his wisdom thinks fit, 340, 341 ; wars and divisions permitted by, for the punishment of wicked princes and people, 378. et seq. ; on want of faith in, 389 ; on the judgments of, 392, 393 ; gives wise ministers of state to that nation he designs to support, ii. 24 ; the disposal of all things proceeds from, 86 ; the wisdom and policy of man of no avail when He chooses to interpose, 120 ; His providence in favour of the French, 148 ; the general voice of the people, the voice of God, 154 ; providence of, 165 ; the conductor of the French in the Italian expedition, 226 ; the power of, shown in affliction, 280.

Gormont, Jean, i. 140.

Goux, Pierre de, chancellor of the duke of Burgundy, i. 108; cancels the charter of Ghent, 109.

Grammont, Michel de, sent ambassador to Castile, ii. 275.

Grandvilliers, granary of, i. 132.

Granada, troublesome to Castile, i. 379.

Granson, besieged by the Burgundians, i. 303; their barbarous treatment, 304; the inhabitants defeat the Burgundians, 305; consequence of Charles's defeat near, 307. *et seq.*; capture of, ii. 381; recaptured, 382.

Crassay, or Grassé, Gilbert de, lord of Champeroux, i. 258; ii. 37.

Grassé, James de, Lord of Yors, i. 258.

Grave, town of, i. 233.

Graville, Louis, lord of, ii. 97.

Gravina, Francisco, duke of, ii. 163.

Grips, in the ports of Albania, ii. 166.

Gruthuyse, Louis, lord de la, i. 193, 194.

Grutuse, lord de la, ii. 75.

Guelders, duchy of, i. 399; seized by the duke of Burgundy, 222; lost and restored, 234. *n.*

Guelders, Arnold, duke of, i. 232; cruelly treated by his own son, 232, 233; is released from prison, 358; invests Tournay, is repelled and slain, 358. *et n.*, 378.

Guelders, Adolphus, duke of, allied to the house of Bourbon, i. 232; his unnatural conduct to his father, 232, 233; his imprisonment and miserable death, 234.

Guelphs and Ghibellines, factions of the, ii. 135. *et n.*, 146.

Guerres, Gratian des, lord of Aubenton, ii. 185.

Guienne, the duchy of, conferred on Charles of France, i. 165, 166; how the English became masters of the, ii. 2. *et n.*; ceded to Louis XI., ii. 359.

Guienne, duke of (Charles of France), is desirous of stirring up a war between Louis XI. and Charles of Burgundy, i. 169; his designs in promoting the war between the king and the duke of Burgundy, 173; his object to marry the duke's daughter, 173. 180.; the war between Louis XI. and the duke of Burgundy renewed through his solicitations, 203. *et seq.*; promises passed respecting the marriage, 206; his death, 210.; and the final peace negotiating between the king and the duke of Burgundy thereby broken off, 210; union established between him and Louis XI., ii. 358, 359; his dissatisfaction, 366.

Guillaume de Bische, i. xxiv.

Guinegaste, battle of, ii. 32.

Guise, Louis, count of, ii. 160.

Guisnes, county of, ceded to the duke of Burgundy, i. 76.

Guns, great, use of, ii. 133.

Guy, town of, ii. 388.

Guy de Brimeu, lord of Rumbercourt, i. 95.

Guynegate, battle of, ii. 216.

H.

Hague, Edward IV.'s arrival at the, i. 194.

Hainault, intended for bestowal by the king on his own subjects, i. 351.

Halles, Olivier, lord des, i. 259.

Hallewin, Madame Jeanne de, her opinion on the projected marriage of the duchess of Burgundy, ii. 11.

Halots, conference at, ii. 59.

Han delivered up to Louis XI., i. 350; his abode at, ii. 365.

Haquelebac gallery, ii. 283.

Harancourt, Guillaume de, bishop of Verdun, imprisonment of, i. 165, ii. 75.

Hastings, William, lord, i. 191; receives a pension from Louis XI.

i. 267, ii. 5; his high character, 4.

Haultbourdin, John, lord of, i. 11;
his bravery, 29, 30; his advice
after the battle of Montlhery, 31.

Heberge, John, bishop of Evereux,
one of the royal commissioners
at Bouvines, i. 227.

Helene des Chambes, married to
Commines, i. xxii.

Henry, a Parisian, employed to
negotiate terms of peace, i. 214.

Henry III. landgrave of Hesse, i.
236.

Henry IV., king of Castile, his
interview with Louis XI., i. 121
—123.

Henry V. king of England, i. 12.
17; qualities of, 22; is offered
the duchies of Normandy and
Guienne, 48; captures Rouen,
273. n.; his death, 22. n.

Henry VI. king of England, i. 22;
his imprisonment, 48; released
from the Tower by the earl of
Warwick, 195; his misfor-
tunes, 393; rebellion against,
ii. 299; reinstated, 363; his
wife and friends visit Paris, and
are royally received, 364; his
army defeated, 366; death of,
i. 48. 201.

Henry VII. king of England, i.
396. (See Richmond).

Herald sent by Edward IV. to
Louis XV.; i. 253; one sent to
Edward, 260.

Herman IV., archbishop of Cologne, 235.

Hermits of St. Pancras, ii. 56.

Herycourt, castle of, besieged, i.
213.

Hesdin, the duke of Burgundy's
arrival at, i. 170; delivered up to
the King, 362.

Hesevare, Cardinal, i. 241.

Hieronymo, Girolamo, Count de,
ii. 28., 133. n.

History, advantages arising from

the knowledge of, especially to
princes, i. 115. et seq.

Holland, Louis XI. intends to
take possession of, i. 351.

Holy Ghost, asserted to be present at the treaty between Edward IV. and Louis XI. i. 279.

Hostages of Liege, their liberation,
i. 96; present the keys of the
city to the Duke of Burgundy,
101; some of them put to death,
106.

Houaste, John de Montespedon,
bailiff of Rouen, i. 70.

Houcs and Cabellans, contentions
between the two factions, ii. 146.

Howard, Lord John, i. 253. 258.
261; master of the horse, 267;
created earl of Norfolk, 282.
ii. 4, 5; the English ambassador
391.

Hugh Capet, the second king
of France, who came collaterally
to the throne. ii. 289, 290.

Hugonet, William, lord of Sail-
lant, and chancellor of Burgundy,
sent as ambassador to Louis XI.
i. 359; arrested by the Gantois,
372; charges brought against,
373; condemned, and publicly
executed, 359. n., 374, 375.

Humbercourt, Guy de Brimeu,
lord of, i. 95; appointed to negotiate with the Liegeois, 101;
takes possession of the city of
Liege, 103; his great abilities
in managing the affair, 104;
gates of the city delivered up to,
105; appointed lieutenant of the
Liegeois, 113; captured by the
rioters of Liege, i. 118; effects
his escape, 119; sent as ambassador to the king, 359, 360;
arrested by the Gantois. 372.;
charges against, 373; condemned
and executed, 374, 375.

Hungary, victories of, against the
Turks, ii. 88, 89; Matthias I.
chosen king of, 89.

Hunniades, regent of Hungary, his wisdom and bravery, ii. 87 ; defeats the Turks at Belgrade, 88. *et n.*

Hunting, the greatest pleasure of Louis XI., ii. 80, 81.

Hure, John de, plundered, ii. 312.

Huye, capture of, i. 93. ii. 346.

I.

Ignorance, the great curse of princes, i. 117.

Imbert de Batorney, Count du Bouchage, i. xlvii. *n.*

Impiety never goes unpunished, i. 234.

Ingratitude often the reward of faithful services, i. 231.

Innocent VIII., his depravity and incapacity, ii. 98. *n.*

Interviews between kings for the settlement of differences often prejudicial, i. 121. *et seq.*; between Henry IV. king of Castile, and Louis XI., 121—123 ; between Charles of Burgundy and the emperor Frederic, 124 ; and other great princes, 124—126.

Isabella, daughter of John, king of · Portugal, and countess of Charolois, ii. 3. *n.*, 9. *n.*, 37. *n.*

Isabella of Castile, i. 333.

Isabella, daughter of Alphonzo II. of Naples, ii. 104.

Isabella, daughter of the earl of Warwick, i. 184.

Ischia, island of, ii. 150. 161.

Isle of France, entered by the Burgundians, ii. 314.

Italians, their nature to side with the strongest, ii. 139. 145.

Italy, the princes of, kept in check by the free states of, i. 379 ; the mission of Commines to, ii. 25. *et seq.*; expedition of Charles VIII. into, 93. *et seq.* ; consists but of three powers, 130 ; league formed in, against Charles

VIII., 179. 183. *et seq.*; the princes of, form various plots in favour of Charles VIII. for the recovery of Naples, and the destruction of the duke of Milan, 264. *et seq.* ; their miscarriage, 266, 267.

J.

Jacqueling, M. Jean, i. 140.

Jacques de Beaumont, lord of Bressuyre, i. xxi. xxii.

Jacques d'Armagnac ; xxv.

James de Pacis, Signor, his conspiracy and death, ii. 27. *et n.*

James of Portugal, duke of Visco, ii. 278.

James III. of Scotland, i. 398. *n.*

James IV. of Scotland, i. 398. *n.* ?

Janly, M. Jean de, i. 140.

Jealousy, passion of, in high stations, ii. 255.

Jean de Beaune, a merchant of Tours, i. xvi.

Jean de Halewyn, i. 96. *n.*, 98.

Jean de la Clite, lord of Commines, i. xii.

Jean Louis, bishop of Geneva, i. 114.

Jerome, the Dominican friar, ii. 189. *et n.* (See Savonarola.)

Jesus Christ, the protector of the French army in Italy, ii 226, 227.

Jewels taken by the Swiss from the Burgundians, i. 312.

Joachim, son of Louis XI., marshal of France, i. 42., ii. 80. 316.

Joan, Prince, of France, death of, ii. 393.

Joan du Bois, ii. 309.

Joanna, daughter of John II. of Arragon, ii. 155.

John, bishop of Cambray, i. 10.

John of Lancaster, duke of Bedford, i. 47.

John, duke of Burgundy, i. 10. *n.*,

298; surnamed " Sans-peur," 72.

John II., king of France, i. 347; the heavy sums paid for his ransom, 390.

John II., duke of Bourbon and Auvergne, notices of, i. 9.

John II. of Portugal, ii. 66. n.

John II., king of Arragon, i. 123; pledges his territories to Louis XI., ii. 65.

Jou, castle of, ii. 23.

Juana, queen of Arragon, i. 122.

Juana, daughter of Henry IV. of Castile, i. 333.

Julian de Medicis, slain, ii. 26.

Julius II., pope of Rome, his character, ii. 98.

K.

Kings, on the wisdom of, i. 229; their jealousies and contests with their own children, ii. 255. 256. (See Princes.)

Kings of France, the early ones, ii. 289, 290.

King's evil, touching for the, ii. 37.

King's nets, adopted by Louis XI., ii. 75.

Knowledge, general advantages of, i. 381.

L.

Labadio, town of, ii. 106.

Ladislaus V., king of Hungary, ii. 88; his cruelties and death, ib.

Lallain, Phillip lord de, i. 21; killed at Montlhery, 12. n., 22. 30.

La Levée, the king contemplates its destruction, i. 353.

Lamoureux, William, i. 132.

Lancaster, royal House of in England, i. 393; their civil contests, 93. 181. et seq.; ii. 365; the

duke of Somerset its greatest supporter, i. 183.

Lancelot of Hungary. (See Ladislaus).

Landais, Pierre, i. 397. n.

Lannoy, Baudoin de, lord of Molembais, i. 225; ii. 60.

Lansquenets, in the French army, ii. 260.

La Rivière, town of, i. 316; the solitary retreat of the duke of Burgundy, i. 321. et seq.

Lau, Antoine, lord de, i. 62; his gallantry, 149.

Lau, Monsieur du, i. 114.

Laurence de Medicis, ii. 25, 26, 29. (See Medicis.)

La Vere, in Holland, i. 192.

Laws, reform of the, attempted by Charles VIII., ii. 282.

Lawyers, illiterate princes often misled by, i. 116, 117.

League, formation of the, between the Venetians and the Pope against France, ii. 179; declared on Palm Sunday, 181; the French forces menaced by the, 202, 203; their formidable force, 209; defeated at Fornovo by the French, 211—214; peace concluded between the, and Charles VIII., 245. et seq.; offensive and defensive, between France and Spain, 359.

Learning, utility of, to princes, i. 117; general utility of, 381.

Leather-money of France, i. 390, 391.

Leghorn, surrendered to Charles VIII., ii. 136.

Leheac, M. de, marshal of France, ii. 337.

Lenoncourt, Claude, bailiff of Vitry, ii. 185.

Le Sauvage, i. 119.

Lescut, Odet, lord of, i. 165; obtains the city of Caen, 84; demands made on behalf of, 223, 224.

Letters, advantages arising from the knowledge of, i. 115. *et seq.*

Librefatta, surrendered to Charles VIII., ii. 136.

Liege, rebellion of, i. xiv.; captured, burnt, and pillaged by the Burgundians, i. xv. 80. 103. 157; ii. 356; the Liegeois compelled to make peace, i. 80; city beleaguered, 100; set on fire, and destroyed, 102; its great strength and population, 104; the duke of Burgundy's triumphal entry into, 105; new laws prescribed, and large sums exacted, 106; the duke of Burgundy again marches against the city, in company with Louis XI., 145. *et seq.*; confusion of the city, 146; the inhabitants sally out and commit great slaughter, 147, 148; its situation and extent, 150; dilapidated state of, *ib.* (See Liegeois.)

Liege, bishop of. (See Louis de Bourbon.)

Liegeois, wars of the duke of Burgundy with the, i. 88. *et seq.*; its causes, 89; a peace agreed to, 92; the peace broken by the, 93; debate concerning their hostages, 95; amount of their forces, 96; defeat of the, 97; great number of slain, 98; consequences of their defeat, 99; divisions among the, 101; their submission, 103; the city of Liege triumphantly entered by the duke of Burgundy, 105; the submission of the garrison, 109; excommunication against the Liegeois, *ib.*; act of treachery, at the instigation of Louis XI., perpetrated by the, 118; murders committed by the, 118; in consequence of which the king is seized and imprisoned at Peronne, 120; the king is

compelled to renounce his league with them, 127 *et seq.*; make vigorous sallies on the duke's forces, by which the duke and the king are placed in great danger, 154, 155; their miseries after the capture of the city, 159; barbarously treated, 161; their treatment justified by their frequent rebellions and cruelties, *ib.*

Liegeois (*continued from Jean de Troyes' Chronicle*). They invade the Burgundian territories, ii. 336; at war with the duke of Burgundy, 341. 346; subdued, 349; massacres committed by the, 354; their city captured by the duke of Burgundy, 355; sustain dreadful slaughter, *ib.*

Ligny, Louis, count of, ii. 147; made governor of Siena, 188.

Lisle, meeting of ambassadors at, i. 1. *et seq.*

Liure, Henry de, ii. 318.

Lodesma, count of, i. 122; afterwards duke of Albourg, 123.

Loheac, André, lord of, 118.

Lombardy entered by Charles VIII., ii. 203.; fineness of the country, *ib.*

Lombes, bishop of, the Spanish ambassador, ii. 391.

Longuejoye, John, count de, ii. 337; appointed royal commissioner, 318.

Lords of France, their conference with the Parisians, i. 50.

Lorenzo de Medici, xxvii.

Lornay, Louis, lord of, ii. 211. *et n.*

Lorraine, John de, ii. 339.

Lorraine, the duke of Burgundy's hostilities in, i. 295; entirely subdued by the duke of Burgundy, 301.

Lorraine, René II., duke of, i. xxxiii. 242. 299; his loss of territory, 315; joins the German confederacy, and defeats the Burgundians, *ib.*; besieges Nancy, 322; takes the field with a powerful army against the duke of Burgundy, 330. *et seq.*; defeats and slays the duke of Burgundy in battle, 335, 336., ii. 383. 386; demands the duchy of Bar and the county of Provence from Charles VIII., ii. 94, 95; sisters of, 95 *n.*; appointed grand chamberlain of France, *ib.*; his claims to Provence disputed, 96; leaves the French court in disgust, 97; the rebels of Naples propose to make him king, 98; how he failed to take advantage of the offer, *ib.*; returns with dishonour to his own country, 99.

Louis de Bourbon, bishop of Liege, i. 91; rebellion against, 118; punished by William de la Marck, 370. *et n.*

Louis de Luxembourg, constable of France, (see St. Paul).

Louis van den Rive, i. 96. *n.*

Louis XI., king of France (*prefatory notices*); his position with regard to Charles the Bold of Burgundy, i. xiii.; the difficulties to which he was exposed before extricating himself, xiv. xv.; induces Commines to leave the service of Charles the Bold, xvi. xvii; his contests with Vicomte Thouars and others respecting the property granted to Commines, xxi. xxii. xxviii. *et seq.*; his munificence to Commines, xxii.; attacked by apoplexy, xxx.; death of, xxxii.; biographical notices of, xlv. Causes of the war between him and the duke of Burgundy, 1. *et seq.*; Charles of Burgundy and several French noblemen raise an army against him, 9. *et seq.*; he marches into Bourbonnois, 15; the noblemen arrayed against him, 16; he fights a battle with Charles at Montlhery, 21; his army retreats, 29; his brothers, the duke of Berry and the duke of Bretagne, take part against him, 34; relieves Paris from the invasion of Charles, 51; his battles near Charenton, 54; a digression on his virtues and vices, 59—61; the extravagant demands made upon him by the allied princes of France, 65; pays a visit to Charles, and enters into conversation respecting their quarrel, 65; visited by Charles, 71; concludes the treaties of Conflans with Charles and others, 73. 80; the great concessions of territory and towns made by him, 74. 76. 78; remarks on the peace into which he had entered, 78; his recovery of what had been given to his brother, 83, 84; makes war in Bretagne on the duke of Burgundy's allies, 110 *et seq.*; he is seized and imprisoned by Charles in the castle of Peronne, 118; renounces his league with the Liegeois, to obtain his liberation, 127; his interview with Henry IV., king of Castile, 121—123; his interview with Edward IV. of England, 126; with Charles at Peronne, 129; enters into a treaty of peace, 129; conditions of the peace, 130. *et seq.*; makes great concessions to the duke of Burgundy, 132. *et seq.*; accompanies the duke of Burgundy in his expedition against the Liegeois, 145. 148; is placed in great danger, 155; returns into France by permission of the duke, 161; his subtlety in acting contrary to the duke's intentions, 165; he seizes the opportunity of waging a fresh

war with Charles, 167. *et seq.*;
assembles the three estates at
Tours, and issues a declaration of grievances against the
duke of Burgundy, 169; seizes
St. Quentin and Amiens, 171,
172; enters into a short truce,
178; assists the earl of Warwick in driving King Edward
IV. out of England, 187. *et
seq.*; renewal of the war between him and the duke of Burgundy, 203. *et seq.*; the final
peace negociating between the
two princes is broken off by the
duke of Guienne's death, 210;
his attempts to outwit the duke,
213; and the duke's attempts to
cheat him, 215; treaty between
him and the duke concluded at
the castle of Crotoy, 216; he concludes a peace with the duke of
Bretagne, and a truce with the
duke of Burgundy, 222—226; a
digression on the wisdom of,
229.; his policy with regard to
the duke, 235; takes the castle
of Trouquoy and various towns
from the duke, 244. *et seq.*;
suspects the constable of France,
247; his territory invaded by
the king of England, assisted by
the duke of Burgundy, 251.
et seq.; his courteous reception
of the English herald, 253;
sends one of his menial servants,
in a herald's coat, with overtures
of peace to the king of England,
259; a truce for nine years negotiated between 'him and the
king of England, 263. *et seq.*;
he entertains the English at
Amiens, 269; the interview
between him and king Edward,
275; enters into a treaty of
commerce with the duke of
Burgundy, 287; arrests the
constable, and executes him,
293. 297; his joy at the defeat

of the duke of Burgundy by the
Swiss, 308. *et seq.*; receives
with joy the intelligence of the
defeat and death of the duke of
Burgundy, 343; seizes Abbeville, 345; his determination to
effect the destruction of the house
of Burgundy, and take possession
of their territories, 350—353;
various cities and places delivered up to him after the
death of the duke of Burgundy,
350—364; his state qualities,
387; cajoles the English after
the death of the duke of Burgundy, under the apprehension
of being interrupted in the conquest of his territories, ii. 1, *et
seq.*; his liberality, 3—5; his
policy, 7; his offers to the king
of England, 8, 9; recovers numerous towns in Burgundy, 18.
et seq.; subjugates the whole
province, 23; his mortification
at his defeat at Guinegaste,
34; enters into a treaty with
the duke of. Austria, 35; is
seized with a dangerous malady,
36; his supposed death, 39; his
state of mind during his illness, 42—45. 56, 57; concludes
the treaty of Arras with Maximilian, duke of Austria, 45;
sends for the holy man of Calabria, in hopes of being cured by
him, 54; strange conduct of the
king, 57; his strange fancies
for different animals, 57, 58;
his great power and prosperity.
65; his behaviour towards his
neighbours and subjects during
his prosperity, *ib.*; presents and
relics for the recovery of his
health sent from all parts of the
world, 66; receives various relics from Pope Sixtus IV.,
66; his character and high
qualities, 68; sends for his son
Charles a little before his death,

ib. ; his precepts and commands, 69 ; a comparison of his sorrows and troubles with those he had brought upon other people, 71. *et seq.* ; his suspicions, 73 ; his cruelties, 75 ; his rigid precautions, 77, 78 ; gives directions for his own funeral, 79 ; his death, 80 ; his habits and character, 81 ; anecdotes of his early life and times, 82. *et seq.* ; his life nothing but one continued scene of troubles and fatigues, 83 ; his exact age at the time of his death, 84. *n.* ; paternal jealousy of, 255.

Louis XI. (*from the Chronicles of Jean de Troyes,* styled " *The Scandalous Chronicle,*" ii. 297. *et seq.*); his accession to the throne, 304 ; his first measures, 304. 308 ; crowned at Rheims, 306 ; his entry into Paris, *ib.* ; his progress to Normandy, 309 ; his visit to Nogent, Tours, &c., *ib.* ; his march towards Angiers and Pont de Ce, 311 ; his contests with the duke of Burgundy, 312. *et seq.* ; marches into Bourbonnois, 312 ; defeats the Burgundians, 318 ; his great bravery, 319 ; his difficulties, 321 ; favours granted to Paris, 322 ; leaves Paris, and visits Normandy, 323 ; review of his forces in Paris, 326 ; his enthusiastic reception in Paris, *ib.* ; makes large concessions to the duke of Berry and Charles the Bold, 332 ; concludes a peace with the Burgundians, 333 ; visits the duke of Burgundy, 334, 335 ; design against his life, 335 ; makes several changes, 336, 337 ; marches into Normandy to reduce it to obedience, 337 ; captures Roan, 339 ; sends an embassy to the king of England, 340 ; issues a mandate for making preparations against England, *ib.* ; appoints royal commissioners to reform abuses, 341 ; makes preparations against the duke of Burgundy, 342 ; proceeds to Roan, and meets the earl of Warwick, 343 ; history of his foreign and domestic relations, 347. *et seq.* ; his territorial and financial arrangements with his brother Charles. the duke of Calabria, and the duke of Bretagne, 353 ; his conference with the duke of Burgundy at Peronne, 354 ; accompanies the duke at the siege and capture of Liege, 355 ; concludes a peace with the duke of Burgundy, 356 ; persuaded to an ignominious peace by cardinal Balue, 356, 357 ; punishes the cardinal of Angiers for treachery, 358 ; establishes a firm union with his brother the duke of Guienne, 358 ; takes possession of the duchy of Guienne, 359 ; prepares for the threatened invasion of Edward IV., and declares the duke of Burgundy an enemy, 360 ; hospitably receives the family of Henry VI. and the duke of Warwick at Paris, 364 ; enters into a truce with the duke of Burgundy, 365 ; again at war with the duke of Burgundy, 368. *et seq.* ; agrees to a truce, 374, 375 ; his interview with Edward IV. at Pecquigny, 378, 379 ; concludes a truce with him, 380 ; his festivities at Lyons, 383 ; assembles a large army in Picardy to reduce the late territories of the duke of Burgundy, 389 ; deceived by the duke of Austria, *ib.* ; agrees to a cessation of arms between him and duke Maximilian of Austria and the Flemings, 390 ; his military operations in Burgundy, 391, 392; prolongs the truce with Edward IV., 392; his illness, 392, 393; his injunctions, 393; concludes a peace with the Flemings, 393, 394; his death, 395; buried in the church of Notre Dame de Clery, *ib.*; his injustice during life, and repentance on his death-bed, 395, 396.

Louis XII. of France, ii. 97. *n.* (see Orleans, duke of,); his accession to the throne, 288; his coronation, 289; at Rheims, *ib.*; the fourth king who came collaterally to the crown, *ib.*

Louppe, M., the physician of the duke of Burgundy, i. 345.

Louvain, town of, i. 93; the duke of Burgundy's army at, 94.

Luce and Grandmont families, contentions of the, ii. 146.

Lucca, city of, receives Charles VIII., ii. 134; visited by him, 194.

Lude, Jean, lord du, i. xxiv., 281. ii. 38; his covetousness and general character, i. 353, 354; occupies the city of Arras, 304.

Ludlow, battle of, i. 49. *n.*

Ludovic, lord of Milan, ii. 101, 102. (see Galeas); visits the king of France at Asti, 125; his letter to Charles VIII., 130; his influence, 131. *et seq.*; seizes and usurps the duchy of Milan, 132.

Luller, Arnold, ii. 337.

Lullier, John, ii. 333.

Lungjumeau, village of, i. 17, 18.

Lusignan, Jacopo de, king of Cyprus, ii. 121.

Luxembourg, invaded by the duke of Burgundy, i. 242.

Luxembourg, Louis de. (See St. Paul.)

Luy, Philibert, lord de, ii. 41.

Lyon, M. de, constable of France, ii. 352.

Lyons, Charles VIII.'s visit to, ii. 121.

M.

Mâcon, salt of, i. 133; bailiwick of, 136.

Madelina, daughter of Charles VII., ii. 89.

Maderey, capt., i. 21. 32.

Madoulet, one of the Liegeois, put to death, i. 159.

Mahomet II., sultan of the Turks, a wise and valiant prince, ii. 87. 90; defeated at Belgrade, 88. *n.*; captures Constantinople, 90; the number of his conquests, 90, 91; his gluttony and death, 91; his wars with the Venetians, 120.

Maine, inundation of the, ii. 302.

Maine, Charles, count of, i. 18, 19, ii. 341; his flight, i. 29; surrenders certain lands and lordships to the count of Dunois and receives others, 82.

Man proposes, but God disposes, i. 215.

Mankind, reflections on the miseries of, ii. 80. *et seq.*

Manniel, Gauvain, beheaded, ii. 340.

Mans, female imposture in the city of, ii. 302.

Mantua, Rodolph, count of, ii. 148, 201, 214.

Marcel, Monsieur Lewis, ii. 187.

Marche, Edward de la, his usurpation, ii. 365, 366.

Marche d'Ardain, Robert de la, ii. 230.

Marck, Everard de la, brother of John de la Marck, i. 373.

Marck, John de la, i. 370.

Marck, William de la, surnamed the Wild Boar of Ardennes, i. 369. *et n.*; slays the bishop of Liege, 370.

Margaret of Austria, married to the dauphin of France, i. 394; and afterwards to the infanta of

Castile, 394. *n.*, ii. 112; her sudden miscarriage, 277.

Margaret of York, married to Charles of Burgundy, i. 38; notices of, *ib. n.*; treaty in favour of, as the widow of Charles of Burgundy, ii. 117.

Margaret, princess of Burgundy, ii. 17; biographical notices of, 16. *n.*

Margaret, countess of Flanders, i. 347; her projected marriage with the dauphin of France, ii. 45. 58. *et seq.*; her reception at Amboise, 61; her marriage, 62. *n.*

Margaret, queen of England, mother to the prince of Wales, i. 202.

Margaret of Anjou, queen of England, ii. 86.

Margaret, princess, of England, ii. 64. *n.*

Margaret, daughter of James I. of Scotland, married to Louis XI., ii. 82.

Margaret, duchess of Savoy, i. 9. *n.*

Margaret de la Tremouille, i. 361.

Margaret, sister of René II., ii. 95. *n.*

Maria, infanta of Spain, ii. 276.

Marriage between the duke of Guienne and the duke of Burgundy's daughter negociated, i. 206; opposed by Edward IV. of England, 208.

Mary, duchess of Burgundy. (See Burgundy.)

Mary de Savoi, death of, i. 247.

Marzano, Giambattista de, ii. 150. *n.*

Marzocchi, figure of the, pulled down, ii. 139.

Mas, James du, slain, i. 23.

Matalon, count de, ii. 163.

Matthias I., king of Hungary, a wise and valiant prince, ii. 87; biographical notices of, 89; his heroic mother, *ib.*; chosen king of Hungary, *ib.*; his victories, *ib.*; his early death, 90.

Mauger, Perrette, burnt alive, ii. 298, 299.

Mauleon, friar John des, ii. 272.

Maximilian, of Austria, son of the emperor of Germany, and king of the Romans, i. 206, 207; ii. 10; his visit to Cologne and Ghent, 13, 14; his character, 13. *n.*; is married to the young duchess of Burgundy, 15; his children, 16, 17; his contests with the French in Picardy, 32, 33; his bravery, *ib. n.*; enters into a treaty with Louis XI., 35. 45. *et seq.*; opposed by the Gantois, ii. 60; marries the daughter of Galeas, duke of Milan, 112; concludes the treaty of Senlis with Charles VIII., 113; his allies, 117; his preparations against Charles VIII., 188; a mortal enemy of the Venetians, 282; enters into a truce with Louis XI., 390; violates the truce, 390, 391.

Mazzara, town of, ii. 155.

Medici, Cosmo di, founder of the family of that name, i. 142.

Medici, family of the, ii. 25. *et seq.*; their contests with the Pacis, 25, 26; the rulers of Florence, 127, 128; the greatest commercial family in the world, 128; thought to be in a declining condition at the time of Peter, *ib.*

Medici, Laurence di, ii. 25; murderous attack on, 26; the chief man of Florence, 29.

Medici, Peter de, ruler of Florence, ii. 127, 128; his government, 128; Charles VIII.'s dislike to, 129; gives up four of his garrisons to Charles VIII., 136; his great courtesy, *ib.*; returns to Florence, 139; his flight and destruction, 140 —142; his palace plundered, 143.

Melfi, Trojanus Caracciolo, duke of, ii. 163.

Melun, Charles de, rewarded by Louis XI., ii. 323; beheaded, 352.

Melun, Charles de, i. 14. 62.

Melun, Philip de, captain of the Bastille St. Antoine, i. 62.

Mely, Albert, ii. 126.

Mendoza, Lorenzo de, ii. 174.

Merchants, importance of, ii. 128.

Merichon, Jean, of Rochelle, i. 259.

Merillano, count de, ii. 163.

Meroveus, the first reigns of the kings of France deduced from, ii. 289.

Merville, lord de, executed by the Burgundians, ii. 352.

Meulane, town of, ii. 330.

Meulant, Oliver, count de, i. 357.

Milan, treaties of alliance between her and France, xxvii.; civil contests in, ii. 101. et seq.; the dukes of, 101. et n.; the duchy of, one of the finest countries in the world, 106; the ducal families of, 112; one of the three powers of Italy, 130; seized and usurped by the lord Ludovic, 132; ambassadors sent to Venice from, 174.

Milan, Galeas, duke of, abandons his alliance with the duke of Burgundy, i. 308; and enters into a treaty with the king of France, 309.

Milan, John Galeas, duke of, ii. 131. 137; interred in the Chartreux at Pavia, 137.

Milan, Louis-Marie Sforza, duke of, protected by the Venetians, ii. 192; his meditated attack on the French, 203; conditions to which he binds himself, 246; refuses a meeting with the king, 247; his equivocal conduct, 248; his tricks and juggles,

250. et seq.; plots of Italian princes for the destruction of, 264; their miscarriage, 266, 267, 269.

Milan, dukes of, (see Ludovic, Sforza, &c.).

Military operations carried on before Paris, i. 55—58, 62. et seq.

Miolans, Louis de, marshal of Savoy, ii. 41.

Miolans, M. de, governor of Dauphiny, ii. 195.

Misfortunes, examples of, that have happened to princes, i. 398—399; history of, which attended the house of Castile, ii. 277—281.

Molins en Gibers, ii. 376.

Money, necessity of, for state purposes, i. 385.

Montagu, John de Neufchatel, lord of, i. 16, 45.

Montague, John Neville, Marquis of, i. 190, 191; slain at the battle of Barnet, i. 201.

Montaigny, lord of, i. 310.

Montauban, John, lord of, i. 19; ii. 83.

Montballon, lord of, ii. 20. n.

Montdidier, town of, ceded to the duke of Burgundy, i. 76; repaired and garrisoned by the duke, 218; capture of, 244; surrender of, ii. 377.

Montefiascone, delivered up to Charles VIII., ii. 144.

Montefortino taken by storm, ii. 160.

Montesecco, Giovanni Battista de, ii. 28.

Montfaucon, Gabriel de, ii. 184.

Montferrat, William VI., marquis of, ii. 124, 125.

Montferrat, marchioness of, ii. 125; visited by Charles VIII., 131; death of, 235; contest for her government, ib.

Montgomery, sir Thomas, i. 267;
sails on a special message to Louis
XI., 286.

Montigny, M. de, i. 141.

Montlhery, duke of Burgundy
encamps at, i. 17, 18, 19; battle
of, xiii. 20. 29., ii. 318; number
slain at, 30; the inhabitants of,
indemnified from loss, 33, 34.

Montmartin, Jacques, lord of, captures the suburb of Beauvais, i.
218.

Montone, count Bernardino di, ii.
209.

Montpensier, Gilbert, count of,
commands the French troops in
Italy, ii. 184; evacuates the
castles of Naples, 230, 231;
enters into the treaty of Atella,
260; his misfortunes after that
event, 262. n.; his death, 261.

Montreuil ceded to the duke of
Burgundy, i. 74.

Moüy, Collard, lord of, i. 101; takes
possession of Tournay, 357, 358.

Moüy, Jacques, lord of, i. 357.

Morat, battle of, i. xxiii.; defeat of
the Burgundians near the town
of, 315.

Mordano, town of, taken by assault,
ii. 133.

Moreul, surrender of, ii. 377.

Moret, in Gastinois, village of, i.
42.

Morialmé, Robert de, murdered
and cut to pieces, i. 119.

Montagne ceded to the duke of
Burgundy, i. 74; signiories of,
133.

Mortara, town of, ii. 197.

Morton, Dr., archbishop of Canterbury, i. 262.

Morton, John, Master of the Rolls,
and Lord Chancellor, memoirs
of, ii. 3. n.

Morvilliers, Pierre de, the lord of
Clary, notices of, i. 1. et n.; ambassador from the king of France,
2. et seq.; his mischievous words,

66; resigns his seals as chancellor, ii. 336.

Mots viere (Mont vieil), explained,
ii. 187. n.

Moulin, Philip du, ii. 212. et n.

Mount St. John, near Naples, taken
by storm, ii. 160.

Multitude of people, seldom formidable unless under proper
command, i. 157; their fury
sometimes terrible, ib.

Munster, Henry of Swartzburg,
bishop of, i. 240.

Myolans, lord de, chamberlain to
Charles VIII., ii. 136.

N.

Namur, to be bestowed by the king
on his own subjects, i. 351.

Nancy, battle of, i. xxiii.; siege
of, 295; surrender of to the
duke of Burgundy, 296. n.; besieged by the duke of Lorraine,
322; surrender of, 324; besieged by the Burgundians, 325.
et seq.; the duke of Burgundy
defeated and slain near, 336, 337;
numbers slain at, 337. n.

Nancy, Jean de Troyes' notices of,
ii. 384; surrendered to the duke
of Lorraine, ib.; to the duke of
Burgundy, 385; retaken, 386.

Nanni, Alexander, bishop of Forli,
i. 241.

Nantes, treaty of, i. 6.

Nanteuil, Margaret de, i. 82.

Nantouillet, Charles de Melun,
lord of, i. 14; high steward of
France, 46.

Naples, expedition of Charles
VIII. against, ii. 93. et seq.;
119. 122. 125. et seq.; the kingdom of, rebels against Ferrand
(Ferdinand), 97; the rebels
offer the throne to René II.
duke of Lorraine, 98; cruelties
committed in, 99; difficulties of

her position, 100. *et seq.* ; state of, at the time of Charles VIII.'s expedition against, 123. ; one of the three powers of Italy, 130 ; royal tyranny in, 152 ; five kings crowned in less than two years, 156 ; Alphonso flies from, at the approach of Charles VII., 153 ; three kings of, died in one year, 154 ; entered by Charles VIII., 161 ; its surrender, 162 ; flight of king Ferrand from, 163 ; Charles is crowned king of, *ib.* ; submission of the nobility to Charles, *ib.* ; the castle of, bombarded, and captured, 164, 165 ; position of affairs at, 184 ; departure of Charles VIII. from, 186 ; castle of, evacuated by lord de Montpensier and the French, 230, 231 ; great difficulties attending, *ib.* ; re-occupied by king Ferrand, 230, 231. *et n.* ; the whole kingdom of lost to the French, 232 ; Charles VIII. receives intelligence of its capture, 257 ; Ferrand the fifth monarch who sat on the disastrous throne of, 263 ; plots of the Italian princes for the recovery of, 264. *et seq.* ; their miscarriage, 266, 267.

Naples, kings of. (See Frederic, Charles, Alphonso, Ferdinand, and Ferrand.

Narbonne, Jean, viscount of, i. 284.

Nassau, Engelbert, count of, ii. 33.

Nations, on the balance of power in, i. 379.

Navarre, factions of, ii. 66. *n.*

Navy of the duke of Brunswick, i. 187. 189.

Nemours, Jacques d'Armagnac, duke of, i. 16 ; swears fealty to Louis XI., 17.

Nepi, town of, ii. 148.

Nerli, Giacopo de, ii. 140.

Nesle, siege and capture of, i. 13 ; in Vermandois, captured and sacked by the duke of Burgundy, 211 ; slaughter of the inhabitants, ii. 368.

Neufchatel, captured and burnt by the Burgundians, i. 222.

Neufchatel, lord of, marshal of Burgundy, i. 45 ; his alarm for duke Charles, 72.

Nevers, John, count of, i. 76. 160.

Neves, Stephen de, ii. 195.

Neville, Anne, daughter of the earl, i. 398.

Neville, George, Archbishop of York, i. 190.

Nice (Nizza della Pagha), Charles VIII.'s arrival at, ii. 225 ; a fleet equipped at, for Naples, 229.

Nicourt, castle of, ii. 372.

Nivernois, taken by the Burgundians, ii. 373.

Nogent, visited by Louis XI., ii. 309.

Noli, Franquein, ii. 26.

Norfolk, John Howard, duke of, ii. 45. (See Howard.)

Normandy, cession of the duchy demanded by the duke of Berry, i. 65 ; refused by the king, 66 ; ceded to the duke of Berry, and its capital occupied by the duke of Bourbon, 69, 70. 78 ; ii. 332 ; declared to be free to all Englishmen of king Henry's party, 303 ; progress of Louis XI. to, 309 ; visited by Louis XI., 323. 339.

Normandy, duke of (Charles duke de Berry), his quarrel with the duke of Bretagne, i. 83 ; renounces his claim to the duchy, 84 ; enters into a treaty of alliance with the duke of Bretagne, 84 ; retires into Bretagne in a poor and disconsolate state, 85 ; signs the treaty of Amiens, 111.

Northumberland, Henry Percy, earl of, i. 275.

Notre Dame de Clery, ii. 67.

Novara, captured by the duke of Orleans, ii. 192, 193 ; the dukes' behaviour in the city of, 191 ; reduced to straits, 228 ; the duke of Orleans and the French reduced to great famine at, 234, 235 ; negociations respecting, 240 ; peace concluded for the preservation of the besieged, 241; sufferings of the duke of Orleans and the garrison, and how they were delivered from the direst misery by terms of accommodation, 242. *et seq.*

Nuz, origin of the wars of, i. 124; a strongly fortified town in the Prussian states, 236 ; besieged by Charles of Burgundy, 236, 239. *et seq.* ; ii. 376 ; the town of, relieved by the Germans and others, i. 240. *et seq.* ; want occasioned by the siege, 242 ; siege of, raised, 250.

O.

Offices, public, dissertation on, i. 47. *et seq.*

Oliver de la Marche, notices of, i. 2. *n.*

Oliver le Mauvais, valet de chambre of Louis XI., i. 350; sent to treat with the citizens of Ghent, 351 ; failed in his designs upon Ghent, 356 ; assumes the title of Count de Meulant, 357 ; secures Tournay for the king, 358.

Olivet, Mount, monks of, ii. 156.

Onofrio de Santa Croce, legate of Rome at Liege, i. 146.

Oppressors, on the punishment of, i. 391.

Orange, William VII., prince of, i. 149.

Orange, Louis de Chalon, prince of, i. 376.

Orange, John II., prince of, reduced to great distress at Novara, i. 234 ; commands the French troops, 236 ; in the service of Louis XI., 376 ; the captured places withheld from, 377 ; abandons his cause, and is banished, 376. *n.* ; chosen to be lieutenant of Burgundy, ii. 18 ; assists in concluding a peace between Charles VIII. and the League, 245. *et seq.* ; excites a revolt, 388.

Orgemont, Charles d', lord of Mery, ii. 309.

Orlando, Charles, cardinal of St. Malo, ii. 191.

Orleans, factions of, ii. 86.

Orleans, Louis duke of, his assassination, i. 273, 274.

Orleans, Louis duke of (afterwards Charles XII.), pretends to the duchy of Milan, ii. 130; captures Novara, 192, 193 ; his behaviour in the city, 197 ; his preparations for battle, 198 ; beleaguered in Novara, 228 ; reduced to great famine at Novara, 234, 235 ; negotiations respecting, 240 ; peace concluded for his preservation, 241 ; how he was delivered from dire misery upon terms of accommodation, 242. *et seq.* ; peace concluded between him and the league, 245. *et seq.* ; next heir to the crown at the death of the dauphin, 254 ; his inconstancy, 266 ; succeeds to the French throne as Louis XII., 97. *n.* 289.

Orleans, Charles, appointed royal commissioner, ii. 341.

Orson, Jacques d', a brave soldier, i. 222.

Orvietto, flight of the Pope Alexander VI. to, ii. 187.

Ostia, town of ii. 147 ; number of troops at, *ib.*

Oudet de Rye, account of, i. 45.

P.

Pacis, family of the, ii. 25. *et seq.*; their contests with the Medicis, 25, 26; their conspiracy defeated, 27, 28.

Padua, subdued by the Venetians, ii. 138.

Paillart, Chrystofle, ii. 323.

Palæologus, Thomas, son of emperor Manuel, ii. 166.

Pallevoisin, Jean Francisco, ii. 102.

Pandone, Camillo, ii. 155.

Paris, the march of Charles of Burgundy upon, i. 13, 14. 17; the duke of, and his allies present themselves before, 45; rencontres at the gates of, 46; entered by Louis XI. while the lords of France are tampering with the citizens, and relieved by him, 50. 52; the Parisians make frequent sallies, 53; heavy cannonading in the neighbourhood of, 55; military operations before, 56—58; negotiations respecting, 65. 67.

Paris (*continued from Jean de Troyes' Chronicle*), public entry of Louis XI. into, ii. 306, 307; magnificent fetes of, 307; defensive preparations of, 313. 317; the Burgundians appear before the walls of, 315; royal favours granted to, 322; review of the king's forces at, 326; the king's reception at, *ib.*; commissioners sent from, to negotiate with Burgundians and Bretons, 325; punishment of the mayor of, 328; quarrels with the military, 331; its vast supplies, 333; proclamation for repeopling, 344; the inhabitants marshalled, 345; great military preparations in, 364; grand review of the inhabitants, 374.

Parties, spirit of, everywhere prevalent, i. 381.

Passes, difficult ones in Milan, ii. 194.

Paul II. pope of Rome, i. 146.

Pavia, visit of Charles VIII. to, ii. 131.

Pazzi. (See Pacis.)

Peace, treaty of, signed at Conflans, i. 73. *et seq.*; the events which followed, 78. *et seq.*; treaty of, signed at St. Maur des Fosses, i. 80; negotiation for, broken off, on the death of the duke of Guienne, 210; negotiations for, 212. 214; negotiations frustrated, 215; overtures for, 223; concluded with the duke of Bretagne, 224; concluded between the emperor of Germany and the duke of Burgundy, 250; entered into between Charles VIII. and the League, ii. 245. *et seq.*; its conditions, 246.

Peers of France, represented at the coronation of Louis XII., ii. 289.

Pembroke, Jasper, earl of, i. 397.

People, the general voice of, the voice of God, ii. 154.

Pequeis, salt of, i. 133.

Perauld, Raimond, cardinal of Gurce, ii. 157.

Peronne ceded to the duke of Burgundy, i. 76; visit of Louis XI. to, 113—115; number of illustrious personages at, 114; Louis XI. is imprisoned by the duke of Burgundy in the castle of, 118. *et seq.*; his release from, effected on his renouncing his league with the Liegeois, 127; treaty of peace concluded at, between Louis XI. and the duke of Burgundy, 130—145; treaty of, confirmed at the castle of Crotoy, 216; delivered up to Louis XI. 350. 359; ignominious peace that resulted therefrom, ii. 357.

Peronne, duke of, i. 112.

Perpignan, surrender of, ii. 377.

Persi, Francis, lord of, ii. 162. *et n.*

Pesaro, Constantine, prince of, ii. 31.

Pescara, Alfonso, marquis, di, ii. 160.

Pescara, Mary of, commands king Ferrand's forces, ii. 163, 164.

Peter di Medici. (See Medici.)

Petillane, count de, his desertion, ii. 217.

Pharamond, the first who was elected king of France, ii. 289.

Philibert, duke, ii. 41.

Philip of Valois, the third king of France who came collaterally to the throne, ii. 289, 290.

Philip, archduke of Austria, ii. 16 ; his treaty of Senlis with Charles VIII., 111. 113.

Philip the Bold, duke of Burgundy, i. 298.

Philip the Good, the duke of Burgundy, godfather of Commines, i. xi.; the brilliant court of, xii. notices of, 2. 9. *et seq.*; speech of, 3 ; death of, 88., ii. 344; his noble treatment of the dauphin, afterwards Louis XI., 82.

Philip the Long of France, ii. 16.

Philip, duke of Bourbon, family of, i. 9.

Philip de la Marche, i. 2. *n.*

Philip d'Oignes slain, i. 27.

Philippe de Luxemburg created cardinal, ii. 159.

Philippa of Lancaster, daughter of John of Gaunt, i. 181. *n.*

Picardy, towns in, ceded to the duke of Burgundy, i. 78. 80; Louis XI. assembles a large army in, ii. 389 ; hostilities in, 392.

Picart, captain, of Nesle, ii. 368.

Piccinino, count James, ii. 151. *et n.*; Nicolo, *ib.*

Picquigny, near Amiens, royal meeting at, i. 126 ; captured by the duke of Burgundy, 176, 177 ; castle of, 272; appointed as the place of interview between Louis XI. and Edward IV. of England, 272, ii. 378, 379; reasons for choosing this place, i. 273; the royal interview takes place at, 275; treaty of, noticed, ii. 7.

Piennes, Louis, lord of, ii. 76 ; chamberlain to Charles VIII., ii. 136.

Pierchon du Chastel, i. 364. *n.*

Piero de Medici, ii. 26. *n.*

Pierre de Bretagne, i. xix.

Pierre-fort, town of, razed, i. 242.

Pietrasanta, surrendered to the French, ii. 136 ; Charles VIII.'s visit to, 194.

Piquart, William, lord of Estelau, i. 70.

Pisa, surrendered to Charles VIII., ii. 136; the inhabitants of, cruelly treated by the Florentines, 138, 191 ; relieved by Charles VIII., 139, 189 ; retained by the king, 189 ; difficulties in the king's march from, 194, 195; delivered up to the Pisans, contrary to the engagement of Charles VIII., 257.

Pittelhane, Nicolo Ursini, count de, ii. 125.

Placentia, visit of Charles VIII. to, ii. 132.

Plague in France, ii. 342.

Plessis du Parc, the residence of Louis XI. during his last illness, ii. 44.

Plessis-les-Tours, fortified by Louis XI., ii. 76 ; Sir Walter Scott's description of, 77, 78. *n.*

Poggibonzi, castle of, ii. 189.

Poictiers, battle of, one of the most

glorious achievements in English history, i. 390. *n.*

Poison, suspicion of, at Fornovo, ii. 204.

Polesan, territory of, taken by the Venetians, ii. 106.

Polignac, John, lord de, ii. 195.

Polleur, village of, i. 163.

Pont St. Maxence, surrender of, ii. 314.

Ponthieu, county of, ceded to the duke of Burgundy, i. 74; fiefs and homages of, ceded to the duke, 132.

Ponthoise, betrayal of, ii. 330.

Pontremoli, Charles VIII.'s march towards, ii. 195; captured, 196; slaughter committed by the Swiss, *ib.*

Popes of Rome, their depravity, ii. 98. *n.* (See Alexander VI., Eugenius IV., Innocent VIII., Julius II., Paul II., and Sextus IV.)

Popoli, Pietro, count of, ii. 151. *et n.*; his release from prison, 163.

Portinari, Thomas, ii. 128. *n.*

Portugal, a political check on Spain, i. 379.

Portunay, Thomas, ii. 128.

Power, balance of, i. 379.

Praguerie, the war so called, ii. 69.

Pretigny, lord of, ii. 323.

Prevost, Mons. Jehan, the king's secretary, i. 101.

Prevost, John, ii. 349.

Priests, illiterate princes often misled by, i. 116, 117.

Princes, how to avoid mutual jealousies and suspicions among, i. 79; the evils they sustain by divisions, 85; different temperaments and dispositions of, 86; evils of ignorance among, 87; ought to have several privy councillors to ensure a correct judgment, 95; on the advantages which they may derive from the knowledge of letters, and especially of history, 115. *et seq.*; instances of treachery and murder which have taken place at the interviews of, 115. *n.*; instances of treachery among, 115, 116; illiterate princes often misled by lawyers and priests, 116; dangerous results of ignorance to, 117; an ignorant prince a great curse to a nation, 117; the meeting of great princes to adjust differences often more prejudicial than profitable, 121. *et seq.*; reasons why they ought never to meet, 126; their want of confidence in each other, 156; the hatred and revenge of, 174; prudent advice and circumspection necessary, 193; ought to be careful of their language, 226; a digression on the wisdom of, with remarks for those who are in authority with, 229, 230; should narrowly watch over the conduct of his governors, 302; the prudence and judgment of Louis XI. a fair example to, 307; wars permitted by God for the punishment of their wickedness, 378. *et seq.*; their rapacity, 382; their tyranny and caprice, 383, 384; their modes of governing and raising taxes, 385; the greatest misfortunes proceed from the most powerful, 388; the sums they are ready to pay for ransom from captivity, 390; examples of misfortunes that have happened to, 393. 399; consequences of their folly and imprudence, ii. 19; the miseries and troubles of, 80. *et seq.*; moderation in all things recommended to, 92; should take upon themselves the conduct of their own affairs, 252;

envy and jealousy of, 255, 256; on the mismanagement of their affairs, 268; their troubles greater than those of inferior persons, 280.

Princes of France, their alliance with the duke of Burgundy, i. 65; their extravagant demands on the king, 65; their departure from Paris, after signing a treaty of peace with the king, 79; sign the treaty of St. Maur-des-Fossés, 80.

Procida, island of, ii. 261, 262.

Proveditors of Venice and Padua, ii. 205, 206.

Provence, duchy of, claimed by René II., ii. 94, 95; will respecting, produced in favour of the French king, 96; refused to René, 97.

Pruce, island of, ii. 229.

Public Good, the Duke of Burgundy raises an army against Louis XI. under pretence of the, i. 9. *et seq.*; confederation so called, 121.

Punishments of criminals in 1490, ii. 298.

Puy, Peter, ii. 337.

Q.

Quanvese, Gerard, his great wealth, ii. 128.

Quarteniers, of Paris, ii. 329.

Quesnoy, possessed by the king, i. 355; restored to the duchess of Burgundy, ii. 17.

Quiers, town of, ii. 232. 248.

Quingy, Simon de, his elevation and honours, i. 28. *et n.*; duke of Burgundy's ambassador at the court of Louis XI., 210.; negociates terms of peace, 212. 214.; enters Verdun with Burgundian troops, ii. 24.

R.

Rabot, Jean, lord of Uppi, ii. 138.

Ranvers, Jean, commander de, i. 317.

Rapalo, town of, ii. 126.; naval engagement off, 129.

Rapine, servant of the constable of France, i. 280, 281.

Rasse, lord de Lintre, i. 100.; declares against peace, 102.; abandons Liége, 103.

Ravenspur, Edward IV. lands at, i. 199. *n.*

Ravestain, Adolphus, lord of, i. 11.; commands the left wing of the Burgundian army, 25.; commands the van against the Liegeois, 97.; his removal from command, 375.

Ravenstain, Philip of, defeated, ii. 3

Rayer, Francis, bailiff of Lyons, i. 96.

Reading, advantages of, i. 117.

Rebellion, Louis XI. endeavours to stir up the towns on the River Somme against the duke of Burgundy, i. 167. *et seq.*; fanned by the constable of France, 168.

Reggio, castle of, ii. 162.

Reindeers, &c., strange fancy of Louis XI. for, ii. 58.

Rely, Jean de, bishop of Angers, ii. 71. *n.* 283.

Renard de Rouvroy, i. 96.

René of Anjou, king of Sicily, abandons his alliance with the duke of Burgundy, i. 309; his interview with Louis XI., 310; surnamed the Good, 396.

René de Brosse, count of Penthevre, marriage of, i. xxxvi.

Revenue of France, in the fifteenth century, i. 386, 387.

Revolutions of England, i. 84. 394. *et seq.*; reflections on, 50; of Spain, 398 (see Civil War).

Rheims, holy vial at, carried to Louis XI., ii. 66, 67. *et n.*

Richard III. of England, i. 396 (see Gloucester).

Richebourg, lord of, ii. 76.

Richmond, Earl of (afterwards Henry VII.), of the house of Lancaster, i. 49. 396.; his vicissitudes and final success, 397., ii. 64. *et n.*; gains the battle of Bosworth, and ascends the throne of England, 65. *et n.*

Richter, John, secretary of the constable, i. 265.

Rieux, John, lord of, ii. 160.

Rimini, Robert, lord of, ii. 30.

Riverol, Geoffroi, lord of, i. 317, 318.

Rivers, Richard Earl, put to death, i. 184.

Riviere, Poncet, lord de la, i. 23. 62. 114. 160.; ii. 337.

Roan, captured by the Duke of Bourbon, ii. 332.; receives the Duke of Berry as governor, 337.; is taken possession of by the king's troops, 339.; visited by Louis XI. and the earl of Warwick, 343.; visited by the Queen of England, 344.

Robert of Bavaria, Count Palatine and archbishop of Cologne, i. 235.

Robertet, Florimont, ii. 208.

Robinet d'Odenfort, i. xxiv. 351.

Robinet le Beuf, i. 333.

Roche, Henry de la, i. 211. *n.*; 223. *n.*

Rochefort, capture of, ii. 22. 391.

Rochefort, William, lord of, the chancellor of France, i. 16., ii. 70,

Rochelle, government of, conferred on Charles of France, i. 166.

Roctaillié, pass of, ii. 194.

Rodolph, count of Mantua, ii. 148. 201; slain, 214.

Rome entered by Charles VII., ii.

149; his stay at, 157; his departure from, 159.

Romefort, Louis, lord of, ii. 242.

Romont, Jacques, count of, i. 114; ii. 33; his territories possessed by the Swiss, i. 301. 303.

Roquebertin, Pierre de, ii. 76.

Rossano, Marino, prince of, ii. 150; his melancholy end, 150. *n*; released from prison, 163.

Rotherham, Thomas of, bishop of Lincoln and lord chancellor, i. 176; memoir of, ii. 3. *n.*

Rottelin, Philip, marquis of, i. 16. 45.

Roualt, Marshal Joachim, lord of Boismenart, i. 13., ii. 329.

Roucy, Antoine, count of, notices of, i. 150.

Rouen, how it was delivered into the hands of the duke of Bourbon for the duke of Berry, i. 69, 70; contentions at, between the dukes of Bretagne and Normandy, i. 83; beleaguered by Henry V., 273.

Roussi, Antoine, count of, ii. 192.

Roussi, Bastard of, ii. 257.

Roussillon, county of, contentions for, ii. 81; rival pretensions to, 272.

Roussy, count of, taken prisoner, i. 247.

Rouville, John de, vice-chancellor of Bretagne, i. 14. 21. 32.

Rouvre, castle of, i. 317.

Rovere, cardinal Giuliana della, pope of Rome, ii. 98, 145 *n.*

Rovigo, town of, ii. 106.

Royal family of France, line of the, ii. 289, 290.

Roye, town of, ceded to the duke of Burgundy, i. 76; invested by him, 217; delivered up to him, 218; royal meeting at, 226; captured by the French, 244; captured by the Burgundians, ii. 368; surrendered to the French, 377.

Rubempré, Bastard of, arrested, ii. 309.

Ryn, William, pensionary of Ghent, ii. 42

S.

Sables, town of, i. xviii. xx.

Salaries, public, dissertation on, i. 47. *et seq.*

Salerno, Antonio, prince of, chief of the house of St. Severino, ii. 104, 147. 163; his escape to France, 99, 100; he endeavours to persuade the king of France to make war upon the king of Naples, 100.

Salic Law of France, ii. 14. 16.

Salins, salt of, i. 133.

Salisbury, Thomas Montague, earl of, i. 22; father of the great earl of Warwick, beheaded, i. 48.

Sallezard, John de, account of, i. 41, 42. *n.*

Sallezard, Robert, lord of Asnoi, ii. 192.

Sallazart, of Beauvais, ii. 370; his bravery, 371.

Sallies out of a besieged town often dangerous, i. 148.

Salt, regulations for the vending of, and levying duties, i. 133.

Salviati, Francisco, archbishop of Pisa, ii. 27: his conspiracy and death, 28.

San Severino, Fracasse de, ii. 225. *et n.* (See Salerno, Galeas, Frederic, and Robert.)

Sancy diamond, taken by the Swiss from the Burgundians, i. 312.

Sansonna, town of, ii. 147.

Sarzana, castle of, ii. 135; surrender of, 136; difficulties of Charles VIII.'s march towards, 194.

Sarzanello, castle of, ii. 192.

Sassenage, lord de, lends money to the dauphin, ii. 83. *n.*

Sausses, town of, captured, ii. 271.

Sauvagière, François de, slays the duke of Gueldres, i. 358.

Savarat, Pierre, the archer, i. 31.

Savelly, cardinal Giambattista, ii. 158.

Savenses, Philip, lord de, brings succours to Charles of Burgundy, i. 71; the prosecution of a decree against published, 141.

Savona, plot for delivering up the town of, ii. 268; its failure, 269.

Savonarola, Jerome, the Dominican friar, memorable preachings of, ii. 189. *et n.*; his predictions, 190; his predictions realised, 208, 285; burnt at Florence by the malice and solicitation of the pope and others, 285. 287; system of persecution carried on against, 286.

Savoy, Charles I. duke of, i. 317.

Savoy, Jacques Louis de, i. 318.

Savoy, Philibert, duke of, i. 206. 317.

Savoy, Yolland, duchess of, abandons her alliance with the duke of Burgundy, i. 309; seized by the duke of Burgundy, 317; and rescued by Louis XI., 319.

Savoyards, always in amity with the Burgundians, i. 114.

Scales, Anthony. lord, i. 191. 241.

Scandalous Chronicle of Louis XI. from 1460 to 1483, ii. 291 *et seq.*; literary history of the, 293.

Scanderbeg, descendants of, ii. 166.

Scotch guards, in the duke of Burgundy's service, valour of the, i. 155.

Scotland, civil war in, i. 398; a check upon England, 379.

Scutari, captured by the Turks, ii. 120; surrender of, 166.

Secco, Signor Francisco, at the battle of Fornovo, ii. 218.

Segre, Jacques, lord of, ii. 37.

Seierre, pass of, ii. 194.

Seine, the duke of Burgundy's army passes over the, by a bridge of boats, 42; great preparations for crossing the, 57 : a second bridge of boats laid over ; inundation of the, 302.

Semur, town of, rebels, ii. 23 ; captured, 24.

Seneschal of Normandy, i. 70.

Senlis, peace negociated at, ii. 110 ; treaty of, between Charles II. and Maximilian I , ii. 113.

Sergine, M. de, i. 149.

Sforza, ducal family of, i. 52 ; the dukes of Milan, ii. 112.

Sforza, Catherine, ii. 133. n.

Sforza, Francis duke of Milan, i. 52.

Sforza, Francesco, duke of Milan, ii. 104. n. ; ii. 112, 113.

Sforza, Louis Marie (See MILAN, duke of).

Sforza, Muzio Attendolo, ii. 112.

Shrewsbury, John Talbot, earl of, i. 22.

Sicily, geographical position and advantages of, ii. 270.

Siena, visited by Charles VIII., ii. 144. 187 ; M. de Ligny the governor of, 188 ; the occupants expelled from, 189.

Sigismund, duke of Austria, and count palatine of the Rhine, his interview with Charles of Burgundy, i. 125 ; concludes a peace with the Swiss, and recovers the county of Ferrette, 243 ; joins the Swiss, 302 ; his character, ii. 18, 19 ; conveys his estates to his nephew Maximilian, 19.

Silver plate taken by the Swiss from the Burgundians, i. 311.

Simon Charles, M. ii. 304.

Sixtus IV. pope of Rome, ii. 25. 107 ; the conspiracy of the Pazzi at Florence promoted by him, 26—28 ; besieges Florence, 29 ; his interest for the health of Louis XI., 66.

Soderini, Paul Anthony, ii. 141.

Soderini, Peter, ii. 127.

Soly, bank of, at Genoa, ii. 94. et n.

Somerset, the noble family of, in England, i. 182 ; the greatest supporters of the house of Lancaster, 183.

Somerset, duke of, defeats the Yorkists at St. Albans, ii. 303 ; defeated at Tewkesbury, i. 202 ; beheaded, 203 ; his two sons slain at Tewkesbury, 202.

Somme, the river, cities, fortresses, &c. of the, ceded to the duke of Burgundy, i. 74.

Sora, Giovanni, duke of, ii. 163. 265. et n.

Sorbier, Lewis, his treachery, ii. 329, 330.

Soubs-Plainville, William de, i. 222, 223 ; pensions granted to, 224.

Spain, Portugal and Granada, checks to, i. 379 ; revolutions in, 398 ; political power of, ii. 100 ; her league with France, 359.

Spezzia, town of, ii. 126.

Spinoli, Laurence, ii. 136.

Spurs, battle of the, ii. 32 n.

Squillazzo, marquis de, ii. 163.

Squibs, confusion caused by, at Escampes, i. 36.

St. Albans, battle of, between the Lancastrians and the Yorkists, ii. 303. et n.

St. André, Monsieur de, captures Sausses, ii. 271.

St. Belin, lord Geoffrey de, slain, i. 30.

St. Clou, captured by the Burgundians, ii. 317.

St. Gengor, bailiwick of, i. 136.

St. Germain, near Naples, ii. 157. 160 ; captured by Charles VIII., 161.

St. Lievin, riot on account of, i. 107.

St. Mathurin de Larchant, village of, i. 42.

St. Maur-des-Fossés, i. 46 ; treaty

of, between the princes of France and Louis XI., 80.

St. Maurice besieged and captured by the French, ii. 313.

St. Omer, captured by the Burgundians, ii. 111.

St. Paul, Louis de Luxembourg, count of, i. 20, 21. 89; commands the left wing of the Burgundian army, 25. 28; his advice after the battle of Montlhery, 31; leads the Burgundian van, 45; appointed constable of France, 79; his fruitless negotiations with the duke of Burgundy respecting the Liegeois, 94; is desirous of stirring up a war between Louis XI. and the duke of Burgundy, 168; forces the inhabitants of St. Quentin to swear fidelity to the king, 171; his designs in promoting the war between the king and the duke of Burgundy, 173, 174; his anxiety to promote the marriage between the duke of Guienne and the daughter of the duke of Burgundy, 203. et seq.; complaints against him, 225; the strong position of his territories, and his wealth and influence, 226; gives the lie to the lord of Humbercourt, which eventually leads to his ruin, ib.; he cunningly escapes the plot laid against him, 227; his interview with the king, 228; a digression on his wisdom, 230; his misfortune, 247; falls under the suspicion both of the king and the duke of Burgundy, 247. et seq.; his great duplicity, 248; his alarm, 249; sends messengers to the king, 265; scheme for detecting his duplicity, 266; sends messages to the king of England, entreating him not to rely on the French king, 270; makes proposals to the king, after the truce with the English, and endeavours to excuse his conduct, 281. et seq.; his traitorous letters to the king of England sent to Louis, 282; the king of France and the duke of Burgundy swear his death, 291; he places himself in the hands of the duke of Burgundy, under a safe conduct, 290; is placed under arrest, 293; reflections on his once powerful position, and the caprice of fortune, ib.; he is taken a prisoner to Paris, 296; is found guilty of treason, and executed, 297. 25. n.; a digression concerning the duke of Burgundy's error in delivering him up to the king, contrary to the safe conduct, 297. et seq.; the sentence upon him, ii. 72. n.

St. Paul (continued from Jean de Troyes' Chronicle), concessions made to, ii. 333; made constable of France, ib.; is reconciled to Louis XI., 375; delivered to the king, and beheaded, 380, 381; his treason and villanies, 381.

St. Paul, Jacques de, his capture at Arras, i. 245. 247; examined and released by the king, 249.

St. Paul, Pierre de Luxembourg, count of, son of the constable of France, i. 372.

St. Peter ad Vincula, cardinal, ii. 145; the town of Savona offered to be delivered up to, 268.

St. Pierre, Jean, lord of, i. 262.

St. Pol, Edward IV. arrives at, i. 198.

St. Priest, Louis, lord of, i. 299.

St. Quentin ceded to the duke of Burgundy, i. 74. 216; the inhabitants forced to swear fidelity to Louis XI., 171; delivered up to him, 174; menaced by the constable's forces, 249; entered by the French troops, 29S; the duke of Burgundy's army assembles at, ii. 349, 350; delivered up to Louis XI., 350; occupied by the constable of France, 374.

St. Riquier, ceded to the duke of Burgundy, i. 74.

St. (or San) Severino, the prince of Salerno the chief of the house of, ii. 104.

St. Severino, lord Francesco de, ii. 103; count of Cajazzo, 103; his great reputation at Milan, 108, 109.

St. Severino, lord Galeas di, meets Charles VIII. at Lyons, ii. 122; his chivalric accomplishments, ib.; meets the king at Suza, 124; in great credit at Milan, 103, 109; his instructions from the duke of Milan, 137; his intrigues, 137, 138.

St. Severino, Federigo, cardinal de, ii. 158.

St. Severino, Robert, lord di, ii. 101, 102; his dispute with Ludovic of Milan, 103; quits Milan, ib.

St. Tron, town of, i. 84; besieged by the duke of Burgundy, 94, 96; surrender of, 100.

St. Vallery, town of, i. 169; captured by the Burgundians, 222; ii. 371; retaken, i. 222.

Stanley, Thomas, afterwards earl of Derby, i. 253, 258, 261; joins the earl of Richmond, 397; ii 65.

Stillington, Robert, bishop of Bath, his eventful life, i. 395. et n.; ii. 63; miserable end of his son, 64.

Suilly, George de, ii. 185.?

Swiss, the, conclude a ten years' alliance with Louis XI., i. 242; come to terms of peace with Sigismund, duke of Austria, 242; their successful military operations, 243; the duke of Burgundy makes war upon the, 301. et seq.; they defeat the duke near Granson, and inflict upon him the greatest misfortunes, 304, 305; their great poverty, 305; enriched by the plunder of the duke of Burgundy's camp, 311; ignorant of the value of the articles captured, 312; list of the spoils taken, 311; take the famous Sancy diamond, 312. n.; presents received by the, from Louis XI., 312; the duke of Burgundy again defeated by the, near the town of Moret, 315; they defeat and slay the duke near Nancy, 336; in the pay of the Burgundians, ii. 18; liberal offers made to the, 21; enter the service of Louis XI., 22; slaughter committed by the, at Pontremoli, 196; assist the French army in transporting their large cannon across the Apennines, 199, 200; their contests with the Estradiots, 201; the finest infantry of the age, 211. et n.; arrival of the, to the relief of Charles VIII. and the duke of Orleans, 244, 245; their tumultuous spirit against Charles VIII., 247; number of, in the French army, 260; their great fidelity, 262; their decisive victories over the duke of Burgundy, 381—386.

T.

Tagliacozzo, county of, ii. 146.

Talbot, Sir Gilbert, joins the duke of Richmond, ii. 65. n.

Talbot, John, earl of Shrewsbury, i. 22.

Talbot, Thomas, apprehends Henry VI. of England, ii. 300. n.

Talmont, principality of, i. xviii. xix. xx.

Talmont, prince de, the title assumed by Commines on his marriage, i. xxii.

Tanneguy, lord du Chastel, i. 3. *n.* 112.

Tarento, surrender of, ii. 162 ; surrendered to Frederic, king of Naples, 249. *et n.*

Tarento, Frederick, prince of, i. 313; ii. 31.

Tassini, Anthony, chamberlain to the duke of Milan, ii. 101, 102.

Taxation of France in the 15th century, i. 386, 387.

Taxes, on the raising of, i. 385.

Ter Veere, in Holland, i. 199. *n.*

Ternant, M. de, i. 140.

Terzago, Ludovico, death of, ii. 105.

Therouenne, invested by the Flemings, ii. 32.

Thibault, marshal of Burgundy, i. 10.

Thiboust, Master Robert, i. xxi.

Thouars, vicomte de, i. xix. ; his family contests, xx—xxii. xxviii.

Thunder and lightning at Paris, ii. 346.

Tiberius, his death predicted by Thrasullus, ii. 75.

Tiercelin, George, lord of Brosse, i. 241.

Tiercelin, John, lord of Brosse, sent on an embassy to the emperor, i. 245.

Tinteville, Gaucher de, ii. 188.

Torcy, Jean, lord of, i. 141. 270.; ii. 33.

Toullois, provostship of, i. 132.

Tournay, bailiff of, i. 133 ; Oliver's visit to, 357 ; secured for the king, 358 ; the inhabitants defeat and repel the Gantois, 378 ; garrison of, ii. 388.

Tours, the three estates assembled at, i. 169. 386.

Tower of London, Henry VI. released from the, i. 195.

Towns ceded to the duke of Burgundy, i. 74.

Trade, royal monopoly of, ii. 152.

Treachery, instances of, among princes, i. 115, 116; existence of, among the duke of Burgundy's retainers, 171.

Treasury, reform of the, attempted by Charles VIII., ii. 282.

Treaties, *passim ;* treaty of alliance between Francis duke of Bretagne and Charles duke of Burgundy, i. 6 ; of alliance between the dukes of Bretagne and of Burgundy, 38 ; of Conflans, 73. *et seq.*; the events which followed, 78. *et seq.* ; of St. Maur des Fossés, 80; of Caen, 84; of Ancenis, 111 ; concluded at the castle of Crotoy, 216 ; between Edward IV. of England and Louis XI., 277.; of Vervins, 285. 287; between Louis XI. and the duke of Milan, 309.

Trebizond, empire of, overthrown by Mahomet II., ii. 91.

Tremouille, George de la, minister of Charles VII., i. xix. xx. 230; family of, despoiled of their property, xxvii ; the property restored, xxxiii.

Tremouille, Louis II., lord de la, ii. 147.

Treves, treaty of, ii. 18. *n.*

Trecate, town of, ii. 198.

Trimouille, Sieur de la, ii. 212. *et n.*

Trino, Charles VIII.'s arrival at, ii. 247.

Tristan l'Ermite, i. xxxiii.

Trivulce, lord John James di, ii. 125. 196. 268; at the battle of Fornovo, 218.

Trivulzio, bishop of Como, ii. 174.

Trouquoy, castle of, captured, i. 244.

Troye, count de, ii. 163.

Troyes, Jean de, Scandalous Chronicle attributed to, ii. 293. *et seq.*; his inducements for writing it, 297, 298.

Truce between Louis XI. and the duke of Burgundy, i. 224. *et seq.*; between the kings of France and England, 263. *et seq.*; terms of the, 267.

"Truth, with its secret counsel," a book written by bishop St. Costade, ii. 154.

Turin, Charles VIII.'s arrival at, ii. 229.

Turks defeated at Belgrade, ii. 88. *n.*; the number of their conquests, 90, 91; dreaded by the Venetians, ii. 120, 121; their treaty of peace with Ferdinand of Arragon and the king of Hungary, 120. *n.*; design against the, by the Venetians, 165; they capture the whole of Albania, 166; send an embassy to Venice, 173.

Tyranny of princes, i. 383, 384.

U.

Ulrich, bishop of Trent, ii. 174.

Unicorn's horn belonging to the Medici family, ii. 143.

University of Paris, its quarrel with the Court of Aids, ii. 300.

Unterbilk, town of, i. 242.

Urbin, Frederigo, duke of, ii. 30; memoirs of, *ib. n.*

Urbino, Anthony d', ii. 209.

Urfé, Pierre, lord of, i. 114; ii. 134; his gallantry, i. 149; his advice for war, 208.

Ursini, lord Charles, surrenders his territories to Charles VIII., ii. 145.

Ursini (Orsini), Giordano, lord of Bracciano, ii. 262. *n.*

Ursini, Paul, lord of Lomentana, ii. 140; his death, 140. *n.*

Ursini, lord Virgil, ii. 125. 262.

Ursins, William Juvenal des, ii. 336; arrested, 310.

V.

Vallée, William de, i. 220.

Vallori, Francisco, murdered, ii. 287.

Valois, Louis of. (See Louis XI.)

Valona, a town in Albania, ii. 165.

Vaquerie, Jean de la, i. 346.

Vaudray, Monsieur de, ii. 22.

Vaudray, Claude de, ii. 388.

Venafro, Marquis de, ii. 163.

Vendôme, Francis, duke of, his death, ii. 237.

Vendôme, Jacques, vidame of, ii. 245.

Venetians, their designs against the Turks, ii. 15; French embassy to the, 119; their contest with the Turks, 120. *n.*; their title to the kingdom of Cyprus, 121; cessions made to the, 121. *n.*; subdue Padua, 138; cabal against Charles VIII., 178; enter into a league with the pope and other confederates against France, 179; their number of forces brought against the French, 203; Charles VIII. sends an embassy to invite them to accept terms of peace, which are refused, 248, 249; towns possessed by, in Apulia, 259; compelled to surrender them, *ib. n.*; enemies opposed to them, 282.

Venice, opinions of the senate of, on the government of Naples, ii. 100; one of the three powers of Italy, 130; on the government of, 168. *et seq.*; entry of Commines into, as ambassador of France, 169; his description of,

170, 171; naval expeditions of, 172; her civil polity, *ib.*; the objects of Commines's embassy to, 173. *et seq.*; various embassies sent to, 173, 174; her friendly intentions towards Charles VIII., 176, 177; doges of, 267.

Vercelli, or Verceil, town of, ii. 233; treaty of, between Charles VIII. and the League, i. xxxv.; ii. 245.

Verdun-sur-Saone, town of, rebels, ii. 23; captured, 24.

Verdun, Guillaume, bishop of, imprisoned, i. 165.

Vere, Walfert, lord de la, i. 359.

Vergy, Guillaume, lord de, i. 76. 362; his various appointments, 362. *n.*; swears allegiance to the king, 363.

Vermandois, revenue of, i. 139.

Vermandois, Herbert II., count of, i. 120.

Vers, sir Stephen de, ii. 70. 108; seneschal of Beaucaire, 93, 94. 96; made governor of Gaeta, 184.

Versé, Pierre, bishop of Amiens, ii. 74. *n.*

Vervins, treaty of, between Louis XI. and the duke of Burgundy, i. 285. 287.

Vidame of Amiens, i. 72.

Vienne, Angelo Cato, archbishop of, the work dedicated to, i. xlv.

Vigevano, town of, ii. 197.

Vignolles, Thevenot de, i. 220.

Vilde, M. Jehan de, i. 147; his death, 148.

Vilheres, Jean de, cardinal of St. Dennis, ii. 157.

Villeneuf, William de, ii. 184. *et n.*

Villeneuve, Louis, baron of Sernon, ii. 147.

Villiers-le-Bel, near Paris, i. 79.

Villiers, Alain, lord de, i. 260.

Villiers, James de, ii. 336.

Villiers, William de, i. 140.

Vimeux, provostship of, i. 132.

Vincennes, castle of, meeting of Charles of Burgundy and the French princes in the, i. 78.

Vingt Escus, the king's guard, ii. 213. *et n.*

Virtues and vices of Louis XI., i. 59.

Visen, Charles de, valet de-chambre to the duke of Burgundy, i. 120.

Visconti, faction of the, ii. 160.

Visconti, the dukes of Milan descended from the family of, ii. 112.

Visconti, Bianca Maria, ii. 112. *n.*

Visconti, lord Galeas de, ii. 108.

Visconti, Francesco Bernardo, ii. 174.

Vitelli, Signor Camilla, at the battle of Fornovo, ii. 218.

Viterbo, visited by Charles VIII., ii. 144.

W.

Wales, Edward, prince of, i. 188, 189; defeated at the battle of Tewkesbury, 202; his death, *ib.*

Wales, prince of, murdered, ii. 366.

War, easily begun between two great princes, but difficult to be composed, i. 113; on the proclaiming of, 205.

Wars, their prevalence in France, i. 209; those which originated from the duke of Burgundy's siege of Nuz, 242; permitted by God for the punishment of wickedness, 378. *et seq.*

Warwick, Richard Neville, earl of, account of, i. 48; the greatest supporter of the house of York, 183; appointed governor of Calais, *ib.*; quarrels with Edward IV., and imprisons him, *ib.*; his great power, 184; defeated by Edward in various battles, *ib.*; flies to Calais and is repulsed, *ib.*; opposed by the duke of Burgundy, 185. 187; proceeds to Normandy, 187; furnished with money by Louis XI., *ib.*; raises a fleet, and sails to England, 190; expels Edward IV., 191; his numerous partisans, 194. *et n.*; releases Henry VI. from the Tower, 195; defeated by Edward, and slain, 201. 48. *n.*; his great political power, 394; the reason of his espousing the interest of the house of York, ii. 86.

Warwick, earl of, (*continued from Jean de Troyes' Chronicle*); he deposes Henry VI. of England, ii. 200; meets Louis XI. at Roan, and is sumptuously treated, 343; flies to Normandy, 360; his return to England, 363; reinstates Henry VI., *ib.*; the countess and her daughter royally received at Paris, 364; defeated and slain, 366.

Wenlock, lord John, lieutenant-governor of Calais, i. 174; repels his captain the Earl of Warwick, *ib.*; complimented by the king of England and the duke of Burgundy, and made governor of the place, 185; his advice to the earl of Warwick, 186; receives the forces sent by the earl of Warwick, 195; entertains Commines, 196, 197.

Westmoreland, Richard, earl of, ii. 85.

Wine, pailful of, drunk by Commines' horse, i. 32.

Wines, scarcity of, in France, in 1490, ii. 298.

Wisdom, a digression on, i. 229.

Withem, Captain Frederick de, i. 162. *n.*

Women, excluded from the throne of France, ii. 14, 16.

Woodville, Elizabeth, her marriage to Edward IV., i. 396. *n.*; ii. 63.

Wool, Calais the staple of, i. 198.

Y.

Yolande de France, the duchess of Savoy, i. 306, 310. *n.*; sister of René II. ii. 95. *n.*; death of, i. xxxi.

York, royal house of, in England, i. 22. 37, 38. 393; their civil contests, 181. *et seq.* (See Edward IV., and Warwick, earl of.)

York, George Neville, archbishop of, i. 190.

York, Richard, duke of, proclaims himself king of England, i. 48; is defeated and slain, *ib.*

Yorkists, defeated at St. Albans, ii. 303.

Ypres, viscount. (See Hugonet.)

Z.

Zizim, brother of Bajazet II., delivered by the pope to Charles VIII., ii. 159; his misfortunes and death, 67. *n.*

THE END.

LONDON:
Printed by SPOTTISWOODE and Co.,
New-street-Square.

Longfellow's Poetical Works. *Twenty-four page Engravings, by Birket Foster and others, and a new Portrait.*

———; or, without the illustrations, 3s. 6d.

——— **Prose Works, complete.** *Sixteen page Engravings by Birket Foster and others.*

Loudon's (Mrs.) Entertaining Naturalist. New Edition. Revised by W. S. DALLAS, F.L.S. *With nearly 500 Engravings.* 7s.

Marryat's Masterman Ready; or, The Wreck of the Pacific. 93 *Engravings.*

——— **Mission;** or, Scenes in Africa. (Written for Young People.) *Illustrated by Gilbert and Dalziel.*

——— **Pirate; and Three Cutters.** New Edition, with a Memoir of the Author. *With 20 Steel Engravings, from Drawings by Clarkson Stanfield, R.A.*

——— **Privateer's-Man One Hundred Years Ago.** *Eight Engravings on Steel, after Stothard.*

——— **Settlers in Canada.** New Edition. *Ten fine Engravings by Gilbert and Dalziel.*

Maxwell's Victories of Wellington and the British Armies. *Illustrations on Steel.*

Michael Angelo and Raphael, their Lives and Works. By DUPPA and QUATREMERE DE QUINCY. *With 13 highly-finished Engravings on Steel.*

Miller's History of the Anglo-Saxons. Written in a popular style, on the basis of Sharon Turner. *Portrait of Alfred, Map of Saxon Britain, and 12 elaborate Engravings on Steel.*

Milton's Poetical Works. With a Memoir by JAMES MONTGOMERY, TODD'S Verbal Index to all the Poems, and Explanatory Notes. *With 120 Engravings by Thompson and others, from Drawings by W. Harvey.* 2 vols.
Vol. 1. Paradise Lost, complete, with Memoir, Notes, and Index.
Vol. 2. Paradise Regained, and other Poems, with Verbal Index to all the Poems.

Mudie's British Birds. Revised by W. C. L. MARTIN. *Fifty-two Figures and 7 Plates of Eggs.* In 2 vols.

———; or, *with the plates coloured,* 7s. 6d. per vol.

Naval and Military Heroes of Great Britain; or, Calendar of Victory. Being a Record of British Valour and Conquest by Sea and Land, on every day in the year, from the time of William the Conqueror to the Battle of Inkermann. By Major JOHNS, R.M., and Lieutenant P. H. NICOLAS, R.M. *Twenty-four Portraits.* 6s.

Nicolini's History of the Jesuits: their Origin, Progress, Doctrines, and Designs. *Fine Portraits of Loyola, Lainès, Xavier, Borgia, Acquaviva, Père la Chaise, and Pope Ganganelli.*

Norway and its Scenery. Comprising Price's Journal, with large Additions, and a Road-Book. Edited by T. FORESTER. *Twenty-two Illustrations.*

Paris and its Environs, including Versailles, St. Cloud, and Excursions into the Champagne Districts. An Illustrated Handbook for Travellers. Edited by T. FORESTER. *Twenty-eight beautiful Engravings.*

Petrarch's Sonnets, and other Poems. Translated into English Verse. By various hands. With a Life of the Poet, by THOMAS CAMPBELL. *With 16 Engravings.*

Pickering's History of the Races of Man, with an Analytical Synopsis of the Natural History of Man. By Dr. HALL. *Illustrated by numerous Portraits.*

———; or, *with the plates coloured,* 7s. 6d.

. An excellent Edition of a work originally published at 3l. 3s. by the American Government.

Pictorial Handbook of Modern Geography, on a Popular Plan. 3s. 6d. *Illustrated by 150 Engravings and 51 Maps.* 6s.
———; or, *with the maps coloured,* 7s. 6d.

Pope's Poetical Works. Edited by ROBERT CARRUTHERS. *Numerous Engravings.* 2 vols.

——— **Homer's Iliad.** With Introduction and Notes by J. S. WATSON, M.A. *Illustrated by the entire Series of Flaxman's Designs, beautifully engraved by Moses (in the full 8vo. size).*

——— **Homer's Odyssey, Hymns,** &c., by other translators, including Chapman, and Introduction and Notes by J. S. WATSON, M.A. *Flaxman's Designs beautifully engraved by Moses.*

Pope's Life. Including many of his Letters. By ROBERT CARRUTHERS. New Edition, revised and enlarged. *Illustrations.*

The preceding 5 vols. make a complete and elegant edition of Pope's Poetical Works and Translations for 25s.

Pottery and Porcelain, and other Objects of Vertu (a Guide to the Knowledge of). To which is added an Engraved List of all the known Marks and Monograms. By HENRY G. BOHN. *Numerous Engravings.*

———; or, *coloured.* 10s. 6d.

Prout's (Father) Reliques. New Edition, revised and largely augmented. *Twenty-one spirited Etchings by Mackise.* Two volumes in one. 7s. 6d.

Recreations in Shooting. By "CRAVEN." New Edition, revised and enlarged. 62 *Engravings on Wood, after Harvey, and 9 Engravings on Steel, chiefly after A. Cooper, R.A.*

Redding's History and Descriptions of Wines, Ancient and Modern. *Twenty beautiful Woodcuts.*

Rennie's Insect Architecture. *New Edition.* Revised by the Rev. J. G. WOOD, M.A.

Robinson Crusoe. With Illustrations by STOTHARD and HARVEY. *Twelve beautiful Engravings on Steel, and 74 on Wood.*

———; or, without the Steel illustrations, 3s. 6d.
The prettiest Edition extant.

Rome in the Nineteenth Century. New Edition. Revised by the Author. *Illustrated by 34 fine Steel Engravings.* 2 vols.

Southey's Life of Nelson. With Additional Notes. *Illustrated with 64 Engravings.*

Starling's (Miss) Noble Deeds of Women; or, Examples of Female Courage, Fortitude, and Virtue. *Fourteen beautiful Illustrations.*

Stuart and Revett's Antiquities of Athens, and other Monuments of Greece. *Illustrated in 71 Steel Plates, and numerous Woodcuts.*

Tales of the Genii; or, the Delightful Lessons of Horam. *Numerous Woodcuts, and 8 Steel Engravings, after Stothard.*

Tasso's Jerusalem Delivered. Translated into English Spenserian Verse, with a Life of the Author. By J. H. WIFFEN. *Eight Engravings on Steel, and 24 on Wood, by Thurston.*

Walker's Manly Exercises. Containing Skating, Riding, Driving, Hunting, Shooting, Sailing, Rowing, Swimming, &c. New Edition, revised by "CRAVEN." *Forty-four Steel Plates, and numerous Woodcuts.*

Walton's Complete Angler. Edited by EDWARD JESSE, Esq. To which is added an Account of Fishing Stations, &c., by H. G. BOHN. *Upwards of 203 Engravings.*

———; or, *with 26 additional page Illustrations on Steel,* 7s. 6d.

Wellington, Life of. By AN OLD SOLDIER, from the materials of Maxwell. *Eighteen Engravings.*

White's Natural History of Selborne. With Notes by Sir WILLIAM JARDINE and EDWARD JESSE, Esq. *Illustrated by 40 highly-finished Engravings.*

———; or, *with the plates coloured,* 7s. 6d.

Young, The, Lady's Book. A Manual of Elegant Recreations, Arts, Sciences, and Accomplishments; including Geology, Mineralogy, Conchology, Botany, Entomology, Ornithology, Costume, Embroidery, the Escritoire, Archery, Riding, Music (instrumental and vocal), Dancing, Exercises, Painting, Photography, &c., &c. Edited by distinguished Professors. *Twelve Hundred Woodcut Illustrations, and several fine Engravings on Steel.* 7s. 6d.

———; or, *cloth gilt, gilt edges,* 9s.

XI.

Bohn's Classical Library.

5s. per Volume, excepting those marked otherwise.

Æschylus. Literally Translated into English Prose by an Oxonian. 3s. 6d.

———, **Appendix to.** Containing the New Readings given in Hermann's posthumous Edition of Æschylus. By GEORGE BURGES, M.A. 3s. 6d.

Ammianus Marcellinus. History of Rome from Constantius to Valens. Translated by C. D. YONGE, B.A. Dble. vol.,7s. 6d.

Antoninus. The Thoughts of the Emperor Marcus Aurelius. Translated by GEO. LONG, M.A. 3s. 6d.

Apuleius, the Golden Ass; Death of Socrates; Florida; and Discourse on Magic. To which is added a Metrical Version of Cupid and Psyche; and Mrs. Tighe's Psyche. *Frontispiece,*

Aristophanes' Comedies. Literally Translated, with Notes and Extracts from Frere's and other Metrical Versions, by W. J. Hickie. 2 vols.
> Vol. 1. Acharnians, Knights, Clouds, Wasps, Peace, and Birds.
> Vol. 2. Lysistrata, Thesmophoriazusæ, Frogs, Ecclesiazusæ, and Plutus.

Aristotle's Ethics. Literally Translated by Archdeacon Browne, late Classical Professor of King's College.

——— **Politics and Economics.** Translated by E. Walford, M.A.

——— **Metaphysics.** Literally Translated, with Notes, Analysis, Examination Questions, and Index, by the Rev. John H. M'Mahon, M.A., and Gold Medallist in Metaphysics, T.C.D.

——— **History of Animals.** In Ten Books. Translated, with Notes and Index, by Richard Cresswell, M.A.

——— **Organon ; or, Logical Treatises.** With Notes, &c. By O. F. Owen, M.A. 2 vols., 3s. 6d. each.

——— **Rhetoric and Poetics.** Literally Translated, with Examination Questions and Notes, by an Oxonian.

Athenæus. The Deipnosophists; or, the Banquet of the Learned. Translated by C. D. Yonge, B.A. 3 vols.

Cæsar. Complete, with the Alexandrian, African, and Spanish Wars. Literally Translated, with Notes.

Catullus, Tibullus, and the Vigil of Venus. A Literal Prose Translation. To which are added Metrical Versions by Lamb, Grainger, and others. *Frontispiece.*

Cicero's Orations. Literally Translated by C. D. Yonge, B.A. In 4 vols.
> Vol. 1. Contains the Orations against Verres, &c. *Portrait.*
> Vol. 2. Catiline, Archias, Agrarian Law, Rabirius, Murena, Sylla, &c.
> Vol. 3. Orations for his House, Plancius, Sextius, Cœlius, Milo, Ligarius, &c.
> Vol. 4. Miscellaneous Orations, and Rhetorical Works; with General Index to the four volumes.

——— **on the Nature of the Gods,** Divination, Fate, Laws, a Republic, &c. Translated by C. D. Yonge, B.A., and F. Barham.

——— **Academics, De Finibus, and** Tusculan Questions. By C. D. Yonge, B.A. With Sketch of the Greek Philosophy.

——— **Offices, Old Age, Friendship,** Scipio's Dream, Paradoxes, &c. Literally Translated, by R. Edmonds. 3s. 6d.

Cicero on Oratory and Orators. By J. S. Watson, M.A.

Demosthenes' Orations. Translated, with Notes, by C. Rann Kennedy. In 5 volumes.
> Vol. 1. The Olynthiac, Philippic, and other Public Orations. 3s. 6d.
> Vol. 2. On the Crown and on the Embassy.
> Vol. 3. Against Leptines, Midias, Androtion, and Aristocrates.
> Vol. 4. Private and other Orations.
> Vol. 5. Miscellaneous Orations.

Dictionary of Latin Quotations. Including Proverbs, Maxims, Mottoes, Law Terms, and Phrases; and a Collection of above 500 Greek Quotations. With all the quantities marked, & English Translations.

———, **with Index Verborum.** 6s. Index Verborum only. 1s.

Diogenes Laertius. Lives and Opinions of the Ancient Philosophers. Translated, with Notes, by C. D. Yonge.

Epictetus. Translated by George Long, M.A. [*Preparing.*

Euripides. Literally Translated. 2 vols.
> Vol. 1. Hecuba, Orestes, Medea, Hippolytus, Alcestis, Bacchæ, Heraclidæ, Iphigenia in Aulide, and Iphigenia in Tauris.
> Vol. 2. Hercules Furens, Troades, Ion, Andromaché, Suppliants, Helen, Electra, Cyclops, Rhesus.

Greek Anthology. Literally Translated. With Metrical Versions by various Authors.

Greek Romances of Heliodorus, Longus, and Achilles Tatius.

Herodotus. A New and Literal Translation, by Henry Cary, M.A., of Worcester College, Oxford.

Hesiod, Callimachus, and Theognis. Literally Translated, with Notes, by J. Banks, M.A.

Homer's Iliad. Literally Translated, by an Oxonian.

——— **Odyssey, Hymns, &c.** Literally Translated, by an Oxonian.

Horace. Literally Translated, by Smart. Carefully revised by an Oxonian. 3s. 6d.

Justin, Cornelius Nepos, and Eutropius. Literally Translated, with Notes and Index, by J. S. Watson, M.A.

Juvenal, Persius, Sulpicia, and Lucilius. By L. Evans, M.A. With the Metrical Version by Gifford. *Frontispiece.*

Livy. A new and Literal Translation. By Dr. Spillan and others. In 4 vols.
> Vol. 1. Contains Books 1—8.
> Vol. 2. Books 9—26.
> Vol. 3. Books 27—36.
> Vol. 4. Books 37 to the end; and Index.

11

Lucan's Pharsalia. Translated, with Notes, by H. T. RILEY.

Lucretius. Literally Translated, with Notes, by the Rev. J. S. WATSON, M.A. And the Metrical Version by J. M. GOOD.

Martial's Epigrams, complete. Literally Translated. Each accompanied by one or more Verse Translations selected from the Works of English Poets, and other sources. With a copious Index. Double volume (660 pages). 7s. 6d.

Ovid's Works, complete. Literally Translated. 3 vols.
Vol. 1. Fasti, Tristia, Epistles, &c.
Vol. 2. Metamorphoses.
Vol. 3. Heroides, Art of Love, &c.

Pindar. Literally Translated, by DAWSON W. TURNER, and the Metrical Version by ABRAHAM MOORE.

Plato's Works. Translated by the Rev. H. CARY and others. In 6 vols.
Vol. 1. The Apology of Socrates, Crito, Phædo, Gorgias, Protagoras, Phædrus, Theætetus, Euthyphron, Lysis.
Vol. 2. The Republic, Timæus, & Critias.
Vol. 3. Meno, Euthydemus, The Sophist, Statesman, Cratylus, Parmenides, and the Banquet.
Vol. 4. Philebus, Charmides, Laches, The Two Alcibiades, and Ten other Dialogues.
Vol. 5. The Laws.
Vol. 6. The Doubtful Works. With General Index.

——— **Dialogues,** an Analysis and Index to. With References to the Translation in Bohn's Classical Library. By Dr. DAY.

Plautus's Comedies. Literally Translated, with Notes, by H. T. RILEY, B.A. In 2 vols.

Pliny's Natural History. Translated, with Copious Notes, by the late JOHN BOSTOCK, M.D., F.R.S., and H. T. RILEY, B.A. In 6 vols.

Propertius, Petronius, and Johannes Secundus. Literally Translated, and accompanied by Poetical Versions, from various sources.

Quintilian's Institutes of Oratory. Literally Translated, with Notes, &c., by J. S. WATSON, M.A. In 2 vols.

Sallust, Florus, and Velleius Paterculus. With Copious Notes, Biographical Notices, and Index, by J. S. WATSON.

Sophocles. The Oxford Translation revised.

Standard Library Atlas of Classical Geography. *Twenty-two large coloured Maps according to the latest authorities.* With a complete Index (accentuated), giving the latitude and longitude of every place named in the Maps. Imp. 8vo. 7s. 6d.

Strabo's Geography. Translated, with Copious Notes, by W. FALCONER, M.A., and H. C. HAMILTON, Esq. With Index, giving the Ancient and Modern Names. In 3 vols.

Suetonius' Lives of the Twelve Cæsars, and other Works. Thomson's Translation, revised, with Notes, by T. FORESTER.

Tacitus. Literally Translated, with Notes. In 2 vols.
Vol. 1. The Annals.
Vol. 2. The History, Germania, Agricola, &c. With Index.

Terence and Phædrus. By H. T. RILEY, B.A.

Theocritus, Bion, Moschus, and Tyrtæus. By J. BANKS, M.A. With the Metrical Versions of Chapman.

Thucydides. Literally Translated by Rev. H. DALE. In 2 vols. 3s. 6d. each.

Virgil. Literally Translated by DAVIDSON. New Edition, carefully revised. 3s. 6d.

Xenophon's Works. In 3 Vols.
Vol. 1. The Anabasis and Memorabilia. Translated, with Notes, by J. S. WATSON, M.A. And a Geographical Commentary, by W. F. AINSWORTH, F.S.A., F.R.G.S., &c.
Vol. 2. Cyropædia and Hellenics. By J. S. WATSON, M.A., and the Rev. H. DALE.
Vol. 3. The Minor Works. By J. S. WATSON, M.A.

XII.
Bohn's Scientific Library.
5s. per Volume, excepting those marked otherwise.

Agassiz and Gould's Comparative Physiology. Enlarged by Dr. WRIGHT. *Upwards of 400 Engravings.*

Bacon's Novum Organum and Advancement of Learning. Complete, with Notes, by J. DEVEY, M.A.

Blair's Chronological Tables, Revised and Enlarged. Comprehending the Chronology and History of the World, from the earliest times. By J. WILLOUGHBY ROSSE. Double Volume. 10s.; or, half-bound, 10s. 6d.

Index of Dates. Comprehending the principal Facts in the Chronology and History of the World, from the earliest to the present time, alphabetically arranged. By J. W. ROSSE. Double volume, 10s. or, half-bound, 10s. 6d.

Bolley's Manual of Technical Analysis. A Guide for the Testing of Natural and Artificial Substances. By B. H. PAUL. 100 *Wood Engravings.*

BRIDGEWATER TREATISES. —
———— **Bell on the Hand.** Its Mechanism and Vital Endowments as evincing Design. *Seventh Edition Revised.*

———— **Kirby on the History, Habits,** and Instincts of Animals. Edited, with Notes, by T. RYMER JONES. *Numerous Engravings, many of which are additional.* In 2 vols.

———— **Kidd on the Adaptation of** External Nature to the Physical Condition of Man. 3s. 6d.

———— **Whewell's Astronomy and** General Physics, considered with reference to Natural Theology. 3s. 6d.

———— **Chalmers on the Adaptation** of External Nature to the Moral and Intellectual Constitution of Man. 5s.

———— **Prout's Treatise on Chemistry, Meteorology, and Digestion.** Edited by Dr. J. W. GRIFFITH.

———— **Buckland's Geology and** Mineralogy. 2 vols. 15s.

———— **Roget's Animal and Vegetable** Physiology. *Illustrated.* In 2 vols. 6s. each.

Carpenter's (Dr. W. B.) Zoology. A Systematic View of the Structure, Habits, Instincts, and Uses, of the principal Families of the Animal Kingdom, and of the chief forms of Fossil Remains. New edition, revised to the present time, under arrangement with the Author, by W. S. DALLAS, F.L.S. *Illustrated with many hundred fine Wood Engravings.* In 2 vols. 6s. each.

———— **Mechanical Philosophy, Astronomy, and Horology.** A Popular Exposition. 183 *Illustrations.*

———— **Vegetable Physiology and** Systematic Botany. A complete Introduction to the Knowledge of Plants. New Edition, revised, under arrangement with the Author, by E. LANKESTER, M.D., &c. *Several hundred Illustrations on Wood.* 6s.

———— **Animal Physiology.** New Edition, thoroughly revised, and in part re-written by the Author. *Upwards of 300 capital Illustrations.* 6s.

Chess Congress of 1862. A Collection of the Games played, and a Selection of the Problems sent in for the Competition. Edited by J. LÖWENTHAL, Manager. With an Account of the Proceedings, and a Memoir of the British Chess Association, by J. W. MEDLEY, Hon. Sec. 7s.

Chevreul on Colour. Containing the Principles of Harmony and Contrast of Colours, and their application to the Arts. Translated from the French by CHARLES MARTEL. Only complete Edition. *Several Plates.* Or, with an additional series of 16 Plates in Colours. 7s. 6d.

Clark's (Hugh) Introduction to Heraldry. *With nearly 1000 Illustrations.* 18th *Edition.* Revised and enlarged by J. R. PLANCHÉ, Rouge Croix. Or, with all the Illustrations coloured, 15s.

Comte's Philosophy of the Sciences. By G. H. LEWES.

Ennemoser's History of Magic. Translated by WILLIAM HOWITT. With an Appendix of the most remarkable and best authenticated Stories of Apparitions, Dreams, Table-Turning, and Spirit-Rapping, &c. In 2 vols.

Handbook of Domestic Medicine. Popularly arranged. By Dr. HENRY DAVIES. 700 pages. With complete Index.

Handbook of Games. By various Amateurs and Professors. Comprising treatises on all the principal Games of chance, skill, and manual dexterity. In all, above 40 games (the Whist, Draughts, and Billiards being especially comprehensive). Edited by H. G. BOHN. *Illustrated by numerous Diagrams.*

Hogg's (Jabez) Elements of Experimental and Natural Philosophy. Containing Mechanics, Pneumatics, Hydrostatics, Hydraulics, Acoustics, Optics, Caloric, Electricity, Voltaism, and Magnetism. New Edition, enlarged. *Upwards of 400 Woodcuts.*

Hind's Introduction to Astronomy. With a Vocabulary, containing an Explanation of all the Terms in present use. New Edition, enlarged. *Numerous Engravings.* 3s. 6d.

Humboldt's Cosmos; or Sketch of a Physical Description of the Universe. Translated by E. C. OTTÉ and W. S. DALLAS, F.L.S. *Fine Portrait.* In five vols. 3s. 6d. each ; excepting Vol. V., 5s.
   • In this edition the notes are placed beneath the text, Humboldt's analytical Summaries and the passages hitherto suppressed are included, and new and comprehensive Indices are added.

———— **Travels in America.** In 3 vols.

———— **Views of Nature; or, Contemplations of the Sublime Phenomena of** Creation. Translated by E. C. OTTÉ and H. G. BOHN. A fac-simile letter from the Author to the Publisher ; translations of the quotations, and a complete Index.

Humphrey's Coin Collector's Manual. A popular Introduction to the Study of Coins. *Highly finished Engravings.* In 2 vols.

13

Hunt's (Robert) Poetry of Science; or, Studies of the Physical Phenomena of Nature. By Professor HUNT. New Edition, enlarged.

Index of Dates. *See* Blair's Tables.

Joyce's Scientific Dialogues. Completed to the present state of Knowledge, by Dr. GRIFFITH. *Numerous Woodcuts.*

Knight's (Chas.) Knowledge is Power. A Popular Manual of Political Economy.

Lectures on Painting. By the Royal Academicians. With Introductory Essay, and Notes by R. WORNUM, Esq. *Portraits.*

Mantell's (Dr.) Geological Excursions through the Isle of Wight and Dorsetshire. New Edition, by T. RUPERT JONES, Esq. *Numerous beautifully executed Woodcuts, and a Geological Map.*

—— **Medals of Creation;** or, First Lessons in Geology and the Study of Organic Remains; including Geological Excursions. New Edition, revised. *Coloured Plates, and several hundred beautiful Woodcuts.* In 2 vols., 7s. 6d. each.

—— **Petrifactions and their Teachings.** An Illustrated Handbook to the Organic Remains in the British Museum. *Numerous Engravings.* 6s.

—— **Wonders of Geology; or, a** Familiar Exposition of Geological Phenomena. New Edition, augmented by T. RUPERT JONES, F.G.S. *Coloured Geological Map of England, Plates, and nearly 200 beautiful Woodcuts.* In 2 vols., 7s. 6d. each.

Morphy's Games of Chess. Being the Matches and best Games played by the American Champion, with Explanatory and Analytical Notes, by J. LÖWENTHAL. *Portrait* and Memoir.

It contains by far the largest collection of games played by Mr. Morphy extant in any form, and has received his endorsement and co-operation.

Oersted's Soul in Nature, &c. *Portrait.*

Richardson's Geology, including Mineralogy and Palæontology. Revised and enlarged, by Dr. T. WRIGHT. *Upwards of 400 Illustrations.*

Schouw's Earth, Plants, and Man; and Kobell's Sketches from the Mineral Kingdom. Translated by A. HENFREY, F.R.S. *Coloured Map of the Geography of Plants.*

Smith's (Pye) Geology and Scripture; or, The Relation between the Holy Scriptures and Geological Science.

Stanley's Classified Synopsis of the Principal Painters of the Dutch and Flemish Schools.

Staunton's Chess-player's Handbook. *Numerous Diagrams.*

—— ... Supplement to the ... Translated ... taining ... the most important modern improvements in the Openings, illustrated by actual Games; a revised Code of Chess Laws; and a Selection of Mr. Morphy's Games in England and France. 6s.

—— **Chess-player's Companion.** Comprising a new Treatise on Odds, Collection of Match Games, and a Selection of Original Problems.

—— **Chess Tournament of 1851.** *Numerous Illustrations.*

Principles of Chemistry, exemplified in a series of simple experiments. Based upon the German work of Professor STOCKHARDT, and Edited by C. W. HEATON, Professor of Chemistry at Charing Cross Hospital. *Upwards of 270 Illustrations.*

Stockhardt's Agricultural Chemistry; or, Chemical Field Lectures. Addressed to Farmers. Translated, with Notes, by Professor HENFREY, F.R.S. To which is added, a Paper on Liquid Manure, by J. J. MECHI, Esq.

Ure's (Dr. A.) Cotton Manufacture of Great Britain, systematically investigated; with an introductory view of its comparative state in Foreign Countries. New Edition, revised and completed to the present time, by P. L. SIMMONDS. *One hundred and fifty Illustrations.* In 2 vols.

—— **Philosophy of Manufactures;** or, An Exposition of the Factory System of Great Britain. New Ed., continued to the present time, by P. L. SIMMONDS. 7s. 6d.

XIII.

Bohn's Cheap Series.

Boswell's Life of Johnson, and Johnsoniana. Including his Tour to the Hebrides, Tour in Wales, &c. Edited, with large additions and Notes, by the Right Hon. JOHN WILSON CROKER. The second and most complete Copyright Edition, rearranged and revised according to the suggestions of Lord Macaulay, by the late JOHN WRIGHT, Esq., with further additions by Mr. CROKER. *Upwards of 50 fine Engravings on Steel.* In 5 vols. cloth, 20s.

Carpenter's (Dr. W. B.) Physiology of Temperance and Total Abstinence, 1s.; on fine paper, cloth, 2s. 6d.

14

Lightning Source UK Ltd.
Milton Keynes UK
UKOW07f0041090316

269875UK00011B/351/P